# AFTER THE ARMADA

# AFTER THE ARMADA

*Elizabethan England*
*and the Struggle*
*for Western Europe*
1588-1595

———

### R. B. WERNHAM

Emeritus Professor of
Modern History in the
University of Oxford

CLARENDON PRESS · OXFORD

Oxford University Press, Walton Street, Oxford OX2 6DP

London  New York  Toronto
Delhi  Bombay  Calcutta  Madras  Karachi
Kuala Lumpur  Singapore  Hong Kong  Tokyo
Nairobi  Dar es Salaam  Cape Town
Melbourne  Auckland

and associated companies in
Beirut  Berlin  Ibadan  Mexico City  Nicosia

Oxford is a trade mark of Oxford University Press

Published in the United States
by Oxford University Press, New York

First published 1984
Reprinted 1985

British Library Cataloguing in Publication Data

Wernham, R. B.
After the Armada: Elizabethan England and
the struggle for Western Europe, 1588-1595.
1. Great Britain—Foreign relations—
1588-1603
I. Title
327.42        DA45
ISBN 0-19-822753-1

Library of Congress Cataloging in Publication Data

Wernham, R. B. (Richard Bruce), 1906-
After the Armada
Includes index.
1. Great Britain—Foreign relations—1558-1603.
2. Great Britain—Politics and government—1558-1603.
3. Great Britain—Foreign relations—Europe.
4. Europe—Foreign relations—Great Britain.  5. Europe—History—
1517-1648.
7. Armada, 1588  I. Title.
DA356.W47 1983        940.2'32        83-8281
ISBN 0-19-822753-1

Printed by Antony Rowe Ltd,
Chippenham

# Preface

My purposes in writing this book are twofold. They are, first, to give juster emphasis to the continental and military side of the Elizabethan war with Spain during the crucial six or seven years following the defeat of the 1588 Armada. Second, I want to suggest how the burdens and frustrations of that war, in Joel Hurstfield's words, 'sapped the wealth and manpower and good temper of the nation' and thereby helped to begin a drifting apart of government and people, of 'court' and 'country', that was to continue and accelerate through the next half century.[1] I should perhaps add that the book is, as its subtitle is intended to suggest, a study of English policies and English operations. It tries to see the struggle for western Europe primarily as it may have appeared to Queen Elizabeth and her advisers rather than from some stratospheric international point of view.

With such purposes in mind, I think there is no need to apologize for treating the subject in a narrative way. Only that can bring out the steady accumulation of burdens imposed by the war; the growth of frustration as decisive victory, several times seemingly just around the corner, eluded England's grasp; and the gradual developments in opinion and sentiment in response to those burdens and those frustrations. Moreover, foreign policy, and especially Elizabethan foreign policy, can hardly be adequately treated in any other fashion. For it was so largely the story of day-to-day responses to the immediate pressure of events and circumstances. No doubt, underlying those responses there was a deep-seated, almost instinctive, sense of English interests and of the basic principles that should guide English actions. But the history of the specific decisions, of their sequence and

---

[1] Like Hurstfield, 'I am of course aware of the revisionist school which has recently emerged and which rejects the notion of a gathering conflict between crown and parliament in the early seventeenth century'. But in addition to the arguments that he adduces to modify this revisionist conclusion, it may be noted how readily conflict developed between Crown and Parliament whenever their relations were subjected to the stress and strain of war, e.g. in the 1620s or 1638–40. J. Hurstfield, *The Illusion of Power in Tudor Politics* (Creighton Lecture, 1978), pp. 19, 20.

timing and more immediate motivation, is of supreme importance to any true understanding of how policy developed.

This is all the more true because the nearness and immensity of the danger during these seven years from 1588 to 1595 imposed something of a lull upon the great debates about policy that had in the rivalry of Leicester and Walsingham with Burghley marked the years before the Armada and that were to be renewed between Essex and the Cecils during the second half of the fifteen-nineties. During those seven years, although the local commanders in Brittany, in Normandy, at Ostend, and in the northern Netherlands, did as it were 'fight their corners', there was little or no disagreement among the Queen's chief advisers about the supreme importance of what was happening in northern France. Indeed, so far as there was debate over general policy, it was between counsellors anxious to give active and timely aid in one way or another to the King of France and a Queen always reluctant to spend money and men and somewhat sceptical of the high hopes of the professional and amateur strategists around her. Policy during these years was therefore even more than usually governed by circumstances, was even more than usually a reaction to events.

The story is, nevertheless, a complex and interwoven one and it has until fairly recently suffered from some distortion of emphasis. The brilliant work of a succession of distinguished naval historians from Sir Julian Corbett, Sir John Laughton, and M. Oppenheim down to J. A. Williamson and Michael Lewis gave an over-great emphasis to the naval and oceanic aspect of the war with Spain. This was of course anyway the more stirring and exciting aspect. It was also the aspect more readily recounted, thanks to the earlier availability in print of the naval records through the *Calendars of State Papers, Domestic series,* and the publications of such bodies as the Navy Records Society and the Hakluyt Society. It is only recently that the primary source for the continental and military side of the war, the Foreign series of English State Papers, has been listed, calendared, and indexed for the years immediately after 1588. This has helped to emphasize once again, as J. A. Froude did over a century ago and as Garret Mattingly did much more recently, that the Elizabethan war against Spain was first and foremost a continental, European, war. It was a continental war against an over-mighty military power that was threatening to dominate western Europe and more particularly the 'invasion coasts' opposite England across the Channel and Narrow Seas. It was, in other words, a war of the same kind as those that England was later to wage against Louis XIV and Napoleon I, against Kaiser Wilhelm II and Adolf Hitler. It involved the whole of western Europe as well as, indeed more than, the Atlantic and Caribbean. The complexity and interdependence of the actions in the various theatres makes it a complicated story. But to tell it in separate parts rather than as an interconnected whole must deprive us of that awareness of what was simultaneously happening in other parts of the field, of that peripheral vision, which so much influenced the thinking and decisions of Elizabeth and her ministers. And this, what Thomas Hardy has called 'the mournful many-sidedness of things', was a particularly marked characteristic of the years between 1588 and 1595.

That many-sidedness was a natural outcome of the causes that had brought Elizabethan England and Spain into conflict. All through the sixteenth century English independence had depended largely upon three factors – upon her own developing sea power and its ability to control the seas around her shores; upon her ability to eliminate, or at least to neutralize, the enmity of Scots and Irish; and upon the maintenance of a reasonable balance between Spain and France, the two great military monarchies of the Continent, so that each knew that if one attacked England the other would come to her defence. During most of the first two-thirds of the sixteenth century danger had threatened from France, closely allied to Scotland, rather than from Spain, the overlord of the Netherlands where English overseas trade found its principal market. From the later 1560s, however, various things happened to complicate and unsettle this traditional situation. In the first place, England's final break with Rome upon Elizabeth's accession made it less certain that either Catholic Spain or Catholic France could be trusted to support her against attack. There were even fears that they might join forces to reimpose Papal authority upon her and that in doing so they might be supported by the still considerable number of Englishmen, and the very much larger proportion of Irishmen, who still clung to the old faith. On the other hand, of course, the success of the Reformation in Scotland at the same time turned the government there and most of its subjects, at least in the Lowlands, from enemies into friends of Protestant England.

The second happening was the arrival of Spain's main field army in the Netherlands in 1567. This northwards shift of the centre of gravity of Spanish military power was the result of Philip II's determination to crush rebellion and heresy among his Low Country subjects rather than of any hostile purpose towards England. Nevertheless, it brought the finest army in Christendom, and a zealously Catholic army at that, to within a score or so of miles of the Kentish coast and not much more than a hundred miles of London. It produced in Protestant English minds a growing suspicion about Spanish purposes. It stimulated accordingly a growing, if cautious and none too trustful, friendship between England and France and an unofficial but none the less considerable encouragement from both countries to the Netherlands rebels. This in turn further strained Anglo-Spanish relations. Moreover, the Netherlands revolt and Spain's efforts to crush it went far to ruin what had been much the most important market for England's overseas trade. English sailors and merchants in their search for alternative 'vents' for their trade came into conflict with Spanish authority and Spanish claims to monopoly in North Africa, the New World, and even the Pacific Ocean. Anglo-Spanish religious differences exacerbated, and were exacerbated by, these maritime and commercial clashes, though by themselves neither maritime and commercial disputes nor religious differences would have brought the two governments to war.

What finally brought that about was the collapse of the French monarchy in the spring of 1585 and the outbreak of what was to prove the last and longest of the French Wars of Religion. By the secret treaty of Joinville at the end of 1584 the Catholic League in France had become the subsidized and dependent ally of the King of Spain. So the French monarchy could no longer play any independent part in international affairs, could no longer fill its wonted role of counterpoise to the power of Spain. The Spanish army in the Netherlands would be free to concentrate upon destroying the rebels there without fear of being stabbed in the back from across the French frontier. And, as the main strength of the League lay in northern and eastern France, this would mean that soon the entire coast from Brest to Emden might be in the hands of Spain or Spain's satellites. To cover all the possible jumping-off places for an invasion along all that length of coast would be beyond the power of England's naval forces. They lacked the numbers for such a task nor, in an area where the prevailing winds blew from south and west, could they sail close enough to the wind to guard at all times all the lee shore of southern England. On land Elizabeth lacked the military forces and the money, and England lacked the manpower, to compete with the King of Spain who controlled the finest army in the Old World and the seemingly inexhaustible gold and silver of the New.

Elizabeth therefore could not afford to let those fall unaided who still stood in arms between Spain and the domination of western Europe. So in August 1585 by the treaty of Nonsuch she took the Dutch into her protection and promised to maintain forces, numbering in all some 7,000 men, to assist in their defence. She perhaps regarded this as merely another way of increasing pressure upon Philip II to restore his Netherlands provinces to the home-ruling and ungarrisoned status they had enjoyed under Charles V and to grant them some measure of religious toleration. But to Philip it was an act of open war and, although neither he nor Elizabeth ever formally declared war upon each other, his direct response was to launch his 'Invincible' Armada against England.

The English navy's victory in 1588 warded off that danger and the successful defence of Bergen-op-Zoom, largely by English troops, later that autumn prevented the Spanish land forces under the Duke of Parma from winning any decisive advantage against the Dutch. But 1589 brought a new crisis. At the end of 1588 the French King Henry III had the League's leaders, the Duke and Cardinal of Guise, assassinated. In April 1589 he joined forces with Henry of Navarre and the Huguenots and together they brought the League to the verge of dissolution. Henry III's own assassination in July averted that. But it also brought the Huguenot Henry of Navarre to the French throne. If he were allowed to establish himself against the League, his next move would almost certainly be to turn upon the League's Spanish paymaster. The position of Spain's main army in the Netherlands, caught between French and Dutch, might then well become desperate. So, although it meant abandoning the initiative against the Dutch, Philip had to intervene openly and militarily in France. He sent his troops from the Netherlands in 1590 to rescue Paris and again in 1592 to save Rouen. The price he demanded for his help was no less than the crown of France for his elder daughter, the Infanta Clara Eugenia. The years from Henry IV's accession in 1589 to his conversion to Catholicism in 1593, which cut the ground from under the League and the Spaniards, therefore brought the struggle for western Europe to the very peak of its intensity. And the storm centre of that struggle was in France.

But it was not only in France that the struggle was now at its fiercest. The Dutch sought with rapidly growing energy to take advantage of the French distractions of their Spanish enemy to work themselves into an almost impregnable position by clearing the north-eastern provinces up to the German border and by seizing the fortress towns along the great rivers that guarded their southern frontiers. Here English troops again played a significant part, while at the same time English assistance to Henry IV of France in both men and money swelled to its maximum. Nor was this all. At sea, too, the war, though largely a matter of privateering, grew to a new intensity. Moreover, after the failure of Drake and Norris in 1589 to complete the destruction of the Armada, English efforts to hamper the rebuilding of Spain's oceanic sea power by stopping supplies of timber, naval stores, and indeed corn too, from the Baltic, brought increasingly strained relations with neutral Danes and Poles and the Germans of the Hanseatic Towns as well as with England's own allies the Dutch. At the opposite end of Europe, England's growing trade to the Mediterranean and the Levant encouraged attempts, prolonged but continuously unsuccessful, to draw the Sultan of Turkey and the 'Emperor' of Morocco into hostilities against Spain.

All these, however, were side-shows. All of them were secondary to the great central struggle in northern France, in Picardy, Normandy, and Brittany, the French provinces where the League was strongest and that were most readily accessible to Spain's army from the Netherlands. Those were also the provinces whose coasts could be, in hostile hands, most menacing to England. It was to defend those provinces and to draw Henry IV and his army to stay in them or near them that England made its greatest effort in the continental side of the war against Spain. During those crucial years that continental war, and not the war at sea, was the centrepiece of the story and it is the hope of this book to show it in something like its proper perspective.

The idea of a book of this sort has, I suppose, been more or less in my mind ever since I was appointed editor of the Public Record Office *Calendar of State Papers, Foreign series* fifty years ago. It would therefore be a quite impossible task to enumerate all those to whose writings, counsel, and kindness I have become so heavily indebted during those years. It would also be invidious to name a few where I owe so much to so many. But my gratitude is assuredly no less sincere for not being particularized. I can only wish that the shortcomings of the book may be forgiven by those who over the years have contributed so much to its making.

Hill Head                                              R. B. WERNHAM

# Acknowledgements

The author is indebted to the Controller of Her Majesty's Stationery Office for permission to reprint Crown copyright material from the Public Record Office, and the *Calendars of State Papers, Foreign series*, volumes XXII and XXIII and to reproduce the plan of Fort Crozon; also to Messrs Longman and the Editors of the *English Historical Review* for material from his two articles in volume LXVI, 1–26, 194–218 on 'The Portugal Expedition of 1589'.

## Dating

Dates are given in Old Style unless otherwise indicated.

# Contents

# Maps

# Abbreviations

| | |
|---|---|
| *Acts P. C.* | *Acts of the Privy Council of England,* new series, ed. J. R. Dasent, vols. XVI to XXIV (1897–1901). |
| *Armada Papers* | *State Papers relating to the Defeat of the Spanish Armada, anno 1588,* ed. J. K. Laughton, Navy Records Society, 2 vols. (1895). |
| Aubigné | T. A. d'Aubigné, *Histoire universelle,* VIII, 1588–93, ed. A. de Ruble (1895). |
| Birch, *Memoirs* | Birch, Thomas, *Memoirs of the Reign of Queen Elizabeth from the year 1581 till her death, from the original papers of . . . Antony Bacon,* 2 vols. (1754). |
| Bor | Bor, Pieter, *Oorspronck, begin, en verfolgh der Nederlandsche Oorloghen,* 6 vols. (Amsterdam, 1595–1601). |
| *Cal. S. P. Domestic* | *Calendars of State Papers, Domestic series, of the Reign of Elizabeth, preserved in the Public Record Office,* II, 1581–90, ed. R. Lemon (1865); III, 1591–4, and IV, 1595–7, ed. Mrs. M. A. Everett Green (1867, 1869). |
| *Cal. S. P. Domestic, Addenda* | *Calendars of State Papers, Domestic series, of the Reigns of Elizabeth and James I, Addenda, 1580–1625, preserved in the Public Record Office,* ed. Mrs. M. A. Everett Green (1872). |
| *Cal. S. P. Foreign* | *Calendars of State Papers, Foreign series, of the Reign of Elizabeth, preserved in the Public Record Office,* XXI, ed. Mrs. S. C. Lomas and A. B. Hinds; XXII and XXIII, ed. R. B. Wernham (1936, 1950). |

Cal. S. P. Irish

*Calendars of State Papers relating to Ireland, of the Reigns of Henry VIII, Edward VI, Mary, and Elizabeth, preserved in the Public Record Office,* IV and V, ed. H. C. Hamilton (1885, 1890).

Cal. S. P. Scottish

*Calendars of State Papers relating to Scotland and Mary, Queen of Scots, 1547–1603, preserved in the Public Record Office, British Museum, and elsewhere,* X, 1589–93, ed. W. K. Boyd and H. W. Meikle (1936); XI, 1593–5, ed. Miss A. I. Cameron (1936).

Cal. S. P. Spanish

*Calendars of Letters and State Papers relating to English Affairs, preserved in or originally belonging to the Archives of Simancas; Elizabeth,* IV, 1587–1603, , ed. M. A. S. Hume (1899).

Cal. S. P. Venetian

*Calendars of State Papers and Manuscripts relating to English Affairs existing in the Archives and Collections of Venice and in other Libraries of Northern Italy,* VIII, 1581–91, and IX, 1592–1603, ed. H. F. Brown (1894, 1897).

Camden

Camden, William, *Annales rerum Anglicarum et Hibernicarum regnante Elizabetha* (Leyden, 1625).

Cary, *Memoirs*

*Memoirs of Robert Cary Earl of Monmouth,* ed. G. H. Powell, King's Classics (1905).

Cayet

Cayet, Palma, *Chronologie Novenaire,* in *Collection complète des Mémoires relatifs à l'Histoire de France,* ed. M. Petitot, XXXIX, XL, XLI (1824).

Collins

*Letters and Memorials of State in the Reigns of Queen Mary, Queen Elizabeth, [etc.], written and collected by Sir Henry Sidney [etc.],* ed. A. Collins, 2 vols. (1746).

| | |
|---|---|
| Coningsby | Coningsby, Sir Thomas, *Journal of the Siege of Rouen 1591*, ed. J. G. Nicholls, in *The Camden Miscellany*, I (1847). |
| *Correspondance de Philippe II* | *Correspondance de Philippe II sur les Affaires des Pays Bas (Deuxième Partie)*, II and III, ed. J. Lefèvre, Académie Royale de Belgique: Commission Royale d'Histoire (1956, 1960). |
| Davila | Davila, H. C., *The History of the Civil Wars of France* (translated from the Italian, 1678). |
| Devereux | Devereux, W. B., *Lives and Letters of the Devereux, Earls of Essex, in the Reigns of Elizabeth, James I, and Charles I, 1540–1646*, I (1853). |
| *Edmondes Papers* | *The Edmondes Papers*, ed. G. G. Butler, Roxburghe Club (1913). |
| *English Privateering Voyages* | *English Privateering Voyages to the West Indies 1588–95*, ed. K. R. Andrews, Hakluyt Society, 2nd series, CXI (1959). |
| *Further Voyages* | *Further English Voyages to Spanish America 1583–94*, ed. I. A. Wright, Hakluyt Society, 2nd series, XCIX (1951). |
| Hakluyt | Hakluyt, R., *The Principal Navigations, Voyages, Traffiques, and Discoveries of the English Nation made by sea or overland ... these 1600 years*, 8 vols. (Dent, 1927). |
| H.M.C. | Historical Manuscripts Commission. |
| *Kronijk* | Utrecht Historisch Genootschap, *Kronijk*, vols. XVI to XX (1860–4). |
| *L. and A.* | *List and Analysis of State Papers, Foreign series, Elizabeth I, preserved in the Public Record Office*, I, II, III, ed. R. B. Wernham (1964, 1969, 1980). |
| L'Estoile | *Journal de L'Estoile pour le Règne de Henri IV*, I, ed. L-R. Lefèvre (Gallimard, 1948). |

| | |
|---|---|
| *Lettres Missives* | *Recueil des Lettres Missives de Henri IV*, III and IV, ed. J. Berger de Xivrey and J. Gaudet (1843–) |
| *Mémoires de la Ligue* | Goulart, S., *Mémoires de la Ligue*, 6 vols. (1758). |
| Meteren | Meteren, E. van, *Histoire des Pays Bas* (French translation from Dutch; The Hague, 1618). |
| *Monson's Tracts* | *The Naval Tracts of Sir William Monson*, ed. M. Oppenheim, Navy Records Society, 2 vols. (1902). |
| Moreau | *Mémoires du Chanoine Jean Moreau sur les Guerres de la Ligue en Bretagne*, ed. H. Waquet, Société d'Histoire et d'Archéologie de Bretagne (1960). |
| Murdin | *A Collection of State Papers relating to Affairs in the Reign of Queen Elizabeth from the Year 1571 to 1596 ... left by William Cecil, Lord Burghley*, ed. W. Murdin (1759). |
| Purchas | Purchas, S., *Hakluytus Posthumus or Purchas his Pilgrims*, 20 vols. (Glasgow, 1906). |
| *Resolutiën der Staten Generaal* | *Resolutiën der Staten Generaal*, VI, VII, VIII, ed. N. Japikse, Rijks Geschiedkundige Publicatiën (1922–5). |
| Rymer, *Foedera, etc.* | *Foedera, Conventiones, Litterae, et cujuscunque generis acta publica [etc.]*, ed. T. Rymer, VII.i (The Hague, 1742). |
| S.P. | State Papers. |
| Thou | Thou, J-A. de, *Histoire universelle depuis 1543 jusqu'en 1607*, XI, XII (French translation from Latin, London, 1734). |
| *Unton Correspondence* | *Correspondence of Sir Henry Unton, Knt., ambassador from Queen Elizabeth to Henry IV, King of France, in the Years MDXCI and MDXCII*, ed. J. Stevenson, Roxburghe Club (1847). |

| | |
|---|---|
| Valdory | Valdory, G., *Discours du Siège de la Ville de Rouen*, ed. E. Gosselin (1871). |
| Verdugo | Verdugo, F., *Commentario de la guerra de Frisa*, ed. H. Lonchay, Académie Royale de Belgique, Commission Royale d'Histoire (1899). |
| Villeroy | *Mémoires d'Estat par Monsieur de Villeroy*, in *Collection complète des Mémoires relatifs à l'Histoire de France*, ed. M. Petitot, XLIV (1824). |

# I

## After the Armada

It was blowing a gale in Dover Roads on the morning of 27 August 1588 and aboard his flagship, the *Ark Royal,* Lord Admiral Howard was in an unusually testy mood. There were, indeed, reasons enough for his testiness, but perhaps the last straw that had snapped his temper was a letter which had arrived overnight from the Queen's Principal Secretary, Sir Francis Walsingham. That letter required Howard to consult secretly with his second-in-command, Sir Francis Drake, about 'the desire Her Majesty had for the intercepting of the King [of Spain]'s treasure from the Indies'.[1]

Now, ordinarily Howard would have gone off to intercept the King of Spain's treasure willingly enough, and Drake more willingly still. After all, it would have been a logical sequel to their recent operations. For it was only a month, or less, since they had 'shuffled' the great Armada of Spain through the Channel, had battered it on 29 July off Gravelines until their own powder and shot ran out, and had then shepherded it northwards until by 2 August it was safely past the Firth of Forth.[2] A couple of days before, on 25 August, they had at last received positive and reliable news that it was to the west of the Orkneys, well past the point of no return and straggling homewards along the back side of Scotland and Ireland.[3] Eight of its fighting ships, they knew, had been sunk or captured in the Channel and Narrow Seas. In this exceptionally rough summer others would hardly avoid shipwreck upon the jagged Atlantic coasts of Scotland and Ireland. Those that did struggle home would long be useless for further service.

[1] *Armada Papers,* II, 167.

[2] The best recent accounts are G. Mattingly, *The Defeat of the Spanish Armada* (1959) and M. Lewis, *The Spanish Armada* (1960). See also I. A. A. Thompson, on the Armada's guns in *Mariner's Mirror,* LXI (1975), 355–71.

[3] *Armada Papers,* II, 137, 150 (where 'young Norris' should read 'young Harris', namely 'young Harris that was sent after the enemy's fleet' – S. P. Domestic, ccxv, no. 47; *Cal. S. P. Foreign,* XXII, 116, 133).

Howard and Drake, therefore, could reasonably reckon that they had deprived the King of Spain of his ocean-going navy at least for months to come. If they could also have caught the homeward-bound treasure ships at the Azores or off the Spanish coast and so have deprived Philip II of his share of the year's silver from the American mines, surely (as Howard himself said) 'that blow, after this he hath, would make him safe'. For the New World was by now the only part of Philip's dominions that regularly produced a revenue handsomely in excess of its local expenditure. He was thus becoming more and more dependent upon this surplus of American silver to equip his navies in Spain and to pay his army in the Netherlands, to keep up his garrisons in Italy, and to subsidize his allies, the rebel Catholic League, in France. Without his ocean-going navy he could hardly attack England; without his American silver he might even have to bow to England's terms.

It did, however, seem to Howard that the landsmen of the Queen's Council, or whoever it was who had put the notion into Her Majesty's head at this time, had very little idea of 'what must be done for such a journey'. For, he went on with mounting sarcasm, 'this is not as if a man should send but over to the coast of France, I do assure you . . . Belike it is thought the Islands be but hereby; it is not thought how the year is spent.'[4]

This irritation may have been, in part, no more than the prickly lassitude that often follows after high endeavour. Howard, it is true, still looked hale and vigorous enough, still had in fact thirty-eight years of life left in him. Nevertheless, he was fifty-two, an age at which in the sixteenth century friends would begin to hint at comparisons with Nestor. Moreover, the past eight months had been peculiarly hard and testing and even now he was getting 'little rest day or night'.[5] And besides being thoroughly weary, he was also a rather disappointed man.

So, indeed, were most of the English sailors. Most of them were at least as irritable as the Lord Admiral and for much the

---

[4] *Armada Papers*, II, 167.
[5] Ibid., p. 168.

same reasons. Sir John Hawkins, the treasurer of the navy, was
snapping back at poor old Lord Treasurer Burghley, who was
himself at his wits' end to scrape up money to pay off the
crews. Sir Martin Frobisher was offering to fight Drake and
Lord Edward Seymour, his wrist sore from hauling on a rope,
was refusing to serve again under him.[6] Part of the trouble was
that all were a little dispirited, and more than a little surprised, at their failure to destroy the Armada in battle. Some
tried to persuade themselves that 'our parsimony at home
hath bereaved us of the famousest victory that ever our navy
might have had at sea'.[7] But most knew in their hearts that it
was the Spaniards' defensive strength and their own tactics
and gunnery that had been to blame, at least until the final
and short-range action off Gravelines – 'so much powder and
shot spent, and so long time in fight, and in comparison thereof so little harm', as master-gunner William Thomas put it.[8]

Further, now that the action was over, reaction was setting
in. These men had been at sea since March; some of them, on
and off, since Christmas. They had endured an unusually
tempestuous summer and the gale was still making it hard
work getting their victuals aboard and their sick men ashore.
They were in addition facing the anticlimax of demobilizing
the splendid fleet in which they had served with a common
purpose that had stilled for the time all personal jealousies
and grudges. Demobilization was work little less demanding
and infinitely more depressing. It was made all the more
depressing by the disease that was raging through the crews.
Over a fortnight before Howard had written that 'it would
grieve any man's heart to see them that have served so
valiantly to die so miserably.' His concern then had been
chiefly with the *Elizabeth Jonas*. She had

had a great infection in her from the beginning, so as of the 500 men
which she carried out, by the time we had been in Plymouth three
weeks or a month there were dead of them 200 and above; so as I was
driven to set all the rest of her men ashore, to take out her ballast,

---

[6] Ibid., pp. 102–4, 108, 175–6, 213–4. 'I do find my Lord [Admiral] and his
company divided in manner to factions', Seymour wrote to Walsingham on
23 August – ibid., p. 146.

[7] Ibid., p. 65.

[8] Ibid., p. 259.

and to make fires in her of wet broom three or four days together;
and so hoped thereby to have cleansed her of her infection; and
thereupon got new men, very tall and able as ever I saw, and put
them into her. Now the infection is broken out in greater extremity
than ever ... so am I driven to force to send her to Chatham.

That was over a fortnight before and Howard had feared
even then that

the like infection will grow throughout the most part of our fleet; for
they have been so long at sea and have so little shift of apparel and
so [few] places to provide them of such wants and no money
wherewith to buy it, for some have been – yea, the most part – these
eight months at sea.[9]

He had proved all too good a prophet. By 22 August he was
writing that 'many of our ships are so weakly manned that
they have not mariners to weigh their anchors'. Nor were
replacements easy to come by, for the supply of experienced
mariners was limited. Demobilization, indeed, had come none
too soon to avert 'the unfurnishing of the realm of such
needful and most necessary men in a commonwealth'.[10]
However, the main obstacle to an immediate raid upon the
King of Spain's treasure from the Indies lay less in the health
or spirit of the English sailors than in the condition of the
English ships. They were, as Hawkins was to confirm a week
later, 'utterly unfitted and unmeet to follow any enterprise
from hence without a thorough new trimming, refreshing, and
new furnishing with provisions, grounding, and fresh men'.[11]
It might be that the defeat of the Armada meant that Spain
no longer had an Atlantic fleet in being. It might be, too, that
the treasure ships had lost their customary escort, since the ten
galleons of the Indian Guard had been pressed into service
with the Armada and were sharing its fate. The raid therefore
would not require the whole, or even a great part, of the
Queen's navy. Probably, as Hawkins had maintained before
he encountered the power of the Armada,[12] half a dozen
royal warships, with the privateers and merchantmen

---

[9] On 10 August – ibid., pp. 96–7.
[10] Ibid., pp. 141, 145.
[11] Ibid., pp. 212–14.
[12] Ibid., I, pp. 358–62.

they would draw after them, would now be an adequate force.

The difficulty was to find even half a dozen royal warships fit to go on the long voyage to the Azores in this tail-end of a stormy summer. All of them, and the privateers and merchantmen too, had grown 'foul and unsavoury' after six, or more often eight, months' continuous sea service. All needed cleansing and fumigating if they were not to breed diseases rapidly among their crews. And, as Howard well knew from the example of the *Elizabeth Jonas,* the cleansing must needs be thorough. Moreover, besides being clean enough internally to keep their crews tolerably healthy, the ships needed also to be clean and sound externally if they were to outsail their enemies and defy the weather. Of the Queen's ships, only a few and those mostly the smaller ones – the *White Bear, Hope, Bonaventure, Mary Rose, Bull,* and the little *Achates* – had leaks and decays serious enough to need long and extensive overhaul in dry dock. But after so many months at sea, every one of them had seams that needed caulking and bottoms that had become thickly encrusted with barnacles and weed. They all needed to be careened, grounded upon a sandy shore and at low tide laid first on one side and then on the other for scraping and tallowing. Most of them also had more or less worn ropes and cables, yards and tackle, some of which needed replacing and all of which needed inspecting; while a number had lost their long boats and half a dozen needed new mainmasts.[13]

For all these reasons this was hardly a moment when the Lord Admiral welcomed suggestions, even from Her Majesty, about sailing off into the Atlantic to intercept the King of Spain's treasure. Accordingly, he at once sent Sir Francis Drake, 'although he be not very well, to inform you rightly of all'. In particular he was to explain that they could not find 'any ships here in the fleet any ways able to go such a voyage before they have been aground, which cannot be done in any place but at Chatham, and now that this spring [tide] is so far past it will be fourteen days before they can be grounded.'[14]

Fourteen days before they could be grounded; certainly

[13] Ibid., II, pp. 161, 241–54.
[14] Ibid., p. 167.

another week or two to careen and cleanse, repair and replenish; add the time required to sail to the Azores and it would be October – with that year's rough weather, probably well into October – before they could get there. By then the treasure ships would already be safe home in Cadiz if they kept to anything like their normal sailing schedule.[15]

The information that Drake brought to court thus, to all intents and purposes, ruled out any attempt that year to intercept the King of Spain's treasure from America. It also goes some way towards explaining why no attempt was made to send a force down Channel to intercept the Armada as it limped across the home stretch between Ireland and Spain. Burghley had seen the desirability of this. Over a fortnight earlier, on 9 August, he had written to Walsingham:

I am not of opinion that the Spanish fleet will suddenly return from the north or the east, being weakened as they are, and knowing that our navy is returned to our coast where they may repair their lacks and be as strong as they were afore. And without a north or east wind the Spanish fleet cannot come back to England. I wish, if they pass about Ireland, that four good ships, well manned and conducted, might follow them to their ports, where they might distress a great number of them, being weatherbeaten and where the numbers of the gallants will not continue on shipboard.

Walsingham had answered, rather unenthusiastically, that 'if it had been thought of in time, they might have been very well employed, but I fear it will now be too late'.[16] So far as catching the survivors of the Armada went, on 9 August it would not have been too late, for another five weeks were to pass before the first of them staggered home, barely able to navigate, let alone defend themselves.[17] Now, possibly in those

---

[15] In fact, although one ship of the 'Peruvian' fleet reached Spain before 27 September, the arrival of the rest was not reported in Madrid until 22 October and even then the Mexican squadron was not yet in – *Cal. S. P. Venetian*, VIII, 398, 409. This, however, was unusually late. In 1587 the whole American fleet, despite delays by storms, was in San Lucar by 27 September, ibid., pp. 308, 312–13. A Dutch flyboat that arrived at Emden on 31 July 1588 had reported that when it left Lisbon on 30 May the American fleet was daily expected – *Cal. S. P. Foreign*, XXII, 156–7.

[16] *Armada Papers*, II, 82, 85.

[17] Cp. Edmund Palmer to Walsingham, from St Jean-de-Luz, 19/29 September – *Cal. S. P. Domestic, Addenda*, pp. 254–5.

five weeks Burghley's four good ships could not have been found or could not have been brought to their station on the coast of Spain. It is true that when the first news came of Spanish ships wrecked on the west coast of Ireland and of Catholic Spaniards roaming loose among the Catholic 'Wild Irish', instructions were given to Sir Walter Raleigh to take three of the Queen's ships and some hastily levied troops to deal with them.[18] That, however, was mid-September and, anyway, Raleigh never sailed. Nevertheless, it does seem a little curious that Burghley's suggestion aroused so little response; that even sailors like Howard and Drake, who a few months earlier had been so eager to encounter the Spanish fleet as it came out of port in all its strength, should now have shown no interest at all in catching it as it returned to port in all its weakness.

This curious lack of interest should remind us of something that historians, particularly naval historians, have sometimes been liable to forget – of how immature and casual naval strategic thinking was in those early days of ocean-going sailing navies. It should remind us also of something else that it is just as important to remember if we want to gain a true understanding of English strategy all through the long Elizabethan war with Spain. It should remind us of how earnestly the eyes of almost all Englishmen were fixed upon the Narrow Seas and, just beyond, upon the great Spanish land army under the Duke of Parma in the Netherlands. Sir John Hawkins might believe that the Queen should keep half a dozen of her ships always upon the coast of Spain and 'have as little to do in foreign countries as may be'. But Sir William Winter's view was by far the more common.

When I consider [he was to write in December 1588] that ships are subject to wind, weather, and other haps, it were not good, as I think, for to build our defence only upon them; for I speak of knowledge, as no person shall be able to prove against it, if the King of Spain had men sufficient at Sluys, Nieupoort, and Dunkirk, with

<hr/>

[18] For Raleigh – S. P. Domestic, ccxv, no. 64; ccxvi, no. 28; *Acts P. C.*, XVI, 280. 'Seeing the condition of the English ships and the terrible drain the campaign had already made on the sea-going population, there can be little question of the wisdom of making no attempt to intercept the perilous retreat' – Sir Julian Corbett, *Drake and the Tudor Navy* (2nd ed., 1899), II, 282.

reasonable shipping to transport them and their provision, the wind being at the north-east and so to the eastward, and Queen's Majesty having an army as great as that which Her Majesty had any time this year, riding, as they commonly do with the like winds, between Blackness [Gris Nez] and Boulogne, the King of Spain's army might be in the Thames and endanger the principal matter before knowledge could be given to our ships lying so upon the coast of France as aforesaid.[19]

Winter knew the North Sea and Narrow Seas. He had led the fleet up to the Firth of Forth through the December and January storms of 1559–60 and he had spent the summer of 1588 aboard the *Vanguard* watching Dunkirk. His opinion should warn us against ridiculing too easily the English fears of Parma's forces. They knew that the Duke had in the Flemish ports 'not above 18 mean ships of the common sort' – or was it 26? anyway, less than 30 – and a lot of flat-bottomed barges that could not face choppy water, let alone the concentration of fighting ships, Dutch as well as English, that was waiting for them outside. Seymour and Winter, and even more the Dutch Admiral Justinus of Nassau, were indeed licking their lips at the thought of catching such a prey out in the open sea. Parma himself had no illusions about it either. He had once, a couple of years before, dreamed of slipping across with his army while the English were not looking. That, however, was before the Queen's navy was mobilized. As things were, he relied upon the Armada to clear the way for him.[20]

Now we know that the action off Gravelines on 29 July had in fact ended any likelihood of the Armada ever commanding the Narrow Seas. But until definite news came on 25 August that it was homeward-bound west of the Orkneys, Howard and his fellows could not feel quite so certain. They had all been greatly impressed by the Spanish fleet's strength and by its capacity for taking punishment. 'I do warrant you, all the world never saw such a force as theirs was', Howard wrote, and he could hardly believe that its power was really broken or that the proud Spaniards would run so ignominiously for

---

[19] J. A. Williamson, *Sir John Hawkins* (1927 ed.), p. 451; *Armada Papers*, II, 311–12.
[20] *Cal. S. P. Foreign*, XXII, 35, 37; *Armada Papers*, II, 114–15, 120, 123, 147; *Correspondance de Philippe II*, III, 105–7.

home. The English sailors had seen it past the Firth of Forth.
They gave little credence, with the winds as they were, to the
rumours that it was reforming in the Moray Firth. Nevertheless, on the other side of the North Sea, though Hamburg and
Emden were reckoned too dangerous for so large a fleet and
such great ships, there were – in theory, at least – havens in
Denmark and southern Norway where it might pull itself
together for a renewed attempt against England.[21] No one,
perhaps, thought this very probable; but the possibility could
not quite be ignored, for as Winter wrote, 'the worst is to
be reckoned of'.[22] This entailed keeping powerful forces in
the southern part of the North Sea and the Straits of Dover.
And with some ships suffering from storm damage and
with sickness beginning to rage in many more, such a
concentration left few warships to spare for operations out in
the Atlantic.

Moreover, even if the Armada did not return, the English
found it hard to rid themselves of concern about what Parma
might do on his own. He had 'powers of intellectual analysis
and organization which lifted the art of war to a level which
the sixteenth century saw but rarely'.[23] The English had
witnessed the effects of those powers at Antwerp in 1585 and
at Sluys in 1587. They were well aware that the Duke was 'a
soldier and will seek all means to deceive' and their respect for
his ability bred a genuine fear that some of his tricks might
succeed. Robert Cecil even suspected that the Armada might
have sailed north to draw the English forces away and give
Parma a chance to make his crossing. Young Cecil was
perhaps as yet no great judge. But Walsingham, too, suspected
that the rumours that Parma was about to turn his army
against the Dutch were a trick to draw the English and Dutch
ships over to Zeeland and give the Duke a chance to slip across

[21] *Armada Papers*, II, 13, 40, 45, 54, 59, 84, 119–20, 123.
[22] Ibid., p. 13. Howard seems to have taken the possibility fairly seriously – ibid.,
p. 92, and Drake was not entirely sure – ibid., pp. 68, 94: indeed on 10 August he was
almost convinced that the Armada must have gone to Denmark – ibid., pp. 97–9.
Sir Roger Williams was also sure that the Armada would refit and return –
S. P. Domestic, ccxv, no. 2.
[23] G. Mattingly, *The Defeat of the Spanish Armada*, p. 55. 'The sailors of those days had
a vast respect for soldiers, a sense of inferiority bred of centuries of subordination' –
Williamson, *Hawkins*, p. 436.

while westerly or southerly winds pinned them on that lee shore. It was, anyway, difficult to keep up a close blockade of Dunkirk and Nieupoort, where Parma's shipping lay. The prevailing winds, the tides, the shoals, and the sandbanks made a continuous watch almost impossible. Indeed, more than once that summer the blockading squadrons had been blown off their station and the exits left open. On the last occasion, with the wind at north-east, they had been left open enough for four small flyboats to creep out to Calais and then on to Spain along the French coast. Small though those flyboats were, their escape seemed to give substance to English fears.[24]

Nor were these merely the panic fears of ignorant landsmen. Winter shared them, as we have seen. So did Drake. 'The Prince of Parma,' he wrote on 10 August, 'I take him to be as a bear robbed of her whelps; and no doubt but, being so great a soldier as he is, that he will presently, if he may, undertake some great matter.' Drake was therefore most anxious for the English fleet to show itself off Dunkirk as soon as possible, 'so as their power may see us returned from the chase and ready to encounter them if they once sally'. A fortnight later, on 23 August, he was still urging that 'we ought much more to have regard unto the Duke of Parma and his soldiers than to the Duke of Sidonia and his ships ... The Duke of Parma should be vigilantly looked upon for these 20 days, although the army of Spain return not this way.'

Apparently what Drake feared was that Parma might land near Lydd, in the estuary of the Rother on a 'half island' of shingle close to the thinly peopled Romney marsh, and then be supplied with victuals and all necessaries by the Leaguers from the French Channel ports that lay upwind of the main English fleet.[25] Rumours of great preparations of men and

---

[24] *Cal. S. P. Foreign*, XXII, 42, 82, 162, 171–2; S. P. Domestic, ccxiii, no. 66; *Armada Papers*, II, 45, 83, 120, 124, 174. In March 1589 Sir Roger Williams wrote of the danger that Spanish galleys, holding the Flemish ports and Le Havre, might slip across in a calm before the English could catch them, and land 30,000 men who would soon be masters of the field and then be in no need of victuals – Lansdowne MSS, lviii, no. 69.

[25] *Armada Papers*, II, 93–4, 99–100, 148. In view of Drake's letter, Laughton's difficulty (ibid., p. 93 note) in believing that he still feared any such landing, seems based more upon some preconceived notion of Drake's genius than upon the evidence of his own words.

shipping at Dieppe and Le Havre gave this some appearance of credibility, with the result, as Howard saw it, that 'we must divide ourselves into parts to prevent all dangers'.[26] With a good many ships, by Howard's own account, already not able to sail for want of crews, such a dividing into parts must have made it even less easy to find forces for operations out in the Atlantic. And these anxieties, which so concentrated English attention upon the Narrow Seas, did not die away until Parma allowed the high spring tides of late August to pass unused; not really, indeed, until he moved off from Dunkirk and Nieupoort to besiege Bergen-op-Zoom early in September.

So almost the whole month of August had been allowed to slip past and now, from the report that Drake took to court on 27 August, it was clear that very little could be done before, at the earliest, October. But by October it would, in all probability, be too late to catch the silver ships from America; it would be, in all certainty, too late to intercept the Armada's survivors as they returned to port. It would anyway be too late for any serious operations at all off the coast of Spain or in the eastern Atlantic. For in those waters the months from October to February were then regarded, by Englishmen and Spaniards alike, as in effect a close season for organized naval warfare.[27] To do nothing now in the early autumn meant, therefore, delaying at least until the early spring of 1589 any English reply to the Spanish Armada of 1588.

This point can hardly have escaped notice in the discussions between Privy Councillors and 'men of war' that followed Drake's coming to court on 27 August. Unfortunately we know next to nothing about those discussions. It is not even clear who took part in them. Burghley and Drake obviously did, and probably Walsingham. Howard, too, when he followed Drake to court on 1 September, could hardly have been left out. Lord Henry Seymour, Lord Thomas Howard, and Lord Sheffield came up with him, but perhaps they came only to court and not to conference, though the latter two had been members of the Lord Admiral's inner council of war

---

[26] Ibid., p. 92.
[27] Cp., e.g., Mattingly, *Defeat of the Spanish Armada*, p. 177; Corbett, *Drake and the Tudor Navy*, II, 115; and Santa Cruz's views in *Cal. S. P. Venetian*, VIII, 321.

during the Armada campaign.[28] Another who was certainly brought into the discussions at an early stage was Sir John Norris, England's best-known and most experienced soldier, who had served long in the Netherlands and Ireland and had been recently chief of staff to the Earl of Leicester in the army gathered at Tilbury. Of the sailors, Hawkins, Winter, Frobisher, and Sir Henry Palmer were left behind at Dover to deal with the remaining stages of demobilizing the fleet and arranging the 'winter guard' for the Narrow Seas – eight or nine of the Queen's ships under Palmer and Frobisher. Hawkins did write to Walsingham urging again his idea of a purely naval 'silver blockade', but as he was still down at Queenborough on 12 September, he can have taken no other direct part in the discussions. As treasurer of the navy, of course, he had more than enough work on his hands paying off the fleet and settling up the accounts for the long Armada campaign.[29] Nevertheless it is at first sight a little surprising that the man who had the longest and most persuasively advocated the intercepting of the King of Spain's treasure from the Indies, should now be left almost unconsulted.

The fact was, however, that after the news which Drake brought to court and the waiting until the spring that it implied, the intercepting of the King's treasure was no longer the first or most urgent objective. Someone – in view of his letter to Walsingham on 9 August, Burghley looks the most likely person – must have insisted and, as we shall see, have convinced the Queen, that the primary objective should now be, not the silver ships out in the Atlantic, but such survivors of the Armada as managed to get back to their home ports. The reasons are obvious enough. Once the annual consignment of American silver for 1588 was safely in Spain, it would be another twelve months before any more was sent across the Atlantic. If the English waited that long before following up their success against the Armada, they would forfeit most of the fruits of their victory. For in twelve months Philip II would have time to repair and make again battleworthy a substantial number of such ships as the Duke of Medina Sidonia managed to shepherd home past Scotland and

[28] *Armada Papers*, II, 185; Williamson, *Hawkins*, p. 428.
[29] *Armada Papers*, II, 184-5, 213-14, 229-30.

Ireland. He might even have time to reinforce them with other galleons newly built in the dockyards of Portugal and northern Spain. By the late summer of 1589, in other words, when the next shipments of American bullion were to be expected, he might well have an Atlantic fleet in being once again; not, indeed, one powerful enough to try another descent upon England, but sufficient to escort the silver ships and even to threaten Ireland. England could then hardly risk leaving her home waters unguarded by sending the bulk of her navy to catch the treasure ships in the Atlantic. Yet to send anything less might well be to send a force not strong enough to face the treasure ships' escort.

It was important therefore that something should be attempted, as soon as the winter 'close season' was over, to prevent the rebuilding of Spanish sea power. By early spring it would still not be too late to go for the Armada's survivors in their home ports, for few of them were likely to be made battleworthy, or even seaworthy, as soon as that. Nevertheless, cutting them out would be a considerably more difficult job by the spring of 1589. It would no longer be just a matter of following defenceless and weatherbeaten 'lame ducks' into ill-prepared and poorly defended harbours. By then the Spaniards would have had time to put their coastal and harbour defences in order and, maybe, to get some of their ships sufficiently manned and reconditioned to add their broadsides to the fire of the shore batteries. Moreover, the natural expectation was that most of the Armada's survivors would make for Lisbon, the main base of Spain's Atlantic naval forces. Now, even Drake never fancied taking his ships unaided up the tricky waters of the Tagus, through the shore defences guarding the narrows on the way into Lisbon.[30] He had shied off it in 1587, when he had not hesitated to sail boldly into Cadiz and when the Spaniards in Lisbon had been hardly more prepared to repel him than they were likely to be in 1589. To destroy Spain's naval forces in the Tagus was not, in short, a suitable operation for ships to attempt on their own. If it was not to be suicidally risky, it required the help of a land force to ease the ships past the shore defences.

---

[30] See the description in Mattingly, *Defeat of the Spanish Armada*, p. 114.

The early association of so distinguished a soldier as Sir John Norris with Drake in command of the enterprise showed that just such a combined operation was now contemplated and that its military component was to be something more than a mere landing party. Again, as we do not know precisely when that association began, this does not help a great deal in tracing the course of the discussions. We do know, however, that as early as 10 September a letter was drafted[31] in which the Queen informed the Sultan of Morocco of her intention to restore the pretender Don Antonio to the throne of Portugal from which he had been driven when the Duke of Alba had conquered the country for Philip II in 1580. Of course, what the Queen wrote to the Sultan of Morocco may have been meant to lure him into open support of Don Antonio rather than to commit her to any action of her own part. None the less, it does look as if by 10 September, at the latest, her original desire to intercept the King of Spain's treasure from the Indies had yielded pride of place to the idea of an amphibious attack upon the main centre of Spain's Atlantic sea power at Lisbon, an attack to be made in sufficient force by land to test the chances of wresting the whole kingdom of Portugal from the Spaniards.

This did not mean, however, that all thought of the treasure ships was now abandoned. They were far too tempting a prize to be so easily forgotten, especially given the impoverished condition of the English Exchequer. For during the past three years of mainly defensive warfare against Spain, the Queen had paid out £400,000 in aiding the insurgent United Provinces to keep the Spanish army in the Netherlands at bay and away from the major seaports there. She had wasted £31,000 on a German levy which had signally failed to bring any real help to Henry of Navarre and the Huguenots against Spain's French allies, the Catholic League. The naval preparations and actions against the Armada had cost her, according to F. C. Dietz's figures, £265,000, quite apart from what her subjects had spent on the musters and in ship money, which might well come to not far short of as much again. The money issued from the Exchequer in the year ending at

[31] E. P. Cheyney, *History of England from the Defeat of the Armada to the Death of Elizabeth*, I, 157.

Michaelmas 1588 totalled well over £400,000, as compared
with an annual average of £167,754 during the last three
years of peace (1582–5).[32]

To meet these extraordinary expenditures, in the three
years of war about £217,000 had come in from direct taxes
granted by Parliament; £30,000 had recently been borrowed
from the City of London; and some £244,000 had been drawn
from the accumulated savings of £299,000 with which the
Exchequer had entered the war.[33] Something more had been
contributed from the ordinary revenues of the Crown; but the
amount must have been limited, for the ordinary revenues did
not greatly exceed £200,000 a year and they had to answer all
the ordinary expenses of government. By comparison, the
cargoes of the treasure fleets looked like wealth beyond
counting. For at this date the annual shipments of bullion, for
the King and on private account, from America to Spain
might be worth, in Elizabethan English money, anything up
to £3,000,000 sterling.[34] It is easy to appreciate how alluring a
prize it seemed to the Queen and her subjects. To destroy the
surviving galleons of the Armada might now be the first
objective, but the silver fleet remained still by far the strongest
attraction.

Thus, when on 20 September Burghley noted down the
proposals as finally formulated,[35] three objectives were named:
'(1) to attempt to burn the ships in Lisbon and Seville; (2) to
take Lisbon; (3) to take the Islands' – and of course, having
Lisbon and the Azores, the English would be ideally placed to
take the silver fleets as well.

This threefold plan has generally been credited to Drake.
One historian regards it as further proof not only of Drake's
precocious understanding of naval strategy but also of his now
taking 'complete possession of the war'. Another sees in it the
triumph of Drake's ideas over those of Hawkins supported by

---

[32] R. B. Wernham, *Before the Armada*, pp. 381, 390–2, 404; F. C. Dietz, *English Public Finance 1558–1641*, pp. 439–41. An abstract of Exchequer issues for the year ending at Michaelmas 1588 gives a total of at least £418,000 – S. P. Domestic, ccxviii, no. 52; F. C. Dietz, *Exchequer under Elizabeth*, p. 101, puts them at £420,300.

[33] These are Dietz's figures – *Exchequer under Elizabeth*, pp. 85–6, 100–1.

[34] The 1587 West Indies fleet brought 13 millions, or in Elizabethan English values £3,500,000 sterling – *Monson's Tracts*, I, 144 note.

[35] S. P. Domestic, ccxvi, no. 33.

Howard and the source of an unhappy estrangement between the Lord Admiral and his recent second-in-command.[36] Now it is true that as long ago as 1581 Drake and Don Antonio had planned an expedition to seize and hold the Azores, though Elizabeth had vetoed the project. But Hawkins himself, in 1584, had suggested organizing a privateering war under Don Antonio's flag. In more recent months others, too, had turned their thoughts to the Portuguese pretender. In February 1588 the Privy Council had considered sending him to Portugal to stir a revolt which might hamper the Armada's preparations. In July Howard had toyed with the idea of using him to raise the country after the Armada had sailed. A little earlier Leicester had helped him to open negotiations through Henry Roberts, the Barbary Company's agent, with Muhammadan Morocco for a loan and a military alliance. Elizabeth's letter of 10 September to the Sultan was written in support of a mission to Morocco by Don Antonio's younger son, Don Cristobal, which was a direct follow-up of those earlier negotiations.[37] Moreover, the earliest dated paper connected with the proposals for the 1589 expedition, was endorsed by Burghley as '19 September 1588: Sir John Norris', with no mention of Drake; and Burghley's rough notes of 20 September were headed 'the notes of the charge of Sir John Norris's journey and Sir Francis Drake'.[38] None of this is conclusive; but taken all together, it does leave the impression that the design to burn the ships at Lisbon, take Lisbon, and then go on to the Azores, could just as probably have been the joint product of a committee of Privy Councillors and 'men of war' as the brain-child of some individual man of genius.

Whatever its parentage, however, it was obviously a very much more complex and ambitious plan than the Queen's first simple idea of a raid on the silver ships. Half a dozen of her warships might still be an adequate nucleus for the naval fighting force. But in the present state of the Queen's

---

[36] Corbett, *Drake and the Tudor Navy*, II, 294; Williamson, *Hawkins*, p. 450.

[37] J. A. Williamson, *Age of Drake*, pp. 212–4, 222; his *Hawkins* (1927 ed.), p. 409 and *Hawkins of Plymouth* (1949), p. 216; Cheyney, *History of England*, I, 156–7; Oppenheim, in *Monson's Tracts*, I, 57–8, 187–8; *Les Sources de l'Histoire de Maroc* (ed. Castries), I, 518–23.

[38] S. P. Domestic, ccxvi, nos. 32, 33.

Exchequer where was the money to come from to levy, equip, pay, and victual so large a land force, an army in fact? Where would the transports be found to carry so many troops? And where the money to hire them? Where, too, could be found the sizeable body of trained troops that was needed to form a reliable hard core to this army? It was against normal government policy to draft for foreign service the substantial citizens and yeomen who composed the trained bands of the city and the counties;[39] and as Parma was just beginning his siege of Bergen-op-Zoom, this was a curious time to think of drawing upon the 7,000 English troops maintained in the Netherlands to support the Dutch, as promised by the Anglo-Dutch treaty of 1585. Yet where else could the Queen find trained and seasoned soldiers in her own service? Trained and seasoned soldiers; transports to carry them; above all, money – how were these essential requirements to be answered in the penurious months after the long Armada campaign?

It was here that Norris and Drake came in. For, even though it looks as if the objectives and priorities of the proposed enterprise may have been settled in committee, it does also look as if it was Norris and Drake who suggested – perhaps were invited to suggest – the ways and means. They could appeal to the commercial ambitions and the military spirit, to the cupidity and the gambling instincts, of the Queen's subjects who, however much they might begrudge taxes and loans and payments for musters or ship money, were still ready to jump at the chance of becoming shareholders in a venture led by England's most distinguished soldier and the prince of privateers. Had not Drake brought home the rich East Indiaman, the *San Felipe,* a prize worth £114,000, even from his raid on Cadiz in 1587, when he had gone out to singe the King of Spain's beard more than to line his own pockets? Drake would draw in, if any man could, those gentry of the southern coastal counties who had long dabbled in privateering and those West Country and London merchants who had also begun to turn to privateering as the war closed down their Spanish trade.[40] From men such as these might come the armed merchantmen needed to reinforce the small nucleus of

[39] L. O. J. Boynton, *The Elizabethan Militia*, pp. 107–8.
[40] For this, see especially K. R. Andrews, *Elizabethan Privateering*.

royal warships; some of the transports needed for the troops; and a good deal of the money needed to float so considerable an enterprise. Even more money might be looked for from those leading City merchants who had long been trying to open ways to the Orient for English trade. Drake's dealings with the Sultan of Ternate in 1579, during his voyage round the world, had done much to focus their eyes upon him. His capture of the *San Felipe* in 1587 had done nothing to shift their gaze. If he could now restore Don Antonio to the Portuguese throne, they might indeed hope that this would settle 'a continual trade for us to the East Indies and the rest of the dominions of Portugal'.[41]

Drake could thus draw in the more adventuring merchants, the mariners, and the privateers. Norris, whose mother was close enough to the Queen to be honoured with a nickname, could attract the courtiers and the soldiering gentry, the Blunts, the Wingfields, the Sherleys, and the rest, so many of whom had served with him or under him in the Netherlands and Ireland. Moreover, in the Netherlands there were many old soldiers of all nationalities, who were lying idle owing to the inability of the Dutch States General to keep them in pay. No one could more easily than Norris recruit from these unemployed but seasoned warriors the trained soldiery that the expedition required. And no one could more hopefully approach the Hollanders and Zeelanders for the transports that could not be found or could not be spared in England.

In short, Norris and Drake between them could reasonably expect to attract the financial and other forms of support which the government, after its efforts and expenses of the past three years, could not provide quickly or on the scale required for an enterprise of this magnitude and moment. Norris and Drake could bring together the Queen, a group of her subjects, and her Dutch allies in a joint undertaking of a size that could not otherwise have been contemplated. Their original plan, it seems,[42] was that the Queen should give £20,000 and 'six of her second sort of ships' with their

. [41] *Monson's Tracts*, I, 178.
[42] S. P. Domestic, ccxvii, no. 79; this undated paper had been placed with the papers of October 1588, but it seems more probable that it was the first proposal or at least the first now extant.

munitions and three months' victuals for their crews. She was also asked to allow the use of two recently taken Spanish prizes, with their guns and tackling; and to supply ten siege guns and six field pieces for the army, besides twenty lasts of powder, 3,000 calivers, and tools for 1,000 pioneers. Norris and Drake further asked for a commission under the great seal, in general terms, 'for the defence of this realm'; and for permission to press 6,000 men in England, at their expense and without calling upon the counties to provide any weapons except swords and daggers. Besides this, they wanted authority to buy or freight shipping, press sailors, and take up grain, victuals, carriages, carts, and post-horses. They also asked the Queen to give free licence to any person of any quality whatsoever to volunteer for the intended service. They wanted her to set down an order for sharing out the profits of the expedition; and also to undertake to victual the entire force if it should be stayed above ten days by unfavourable weather and to bear the whole cost of it if it were countermanded by her order.

For their remaining needs, Norris and Drake proposed to ask the Dutch for leave to levy 2,000 to 3,000 'shot' (that is, troops equipped with firearms) in the Netherlands. They also wanted the Dutch to provide the transports for these troops as well as ten hulks to carry horses, six siege guns, and a good quantity of powder. The value of these contributions was reckoned to be about £10,000. From London and other English towns they hoped to obtain another twenty good ships of 150 tons and upwards, victualled and supplied like the Queen's six warships.

These first proposals were a little modified in the discussions that apparently followed upon their offer. Certain points were referred to the Queen herself for decision. Thus, she ruled that the commanders' commission was not to be in general terms, for the defence of the realm, as they had asked, but for 'some special service to be done' as had been 'resolved with you two by advice of our Council'.[43] She also appointed Norris himself to go to the Netherlands to arrange for the troops, shipping, arms, and munitions that they hoped to get from the Dutch.

---

[43] 'Certain Points to be resolved by Her Majesty' (undated) – S. P. Domestic, ccxvi, no. 15; Commission enrolled on Patent Roll, 30 Elizabeth I, part iv dorse.

Either the Queen or Burghley[44] further pointed out that she could not be expected to bear the cost of the expedition if it fell through from any default on the adventurers' part. It was presumably in answer to this that Norris on 19 September offered that, if the Queen would name a treasurer for the whole adventure and give him £5,000 at once, the adventurers would not ask for her remaining £15,000 until they had put the whole of their £40,000 into his hands. Moreover, they would give security to repay the £5,000, or sell back at London market prices any armour, etc., bought with it, if they failed to pay up their share and the voyage fell through as a result.[45]

Next day Burghley jotted down a memorandum of the proportion of men and shipping and other preparations out of England and abroad.[46] This shows that by then a few further modifications had been made to the original proposals. The six Queen's ships were to be furnished with masters, mariners, and gunners at the adventurers' charge, though this was probably a clarification rather than an alteration of the first proposal. No more was said about taking the two Spanish prizes, though four of the best guns and the powder from one of them were later delivered to Norris and Drake.[47] The artillery was cut down to six pieces of battery, with forty lasts of powder. The land forces were to be made up of 8,000 troops from England and 4,000 (instead of 2,000 or 3,000) from the Netherlands. Of the English levies, 4,000 (instead of 6,000) were to be men pressed in the counties, but with arms supplied by the adventurers, and none of them were to be men from the trained bands. The whole force was to be victualled for four months, and they hoped to have wheat for another three months, as well as arms, munitions, and powder (but no longer, it would seem, any siege guns) out of Holland.

In short, what was now decided upon was a naval force of six royal warships and twenty armed merchantmen together

[44] The comment was added by Burghley to another copy of the 'Certain Points' – S. P. Domestic, ccxvi, no. 60.

[45] Ibid., ccxvi, no. 32.

[46] Ibid, ccxvi, no. 33; ccxix, no. 37.

[47] *Acts P. C.,* XVII, 89. Of the two prizes, one was unseaworthy and the other was wrecked off Studland in November – *Armada Papers,* II, 296–8, 384.

with the transports and supply ships needed for the land army of 12,000 soldiers, with 1,000 pioneers, a small siege train of six heavy cannon, and victuals for at least four months.

This was still substantially what Norris and Drake had originally proposed and in the last days of September they began their preparations with high hopes of eventual success in all their purposes. By the time their commission passed the great seal on 11 October, Norris was on his way to Holland and Drake had already started gathering money, ships, and supplies at home in the expectation of all being ready to sail by 1 February.

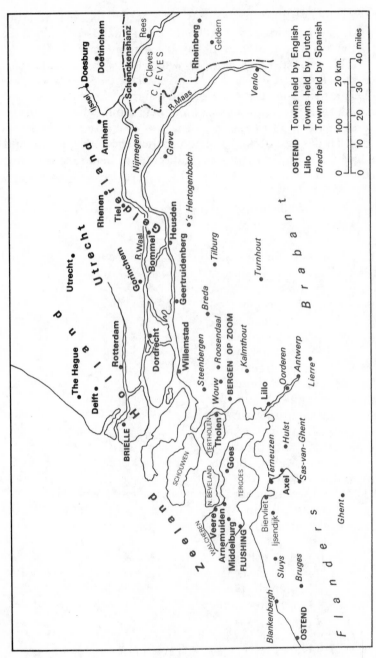

Map 1. The United Provinces' Southern Front (late 1588).

# II

# Victory at Bergen-op-Zoom

From the day late in August 1588 when Howard sent Drake up to court, it had taken less than a month to transform 'the desire Her Majesty had for the intercepting of the King [of Spain]'s treasure from the Indies' into a grand design to destroy the remnants of his ocean-going war navy and to rob him of some of his recently won Portuguese dominions as well. For a sixteenth-century nation, with no regular general staff or planning organization, this was quite an impressive achievement. It was no less remarkable that a queen as notorious as Elizabeth was for her hesitations, should have accepted so readily such a bold and far-reaching transformation of her original purpose.

Her ready agreement to that transformation becomes the more surprising when we consider it in the broader context of the military and political situation on the Continent. Northern France and the Low Countries were, after all, always and by far the most urgent concerns of Elizabeth's foreign policy. It was dangers in those quarters that had finally dragged her into war against Spain three years before.[1] The Netherlands' rebellion against Spain had then looked to be on the verge of collapse after the assassination of William the Silent (July 1584) and the fall of Antwerp (August 1585). The French monarchy, too, had been brought near to total breakdown when the death of Francis of Anjou (May 1584) left the Huguenot Henry of Navarre as heir presumptive to the throne and in March 1585 the Catholic League had revolted against the horrifying prospect of a Protestant succession.

Together these collapses in France and the Netherlands had seemed likely to clear the way for a most menacing overgrowth of Spanish power in western Europe. They had threatened to set free Spain's army in the Low Countries and

---

[1] R. B. Wernham, *Before the Armada*, ch. 26.

to give Spain and Spain's satellites control of the southern shores of the Channel and North Sea all the way from Brest to Emden. Now, Elizabeth's government, like later English governments all through the succeeding centuries, could not view without very great alarm such a domination of western Europe by a single over-mighty power. Even if ships had been a far surer defence than Sir William Winter reckoned; even had there been no Armada gathering in Spain; even then, any attempt to cover England against invasion from so long a string of potential bases must have stretched the country's naval resources far past their breaking-point. It was to avert such a danger that Elizabeth had taken the insurgent United Provinces of the Netherlands into her protection by the treaty of August 1585 and had kept so close a watch upon the affairs of France. To keep the Spaniards and their allies out of the Channel and North Sea ports, and so to prevent the posing of an almost insoluble problem of national defence, had been the chief reason for England's entry into the war in 1585. It remained in 1588 as much as ever the first concern of her policy, with the first call upon her already strained resources.

Now, in September 1588 the situation in northern France and the Low Countries was still full of menace. The Continental calls for further English commitments there were not much less loud and strong than in 1585. In France the royalist governors of the Channel ports, Le Havre excepted, had not yet submitted to the Catholic League; but it was doubtful if they could stand out much longer. For in July King Henry III himself had capitulated to Duke Henry of Guise and the Leaguers,[2] who already controlled nearly all the rest of northern and eastern France. Away south of the Loire, the third of the three Henrys, Henry of Navarre, still stood with his Huguenots defiantly in arms, but they were too far off to succour the Channel ports. Moreover, if the Catholic clergy, nobles, and deputies now assembling for the States General at Blois were to get their way, the Huguenots would soon be fighting for their lives against the combined forces of the monarchy and the League. In that event England would

---

[2] Dumont, *Corps universel diplomatique*, V, i, 476–7; *Cal. S. P. Foreign*, XXII, 4.

hardly be able to stand by and let the Channel ports succumb, the Huguenots be crushed, and the government of France pass entirely into the hands of Spain's Catholic allies.

However, it was still in the Netherlands that the dangers looked most urgent. It needed no great insight to foresee that in what was left of the campaigning season Parma would want to put to profitable use the great army he had held inactive so long in Flanders awaiting the hoped-for invasion of England. In terms of a later war, Parma would want to win his Austerlitz now that Medina Sidonia had met his Trafalgar. The Dutch must therefore expect, and indeed did expect,[3] soon to feel the full force of the blow that Howard and Drake and the Queen's ships had turned away from England. And, sure enough, as early as 24 August definite news came that Parma was breaking up his camp around Dunkirk and moving off east. Five days later – two days after Drake went up to court from Dover – the Duke had 12,000 of his horse and foot within little more than twelve hours' march of Bergen-op-Zoom. On 2 September English patrols from that town brushed against his vanguard only three Dutch miles away at Kalmthout.[4] Prisoners said that his purpose was to besiege Bergen, but some thought that he might merely blockade that town while he thrust across into the nearby island of Tholen. And indeed on 7 September the Marquis of Renti with his vanguard did try to force a crossing into the island at Vossemeer. When their attempt failed, Parma with his full army of at least 24,000 men did at last sit down before Bergen.[5]

Bergen-op-Zoom in 1588 was no longer the great cloth-marketing centre that barely a century ago the English Merchant Adventurers had been able to play off against Antwerp itself. Yet although it had lost its commercial eminence, it was still a place of first-rate strategic importance. It was one of a thin line of Dutch outposts, stretching from

[3] Ibid., p. 117.

[4] Ibid., pp. 158, 164, 180–1; S. P. Domestic, ccxv, no. 47.

[5] *Cal. S. P. Foreign*, XXII, 180,188, 197, 215, 251; *H. M. C., Ancaster MSS*, pp. 184–6; *Correspondance de Philippe II*, III, 353, 362, 366–8; L. van der Essen, *Alexandre Farnèse, duc de Parme*, V, 243–4.

Axel on the northern verge of Flanders, round the northern rim of Brabant from Lillo on the Scheldte to Willemstad, Geertruidenberg, and Heusden on the Maas, and Bommel on the Waal. These outposts provided potentially useful bridgeheads on the far side of the Scheldte estuary, the Maas, and the Waal, the great triple water barrier that formed the main southern defence line of the United Provinces. Much more important, their occupation by the States denied to the Spaniards almost the only really suitable jumping-off bases for an invasion across the rivers into the provinces of Holland, Zeeland, and Utrecht, the central core of the United Provinces.

The especial significance of Bergen in this line of outposts was that, if it were lost, Axel and Lillo would become untenable and the great arc of the mainland coast of the Scheldte and Maas estuaries between Ostend and Willemstad would fall under Parma's unhampered control. From Bergen then he could easily thrust in great force at the islands of Ter Tholen, Duiveland, and Schouwen, so threatening not only to split Zeeland through the middle but also to take in rear its southern islands of Walcheren and Ter Goes (or Beveland), from which the Zeelanders maintained their stranglehold on the waterways up to Antwerp. The capture of Bergen would thus be one of the severest blows that Parma could hope to deal the United Provinces in the remaining weeks of the year's campaigning season.

To defend the town against such an army as was now approaching it was no mean task. The two-mile circuit of its walls still recalled its former prosperity. And beyond the walls was an area of twice that circuit, embracing the forts that commanded the landward approaches and guarded the entrance to the haven. This area, too, must be defended if the enemy was to be prevented from coming close enough to breach the town walls with his cannon or to stop supplies and reinforcements coming in by sea. It was hardly less important to hold the neighbouring islands of Ter Tholen and Ter Goes, which commanded the waterways leading up to the haven from Zeeland. Lord Willoughby, the lord general of the English 'auxiliary' forces in the Low Countries, considered that 3,000 men were needed for this and as many again for Bergen and its forts.[6]

It was particularly unfortunate therefore that Bergen had not been 'so meanly manned this great while' as it was in August 1588. Its garrison at that time consisted of two troops of horse and nine foot-bands drawn from the English auxiliary forces. Their nominal strength was 300 horse and 1,450 foot. But, as with all the Queen's forces in the Netherlands, ten 'dead pays' in every hundred were allowed to the captains to reward – at least that was the theory of it – old soldiers, corporals, gentlemen volunteers, and such like. So at their best the horse could not be in reality more than 270 nor the foot more than 1,305. And in August 1588 both were far short of their best. Of the foot, 364 had gone to England as part of the nominal 1,000 – in reality about 800 – 'shot' from the auxiliary companies that Sir Thomas Morgan had taken over to help defend their own country against the Armada and Parma. Besides these, another 139 foot and 76 horse were absent or deficient. The effective garrison therefore, even assuming that its latest musters on 4 August had been free from the usual frauds, was no more than 194 horse and 802 foot – a bare third of Willoughby's required 3,000.[7]

To find the other two-thirds, the other 2,000, not to mention 3,000 for Tholen, and to find them quickly, was by no means easy. It would be difficult to get more than a few hundred from the rest of the forces in the Queen's pay. It did not greatly matter that the States had just sent most of the English horse-bands off with Colonel Schenk to relieve Bonn, one of the few Rhineland towns still held for the Protestant ex-Archbishop Elector of Cologne, Gebhard Truchsess. What Bergen needed was infantry. Now there were nominally 6,400 foot soldiers in the Queen's pay in the Low Countries.[8] But from these we must, of course, knock off ten per cent, or 640, for the dead pays. Then from the remaining 5,760 must be deducted another 1,305 'cautionary' troops, paid by the Queen to hold Flushing (855) and Brielle (450) for her, according to the 1585 treaty, as pledges for the States'

[6] *Cal. S. P. Foreign*, XXII, 143, 205, 215, 251; *H. M. C., Ancaster MSS*, p. 181.
[7] *Cal. S. P. Foreign*, XXII, 136–8, 159; XXIII, 378.
[8] Ibid., XXII, 137–8.

repayment of her expenses at the end of the war. With those 1,305 not available for service outside those two 'cautionary towns' and another 1,305 of the 4,455 'auxiliary' foot already allotted to Bergen, there could be no more than 3,150 from whom reinforcements might be drawn.

Moreover, according to musters taken during the first half of August, the companies outside Bergen were 138 short of their proper numbers and had 648 absent for more accountable reasons (310 of them in England with Sir Thomas Morgan). That left 2,364, if the commissaries of musters were honest and their figures reasonably trustworthy. But few believed then, and we can hardly believe now, that they were all honest and trustworthy. The States asserted that the foot-bands were at no more than half strength. The English overseer of musters, James Digges, accused the captains of passing off camp-followers as soldiers at the musters, bribing those present to answer to the names of those absent as well as to their own, and of defrauding both the Queen and their men in a host of other ways. Commissaries, too, were allowed to stay long enough in one garrison to become over-friendly with the captains. Some even accepted a weekly allowance from them, while one at least was said to admit that 'he cannot skill to keep any reckoning'.[9]

The States had, of course, an obvious interest in putting the numbers as low as possible, for the treaty bound them to repay eventually what those numbers cost. Digges, too, was a new broom, over-anxious to create an impression of clean sweeping – or perhaps to cover his own activities in a cloud of dust.[10] Yet Henry Killigrew, the Englishman who in accordance with the 1585 treaty represented the Queen in the Dutch Council of State, believed that the foot-bands might be 1,000 men below establishment.[11] And indeed there was plenty of temptation for captains and other officers to fiddle the musters. They were living from hand to mouth upon weekly 'lendings', weekly advances of a portion of their pay; and it was nearly two years since their accounts had been made up and the balances paid over to them at a 'full pay'. The Queen had thereby saved, or

[9] Ibid., pp. 14, 141–2, 215, 229, 241, 293–4.
[10] Ibid., pp. 109–10, 159.
[11] Ibid., p. 141.

rather had put off paying, some £70,000,[12] a notable relief to her harassed Exchequer in this expensive Armada year. But any captain who kept his company up to strength was left, despite his dead pays, with very little money for replacing lost men and equipment, relieving his sick, and ransoming prisoners.[13] To meet those expenses he might have to pledge not only his personal credit but also part of his company's equipment with the citizens of the town where he was in garrison. That made it difficult to move away from the town and was embarrassing in many ways. The easier course was to let the company grow weak but still qualify fraudulently for full lendings by mustering camp-followers and bribing the commissary to enter non-existent soldiers on his rolls. An even more drastic course was to go off to England, where experienced officers were so scarce that, until the danger from the Armada was past, the government winked at the influx from the Low Countries. Many, if not indeed most, of the captains were thus absent from their Netherlands posts in August 1588, leaving their lieutenants to struggle along as best they could; sometimes apparently even farming out the company to the lieutenant for a yearly rent.[14]

The temptation to such courses was all the greater because that summer even weekly lendings were hard to come by. The £18,000 issued to Sir Thomas Sherley, the treasurer-at-war, on 27 May was all used up by August and for some weeks the garrison of Brielle had to borrow its lendings from the town revenues, while the Bergen and Ostend troops were victualled from the States' magazines. A further £12,000 was issued from the Exchequer in August, but there was some delay before it could reach the troops, who were by now 'in extreme misery by the long delay of full pay'.[15]

Yet even if the musters figures had truly stood for real live soldiers, it would still not have been possible for the English auxiliary foot-bands (as distinct from the 'cautionary' bands) to provide anything like the 2,000 extra men that Bergen and

[12] Ibid., p. 277.
[13] Ibid., pp. 134, 162.
[14] Ibid., pp. 54–5, 68, 162.
[15] Ibid., pp. 68, 122, 137, 144, 171, 297. 'Here is not one whit of treasure left', Willoughby wrote to the Privy Council on 6 August – ibid., p. 113.

its forts alone needed. There were, after all, even according to the musters only 2,364 auxiliary infantry outside Bergen – 1,245 at Ostend, 913 in Flushing and Brielle, and 206 at Utrecht. At Utrecht local political tensions made the town's ruling faction exceedingly loath to part with any of the English soldiery and, anyway, 206 would not go far to satisfy Bergen's need. The presence of 913, or indeed of any, of the auxiliary troops in the cautionary towns was naturally looked upon by the States as a great abuse.[16] Yet to get them out was far from easy. The cautionary town governors held commissions independent of the lord general's authority and, as they were acutely conscious of the dislike which the burghers felt for their heavily indebted foreign garrisons, they would never allow those garrisons to be weakened except upon specific orders from the home government. This was especially true of Sir William Russell at Flushing who until shortly before this time had been on bad terms with Willoughby and was on worse terms with the Dutch commander, Count Maurice of Nassau. Russell was always ready to see in any untoward incident a deep plot by the States of Zeeland and the Flushing burghers to rid themselves of their English garrison. He and Lord Burgh at Brielle would not readily yield up their 913 auxiliary infantry. And even if they did, that would be only half the number Bergen required.[17]

There remained Sir John Conway at Ostend. He, no doubt, would gladly have seen the backs of many of his 1,245 auxiliary infantry. For in late August and early September they broke into a 'wonderful dangerous mutiny' over delays in pay and over victuals that they complained were 'neither wholesome, savoury, nor man's meat'.[18] They had thrown the victualler's man into the harbour and pelted him with clods and stones as he clambered out. They had trained their weapons upon Conway and their officers. They had then carried off the lot of them to the common gaol. According to Conway, never a belittler of his own hazards, ten or twelve of them had even fired their muskets at him – and missed from

---

[16] Ibid., p. 142.
[17] Ibid., pp. 48–9, 134, 163–4, 187–8, 379.
[18] For the Ostend mutiny, see preface to *Cal. S. P. Foreign*, XXII, xxxvi–xxxix and references there.

six yards' range! Their petitions to the Queen, however, were dutiful enough and the Queen and Privy Council responded by sending back one of the absent captains, Sir Edward Norris, with promises of prompter lendings, more palatable victuals, and a full and fair enquiry into all grievances. Lord Willoughby was also ordered to see that these promises were performed. Sir Edward Norris, Sir John's younger brother and the least sensible of a hot tempered soldiering family, almost provoked another outbreak by some tactless blustering. But the arrival of letters from Willoughby calmed things again and by mid-September order was more or less restored. Two hundred men (among them six or eight of the most troublesome in each company) were sent off to Bergen. But that left only 1,045 at Ostend and clearly not many more could be spared, even though when it was in the States' hands its garrison had never numbered above five or six hundred.

Thus, although Sir Thomas Morgan brought his 800 men back from England early in September,[19] it was unlikely that the English auxiliary forces would be able to provide much more than half the reinforcement needed for the garrison of Bergen. Nor was it by any means certain that the Dutch could, in the time, provide the other half and a sufficient force for Tholen as well. There were soldiers enough on their pay rolls, more indeed than they had the money to pay.[20] Their greatest lack, however, was a lack of central authority. The quarrels between the States and the Earl of Leicester had left the United Provinces without an effective high command for military affairs and without any proper political executive organ.[21] By the 1585 treaty the English lord general and the Council of State, over which he had presided and in which another Englishman sat as a member, should have provided both. But the lord general's authority, particularly since Leicester had handed it over to Lord Willoughby, had become more and more restricted to the English forces alone.[22]

The gap thus created had not yet been filled by any Dutch

[19] Ibid., p. 192.
[20] Ibid., pp. 91, 119.
[21] Wernham, *Before the Armada*, ch. 27.
[22] *H. M. C., Ancaster MSS*, pp. 181–2, 218.

commander. For although Count Maurice commanded the joint forces of Holland and Zeeland and those two Provinces had tried to get the rest to accept him also, the most that they had been able to obtain was that he should command the forces in Brabant as well as their own.[23] At the same time the States allowed the Council of State no control over the Provinces' revenues. The Council therefore could only pay their forces by bills upon particular Provinces or towns. This meant that there was no longer an army in the field. For once a company was put into garrison or winter quarters in a town, it became very reluctant to disregard its local paymasters or to move far away from them.[24] Nor was it easy to overcome such obstinacy now that military and political authority was to a large extent fragmented among these local paymasters, among the States of the various Provinces, their stadholders, and even the magistrates of the towns.

There was, it is true, the States General, sitting at The Hague and steadily usurping more and more of the executive functions of the Council of State. But the States General, an assembly of provincial delegates bound hand and foot by their instructions from their provincial States, could make few decisions of importance, particularly in money matters, without referring back to their principals. That usually entailed much negotiation and, even though distances in the Netherlands were short, the resulting delays were often long. Moreover, at the beginning of September the States General broke up and did not reassemble until December.[25] And at the beginning of October the only other central authority, the Council of State, also 'divided some into one quarter, some into another'. The Friesland and Overijsel representatives had anyway not yet been appointed. Now, when those of Utrecht went home after the 'brabble' there, three other Councillors went with them and yet another three went off to assist Count Maurice in Tholen. So those remaining at The Hague were very few.[26]

[23] *Cal. S. P. Foreign*, XXII, 185.

[24] Ibid., pp. 155, 197; *H. M. C. Ancaster MSS*, p. 179.

[25] *Cal. S. P. Foreign*, XXII, 183. For this and for the next two paragraphs, see in particular George Gilpin's letters of 13 July and 23 August and Henry Killigrew's of 4 September – ibid., pp. 42–3, 154–5, 184–5.

[26] Ibid., pp. 215, 233, 254; *H. M. C., Ancaster MSS*, p. 195.

This fantastic method of waging war by an impotent executive Council and a sort of international conference that half the time was not in session, could well have proved fatal to the 'United' Provinces had it not been for the predominance of Holland, the wealthiest and most populous of them. Holland paid nearly two-thirds of every general contribution. Hence, in the States General 'Holland beareth the sway and this proceedeth because they have the greatest purse'.[27] They had also in their Advocate, Jan van Oldenbarnevelt, the ablest statesman.[28] The best hope of getting anything done was therefore to get it backed by the States of Holland sitting, like the States General, at The Hague. Nevertheless there were distinct limits to the willingness and authority of the States of Holland. Their members also were delegates. They, too, had to refer most matters of importance back to their principals, the towns. So 'in this popular government such present order cannot be taken as in other governments'.[29] Moreover, the States' government was not all that 'popular'. Indeed, in dealing with their towns the States of Holland – and the States of Zeeland who generally went along with them – had at this time to walk very cautiously. It was only within the previous few months that they had mastered the opposing faction of militant Calvinists, disgruntled refugees from the subjugated south, and malcontent soldiery, that had gathered around the Earl of Leicester. It was as recently as 19 July that, by the mediation of Lord Willoughby and at a cost of £26,000, they had appeased for a time the last of their mutinous garrisons, at Geertruidenberg. Even within their own Provinces, therefore, the States of Holland and Zeeland dared not yet carry matters with too high a hand.

With the other Provinces they had to walk even more warily. In Friesland the stadholder, Count William Louis of Nassau-Dillingen, and the States party had won the upper hand and exiled their opponents or driven them from office.

---

[27] *Cal. S. P. Foreign*, XXII, 155. In the provisional 'state of wars' agreed upon on 18 May Holland's quota was over 120,000 livres, Zeeland's 31,000, Friesland's 24,800, Utrecht's 11,373, Overijsel's 4,669, and Gelderland's 3,794 – *Resolutiën der Staten Generaal*, VI, 187, note 2.

[28] J. den Tex, *Oldenbarnevelt* (5 vols., 1960–72; shortened English translation, 2 vols., 1973).

[29] G. Gilpin to Walsingham, 8 August – *Cal. S. P. Foreign*, XXII, 119.

Yet the opposition there and in Gelderland and Overijsel retained sufficient influence and organization to obstruct the election of representatives to the Council of State and to hinder until the end of August the voting of the provincial quotas of taxes. In all three Provinces, and especially in the largely Catholic Gelderland and Overijsel where the stadholder, Count Mörs, was but slowly securing control, the people were 'wearied with long wars' and ready to go over to the enemy if pressed too hard, or tempted too far.[30] Utrecht was worse, bitterly divided by the still unsettled dispute between the country gentry, led by their stadholder (Count Mörs here also), and the Leicestrian faction under burgomaster Deventer, which controlled the city and the provincial States.[31] These landward provinces, poor, weak, and exposed, had hardly begun to acquiesce in the leadership of Holland or to co-operate through the States General and Council of State, when Parma sat down before Bergen. To draw forces and funds from them would be even slower and more difficult than from the towns of Holland and Zeeland.

What made it the more difficult everywhere was that until Parma actually sat down before Bergen the States could not be absolutely sure about where he would strike. Bergen or one of the islands of Zeeland might seem the most likely. But it was only sensible to send reinforcements and supplies also to Axel, Heusden, and Arnhem. There was also the possibility that Parma might move across east to join Count Charles Mansfelt and Colonel Verdugo who were besieging Bonn and blockading Rheinberg. The loss of those two places would lay Gelderland and Overijsel wide open to invasion from the east and put Utrecht at risk as well. So, late in July the States General had felt compelled to vote £3,000 to Colonel Martin Schenk and, early in August, to despatch him to the relief of Bonn. He was too late to save Bonn, though in a brilliant little campaign he revictualled Rheinberg and made the eastern frontier safe at least against the weak and ill-ordered forces of Mansfelt and Verdugo.[32]

[30] Ibid., pp. 42–4, 134–6; *Resolutiën der Staten Generaal*, VI, 9–10, 80–1, 187–206, 223–7, 237–8, 252.

[31] *Cal. S. P. Foreign*, XXII, 70, 134–6; Bor, xxiv, fos. 108–13.

[32] *Cal. S. P. Foreign*, XXII, 43–4, 90, 215, 235–7.

All this made it more difficult still for the States to scrape together the forces and supplies to assure Bergen. Yet if Bergen were lost, Holland and Zeeland must soon become too preoccupied with their own defence to spare even the little that they now spent upon the defence of the Provinces to the east of them. Utrecht, Gelderland, Overijsel, maybe even Friesland, would then grow war-weary to the point where 'if the Prince of Parma should bend his forces that way . . . all were gone'.[33] To save Bergen was thus a matter of the first importance; but its salvation seemed to depend upon the Queen of England's willingness to increase substantially her military and financial aid to the tottering United Provinces.

That had been the refrain of almost every letter from the Netherlands since early in August. In the middle of the month Willoughby had warned the Privy Council that Bergen was 'not in any sort tenable' without immediate supplies and reinforcements and on 17 August the States of Zeeland wrote to the Queen that they must perforce cast upon her the burden of providing for the town's needs.[34] To this Elizabeth's first reaction was to instruct Willoughby on 1 September to inform the States that she did not regard the defence of Bergen as in any sense her responsibility. If they were careless of the place's security, she would call away all her subjects who were in garrison there. She did send back Sir Thomas Morgan with his 800 'shot' and with her commission to be governor of Bergen instead of the less experienced Sir William Drury, whom the States and Willoughby had just appointed to that post. She also ordered to Bergen two of her foot-bands from Flushing, one from Brielle, and three from Ostend. But she held out absolutely no hope that she might do anything more. As the Privy Council remarked, the time – five days after Howard had sent Drake up to court – was 'not seasonable to urge Her Majesty to any increase of disbursements'.[35]

With Elizabeth, it may be, no time ever was seasonable; but certainly this time was less seasonable than most for any generous loosening of her purse-strings. It does, however, also

[33] Ibid., p. 65.
[34] Ibid., pp. 136, 142.
[35] Ibid., pp. 176, 178–80.

seem clear that at first she and her Councillors felt reasonably confident of the States' ability, with the help of the English auxiliary forces, at least to defend the vital coastal areas until winter put a stop to serious military operations. Walsingham, indeed, was convinced 'that so long as we shall be the strongest by sea, it is not likely the Duke of Parma will attempt any maritime places'.[36] It is true that when Parma, by sitting down before Bergen, had proved Walsingham wrong, the Queen's attitude did appear to change somewhat. But the change was perhaps not altogether due to a loss of confidence in the States' ability and will to hold the place without additional help. There may well have been another motive. After all, the news arrived just when Sir John Norris was being sent over to ask the Dutch to contribute to the great expedition that he and Drake were preparing. On such an errand and at such a moment he could hardly be sent over entirely empty handed.

A rumour had reached Flushing as early as 22 September 'that Her Majesty hath a determination to send some more forces into these countries'. This, however, was probably guesswork. For it was only on 23 September that the Privy Council wrote to tell Willoughby that Sir John Norris, who was going over on other business, would be taking with him 1,500 footmen to reinforce Bergen, while Captain Nicolaas van Meetkerke was to take another 500 levied by the refugee Protestant churches in England. The States were to be required to promise repayment of the cost of levying, arming, transporting, and paying the 1,500. If they refused, they were to be told, in a formal protest, that Her Majesty would withdraw an equivalent number of her auxiliary troops and would give the Provinces no help in any future necessity. Furthermore, if they failed to supply the men, munitions, and victuals that Bergen needed, if they neglected it as they had neglected Sluys in 1587, she would withdraw her forces from that garrison. Finally since it must take time to levy and transport Norris's and Meetkerke's men, and as Bergen's need was pressing, one of the English auxiliary companies already in

---

[36] Ibid., pp. 176–7.

Brielle, two of those in Flushing, and two more in Ostend were to go there at once.[37]

In the event Norris did not leave London until after 9 October and did not reach Flushing until the 20th, although some of his men landed in Zeeland a few days earlier.[38] By that time the crisis of the siege was already passed. The States, with the help of Willoughby and the English auxiliary forces, had managed after all to hold this maritime place. Nevertheless it had been a near thing and the outcome owed at least as much to the skill and courage of the English garrison as to the slow and stumbling efforts of the States to support them. As early as 23 August the States had asked Willoughby to take order for the defence of Bergen and had promised to send five companies of Flemish old soldiers to him there, along with victuals and munitions.[39]

Willoughby was at Bergen the next day and was plainly dismayed at the weakness and wants of the garrison. He hurried back to Middelburg to try to goad the States of Zeeland into action and to see what help he could get from Sir William Russell at Flushing. Then, while he himself went back to Bergen at the end of August, he sent George Gilpin off to The Hague to stir up the Council of State and the States of Holland. The Council had, indeed, already written to the States of Zeeland for reinforcements and provisions, while the States of Holland promised to 'strain themselves to the uttermost'. But they did all things so slowly and so weakly that Bergen felt little benefit. Their intentions were good, but their authority over their towns, their garrisons, and their merchants was sadly defective. Thus the Council of State ordered to Bergen and Tholen the soldiers now coming off their ships as the fleet was discharged. The soldiers, however, slipped away to their garrisons, to the towns that were their normal paymasters. The Council therefore had to levy and equip new companies in their place, something that could not be done in a day or two.[40]

In fact almost all the help that reached Bergen in the first

---

[37] Ibid., pp. 217, 220, 247; *Acts P. C.*, XVI, 288–90.
[38] *Cal. S. P. Foreign*, XXII, 266–7, 273.
[39] Ibid., p. 155; *H. M. C., Ancaster MSS*, p. 180.
[40] *Cal. S. P. Foreign*, XXII, 160, 183; *H. M. C., Ancaster MSS*, pp. 179–82.

three weeks of September came from the other English garrisons or was paid for, to the tune of almost £2,000, out of Willoughby's own purse and credit. The States and magistrates of Utrecht refused to release either of the English companies there although, like Geertruidenberg, they did send 100 musketeers; but Russell sent Captain Richard Wingfield with 150–200 harquebusiers from Flushing, Lord Burgh sent Lieutenant Turner with another 100 from Brielle, and by mid-September the 200 from the mutinous Ostend garrison had also arrived. By then, too, Sir Thomas Morgan had brought back the 'shot' from England. Before that, on 4 September Willoughby was again at Middelburg, badgering the States of Zeeland and sending his secretary Jean Houfflin to jog the memory of the Council of State at The Hague. His hopes were not high and 'having no means of men, money, or provision to succour them from the States of this side. I can conceive no certain way', he wrote to the Queen, 'to encourage or relieve them but with community of the peril to spend my life together with them' in Bergen. Two days later he received the Privy Council's letter of 1 September. He doubted whether the States would take very seriously the Queen's threat to withdraw her troops from Bergen if they neglected it, but at least he now had another excuse for putting pressure on them. So off he went again to The Hague on 8 September to inform the Council of State and the States of his latest instructions. They assured him that they would furnish all Bergen's needs; urged him to hold good correspondence with Count Solms, the commander of such forces as they had scraped together in Tholen; and promised to send to Bergen the foot-bands of Captains Heraugières, Traile, and Christal, as well as 500 men recently come down from Friesland.[41]

By the time Willoughby had returned to Bergen on 14 September, the enemy were encamped around it on every side within cannon shot. The siege had begun. That afternoon the garrison sallied out to prevent the besiegers from occupying a place of some advantage near the Steenbergen gate, on the north side. A long skirmish resulted in the enemy being forced

[41] *Cal. S. P. Foreign*, XXII, 188, 192–3, 205, 251, 265; *H. M. C., Ancaster MSS*, pp. 181–7, 191–2.

to retire, with considerable loss. After that, although on the next day, Sunday, there was some light skirmishing near the Wouw gate, the first week or so passed fairly quietly. Indeed, Willoughby's chief difficulties came from his own side. It was only after two days of argument, and finally of threats, that on 16 September he persuaded the town magistrates to let him set the burghers to work on the fortifications, throwing up a 'fausse braie' between the Wouw gate and the water gate and 'a "strada comperta" with a traversing line flanking the mount, the north fort, and the haven'.

Then, no sooner had the burghers been got to work than more trouble arose. On 18 September Sir Thomas Morgan arrived with the States' commission, given him at the Queen's request, to take Drury's place as governor of Bergen. Drury, obediently though sadly, let himself be put 'out of the hall into the kitchen'; but the irascible and opinionated Morgan at first claimed absolute command of all Her Majesty's forces there, overriding even the authority of Lord Willoughby, the lord general. It required the mediation of Count Solms and Marshal Viliers, who had come over from Tholen, to persuade him to a reasonable compromise and eventually, on 21 September, to agree to leave the English companies in the forts to Drury and content himself with the command of the town, while Willoughby remained in charge overall. This arrangement, and a rumour that the captains in the forts refused to obey Morgan, somewhat alarmed the Council of State but Willoughby did in fact manage to keep the two men pulling together fairly well in their double harness.[42]

By now the arrival of the English reinforcements from Brielle, Flushing, and Ostend, and of the States' musketeers from Geertruidenberg and Utrecht, made it possible to put seven foot-bands into the forts and so provide some more adequate defence for the wider perimeter. Willoughby, upon his own credit, had also provided 12,000 lbs of cheese and 25 lasts of oats. But apart from a small quantity of weapons, munitions, tools, and timber from Zeeland, little or nothing of the supplies promised him by the States had yet arrived

[42] *Cal. S. P. Foreign*, XXII, 204–7, 210–1, 228–9, 272; *H. M. C., Ancaster MSS*, pp. 187, 201–3.

and the handful of their troops who had trickled in were already more than half mutinous for lack of pay. Although Willoughby had been writing and sending every other day for the previous week to hurry them along, all that he received from the Council of State was exhortations to patience, excuses blaming wind and weather for the delays, and urgent entreaties to use the supplies as sparingly as possible when they did arrive. The economy was even to extend to the consumption of gunpowder and since 'it was reasoned that musket shot would annoy the enemy so much as greater', he was to avoid using the cannon except in extreme necessity![43]

This waging of war upon a shoestring was all the more exasperating to Willoughby because, now that action was joined, his spirits were rising. On 20 September he had led out a portion of the garrison in another elaborate two-hour skirmish and for the second time had returned 'though not a conqueror, yet no loser'. He was beginning to feel that, if only he could have 5,000 men in Bergen and its forts and Solms could have another 2,000 or 3,000 in Tholen, there would be a fair chance after all of overthrowing the enemy's great army that 'hath seemed to threaten all those of the reformed religion throughout Europe'. Admittedly it was very doubtful whether the States and the English auxiliary forces could between them provide troops on this scale. Killigrew did not see how they could find even 3,000 for Tholen and 3,000 for Bergen and when, a little later, the Council of State heard from Morgan that the two places together needed at least 9,000 or 10,000 men for their defence, 'some smiled, saying that if there were so many men they might meet the enemy in the field'.[44]

Nevertheless, Willoughby decided that one final effort at persuasion might produce at least some of the men and supplies that Bergen needed. So, on 22 September he set off again to see what his personal entreaties might achieve at Middelburg and The Hague. The need had now grown more urgent still, for during the night of 20–21 September the enemy had crept up and 'entrenched himself within caliver

[43] *Cal. S. P. Foreign*, XXII, 210, 297; *H. M. C., Ancaster MSS*, pp. 189, 202, 204.
[44] *Cal. S. P. Foreign*, XXII, 209, 215, 220; *H. M. C., Ancaster MSS*, p. 195.

shot of the Wouw gate' on the eastern, landward, side of Bergen. By this 'were our sallies cut off from that quarter where otherwise we might have cut off their passage from one camp to another', from their main camp on the southern and south-eastern quarter of the town to their other camp on the northern side. As some of the enemy had been seen, only three days before, coming down to view the north dyke, the move seemed to presage an attempt to cut Bergen's lifeline to Zeeland by seizing the dyke and the north fort which commanded one side of the entrance to the haven.[45]

It must therefore have been with some excitement that Willoughby, the day before he embarked for Middelburg, listened to an offer to entrap the enemy in just that attempt. The offer was made by William Grimston, ensign of Captain Baskerville's company in the north fort, and in view of his subsequent behaviour it would perhaps be a little ungenerous to suggest any doubts about his motives in coming forward now. Nevertheless, earlier that very day Willoughby had received warnings from both Count Maurice and the Council of State about prisoners' tales of the enemy having dealings with persons in the town. He had at once issued a proclamation offering a thousand gulden (and, if necessary, a pardon) to anyone who could reveal any such practice or conspiracy.[46] It was after this that Grimston came forward and the story that he had to tell certainly came very pat to the occasion. He had it, he said, from an acquaintance, Robert Redhead, in whose house two prisoners of war were lodged. One was a Spaniard called Pedro de Lugo, the other supposedly an Italian, going by the name of Cosimo d'Alexandrini. Redhead, however, had noticed in his conversations with Alexandrini that, when their Latin broke down, Alexandrini· 'used some English words wherein his perfect pronunciation gave great suspicion'.

So, the better to discover him, Redhead professed to be very well affected to Sir William Stanley, the English renegade who had betrayed Deventer to Parma in 1587 and who now commanded a regiment in the northern camp of the besieging

[45] *Cal. S. P. Foreign*, XXII, 211; *H. M. C., Ancaster MSS*, pp. 204-5.
[46] Ibid., pp. 190, 205.

army. Alexandrini thereupon confessed, under pledge of
secrecy, that his real name was Thomas Suigo and that he was
an Englishman born in London. He went on to tell Redhead
that if 'he could find out anyone that either could assure any
port of the town, any fort, or any piece of ground of
advantage, it should much both advance his reputation and
put good food of crowns in his purse to maintain him like a
gentleman'. Such was Redhead's story and on hearing it
Willoughby at once sent Grimston to confer with Suigo and de
Lugo. With them Grimston concocted letters to Parma and
Stanley, 'assuring that Grimston was a very good Catholic'
and was willing to render the north fort to the besiegers.
Grimston brought the letters to Willoughby the next morning,
just as he was ready to embark for Zeeland. So Willoughby
took him along too, had copies made of the letters to send to
the Privy Council, and then sent him back with the originals,
'appointing when and in what sort they should be sent by
Redhead to the camp'.[47]

With Grimston's stratagem thus in train, Willoughby
was more than ever anxious to get the supplies and reinforcements that Bergen needed. He was also anxious to concert
plans with the States' commanders and their forces in Tholen.
The States, however, both in Zeeland and in Holland, gave
him a rather chilly reception. Indeed, at The Hague on
24 September he was told that 'they had committed the
charge and care of the place to Sir Thomas Morgan and that
therefore his lordship should not need to meddle in it'.[48] This
coolness was the more riling because, while such inadequate
supplies were dribbling into Bergen, considerable quantities
of victuals were being shipped daily to the enemy's camp,
where prices were at scarcity level. Deserters from Stanley's
regiment reported that in one day 300 tuns of beer, besides
cheese, butter, bacon, etc., had come from Holland through
Steenbergen. In the north camp, according to another
prisoner, they had almost no victuals but those that came
from Holland. Willoughby himself believed that without the
victuals, etc., whose transportation the States continually
licensed, the enemy could not possibly stay in the field. Yet the

[47] Ibid., pp. 205–6.
[48] Ibid., p. 207.

Council of State at this very time protested loudly to him when the garrison of Geertruidenberg seized a couple of Holland ships and diverted to Bergen the victuals they were carrying to the enemy. The States, the Council said, had long since forbidden all traffic to Breda, Zevenbergen, Steenbergen, Roosendaal, Antwerp, and such places, but trade up the river to 'sHertogenbosch and eastward was allowed by passport and must not be interfered with. They did not explain how the two ships came to be carrying the States' passports licensing them to take victuals to the enemy at Steenbergen and Roosendaal, passports which the governor of Geertruidenberg, Sir John Wingfield, had sent to Willoughby.[49]

From The Hague Willoughby went to Geertruidenberg for a couple of days. He then came back to Dordrecht to meet Count Maurice and discuss with him plans for the defence of Bergen and for exploiting Grimston's plot. All this, and a contrary wind, held him longer than he expected and it was not until late on 3 October that he got back to Bergen, bringing Count Maurice with him. Next morning he found that the plot had progressed considerably during his absence. Parma had risen to the bait and sent his patent promising Grimston 7,000 gold crowns and a captain's pay in Stanley's regiment, besides 1,200 crowns and thirty crowns a month to Redhead, a captain's pay to Suigo, and four months' pay to any soldiers who helped them.[50] Expecting Willoughby back earlier, Grimston had arranged for the action to be performed that very night, 4 October. This, of course, was now out of the question, for Willoughby could not concentrate the required forces and make all the preparations needful in so short a time. Grimston therefore had to send Redhead back with fresh letters from Suigo and de Lugo to excuse the delay. To lull suspicion still further, on the night of 6 October he himself slipped out and saw Stanley and Parma. They seemed quite satisfied with his explanations and Parma gave both him and Redhead gold chains. In return Grimston promised to let the Spaniards into the north fort the next night, 7–8 October.

[49] Ibid., pp. 207–8; *Cal. S. P. Foreign*, XXII, 234, 254.
[50] *Cal. S. P. Foreign*, XXII, 258; but the patent must be NS – see *H. M. C., Ancaster MSS*, pp. 208–9, though the copy at ibid., p. 199 is given as OS.

When the two plotters got back to Bergen they found that once again they had promised too precipitately. Willoughby insisted that they put it off until the night of 10 October. For, a few days earlier the enemy had won a foothold on the north dyke and planted artillery there to command the harbour entrance and 'to impeach our passages by water'. They had shot through several boats, killed some of the people in them, and 'made it very dangerous to come in or out, in such sort as few durst enter but in the night'. Willoughby succeeded in countering this move by planting a couple of cannon and a culverin near to the north fort, while Count Maurice sent some of the States' great artillery 'to scour the north dyke' from a sconce his troops had built at Guisegate at the seaward end of the dyke. But until this threat to Bergen's supply line had thus been dealt with, Grimston and Redhead had to wait. Besides, one or two weak points had to be strengthened so as to assure the place against surprise. For Willoughby was still a long way short of the 5,000 men he wanted and in order to gather the strength needed to back up Grimston at the north fort, he had to leave the rest of the defences all too slenderly manned. It is true that the companies of Heraugières, Traile, and Christal had arrived by then and presumably those from Friesland also, besides more English from Ostend and, under Russell himself, from Flushing. Even so Willoughby had at his disposal less than 3,400 infantry all told, a bare 2,000 in the town and under 1,400 in the forts. He needed to add at least 500 of the town's 2,000 to those that he could draw from the other forts to the north fort. And until he could feel reasonably sure that the town and the other forts would be safe against a surprise attack when those numbers were drawn from them, Grimston had to wait.[51]

Nevertheless this second delay aroused the enemy's suspicions and made Grimston's part very much more dangerous.

[51] *H. M. C., Ancaster MSS*, pp. 208–10. Exact figures for the defenders' numbers are difficult to arrive at. On 3 October Morgan wrote that there were 2,260 horse and foot in the town – *Cal. S. P. Foreign*, XXII, 237. On 10 October he and the town's sergeant-major reckoned that there were 2,125 foot and four troops of horse – *H. M. C., Ancaster MSS*, p. 211. A list endorsed merely as October shows 1,355 foot in the forts, 2,028 foot and 340 horse in the town, but as Heraugières with 75 men and Hay with 60 are listed as in both the town and the forts, perhaps one or other of these figures for the foot should be reduced by 135 – *Cal. S. P. Foreign*, XXII, 290–1.

Indeed, when on the night of 10 October all was at last ready and Willoughby 'about eleven of the clock sent forth Grimston to draw on the enemy', they vehemently accused the ensign of treachery. Although he no less vehemently protested his faithfulness, 'they tied fast his hands, [and] he was so led by a Spaniard with halberds, drawn swords, and daggers'. Thereupon – but let Lord Willoughby now tell the tale in his own words:

They marched forward and brought him so bound and guarded to the fort and in the meantime the enemy gave great alarms on all sides of the town to keep them busy there . . . When they came to the fort, Grimston being so led in the first rank by a Spanish sergeant, he called to the sergeant that stood at the port to open the gate, which he did accordingly. The Spanish sergeant was the first that entered and Grimston offering to follow him, the Spaniard put him back, whereupon Grimston called to the sergeant within the fort to pull him in by the hand or otherwise he were but a dead man. And so striving forward and being thrust by those that were behind, he got within the port.

Our men within lying close and the enemy being entered to the number of thirty or above, thinking all sure, went about to loose Grimston, while in the meantime the portcullis being let down by Captain Buck, Mr Wilsford with those under his command charged and so recovered the entry of the port and so Grimston, sorting himself amongst our men, escaped with great danger.

The Spaniards, being then in great number about the fort and under the ramparts, after they had continued in fight at push of pike about an hour and a half, were driven to retreat, yet returned again and with great force brake down the palisade forty pace wide and assaulted the place with great vehemency, continuing at the push of pike above half an hour, yet driven again to repulse. In their retreat there were many drowned because the water at their coming over, though it was low was yet flowing. Many also, whereof divers of good quality, were slain and taken prisoners.[52]

Next day Willoughby, with Russell and the other captains and gentlemen, celebrated their triumph in good sixteenth-century fashion. In the morning they 'went to the church to give God thanks for his goodness and their good success'. In

[52] *H. M. C., Ancaster MSS,* pp. 212–13. According to Captain Thomas Maria Wingfield, who was also present, part of the palisade was 'shaked down' by the first shot of the fort's own cannon – *Cal. S. P. Foreign,* XXII, 307.

the afternoon 'Suigo and Pedro de Lugo were hanged for their practising for the north fort'. Grimston, on the other hand, was given one of the best prisoners to ransom, was promised a captain's place, and was sent off home with a letter from Willoughby and a discourse of the action to show 'how worthily and with what resolution he hath performed it'.

Willoughby and his captains certainly had reason to feel pleased. They had taken prisoner fourteen captains and gentlemen, and thirteen soldiers from the most famous regiments of the Spanish army. Estimates of the number of enemy killed or drowned varied between 400 and 800, among them being Don Alonso d'Idiaquez, son of the Spanish secretary of state.[53] Most important, they had dashed Parma's hopes of quick success against Bergen or its forts. Nor had he now much chance of getting a foothold in Tholen, for a second attempt to force a crossing into that island had been repulsed on 6 October with the loss of another 500 men. These two setbacks, at Tholen and at the north fort of Bergen, in fact marked the end of all Parma's hopes for that year. On the night of 15 October he withdrew Renti's 4,000 troops from their trenches opposite Tholen and sent them off with many small boats into Flanders to invade Ter Goes from Terneuzen. Within the week the unlucky, or unenterprising, Renti was back without even making the attempt.[54] Then about midnight on 20 October Willoughby, watching from Bergen's water gate, 'perceived that they were retiring from the north dyke the artillery which they had placed there to impeach the passage by water' – and for further encouragement he also 'did clearly discern a fair great rainbow, which was held strange to be seen at that time of the night'.

When morning came, the rainbow's promise was fulfilled, for the States' troops from Tholen were able to occupy the north dyke without opposition. In the afternoon Willoughby, not to be outdone, led some of the Bergen garrison out from the Steenbergen gate and in the ensuing skirmish was himself 'lightly shot in the heel with a musket bullet which before had grazed'. He could not, however, draw the enemy from their trenches. By this time Sir John Norris was in Zeeland with his

[53] Ibid., pp. 264–5, 307; *H. M. C., Ancaster MSS*, p. 213.
[54] Ibid.; *Cal. S. P. Foreign*, XXII, 254, 271, 278; *Correspondance de Philippe II*, III, 367.

1,500 men from England. Supplies were beginning to flow rather more freely, since on 8 October the States of Holland, finding the proportion appointed for Bergen 'not so ample as could have been required, of their own accord increased the same and have given order for all things in very good measure'. The weather was as bad as ever. Great storms early in October had washed a number of ships on to the coasts of Holland and Zeeland, while around Bergen 'the ways were so deep that no provision could be brought to the [enemy's] camp and every pound weight cost 1*d.* for freight'.[55] With winter close at hand, Parma could not keep the field much longer. On 3 November Willoughby was able to send home Francis Vere (newly knighted for his services) with the triumphant news that 'the town, God be praised, is quitted of the siege'.[56]

[55] *H. M. C., Ancaster MSS*, pp. 213-14; *Cal. S. P. Foreign*, XXII, 253, 273, 330; *Correspondance de Philippe II*, III, 367, 373.

[56] *Cal. S. P. Foreign*, XXII, 300. The news reached England on 10 November – ibid., p. 311.

# III

# Widening Commitments

With Parma's repulse before Bergen the King of Spain had received, as Elizabeth had hoped, 'no less blemish . . . by land than he hath done by sea'. Not less important, Parma himself had lost his reputation of invincibility. He had, it was remarked, taken no place in the United Provinces since his capture of Sluys in July 1587. What was more, he had now tried to take one and been beaten off. Perhaps he had not shown before Bergen the energy and determination that he had shown before Sluys.[1] Perhaps he was discouraged by the discontent among his troops and by Spanish allegations that he had been unready and unwilling to help the Armada. Perhaps he had never intended to commit himself to a regular siege at all, but had only meant to mask Bergen while he thrust through Tholen at the main isles of Zeeland.[2] Yet whatever the reasons, the fact plain for all to see was that he had been repulsed both before Tholen and before Bergen. Moreover, if the *greffier* of Antwerp could be believed, he had lost 10,000 men killed or dead from sickness.[3]

The Dutch and the English auxiliary forces had won this double success almost entirely by their own efforts. For although the arrival of Norris's 1,500 men may have helped Parma to decide upon a withdrawal, they had come too late to take any active part in the operations. Nevertheless, it had been a very close run thing and the States had had to lean heavily upon Willoughby and his Englishmen. Out of the 3,248 infantry in Bergen and its forts at one point in October, no less than 2,312 were in the Queen's pay.[4] Add to these the 1,500 brought over by Norris and clearly the Queen's forces involved must have been just about as numerous as those which the States had in Bergen and Tholen. Of course, the

[1] *Cal. S. P. Foreign*, XXII, 249, 267; van der Essen, *Alexandre Farnèse*, V, 244.
[2] *Cal. S. P. Foreign*, XXII, 98, 108, 146; *Correspondance de Philippe II*, III, 362, 366-7.
[3] *Cal. S. P. Foreign*, XXII, 323; cp. *H. M. C., Ancaster MSS*, p. 237.
[4] *Cal. S. P. Foreign*, XXII, 290-1; and note 51 to chapter II above.

1,500 were destined to go off with Norris and Drake and the States were to be required to promise the eventual repayment of the cost of their levy and transportation as well as of their pay while they were in the Low Countries. But even if the States gave that promise, the repayment would not be due until the end of the war. Meanwhile the charge – probably between £4,000 and £5,000 – had to be carried by the Queen's Exchequer.

Now £4,000 or £5,000 was no great sum, even for Elizabeth's government in 1588 and after all the expenses of the Armada campaign. But it was a reminder of how easily she might be drawn into the Netherlands wars well beyond the limited liability of £126,000 or so that she had undertaken there by the 1585 treaty. And deeper involvement in the Netherlands was something that she would now more than ever be anxious to avoid. For after the Armada, although neither side made any formal declaration, there could be no blinking the fact that England and Spain were openly at war. On Elizabeth's part it was no longer merely a matter of helping the Dutch to hold the Spanish army back from the Netherlands ports and of periodically aiding and abetting the English sea-dogs. Henceforth she had, in addition, to face the threat of direct Spanish attack upon England or Ireland. This meant some reinforcement of the Irish garrisons. It meant also increased expenditure on exercising and equipping the counties' trained bands in England; and although this expenditure fell more upon the counties than upon the Exchequer, the central government could not ignore its possible political consequences. Lord Treasurer Burghley was already well aware of the murmurings among the people over these burdens.[5]

The threat of direct Spanish attack must also call forth efforts, such as the expedition that Norris and Drake were even then preparing, to destroy the necessary instrument of any seaborne invasion, the enemy's ocean-going naval forces in the western ports of Spain and Portugal. It must call for more support for the English seamen's efforts to cut the Spanish empire's vital sea communications. It added weight

[5] S. P. Domestic, ccxii, no. 63.

to Hawkins's pleas for a more regular 'silver blockade' on the Atlantic routes. The Channel Guard squadron, too, was needed, not only to watch Dunkirk, but also to intercept the flow of naval stores and corn from the north German and Baltic ports to Spain and Portugal. For without those supplies, the King of Spain would be hard put to it to find masts and rigging for his ships, biscuit for their crews, even perhaps bread for his people.

Nor was that all. French affairs, as we have seen, also showed signs of developing in a manner that might before long require new, and possibly large-scale, English commitments there. Henry III of France had just submitted again to the Guises and the Catholic League. He had summoned a States General to meet at Blois in September to agree upon – and, the Guises hoped, to finance – a joint crusade to crush the Huguenots once and for all. If that crusade were indeed to be launched, then by the spring of 1589 massive English aid for the Huguenots might well become necessary. True, Elizabeth with the Armada on her doorstep had in July turned a very deaf ear to Henry of Navarre's pleas for money to help him to hire another army in Germany.[6] Even after the Armada's defeat she remained obdurate against undertaking any substantial commitments to the Huguenots. In part this was because they were not for the moment in much danger. The operations of their enemies were seriously cramped by lack of money and by the bitter jealousies among the Catholic nobles, while winter would soon close down large-scale operations altogether until the spring.

Besides this, however, Elizabeth had reason to believe that Henry III still hated the Guises as much as ever and that their seeming reconciliation might well not last until spring. Sir Edward Stafford, the English ambassador, was reporting even in July that 'though there be an union made in protestation and writing, I never saw minds more disunited nor anything more laughed at'. He was assured 'that we shall ere long see a great change' and that 'the King hath some marvelous design'.[7] There were plenty of straws to justify Stafford's view of the way the wind was blowing. Henry

6 *Cal. S. P. Foreign*, XXII, 6, 53–4.
7 Ibid., pp. 62, 90, 99.

was assiduously courting the Catholic princes of the blood
– the Duke of Montpensier, the Count of Soissons, the
Cardinal of Vendôme – and the moderate Dukes of Nevers
and Longueville. He was still secretly in touch with the
hated Duke of Épernon and indirectly through Épernon with
such southern *politiques* as Montmorency and La Valette, even
with Navarre and the Huguenots. He steadily refused to
return himself, or to transfer the States General, from
provincial Blois to Leaguer Paris or anywhere near Paris.
Then at the end of August he suddenly dismissed all his
leading ministers – Cheverny, the Chancellor; the Secretaries
of State Villeroy, Brulart, and Pinart; Bellièvre, the Superintendent of Finances; and the *trésorier de l'épargne,* Le Roy. In
their places he put lesser-known men, who owed all to himself
and who could be trusted with his secrets, 'men of great
integrity but such as were not of too high an understanding'.
There was the lawyer (honest, we are told) Montholon as
*garde des sceaux*; Robert Miron, sieur de Chenailles,
brother of his own physician, as Superintendent of Finances;
Épernon's henchman Louis Revol as Secretary of State.
The exact meaning of these dramatic changes was perhaps
not altogether obvious, but they clearly boded no good
to the Guises and they strongly corroborated Stafford's
predictions.[8]

All this encouraged Elizabeth to think that, if she were to
rush to the aid of the Huguenots now, the effect might simply
be to drive Henry III back farther into the arms of the League
and to stir the League-dominated States General to open wide
its purse strings. So for the remainder of 1588 the chief
concern of English policy in France was to detach Henry III
from the League, to commit him at least to occasional gestures
against the League's Spanish allies, and to encourage him
towards an understanding with Navarre. Unfortunately, from
this point at the end of August until the middle of December
not one of Stafford's despatches has survived.[9] The drafts,
preserved in the British Library, of one letter from the Queen
to the ambassador and of some half-dozen to him from Sir

---

[8] Ibid., pp. 61–2, 125–6, 178; Davila, p. 357.

[9] Except for one about the financial affairs of Anthony Bacon – *Cal. S. P. Foreign,*
XXII, 332–3.

Francis Walsingham,[10] are all that we have to help us in charting the course of English diplomacy during these critical months when Henry III was maturing his plans against the Guises. Nevertheless it is clear that little or nothing happened to change the Queen's mind. Stafford was not, apparently, able to make much headway in drawing the French King and the King of Navarre towards an understanding. He did get the export of French corn to Spain prohibited, even though it was done on the ground that it was needed for the armies preparing against the Huguenots. Above all – though there is no reason to attribute this in any detectable degree to English encouragement – Henry III did on 13 December have the Duke of Guise stabbed to death at the door of the royal cabinet in the château of Blois. At the same time he arrested the Cardinal of Guise, brother to the Duke, and other prominent Leaguers who were at Blois for the States General. Next day, Christmas Eve by the new style (the Gregorian calendar that Pope Gregory XIII had introduced in 1582 and that most Catholic countries had since followed), the Cardinal too was assassinated.[11]

These were staggering blows to the League. But they did not necessarily end all possibility of Elizabeth having to involve herself, perhaps involve herself deeply, in the affairs of France. For as an English observer in Venice remarked: 'if the King of Spain cannot find means to set again on foot in France the remnant of the Guises' faction, then by all men's judgement his affairs will be in a very evil estate.'[12] Spain was likely therefore to come openly and in force to the aid of the League, whose chief strength and support lay in just those northern and north-eastern regions of France that were most dangerous to England's security. In that event Elizabeth would hardly be able to avoid getting drawn in herself.

This prospect made it the more necessary both to limit England's other commitments and to distract Spain's energies. Before the spring of 1589 everything possible must be done to make the Dutch capable of holding their own with no more help from England than that already promised by the

[10] Cotton MSS., Galba E. vi; Harleian MSS, cclxxxvi, fo. 155.
[11] Stafford's account is printed in *Hardwicke State Papers* (1778 ed.), I, 266–96.
[12] *Cal. S. P. Foreign*, XXII, 393.

1585 treaty. It was no less important to get Norris and Drake's expedition away and in action before the armies took the field again in northern France and the Low Countries. During the final months of 1588 quite good progress was made in both these directions. In the Netherlands perhaps the most important single step forward was a change of government at Utrecht. Early in August Killigrew and deputies from the States General had managed to patch up an agreement there between the stadholder, Count Mörs, and the Leicestrian faction led by the burgomaster Deventer who controlled the city and the provincial estates.[13] However, with the annual elections of the city magistrates and militia captains due on 1 October, this truce could hardly last. In the event its breakdown was precipitated by the desperate action of the present magistrates in summoning their exiled opponents to appear before the provincial court to stand their trial for treason at about the same time as the elections. This forced the exiles to act quickly, both to prevent the re-election of their enemies and to save themselves from conviction. It made a conflict imminent as well as inevitable, and in that conflict the odds would be against Deventer unless he could obtain outside help to overmatch his enemies, who could rely upon at least the acquiescence of Mörs and the sympathy of Holland.

Outside help could only mean English help and in August Deventer's faction had already despatched Captain Nicolaas van Meetkerke to England to entreat the Queen to keep four – and in times of emergency, ten – companies of her auxiliary forces and 100 horse in the Province and under their orders. He was to persuade her to send them 3,000 more men, paid for by a tax upon the Low Country refugees in England, ostensibly to secure Utrecht by expelling the Spaniards from Gelderland. He was further to get letters from her recommending the re-election of Deventer and the present magistrates. Finally, he had a secret commission to find whether or not she would listen to a fresh offer of the hereditary sovereignty, or of a temporary protectorate, over the United Provinces. Not long after Meetkerke's departure the captains of the city militia resolved to stay in office for another year,

---

[13] Ibid., p. 109. The following account of the alteration at Utrecht is based, apart from the State Papers, chiefly upon Bor, xxiv, fos. 113–5 and xxv, fos. 14–16, 24–6.

and when on 20 August the city council approved their resolution, they showed their gratitude by sending one of their number, Frans Gerritsz., to join Meetkerke in urging Elizabeth and Leicester to recommend the re-election of Deventer and the present magistrates.[14]

Given the general trend of Elizabeth's policy at this time, there can have been no likelihood at all of her accepting the new commitments that Meetkerke was to invite her to shoulder. And, indeed, he and Gerritsz obtained nothing from her except letters recommending the reappointment of Deventer as burgomaster. Walsingham disapproved even of this and in writing these letters Elizabeth apparently acted upon the advice of Leicester alone – it must have been almost the last counsel that he ever gave her, for by 28 August he was on his way to take the waters at Bath and on 4 September he died. Nevertheless, in her letters the Queen was careful to explain that she was writing in this way only because Mörs and the States had both repeatedly assured her that all their differences were at an end and because she understood (from Leicester presumably) that Deventer was a man of skill and experience in government.[15] What she intended was thus not a declaration in favour of the Leicestrian faction, but an exhortation to concord. It looks, in fact, as if Mörs by his subtlety may have defeated his own purpose. His assurances that all their quarrels were over, were probably meant to keep Elizabeth from making any pronouncement at all until Deventer was overthrown and it was too late for her to intervene. The request, which he made in the same letters, that she should come to no decision upon any complaints made against him until she had heard his side of the case, certainly suggests that his intention was merely to checkmate the efforts of Meetkerke and Gerritsz.[16]

As it was, Leicester, true to form, by his last counsel brought conflict to the United Provinces and disaster to his friends there. For when Gerritsz got back to Utrecht with the Queen's

---

[14] *Cal. S. P. Foreign*, XXII, 86, 134–6; Bor, xxiv, fos. 113–15.

[15] *Cal. S. P. Foreign*, XXII, 181–2; there are also two drafts, dated 23 September, of a letter to Mörs and the States of Utrecht in which the recommendation of Deventer is crossed out – ibid., p. 217; but the other letters, including the recommendation, were sent – ibid., p. 316; *H. M. C., Ancaster MSS*, p. 194.

[16] *Cal. S. P. Foreign*, XXII, 109, 157.

letters on 13 September, Mörs promptly opened a correspondence with the exiles and malcontents. He also induced a section of the provincial States to join him in writing a protest to Elizabeth, and on 16 September he protested formally to the city council, against the militia captains dealing with the English without his knowledge and consent. Next day the city council took up his challenge by voting their approval of what the captains had done. Thereupon open hostilities began. All through the following week the city was agitated by panics and wild rumours. The exiles assembled outside the walls, little groups of them met in private houses in the city, and others tampered with Captain Cleerhagen's company of foot in the Vaert fort. The Leicestrians likewise held secret meetings and Deventer wrote to Willoughby begging him to come and protect them. He called Cleerhagen's company into the city on 20 September, waylaid Christopher Blunt's English horse-band which was on its way to join Colonel Schenk for the relief of Bonn, and refused to send Champernon's English foot-band to help Willoughby in beleaguered Bergen.

Then on 24 September Gerritsz. and the other militia captains decided, without informing Mörs, their stadholder, to change the stations of the watch and to practise an imaginary alarm that evening. That night Mörs stayed quietly at home but, apparently by his orders, some of the malcontents kept counter-watch in their houses. The officer of the city watch discovered some of them in the house of one Gijsbrechtsz. and at once, about four o'clock in the morning, summoned Deventer and certain of the council to the town hall. Four cannon were placed in front of the building, Blunt's troopers were called up from the outskirts of the city, and the schout, Trillo, was sent to arrest the suspects. By the time he brought them to the town hall, most of the already nervous burghers had rushed into the streets in panic. They seemed very hostile to Deventer and made it impossible to bring up powder for the cannon. They easily persuaded Blunt's no doubt sleepy troopers to remain inactive and they rabbled, wounded, and arrested Cleerhagen, whose leaderless and bewildered soldiers allowed themselves to be thrust out of the city. By noon Deventer, Trillo, and Gerritsz. were also prisoners and their more notable supporters had fled over the walls. Thereupon Mörs took charge and next day, with the consent of the remaining magistrates and deputies of the provincial States, named a new city council and new militia captains, all of them his friends and followers. He then made an agreement with those outside the city, recalled the exiles, and published an amnesty for all except the opposing leaders. A little later, as if to emphasize the real significance of the alteration, the States of Holland sent an Amsterdam foot-band into the city. This, and reiterated assurances from Mörs and the new magistrates that they intended no change in religion, also gradually lulled the fear that the government of Utrecht might have fallen into Papist hands.[17]

The worst obstacle to a firm union of all the Provinces under the States General had thus been removed. A party devoted to Mörs, ready like him to co-operate closely with Holland, had gained full control over the machinery of government and over the armed forces of the one province and city where hitherto the opposition had held those advantages. That opposition, deprived of the forces and the influence and organization which such a constitutional base alone could give to their party, rapidly broke in pieces now that they could no longer lean upon the support of England. For Elizabeth during this autumn made it abundantly clear that opposition to the States could look for no support from her. At Utrecht, during the alteration there, 'such of our English companies as were in the town held themselves "neuter", which hath bred a good opinion of their uprightness', Killigrew reported on 8 October.[18] And in holding themselves 'neuter', those English companies had accurately reflected the attitude of the English Queen. She did write, as we have seen, very guardedly in favour of Deventer. But she paid no heed at all to Meetkerke's other proposals, if indeed he ever got so far as to put them to her. Nor would she listen to another project (obviously the work of those whose devotion to Leicester had marred their prospects in the northern provinces) for the reconquest of Flanders by a force of 6,000 or 7,000 men similarly paid for by

[17] Ibid., pp. 225, 245, 253-4, 257, 270-1, 302, 317; *H. M. C., Ancaster MSS*, p. 187; *Kronijk*, XVI, 181-2.
[18] *Cal. S. P. Foreign*, XXII, 253.

the Netherlands refugees in England. She gave at least as cold a reception to a suggestion from the Frisian opposition that she should send 4,000 foot and 500 horse, in her own pay apparently, to bring Friesland, and perhaps Groningen too, under her rule. She very firmly refused to take the turbulent German garrison of Geertruidenberg into her pay, even though they insisted upon having Sir John Wingfield, Willoughby's brother-in-law, as their nominal commander.[19]

By now, indeed, most of Leicester's defeated followers had themselves come to realize that they could hope for little more from Elizabeth than diplomatic intercession to get them a fair settlement and a free discharge. Most of them merely asked that she would use her influence to clear them of the accusations brought against them and to secure the payment of their arrears. Such were the requests of Colonel Sonoy, of Adrian Saravia and the exiles of Leyden, even of Deventer and Cleerhagen. Others, like Colonel Fremin and young Meetkerke, asked to be taken into the Queen's pay. Sonoy was not above hinting at his need of a pension, Noël de Caron obtained one, and Lucas Engelstedt asked for a licence to do a little gun-running for his own profit and the assistance of the opposition in Friesland. The States had nothing much to fear from men in this defeatist frame of mind.[20]

The alteration at Utrecht thus practically ended that serious provincial opposition to the States General and Holland which had been the legacy of Leicester's governor-generalship. As early as 1 October Killigrew could write that 'the controversies for which it pleased Her Majesty to continue my service here the longer, are all appeased save this new brabble at Utrecht'.[21] Soon afterwards Friesland at last sent its deputies to the Council of State and Utrecht promised to do the same. When the States General began to come together again at the end of November, there were unwonted signs of harmony, although the Utrecht deputies had insufficiently full instructions and Gelderland was still rather restless. How successfully the Hollanders had established their ascendancy, which alone could make the general union effective, is shown by Gilpin's remark that 'the 19th article of the treaty, concerning the equality of government and councils, must be looked to and maintained or else new controversies and divisions will still fall out'.[22]

For the other provinces, of course, remained jealous of Holland and this jealousy still prevented any reform of the slow and cumbrous federal administration. Nevertheless, although Holland and Zeeland could not get the other provinces to accept Count Maurice as their governor and commander, he was coming to be generally regarded as 'chief of the wars'. Fortunately, too, he was able to work in close concert with Count Mörs, the governor of Utrecht, Gelderland, and Overijsel, and with Count William Louis of Nassau-Dillingen, the governor of Friesland. This triumvirate was now free from serious rivals since Count Hohenlohe had gone on a lengthy mission to Denmark and Germany.[23] They were moreover all good friends of Holland, obedient servants of the States, and on good terms with Jan van Oldenbarnevelt whose influence was now becoming more and more dominant there. So the authority of the States General, whatever the defects of its machinery, was becoming firmly established throughout the United Provinces and those Provinces were made that much the more capable of holding their own against Spain.

Elizabeth had already contributed substantially to this improvement. Her refusal to assist or to countenance the designs of the Leicestrian opposition against the States had done much to damp down the faction strife that had so enfeebled the Provinces in recent years. The breaking-off of the Bourbourg peace negotiations and the defeat of the Armada had restored Dutch confidence in the sincerity of her commitment against the Spaniards. The leading part played by Willoughby and his troops in the successful defence of Bergen had cleared away much of the suspicion and ill will that Stanley and Yorke's treasons in 1587 had brought upon all Englishmen. And Sir John Norris's arrival with another 1,500 English soldiers had manifested the Queen's continuing readiness to help the Dutch in their hours of need.

Norris, moreover, brought with him more than just a relief

<hr>

[22] Ibid., pp. 253, 270-1, 342; *Resolutiën der Staten Generaal*, VI, 18-20, 91-3.
[23] *Cal. S. P. Foreign*, XXII, 186-7, 302.

force of English soldiers. He brought also an invitation to the States to co-operate in the great counterstroke to the Armada that he and Drake were preparing. And he brought further instructions designed to smooth away old animosities and to give the Anglo-Dutch alliance a fresh start. He was to urge fair treatment for Leicester's defeated followers as a means to a general reconciliation between all the Provinces and all the parties. He was also to press the States to prohibit trade with the enemy; to provide money to repair Ostend's defences; and to undertake to repay the Queen's extra expenses in sending additional forces to their assistance, as to Sluys last year and Bergen this. But in return he might repeat the promises, most of them already made to the States' agent Ortel, to remedy the States' grievances. All the auxiliary companies in the Queen's pay were henceforth to be kept up to strength and 'employed to the field', provided that they were not sent upon desperate services and that the places from which they were drawn were left with adequate garrisons. The States would not again be called upon to advance lendings or provide victuals to the English companies and whatever they had advanced or provided would be repaid as soon as the accounts between them and the Queen for the past two years were completed and agreed. Norris was also to concert with Willoughby measures to assure Geertruidenberg to the States and to remove its still mutinous garrison.[24]

These instructions did suggest a real desire on Elizabeth's part to seek a better understanding with her Dutch allies and to make her aid to them fully effective. Norris, of course, during the few busy weeks that he was in the Low Countries, could hardly do more than sketch out the Queen's intentions, and the replies of the States of Holland and the Council of State showed clearly that better understanding would come but slowly, after long argument and tough bargaining. Old grievances and old suspicions had burned too deep for quick erasure. Norris therefore had to leave these matters for Thomas Bodley to pursue when he came over in mid-December to take Henry Killigrew's place in the Council of State.[25] Nevertheless the discussions that Norris initiated did

---

[24] Ibid., pp. 247–50; *Resolutiën der Staten Generaal*, VI, 86.
[25] *Cal. S. P. Foreign*, XXII, 318, 381; *Kronijk*, XVI, 181–2.

promise to set the Anglo-Dutch alliance on the road to recovery from the false start made in Leicester's time, to set it on a course that might eventually make the Provinces united and strong enough to defend themselves with no greater English assistance than that promised in the 1585 Treaty.

Indeed, before Norris went back to England in mid-December, he had already persuaded the States to manage for a time with even less than the promised amount of English aid. This had not been the Queen's original intention. She had, it is true, authorized Norris to threaten that, if the States would not undertake to repay the charges of the 1,500 men he brought to the relief of Bergen, she would withdraw the same number from her auxiliary companies and would not help in any future necessity.[26] Elizabeth's bark, however, was usually a lot worse than her bite and there is no reason to suppose that this threat would have proved an exception to the rule had it not been for Norris. His first talks with Count Maurice and Oldenbarnevelt, and others of the Holland and Zeeland States and the Council of State, gave him high hopes of getting 'a very honourable assistance' from them for his Portugal expedition. He could not get final answers, of course, until the States General reassembled at the beginning of December. But as early as 26 October the States of Holland and the States of Zeeland agreed to give their deputies authority to consent, when the States General did meet, to up to £10,000 worth of assistance. Out of this £10,000 Norris understood that

they intend to set forth ten of their greatest ships of war, furnished with victual and munition for six months. They will also set forth 2,000 shot, armed, entertained, and victualled for the like time, under the conduct, as it is thought, of the Count Philip. They will give me assistance also to levy 2 or 3,000 shot of these country men and permission to freight shipping for their transportation. They will be content that I shall freight ten of their best ships, that are fittest, to carry horses. It is told me that the States of Holland will yield to somewhat more from themselves, but what not yet resolved of.[27]

However, as against these high hopes – not all of them to be realized – it was clear to Norris from the very first that there

[26] *Cal. S. P. Foreign*, XXII, 247.
[27] Ibid., pp. 284, 288, 312; *Kronijk*, XVI, 188–9.

was no likelihood at all of the States undertaking to repay the charges of the 1,500 men he had brought over for the relief of Bergen. Those 1,500, he was told, had not been asked for; they were no more than were needed to bring the decayed auxiliary bands up to strength; and anyway the States' extraordinary expenses for the defence of Bergen and the islands made them quite unable to shoulder such an additional burden. Accordingly, as early as 29 October Norris was writing home that 'Her Majesty shall not have any so good means to prevail herself of that charge as to give us leave to have ten of the old companies with us' for the Portugal expedition. A fortnight later he sent Sir Roger Williams with a formal request for them and for some of the horse-bands as well. The Queen agreed, provided that the States consented. But long before he received her answer, Norris had asked the Dutch on 16 November not for ten but for thirteen of the English auxiliary foot-bands (2,000 men) and for six of the horse-bands (600 men) as well.[28]

When the States General at length reassembled early in December, they agreed without much difficulty to this request, though on condition that the troops were to be back in the Provinces by 1 June and that in the meantime the English would keep 2,000 foot (thirteen companies) and 200 horse in Bergen, 1,000 foot (seven companies) in Ostend, and another 200 horse on the eastern frontiers. With their own troops they were less generous. At first they offered only eight of their foot-bands. By 14 December Norris had persuaded them to increase these eight to ten and to make one of them 200 strong instead of the usual 150. They were to get a month's pay and a bonus of 400 to 500 gulden (£40 or £50) a company to wipe off some part of the arrears due to them by the States, but thereafter they would be at the Queen's charge. Besides these, the States agreed, no doubt with alacrity, that Norris might take at the Queen's charge the 350 foot and 300 horse of the unruly Geertruidenberg garrison – if he could persuade them to go. But he was not to be allowed himself to raise any other companies in the Provinces.[29]

[28] *Cal. S. P. Foreign*, XXII, 244, 288, 293, 313, 336.
[29] Ibid., p. 402; *H. M. C., Ancaster MSS*, pp. 221-2, 227; *Resolutiën der Staten Generaal*, VI, 50-1, 84 note 5, 89-91, 178-9, 210-11; *Kronijk*, XVI, 196-7.

In addition to these promises about troops, the States General confirmed the earlier undertaking to give Norris up to £10,000 worth of assistance, and Friesland and Utrecht promised to join Holland and Zeeland in contributing their quotas to this expenditure. They promised to lend him 12,000 to 14,000 lb. of gunpowder and to let him buy and take away, duty free, large quantities of victuals, arms, and munitions. They granted his request for leave to hire, at his own expense, twenty-four transports. Later they agreed that instead of ten of these he might hire, for transporting horses, five 550-ton 'furlangers' from Amsterdam and Hoorn if he could persuade the owners to let them go and if frost and contrary winds did not prevent them coming round from the Zuyder Zee. The Zeeland States further promised to furnish fourteen ships, with a warship for escort, to take back the 1,500 men he had brought from England. This may perhaps have been the source of his mistaken impression that he was promised four warships from the States General and another ten from Flushing. The States altogether denied any such promise, although they did later agree to provide four, and eventually six or seven, 150-ton warships and a couple of pinnaces, victualled and equipped for four months.[30]

With these promises Sir John Norris returned to England, leaving his brother Sir Edward to complete the gathering in of the troops, ships, and supplies and to see to their despatch to England, he hoped by the end of the year. His mission had taken almost nine weeks, a good deal longer than he had anticipated and just about twice as long as the earlier discussions with the Queen and in the Privy Council. Nevertheless he could return home feeling reasonably well satisfied. During those nine weeks Parma had suffered a most damaging set-back before Bergen; discussions had been started between the Queen and the States to clear away the disputes and difficulties that had hindered the efficient working of their alliance; and the States had promised a substantial contribution towards the Portugal expedition. They had, besides, acquiesced in the withdrawal of two-fifths of the English auxiliary forces for service in another theatre,

---

[30] *Cal. S. P. Foreign*, XXII, 402; *H. M. C., Ancaster MSS*, p. 227; *Resolutiën der Staten Generaal*, VI, 50–1, 84 note 5, 89–93, 96, 365–73, 450, 550, 573–7.

even if it were only for five months that mostly fell within the close season for large-scale military operations in the Low Countries. With the Catholic League in France staggering from the blow of the Guises' assassinations, the outlook for the English counterstroke against Spain and Portugal seemed set fair.

The preparations in England for that counterstroke, too, were well advanced by the end of the year. While Norris had been arranging for the troops, ships, and supplies from the United Provinces, Drake had made equally good progress in England. He had indeed been paying out faster than his fellow adventurers had been paying in and barely a fortnight after the sealing of his commission he was already begging the Queen for help. He and Norris, it will be remembered, had promised on 19 September that they would not call upon the Queen for more than £5,000 of her £20,000 until the private adventurers had paid their £40,000 in full. Thereupon she had promptly contributed £3,000. Yet now on 23 October Drake asked for the immediate payment of the remaining £17,000, to cover the cost of the first two and a half months' victuals which he had begun to purchase. By then private contributions of £43,000 had been promised but very little of it had so far been paid. Indeed, one of Drake's reasons for asking for the Queen's remaining £17,000 was that it would 'induce the adventurers to bring in their adventures with greater readiness and expedition'.[31]

Elizabeth, it seems, was inclined to hold Norris and Drake on this point to the strict letter of their bargain. But Lord Treasurer Burghley either over-persuaded her or else quietly ignored her wishes. 'Her Majesty', he wrote to Walsingham later, 'did persist to have the same performed and so commanded me to follow that course in delivery of her money, which if I had done, had been a hindrance or rather an overthrow of the journey.' At all events, the full payment had been warranted by 29 October and the Exchequer had paid over £17,000 by Christmas and the full £20,000 by the end of January. Thus assisted, Drake's preparations went steadily forward. During November and December 1,200 mariners or

<hr/>

[31] S. P. Domestic, ccxvii, nos. 55, 56.

more were busy rigging and fitting out the ships. At the same time James Quarles, the surveyor of victuals for the Queen's navy, and his assistant Marmaduke Darrell, were completing the collection of the three months' store of victuals that the expedition was to carry with it to sea and the additional supply to feed them 'for fourteen days which by estimation they may remain together before their going to sea'.[32]

By the time that Norris got back from Holland therefore, everything was so well advanced that on 30 December the Privy Council sent out its letters to the lord mayor of London and the lords-lieutenant of twenty-five English and Welsh counties for the levy of the troops that were to be raised at home. The local authorities were to select, as near as might be, 'strong and serviceable persons' who were willing to go; and they were to provide them with swords and coats, but no other arms or armour, and with enough conduct money to get them to the seaside by 20 January. By that date Norris expected to have the Netherlands contingents, ships, and supplies over as well. What was more, the 2,000 foot and 600 horse from the English auxiliary forces would cost him nothing. For during the five months for which they were promised to him, they were to remain in the Queen's pay just as if they were still in the Netherlands. Apparently, too, the customary defalcations (deductions for defects in numbers and so forth) were not to be made during those five months. On top of this, the Queen now sent over an additional £4,000 to enable Norris to prepare the companies for the voyage.[33] This time it was Burghley who felt a little uneasy about the extra cost to the Exchequer.

I see [he wrote to Walsingham on 30 December] that the bargain first offered to Her Majesty shall be much altered to the burden of Her Majesty and the disburdening of Sir John Norris and Sir Francis Drake. For they offered, having £20,000 in money and the six ships of Her Majesty, to levy 8,000 men in England and 4,000 in Holland. And now they will charge Her Majesty with 2,000 footmen and 600 horse, the charges whereof seemeth to come to the sum of £14,511, besides such a further sum to be paid as it is in your letter

---

[32] Ibid., ccxix, nos. 37, 49; ccxxii, no. 40; *Acts P. C.*, XVI, 334; *Cal. S. P. Foreign*, XXII, 311; S. O. Docquets, I, fo. 169b.

[33] *Acts P. C.*, XVI, 418–19; S. P. Domestic, ccxix, no. 47; ccxxii, no. 45; ccxxiv, no. 53.

comprised, which may come to £4,000; so as they are to be relieved further than was at first offered to the sum of £18,511, a matter worthy consideration.[34]

Burghley then went on, however: 'these doubts I move not as unwilling to further the voyage', and a postscript to the letter vindicates his sincerity. 'I have', he there wrote, 'taken some pain in writing hereof with a sore hand, because I would not make any other acquainted with the matter.' This picture of the old Lord Treasurer writing painfully with his own gouty hand so that not even his confidential clerk should be aware of his anxiety, differs considerably from the traditional one of the chief 'scribe', by whose hostility the 'men-of-war' were balked at every turn. There is, indeed, little or no evidence that so far either Burghley or the Queen was anything except enthusiastic about the expedition and eager to hasten it on its way, whatever doubts Hawkins and perhaps Howard may have felt. And there was every reason to hope that it would be ready to sail, as planned, by 1 February, ready to strike a decisive blow in Portugal and Spain long before the campaigning season opened in northern France and the Low Countries.

[34] Ibid., ccxix, no. 45.

# IV

## Delays and Complications

About Christmas 1588 English hopes of decisive success against Spain were higher than they had ever been before. They were also higher than they were ever to be again. For during the following six or seven months the prospect of speedy victory was gradually eclipsed by a growing likelihood that the war would be a long-drawn-out and increasingly burdensome affair. The first disappointments came over the expedition that Norris and Drake were preparing. To begin with, instead of sailing from England on 1 February as planned, it did not get away until 18 April. Many historians have put the blame for this upon Elizabeth and her civilian advisers, her 'scribes', Lord Treasurer Burghley in particular. 'Week after week passed by', one alleged, 'while differences of opinion in the Council and changes of inclination on the part of the Queen threatened the stay of the expedition'.[1] But the records provide little or no evidence for anything of the sort and, although Elizabeth was indeed in part to blame, it was not quite in that way.

The primary cause of the delay was not ill will on the Queen's part but an unfortunate quarrel with the Dutch that flared up when Willoughby on 9 January informed the States General of her orders for the despatch of the thirteen foot-bands and six horse-bands from the English auxiliary forces. In those orders she instructed Willoughby to have the troops ready to embark as soon as Sir Edward Norris gave the word. At the same time, however, he was to make it clear that she would never have withdrawn any of her auxiliary forces if the States had not first agreed to it and if they had not promised to supply in any emergency the places of the absent Englishmen with their own troops at their own charges. Anyway, he was to add, as Ostend was to be abandoned owing to the States' failure to repair its defences, its nine foot-bands

[1] E. P. Cheyney, *History of England,* I, 161.

would be available elsewhere and Norris's withdrawals should not therefore much disfurnish any place. Five of the Ostend bands were to go with Norris, leaving the other four to replace the five from Bergen that, with three from Flushing and one from Brielle, were, according to the Privy Council's curious arithmetic, to make up his thirteen companies.[2]

Now although the Queen's orders did not reach Willoughby until 8 January, they had been sent off on 23 December, just about as soon as possible after Sir John Norris got back to England. The promptness, indeed the hastiness, of their despatch certainly does not suggest any hesitation or ill will on Elizabeth's part. And it must mean, almost as certainly, that her orders were based wholly upon Norris's account of his agreement with the States. If so, then he must have seriously misunderstood or seriously misreported the terms of that agreement and much of the blame for the ensuing quarrel with the Dutch must be laid at his door.

For the States, as they were quick to protest, had never given any promise to provide troops of their own to fill the places of the Englishmen Norris was to take away. On the contrary, they expected any lacks to be made good out of the English auxiliary companies that were lying in the cautionary towns in breach of the 1585 treaty. Indeed, to get those auxiliary companies out of the cautionary towns was transparently the purpose of the main condition that the States had made when they agreed to Norris's proposals. For, to provide 2,000 foot in Bergen and 1,000 in Ostend would require all, or more than all, of the 3,000 auxiliary footmen who would nominally remain after Norris took his 2,000.[3]

This was a matter on which the States were now particularly sensitive, since they felt that they had just been let down badly by their English allies in their efforts to succour

---

[2] *Cal. S. P. Foreign*, XXII, 389–91; XXIII, 29–31; *Kronijk*, XVI, 205–6. Possibly the mistake in arithmetic was discovered and the Privy Council's letter held back for correction, for although both the minute in the State Papers and that in the Council register (*Acts P. C.*, XVI, 410–11) are dated 23 December, the letter and list of companies that Willoughby received were dated 31 December and arrived a week later than the Queen's instructions – *Cal. S. P. Foreign*, XXIII, 40, 54.

[3] Ibid., XXII, 329; XXIII, 30, 45–6, 60–1; *Resolutiën der Staten Generaal*, VI, 375–80.

Wachtendonk and Rheinberg. Those two places, although they lay beyond the frontiers of the United Provinces, were important for the cover they gave to Gelderland and Overijsel against a flank attack down the Rhine. Yet when the enemy with 1,500 horse and 5,000 foot under Count Charles Mansfelt, after taking Bonn besieged Wachtendonk, the most that the States and Count Mörs could scrape together for its relief was 640 horse and 1,300 foot. So, at the end of November they begged Willoughby to assist them with 400 English horse and 1,000 English foot. He seems to have agreed readily enough and at a conference held on 5 December to settle ways and means, he promised to go himself to join Mörs with six of the English horse-bands, four foot-bands from Bergen and three from Ostend, to which Norris allowed him to add three of the new foot-bands that he had brought over for Bergen. These last three were added on the ground of the weakness of the companies in the English garrisons; and if it really took ten foot-bands – each nominally of 135 men even after deducting the dead pays – to make up 1,000 men, then the States had good reason to complain that the Queen was not keeping her auxiliary forces up to the strength promised by the 1585 treaty.

For the moment, however, they were glad enough of the help, even though they were not prepared to advance the English any lendings or to appoint them garrisons to return to. Later the States did accuse Willoughby of causing them to delay the relief operations for more than a fortnight, but Willoughby denied this and a fortnight does not seem an excessive time for collecting troops and shipping and mounting such an operation in midwinter. In the event, Wachtendonk surrendered on 16 December, the day before the relief forces were due to assemble at their rendezvous. That made it more than ever necessary to revictual and reinforce Rheinberg before the enemy moved on to besiege that place. Willoughby still seems to have been willing enough to help. But ten days earlier, without his knowledge, the States and Norris had made their agreement about the withdrawals for the Portugal expedition. So, on 12 December Norris informed Willoughby that all the companies appointed to be withdrawn, new and old, must be at their ports and ready to embark by 31 December. This meant, of course, that not only were the three new companies he had promised for the relief force no longer available, but also that none of the new companies could any longer be counted upon to provide temporary replacements for the four old companies from Bergen or the three due from Ostend. It was at this point, too, that Willoughby learned for the first time of the States' requirement that 2,000 footmen be left in Bergen and 1,000 in Ostend. He reckoned that in fact Bergen would now be left with only 800, a quite inadequate garrison. So, as the cautionary town governors refused to send him any troops, he called upon the States to accept responsibility for Bergen's safety until he and his companies got back from Rheinberg.

That really put the States' backs up. On 19 December they sent the English companies back to Bergen in order that, as they angrily told Willoughby, with Wachtendonk lost and Rheinberg in danger they should not also lose Bergen, where until now they had believed, and where they still expected, 2,000 English soldiers would be left after Norris made his withdrawals.[4] Willoughby at once protested that his commission did not give him powers to cashier, conflate, or reform companies so as to bring the Bergen and Ostend garrisons up to the required numbers. If the States wanted that done, they must apply to Her Majesty. This they at once did, on 20 December, by letters sent to Elizabeth and by instructions to their agent Ortel. On the same day they wrote formally requiring Willoughby, Morgan, and Conway to see to it that there were the required 2,000 foot and 200 horse in Bergen and 1,000 foot in Ostend. Two days earlier they had resolved to keep in service ten of their own supernumerary foot-bands. These were bands which, like the other ten promised to Norris and like most of the States' soldiers on the frontiers, had been 'upon no repartition of any province' but lived upon the contributions that they could exact from the districts where they served. The ten were now put upon the regular pay rolls of Holland, Zeeland, and Friesland and given a month's pay. They were to be employed to assure and strengthen the

[1] *Cal. S. P. Foreign*, XXII, 374; *H. M. C., Ancaster MSS*, pp. 224–5, 229–33; *Resolutiën der Staten Generaal*, VI, 36, 40, 42–6, 48–9.

eastern frontiers in place of the companies from the Queen's auxiliary forces that Norris would be withdrawing.[5]

That was how matters stood on 9 January, when Willoughby informed the States of the Queen's instructions for the despatch of the companies for Portugal and of her request that they would at need make good any gaps those withdrawals created in the English garrisons. And hard on the heels of this came the threat to abandon Ostend. Threat rather than firm and absolute decision, for although on 23 December the Queen wrote so decidedly, she also wrote in haste and rather carelessly – she apologized for the disorderliness of her letter, 'as setting the cart before the horse'[6] – and this seems to have been another instance of her bark being worse than her bite. In other letters, written a few days earlier but despatched at the same time, the threat was conditional. Willoughby was to inform the States that, if they did not immediately put the necessary repairs in hand, she would withdraw Ostend's garrison to Bergen. And that was how Willoughby put it to the States on 10 January.[7] Now Ostend's defences, both against the enemy and against the sea, were certainly in a dangerously dilapidated condition and the States had been exasperatingly dilatory in answering repeated calls for their repair.[8] But dilatory people hate being spurred on and Elizabeth's threat of unilateral action over Ostend made the States more angry than ever at what seemed to them her high-handed attitude. They did despatch a commissary to see to the repairs, but they flatly denied that the place was untenable and they protested that they could in no wise consent to its being abandoned. At the same time in strongly worded declarations they absolutely forbade Willoughby and the other English commanders either to order or

---

[5] *H. M. C., Ancaster MSS,* pp. 232, 234; *Cal. S. P. Foreign,* XXII, 388; *Resolutiën der Staten Generaal,* VI, 178–9. The ten supernumerary bands were retained 'in plaitsse van het volck uuyt het secours van Hare ma.' tot hetselve exploict geconsentert . . . om daermede dies te betere op de versekeringe end versterckinge van de frontieren te moegen versien' – ibid., p. 178. The States had been talking about doing this before Norris left The Hague – ibid., p. 36. Could he possibly have mistaken this talk about supplying the eastern frontier places for a general promise to replace the English wherever and whenever necessary, e.g. at Bergen and Ostend as well?

[6] *Cal. S. P. Foreign,* XXII, 389.

[7] Ibid., p. 380; *Resolutiën der Staten Generaal,* VI, 440.

[8] *Cal. S. P. Foreign,* XXII, 340–1, 376–7.

to permit any of the auxiliary companies to be withdrawn from Bergen and Ostend until others had arrived to replace them and to provide the specified numbers in the two garrisons.[9]

The States' anger was obviously a very serious threat to the expedition's prospects. If not quickly appeased, it might stop all the expected contributions from the Netherlands, upon which so much depended. Elizabeth recognized this and once she was made aware of the storm that her orders to Willoughby had aroused, she was quick to do all she could to put matters right. As soon as she received full reports from Willoughby and from Ortel, and from the States' own letters, she hastened to despatch on 27 January a fresh set of instructions and a fresh list of the companies to be withdrawn. These did meet practically all the States' demands. The Queen still believed, and was to go on believing, that they had promised to make good at need any gaps caused by the withdrawals. But she now cut down the number of English foot-bands that were to be withdrawn from thirteen to ten, the number Norris had first thought of. Some auxiliary companies at least were to be sent from the cautionary towns to Bergen and the new list explained in detail how the States' conditions were to be satisfied there and at Ostend. And Ostend, about which Her Majesty had now received more reassuring reports, was no longer to be abandoned.[10]

That should have settled it. But when on 8 February Willoughby informed the States General of these new orders, he added a letter of his own, painting in the blackest colours the effects that they would have upon the forces under his command. By some quite incomprehensible arithmetic he contrived to satisfy himself that he would be left with no more than 1,000 or 1,100 English foot to defend both Bergen and Ostend.[11] Whether he did this out of malice or from the exaggerated obsession of a local commander with his own theatre of operations, is hard to tell. Certainly he was weary and homesick, suffering from an attack of jaundice, and on

[9] Ibid., XXIII, 30, 40, 45–6, 57–8; *Resolutiën der Staten Generaal*, VI, 375–83; *Kronijk*, XVI, 207–9.

[10] *Cal. S. P. Foreign*, XXIII, 22, 71–2.

[11] Ibid., pp. 99–100, 110–12; *Resolutiën der Staten Generaal*, VI, 389.

bad terms with the Dutch. He had not been privy to the agreement with the States and he was intensely jealous of Norris and Drake who, 'glorying with Artaxerxes over a few ships', were reducing his own forces far below what he considered the margin of safety. He particularly resented their taking away his own chosen captains and officers. 'I had hoped', he protested, 'my Lord Willoughby, being lord general for Her Majesty in a certain war near England, had had as good reason to hold those he had advanced as others, in a removed war of hope, not only to create new but to choose whatsoever they listed.' He had even put forward a counter-project of his own for an offensive in Flanders, especially to take Dunkirk, and offered to adventure £10,000 in it. Such a project was to have its attractions eighteen months or so later, when the bulk of the Spanish army was on its way to relieve Paris and the remainder was being severely stretched to hold its own against Dutch and English on the Maas and Waal. But in February 1589 the idea of thus assaulting Parma's still undivided army head-on and on its home ground was not likely to appeal very strongly to Elizabeth or her Council. None the less, it is understandable that 'the brave Lord Willoughby', after his notable triumph at Bergen, should resent having two-fifths of his forces snatched away and being himself used as 'a commissary to post men from one to another'.[12]

Understandable, but very unfortunate: for his letter utterly spoiled the effect of the Queen's revised instructions. The States were only too ready to believe any tale of the English companies' weakness and so this letter went far to kill their already waning enthusiasm for the expedition. They did eventually allow six of the promised ten Dutch foot-bands to embark, but they made no serious effort to get the other four off or to get ready their six warships or the transports.[13] Their hostility also seriously weakened and delayed the English contingents. Sir John Conway at Ostend and Sir Thomas Morgan at Bergen both feared enemy attacks and welcomed the States' repeated orders not to send away any of their

---

[12] *Cal. S. P. Foreign*, XXIII, 37, 54–5; *H. M. C., Ancaster MSS*, pp. 237–9, 262.
[13] *Cal. S. P. Foreign*, XXIII, 168; Anthony Wingfield's account of the Portugal Voyage in Hakluyt, IV, 310.

troops until others arrived to replace them. The still unre-paired defences of Ostend gave Conway continuing cause for nervousness, while Morgan had more personal reasons for wanting to please the States. He and Sir Thomas Knollys had just carried off from Dordrecht to Bergen the two daughters of the Baroness of Merode-Petershem. They did marry the girls, who clearly were by no means unwilling. 'But', Morgan wrote, 'forasmuch as it hath been done without the knowledge and liking of the mother, therefore are the States greatly incensed against me' – all the more, presumably, as the young ladies' father was living on the enemy's side. Being on bad terms with Willoughby ever since replacing Drury at Bergen, Morgan could not afford to antagonize further the States from whom he held his commission as governor.[14] Individual captains, too, followed their superiors' example by seeking to extract a long overdue full pay or a substantial imprest as the price of setting their companies on the march.[15]

In the end, the four companies from the cautionary towns were released fairly readily and Sir Edward Norris got his own band out of Ostend easily enough. But it took repeated orders from the Privy Council to extract a mere forty men of Anthony Wingfield's company from that town, whilst none of the three bands appointed to come from Bergen ever left their garrison. The tenth foot-band and the horse-bands had gone after all with Count Mörs to the relief of Rheinberg and did not get back, considerably weakened, until late in January. When they reached their ports of embarkation early in February they found that, through the hostility of the Dutch officials and the negligence of the purveyors appointed by Sir Edward Norris, no transports had been provided to carry them to England. These bands, and the States' footmen, were delayed further by the freezing of the harbours and it was the middle of February before they embarked. Even then they and the foot-bands from the cautionary towns were still further delayed until early March by contrary winds.[16]

[14] *Cal. S. P. Foreign*, XXIII, 40–1, 51; *H. M. C., Ancaster MSS*, pp. 242–3; *Correspondance de Philippe II*, III, 359.

[15] *Cal. S. P. Foreign*, XXIII, 52, 59; *H. M. C., Ancaster MSS*, pp. 226, 233.

[16] *Cal. S. P. Foreign*, XXIII, 100–1, 103, 167, 377; *Resolutiën der Staten Generaal*, VI, 449, 454.

So the seasoned infantry expected from the Low Countries were reduced from twenty-three companies (3,500 men) to twelve companies (1,800 men).[17] The seasoned cavalry vanished altogether, for one of the six English horse-bands existed only on paper and the other five had been so weakened by their Rheinberg operations that when they landed in England they were little more than half strength and had to be discharged. The only horsemen to go were thus the single raw troop that Sir John Norris had raised.[18] The Low Countries' shipping and supplies were similarly diminished and delayed. None of the States' warships and very few of their transports ever came; and out of £9,000 worth of arms and munitions that Norris had ordered from Holland, £4,651 worth never reached him, while the rest did not arrive until late in March.[19]

Even more serious than the deficiencies was the delay in the arrival of those forces and supplies which did come. For want of them, as the commanders told Elizabeth, the whole expedition was fain to stay. Elizabeth did her best to hurry matters along. For example, when Ortel on 11 February reported that the States' footmen and the English cavalry were held up by the freezing of the waterways, she gave orders for Norris and Drake to be informed that they must not wait, but must arrange for these forces to follow them. Norris and Drake, however, were most unwilling to sail without their cavalry, their full contingents of seasoned infantry, and so considerable a portion of their supplies. They were also, either from underestimation or through defaults in the Netherlands, very short of transports.[20]

It was the middle of March before these hindrances were removed. By then the depleted Netherlands contingents had arrived and the whole force was assembled at Dover and other

---

[17] Six instead of ten Dutch, six instead of thirteen English (Wingfield's forty men could not be counted as a company) – Hakluyt, IV, 310. These figures, of course, exclude the 1,500 men Norris took from England to the relief of Bergen.

[18] *Cal. S. P. Foreign*, XXIII, 142–3, 158–9; *Acts P. C.*, XVII, 116.

[19] S. P. Domestic, ccxix, no. 56; *Cal. S. P. Foreign*, XXIII, 246.

[20] *H. M. C., Salisbury MSS*, III, 233; *Cal. S. P. Foreign*, XXIII, 128; S. P. Domestic, ccxxii, no. 79. 'The cause of our stay here will be the want of some part of our munition which must come out of the Low Countries', Drake wrote from Plymouth on 20 March – ibid., ccxxiii, no. 24.

south-eastern ports. The problem of transports was solved at the same time by a lucky chance – the arrival in Dover harbour of sixty Dutch flyboats on their way in ballast to the western ports of France. By impressing these reluctant allies, Drake was able to embark his forces and carry them down Channel to Plymouth, where he arrived on 19 March.[21] Yet nothing could alter the fact that it was now the middle of March instead of the beginning of February, and at Plymouth a further consequence of the long delays developed. The fleet had missed its wind and was now penned in the Sound for another month by the strong and persistent south-westerly gales of late March and early April.

During that month, of course, the men had to be fed. And there were by now a lot more men than Norris and Drake had reckoned on. They had budgeted for a force of 10,000 or 12,000 soldiers, besides sailors and pioneers. For these they had provided £28,377 7s. 9d. worth of victuals, sufficient they estimated to last them for four months. At Plymouth, however, they allowed popular enthusiasm for the expedition to upset all their calculations. 'Since our first assembly of the determined number of men for this service', they wrote to the Privy Council on 3 April, 'the army hath been almost doubly increased, especially of late since the bruit of the taking of the flyboats, by the repair of many gentlemen and divers companies of voluntary soldiers offering to be employed in this action whom, both for their satisfaction and the advancement of the service, we could in no sort refuse to entertain.' In fact according to the muster rolls which they both signed on 8 April, they then had, not 10,000 or 12,000, but just on 19,000 soldiers to feed, besides 290 pioneers and 4,000 English and Dutch sailors. As a result, since arriving at Plymouth on 19 March, they had been 'forced, the country not being able by far to furnish the daily expense of victual, to sustain the army out of the bulk of our sea store'. By 1 April £8,885 of the £28,377 7s. 9d. worth of victuals in that sea store had already been consumed. At such a rate the remaining £19,492 7s. 9d. would last barely another six weeks, to about 10 May the commanders estimated. And still the winds

<hr/>

[21] Ibid., nos. 24, 57.

remained contrary, keeping the whole force weather-bound at Plymouth.[22]

For Norris and Drake the situation was already verging on the desperate. The swollen numbers that they had too light-heartedly welcomed were rapidly consuming in harbour the supplies that they had laid in for the voyage. They had no money to buy more, for they had already spent £96,324 10s. 8d. instead of their budgeted £70,000 and, with their mounting debts, their credit, too, was exhausted.[23] In this extremity, they turned again to the Queen for help. On 3 April they reminded her that, in accepting their original project, she had agreed to victual the expedition if it were stayed by contrary winds for longer than ten days. Accordingly they asked her now to victual their entire force until they sailed and also to arrange for 'a convenient proportion of victual' to be sent after them when they did get away – this regardless of the fact that, by their own admission, their numbers were 'almost doubly increased' from those specified in that original project. They reiterated these requests with even greater urgency on 8 April, immediately after the weather had again frustrated an attempt to get to sea.

If the wind continue against us [Norris wrote on that day to Burghley] we are utterly unable to supply ourselves and, the voyage breaking, we cannot think what to do with the army. For, upon failing of the voyage, every man will call for pay from Her Majesty, being levied by Her Highness's commission. And if they have it not, the country will be utterly spoiled, robberies and outrages committed in every place, the arms and furniture lost, besides the dishonour of the matter.[24]

The Queen must have found this cool attempt at blackmail peculiarly irritating. She had already contributed almost twice as much as her original undertaking of £20,000. For besides handing over that £20,000 and her six ships, she had given Norris credit for the five months' pay of the auxiliary companies from the Low Countries. That, with a supply of

[22] Ibid., ccxvii, no. 55 (Drake's estimate, 23 October); ccxxiii, nos. 56 (his account 1 April), 59 (Norris and Drake to the Privy Council, 3 April), 74 and 75 (musters).
[23] Drake's account, 1 April, totalled £51,188 14s. 8d., Norris's £45,135 16s. – ibid., nos. 56, 64.
[24] Ibid., nos. 59, 71, 72.

apparel for them, came to £11,678 8s. Of course she would be saving that sum in the Netherlands; but nevertheless for Norris and Drake it was an uncovenanted addition to what they had at first looked for from her. Moreover, on top of it she had also given Norris £4,000 to make those companies ready and another £2,500 besides. Norris and Drake had thus already drawn from her £38,178 8s. instead of the £20,000 she had originally promised. Yet here they were asking her – before they had even got to sea – for supplies for almost double the determined number of men, supplies that the Privy Council reckoned would cost another £14,000 or £15,000.[25]

The demand came, too, at a moment when the Queen's own financial position was by no means comfortable and when the approach of the continental campaigning season threatened to impose fresh burdens upon her both in the Netherlands and in France. The Armada campaign had left the Exchequer almost empty and in September – despite Burghley's misgivings[26] – the writs had to go out for a new Parliament. Had that Parliament assembled on 12 November as the writs required, the first instalment of the subsidies it granted might possibly have been coming in during the early summer of 1589.[27] But on 15 October the meeting was postponed until 4 February. The prorogation was no doubt politic. Tudor Englishmen were not accustomed to paying taxes as regularly, year after year, as they had been doing since 1585 – and not only parliamentary taxes, but also ship money in many coast towns and regular local subsidies for musters and training of soldiers in all the counties. A good many, enough to give grounds for Burghley's misgivings, were

---

[25] Ibid., nos. 89, 90. The pay of the six discharged horse-bands was to be used to pay twelve foot-bands – *H. M. C., Ancaster MSS*, pp. 261–2. An abstract of Exchequer issues for the period Michaelmas 1588 to Easter 1589 shows £26,500 paid to Norris and Drake – S. P. Domestic, ccxxv, no. 52; Sherley's note of payments to them for the six horse-bands and six foot-bands from the Netherlands totals £11,678 8s., excluding £1,200 for the pay of Norris's horse-band noted by Burghley as 'denied' – *Cal. S. P. Foreign*, XXIII, 129, 148. Dietz, *English Public Finance*, pp. 61, 444, ignores the five months' pay and puts the Queen's contribution at this point as £25,000 or £26,000. Burghley noted 'double the number' in the margin of the commanders' letters of 13 April.

[26] R. B. Wernham, *Before the Armada*, pp. 403–4.

[27] J. E. Neale, *Elizabeth I and Her Parliaments, 1584–1601*, p. 302.

already grumbling about it and dragging their feet. Devon men were not the only ones to seek a cut in their local taxes by alleging that money for musters and training had gone to line officials' pockets nor was York alone in refusing to help out a neighbouring town with its ship money, while not a few well-to-do Londoners had slipped off to the country to dodge assessment for the earlier city loan. In this atmosphere, and with the final third of the 1587 Parliament's grant due to be collected in October and November, mid-November was hardly the best time to ask the Commons to open their purse-strings afresh and even wider. There was a lot to be said for letting the customary celebrations of the Queen's accession on 17 November, and the special nation-wide thanksgivings for the Armada's defeat, led by the Queen herself at St Paul's a week later, reanimate men's patriotism and soften the memory of what victory had cost them.[28]

Nevertheless the prorogation did create considerable financial problems. In November Burghley made a list of the money needed to pay 'necessary debts' – the Low Countries £75,000, naval supplies £10,000, the Household £11,000, the Ordnance £8,000; besides £20,000 for a store of 200 lasts of powder, £50,000 to repay the city of London, and an unspecified sum for repairing ships and building new ones. To find this money the means must be many – a loan of £100,000, the sale of some Crown lands, borrowing overseas, and calling in of debts due to the Queen, in addition to a subsidy from Parliament. Recourse to one of these means soon became necessary and in January 1589 letters under the privy seal were distributed through the lords-lieutenants, requiring loans from the more affluent inhabitants of the counties and towns outside London. Despite a certain amount of resistance, this brought in about £76,000 – £46,925 of it by the middle of June 1589. But this, like the earlier loan from the city, was due to be repaid (and was repaid) after one year. Added to the probable burdens of the coming summer, it meant that when Parliament did meet on 4 February 1589 the government

---

[28] *Acts P.C.*, XVI, 281-2, 284-5, 352-3; XVII, 45-6, 94-5, 108, 117; Murdin, p. 632. For the thanksgiving at St Paul's, see Cheyney, *History of England*, I, 3-4.

could not be content with the customary grant of one subsidy and two fifteenths and tenths, say roughly £160,000.[29]

A rousing oration from Lord Chancellor Hatton at the opening of the session, another impressive speech from the Chancellor of the Exchequer, Sir Walter Mildmay, and no doubt much steady pressure from the other Privy Councillors, did move the Commons to vote two subsidies and four fifteenths and tenths, or twice the customary grant. But the manner and terms of their giving were as important as the total amount. They were, of course, anxious that the size of their grant should not become a precedent and their committee accordingly charged Francis Bacon to draft a safeguarding clause. That was natural enough; and anyway, 'the very mild, ineffective words, finally incorporated in the preamble appear to have been composed by Burghley'. But there was also clearly a good deal of discussion, even some opposition, over the amount. For at the bill's third reading Henry Jackman, a London cloth merchant sitting for Calne in Wiltshire, framed a speech opposing the second subsidy. 'Our country' [he protested] 'is at this present in no such desperate or dangerous case . . . , the teeth and jaws of our mightiest and most malicious enemy having been so lately broken'; and such a tax, on top of all the past year's burdens, would breed discontent, especially among the less well-to-do. Whether Jackman actually delivered his speech, or whether other members supported him if he did, we do not know, for unfortunately this is one of the more poorly documented of Elizabethan Parliaments. Nevertheless, in the opinion of Sir John Neale, the most authoritative historian of those Parliaments, this one was 'clearly more intransigent . . . than our sources permit us to know'. And even if 'the subsidy bill caused no real trouble', the debates upon it must have warned the Queen against pressing her faithful Commons too hard. They should also warn us of how limited was the elasticity of parliamentary taxation.

For a government in urgent need of cash, however, the most disappointing feature of the grant must have been that, although the Commons promised to pay twice the normal

---

[29] For what follows, and for this Parliament in general, see Neale, *Elizabeth I and Her Parliaments, 1584–1601*, pp. 193–239.

sum, they also spread the payment over twice the normal length of time and did not make even the first of its four instalments payable until the following November. Thus although it did eventually bring in about £320,000, the amount coming into the Exchequer in any one of the following four years was to be little more than that brought in annually during the previous two years by the normal, one-subsidy grant of the 1587 Parliament. And none at all was to come in until November 1589.[30] Nor was Convocation's grant of a double subsidy from the clergy, worth another £40,000 or so, of much immediate help; for the payment of that was spread over an even longer period -- over six years – and was not to begin until 1591.[31]

The Queen therefore must have smiled somewhat wryly when Mr Speaker, at the closing ceremony on 29 March 1589, presented to her a joint petition from the two Houses of Parliament begging her 'to denounce open war against the said King of Spain' and 'to use all honourable means, as well offensive as defensive', against him and his adherents. For, to find the means was the very heart of the problem and it is small wonder if she answered Mr Speaker tartly that 'many come hither *ad consulendum qui nesciunt quid sit consulendum*', that many come hither to counsel who have no idea what counsel means.[32] The sources of the Crown's 'ordinary' revenues were already being exploited more and more thoroughly. It was in this financial year 1588-9 that the rents of the Crown lands began to show a marked increase; that on the expiry of Thomas Smith's lease of the London customs duties their direct collection brought in over £35,000 instead of the £30,000 that he had been paying as rent; that there was a sharp calling in of 'stalled debts'; and that recusancy fines rose

[30] F. C. Dietz, *English Public Finance*, p. 392 note 23, gives the total for the double grant as £316,026; but elsewhere he gives £322,980 1s. 6d. as the amount collected in the four years to Michaelmas 1593, namely £95,316 9s. 2d. in 1589-90, £72,038 13s. in 1590-1, £91,998 4s. 11d. in 1591-2, and £63,626 14s. 5d. in 1592-3 – *Exchequer under Elizabeth*, pp. 86-7. Burghley told the 1593 Parliament on 1 March 1593, i.e. just after the final instalment fell due on 12 February 1593, that the 1589 grant had brought in only £280,000 so far – Neale, *Elizabeth I and Her Parliaments, 1584-1601*, pp. 241, 302.

[31] Dietz, *English Public Finance*, p. 395.

[32] D'Ewes, *Journals of all the Parliaments of Elizabeth*, p. 459.

to over £8,000.[33] Yet, notable though these increases in the 'ordinary' revenues may have been, they too came in slowly and, all told, they can hardly have provided much more than the sum needed to pay back the London loan of the previous summer. Of the 'extraordinary' revenue just voted by Parliament, none would be available before the late autumn; and it was too soon to think of any further borrowing at home.

Almost in desperation the government turned to the foreign moneylenders – a fact apparently unknown to such contemporary critics as Raleigh and Monson and of which modern historians have until recently been equally unaware.[34] At the end of February, just when the subsidy bill, its terms already settled, was coming up for its second reading, the Queen decided to send one of the leading Merchant Adventurers, William Milward, over to Germany to try to borrow £100,000 for her, at not more than ten per cent interest. Milward was to carry himself at first as a private merchant coming for his own trade. He was not to use the Queen's name lest it raise the interest rate. For the same reason, he was to take up the money in portions and at several times. As security he might offer bonds of the Merchant Adventurers, who themselves would be given counter-bonds under the great seal. If the Adventurers' bonds proved unacceptable, he might offer bonds of the city of London, or as a last resort the Queen's bonds under her great seal.[35]

The mere fact that the Queen was attempting to borrow money abroad indicates clearly how serious her financial problems were. For the trials of raising foreign loans during the first fifteen years of her reign had been so chastening that none had been even attempted since 1574.[36] And that she should have been seeking now a loan of no less than £100,000 – the largest attempted either at home or abroad during her reign – is startling evidence of how dark the outlook for the coming summer already seemed to be.

Milward left England on 30 March and before his first,

[33] Dietz. *English Public Finance*, p. 63.
[34] See my Preface to *Cal. S. P. Foreign*, XXIII, lvi.
[35] *Cal. S. P. Foreign*, XXIII, 127–8.
[36] R. B. Outhwaite, 'The trials of foreign borrowing: the English crown and the Antwerp money market in the mid-sixteenth century', in *Economic History Review* (2nd series), XIX, 288–305.

none too encouraging, report of 4 April from Stade arrived,[37] the general outlook had grown gloomier than ever. In the Netherlands the last days of March brought fresh alarms and a dangerous military set-back. Reports of enemy troops gathering for an attack upon Ostend caused the Privy Council on 28 March to order the levying in haste of 1,500 men to reinforce the garrison there. The danger passed within a few days and the levy was countermanded, but the captains of it were kept standing by, for there was still considerable anxiety about the state of the town's defences.[38]

Meanwhile worse was happening farther east, at Geertruidenberg. That town was garrisoned by 300 horse and 350 foot, Germans for the most part, put in by Count Hohenlohe and in the States' pay. Along with other garrisons they had mutinied in 1588. They had then renounced their allegiance both to the Count and to the States. Elizabeth, as we have seen, had very firmly refused their demand to be taken into her pay; but when Willoughby helped Maurice to patch up an agreement with them in July 1588, they had insisted on having an Englishman as their commander, Willoughby's brother-in-law Sir John Wingfield. This has fostered one of the more ineradicable of historical legends, repeated even in the latest English works,[39] the legend that this was an English garrison and that Sir John Wingfield was another Sir William Stanley or Rowland Yorke. In fact he never had any real authority in Geertruidenberg and, as he was 'not anywise languaged in French or "Dutch"', even communication cannot have been all that easy! Perhaps, as Gilpin said, he would have been wise not to hazard his honour and credit by staying on when he could not establish discipline.[40] Yet as an Englishman he was the last remaining link with any outside authority for which the troops had even a modicum of respect.

Nevertheless, as the winter wore on, their disorders and depredations grew worse. In February 1589 Willoughby, on

---

[37] *Cal. S. P. Foreign*, XXIII, 197–8.

[38] Ibid., pp. 187, 192–3, 199, 293–4; *Acts P. C.*, XVII, 118–19.

[39] C. Wilson, *England and the Netherlands*, pp. 107–8; G. Parker, *The Dutch Revolt*, p. 222.

[40] *Cal. S. P. Foreign*, XXIII, 65, 137, 169.

the Queen's instructions, tried in vain to mediate a fresh agreement and there were rumours that some of the garrison were treating with the enemy.[41] Accordingly on 5 March Count Maurice attempted to surprise the town. The attempt misfired. The garrison refused a summons to surrender. They made Wingfield virtually a prisoner and transferred effective command to a council of captains. Maurice therefore had to sit down to a regular siege. He brought up artillery and on 23 March, after a few days' bombardment, launched a full-scale assault. It was repulsed with some loss and he was forced to draw off. By then the garrison really were treating with the enemy and on 31 March they agreed to yield the town to Parma. Within another week the Spaniards were in full possession of Geertruidenberg.[42]

This meant that Parma had breached the line of outposts covering the States' main southern defences; that he had been presented with one of the main launching-points for an invasion across the Maas and Waal which he had so signally failed to secure at Bergen-op-Zoom in the autumn. It is true that he, too, was in serious financial straits. His enemies knew that. But they did not know how serious those straits were. Equally, although they knew that a considerable sum of money was on its way to him from Spain, they did not know that King Philip had earmarked part of it for assisting the League in France and had in other ways severely restricted Parma's employment of it.[43] As it appeared to them, he had plenty of troops to exploit the breach opened at Geertruidenberg and at least enough money coming to pay them. In Flanders there was La Motte with the 4,000 to 6,000 men who had so recently threatened Ostend. Between Breda and 'sHertogenbosch Count Charles Mansfelt had the six regiments of foot and fifteen troops of horse which had just secured Geertruidenberg. Away to the east, around Rheinberg, Warembon had another 6,000 men threatening the frontiers of Gelderland and Overijsel. Northwards, in Groningen, was Verdugo with more troops. Behind all these

[41] Ibid., p. 21; *H. M. C., Ancaster MSS*, pp. 229, 247–8, 255, 258–60.
[42] *Cal. S. P. Foreign*, XXIII, 154–6, 167–8, 186–7, 194–5; *H. M. C., Ancaster MSS*, pp. 265, 505; Bor, xxvi, fos. 5–7; *Correspondance de Philippe II*, III, 410.
[43] Ibid., pp. 398–9, 412–3; van der Essen, *Alexandre Farnèse*, V, 250–62.

were the famous Spanish *tercios,* still in winter quarters in Brabant and Flanders and able quickly to reinforce La Motte or Mansfelt or even Warembon.[44]

Against these forces the States' means looked woefully inadequate. It was impossible for them both to strengthen their garrisons sufficiently to insure against a decisive initial defeat and at the same time to assemble any army capable of confronting the enemy in the field. Those garrisons already cost them £50,000 a year more than the ordinary monthly contributions from the Provinces brought in, and £50,000 was about all that they could get by way of extraordinary contributions. Maurice, indeed, in gathering a mere 4,000 men to attack Geertruidenberg, had so depleted the other garrisons that some had barely thirty men left to watch at night. Even if, as the States hoped, Mörs and Schenk could spare him 1,000 men from the eastern frontiers and money could be found to levy another 2,000, he would still have no more than 7,000, hardly more than any one of the enemy groups under La Motte, Mansfelt, and Warembon, not to mention the Spanish *tercios.*[45]

Moreover, if the military prospects were gloomy, the political outlook was not much brighter. Behind the great rivers there was confusion as well as weakness. John Gylles wrote a few weeks later that he had never seen Holland in so ill a state. Eastwards, Bommel and the little towns in the Betuwe were ready to compound with the enemy and Utrecht was still torn by domestic quarrels. This could well let Parma, once he was past Heusden and the great rivers, right through to the Zuyder Zee and Amsterdam. Things were no better in Gelderland and Overijsel, where the States' troops were so ill supplied and disorderly that some towns would not admit a soldier within their walls. In Friesland Verdugo levied almost as large a contribution as the States' governor, Count William Louis. Altogether, as Bodley wrote on 1 April, 'the state of these Provinces is weaker at this present than it hath been these many years and unless by Her Majesty's extraordinary

---

[44] *Cal. S. P. Foreign,* XXIII, 188, 202, 211, 218, 270–1; van der Essen, *Alexandre Farnèse,* V, 261.

[45] *Cal. S. P. Foreign,* XXIII, 155, 238; *H. M. C., Ancaster MSS,* p. 267; *Resolutiën der Staten Generaal,* VI, 565.

assistance and counsel it be presently holpen, there is little appearance that they can hold it out long'.[46]

It seemed likely, too, that English help would have to take the form of 'extraordinary assistance' rather than of mere 'counsel'. Admittedly, the Geertruidenberg affair had convinced the Queen and Privy Council more than ever of the political and military incompetence of the States' leaders, Maurice and Oldenbarnevelt in particular. Those two had planned and launched the attack without a word to Willoughby, Bodley, the Council of State, or even the States General. They had ignored the prompt protests of Willoughby and Bodley against their 'forcible course'. They had refused, until it was too late to listen to Bodley's offers of mediation. It was certainly unfortunate that he had to make those offers without the support of Willoughby, who was already on his way home to England when the siege began. It was more unfortunate still that he had to make them on his own initiative, without any directions from the Queen or Privy Council. That, however, was not the Queen's fault. During the first two weeks of March westerly gales had stopped all sailing from Holland and Zeeland to England. Willoughby himself was weatherbound all that time at Flushing.[47] As a result it was not until 14 March, nine days after Maurice appeared before Geertruidenberg, that reliable news of the siege reached the English court. Elizabeth then acted promptly enough. On 16 March she wrote to Maurice and the States, as well as to Bodley and Geertruidenberg, protesting strongly at the States' resorting in such secrecy to such desperate remedies and requiring them to 'surcease all violent actions' and with Bodley's help to seek some reasonable settlement whereby the town might 'be preserved from the enemy and reduced to be under your government'.[48]

It is just possible that Bodley's intervention at this stage might have been effective. The garrison's respect for the English was not utterly destroyed until Maurice, after his repulse on 25 March, revealed to them Willoughby's ancient promise of 4 June 1588 to secure the town for the States. Only

---

[46] *Cal. S. P. Foreign*, XXIII, 140–1, 184, 195, 271–2.
[47] Ibid., pp. 154–5, 167, 194–5.
[48] *H. M. C., Ancaster MSS*, 266–7, 269, 272.

after that did they begin to answer Parma's signal fires and send envoys to treat about delivering the town to him.[49] Until then there was perhaps a tiny hope that they might listen to Bodley. And the Queen's urgent letters might have moved the States to give Bodley his chance. Alas, the messenger carrying those letters, Sir Francis Vere's servant Edward White, had his crossing delayed for days by the slackness of Captain Scott of the Queen's pinnace *Spy* and Captain Riggs of the *Achates*, who were hoping to turn a more or less honest penny by convoying some merchantmen at the same time. As a result, though White was at Gravesend ready to embark on 20 March, he did not reach Bodley until 2 April, by which time Geertruidenberg had already come to terms with Parma. Whatever slight chance of success Elizabeth's 'counsel' might have had, had been destroyed by the nine days' delay in the arrival of the first news of the siege and by the fifteen days' delay in the delivery of her letters, by a most un-Protestant wind and a couple of lazy sea captains.[50]

So the States' leaders had enjoyed a free hand. The outcome confirmed the English conviction that 'extraordinary assistance' alone would not suffice. They must also 'counsel', and indeed bring about, reforms in the Provinces' government that would strengthen the central executive organs by restoring the authority of the lord general and the Council of State. This, incidentally, may well be the reason why the Queen and Privy Council now lost interest in Ortel's suggestion that she should pay the States an annual subsidy in place of her troops. They did not feel that they could trust the Dutch leaders' competence to direct successfully the defence of the Provinces against Parma.[51]

Yet the Geertruidenberg affair made it clearer than ever that it would be no easy matter to get the Dutch leaders to swallow 'counsel' of this sort. For they had not only ignored Willoughby and Bodley before and during the action. After it was over, Maurice and Oldenbarnevelt also tried to cover their own failure by blaming it on their English allies. They encouraged the suspicion that everything in Geertruidenberg

[49] Ibid., pp. 273–4; *Cal. S. P. Foreign*, XXIII, 195.
[50] *H. M. C., Ancaster MSS*, pp. 273, 278–80.
[51] *Cal. S. P. Foreign*, XXIII, 144, 191, 200, 229–30; *H. M. C., Ancaster MSS*, p. 274.

had been done with Her Majesty's good liking. They hinted that all places held in her name would suffer a like fate. And in their placard outlawing the Geertruidenberg garrison they not only blamed Willoughby and Bodley but listed Sir John Wingfield and, by a reluctantly confessed error, Sir Francis Vere among the traitors.[52]

Anglo-Dutch relations, it seemed, were slipping back into the bad old pattern of Leicester's day. and if the Dutch would not accept English 'counsel', the Queen and her advisers were more than ever afraid that the situation, military and political, in the Low Countries would soon deteriorate to such an extent that very 'extraordinary assistance' would be needed from England before the summer was far advanced.

In France just that sort of situation was already developing. Henry III, having failed to listen to Elizabeth's counsel, was by April begging for her extraordinary assistance. English hopes of him had at first run high. 'Your late news of the death of the Queen Mother and the killing of the Duke of Guise was most welcome unto Her Majesty', Walsingham wrote to Stafford on 24 December. So welcome, indeed, that Her Majesty meant 'to send a gentleman over to comfort the King to proceed thoroughly as well to a severe correction of his corrupt subjects at home as also to prosecute his enemies abroad in princely sort', particularly the arch-enemy Spain. If the humours there, Walsingham added, were 'as well disposed to embrace such a course as they are here, it will then prove a match'.

Almost immediately, however, a letter from Stafford damped this enthusiasm. 'Finding the French King by your late letter', Walsingham wrote again on 29 December, 'nice in having the intelligence between them known to the world for a season, the Queen held it best to forbear to send an express messenger unto him.' Instead, Stafford should inform him that she would have sent had it been welcome. At the same time the ambassador was to 'renew unto the King the former motion for the restraint of grain' and to do what he could to bring him and the King of Navarre together. Significantly, Walsingham added that the Queen still 'showeth by speeches

[52] *Cal. S. P. Foreign*, XXIII, 200, 205–8, 272; Bor, xxvi, fos. 10–14.

to be most ready to assist the French King; but the assistance that she can give is to entertain the King of Spain by sea, which in very truth may most annoy him'.[53]

Henry III, however, was far from showing 'a princely resolution to go thorough with the matter'. He was much cast down by his mother's death. He was also having a bad time with piles, which discouraged him from getting on his horseback to follow up his blow against the League's leaders by vigorous midwinter action against their momentarily bewildered supporters.[54] It may well be, too, that he was bent upon a very different policy from that alliance with Navarre which Elizabeth was urging. For it looks very much as if he hoped to step into Guise's place, make the League a royal and national instead of a factional organization, and use it to re-establish both royal authority and religious unity in his kingdom.[55]

For weeks therefore Stafford made little headway. In common with all the other ambassadors he was not allowed to come to court or receive audience, although his servant William Lyly was permitted to remain at Blois. Stafford was able on 17 January to send the Queen's letters to the King, but only to receive, somewhat tartly at the very end of the month, the same damping response as in December. Henry III raised no objection to the arrest of six French ships that had been caught carrying corn to Spain, or to the owners being required to sell their cargoes in England. But he would not reimpose his ban on the export of victuals to Spain, for nobody would observe it if he did. Moreover, he returned the Queen's letter and sent Stafford word 'that he would not for anything in the world it had been found, and showed that he was half discontented that in this time Her Majesty would write unto him, having no cipher, that which, being taken (as everything now, is subject unto that), that which they mought make their profit of, as they do'.[56]

Stafford's report naturally put a stop to Elizabeth's renewed

---

[53] Cotton MSS, Galba E. vi, fos. 374–5.

[54] Ibid., fo. 371; *Cal. S. P. Foreign*, XXIII, 80–1.

[55] Cp. his instructions to governors – ibid., p. 7; also, e.g., Davila, pp. 381–92.

[56] Cotton MSS, Galba E. vi, fos. 376–7; *Cal. S. P. Foreign*, XXIII, 80–1, 93, 95; *Acts P. C.*, XVI, 415–16.

proposal to send 'some well chosen gentleman' – it was to have been Edward Wootton – to spur Henry III on to an alliance with Navarre, the German princes, and any Italian states that might be willing to oppose the ambition of Spain. Just what happened between this point and mid-March is unclear, for there is again here an almost total lack of English papers about French affairs, except for two or three from the Channel ports and two or three from the French ambassador, Châteauneuf. Possibly Stafford did not risk writing often. At least one of his letters was intercepted in February and somewhat later two couriers were captured by the Leaguers – John Tupper in March at Rennes, and John Wells in early April at Rouen, where he was to remain a prisoner for nearly two years, sending home a steady stream of letters whose eccentric spelling, atrocious handwriting, and often quite remarkably inaccurate news go a long way towards destroying our natural sympathy for his plight.[57]

The state of affairs north of the Loire, however, had begun to alarm Henry III, as well as to endanger English couriers, weeks before Tupper and Wells were captured. The King's inactivity had allowed Guise's brother, the Duke of Mayenne, and other League chiefs who had escaped execution or arrest, to recover their nerve and rally their followers. The Catholic populace in the cities of the north and east, Paris, Orléans, Chartres, Rouen, Reims, Amiens, Dijon, Lyons, had risen to join them and there were 'few towns but are either against the King or will have no garrison at all'. Meanwhile south of the Loire the King's army facing the Huguenots had largely disintegrated; its commander, the Duke of Nevers, and many Catholic nobles had withdrawn into a sulky neutrality or, like La Châtre, gone over to the League; and the King of France was being reduced to little more than a King of Blois. By the middle of March the League army that Mayenne was gradually gathering west of Paris, around Étampes, was already little inferior to the remnants of Nevers' army around the King.[58]

[57] *Cal. S. P. Foreign*, XXIII, 85–6, 91–2, 97, 182, 203; Cotton MSS, Galba E. vi, fo. 379; *Cal. S. P. Spanish*, IV, 510, 532–3; *H. M. C., Salisbury MSS*, III, 397.
[58] *Cal. S. P. Foreign*, XXIII, 97, 126; *H. M. C., Salisbury MSS*, III, 397–8, 405; Davila, pp. 380–1, 385; Aubigné, VIII, 22–38; M. Wilkinson, *History of the League*, pp. 74–83.

Now, at last, Henry III began to adopt the course that Elizabeth had so long counselled. The first hints of intelligence between him and Navarre came early in February, although 'it is marvellous secretly kept if it be'; and when Stafford did eventually secure audience a couple of weeks later, nothing much seems to have eventuated. But another audience, or perhaps several audiences, early in March produced more results. Stafford apparently then offered the Queen's good offices to obtain a levy of German mercenaries for the King and reiterated her determination to seize French ships trading in Spain. This time Henry III was more ready to listen. He wrote to Stafford on 12 March that, although it would be useless for him to forbid his subjects to trade to Spain, they could hardly complain if they took the risk and were caught. He also welcomed the Queen's offer of her good offices in Germany. Furthermore he asked Stafford to press her for a loan of 150,000 crowns to levy 5,000 horse and 6,000 foot there. Later he talked about raising this to a higher figure, to provide 8,000 horse and 14,000 foot; but at this stage that does not seem to have been a definite request. Thereupon he gave Stafford leave, ostensibly for private reasons, to return to England. On the way home Stafford spent three weeks with the King of Navarre. Whether he played any part in the secret negotiations that were going on between the two Kings during those weeks, it is impossible to say. But before he sailed from La Rochelle he was informed by du Pin of the terms of the agreement signed on 24 March, by whose secret articles Henry III and Henry of Navarre undertook to turn their combined arms against the League. This alliance of the two kings was, of course, good news, but their position, especially Henry III's, was still very precarious. How precarious was clear from the fact that Stafford was bringing a request from him for English help to the tune of at least 150,000 crowns, or £45,300.[59]

All the possible continental complications that Elizabeth had been able to discount when she authorized Norris and Drake's enterprise in the previous autumn, were thus developing now simultaneously. Indeed, it would be no great exaggeration to say that they all came to a head on the same

[59] *Cal. S. P. Foreign*, XXIII, 94, 96, 171, 177–8, 209, 321; Cotton MSS, Galba E. vi, fo. 381; *Cal. S. P. Spanish*, IV, 516, 528–9.

April day. For it was on 8 April that a very seasick Stafford landed at Dartmouth. On that same day news reached the English court of the betrayal of Geertruidenberg to Parma.[60] It was also the day after Norris and Drake had been forced back to Plymouth by contrary winds; the very day that Norris wrote his letter requiring the Queen to take over the victualling of their forces and to make good their depleted sea stores. And it was only two or three days earlier that the young Earl of Essex, defying the Queen's prohibition and hoping to find fame and fortune with the expedition, had stolen away from court and put to sea with Sir Roger Williams in the *Swiftsure*.

[60] *Cal. S. P. Foreign*, XXIII, 172, 209.

# V

## Norris and Drake's Instructions

From the time when Essex ran off to join Norris and Drake, one sober historian tells us, 'the Queen's unfavourable attitude to the expedition was transformed into actual hostility'. She was, so another alleges, 'much more interested in recovering the victim of her elderly charms than in the needs of the army'.[1] The first of these statements is manifestly not true, the second, though romantic, is also wrong. We have seen already that the story of Norris and Drake's preparations lends little support to the charge that Elizabeth's attitude was unfavourable before the beginning of April. She had accepted their plan promptly. She had paid over her £20,000 in full and earlier than she had covenanted. She had agreed readily to Norris's request for the auxiliary companies from the Netherlands and had ordered the levies at home as soon as the vital Netherlands contingents seemed assured. She had hastened to clear up the misunderstanding with the States over those contingents and, as soon as they were on their way, she had on 23 February prepared the commanders' instructions.

Of course she had not done quite everything that the commanders asked. She had not granted Norris's request in October for the *Victory* to carry Don Antonio and his suite; but the 800-ton *Victory* could hardly be called one 'of her second sort of ships'.[2] Again the two generals, in trying to explain in February why they found it difficult to meet their expenses, did complain of the long time the Queen had taken to resolve about the matter. Their commission, they said, had been stayed ten days at the seal after its warrant was signed and this caused many adventurers to withdraw their promises of contributions. Yet from 19 or 20 September, when the scheme

---

[1] E. P. Cheyney, *History of England*, I, 167; Oppenheim, in *Monson's Tracts*, I, 193, echoed by Cheyney (I, 188).

[2] S. P. Domestic, ccxvii, no. 25. A little later the *Victory* was lent to the Earl of Cumberland for another privateering venture – Hakluyt, IV, 355–80.

was finally formulated, to 11 October, when the commission passed the great seal, does not seem an unduly long time to resolve upon so important an undertaking. Even if we go back three weeks, to the day when Drake came up to court, the delay still does not look unreasonable.[3] As for the adventurers going back upon their promises, the only one that the generals named was the Earl of Northumberland who, by their account, stayed his going and his £2,000 adventure at the Queen's command. Anthony Wingfield did say later that they wanted '£20,000 of their adventure'; that £10,000 of this was money promised by courtiers who had withdrawn their offers; and that another good sum was spent on three months' pay for the 1,500 sent to Bergen.[4] But all this was very much exaggerated. Drake's account to 1 April shows that he had received £18,070 1s. 8d. from other private contributors, while as early as 8 February Norris had collected £7,000. As Drake was putting up £3,000 himself and the army captains were reckoned to have contributed £5,000 towards levying their companies, the private contributions came to at least £33,070 or only £6,930 short of the £40,000 originally expected – and that without counting anything from Norris. The pay of the 1,500 from 1 December to 1 April comes to another £6,757 10s., but against that we must set the extra £6,500 which the Queen had added to her original £20,000. All this hardly justifies Norris's bitter complaint to Burghley on 8 April that 'we have never received any favourable answer of any matter that was moved by us, were it never so just or reasonable, but contrarily threatenings and chidings.' Black John Norris was a notoriously rough tempered and quarrelsome man and on 8 April, the day he had just been blown back into Plymouth

---

[3] *H. M. C., Salisbury MSS*, III, 233 (for the date of this letter, see Sir Julian Corbett, *Drake and the Tudor Navy*, II, 299 note); Patent Roll, 30 Elizabeth, part iv dorse. Corbett (II, 307) and Cheyney (I, 162) seem to think that there was a second commission in February, presumably because there is a literal, undated copy placed with the commanders' draft instructions of February among the State Papers – S. P. Domestic, ccxxii, no. 88. But the Patent Rolls are the only and natural proof for the actual issue of a commission (apart from the commission itself) under the great seal and on the Patent Rolls there is only one commission to Norris and Drake, that of October.

[4] Hakluyt, IV, 310. Can Wingfield have transformed into actual promises by courtiers Norris's request of 16 October to Walsingham to move the Privy Councillors to contribute? – S. P. Domestic, ccxvii, no. 25(i).

Sound, cannot have been one of his gayer days. Clearly in this case what the soldier said is hardly evidence.[5]

Nor is there much better evidence that Essex's escapade turned the Queen hostile to the whole expedition or that her anger against him made much real difference to its fortunes. After all, Norris and Drake were not prevented from getting to sea as soon as the wind turned favourable on 18 April, a full fortnight after Essex left the court. That they then sailed with only three weeks' victuals aboard, was likewise not due to any refusal on Elizabeth's part to advance the money for a further supply. Marmaduke Darrell, the expedition's treasurer, sent off from Plymouth his estimate of their needs on 8 April. Within nine days the Privy Council had ordered the despatch of £14,000 to pay for it, £10,000 of it to be sent down in carts from London and £4,000 to be handed over by the Cornwall and Somerset collectors of the privy seal loan. It is true that some economies were made on these figures. By cutting out beer and substituting fish and pease for beef, the cost to the Exchequer was kept down to £11,101. But apart from the beer, this altered the kinds rather than reduced the quantity of the victuals. Moreover, as it raised the Queen's paid-up contribution to over £49,000, almost two-and-a-half times what she had originally promised, it is not surprising that she informed the two generals that 'she looketh to be satisfied again hereafter for this present supply of victuals'.[6]

That the supply did not reach the fleet until 9 June and then 'little answered our expectations', was again not directly the Queen or Council's fault. Norris himself blamed the deficiencies on the mayor of Plymouth and William Hawkins. They had, he alleged, received £12,000 from Her Majesty and the generals to supply victuals and pay debts, yet 'the army hath never received thereof the worth of £1,000' – in fact it looks as if most of it may have gone to pay the debts. The delay, too, was partly due to the scarcity of victuals in the west country, partly to a dispute between Captain Crosse and

---

[5] Ibid., ccxxii, no. 66; ccxxiii, nos. 56, 64, 71. For Norris's ill temper, see *Dictionary of National Biography.*

[6] *Acts P. C.*, XVII, 134–5, 159; S. P. Domestic, ccxxiii, nos. 69, 91–2, 94, 101–2; ccxxiv, no. 8; ccxxv, no. 52. The £11,101 for the victuals was, of course, additional to the sum stated at p.77 above.

Captain Plott as to which should take them, a dispute eventually settled by Lord Chancellor Hatton's simple device of sending both captains. The story of this extra supply of victuals certainly does not suggest any marked change of heart or any obvious hostility in the Queen.[7]

That is not, however, to say that the Queen and the two generals saw eye to eye about the primary aims of the expedition or that Essex's flight may not have aggravated the divergence between their views. It will be remembered that the aims agreed upon in September had been: '(1) to burn the ships in Lisbon and Seville, (2) to take Lisbon, (3) to take the Islands.' Now Elizabeth clearly looked upon the burning of the ships as the first and by far the most important task. For her, Norris and Drake's enterprise was the cutting edge of a wider strategy designed to destroy what was left of the 1588 Armada and to prevent any revival of Spain's Atlantic sea power. It had taken Philip II seven years to prepare that Armada. Half of it was already lost. Were the remaining half now destroyed, he must start upon his seven years' labour all over again and with much less hope of success. For while he was so engaged, the English would be able to keep their squadrons – fleets would hardly be necessary – at the Azores in perfect safety. At least for several years there would be no Spanish navy to prevent them from systematically capturing or blockading the American silver fleets. Philip might then well lack the means either to rebuild his navy or to pay his army in the Netherlands or to subsidize his Leaguer allies in France. He would certainly have no power to invade England. To make doubly sure, Elizabeth aimed also to deprive him of the vital supplies that he drew from France and the Low Countries and, more especially, from north Germany, Scandinavia, and the Baltic lands.[8] But the first essential was to destroy the half of the 1588 Armada that had managed to get back to Spain.

Now had those Armada survivors returned, as they should have done, to Lisbon or even to Coruña, Ferrol, or Cadiz,

---

[7] Hakluyt, IV, 34; S. P. Domestic, ccxxiii, no. 95; ccxxiv, nos. 25, 43, 51; ccxxv, no. 30. For demands from various ports for payment of debts – ibid., ccxxiii, nos. 30, 42–5; ccxxiv, no. 27.

[8] See below, chapter XI.

Norris and Drake might have found no great difficulty in accepting the Queen's order of priorities. Lisbon, after all, was the gateway and key to Portugal. Like Coruña, Ferrol, and Cadiz, it was also on their direct way to the Islands. Unfortunately, however, as early as the end of September news began to come in that Medina Sidonia, and the fifty or more battered and storm-strained vessels with him, had not been able to make those western ports, not even Coruña or Ferrol. Instead they had been blown far to the east, to Santander and San Sebastian, two ports deep in the leeward corner of the Bay of Biscay.[9] This posed a more difficult problem for Norris and Drake. To take a large fleet so far to leeward in the Bay of Biscay, especially in such a stormy season of westerly gales, would be a tricky undertaking. To take it out again on the long beat to windward before Cape Finisterre could be rounded, might be no less testing. It might weaken their forces; it must give the Spaniards in Portugal advance warning to put their defences in order; and it could bring the expedition's backers little or no financial gain.

Nevertheless the fact that those fifty Armada survivors had returned to the wrong ports, did not make their destruction one whit the less desirable. Every report spoke of Philip's determination to refit and rebuild his navy and to send it once more against England. With half his 1588 Armada as a nucleus he might still hope to do that. Even if he could not hope to renew the Enterprise of England in 1589, he could reasonably hope to provide by the late summer some sort of escort for the American silver ships. And if the 1589 treasure came safely home to Spain, there might well be a new Armada in 1590 or 1591. Yet the condition of those fifty or more vessels that had returned still offered England a unique and glorious opportunity. Battered and torn, they rode defenceless, forty of them huddled together in Santander and another dozen in San Sebastian. The whole remaining navy of Spain lay helpless in those two ports. There were not enough sailors to man them, not enough workmen to refit them speedily, and their soldiers had dispersed to winter quarters twelve leagues

[9] E. Palmer, from St Jean-de-Luz, 19/29 September – *Cal. S. P. Domestic, Addenda*, p. 254.

inland.[10] For months the ships must lie there, powerless to move or to fight. And their destruction, let it be said again, would complete the work of 1588 and crush Spanish naval power, Spain's capacity to invade England, past all hope of recovery.

Ideally, of course, the proper way to accomplish their destruction would have been to fit out a special, government-financed, task force. But, as we have seen, the Queen's resources at this time would hardly run to that. She had to leave it to Norris and Drake. She was, as we shall see, fully alive to the dangers of this and did her best to minimize them. Yet given the method perforce adopted for financing Norris and Drake's expedition, she had rather to ask than absolutely to command. She did the best she could, by insisting as strongly as possible that the attack upon Santander must come first and the operations in Portugal take second place both in time and in importance.

This was precisely the aim of the instructions which the Queen had prepared for Norris and Drake on 23 February.[11] They began by laying down very clearly that the expedition had two, and only two, essential objects: 'the one to distress the King of Spain's ships, the other to get the possession of some of the Islands of Azores thereby to intercept the convoys of the treasure that doth yearly pass that way to and from the West and East Indies.' It was emphasized very strongly that only after the King of Spain's ships had been destroyed was the rest of the programme to be attempted. Before attempting anything else Norris and Drake must

first distress the ships of war in Guipuzcoa, Biscay, Galicia, and in any other places ... to the end that they may not impeach you in such enterprises as you are to execute upon his dominions; as also, the said ships remaining entire and undistressed, they may not ... take encouragement in the time of your absence to attempt somewhat against this our realm or our realm of Ireland.

[10] Ibid.; also *Cal. S. P. Venetian*, VIII, 426, 435.

[11] S. P. Domestic, ccxxii, no. 89. This is a very messy draft in two different hands, with many erasures and insertions. But Elizabeth's letter of 20 May 1589 (ibid., ccxxiv, no. 53) makes it almost certain that these were substantially the final instructions. Oppenheim's doubts on that point (in *Monson's Tracts*, I, 195) seem based upon no more than an intuitive conviction that the Queen could not have remained so long of one mind.

Furthermore, if they found the Spanish forces 'at Santander, the Groyne,[12] or at Lisbon, or any other place' too strong for them to make head against or distress in their havens, they were either to stay and watch them while their own victuals lasted or else, if they felt themselves too inferior in strength, to return home.

To make the priorities doubly clear, an invasion of Portugal, although not ruled out, was relegated to a very subordinate place and permission to attempt it was hedged around by many safeguarding clauses. After, and only after, destroying the Spanish ships of war in the north, Norris and Drake might visit Lisbon to destroy the shipping in the Tagus. While there, they might cautiously test the affections of the Portuguese to Don Antonio and find out the strength of the Spanish forces. If then

upon enquiry you shall-find that neither the love borne unto him is so great as he pretendeth and that the forces of the King of Spain are such as nothing can be attempted without very great hazard, our pleasure is that you shall then forbear to attempt anything towards Lisbon other than the destruction of the ships there. But in case you shall find upon good ground that the party Don Antonio hath there is great, and that they stand so well affected towards him as he pretendeth, and that there will be a party of the Portugal nation that will be ready to aid the King and join with his forces against the Spaniards – you may proceed to make a descent there without any great hazard.

They might then stay long enough to see Don Antonio settled and his frontier defences provided for, before going on to their more important work at the Azores.

The most simple 'man-of-war' must surely have been capable of understanding from these clear and emphatic instructions what, in the Queen's view, were the essentials of the campaign – even if those instructions have seemed beyond understanding to some naval historians. Moreover, Elizabeth was not content merely to state her views this once. During the long weeks that followed before the expedition finally sailed, she continued to insist upon them. With good reason. For on 4 March Palmer reported from St Jean-de-Luz that the treasure

---

[12] Elizabethan English for Coruña.

fleets were expected within three months and that forty-one ships and sixteen pinnaces were making ready in the Biscayan ports to escort them home, although mariners were very scarce in Spain. A little later news was sent from Stade that seventy-three well-armed Hanseatic ships were ready to sail round Scotland for Spain with guns, munitions, and naval stores. On 6 April Richard Geste, freshly escaped from Lisbon, reported that two of the Santander galleons were already at sea and another dozen large ships ready at Lisbon.[13] Everything pointed to the Santander and San Sebastian galleons being ready by June or July to go to escort the treasure fleets. Against those fifty or sixty sail, Drake's six Queen's ships and gaggle of armed merchantmen – of which it is very doubtful if more than six or seven at most were large enough to take their place in the line of battle[14] – would be a distinctly inadequate force and a more powerful fleet than the Queen could easily afford might soon be required to accomplish her purposes.

Every week that passed thus increased her anxiety to see the Santander forces destroyed while they were still immobilized and unable to defend themselves. Her anxiety was reflected in further attempts to make sure that Norris and Drake understood and obeyed her instructions. In March, for example, she gave Anthony Ashley, one of the clerks of the Privy Council, detailed verbal orders 'to go with the commanders on the expedition, to observe their actions, use his influence and counsel with them, and report by letter the progress of affairs'.[15] In a later letter she was also to remind Norris and Drake that 'before your departure hence you did at sundry times so far forth promise as with oaths to assure us and some of our Council that your first and principal action should be to take and distress the King of Spain's navy and ships in ports where they lay, which, if ye did not, ye affirmed that ye were content to be reputed as traitors'.[16]

[13] *Cal. S. P. Foreign,* XXIII, 151, 202–3; S. P. Domestic, ccxxiii, no. 66.

[14] *Monson's Tracts,* I, 182–5; S. P. Domestic, ccxxii, no. 55.

[15] Cheyney, *History of England,* I. 162.

[16] S. P. Domestic, ccxxiv, no. 53. The next sentence in the draft, crossed out, ran: 'whereby his force might be cut off and so far weakened that he should be utterly made unable to annoy us and our realm any more for a long season or to impeach any your further attempts in Portugal'. Was the Queen's failure to provide the promised

There can be little doubt that the generals did protest too much. For if by then they were not already resolved to go to Portugal first, they were certainly becoming more and more enamoured of their Portuguese project. The terms of an agreement they made with Don Antonio in February, for example, suggest that its attraction had already grown dangerously strong.[17] He there promised, as they required, to take their whole army into his pay ten days after it landed in Portugal and, if possible, to give it three months' pay then and there, with the promise of regular monthly payment in advance after those three months ended. At least the possibility of keeping the whole army in Portugal, and making the operations there of primary importance, must have been in the generals' minds when they exacted this promise. And this may perhaps explain their curious complacency about the sudden doubling of their land forces after their arrival at Plymouth in mid-March. That, of course, in its turn gave all the more emphasis to the military, that is the Portuguese, aspect of the expedition. It must also have made the sailors more than ever hesitant about taking their swollen and unwieldy crowd of shipping to Santander and San Sebastian. There was, too, a further clause in the agreement with Don Antonio that may be significant. In it he asked that, if they could not land in Portugal, they would take him to some other part of his dominions. If he wanted to stay there and they wanted to go on to reduce his East Indies, they should leave him 4,000 men and ten ships. This, with its echoes of Drake's dealings with the Sultan of Ternate in 1579 and Edward Fenton's abortive voyage to follow it up in 1582, suggests that Norris and Drake, and probably some of their backers, had thoughts far more grandiose than merely cutting out the King of Spain's battered galleons.

It was this that made Essex's unauthorized presence with the expedition so disturbing to Elizabeth. Leicester, his stepfather, had demonstrated in the Netherlands in 1586 what a peer of the realm, once he got away from England's shores,

---

siege guns perhaps another device to prevent the purely military operations from becoming too attractive?

[17] *Cal. S. P. Foreign*, XXIII, 138–40.

could do to warp and defy the Queen's most explicit instructions. Young Essex might well do just that again. At twenty-three he was already a good deal more attractive and popular a figure than Leicester had ever been. Handsome and moody, he had all the charm and magnetism of romantic and self-centred youth, all its brilliant promise, its intolerant idealism, its self-willed impatience of control or restraint. He was particularly attractive to, and attracted by, soldiers. For, having inherited his father's crippling debts and Sir Philip Sidney's best sword, his head buzzed with notions of winning both fame and fortune by knightly prowess in military adventure.

The Queen, well aware of both the promise and the peril in his make-up, had been trying to mould him into a responsible public servant for two years and more, ever since she had taken him up as someone to talk to after Mary Stuart's execution, when she was hardly on speaking terms with any of her Councillors. Yet even in that first flush of royal favour, Essex remained restive. He plunged into some deep and dark design with Drake, perhaps to run off and join him in 'singeing the King of Spain's beard'.[18] Then in defiance of a royal prohibition, he actually got as far as Sandwich in an attempt to join Leicester in trying to save Sluys from Parma. At court, despite being appointed Master of the Horse and a Knight of the Garter, he quarrelled like a jealous schoolboy with Sir Walter Raleigh, Sir Charles Blunt, and others with whom the Queen made him share her favour. With Blunt it even came to a duel in Marylebone Park, where Essex was both worsted and wounded – which drew from Elizabeth the comment, 'by God's death, it were fitting someone should take him down and teach him better manners, or there would be no rule with him'.[19]

'No rule with him': such was the young nobleman who galloped off between five and six o'clock on Thursday evening, 3 April, to sail with Norris and Drake. That afternoon two posts had brought him word from Plymouth that the expedition would be putting to sea next day and that a pinnace would be left to bring him out to them. Thanks to the

[18] Corbett, *Drake and the Tudor Navy,* II, 122–4.
[19] Devereux, I, 194.

relays of post-horses the posts had arranged for him on their way up and thanks also to some hard riding, he was at Plymouth before dawn on Saturday, 5 April, after covering 220 miles in a bare thirty-six hours.[20] He found the fleet still windbound, but the pinnace *Marleon*[21] was there to whisk him off to join his brother Walter Devereux, Sir Roger Williams, and other friends aboard the Queen's galleon *Swiftsure*. There, it would seem, he lay low until darkness fell and the wind began to turn more favourable. The *Swiftsure* and the little *Marleon* then crept out of Plymouth Sound and made for the open sea. By next morning the wind was fair enough for the whole fleet to begin moving out.[22]

It was amid all that busy confusion that young Sir Francis Knollys rode in with the Queen and Council's strict commands for Essex to be sent back to court immediately. Norris and Drake, with almost too bland an air of innocence, wrote back to the Council on the Monday that 'understanding a ship of Her Majesty's, called the *Swiftsure*, was gone forth to sea that [i.e. Saturday – Sunday] night, we entered into some mistrust of the Earl's departure to sea in the said ship; whereupon we presently sent forth a pinnace to follow the said ship, wherein Sir Francis Knollys went'. Or perhaps not so very 'presently': for by the time they got Knollys off, the wind had swung back southerly, the pinnace could not weather Rame Head at the harbour entrance, and the whole fleet was penned back in the Sound once more. On 7 April, the sea was a little calmer and they sent Knollys off again in another pinnace. He had hardly got aboard when the Earl of Huntingdon came posting in with yet more imperative orders from the Queen. Thereupon, the generals wrote, 'we have again written to the Earl [of Essex] and Sir Roger Williams who is gone with the Earl' – words that seem to betray a rather more definite knowledge than they had professed to have in the earlier part of their letter.

Yet even now the Queen's orders do not seem to have got

---

[20] Ibid., pp.196-7.

[21] According to *Acts P. C.*, XVII, 131-2, though no *Marleon* appears in the 9 April list of ships in *Monson's Tracts*, I, 182-5. The *Marleon* was one of the new pinnaces built since the Armada actions – S. P. Domestic, ccxxxiii, no. 47.

[22] Devereux, I, 198; S. P. Domestic, ccxxiii, no. 64.

through to the runaways. This is odd. For the *Swiftsure* and *Marleon*, too, were forced back when the wind turned. They managed, however, to fetch up in Falmouth instead of Plymouth, Essex hoping there to 'avoid the importunity of messengers that were daily sent for his return and [having] some other causes more secret to himself'. And, indeed, there he did avoid the messengers' importunity for the next ten days, until the wind again turned favourable. Yet Falmouth, whatever the weather at sea, was little more than sixty miles by land down the old London to Lands End road – not a very good road, maybe, but even in a wet and windy April surely not altogether impassable for man and horse, even for a troop of horse?[23]

All this, taken together, makes it hard to resist the conclusion that Norris and Drake were pretty well aware of Essex's intentions long before Knollys and Huntingdon came posting down to tell them. There are, indeed, some hints that they may have been hand-in-glove with him from the first. There is, for instance, that curious request in their very first proposal, the request that the Queen should promise to give free licence to any person 'of what quality soever' to go with them on the voyage. But if Norris and Drake were aware of Essex's plans, he must have been aware of theirs. Certainly there does seem to have been quite a close contact between them. Essex himself wrote some years later, with his accustomed modesty, that 'I engaged my means, kinsfolk, friends, and followers, else neither the adventure had been made up nor the journey performed.'[24] Even if we discount this boast, the 1587 episode shows that he was no stranger to Drake. He had also served alongside Norris in the Netherlands in 1586. Above all, he had adopted as his military mentor and companion in arms that gallant old Welsh warrior Sir Roger Williams, one of England's most professional and experienced soldiers and one as fluent with his pen as he was ready with his sword. Now, on 23 February Williams, with the rank of colonel-general of the infantry, had been appointed to succeed

---

[23] Devereux, I, 198–9; Hakluyt, IV, 327; *Acts P. C.*, XVII, 131–3. The Archbishop of Canterbury blamed the foul weather of this April for his cold – *H. M. C., Salisbury MSS*, III, 406.

[24] In his 'Apology' after the 1596 Cadiz voyage, quoted in *Monson's Tracts*, I, 190.

Norris in command, as Thomas Fenner was to succeed Drake, in case of accident happening to either. We may well believe Essex's later claim that his influence secured this appointment. Anyway Williams, as in effect second-in-command of the land forces, can hardly have been ignorant of the generals' intentions. And what Williams knew, Essex must have known also.[25]

That being so, it is highly significant that when the *Swiftsure* finally got away from Falmouth on 17 or 18 April, she made straight for Lisbon. This must surely suggest that when Essex and Williams left Plymouth on 5 April the generals were already resolved to ignore the Queen's orders and, leaving the Santander galleons for later treatment, to go first and direct against Lisbon. That, after all, had been the idea behind their original proposals, before it was known where the Armada survivors had made port. It was natural enough for them to cling to it as much as they could in the altered circumstances. It was natural enough that they should do their best – or their worst – to prevent that original idea from being eroded by the Queen's insistence upon Santander. It was all the more natural because it was the Portugal side of the enterprise that pulled in the subscribers. One of them at least, Robert Flick, subscribed £1,000 and furnished twenty musketeers, 'upon foundation only of a direct course and voyage to Lisbon or the Islands'. Then, too, in March Manuel d'Andrada, a trusted confidant of Don Antonio but also a Spanish spy, despatched to Mendoza, the Spanish ambassador in Paris, a remarkably accurate summary of the generals' agreement with the Portuguese pretender and along with it information that the fleet would go straight to Portugal and land the army at Peniche, the very place that in the event it was to land at.[26] About the same time there is among the English state papers another memorial advocating not only that the expedition should go straight to Lisbon without attempting any other service on the way but also that they should sail straight up the Tagus, using two smoke ships to screen them past the guns of St Julian's castle, and land the army in Lisbon itself, the ships' guns battering a way for the troops' assault. Whoever

<hr/>

[25] Hakluyt, IV, 341; S. P. Domestic, ccxxii, no. 90; *Monson's Tracts*, I, 222 note 116.
[26] Hakluyt, IV, 327; *Monson's Tracts*, I, 205 note 70; *Cal. S. P. Spanish*, IV, 524.

wrote this paper – and Sir Roger Williams, who all along had strongly advocated getting a foothold in the Peninsula, was to express very similar views after the expedition's return – it implies that what debate there was, was really about which way to approach Lisbon – overland or up the Tagus? – rather than about whether to go there first of all.[27]

There can be little doubt as to what course would win the support of the young Earl of Essex, twenty-three years old, £23,000 in debt,[28] and itching to make a great name for himself as a soldier. Where the treasure and the glory lay, there would his heart be also; and the glory and the treasure were obviously to be sought in Portugal and around the Azores, not at Santander and San Sebastian. All the very considerable influence that he had, as an earl and as one of the most popular young men in England, would be exerted in favour of putting those things first and of going straight to Lisbon despite the Queen's instructions. Nor could there be much doubt that he would use that influence to the full. As he said later, 'though I had no charge, I made my brother general of the horse and my faithful friend Sir Roger Williams colonel-general of the infantry, seven or eight of my fast friends colonels, and twenty at least of my domestics captains, so as I might have authority and party enough when I would.'[29] It is small wonder that the Queen was alarmed and bitterly angry at the prospect of all that 'authority and party' being thrown enthusiastically into the scale to encourage the disobedience of two generals who were already only too inclined to disregard her most emphatic instructions. It is surely unnecessary to invoke the psychology of ageing virginity, or the doting sentiments of maiden aunts, to explain her anger. Her fears that the enterprise of Norris and Drake might be perverted from its primary purpose must have been immeasurably increased by the presence of Essex in their fleet. For it was his presence with them, not his absence from her, that so perturbed Elizabeth.

---

[27] S. P. Domestic, ccxxiii, no. 50. For Williams's views, see *Cal. S. P. Foreign,* XXII, 409–11; XXIII, 186; Lansdowne MSS, lviii, no. 69.

[28] Devereux, I, 206.

[29] In his 'Apology', quoted in *Monson's Tracts,* I, 222 note 116.

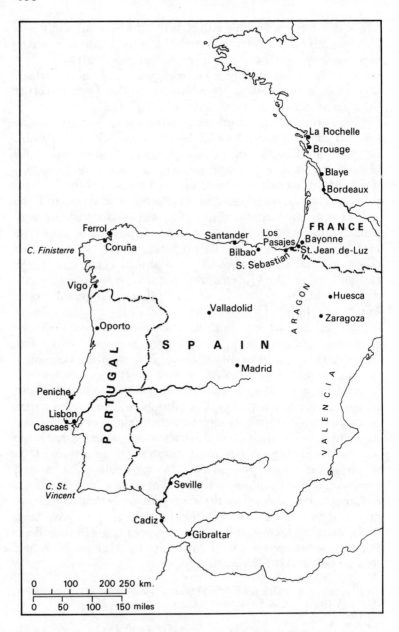

Map 2. Western Spain and Portugal and South-Western France.

# VI

# Failure in Portugal

Elizabeth's fears were all too soon justified. She could not, however, blame Essex for the expedition's first, and perhaps most disastrous, aberration. For, as we have seen, Essex and Williams, when they slipped out of Plymouth aboard the *Swiftsure* on the night of 5 April, probably expected Norris and Drake to sail direct to Lisbon. They must certainly have been under that impression when they finally got to sea from Falmouth on 17 or 18 April, or they would hardly themselves have sailed straight to the mouth of the Tagus. Yet when they got there, and for the next two or three weeks, they found no sign of the rest of the expedition. They cruised as far south as Cadiz. They 'lay up and down about the south cape' [Cape St Vincent], where they took a few corn ships. Moving back north, they landed a raiding party near the Bayona Isles. But it was only on 13 May and further north still, off Cape Finisterre, that at long last they made contact with the rest of the fleet.[1]

What had happened was that Norris and Drake, instead of going straight to Lisbon as Essex and Williams seem to have expected, had gone first to Coruña and spent a fortnight there. They apparently decided on this change of plan the very day after the *Swiftsure* left Plymouth. For on that Sunday, 6 April, they wrote to the Privy Council that '*200 sail of ships* of divers nations' were credibly reported to have arrived

at the Groyne ·and other ports of Galicia and Portugal with a store of munition, masts, cables, and other provisions for the enemy. And therefore we resolve with all speed we may, if the wind will not suffer us to bear *with Biscay* and those parts, to attempt the destroying of the shipping in the foresaid coasts of Galicia and Portugal, both in

[1] Sir Roger Williams, *A Briefe Discourse of War*, pp. 12–13, in *The Works of Sir Roger Williams*, ed. J. X. Evans; Hakluyt, IV, 327–8; S. P. Domestic, ccxxiv, nos. 85, 86; Harleian MSS, clxvii, fo. 114v; *Cal. S. P. Foreign*, XXIII, 273, 282.

respect of the most annoyance of the enemy and of hope to supply somewhat of our needs.[2]

The tone of this letter can only strengthen our suspicion that Norris and Drake had already made up their minds to ignore the Queen's reiterated instructions about going first to Santander. It looks as if that, too, was the impression it gave Burghley. For when it came to his hands he underlined the words here printed in italics, and also the commanders' request for a good supply of victuals to be sent after them 'to *Cape Finisterre* or the *Isles of Bayon*'. And, indeed, after their return to England, they were to excuse their disobedience by alleging that the wind did not suffer them to bear with Biscay. By the morning of 22 April, they then said, it had gone round from NNE so 'far easterly' that they could not have made Santander. Yet on 7 May they had written that the 'prosperous wind' which got them away, had continued at least until they made their landfall at Cape Ortegal late on 23 April. Other evidence also suggests that for at least six days after 21 April the wind was never so far easterly as to rule out setting a course for Santander.[3]

It is true, of course, that by going first to Coruña Norris and Drake made a visit to Santander, eastwards along the rough northern coast of Spain, an even less attractive enterprise. But it is very doubtful whether the decision to go to Coruña had much to do with the decision not to go to Santander, for as we have seen the commanders' minds seem to have been already set upon Lisbon – that was probably their reason for not calling a council to discuss their course.[4] Now, in that context there was something to be said for a quick visit to Coruña. It was on the way to Lisbon. And if those two hundred ships of divers nations did exist – as some at least did, for Drake was to catch eighty of them off the Tagus – to have caught them at Coruña within a few days of the expedition leaving Plymouth would have notably raised everyone's spirits and gone some way towards relining the pockets of those who had invested in the enterprise.

    [2] S. P. Domestic, ccxxiii, no. 64.
    [3] Ibid., ccxxvij, no. 35; Lodge *Illustrations of British History*, II, 379; *Monson's Tracts*, I, 198–9.
    [4] S. P. Domestic, ccxxxviii, no. 45.

When, however, Norris and Drake arrived off Coruña on the afternoon of Thursday, 24 April, they found in the harbour only five ships instead of two hundred. All that were there were the dilapidated galleon *San Juan,* from the Portugal squadron of the 1588 Armada; a 600-ton Flemish hulk, also from the 1588 Armada; a 1,000-ton Biscayan; another 'great ship upon the careen'; a smaller vessel, laden with pikes, muskets, and calivers; a few small craft; and a couple of galleys.[5] This mere handful of shipping was not worth any long stay and in fact, although the English went about the job in a somewhat ponderous fashion, they did in a couple of days deal with the stores ashore as well as the ships afloat. Late on that Thursday, 24 April, they disembarked 7,000 troops about a mile east of the town in barely three hours – a very smart piece of work. Next morning they landed some artillery to cover them from the guns of the *San Juan* and her consorts which for some reason or other Drake and the sailors made no attempt to attack from the sea. That evening Norris and his soldiers stormed and occupied the lower town, which was built upon the narrow neck of land that joined the walled upper town to the mainland. They captured a few ransomable officers and cut the throats of perhaps five hundred unransomable men. Then they fell to plundering the 'abundant store of victuals, salt, and all kind of provision for shipping and the war' which they found there and which a captured commissary of victuals assured them was 'the beginning of a magazine of all sorts of provisions for a new voyage into England'. Unfortunately they also found 'every cellar full of wine' and promptly fell to 'inordinate drinking', with the disastrous consequences that free wine usually had upon the beer-drinking English soldiery. With the lower town lost, the Spaniards on Saturday morning, 26 April, set fire to the *San Juan* and abandoned their other vessels. The two galleys had already crept away to Ferrol. From the ships and the shore the English collected 150 brass cannon, a 'shipload' of small arms, and whatever supplies they could be bothered to carry away.

---

[5] For the Coruña operations, see Hakluyt, IV, 317–27; S. P. Domestic, ccxxiv, nos. 13–15, 22–4, 44, 47–8; ccxxv, no. 42; Harleian MSS, clxvii, fos. 113–14; *Cal. S. P. Foreign,* XXIII, 353; *Cal. S. P. Spanish,* IV, 537–8, 544; *Cal. S. P. Venetian,* VIII, 434–41, 443–4.

All this had been done by the morning of 26 April, and it was all that usefully could be done at Coruña. Yet it was another fortnight before the expedition got away. For after seizing the lower town and easily repulsing a relief attempt by 2,000 ill-disciplined local levies, Norris and the soldiers proceeded to attempt the upper town. A drum was sent to demand its surrender. He was shot at, whereupon the garrison promptly hanged the soldier who had fired the shot. But 'they listened not greatly' to the summons to surrender. So Norris had either to call off his attack or to sit down to a regular siege. He decided upon a siege, but as the Queen had not provided the siege train for which he had asked, he had to do the best he could with two culverins and two demi-cannons, one of which 'brake in her carriages' at the very first shot. Nevertheless, by 2 May the remaining three pieces had made a practicable breach and in addition a mine was sprung beneath a tower a little distance along the wall (at the second attempt: at the first 'the powder brake out backwards'). The besiegers assaulted both places enthusiastically but, as Ashley re-marked, 'the English common soldier is not well acquainted with matters of breach'. Thus one party rushed forward as soon as the mine brought down half the tower, only to find the other, more slowly-toppling half falling on their heads. Thereupon they took to their heels, leaving behind twenty or thirty dead, and poor Captain Sydenham who was held fast 'by three or four great stones upon his lower parts'. Meanwhile 'the breach made by the cannon was wonderfully well assaulted by them that had the charge thereof, who brought their men to the push of the pike at the top of the breach'. But too many rushed up at once and the rubble over which they climbed, 'with the weight of them that were thereon, slipped outwards from under their feet, whereby did appear half the wall unbattered'.

That virtually ended English hopes of taking the upper town, all the more as Drake had left the seaward side open and allowed the two galleys to run in supplies from Ferrol. Before, however, Norris could call off his siege, he had to deal with another relief force, of some 8,000 men, that had gathered six miles to the east at Puente de Burgos. So, leaving about a third of his soldiers to look after the upper town, on the morning of 6 May he led the rest against this relief force. The raw enemy levies again put up a poor resistance, except at a bridge 'the further end whereof was barricaded with barrels' and flanked on both sides by their shot. Here there was a brisk brief action in which, before the bridge was won, Captain Hendar had his casque shot off and received five sword wounds in the head and Captain Fulford was shot in the arm and Captain Barton hurt in the eye. Sir Edward Norris, too, 'charging the first defendant with his pike, with very earnestness in over-thrusting fell and was grievously hurt at the sword in the head but was most honourably rescued by the General, his brother', fighting, we are told, without armour in doublet and hose. The relief force thus disposed of, Norris then burned the lower town of Coruña and on 8 May re-embarked his troops. Next day the expedition at long last set sail again.

By then, however, the enemy had been given an invaluable fortnight to prepare himself in both Portugal and Biscay and the chance of surprising him had been thrown away. Four English captains and several hundred soldiers had fallen in action. A very much larger number was sickening with diseases bred of orgies in Coruña's wine cellars and of infection from the rotting clothes and baggage of the previous year's Armada. Besides this, a couple of dozen transports – most of them impressed Dutchmen – with close on 3,000 troops had found various pretexts for returning to England or for putting into La Rochelle before the fleet reached Coruña. Now another 2,000 men slipped away as it left.[6]

Of course the commanders once again put the blame for the delay upon the wind, now turned westerly. But it did not turn before 26 April or perhaps later and it was still westerly when they left on 9 May.[7] Nor can their low stock of víctuals, of which they all complained and which Don Antonio later gave as the reason for visiting Coruña,[8] have required them to stay there a fortnight. The supplies captured in the lower town on 25 April could, with proper organization, have been taken aboard in very little time and, on Wingfield's evidence, the cannon of the upper town could do nothing to prevent the

[6] *Acts P. C.*, XVII, 188-9, 226-9, 245; Corbett, *Drake and the Tudor Navy*, II, 306, 318.
[7] See the discussion by Oppenheim, in *Monson's Tracts*, I, 198-9, 203-4.
[8] *Cal. S. P. Spanish*, IV, 553.

more provident captains from transferring those stores from shore to ship. Whatever the true explanation of the delay, the whole proceedings had an air of casualness and slack purpose that augured none too well for the future.

Moreover when they did leave Coruña, Norris and Drake set course for Lisbon, not for Santander. Once again the wind was made their excuse. At a council of war held to discuss their next move, they called in Thomas Drake and Thomas West, the captain and shipmaster of Sir Francis's flagship, the *Revenge*, and Captain Sackville and Master Robert Wignall of the *Nonpareil*. These nautical experts obligingly, and perhaps not altogether unexpectedly, advised that to go eastwards to Santander 'was a thing unfit and most dangerous in respect there was no safe harbour on that coast where such a fleet might ride in safety before the army should be landed'. This was, of course, an argument against ever going to Santander at all; and as West and Wignall refused 'utterly to undertake the conduction of the navy thither' from Coruña, the council readily enough, 'the wind being west, thought meet to leave the intended enterprise of Santander'.[9] And the wind apparently stayed westerly for another week[10] – though it is perhaps not altogether obvious why a west wind should not serve reasonably well for sailing eastwards.

It is also a little curious to find Drake thinking in terms of sending the army in to do the work while the fleet rode in safety outside. He was, of course, much cluttered with transports and supply ships, with a fleet of 83 sail all told, besides the Dutch flyboats. And the soldiers provided another excuse. 'We find by experience', Norris wrote to Burghley on 8 May, 'it is very hard to distress any shipping that is guarded by the ordnance of a town, except we were able to take the town', which they could hardly hope to do without their siege cannons. Ashley elaborated the argument. 'Santander', he

---

[9] S. P. Domestic, ccxxvii, no. 35.

[10] So Sir William Knollys reported to the Queen – ibid., ccxxiv, no. 53. Windebank's statement that the Queen understood 'they had eight days fair wind to have gone to those two places [Santander and San Sebastian] *before* they came to the Groyne' seems to be a misunderstanding of what she said or of what Knollys reported – ibid., ccxxiv, no. 53. Evesham said that the wind turned northerly by 14 May – Harleian MSS, clxvii, fos. 113–14; Wingfield that it took them nine days to reach the Berlengas – Hakluyt, IV, 327.

wrote, 'is by report as strong as the higher town of the Groyne, whereunto the cannon must of necessity be brought if we shall prevail according to the generals' instructions. The entry to the haven is straiter than this, where notwithstanding the fleet hath rid it out in contempt of the cannon, yet hath been somewhat endamaged.'[11] The experience of distressing ship- ping at Coruña had perhaps been somewhat limited, and the English ships had in fact rid it out in contempt of the cannon with no loss and very little damage. Certainly, too, Drake's experience had been very different in 1587 when he had sailed boldly into Cadiz without waiting for an army to land and past defences quite as lethal as any at Coruña or Santander in 1589. But Drake's cautious, almost timid, conduct of the naval forces is throughout one of the more puzzling features of this expedition. His blindness to the supreme strategical impor- tance of the galleons at Santander is equally surprising. For, like everyone else, he professed to have been convinced by the visit to Coruña that the King of Spain had been preparing to put a new Armada to sea within a few months. Can he or any of them really have been sincere in their protestations that by destroying four or five ships and a townful of half-rotten stores they had disrupted those preparations?

The fact would seem to be that the experience at Coruña, whatever lessons it taught about distressing shipping, had revealed the remarkable military weakness of the Spaniards in their own countryside. English raiding parties had roamed for miles round Coruña, burning and plundering, and the Spaniards' two relieving attempts had been easily shattered. 'An army of 10,000 good soldiers', Ashley wrote on 7 May 'may pass through the whole realm without great danger.'[12] What an opportunity, therefore, might await them in Portugal if they could get there promptly and if there were any foundation for Don Antonio's assurances of a Portuguese national rising! Norris, carried away by that prospect, wrote excitedly to Burghley:

A supply of 30 companies out of the Low Countries would serve to continue the war here all this year, which (under correction) were a

---

[11] S. P. Domestic, ccxxiv, nos. 14, 22.
[12] Ibid., no. 14.

more safe and profitable course than to attend the enemy at home. And this I do assure your lordship, that if Her Majesty do repose trust in the new-trained companies of England, they will deceive her when there shall be most need, which we have found by experience. It is most necessary that Her Majesty breed soldiers both here and in Flanders and give encouragement to men of account to follow the wars, otherwise she shall miss them when it will be too late to wish for them.[13]

To expect the impecunious Virgin Queen to 'breed soldiers' on that scale in both Portugal and the Netherlands was hardly reasonable, and the withdrawing of another thirty companies – the whole of the English auxiliary forces – from the Netherlands a bare month after the loss of Geertruiden-berg was obviously neither practical politics nor feasible strategy. Nor was Elizabeth likely to agree to so revolutionary a change in the whole character and purpose of Norris and Drake's expedition. For nothing had happened either to diminish the importance of destroying Spain's war navy and cutting off her American silver supplies, or to make it certain that the Portuguese would rise in strength. Even if they did so rise, a new commitment to large-scale operations in Portugal would place a new and increasing strain upon England's already stretched financial and military resources. Elizabeth could hardly do other than reject this proposal to turn the sideshow into the main campaign and tell the generals firmly that in the Netherlands 'there are few enough for the cause which we have undertaken and therefore not much to be diminished'.

Nor is it altogether surprising that, on receiving Norris and Drake's letters from Coruña, she remarked 'that they went to places more for profit than for service'. Ashley, after all, was of very much the same opinion. He had written on 7 May:

if this opportunity be taken and speedy supply sent, I see no doubt of very good success, of which otherwise there will be very little hope, for such persons as are deeply interested herein I find already disposed to seek by all means possible to recover themselves in their

---

[13] Ibid., no. 22. Ashley, too, wrote that the brunt of the action at Puente de Burgos on 6 May had to be borne by a small proportion of veteran captains and troops.

particular, which if they cannot (through want of things needful) timely supply in Portugal, I perceive, whatsoever advice be given, they will attempt the Islands or take in hand some such matter.[14]

This may have been unkindly put, but it was perhaps not altogether wide of the mark. Norris and Drake had themselves invested heavily in the enterprise and there were many with them who, as Williams had said earlier,[15] would be ruined by its failure. Besides these, there were backers at home – Elizabeth among them – who looked for a substantial return upon their investments. And a very substantial return might now be needed to buy off the Queen's inevitable wrath at their failure to visit Santander. They would be therefore more anxious than ever to intercept the treasure fleets. Moreover, with one eye on the Azores and the treasure fleets, they were not likely to take great risks in Portugal unless success was reasonably assured by a prompt and general Portuguese revolt and by a promise of further support from home.

Nor was it by any means easy for Norris and Drake to assess at all accurately just how much Portuguese assistance they could rely upon. For neither they nor the English government had direct contacts with the resistance movement in Portugal and it had been left to Don Antonio to make whatever efforts were made to prepare and organize an uprising. There was, of course, no doubt that a resistance movement did exist or that its members were in secret correspondence with Don Antonio.[16] It was they, apparently, who suggested the idea, which Lord Admiral Howard toyed with in July 1588, of the Pretender landing with troops to raise a national revolt once the Armada had departed. Again, in late October a Spanish spy had noticed that one of Don Antonio's Portuguese adherents, Juan Vaz, had disappeared – to Portugal, it seemed, to visit his father, a rich Lisbon merchant and adherent of the Pretender.[17] The movement had the sympathy of many of the populace and a fair number of the nobles and gentry, who resented Spanish rule; of some of the wealthier merchants, who grumbled at Spain's inability to protect their

[14] Ibid., nos. 14, 50, 53.
[15] *Cal. S. P. Foreign*, XXIII, 186.
[16] S. P. Domestic, ccxxii, no. 27; *Cal. S. P. Venetian*, VIII, 331–2, 335, etc.
[17] *Cal. S. P. Spanish*, IV, 485.

seaborne commerce against the English; and particularly, if somewhat surprisingly, of many friars and other ecclesiastics, who were said to be the most turbulent of all. Don Antonio therefore received plenty of promises and he was correspondingly lavish with his own assurances to Norris and Drake. But as the Venetian ambassador in Spain remarked, 'the hopes of exiles are usually higher than the inclination of the populace will warrant'. And promises to a 'king over the water' are more often made as insurances for their givers than as guarantees of active help for their receivers.[18]

Nevertheless it is possible that the best way of transforming promises into deeds might have been for the expedition to seek an early and resounding success by a rapid direct attack upon Lisbon. For even now the Spanish governor in Portugal, Philip II's able young nephew the Cardinal Archduke Albert, had barely 7,000 troops and of those some 4,000 were disaffected and unreliable Portuguese. One Spanish report reckoned that he had no more than 1,500 men that he could fully trust.[19] With such a force it was not easy to man Lisbon's extensive perimeter and hold down its restive population. To keep the field against an English army of equal or superior numbers was out of the question altogether. The way was thus open for a bold and rapid English thrust. The boldest approach would have been that suggested earlier by Sir Roger Williams (if he it were) of sailing straight up the Tagus and landing in the city itself. If that were still regarded as too bold, there was another way. Norris and Drake, like Alba and Bazan in 1580, might land their army near Cascaes at the mouth of the Tagus and hasten the sixteen miles up the right bank of the river to Lisbon, with the fleet in close support. Army and fleet would then keep in constant and visual contact. The troops could ease the fleet's passage past the castles of St Julian and Belem. The ships' guns could support the soldiers' assaults upon those castles and upon the city itself. And with so short a distance to cover, the entire force might be at the gates of Lisbon before the defence became

[18] *Cal. S. P. Venetian*, VIII, 445, 461–2: *Cal. S. P. Foreign*, XXIII, 23–4.
[19] *Cal. S. P. Venetian*, VIII, 441, 457; *Cal. S. P. Foreign*, XXIII, 336; S. P. Domestic, ccxxiv, no. 78; Hakluyt, IV, 336–7.

fully organized and while Don Antonio's friends still had a chance to play their part.

On 15 May the expedition, it seems, was ideally placed for just such an operation, having made its landfall at Cape la Roca, the 'Rock of Lisbon', a few miles north-west of Cascaes. There a council of war was again held, 'who delivered their opinions with relation to landing, which was at last determined to be at Peniche'.[20] Now Peniche, as we saw, was probably the landing-place decided upon before the expedition left England. Nevertheless, those two words, 'at last', do suggest another considerable debate. Did Sir Roger Williams, who with Essex had rejoined the fleet two days before, perhaps again argue for a bolder course? It would be surprising if he did not, for he was an argumentative fellow and Peniche was no place from which to launch a quick thrust at Lisbon. Not only was it '45 long English miles'[21] to the north-west of the capital, but also a landing there must make close co-operation, even communication, between fleet and army exceedingly difficult. The decision to land at Peniche is, in short, hardly intelligible except upon the assumptions that it was designed as a reconnaissance in force to test Portuguese feeling and that it was not regarded as at all necessarily implying a thrust at Lisbon.

The whole conduct of the operations which followed, bears out these assumptions.[22] On the afternoon of 16 May some 6,000 troops were landed about a mile from Peniche. They disembarked quickly, in a mere four hours, even though they had to go in through heavy surf that overturned one boat, drowning twenty-five of Captain Dolphin's men. They then had to wade through water up to their waists – except for Essex who, to be first ashore, must needs plunge in up to the shoulders. Don Pedro de Guzman, with a mixed force of

[20] If we may trust William Fenner, who was not present at the time but joined three weeks later – Birch, *Memoirs,* I, 59. It seems clear from the context that by the Rock of Lisbon he meant Cape la Roca and not Cape Carvoeiro, which was sometimes called 'the young Rock', just north of Peniche. Unfortunately there seems to be no other evidence about either the landfall or the council.

[21] Stowe MSS, clix, fo. 371.

[22] For the Peniche and Lisbon operations – Hakluyt, IV, 328–39; S. P. Domestic, ccxxiv, nos. 77–9, 85–6; ccxxv, no. 42; Stowe MSS, clix, fos. 370–1; Harleian MSS, clxvii, fos. 113–16; Birch, *Memoirs,* I, 59; *Cal. S. P. Foreign,* XXIII, 353–4, 362–3; *Cal. S. P. Venetian,* VIII, 445–50, 453–4, 456–8.

Spaniards and Portuguese, did try to oppose their landing but, although it came to push of pike, his Portuguese ran away and his heavily outnumbered Spaniards were soon forced to withdraw likewise. Yet no serious attempt was made to pursue him and all next day the invaders sat idly around while Peniche castle gave itself up without a shot fired and some friars and peasants, shoeless and hoseless, came to Don Antonio promising 'that within two days he should have a good supply of horse and foot'.

These few poor swallows hardly made a summer; but they were sufficient to persuade Norris to 'think it most convenient speedily to march to the principal place, thereby to give courage to the rest of the country'. Ralph Lane would have waited a few more days yet, to give Don Antonio time to publish his arrival and his friends time to rally to him. The generals, however, now decided that Norris and the army should march the forty-five miles across country to Lisbon, Drake promising 'to meet him in the river thereof with the fleet'. The sick and wounded were left in Peniche castle, with a company of foot to guard them.[23] Six more companies stayed on board ship with Drake. The rest marched away with Norris next morning, 18 May, Drake standing on a hillside to see them off and wish them well.

Yet convenient though Norris thought it to march speedily to Lisbon, the advance even now was leisurely enough. True, the first day for want of carriages 'they were enforced to carry their munition upon men's backs', though this was remedied next day. True, the mid-May heat was very oppressive and on the later stages Essex had all his stuff cast out of his carriages to make room for some of the many who fell sick or fainted by the way. True, again, on the second day's march the men were short of victuals, especially bread, since plundering was strictly forbidden now that they were in Portugal, while Don Antonio's friends had not yet organized a regular flow of supplies. Even so, the army took six days to cover the forty-five miles, which hardly amounts to forced marching. Nor was the pace slowed by enemy opposition. A mixed force of some 300

---

[23] According to William Fenner, their commander Captain George Bertie went off home on a French ship and his men were afterwards all put to the sword by the Spaniards when the expedition left – Birch, *Memoirs*, I, 59.

Spanish horse, pikemen, and harquebusiers, under the promisingly named Don Sancho Bravo, did skirmish with them occasionally, if a little gingerly. The Count of Fuentes, too, marched out on 17 May with about half the Lisbon garrison. But his Portuguese ran away, too, and as the Cardinal Archduke warned him of plots within the city he gave up the idea of making a stand either on the hills over Torres Vedras or at the bridge at Lores. On 22 May he withdrew into Lisbon.

Next night Essex and Williams tried in vain to tempt him out and into an ambush. Then on 25 May 'we came to the suburbs of Lisbon'. That evening Williams, with Anthony Wingfield and thirty shot, scoured the streets of the northern and western suburbs, Santa Caterina and San Antonio, but found there 'none but old folks and beggars crying *viva el Rey Don Antonio,* and the houses shut up, and [the enemy] had fired some houses by the waterside full of corn and other provisions of victuals'. Unwisely perhaps, the Spaniards had also poured away all the wine. Now, more sensibly, they burned all the houses that stood or abutted upon the city walls. Next morning, 26 May – a month after they had taken the lower town at Coruña – the main body of the English army moved into the northern and western suburbs of Lisbon, while Williams just failed to beat the enemy in a race to occupy the church of San Antonio which adjoined the city wall and might have provided the besiegers with a covered way in. Then the English troops, weary from their six days' march and the last night's watching in the fields, settled down for a siesta during the noonday heat. The Spaniards, learning of this, promptly sallied out upon them at three different points. Colonel Brett, roused from sleep, and Captain Carsey were killed and Captain Cave wounded before the attackers were put 'to a sudden foul retreat', with Essex and others pursuing them 'even to the gates of the high town'. During the following night, none the less, another attack, a *camisado,* had also to be repulsed.

Essex in his pursuit had knocked on the gates of the city, but that was as far as he could get, for the English had no means of forcing an entry. They had brought no artillery with them. They had not enough 'powder and match to maintain a fight half a day'. They had lost by sickness and by wounds getting on for 2,000 men, perhaps a third of the total force that had set out from Peniche.[24] Above all, the Portuguese had not risen. A good many friars had, indeed, shown great devotion to Don Antonio. The villagers of Torres Vedras had come out with a canopy to welcome him as their king. One gentleman had brought him a basket of cherries and plums. But in general, as Wingfield said 'the laity did respite their homage till they might see which way victory would sway'. Altogether, not more than 200 Portuguese had joined, and 'those the greatest cowards that ever I saw', Williams grumbled. We can, however, hardly blame the others for not coming into the open and risking their necks for a Pretender who, with a mere 4,000 fit men and no artillery, was attacking a great city whose garrison equalled, if it did not by now outnumber, the besiegers.

They were the less willing to declare themselves because the Cardinal Archduke appeared to have an uncanny foreknowledge of contemplated treasons. He owed much of it, in fact, to spies in Don Antonio's own ill-paid household. For some of the Pretender's most intimate and trusted servants and friends regularly passed on all they knew to Philip II through the Spanish ambassador in France, Bernardino de Mendoza. And there was little in Don Antonio's correspondence that was not soon known to such confidants as Antonio de Escobar, his agent in France, or Manoel de Andrada – who appeared as Sampson and David in Mendoza's correspondence – or the egregious Antonio de Vega. In addition, if we may believe the Venetian ambassador in Spain,[25] a Portuguese nobleman, who had been with Don Antonio in England, managed to slip away at Coruña and reveal to Philip himself a number of conspiracies involving some of the leading people in Lisbon. Juan Vaz's father, a man 'of vast and famous riches', escaped to Africa but a number were executed, while others were imprisoned, and some tortured, to discover their accomplices. As many Portuguese notables had already been deported or

---

[24] A muster at Cascaes on 2 June showed 5,735 serviceable men and 2,791 sick, but these figures include the companies with Drake – S. P. Domestic, ccxxiv, no. 78(i). Evesham put their losses at 2,000 – Harleian MSS, clxvii, fo. 115*v*; Williams said that they were down to 4,000 effectives when they left Lisbon – S. P. Domestic, ccxxiv, no. 77.

[25] *Cal. S. P. Venetian*, VIII, 442.

inveigled to Spain earlier, the Cardinal Archduke's swift severity now not only cowed the Lisbon populace but robbed them of their remaining leaders as well.

In these circumstances it needed more than a knocking at the city gates to give courage to any would-be helpers inside. For the plain facts were that the Portuguese would not revolt until the English took Lisbon and the English could not take Lisbon unless the Portuguese first revolted. It might be that Coruña had taught them – and Williams, for one, still believed it – that 10,000 good soldiers might march through the King of Spain's realm without much danger. But it had also taught them that to march through his realm was a very different matter from storming his fortified cities. Anyway, Norris had only 4,000 fit men, not 10,000. Even if he had had 10,000, with ample powder and shot, he must have hesitated (as Henry IV of France was to hesitate the following year before Paris) to plunge them into that labyrinth of streets and alleys unless he knew for certain that they could depend upon the citizens' prompt and whole-hearted support.

Meanwhile the position of those 4,000 was fast growing critical. So, on 28 May Norris called a council of war to discuss what should be done. Some, like Ralph Lane, were for hanging on a few more days in hopes of the Portuguese rallying to them. Others had by now no faith at all in Portuguese promises and wanted to 'march wholly away'. In the end it was decided to wait until the next morning to see whether there was any substance in Don Antonio's last desperate assurance that 'he should have that night 3,000 men armed of his own country'. If those 3,000 turned up, Norris would send the same number of English to bring up their artillery and munitions from the fleet and then 'try his fortune for the town'. If the 3,000 did not appear, he would retire from Lisbon next morning. They did not appear; and so next morning, 29 May, the army marched away to join the fleet at Cascaes.

For the fleet was still at Cascaes. Drake had not kept his promise to meet the army at Lisbon. He had reached Cascaes on 20 May. There he held another council of war and decided to wait for news of the army before moving into the Tagus. This caution was reasonable enough, for accurate timing was essential now that the landing at Peniche had put land and sea forces out of contact with each other. Yet when the news came, Drake showed no great alacrity to rush the Tagus defences. He said later that he again consulted the council of war on 26 May and on its advice at once prepared to take two-thirds of the fleet in with the first fair wind, 'which had accordingly proceeded had not Sir John Norris returned to Cascaes with the army'. But by his own account the fair wind came on 27 May, giving him two full days before the army began its retreat. According to the great contemporary historian William Camden, he also pleaded the danger of taking the fleet past St Julian's without the support of the land forces. Don Antonio added that the Queen had forbidden Drake to risk the ships in the Tagus.[26] And, indeed, her instructions had made operations in Portugal conditional upon their being 'without any great hazard'. The two generals, however, had shown no great reluctance to ignore their instructions when it suited them to do so and there is no reason to suppose that Drake suddenly became all obedience now. Nor need we suppose that he lost his nerve, or that his powers were failing, even though on 2 June, thinking back to happier days off Lisbon, he did misdate his letter as 1587.[27]

After all, Drake and Norris had not yet attempted the third and, they hoped, by far the most lucrative part of their enterprise. They had also failed to perform the first, and in the Queen's view the most important, of their tasks. If the fifty or more Armada ships which they had left unmolested at Santander should go to escort the treasure fleets as Palmer suggested, Drake would need every fighting ship he could muster to accomplish his final purpose at the Azores. He might have been ready enough to sail up the Tagus and join the army in taking delivery of Lisbon if the river's banks had been lined by cheering Portuguese risen to welcome Don Antonio. When the Portuguese had not risen, he dared not lightly risk losing even a few of his fighting ships to the forty

---

[26] Harleian MSS, clxvii, fo. 115; S. P. Domestic, ccxxvii, no. 35; *Cal. S. P. Spanish*, IV, 554: Camden, pp. 553–4.

[27] S. P. Domestic, ccii, no. 7. See Oppenheim's discussion in *Monson's Tracts*, I, 221–3 and Drake's letter of 2 June in J. Strype, *Annals* (1824 ed.), IV, 11.

cannon of St Julian's and the twelve galleys lurking under their shelter. Nor, it seems fairly certain, did Norris think very differently; for he himself reminded his council of war on 28 May that 'the expedition of Portugal were not the only purpose of their journey, but an adventure therein (which if it succeeded prosperously might make them sufficiently rich and wonderful honourable)'.[28] He, too, had one eye on the Azores and the treasure ships and therefore was not inclined to risk too much at Lisbon.

This hesitating caution in Portugal, coming on top of the failure to go to Santander and the pointless delay at Coruña, proved fatal alike to the Queen's purposes and to Norris and Drake's adventure. For the retreat from Lisbon virtually ended the expedition's serious operations. They did hang about at or off Cascaes for another ten days, from 30 May until 8 June, for they were reluctant still to abandon hope of Lisbon altogether.[29] At Cascaes, too, especially after they had taken the castle, both fleet and army were reasonably safe. There they might wait a little longer to see if a Portuguese revolt would develop, or if they could expect help from Morocco, or if the Queen would send them their siege train and promise them their thirty companies. The enemy made no serious effort to molest them. The Cardinal Archduke's troops once advanced gingerly in their direction, but refused to stay for a battle. Norris tried to taunt Spanish pride by sending a trumpet to challenge the Count of Fuentes to stay and fight. Essex, not to be outdone and 'full of high spirits and hot youthly blood',[30] sent 'a particular cartel offering himself against any of theirs, if they had any of his quality; or if they would not admit of that, six, eight, or ten, or as many as they would appoint'. Fuentes was still not to be drawn. He could not trust his Portuguese, he dared not draw too many Spaniards out of Lisbon, and he took no notice of the challenges. Nor did the Spanish galleys show much more spirit after 'the long and good fight' that Captain Minshaw and the

---

[28] Hakluyt, IV, 334.

[29] For these final operations – Hakluyt, IV, 338–45; S. P. Domestic, ccxxiv, nos. 78–9, 85–6; ccxxv, nos. 5, 27; ccxxvii, no. 35; Harleian MSS, clxvii, fos. 115–16; Stowe MSS, clix, fo. 371; Birch, *Memoirs*, I, 59–61; *Cal. S. P. Foreign*, XXIII, 354, 363, 383–4; *Cal. S. P. Venetian*, VIII, 451–2, 455, 457–62.

[30] J. Speed, *History of Great Britain* (1632 ed.), p. 190.

crew of one of the hulks put up, 'who fought with them to the last, yea, after his ship was on fire'.

Meanwhile the English fleet was able to do a little towards covering expenses by 'fetching in' twenty French and sixty Hanseatic ships which happened now to arrive off the Tagus, some in ballast, 'of great burthen wonderful well builded for sailing' and apparently intended for service with a new Armada, others laden with grain and naval stores. But although the captain of St Julian's did offer, sincerely or otherwise, to yield to a show of force, there was still no sign of a Portuguese revolt. Nor was there any longer hope of help from Morocco. Earlier in the year Mushac Reyz, an envoy from Mulay Ahmed el Mansur, the Sultan, had promised the Queen that her fleet should 'have all needful relief of victuals and other necessaries out of his ports and havens in case they shall have need to use the same'. Mushac seems also to have led Don Antonio to expect money, munitions, and even men. So, as soon as a landing was made in Portugal, Don Antonio sent him off, with his own servant Cipriano de Figueredo and with Captain Ousley from the generals, to inform Mulay Ahmed. But whatever hopes Mushac Reyz had given, Mulay Ahmed was much too preoccupied with African affairs, and too nervous about Turkish encouragement of a young pretender to his own usurped throne, to rush into a quarrel with Spain. Thus it was that Cipriano and Ousley, with another Moroccan agent, now returned to Don Antonio and the generals at Cascaes with an answer that brought them no comfort at all.[31]

No answer had yet come from the Queen either. So on 3 June Norris re-embarked his troops and on 5 June he and Drake decided to leave. If the wind were favourable, they would sail for the Azores to attempt the last of their purposes there and, in Drake's phrase, find 'some comfortable little dew of heaven' for themselves. If it blew southerly, they would beat up and down the coast of Portugal. Leaving it to the wind to blow them where it listed sounds a dispirited sort of decision. However, next day two small vessels arrived from England,

[31] Hakluyt, IV, 341; *Cal. S. P. Foreign*, XXIII, 125, 130–1, 193; *L. and A.*, I, 830; *Cal. S. P. Spanish*, IV, 516, 523, 550; *Cal. S. P. Venetian*, VIII, 447, 458–9; D. Yahya, *Morocco in the Sixteenth Century*, pp. 133–9.

bringing news that Crosse and the victuallers were close at hand and bearing the Queen's letters of 20 May written in answer to their requests from Coruña.[32] Those letters, refusing both the artillery and the thirty companies, settled it. On 8 June, after sending home the latest prizes with the sick and the Earl of Essex, and releasing the Dutch flyboats to finish their long-interrupted voyage to France, the expedition left Cascaes for the Azores.

The last and worst unkindnesses of the weather then smote them. A fierce southerly gale prevented them from seeing the Azores or the treasure ships. Young William Fenner, who had come out with the victuallers from England, got separated from the rest and after 'wandering as a lost ship in search of the generals', fetched up at Porto Santo in the Madeiras. There he met Crosse and seven more of the victuallers. Together they took the island and ransomed the town before sailing for home.[33] Meanwhile the rest of the expedition had been forced back by the gale as far to the north as Vigo. There a landing was made and the town sacked on 20 June. By now, however, the delays and diseases incurred at Coruña and the losses and disappointments suffered at Lisbon were having their effect. Less than 2,000 soldiers were fit for duty and some of the ships were strained and leaking besides having only a handful of sailors able to work them.[34] It was therefore agreed that Norris should take home all but twenty of the best vessels. With those twenty Drake was to make a last desperate dash for the Azores. Once more, however, a fierce southerly gale sprang up and scattered the expedition as it was getting to sea. Drake's flagship, the *Revenge*, sprang a leak and he joined the rest in running for home. By the end of June all but a very few were back in Plymouth or other south coast ports.

They were distinctly anxious about the reception that they would receive. Essex, who arrived ahead of the rest on 24 or 25

[32] S. P. Domestic, ccxxiv, no. 53.

[33] Birch, *Memoirs*, I, 60. This William Fenner is not to be confused with the William Fenner, captain of H. M. S. *Aid* and rear-admiral in the expedition.

[34] The vice-admiral, Thomas Fenner, on the *Dreadnought*, had 150 of her crew of 300 sick at one time and only eighteen able to work: 114 had died and only three escaped the sickness – S. P. Domestic, ccxxv, no. 27. On the *Gregory* of London there were at one point only eight men to trim the sails according to John Evesham who served in her – Harleian MSS, clxvii, fo. 116*v*.

June, at once sent his brother Walter to sue for the Queen's pardon. A few days later, after Drake and Norris were home, the Earl himself rode off to court along with Ashley, who carried letters from the generals and Don Antonio. Then on 4 July Sir John Norris sent his brother, Sir Edward, with a letter to Walsingham and ten days later Thomas Fenner, the vice-admiral, also wrote to the Secretary, both explaining that only a virulent outbreak of disease among the troops and sailors had prevented them going to the Azores as intended.[35] Ashley must have glossed over the facts very effectively, for his report of their good success pleased the Queen enough for Walsingham on 7 July to draft a letter in which she thanked them for their service and acknowledged 'that there hath been as much performed by you as true valour and good conduction could yield'.[36] Yet even this early there were hints that the pleasure was not unalloyed. On the same day the Privy Council sent down commissioners to take charge of the prizes, appraise and sell the corn, etc. in them, and from the proceeds pay off the shipowners, sailors, and soldiers who had been imprested by the Queen's commission. And besides thus taking all this out of the generals' hands – to their considerable annoyance – the Privy Council also required them to report on the state of their ships, on the numbers of soldiers and mariners safely returned, and how many ships and men might be 'set forth again for the following of this action to destroy the King of Spain's ships and to intercept his fleet coming from the Indies'.[37]

It very quickly became apparent that the expedition had not only left undone those two things that it ought to have done, but also that it was in no state to set forth again to do them. Even the hope that it would pay its way soon faded.[38] Thereupon the official attitude grew more critical until, first, the winding-up of the expedition's finances was handed over to a commission headed by Sir John Hawkins, and then in the autumn Norris and Drake were called before the Privy

[35] S. P. Domestic, ccxxv, nos. 5, 27; *Cal. S. P. Spanish*, IV, 549–50.

[36] S. P. Domestic, ccxxv, no. 15; Oppenheim (*Monson's Tracts*, I, 217) thinks the letter was never sent, but the Privy Council referred to it in a letter of 7 July – *Acts P. C.*, XVII, 352.

[37] Ibid., pp.358–61; cp. also S. P. Domestic, ccxxv, nos. 24–5, 43.

[38] See below, pp.127, 140.

Council to answer for their failure to carry out the Queen's instructions.[39] They seem to have defended themselves well enough to avoid actual censure, but by this time dissatisfaction with their achievements had spread far beyond government circles. To begin with, about all the plunder they had managed to collect was the guns taken at Coruña and the hulks taken off the Tagus and to avoid undue international complications, the Privy Council soon ordered the release of all the captured ships except those (like the *Peter* of Lübeck) built for the King of Spain, and the restitution of the goods taken in them except for munitions and victuals. Merchants, shipowners, and others who had invested in the enterprise found themselves with little or nothing to show for it. Even vice-admiral Thomas Fenner reckoned that he was £1,000 worse off for his adventure, and there were ships' captains still begging for a settlement of their accounts in October.[40] As for the rank and file, Wingfield says that the generals gave 'every soldier five shillings in money and the arms he bare to make money of, which was more than could by any means be due unto them'. Yet there were enough of them discontented to riot at Bartholomew Fair in London and to terrorize some country districts.[41]

In the nation at large there was disappointment, almost disillusionment. There was grief for the loss of men as well as for the loss of money. Wingfield tried to make out that no more than 3,500 were lost. Young William Fenner, however, understood that 11,000 had been killed or had died of sickness, among them 750 of the 1,100 gentlemen of name. Remembering that no more than 2,000 soldiers were fit for duty at Vigo and that Thomas Fenner lost 114 of the *Dreadnought's* crew of just under 300, we should be probably not far wrong in guessing that the true number was rather nearer Fenner's estimate than Wingfield's.[42] That would be more than the total number of the English auxiliary forces in the Netherlands.

---

[39] *Acts P. C.*, XVIII, 46–8; S. P. Domestic, ccxxvi, no. 4; ccxxvii, nos. 32, 35.
[40] S. P. Domestic, ccxxv, no. 27; ccxxvii, nos. 50, 53.
[41] Hakluyt, IV, 345; *Acts P. C.*, XVII, 387, 416, 420–1.
[42] Hakluyt, IV, 314; Birch, *Memoirs*, I, 61; S. P. Domestic, ccxxv, no. 27; *Cal. S. P. Domestic, Addenda*, p. 287.

Some of the survivors made matters worse by criticizing the conduct of the expedition in their attempts to explain its failure. There seems to be no English evidence to support the story current in Spain that Norris and Drake now became open enemies, Norris blaming their lack of success upon Drake's failure to bring the fleet up the Tagus to Lisbon.[43] Yet even if Norris did not blame Drake, plenty of others did. Ralph Lane, writing to Walsingham on 27 July, sharply criticized both generals, 'two so overweening spirits contemning to be advised and disdaining to ask advice'. But he singled out Drake's failure to 'pass St Julian's and meet us with the fleet at Lisbon' as one of the more disastrous errors. Sir Roger Williams, writing also in July to urge (somewhat belatedly!) an attack on Santander, seems to be pointing at Drake when he added that 'your captains must be resolute and valiant, else excuses will be made'. In his *Briefe Discourse of War*, published the following year, he put it more bluntly: 'when we arrived, had our navy entered, we would have entered the town.' That was also Anthony Wingfield's published opinion. Indeed, according to another contemporary, Sir William Monson, Drake 'was much blamed by the common consent of all men, the overthrow of the action being imputed to him'.[44]

It was all very well for Norris and Williams to prate that, although their journey had not brought them great profit, it had done much for the Queen's honour and the country's reputation. It was all very well for Anthony Wingfield to rush into print with boasts that they had routed the Spaniards even upon their own dunghill; that they had 'won a town by escalade, battered and assaulted another, overthrown a mighty prince's power in the field, landed our army in three several places of his kingdom, marched seven days in the heart of his country, lain three nights in the suburbs of his principal city, beaten his forces into the gates thereof, and possessed two of his frontier forts.'[45] They had done all this and more. They

[43] *Cal. S. P. Venetian*, VIII, 467.

[44] S. P. Domestic, ccxxv, no. 42; *Cal. S. P. Foreign*, XXIII, 411; Williams, *Briefe Discourse of War*, p.13; Hakluyt, IV, 335; *Monson's Tracts*, I, 178.

[45] S. P. Domestic, ccxxv, no. 5; *Cal. S. P. Foreign*, XXIII, 409–11; Hakluyt, IV, 307, 309.

had distracted a few of Parma's regiments from the Low Countries and forced Philip to raise others in Italy. The destruction of the Lisbon granaries and the seizure of the Hanseatic ships were serious blows to Spain's food supply as well as to her naval preparations.[46] The mutiny in Parma's army, which saved the Dutch from a threatening attack in August, was due to lack of pay; and that lack arose largely from the expenses, and the delay and uncertainty about the safe arrival of the American treasure, which Norris and Drake had caused.

Yet humiliating and painful as these things might be to Spain, they were not fatal. Norris and Drake had set out to light a fire in the King of Spain's own house. All that they had succeeded in doing was once again to singe his beard. Nor could they convincingly blame the Queen or Privy Council for their failure. It was a pity that her purse had not been full enough for her to find the whole of the £100,000 that the expedition cost. It was a pity that her hasty orders had annoyed the Dutch. Yet financially she had contributed or advanced nearly two and a half times as much as she had originally been asked for. She had done her best to soothe the Dutch and to shorten the delays. If victuals were short and impressed Dutch transports unreliable, it was because the generals had allowed volunteers to swell the land forces to 'double the determined numbers'. Her lack of sympathy with their Portuguese dreams had not, after all, prevented them from providing themselves with land forces of a size that could only be justified if the object was a full-dress invasion of Portugal. Yet they both planned and conducted their Portuguese campaign as if they agreed with the Queen in regarding it as a subsidiary and experimental side-show, in which they dared not involve their forces at all deeply unless an immediate and wholesale national rising made success certain from the start.

It is true that had they trusted to their own strength and to the capacity for surprise which its mobility gave to a seaborne force, they might perhaps have rushed the defences of Lisbon and so given a Portuguese revolt a firm back to lean against.

[46] *Cal. S. P. Foreign*, XXIII, 16, 132, 289, 302–4, 363, 384; *Cal. S. P. Venetian*, VIII, 435, 447, 453, 462.

But they had not grasped this possibility beforehand any more than Elizabeth had. It was not until 2 June that Drake wrote – and others were soon to echo him – 'if we had not been commanded to the contrary, but had first landed at Lisbon, all would have been as we desired it'.[47] That may have been true, although it is by no means completely certain. But it was not the Queen's instructions that prevented them from landing first at Lisbon; and there was nothing in her orders to compel them to waste a fortnight or more at Coruña letting the soldiers display their prowess in that almost empty port. It was only after their experience at Coruña that they realized how weak and thinly spread the Spanish defences were and even then, the lesson sank in too slowly to avert the choice of Peniche as the army's landing place. When, therefore, we read their claim that they had 'discovered [the Spanish] government's ability, means, and weakness, and how to undo them',[48] we must remember that they made this discovery too late to be able to profit by it, that their wisdom was at best wisdom after the event.

Indeed, we may well doubt whether it was truly wisdom even then. For the real tragedy of Norris and Drake's expedition was not their failure at Lisbon nor even their failure to intercept the treasure ships. The real tragedy was that they missed a unique opportunity to cripple Spain's naval power past hope of recovery. In the first half of 1589 the key to final victory lay not at Lisbon, not at the Azores, but at Santander. As Edmund Palmer wrote from St Jean-de-Luz on 15 July:

If Sir Francis had gone to Santander as he went to the Groyne, he had done such a service as never subject had done. For with 12 sail of his ships he might have destroyed all the forces which the Spaniards had there, which was the whole strength of the country by sea. There they did ride all unrigged and their ordnance on the shore and some 20 men only in a ship to keep them. It was far overseen that he had not gone thither first.[49]

[47] S. P. Domestic, ccii, no. 7; cp. also ibid., ccxxiv, nos. 77, 79; ccxxv, no. 42.
[48] *Cal. S. P. Foreign*, XXIII, 411.
[49] Ibid., p. 383.

# VII

## Crisis in France

Edmund Palmer was surely right. Even so enthusiastic an apologist for the Portugal adventure as Sir Roger Williams began to realize that, once he was back in England and had leisure to reflect on the situation. 'It were necessary', he wrote to Hatton, Burghley, and Walsingham sometime in July,

> to send six of Her Majesty's good ships, with twelve good merchants and some six pinnaces, with store of fireworks in some six old vessels, resolutely conducted, into Santander, there to burn their 58 'armathoes'. Then are you sure from Spanish forces, I mean out of Spain, this two years ... If your honours send, it must be out of hand. But all your captains must be resolute and valiant, else excuses will be made. The island and castle is mended since we saw it last.[1]

In view of his part in Essex's escapade, Williams was not a man whose advice was likely to carry much weight with the Queen at this moment. He was in fact more or less confined to barracks and wrote his letter 'from my purgatory garrison'. Nevertheless the Privy Council must have been thinking along much the same lines when they enquired of Norris and Drake on 7 July how many of their ships and men could set forth again at once 'to destroy the king of Spain's ships and to intercept his fleet coming from the Indies'.[2] It comes therefore as something of a surprise, all the more after the fuss that Elizabeth had made earlier, to find that this enquiry seems to be the last suggestion from Queen or Council of any plan for a further attempt upon those galleons at Santander. How was it that a project, which so recently had been deemed of such vital importance, was so rapidly and so completely put aside?

Doubtless part of the explanation, now as after the Armada's defeat, was lack of ships. The Queen's navy at this

---

[1] *Cal. S. P. Foreign*, XXIII, 409–11.
[2] *Acts P. C.*, XVII, 358–61.

time consisted of twenty-one first-rate warships, 'good ships' of 200 tons and upwards; three second-liners of 100–150 tons; and five pinnaces of 40–60 tons.[3] Of the twenty-one first-line warships, the six that had just come back with Norris and Drake needed overhaul before they could undertake any further service; a seventh, the *Victory*, had sailed off on 18 June for a privateering cruise under the Earl of Cumberland; an eighth, the *Mary Rose*, was in dockyard hands, being modernized; another five, with two of the second-liners and three of the pinnaces, formed the Channel Guard or, in effect, the Home Fleet; and another three, the *White Bear, Elizabeth Jonas,* and *Triumph*, the only old first-line ships that had not been modernized, were always looked upon as too big and old fashioned, too high built and clumsy, for Atlantic service, let alone for operations in the leeward corner of the Bay of Biscay. That left only five first-line fighting ships. If those five were sent off, there would only be the three old-fashioned 'great ships' to reinforce the Channel Guard at need. Little enough, for the Channel Guard had to cover not only the Channel and Narrow Seas but also to keep an eye on Scotland where Huntly and other Catholic lords were restive and known to be in correspondence with Parma. As it was, the English trading community were already grumbling that there were too few of the Queen's ships in the Narrow Seas to repress the Dunkirk privateers, and Burghley had even wondered about the prospects of obtaining Danish naval aid in those waters.[4]

It was a question, too, whether five of the Queen's ships, even if they could be spared, would now be enough to deal with the Armada shipping. Williams had suggested six, with twelve good merchantmen; and he was clearly thinking in

[3] For a detailed list, with names, tonnages, etc. – *Armada Papers*, II, 324–38. Another (contemporary) list divides them, as here, into 'good ships' of 200 tons and upwards, 'mean' of 100 to 150 tons, and 'pinnaces' under 100 tons – ibid., p. 5. See also, M. Lewis, *The Spanish Armada*, p. 67. G. Mattingly, *The Defeat of the Spanish Armada*, p. 175, makes the division between 'good' and 'mean at 300 tons. The *White Lion*, 140 tons, and the pinnaces *Charles, Cygnet,* and *Disdain* were sometimes listed among the Queen's ships (e.g. *Armada Papers*, II, 66, 241, 325, 338) but belonged to the Lord Admiral – Sir Julian Corbett, *Drake and the Tudor Navy*, II, 66, 148; K. R. Andrews, *Elizabethan Privateering*, p. 89 note. For the Channel Guard – *Monson's Tracts*, I, 238; S. P. Domestic, ccxxv, nos. 1, 2, 32–4; ccxxvi, nos. 83–4, 88.

[4] Lansdowne MSS, ciii, no. 52.

terms of an operation to burn 'armathoes' more or less immobilized in harbour. As early as 15 July, however, Palmer was reporting that eleven ships at San Sebastian were ready for sea and perhaps another forty at Santander. And on 27 July forty large and twenty smaller vessels actually set sail from those ports for Coruña. Maybe no more than half, even of the forty, were fighting ships; maybe they were all 'manned with cobblers, tinkers, and shoemakers, and horse boys and labourers, for that all his country is destroyed for mariners'.[5] But they were at sea again and Spain once more had a fleet in being, a fleet that would have to be fought with rather than cut out as it lay helpless at its moorings. England's golden opportunity to destroy Spain's naval power easily and beyond hope of recovery had already passed.

As a result, although in mid-July it was decided to send out a squadron under Sir Martin Frobisher, his business was not to be with the Armada survivors, but with 'the fleet coming from the Indies'.[6]

There was nothing surprising in this revival of Her Majesty's desire to intercept the King of Spain's treasure from the Indies. Money was now tighter than ever for the government. The privy seal loan from the counties was coming in reasonably well, but the 1588 London loan was at the same time falling due for repayment, and was in fact repaid. As for Parliament's grants, the commissioners were only just starting to make the first assessments and nothing at all could be expected from that source before November. Nor were Milward's reports very encouraging about the prospects of borrowing in Germany. Money was very scant at Hamburg because of the great preparations recently made to send corn and munitions to Spain – incidentally, 'a trade maintained only with Netherlanders' purses'. Elsewhere men waited to see the outcome of Norris and Drake's enterprise and how the Dutch would fare against Parma. There was little likelihood of any immediate lending, though perhaps something might be had at Frankfort mart in September or at Kiel around

<hr />

[5] *Cal. S. P. Foreign*, XXIII, 383; *Cal. S. P. Domestic, Addenda*, p. 288; *Cal. S. P. Venetian*, VIII, 467.

[6] S. P. Domestic, ccxxv, nos. 28, 32; and see below, ch.11.

Twelfthtide or at Augsburg at some more indefinite future date.[7]

While there was so little elasticity about the Queen's income, her extraordinary expenditure, actual and prospective, was mounting at an alarming rate and 1589 already threatened to prove just as costly as 1588 had been.[8] The counties could be left to pay, as usual, for the summer's general musters and for the more regular local exercising of the trained bands. The lord deputy in Ireland could be told to make shift without the usual subsidy from the English Exchequer.[9] It proved possible to cut back expenditure on the Queen's navy by about a quarter as compared with 1588, though the figure for the year was still to be around £60,000, at least five or six times the normal pre-war cost. Besides, after the 1588 experience, it was felt necessary to strengthen the navy by building three more first-line warships of 500 to 800 tons, four 200-ton 'cromsters' and half a dozen 'great boats', at a cost of over £14,000.[10]

As for external commitments, £3,000 was sent to James VI of Scotland in May. After the £5,000 paid in 1588, that might be regarded as squaring his account, if he would overlook the fact that in 1587 no payment at all had been made towards the £4,000 a year pension promised to him by the 1585 treaty.[11] In the Netherlands, too, the Queen's troops could be kept on weekly imprests and made to wait a while longer for their full pay. Even so, by the middle of July the Exchequer had already issued £85,800 5s. 10d. to the treasurer-at-war, Sir Thomas Sherley, during the nine months since the previous Michaelmas and Sherley had in fact spent £86,285 17s. 2d. in that period.[12] This suggested a total for the year ending at Michaelmas 1589 of about £115,000, £27,000 more than the previous year but still £11,000 or so below the estimated

---

[7] *Cal. S. P. Domestic, Addenda*, p. 273; *H. M. C., Salisbury, MSS*, III, 429; *Cal. S. P. Foreign*, XXIII, 232, 269–70, 279, 331.

[8] F. C. Dietz's figures (*Exchequer under Elizabeth*, p. 101) for Exchequer issues are £420,300 15s. 11d. for 1588 and £426,513 5s. 3d. for 1589.

[9] *Acts P. C.*, XVII, 73–5.

[10] Corbett, *Drake and the Tudor Navy*, II, 291–3 and *Successors of Drake*, pp. 56, 416; Dietz, *English Public Finance*, pp. 440–1. The new first-line ships were the *Merhonour*, *Garland*, and *Defiance*; the cromsters were the *Advantage, Answer, Crane*, and *Quittance*.

[11] Conyers Read, *Mr Secretary Walsingham*, III, 322–3, 337–44.

[12] *L. and A.*, I, 214; II, 170.

charge under the new establishment framed in March 1588. Nevertheless, in July and August 1589 both the Queen and her servants must have looked upon even that as an outcome too good to be true. For the loss of Geertruidenberg had confirmed and deepened their grave and long-felt doubts about the ability of the United Provinces to survive without very substantially more English assistance as well as a thorough reformation of their government.

However, fortunately for the States, Parma too had his troubles. From the end of April onwards he himself had to retire to Spa to seek a cure for dropsy. There he was for a time too ill to transact even essential business. All through the summer he had to leave the command of his troops to inferior leaders who lacked his authority and his genius.[13] To make matters worse, his troops were on the verge of mutiny for lack of pay and he was almost as hard pressed for money as they were. The King did promise, and eventually send, 1,200,000 crowns but 300,000 of these were earmarked for subsidies to the Leaguers in France and the rest was wholly inadequate to Parma's needs. Moreover, none of the rest was to be used to repay the 430,000 crowns that he had had to borrow in the previous December from the Antwerp bankers, who would not lend another crown until that was repaid.[14] Then, on top of it all, the King kept pressing Parma to provide, out of the same money, for an expeditionary force of 6,000 men, with flyboats and small craft, to invade England (the Isle of Wight for preference) so as to divert Norris and Drake's forces from Spain and Portugal and prevent English aid to Henry III in France. Perhaps, in view of Drake and Winter's fears in August 1588, Philip's idea for a diversion was not quite as silly as it sounds. At all events, it may have helped a little to put a brake on operations in the Netherlands; for Parma, although he showed no striking enthusiasm for a dash across the Narrow Seas or down the Channel in flyboats and barges, did take it seriously enough to hire some shipping in northern France.[15] The principal impediments to action in the

[13] Van der Essen, *Alexandre Farnèse*, V, 256–8.
[14] *Correspondance de Philippe II*, III, 377, 398–9, 401, 412–13; van der Essen, *Alexandre Farnèse*, V, 258–61.
[15] *Correspondance de Philippe II*, III, 399, 404, 414, 417–18.

Netherlands, however, were Parma's ill health and his lack of money to appease his near-mutinous soldiery. For those reasons the betrayal of Geertruidenberg 'waked the sleeping dog'[16] much more slowly than most people anticipated. April, May, and June passed with only some desultory operations by Count Charles Mansfelt on the lower Maas around Heusden and, farther east, Warembon's capture of Blienbeck, a minor enemy success that was promptly offset by Colonel Schenk and Sir Francis Vere's skilful relief of Rheinberg.[17]

Then, however, Parma, disregarding Philip's strict instructions, managed to come to an arrangement with the Antwerp bankers. With the money they made available he was able to give his Spaniards and Italians two months' pay and on 29 July send them off to join Mansfelt before Heusden.[18] Count Maurice, in this 'the first enterprise wherein he commanded in person as chief', did put some reinforcements and supplies into the town, at the cost of some losses, just before the enemy's main forces arrived. Yet after gathering troops for a month, he still had barely 1,500 men. Half of these were 'dispersed alongst the river Waal, fronting the Bommelerwaard, to impeach the enemy's passage into the Betuwe'. Of the 800 or so remaining available for field operations, 600 were English commanded, in Lord Willoughby's absence, by Sir Francis Vere, their new sergeant-major-general. Those 600 were about all that could be drawn from the English garrisons until the companies from Portugal returned. And Bodley thought that the States' garrisons could not spare more than another 1,300 foot and 500–600 horse. Schenk's death in a characteristically rash attempt to surprise Nijmegen on 31 July further disordered their affairs, for on his death his troops dispersed to various garrisons and some of them even disbanded.[19] When, therefore, Mansfelt on 24 August, leaving Heusden to one side, embarked his Germans and Walloons to cross the Waal between Bommel and Woudrichem, there was little,

[16] *Cal. S. P. Foreign*, XXIII, 218.

[17] Ibid., pp. 276, 311, 338–9, 391–2, 400; Bor, xxvi, fos. 22, 31, 41; Meteren, 317.

[18] *Correspondance de Philippe II*, III, 412–14, 419; van der Essen, *Alexandre Farnèse*, V, 260, 262–3.

[19] *L. and A.*, I, 3, 7, 78–9; Sir Francis Vere, *Commentaries* (1657), pp. 1–2; Bor, xxvi, fo. 42; *Resolutiën der Staten Generaal*, VI, 323.

frighteningly little, to stop him from thrusting on northwards across the Lek to Utrecht or even beyond Utrecht to the Zuyder Zee and Amsterdam. At the very least it looked as if he might easily (as he hoped to do) block the rivers against Dutch trade and quarter his troops where they might live off rebel country. In the event, however, the Spanish 'old *tercio*' refused to follow Mansfelt across the Waal and their mutiny put an abrupt end to his offensive. Nevertheless, all through July and August it had seemed, as Vere wrote on 27 July, that 'if Her Majesty help them not with more men, this winter the enemy will have good footing in Holland'.[20]

Yet whatever were the dangers in the Netherlands and whatever the opportunities at sea, it was more and more the situation in France that came to take first place in the thoughts of Queen and Council during these summer months of 1589. It was the need to spend there that finally ruled out any major naval operations against the now mobile Santander shipping. The French King had not immediately followed up the requests that he had sent over by Stafford early in April. Presumably he was no more anxious to make known his appeal to the Protestant Queen of England than he was to make public his accord with the Protestant King of Navarre. At all events it was not until early May that he despatched Pierre de Mornay, seigneur de Buhy, to ask formally for English assistance and it was the beginning of June before de Buhy got as far as Dover.[21] By then the situation in France had altered completely. In April the advance of Mayenne's army had compelled Henry III to publish his truce with the Huguenots and stage a public reconciliation with Henry of Navarre at Plessis-les-Tours. Eight days later, on 28 April, the Count of Châtillon with the vanguard of the Huguenot army foiled Mayenne's attempt to capture Henry III at Tours. Next morning the League's forces 'parted like nobody without sound of trumpet or drum'. Their retreat marked the turn of the tide. Soon afterwards Mayenne was recalled to the Île de France to steady Parisian nerves, badly shaken by the Duke of

---

[20] *L. and A.*, I, 4, 9, 10, 12; *Correspondance de Philippe II*, III, 431, 436; Bor, xxvi, fos. 48–9; *Cal. S. P. Foreign*, XXIII, 400; Van der Essen, *Alexandre Farnèse*, V., 263–5.

[21] *Lettres Missives*, III, 481–3; *Cal. S. P. Foreign*, XXIII, 297.

Longueville's defeat of their governor, Mayenne's younger brother, the Duke of Aumale, at Senlis on 7 May.[22]

Thenceforward the League had no organized army in the field. The King became master of the country between the Loire and the Seine and everything took on a new look. On 13 June the royal armies stormed over the Loire at Jargeau; on 15 June they took Pluviers. Chartres thereupon opened its gates, leaving Orléans isolated. At that moment news that Mayenne was marching east to attack Longueville spurred the Kings to an immediate advance to Étampes, where their presence threatened Paris itself. This brought Mayenne rushing back, but with his forces weakened by desertions, he dared not risk a battle. Once again he drew off and on 20 June Étampes, too, was stormed. By then Longueville had been reinforced by 13,000–14,000 Swiss troops raised by Sancy with money lent by the Protestant Cantons. So Paris now had superior forces advancing upon it from the east as well as from the west. Everywhere else, except perhaps in Brittany, the King's supporters were more than holding their own.[23]

Henry was therefore no longer in desperate need of help by the time that de Buhy reached the English court. Nevertheless, upon reports that the League was intending to hire troops in Germany, he had decided to double his own German levy and to bring it up to the 8,000 reiters and 14,000 landsknechts that he had talked of to Stafford. This put the cost of the levy up from £45,300 to between £77,000 and £80,000. Accordingly the request that de Buhy now brought was not for 150,000 crowns but for 250,000, or about £78,000 sterling. It was a staggering demand and it came at a time when, as we have seen, the Queen simply could not lay her hands on anything approaching such a sum. The Privy Council had to tell de Buhy this on 14 June, explaining that she already had to maintain two armies, one at sea and the other in the Low Countries, in addition to her expenses in Ireland and Scotland. As a result, the best she could offer was to send someone – Dr Daniel Rogers was the man first thought of – to

[22] Ibid., pp. 236–7, 244–5, 291.
[23] Ibid., pp. 334–6, 351; Thou, X, 666; Davila, p. 403; Cayet, XXXIX, 137; Aubigné, VIII, 46–70. For Brittany, see also *Cal. S. P. Foreign*, XXIII, 285; for the Channel ports – ibid., pp. 202–3, 211–12, 220–1, 227–8, 230–1, 260, 275, 342, 363.

Germany to join with the King's ministers there in borrowing 150,000 crowns, for whose repayment in one year she would bind herself jointly with the King.

De Buhy scornfully rejected this offer. He would not have his master risk his state on credit. He had no faith in German generosity and if he could not have ready money, he must return to France at once. Elizabeth's reaction was curiously mild. She was obviously anxious that the negotiations should not be broken off. So she kept de Buhy in England for another ten days while she enlarged her offer a little. For when he eventually started back for France on 28 June, he took with him a letter to Henry III, written in the Queen's own hand. In this letter, although she did complain of de Buhy's stiff tactlessness, she repeated her promise to send an envoy at once to Germany and she also offered to pledge her credit there not merely for 150,000 crowns but for the entire 250,000 that he had required.[24]

Henry, it seems, was less intransigent than his ambassador. Indeed, he could now afford to be. He may not have known that the German princes were prepared to lend him a handsome sum (perhaps as much as 300,000 crowns) and were only waiting for his long-delayed envoy, the Count of Schomberg, to get on with the levy. He did know, however, that the Grand Duke of Tuscany, who had just married the Queen of France's sister, had promised him 200,000 crowns. Moreover, half that sum was already on its way to Augsburg, sent in cash by pack mules so as, for secrecy, to avoid putting it through bankers' books.[25] Accordingly when we next meet de Buhy, now back with his master outside Pontoise, his tone was a little more accommodating. On 3 July he wrote begging Burghley to persuade Her Majesty at least to lend 100,000 crowns in cash. That would pay the German levies' *anreitgelt*, or earnest money, and leave the King time to seek the rest of their pay before their muster three months later.[26] Elizabeth,

---

[24] Cotton MSS, Galba E. vi, fos, 387, 389; *Cal. S. P. Foreign*, XXIII, 321, 330, 340–1. For Rogers – ibid., p. 362 and *Cal. S. P. Domestic, Addenda*, p. 287 (the date is almost certainly early July, not September). De Buhy's passport passed the signet on 27 June – S. O. Docquets, I, under date.

[25] *Cal. S. P. Foreign*, XXIII, 364, 395; *L. and A.*, I, 706; Thou, X, 630; Davila, p. 392.

[26] *Cal. S. P. Foreign*, XXIII, 360. The letter was dated from Martine abbey, probably St Martin's abbey outside Pontoise.

who of course knew nothing of the Grand Duke's promise, was partly persuaded. She, or some of her advisers, consulted Sir Horatio Palavicino, the Genoese financier who had made his home in England and who had conducted the last negotiations in Germany for Navarre's 1587 levy. Palavicino agreed that de Buhy ought not to ask the Queen to foot the entire bill for so large a levy, especially as the latest advices said that the German Protestant princes were very well disposed to give substantial help towards it. He did, however, suggest, that as an assurance of her sincerity, her envoy to Germany should take 50,000 crowns in bullion with him and instructions for the Merchant Adventurers at Stade to provide another 50,000 by exchange upon his demand.[27]

This was near enough what de Buhy was now asking for, and Palavicino's advice may have helped to move the Queen towards granting it. Even more persuasive, we may guess, was the return of Norris and Drake just as this time with their eighty prizes from whose sale she might look to be soon repaid the £49,000 which she had invested in that enterprise. At all events, when de Buhy came back to England he found the Queen prepared to meet his modified demands rather more than halfway. On 13 July she agreed not only to send an envoy to Germany but also to send £20,000 (70,000 crowns) in cash, if the King gave his bond to repay it with interest in a year's time. In addition she offered 'her bonds in the largest manner that can be devised' for the remainder of the 250,000 crowns, if Henry's bonds were not acceptable in Germany.[28]

Ten days later the Queen was hesitating again. This was nothing unusual, for once Elizabeth had made up her mind it took very little to start her wondering whether she might not have made it up wrongly. And it was just at this time that the Privy Council decided that, on both legal and political grounds, Norris and Drake's eighty prizes and a part at least of their cargoes ought to be restored to their Hanseatic and other owners. There went Elizabeth's hopes of getting back her £49,000. There, too, might go Henry III's hopes of getting his £20,000. For on 15 July Walsingham found Elizabeth not

[27] Ibid., pp. 349, 362, 395. For Palavicino, see the biography, *An Elizabethan*, by L. Stone.

[28] Lansdowne MSS, lx, no. 55; also *Cal. S. P. Domestic, Addenda*, p. 287.

only very angry at the Privy Council's unwelcome recommendation, but also beginning to hesitate about de Buhy's despatch, although so far she still 'showeth herself inclined to perform her promise touching the £20,000'. Walsingham, 'without urging her in any particular touching that point', did his best to make her flesh creep with tales of the doubtful state of Scotland, the great designs of Spain against her for 1590, and her own 'weak means at home to make head against them' unless she took 'so good an opportunity to strengthen herself as was offered her by the request of the French King'. He believed he had 'wrought some impression in her'.[29]

We may be sure that almost all her other advisers did their best to strengthen that impression. Burghley might find that 'the state of the world is marvellously changed when we true Englishmen have cause for our own quietness to wish good success to a French King and a King of Scots'. Nevertheless the old Lord Treasurer recognized, as clearly as Churchill with Stalin in 1941, that 'seeing both are enemies to our enemies, we have cause to join with them against our enemies'.[30] Lord Chancellor Hatton, whose influence had grown markedly since Leicester's death, was on close terms now with both Burghley and Walsingham and would assuredly be of one mind with them over de Buhy's mission.[31] Lord Admiral Howard, with his anxieties about the Channel ports and Narrow Seas, must have been on the same side even if he was also attracted by Hawkins's treasure-hunting schemes. These four – Burghley, Walsingham, Hatton, and Howard – were now by far the most influential of the Queen's Councillors, particularly in foreign affairs. Outside the Privy Council, with Essex, Drake, and Norris in disgrace, there was no one who counted for much except Sir John Hawkins and perhaps Sir Walter Raleigh and while Raleigh generally went with the Lord Admiral,[32] Hawkins's wish to 'have as little to

[29] Harleian MSS, 6994, fo. 187.

[30] Lodge, *Illustrations of British History*, II, 373.

[31] In February he asked Burghley to look over and amend the draft of his speech to Parliament; in September he submitted to him a memorial on public business – S. P. Domestic, ccxxiii, no. 33; ccxxvi, no. 4. For his good relations with Walsingham, *Cal. S. P. Spanish*, IV, 431; Conyers Read, *Mr Secretary Walsingham*, III, 336.

[32] R. W. Kenny, *Elizabeth's Admiral: the Political Career of Charles Howard, Earl of Nottingham, 1536-1624*, pp. 164-5.

do in foreign countries as may be' was not very likely to prevail against the unanimity of the leading Privy Councillors.

Nor did it prevail. On 20 July de Buhy's passport for his return to France was sealed and on 24 July a warrant passed the signet for £20,000 to be taken to Germany by Palavicino, who was now to be the Queen's envoy instead of Rogers. On the previous day the Privy Council informed the lord mayor of London that Her Majesty required the city's bond for £60,000 which she intended to take up in Germany 'for some special purpose'.[33] Elizabeth had held, or had been held, to her course. The cash and loan, £80,000 together, would fully cover the 250,000 crowns that Henry III's levy was estimated to cost. The English were certainly making a very considerable effort to meet the French King's demands.

They were, moreover, making this effort at a time when Henry III's need for immediate help must have appeared even less urgent than in June. Sweeping round west and north of Paris, he and Navarre had taken Poissy on 28 June, had crossed the Seine on the 'brave and spacious bridge' there, and then on 15 July secured the Oise crossing by taking Pontoise. Longueville and Sancy followed, reaching Poissy on 16 July. On 19 July the combined armies, upwards of 40,000 men, took up their assault positions in the suburbs of Paris. All that Mayenne could muster against them was a bare 5,000 French foot, some mutinous Germans, a Walloon regiment, and 600–700 good horse. There were royalist plots inside the capital, food was scarce there, and even if the impending assault could be repulsed, the city could hardly hope to hold out for more than a very few weeks. Indeed, Balagny, the governor of Cambrai and one of the League's commanders, gave it no more than ten or twelve days. Nor, although Meaux and Melun still kept roads open to the south and east, was there much prospect of deliverance from outside if time was as short as that. The League's foreign friends, even Parma, were too far away and too unready. Its only field army was already shut up in Paris. Its forces in the provinces had been split into fragments, each fully occupied in its own local struggle for

---

[33] S. O. Docquets, I, fos. 199, 200; *Acts P. C.*, XVII, 419–20.

survival. Cut off from Paris, these scattered fragments could neither succour the capital nor long outlive its fall. For Paris was not only the head and heart of the League but also the vital link between its various parts.[34]

Why, then, should Elizabeth and her advisers have been willing to strain their country's resources so far to help Henry III at this juncture? Why, in particular, when the German levy was altogether unlikely to reach him before Paris had fallen and the power of the League had already been broken? We may, I think, see the answer in an unfinished paper by Burghley dated 13 July and headed 'Instructions for a league with France'.[35] This started off with the proposal to promise the King £20,000 cash and £60,000 credit. In return Henry should explicitly assure the Queen in a private letter (as Charles IX had done in 1572) that he would at need aid her against Spain and even against the Pope if they attacked her. He should also forbid the export of grain from France to Spain and Portugal and of victuals to the Spanish Netherlands, prohibitions that would violate no Franco-Spanish treaties and could be justified as domestic wisdom in view of the devastation caused by the civil wars. Then followed a proposal of much more far-reaching nature – that Henry III should join in a straight defensive and offensive alliance with Elizabeth and all princes who feared Spanish aggression and who wanted to prevent the King of Spain becoming 'a tyrant or monarch of the greater part of Christendom'. All German princes who feared Spain should be invited to join, along with Denmark, Scotland, and possibly Venice, Tuscany, and other Italian states. Their aims should be only to restrain Spanish aggression and to induce the King of Spain to an accord with his people in the Low Countries, granting them their liberties and withdrawing his troops. So 'all Christendom may enjoy an universal peace'; its arms could be turned upon the Turks; the seas could be freed of men-o'-war and pirates; and trade might again flourish.

[34] *Cal. S. P. Foreign*, XXIII, 335–6, 357–9, 375–6, 385–90; Davila, pp. 402–4; *Correspondance de Philippe II*, III, 431.

[35] Lansdowne MSS, lx, no. 55; civ, no. 26; cp, also *Cal. S. P. Domestic, Addenda*, p. 287. Similar, but less definite, proposals for the wider alliance had been suggested in the instructions for Wotton in February – but Wotton did not go – *Cal. S. P. Foreign*, XXIII, 91.

Some of this, particularly the last few pious aspirations, may have been mere window-dressing. The main proposals, however, were a serious attempt to look beyond the French civil wars, beyond 1589 or even 1590, to the re-establishment of a stable west European political system. That was something well worth paying for, much more worth paying for than any alternatives that could be offered by soldierly advocates of Peninsular wars such as Anthony Wingfield and Sir Roger Williams or by such 'idolaters of Neptune' as Sir John Hawkins. That was why the attention of the Queen and her Councillors was now so much concentrated upon France. The destruction of Spain's war navy, the occupation of Portugal even, might for the time being insure England against invasion from Spain. The interception or interruption of the flow of silver from America might bring King Philip to accept reasonable conditions of peace. Yet these were short-term, war-winning, measures. When peace returned, the American silver would flow again and there would be no way, short of renewed war, to stop Spain rebuilding her navy. More durable, peace-preserving, guarantees were needed.

Now all through the sixteenth century England's peace and independence had depended largely upon the two great military monarchies of the continent, France and Spain, being too jealous of each other and too evenly matched in strength for either to commit itself to an attack upon her. England had, almost always, been able to count upon the goodwill of one of the two continental Leviathans whenever the other turned unfriendly. The collapse of the French monarchy in the spring of 1585, by destroying that balance, had freed Spain's hands for the Armada. The recovery of the French monarchy, by restoring that balance, would go a good way towards providing England once again with a long-term guarantee against 'the envy of less happier lands' across the seas.

It was not, however, quite as simple as that. Even in the days of Francis I, France had hardly proved an equal match for Habsburg power, nor was she to prove so for another half-century after Elizabeth's death. Yet at the same time she was always looked upon as herself a dangerously aggressive power; aggressive, too, towards some areas, such as the Low Countries and Scotland, where England was especially sensitive. When to all this was added the religious divisions, the civil wars, and the feebleness of government under the last two Valois kings, it was small wonder that Elizabeth and her Councillors placed small faith in the constancy of French policy and had less than complete confidence in France's reliability as a bulwark against Spain. The remedy that they were now considering was that which was to become in later centuries the traditional English answer to an over-mighty power that threatened to dominate the Continent – the policy of the Grand Alliance. They proposed to call in the lesser powers to strengthen France into an adequate counterpoise to Spain and at the same time by grouping her among them to lessen her opportunities for independent aggression.

This reinforcement would, moreover, be very much needed in the immediate future. For it was not likely that France would be allowed to recover unmolested. The King of Spain, his son-in-law the Duke of Savoy, and his henchman the Duke of Lorraine might not be able to save Paris, but they would undoubtedly do their utmost to prolong the resistance of the League's followers in such outlying provinces as Picardy, Brittany, and Dauphiné. The first two were of vital concern to England; and English statesmen certainly suspected, if they did not know for certain, that Philip II was already aiming to get possession of the Breton and Channel ports, as well as the Somme towns and Cambrai, in return for his help to the League.[36] They were far less sure that the weak and inconstant Henry III could be trusted to resent such provocations and allow himself to be drawn thereby from civil into foreign wars unless he felt confident of substantial foreign support. Already those around him, fearing Spanish designs in Picardy, were anxious to see English forces sent into Flanders 'and for this and divers other considerations would enter into a perpetual league with Her Majesty. All the greatest,' Lyly said, 'counsel this as necessary for both sides, and the time fit.'[37] The time was indeed fit and had all this come to pass, 1590 might well have brought the victorious peace that had been so lamentably missed in 1589 at Santander and Lisbon.

[36] *Correspondance de Philippe II*, III, 403, 447; *Cal. S. P. Foreign*, XXIII, 202, 297; *L. and A.*, I, 564–8.
[37] *Cal. S. P. Foreign*, XXIII, 376.

It was not to be. For there now occurred one of those 'frantic accidents' which William Lyly had long feared were an inescapable flaw in France's destiny.[38] While the Kings' forces were preparing for the assault that was to be launched on 23 July, a Jacobin friar named Jacques Clément came to the camp with an offer to render one of the gates of Paris. About seven o'clock on the morning of 22 July he was brought into Henry III's chamber at St Cloud. The King was not yet fully dressed, being 'still without his buff coat (which by reason of his arms he was wont to wear) and having on only a thin taffeta doublet all untrussed'. What happened next was described by William Lyly in a letter which he dashed off immediately to Elizabeth. Clément approached the King and

in making him a monastical reverence, with a knife which he held in his sleeve struck the King under the short ribs, to have pierced his bowels; which the King with his own hand, seeing the motion, did in part rebate so as no one of them was pierced; and with great courage and force got the knife from him and therewith gave the Jacobin two blows, the one on the face, the other in the breast, with which and the servants' assistance the felon was presently slain.

Very soon afterwards Lyly managed to see the King, who said to him 'I am sure the Queen your mistress will be sorry for this, but I hope it shall quickly be healed and so I pray you write her from me.' Lyly wrote off at once, but the ink on his letter was hardly dry before it became clear that the wound would not be healed. Had Henry III's reflexes been a little faster, or perhaps if he had had time to put on that buff coat, he might indeed have suffered no more than a nasty scratch. As it was, he had not been quick enough to 'rebate' the blow and Clément's sharp new knife had in fact 'pierced his bowels'. By evening he was in a high fever and by two o'clock that night he was dead.[39]

Upon such tiny hinges did the destiny of France, and of western Europe, turn. For Clément's knife achieved what neither Mayenne nor the League's soldiers, neither Philip of Spain nor Parma's army, could have accomplished. Paris was

[38] Ibid., p. 335.
[39] Ibid., p. 394; Davila, pp. 404–5; Thou, X, 669.

saved and within a very few weeks it was not Paris and the Catholic League but the new Protestant King of France, Henry IV, who was fighting desperately for life. First reports from the royal armies had been moderately reassuring.[40] Sancy had persuaded the Swiss to continue their service. The Catholic princes and nobles who had obeyed Henry III swore allegiance to Henry of Navarre as King Henry IV of France on 25 July, after he had made an agreement – it might also be called a treaty – with them by which he promised to submit himself in the matter of his religion to the decision of a general or national council within six months, if possible. Meanwhile he undertook not to alter or innovate anything to the detriment of the Roman Catholic Church and faith. What he would not do was to turn Catholic on the spot. He wanted to win his inheritance rather than to buy it. Besides, apostasy, to be convincing, required a decent interval.

Thus, for the time being at least, the Most Christian King of France remained a Protestant. That was a fact which, when once the emotions roused by Henry III's assassination quietened down, most Catholic royalists needed time to think about and get used to. To that extent Buzenval was right when he warned Elizabeth 'qu'il n'y a guère papiste bien superstitieux qui n'ait quelque partie de l'âme capable à recevoir des impressions ligueuses'.[41] Moreover the harvest was ripening and the gentry, Huguenot as well as Catholic, were anxious to get home and see it all safely gathered in. The Huguenot La Trémouille departed as well as the Catholic Épernon, and within a week the great army that had been the terror of Paris was reduced by a half. Nor was the half that remained much to be relied upon by a new king who had little enough money of his own and who had just inherited an empty treasury and a bankrupt state. For while nobles and gentry were riding homewards, the infantry, the permanent hard core of any sixteenth-century army, were crying out for pay. The French foot companies were weak and ragged; the

[40] *Cal. S. P. Foreign*, XXIII, 402–4, 407, 409. For what follows: *L. and A.*, I., 367–9, 376–82; Thou, XI, 1–25; Davila, pp. 407–18; Aubigné, VIII, 80–90, 147–65; Cayet, XL, 194–207; *Mémoires de la Ligue*, VIII, 29–58; also Lavisse, *Histoire de France*, VI, i, 304–7; M. Wilkinson, *History of the League*, pp. 92–6; P. de Vaissière, *Henri IV*, pp. 327–42.

[41] *Cal. S. P. Foreign*, XXIII, 405.

Swiss and Germans were mercenaries who would not serve long nor fight willingly without money; and those few English who had run into La Rochelle and joined Navarre instead of going to Portugal, had not received a penny in four months' service.

It was manifestly impossible to go on besieging Paris with an army such as this. So on 2 August Henry IV raised the siege. He sent off the forces of Picardy under Longueville and those of Champagne under Marshal d'Aumont to rest awhile at their homes. Montpensier likewise took off some of the Norman forces, though in mid-August these rejoined the King in making threatening gestures against Rouen. By then, as the spirits of the League revived, Mayenne was again getting an army into the field. By 22 August his troops were at Mantes, on both sides of the Seine and in strength enough to make Henry give up whatever he was attempting against Rouen. At first the King tried to fall back to Picardy, to pick up Longueville's forces and possibly d'Aumont's as well. But again the Leaguers proved too strong for him. With a mere 7,000–8,000 men he could not face Mayenne's 25,000–30,000 in the open field and at the end of August he withdrew to a strongly fortified position at Arques, just in front of Dieppe. He was more than ever in desperate need of money. He had hardly any more hope of help from elsewhere in France than Paris had had in July. The nearest other royalist forces were Longueville's, who was twenty-five leagues away and had the enemy's main army between him and the King. A thousand or more Scots had reached Dieppe from Dundee on 22 August, but in very ill order. In short, Henry desperately needed money to retain the forces he already had, and infantry to reinforce them; and there was little hope of getting either men or money quickly from anywhere except England.

Nevertheless it was not until the middle of August that he despatched one of his more trusted Huguenot councillors, Jean de la Fin, seigneur de Beauvoir la Nocle, to be his resident ambassador in England and to join his agent Buzenval and Henry III's envoy de Buhy in asking Elizabeth for money and munitions. In all the confusion and the press of business accompanying the King's accession it was 13 August before the new ambassador received his commission, though four days earlier Henry had written commending him to Walsingham. It was not until 21 August that he embarked at Dieppe for England.[42]

While waiting for his arrival, Elizabeth had taken steps to persuade the governors of the Channel ports to support their new king. These efforts were hardly assisted by the depredations of the English privateers, and even Her Majesty's own warships, upon merchant shipping and fishing vessels from those ports. Nor did Walsingham's somewhat dubious agent, Solomon Aldred, manage to dissuade Villars at Le Havre from declaring for the League and taking with him Honfleur, just opposite on the other bank of the Seine. At Dieppe, however, a letter from the Queen delivered by Ottywell Smith, an English merchant who had moved there when Rouen declared for the League, encouraged the governor, Aymar de Chatte, to make the burghers swear and sign to hold the town for Henry IV. At Boulogne the governor, Bernet, had been reinforced only three months before by a company of 169 'Walloons', under a Dutch captain, Hans van Loo, raised among the Protestant refugee congregations in England with a month's pay from the Queen. Now Walsingham wrote to Captain Captot, who had negotiated van Loo's levy, to assure Bernet of continued support, although as Épernon's henchman Bernet needed no great encouragement to oppose the Leaguers. At Calais Walsingham already had an agent, Thomas Mills, seeking intelligence of Parma's intentions and of troop movements in the Spanish Netherlands. As soon as the news from St Cloud came through, Gourdain, the governor of Calais, at once declared strongly for Henry IV and on 2 August sent Mills home to urge that money be promptly sent to the King by the shortest route, through Dieppe.[43]

Mills reported this to Walsingham, who sent him on to see Burghley and eventually to Elizabeth herself. They all agreed with Gourdain, and the Queen assured him that she was 'resolved to yield the King all possible support'. But although

[42] *L. and A.,* I, 466; *Lettres Missives,* III, 25–7, 29–31.

[43] *L. and A.,* I, 371–4, 465, 467–8; *Cal. S. P. Foreign,* XXIII, 397, 402–3, 405, 409; *Cal. S. P. Domestic, Addenda,* p. 281. For O. Smith moving to Dieppe – *Cal. S. P. Foreign,* XXIII, 43–4, 153. For van Loo's company, see ibid., pp. 260, 275; S. P. Domestic, ccxxiii, no. 98.

Lyly had written that Henry was sending Beauvoir to her, she had not yet heard from him and must await his arrival before she could decide on what aid she should send.[44] Meanwhile she moved down to Rye in case Henry was able to come across from Dieppe for a few days to explain his needs in person. That did not happen, but by the last week of August Beauvoir was in England. His instructions were to ask for money and munitions; to request continued English help, financial and diplomatic, towards a levy in Germany; and to urge the formation of an offensive and defensive Protestant counter-league of England, France, Scotland, Denmark, and the German Protestant princes. He had full powers, in conjunction with de Buhy and Buzenval, to bind the King and his heirs to repay any loan that the Queen might grant. These instructions said nothing about troops, but already Lyly had warned Walsingham that in face of the rapid build-up of Mayenne's army Henry might soon be asking for men as well as money and that it might be well to have 3,000 foot ready at the ports. Lyly wrote on 22 August, just as Beauvoir was crossing from Dieppe. Only two days later the King asked him to get Burghley and Walsingham to persuade the Queen to send him for a month or two the 400 English horse from the Netherlands and 4,000 foot from England. They would do him more good now than an army of Germans later.[45]

This last suggestion made it somewhat easier for the Queen to agree to the French demands. For it indicated that she might reasonably defer the despatch of money to Germany; indeed it almost invited her to switch to Henry at Dieppe the £20,000 that she had been about to send with Palavicino to Stade. If that were done, then she might afford both the money that Beauvoir was asking for and the men that the King requested. Lyly apparently came over himself with the King's request and on 31 August delivered express letters to Beauvoir, Buhy, and Buzenval as well. Next day the three envoys begged urgently to speak with Burghley and to have audience with the Queen. Only a few days earlier, on 27 August, Burghley had been moaning to Walsingham: 'God help us, for we shall lack money forthwith to do necessary

[44] S. P. France, xix, fo. 231.
[45] *L. and A.*, I, 470–1.

things, except the residue of the loan will come in.' Now, on
2 September, Hatton noted in a memorial for the Lord
Treasurer that they should 'speak with the aldermen for
money'. Five days later, at Burghley's house in the Strand,
Burghley, Howard, and Walsingham, in the Queen's name,
concluded an agreement with the three French envoys. The
Queen was to lend Henry IV £20,000 in cash, £350 worth of
shot, and twenty lasts of powder worth another £2,000. The
envoys gave their bond for the repayment of the powder
within six months and of the rest in a year. The King and
his supreme Parlement were to ratify the agreement within
four months. On the day the agreement was concluded,
7 September, the £20,000 was paid over to 'Stample the
Frenchman' by the tellers of the Exchequer, £9,000 by
Killigrew and aother £9,000 in silver in ninety bags by Freke,
Stoneley, and Taylor, with the remaining £2,000 in angels,
francs, and pistolets. The powder and shot could not be
provided quite so quickly, but were to be shipped from
London by 20 September.[46]

It is not clear whether Henry's request for English troops
was also agreed to on 7 September. It rather looks as if it was
not granted then. However, on that day or the next news came
from Ottywell Smith and de Chatte that the League army,
outnumbering the royalists by three or four to one, was closing
in on Dieppe and that Henry had to sell his gold chains to
pay his Swiss infantry, without whom all would be lost.
The possibility that the King might therefore soon be driven
into the sea brought remarkably rapid English action. On
8 September the Queen urgently summoned Burghley,
Hatton, and Walsingham to be at court by noon next day to
consider what should be done.[47] And on that day a stream of
letters went out from the Privy Council, to the lord mayor of
London and the lords-lieutenant of Kent, Sussex, and
Hampshire to levy 1,000 men apiece for the relief and succour
of the King of France; to the master of the ordnance to
provide munitions; to Hawkins to prepare the *Vanguard*; to
Lord Willoughby to come up and take command of the 4,000

---

[46] Ibid.; Lansdowne MSS, ciii, no. 62; *Cal. S. P. Domestic, 1581–90*, p. 614;
S. P. Domestic, ccxxvi, no. 20.
[47] Lansdowne MSS, lxi, no. 62; *L. and A.*, I, 380–2, 470.

troops. They were to embark at London, Dover, Rye, and Portsmouth and all to rendezvous at Rye by 20 September – quick work indeed if it could be done. Time was saved, of course, by drawing all the men from London and the three counties nearest to Normandy, an arrangement that incidentally enabled the companies to be grouped into four 'county' regiments.[48]

Yet despite the haste, the Privy Council did its best to ensure that these troops should be well chosen, well equipped, and well led. The sergeant-major-general was to be Sir Thomas Baskerville and the colonels of the four regiments were to be Willoughby himself for the Londoners, Sir Thomas Wilsford for Kent, Sir John Burgh for Sussex, and Sir William Drury for Hampshire, all of them well tried in offices of command in the Netherlands. In each regiment, too, the companies were to be commanded by some of 'the best experimented captains that have served in the Low Countries'. These captains, selected by the Privy Council mostly from a list drawn up by Willoughby, were to replace the inexperienced county gentlemen named by the lords-lieutenant. Of the rank and file, some were 'loose and masterless men' swept in by the press gang, but some at least were taken from trained bands, whose accustomed immunity from foreign service was ignored in this emergency. All of them were to be armed with modern weapons (firearms or pikes), the captains signing indentures with the county authorities for the return of their soldiers' arms and armour at the end of their service. And if the Sussex experience with the fussy Captain Cosby is anything to go by, the experimented captains from the Low Countries were not too easily satisfied with the somewhat motley assortment of weapons and harness that the county authorities could supply. Nor did the counties' provision of clothing – we can hardly call it 'uniform' – altogether meet with their approval. Sir William Drury found many of the Hampshire men ill chosen, short of their quota of muskets and corslets, some with coats and some without until the lord-lieutenant, the Earl of Sussex, himself remedied the deficiencies. Willoughby, too, was a little later to describe the

---

[48] *Acts P. C.*, XVIII, 86–9; *Cal. S. P. Domestic, 1581–90*, pp. 615–6.

Sussex and Hampshire bands as 'ill furnished, ill chosen, and badly armed'. Captain Leveson's Kentish band, he said, upheld England's reputation, but the French swore that 'we have let all our ploughs stand for the rest'.[49]

It is hardly surprising if the local authorities were less zealous and less efficient than the Privy Council. After all, the standards aimed at in the part-time trained bands, a sort of territorial home guard, were bound to be lower than in the old veteran companies that Willoughby and Drury had commanded at Bergen the previous autumn. We must remember, too, that these new demands came on top of the heavy burdens of the Armada year and of the Portugal expedition levies. It is true, of course, that the counties were supposed to get their arms and armour back at the end of the campaign – and according to Willoughby did on this occasion get back more than usual – but some part was sure to be lost or broken or worn out in service. It is also true that the local authorities could claim back coat and conduct money and such things from the Exchequer. But the Exchequer allowance was only 4s. for a coat which might cost 12s. to 16s., and a halfpenny a mile for conduct to the port of embarkation which for the Sussex men worked out at barely half the cost. The counties seem to have lost similarly over the ten days' victuals they were required to provide, for while they were allowed 6d. a day for each man, each man's daily ration – a pound of biscuit, a penny loaf, a pottel of beer, a quarter stockfish, half a quarter of butter, and a quarter pound of cheese – was fixed as 10d.[50]

It was not, however, primarily the counties' fault that the Privy Council's hopes for a speedy embarkation proved too ambitious. Buckhurst, indeed, was getting the Sussex contingent ready well up to time and was much put out when on 14 September the embarkation date was put back from 20 to 24 September. This was done because the 'best experimented' captains of Low Country experience could not be got together and could not make themselves ready so soon,

[49] *Acts P. C.*, XVIII, 88, 96–7, 100, 113–15, 117–19, 123, 173; *Cal. S. P. Domestic, 1581–90*, pp. 615–17, 620–1.

[50] *Acts P. C.* XVIII, 99, 114, 117, 119, 127, 132–3, 139; *Cal. S. P. Domestic, 1581–90*, pp. 618, 620–1; *H. M. C., Ancaster MSS*, p. 312.

neither could shipping be found and naval escort provided so speedily.[51] In mid-September, too, much better news came from Dieppe; the best possible news, wrote Beauvoir, who had not yet learnt the dangerous effects of ambassadorial optimism upon the Queen of England. Mayenne's attempt to turn the King's left flank, by attacking the Pollet suburb of Dieppe, had been repulsed on 7 September. Then, after another three days' sparring, his frontal attack on the main position at Arques on 11 September ended in defeat, despite the double treachery of his German landsknechts who first went over to the King and then in the heat of the battle deserted back to the League. Whatever the fires and strange sights seen in the sky during the battle presaged, they surely carried no happy omens for the League – did not the changing figures appear 'first like a racket and then like a crown'? And with Longueville and d'Aumont's combined forces only a few days' march away, Henry IV's position was no longer desperate.[52]

Now, as Henry himself recognized, Elizabeth's intention in getting ready her 4,000 troops 'was but to succour his present necessity of besiegement'. At the very outset Sir Edward Stafford, when he was sent back again to France as resident ambassador on 9 September, was instructed to make this quite clear to the King. He was also to inform the Privy Council if Longueville's approach made English help unnecessary, so that they might stay the troops' departure. And on 15 September, when the League army drew back somewhat, Stafford did send William Stallenge to stay them. Elizabeth in fact had already decided not to send them even to their ports of embarkation until she heard from Stafford that the King had very great need of them. Walsingham, in a letter written on that same 15 September, warned the ambassador that Her Majesty was 'very loath to send any unless there shall be very apparent and urgent necessity to employ them'. He should therefore be 'very wary in putting them in comfort there' or in giving greater hopes 'than may stand with the weakness of our resolutions, which are subject to many changes when they are

[51] *Acts P. C.*, XVIII, 95–6, 98–9, 113, 115, 125–7; *Cal. S. P. Domestic, 1581–90*, p. 618; *L. and A.*, I, 473.
[52] Ibid., 383–5.

accompanied with matter of charge'. That was one way of putting it, though Elizabeth might have claimed that she was merely being constant to her original resolution now that Henry's victory at Arques had removed the danger of Dieppe being lost and the King himself being driven into the sea.[53]

This did not mean that the preparation of Willoughby's force came to a standstill. It did mean, as Walsingham feared, that the troops could not be ready to embark until almost the end of September. But the shipping and victuals were kept in readiness, and imprests were sent down to keep the sailors from deserting. Sir Henry Palmer with the ships of the Channel Guard was instructed to convoy them, as Leaguer and Dunkirk privateers were prowling off the French coast. He sent the *Aid* and the *Moon* to Portsmouth and the *Swiftsure* and *Tramontana* to Rye for that service. The army captains went to the ports to take over their companies and the Exchequer on 19 September issued £6,000 to the treasurer-at-war, Thomas Fludd, for their month's pay and other expenses. On the same day warrants went out to take up 48 drummers, 24 fifers, and 24 surgeons, while two days later the Archbishop of Canterbury and the Bishops of London, Chichester, and Winchester were each called upon to provide a chaplain at twenty shillings a day, the money to come from a levy upon the clergy.[54] On 20 September Willoughby received his commission and instructions. He was to assure Henry that Elizabeth would have sent greater aid if her circumstances had permitted. As it was, after all the burdens she and her subjects had borne in making head against the King of Spain in England, Ireland, and the Netherlands, without any help from fellow Protestants, she could only afford to pay the 4,000 men for one month. After that they must come home, unless Henry could pay them at English rates for a longer period. Willoughby and Stafford were 'to feel his mind therein betimes'. Willoughby, besides being given the usual authority of a general to make and enforce orders for his troops' discipline and to issue warrants for their pay, was also, at the

Queen's command, particularly admonished by the Lord Chancellor and others of the Privy Council to see that sundry disorders committed of late years by captains and officers were now avoided. He was also to see that his men gave no offence in matters of religion and that the victuals provided for their transportation were not wasted.[55]

While Willoughby was receiving these instructions, Stafford was writing to urge that the troops be hastened across after all. The enemy were still close to the King at Arques and their artillery had just killed his cook as he prepared the King's broth. But they were very cowardly and might be utterly undone if Willoughby's men could be landed and refreshed by the time Longueville and Aumont came up. A few days later, however, on 26 September Stafford had to report that Mayenne had finally dislodged. According to his instructions, therefore, he again wrote to stay Willoughby till the Queen's pleasure could be known. Willoughby was about to embark at Dover when the ambassador's warning arrived. He decided to ignore it, put to sea, and reached Dieppe with most of the Kentish troops in the morning of 28 September. Most of the Sussex and Hampshire companies, too, had embarked before countermanding orders arrived, so they were at Dieppe soon afterwards. By 2 October all had landed except the Londoners, who turned up two days later, and Captain Cosby, who was presumably still fussing over the variety of his company's morions and the old-fashioned cut of their flat-bellied corslets.[56]

Once again Elizabeth reacted more mildly than might have been expected. After reading Willoughby's excuses, she did not disallow his crossing, though he ought to have waited for orders. As for the future, if the King did not need his troops, they were to return at least within the month and meanwhile Stafford was to report what the King's needs were.[57] Once again Elizabeth had been better than her promise. She had promised 4,000 men, paid for one month, only to relieve

[55] *L. and A.*, I, 475, 532; *Cal. S. P. Domestic, Addenda*, pp. 283–4; *H. M. C., Ancaster MSS*, pp. 289–91.

[56] *L. and A.*, I., 385–6, 476, 478, 534; *Cal. S. P. Domestic, 1581–90*, pp. 620–1; *Cal. S. P. Domestic, Addenda*, p. 286; *H. M. C., Ancaster MSS*, pp. 288–9.

[57] *Acts P. C.*, XVIII, 144–6.

Dieppe and raise the League's siege. In the event, the men arrived after the siege was already raised and they were to campaign, not for one month, but for three, not just around Dieppe, but through half of northern France.

Map 3. Willoughby's Expedition, 1589.

# VIII

# Willoughby's Expedition

It was chiefly thanks to Willoughby that the 4,000 English soldiers, sent under him to Dieppe only to succour Henry IV in his 'present necessity of besiegement', stayed on to serve in a three months' campaign that was to carry them past Paris to the Loire and back again. Stafford's dutiful report of the League army's withdrawal no doubt spurred Willoughby on much more than it held him back. As lord general of the Queen's forces in the Netherlands he had been intensely jealous of Norris and Drake's expedition. He was still smarting from some uncomplimentary insinuations in the Dutch States General's placart about the betrayal of Geertruidenberg.[1] He coveted martial fame no less than did those English gentlemen – Essex's brother Walter Devereux, Sir William Sackville, Sir Roger Williams, and the rest[2] – who were hurrying over to serve as unpaid volunteers under the new, Protestant, King of France. And now, surely, with the League army dislodging and Henry IV going over to the offensive, 'the brave Lord Willoughby's' turn had come. Moreover, like many another Elizabethan commander, the farther he moved away from Queen and Council, the less heavily he felt their instructions weigh upon him. Thirty-four years old, in the prime of his vigour yet with testing diplomatic and military experience behind him, he was not afraid to back his own judgement. He had taken his own line in leaving Dover; he was hardly going to be less independent at Dieppe. Thus Henry and he soon came to an agreement that the English troops should stay, not just for the 'Queen's month', but also for a second month in the King's pay. And on 11 October they set out with the rest of the royal forces upon their southward march towards Paris, leaving Sir Edward Stafford to return to England to inform the Queen of the agreement and to persuade her to approve it.

[1] *L. and A.*, I, 257; *H. M. C., Ancaster MSS,* pp. 280–8.
[2] *L. and A.*, I, 384, 470, 536. Walter Devereux was a volunteer, not one of Willoughby's officers as, e.g., *Mémoires du duc d'Angoulême*, p. 579 implies.

Elizabeth was none too pleased. For one thing, she had just ordered Stafford himself to stay in France. He pleaded that there was nothing for him to stay for. He could not accompany the King because it was impossible to buy or borrow a horse at Dieppe. He was, he said, living 'almost like a lackey'. He had 'neither coat, shirt, nor any provision'. Nevertheless, his coming back, like Willoughby's going over, was another breach of the Queen's instructions. More serious, however, was 'the doubt she conceiveth how the King will be able to pay them, for that at this time he doth earnestly press her for the loan of a further sum of money'. And indeed yet another French envoy, Philippe Canaye, seigneur de Fresnes, had come over with Stafford to beg for the immediate loan of a further 50,000 crowns, which the King urgently needed to pay his Swiss. De Fresnes was to point out that without the Swiss infantry Henry would be quite unable to follow up his success at Arques. For the unpaid French, foot as well as horse, ebbed and flowed as their whims and their purses might dictate. Apart from Willoughby's English, only the Swiss and some German reiters and landsknechts would keep soldiering on, and they only if the money was forthcoming to pay them with reasonable regularity. Yet it was all too obvious that Henry could not lay hands on such money. For the moment he had around him a fine powerful army, whose numbers some put as high as 30,000. Yet how long would most of those 30,000 stay with him? Even with the help of Elizabeth's first loan of £20,000 – more money, Henry said, than he had ever seen in one place at one time – he could scrape together only a fortnight's pay for the Swiss and his other foreign infantry. Many of the French were already, from mere want, having to leave him. He himself and his nobles had hardly money enough to buy victuals, and three of the princes of the blood royal were reduced to seeking loans of 500 crowns apiece from Ottywell Smith.[3]

But Elizabeth, too, hardly knew where to turn to find money for her own needs, let alone for Henry's, 'to whom', as Walsingham wrote to Willoughby, on 18 October,

---

[3] *L. and A.*, I, 388, 479–81; *H. M. C., Ancaster MSS*, p.291; *Lettres Missives*, III, 60–1; Camden, p. 559.

though Her Majesty carrieth a very good inclination, yet such is the necessity of her own estate as her means will not stretch to yield him that relief that he desireth ... I fear that the troops serving under your lordship, for lack of pay shall endure some extremity and therefore in my poor opinion, if your lordship shall see the King's means fail, you shall do well to urge him that you may retire betimes. Good my lord, have care of the preservation of the armour; you shall hereby greatly content both Her Majesty and her realm. The ambassador hath not yet had audience, but here nothing will be gotten.[4]

For Walsingham to write thus of the Queen's shortage of money without insinuating that it was no more than a mere excuse for saying no, is something so uncommon in his correspondence as almost to be termed unique. If he wrote so acceptingly of her financial difficulties, they must have been serious. And, indeed, it is quite clear that at this point Elizabeth was faced by an empty Exchequer and small hopes of immediately replenishing it. The most convincing proof of this is that she was now driven back to 'the vicious policy of selling Crown property to provide cash in emergencies', a desperate remedy that she had managed to avoid for a quarter of a century. On 21 October, three days after Walsingham wrote his letter to Willoughby, a commission passed the great seal for the Lord Chancellor, the Lord Treasurer, Walsingham himself, and four others to sell Crown lands. During the ensuing year they were to do so to the tune of £126,000.[5] Nevertheless these sales took time to negotiate. They brought little, if any, immediate relief in October and November 1589. Nor did the general tightening of financial administration help immediately. The sharper collection of debts brought only slow returns. The Earl of Essex, for example, also had to sell lands before he could repay the £3,000 loan that the Queen called in early that October. The gains from direct Exchequer control over most of the customs administration, after Thomas Smith on 16 October declined to renew his farm at a higher rent, gave little help in October and November 1589.[6]

[4] *H. M. C., Ancaster MSS,* pp. 291–2.

[5] F. C. Dietz, *English Public Finance,* pp. 19, 63–4; S. P. Domestic, ccxxvii, no. 31; ccxxviii, no. 3; ccxxix, no. 11; ccxxxviii, no. 30.

[6] Devereux, I, 207; Lansdowne MSS, lx, no. 81; S. P. Domestic, ccxxvii, no. 22; Dietz, *English Public Finance,* 63 note 29.

From all this it is obvious that, as Walsingham said, at this juncture Elizabeth's means would not stretch to yield what Henry asked for. Yet on 30 October we find Beauvoir and de Fresnes signing new bonds promising that Henry would repay both his earlier borrowings and a new English loan of £15,000 (50,000 crowns). What had happened was that, although the ambassadors' bond was made out to the Queen, the money came from some of the leading citizens of London. Elizabeth had used her credit and her influence to persuade them to lend her what her Exchequer could not provide. The persuasion, by the look of it, was not altogether easy. For unlike the earlier loan of £20,000, this £15,000 was to be repaid by Henry after six months instead of twelve and with £750 interest, equal to a yearly rate of ten per cent.

Even so, ten per cent interest was less than a borrower as impecunious as Henry IV could reasonably expect from any other lenders. For his ambassadors, the outcome quite surpassed their hopes and they had a special word of thanks for Burghley. He, as Lord Treasurer, must have played the leading part in persuading the Londoners, in once again 'speaking with the aldermen for money'. Of Walsingham's help, too, there can be no doubt. Indeed, his biographer would have us see in this and in Willoughby's expedition 'the final triumph of Walsingham's French policy'.[7] This is going too far. It is true that the Secretary had long been clamouring for more active help for Henry of Navarre and the Huguenots, whereas the Queen, with the apparent approval of Burghley, had preferred to put her money on a Catholic French King rather than upon a Protestant minority faction among his subjects. It is true, too, that she was now, at last, backing Henry of Navarre with men and money as Walsingham wished. But she was backing him, not as Henry of Navarre, the Huguenot chieftain, but as Henry IV, the lawful King of France, leader of Catholic royalists as well as loyal Huguenots. What she was doing was a logical extension of her own previous policy, with which changing circumstances had now brought Walsingham's ideas into line. As a result, though,

---

[7] *L. and A.*, I, 483; II, 455; Conyers Read, *Mr Secretary Walsingham*, III, 368, who, misled by E. P. Cheyney, *History of England*, I, 217, makes this into two loans of £15,000, one from the Queen and the other from London.

Queen and Secretary now saw eye to eye; indeed, Queen and Councillors were pretty well unanimous in their goodwill towards the King of France. All they lacked was the financial wherewithal to give him the help that he needed.

What then happened between 18 October, when Walsingham was so certain that 'nothing will be gotten', and 30 October, when Beauvoir and de Fresnes were able to acknowledge the loan of £15,000? What provoked the approach to the city of London, which transformed mere goodwill into substantial assistance? Perhaps part of the answer may be found in a particularly cogent memorial that Beauvoir sent in on 22 October.[8] In this he emphasized that if the King's army were to break while Mayenne's was still in the field, all France north of the Loire would be lost. That, of course, meant all the Channel coast, all the Channel ports. For few royalist towns or strongholds could hold out without strong field forces to support them against the great League cities and such an army as Mayenne had. Nor would they have the will. After all, most of the King's Catholic supporters had joined him more from a desire to avenge Henry III than out of affection for a still Protestant Henry IV and very few even of the northern Huguenots would abandon family and property to follow him across the Loire. Nor would he there be able to rely on hired foreign troops unless he could pay them. And where could he find the money to do that? All the provinces beyond the Loire had their own local wars. Their garrisons cost twice as much as the local royal revenues brought in. In none was the King absolute master. Nowhere could nobles or people bear greater expense. For all these reasons it was vital for the King to keep his army in the field and north of the Loire, at least until winter came when the enemy would disband. Fifty thousand crowns now would therefore do more than ten or twenty times as many later. Moreover – so Beauvoir wound up, in a burst of desperate optimism – this would be Henry's last request, because if he failed during the next month or two to make secure what he already possessed, he would never have a chance to regain it.

Elizabeth and her Councillors may well have doubted the

[8] *L. and A.*, I, 482.

finality of Henry's latest appeal. But they needed no reminding of the dangerous consequences for England that might ensue if he abandoned northern France to the Catholic League and its Spanish allies. Nor, probably, did they need telling that the Protestant Henry IV might always be more tempted than the Catholic Henry III could have been to retire beyond the Loire, to fall back upon those southern and western provinces where the Huguenots' greatest strength lay. At this precise moment, too, it looked very much as if that temptation was about to prove irresistible. For Henry and his army, after a somewhat half-hearted attempt against Paris, were between Étampes and Vendôme marching away south-westwards and already not much more than twenty miles from the Loire. His true intention, as he had told Buzenval in mid-August, was only to visit Tours to establish his government and courts there. After that he meant to swing northwards again to secure the provinces between Loire and Seine, preparatory to a more serious attempt upon Paris. Elizabeth and her Councillors, however, could not feel sure of this, even if they had been told of it. What they *saw* was the French King and his army, Willoughby's English among them, moving steadily away from the Channel coast and even from Paris, moving towards Tours and the Loire and perhaps even (as Willoughby feared) to La Rochelle.[9] This was the danger that spurred them on to adopt the unusual expedient of getting the city of London to supply the Exchequer's deficiencies. And as if to underline their motive, they persuaded Beauvoir and de Fresnes to sign a declaration, drafted apparently by Burghley, in which the ambassadors promised to urge their master 'de regagner les rivages de la mer de Picardie et Normandie de la possession de ses rebelles et de ne point retirer de là toutes ses forces si ce n'est pour le recouvrement de ses villes de Paris et Rouen'. They were to point out to him that if he failed to recover the coasts of those two provinces (and of Brittany, Burghley added to the draft), his enemies and rebels would soon be masters of the sea and of the chief maritime places of the country. That would do him more harm than the loss of two or three other provinces.[10]

[9] Ibid., 389–90, 397-8, 538; *Lettres Missives*, III, 29–31.
[10] Lansdowne MSS, lx, no. 56; S. P. France, xx, fo. 154; *L. and A.*, I, 483.

Meanwhile, what had been happening to Willoughby and his 4,000, or rather (deducting the usual ten per cent for dead pays) his 3,600 men and their 200 officers?[11] His moans, and those of such professionals as Captain Cosby, about their quality and equipment, seem to have been somewhat overdone. At any rate when Henry and his nobles saw them in battle order, and later on the march, they commended them as proper men and well appointed, 'for they never saw men better armed ... for so many together'. This could have been merely French politeness, a politic desire not to look gift horses in the mouth. Nevertheless, desertions were comparatively few, at least in these early days, and discipline was good. The only untoward incident was when, in full view of Willoughby and close to the King, Anthony Sherley cudgelled Captain Swan and Swan, drawing his sword, wounded Sherley. Willoughby was much upset by the affray; but the two men were volunteers, not members of the Queen's forces, and to judge from the letter that gallant old one-armed Huguenot warrior François de la Noue wrote when Sherley went home, the French again showed great politeness about it. With no more excitements than these, the first seven days' marches, at about eight miles a day, along the higher ground east of the Seine brought Willoughby and his men to Meulan. There on 17 October they crossed the river. Another four days' marching along its west bank, through St Germain-en-Laye and St Cloud, brought them to the southern suburbs of Paris, so close indeed that on the march two or three of them were killed by the city's great ordnance.

After this baptism of fire, Willoughby's men saw their first action in the attack on the southern suburbs of Paris on 23 October. Along with a Swiss regiment and two regiments of French infantry they formed the right wing under Marshal Biron, who had especially asked to have them attached to his command. While La Noue and Châtillon's Huguenots on the left were storming the faubourg St Germain to shouts of 'St Bartholomew', and Marshal d'Aumont's group attacked St Michel and St Jacques in the centre, the English by 9 a.m. had

[11] For this and the next two paragraphs – ibid., 389–90, 535–6; Cotton MSS, Galba E. vi, fo. 411; Thou, XI, 33–5; Davila, p. 424; Cayet, XXXIX, 289–95; also P. de Vaissière, *Henri IV*, pp. 343–8.

won the faubourg St Marceau, burned down one gate and won a piece of street leading to another. Had the King supported them with artillery, as Willoughby asked, they believed they could have lodged themselves in the University under cover of the morning mist. As it was, they stayed the rest of the day and the following night in the suburbs, with small losses in spite of continual shooting by both sides. They had taken four ensigns and conducted themselves with a bravery that, according to Willoughby and Lyly, drew praise even from the French 'who confess nothing' – though in fact both the King and La Noue wrote warmly of their good service. Williams, Sackville, and the other English voluntary gentlemen had distinguished themselves no less under La Noue on the other flank.

However, at noon the next day, 24 October, news came to the King that the Duke of Nemours with 600 League cavalry had entered Paris from the north and that Mayenne with the rest of the League army was only a few miles behind him at St Denis. In Paris the royalist supporters were being rounded up and any hope of surprising the capital by their help was fading fast. To launch a full-scale assault supported by artillery, which La Noue as well as Willoughby had urged, appeared too dangerous, 'for fear to engage in an abyss and against his subjects'. Anyway, even if it succeeded, it could only gain him the south bank. The main city on the north of the Seine would still be in enemy hands, its communications open, and the river between it and the King's army. There was nothing for it but to give up the attempt and, after consulting his nobles, Henry withdrew his troops from the suburbs and marched off south-westwards towards Étampes which was now again in League hands.

The English marched along with him, but took no part in the capture of Étampes on 27 October or of Janville on 31 October.[12] By then the 'Queen's month' was up and even the ever-hopeful Henry had to confess that he saw no means of keeping his promise to pay them for a second month. They

---

[12] For this and the next two paragraphs, – *L. and A.,* I, 397 – 9, 402, 502, 537–41, 551; *H. M. C., Ancaster MSS,* pp. 294–6; S. P. Domestic, ccxxviii, no. 30; *Acts P. C.,* XVIII, 210–1, 245; Thou, XI, 58–71; Davila, pp. 424–6; Cayet, XXXIX, 298–302.

had now neither weekly lendings nor daily bread rations and there were great complaints if they helped themselves. So, immediately after the taking of Étampes, Willoughby asked the King to release them and send them back to Dieppe. It seemed an appropriate moment, for Henry was proposing to let Longueville and La Noue take their troops home again to Picardy and Aumont his to Champagne. The English could therefore go in company of considerable forces for at least a part of the way. The King agreed, though he suggested that it would be more practicable to go by Caen rather than to Dieppe. Accordingly, on 29 October Willoughby wrote off to ask the Privy Council to have shipping ready for him at Cherbourg or Granville. The Council replied very promptly on 8 and 9 November that shipping would be there for him in six or seven days. Six hoys, with a week's victuals for 3,000 men and escorted by four of Her Majesty's ships and two of her pinnaces, were at once ordered away, at an estimated cost of another £1,197. It was largely money wasted, for contrary winds kept some of the shipping in the Thames and drove the rest into Portsmouth. Then, by the time the wind changed, Willoughby's return had been again deferred and the shipping had to be discharged.

For Henry IV, as usual, had proved much readier to promise than to perform. In early November Willoughby found himself still near the Loire and by the end of the first week of November his men were fully committed to the siege of Vendôme. They took the St Georges suburb, between the town and the castle, by surprise and escalade at ten o'clock on the night of 6 November. Next day they entrenched themselves within pistol shot of the castle. Two days later, on 9 November, after the artillery had played most of the morning, they stormed the town while the French dealt with the castle. The defenders put up only a weak resistance, but Willoughby's men bore themselves well, 'wading through the river and ditches and climbing over the walls in most valiant manner'.

They were, none the less, eager to go home. Now that they lacked pay, 'to fill the hungry belly they are fain, after the licentious fashion of wars, to spoil'. This embittered relations with the French and increased 'the ancient malice and pique of our nations'. They were also feeling the effects of long marching in bad weather, passing 'the children of Israel's march in the land of Egypt'. Their clothing, and especially their shoes, were fast wearing out and many of their weapons were broken. Willoughby therefore hardly needed Walsingham's letter to send him again to the King to ask for their release. Henry put him off, first until they should meet before Vendôme; then until the town was taken; and then, when it was taken, he slipped away to Tours without giving Willoughby a firm answer.

The King's reluctance to part with the English contingent is understandable. Its regiments were still 'reasonably fair for numbers and arms'. Only a few men had been killed and although some had been wounded and a good many were sick, these were carried along on the officers' horses, in Willoughby's coach, and in commandeered carriages. None had been left behind and those who recovered took their places again in the ranks. Thus they were still an effective fighting force. Indeed, as late as 14 November Willoughby could suggest in a letter to Burghley that, under colour of being transported home, they should sail to Spain to burn the King of Spain's ships or else join the troops in the Low Countries in surprising Dunkirk. Moreover they formed an increasingly significant fraction of Henry IV's forces. Lyly went so far as to say that without them the King would have no form of an army. He was having to let Givry go back to Brie with his troops and Châtillon to Languedoc, as well as Longueville and La Noue to Picardy and Aumont to Champagne. The French regiments that remained were down to 400 men apiece instead of 1,500. Happily the Swiss just now received directions from their Cantons to continue in the King's service but they were even more reduced than the French, besides being reluctant to fight unless paid. There were also a few German landsknechts, no less mercenary. Thus Willoughby's Englishmen, even if effectively they were at not much more than half or two-thirds strength, could make an important and perhaps a decisive difference. Without them, Henry might yet be tempted to withdraw across the Loire, with all the disastrous consequences that Beauvoir had predicted would follow such a move. With them, he might still keep some sort of an army in the field and use these winter months to build up his strength between Loire and Seine while the League's forces were in hibernation.

It is not surprising therefore that when Willoughby did catch the King at Tours on 13–14 November he found him still anxious to draw some further service from the English, although he had no idea when, or if, or how much he might be able to pay them. He told Willoughby that he meant next to bend his forces towards Normandy. He hoped that Willoughby's men might help him to win Le Mans on the way. After that, they could accompany Montpensier and the Norman troops until they reached the coast. There in some Norman port they might wait, either for supplies and clothing to be sent to them from England or for shipping to transport them home, whichever the Queen should decide. Henry hoped, however, that 800 of them might remain with him, even if the rest were called home.[13]

On receiving Willoughby's account of these proposals the Privy Council wrote to him on 30 November that Her Majesty, 'tendering the weal and safety of her good subjects', thought it expedient that he should now bring them home. She had therefore again ordered shipping to go to Cherbourg to convey them. If the King desired to retain any part of them, and if 'some eight hundred or a thousand (which we wish to be of the regiment levied in London) shall of themselves like to continue in the service, which Her Majesty doth wholly refer to their election', they might remain. But they must 'content themselves with such chance as may befall them for their pay and maintenance to be had from the King, and not to rely upon Her Majesty or to look for satisfaction at her hands in case the King shall not be able to perform his promise'. Finally, 200 able and well-armed men were to be sent direct to Dieppe, whose governor feared an attack by Spanish forces that were moving up to the Netherlands frontier.[14]

This last order was revoked next day on news from the governor that the Spanish troops had gone back to Flanders.[15] It does nevertheless illustrate how anxiously the English

[13] *L. and A.*, I, 539.
[14] *H. M. C., Ancaster MSS*, pp. 296–7.
[15] Ibid., p. 297; *L. and A.*, I, 491.

government watched over the French Channel coast. It also helps to explain why Elizabeth was persuaded by Beauvoir and de Fresnes to revoke her order of 30 November for Willoughby's return. On 28 November the two ambassadors had sent Walsingham a discourse designed to prove that the Spaniards and their allies would concentrate their efforts the following year upon France, not upon England. If that were so, Henry's friends should not only prepare to help him then, but should also make sure that he did not now have to abandon the provinces north of the Loire. Therefore Her Majesty should order Willoughby and his troops to stay with the King for as long as he needed them. These were arguments well calculated to impress the Queen and her Council. The discourse, however, went on to urge that the Queen should help Henry to pay her troops, and his Swiss as well, if he could not find the money himself. A suggestion as unwelcome as this could well have nullified the effect of all the previous arguments and the ambassadors were apparently persuaded to drop it, perhaps by Lord Treasurer Burghley, to whom they had asked Walsingham to show their discourse. At all events, when they had their audience with Elizabeth on 4 December, they said nothing about further financial aid for those purposes. Instead, they suggested that if she would let Willoughby and his men stay for another month, the King would make them a month's pay out of the £15,000 loan. It would, of course, still mean that the troops received only two months' pay for three months' service, unless Henry found some unexpected supply of cash.[16]

Nevertheless, despite some misgivings, Elizabeth very soon accepted this offer and agreed to her troops staying for another month. She herself seems to have been a little surprised by her own graciousness. 'We were, we know not how, overcome and enchanted by the King to yield thereunto', she wrote to Willoughby on 6 December. Perhaps, however, what had moved her most was not the French King's enchantments, but her own pride and satisfaction at the way this small force had, as she put it, given the lie to 'such as have conceived an opinion either of our weakness or of the decay and want of courage or other defects of our English nation'. She asked Willoughby to pass on her thanks to 'the whole company of our soldiers there' for their 'forward endeavours and valour'. Then, with one of those small touches that make it easier to understand the devotion that, with all her exasperating faults and foibles, she so often inspired in those who served her, she added at the head of the letter:

My good Peregrine, I bless God that your old prosperous success followeth your valiant acts and joy not a little that safety accompanieth your luck. – Your loving sovereign, Elizabeth R.[17]

To these comfortable words letters from the Privy Council and the Lord Treasurer added the more material comfort that, if the troops remained in France, Robert Bromley, a London merchant who specialized in army contracting, was to take over to them £1,000 in cash and £825 worth of apparel. This was to come from the £4,657 4s. for one month's pay, handed back by the French ambassadors out of the £15,000 loan. In addition Bromley might take £425 worth of apparel as a private venture of his own.[18]

Willoughby received these letters from the post John le Roye on 15 December at La Roche-Mabile, six miles from Alençon. They were indeed the first letters to reach him since he left Paris. For from the time that he and his troops left the Paris suburbs on 24 October until they re-entered Normandy in mid-December they virtually lost all contact with home. Burghley complained that it was easier to hear from Venice than from them. To this Willoughby retorted that he would rather travel from Venice, for the ways between the Channel coast and the Loire were so dangerous. They were infested, here and there by League partisans, almost everywhere by infuriated peasant guerrillas who plundered, and often murdered, likely-looking travellers and stragglers of whatever party, creed, or nation. Lyly added that, until they approached the seaside, it was impossible to find a man who would travel two leagues from a town, the enmity of the

[17] Ibid., 506, 546; *H. M. C., Ancaster MSS*, p. 297.

[18] *L. and A.*, I, 501–2, 547, 559; *Cal. S. P. Domestic, Addenda*, pp. 292–3; *H. M. C., Ancaster MSS*, pp. 298–9. The figures for apparel vary somewhat in these various documents. Those given above are from the Exchequer teller, Robert Freke's note.

peasants for soldiers made the ways so unsafe. Even an embassy sent by the Dutch States General to congratulate Henry IV on his accession and take him a loan of 20,000 crowns (about £6,000), could get no farther than Dieppe.[19]

It was while they were thus lost to English view that Willoughby's troops rendered Henry their greatest service. 'Whether it be surprise or approach we have our part, though they, [the French] will borrow the greater part of the honour and profit from us', Willoughby wrote on 14 November, soon after the taking of Vendôme. Since then they had played a no less prominent role in the capture, first of Le Mans, and then of Alençon. At Le Mans, after the King and Châtillon had taken the St Vincent suburb on 18 November, the English next day got themselves across the river Sarthe, many 'being carried over on horseback behind the gentlemen that attended the King and some behind the King himself'. Once across they occupied the Le Pré and St Jean suburbs and went on in the evening to seize the other 'inward suburbs' and a fortified gate. Again, it looks as if they met little opposition and three days later the 2,000 defenders of Le Mans tamely surrendered after the King's artillery had thrown 800 shot at their walls – and incidentally had only 450 rounds left. The English were thereby denied the chance to approach the town on 'float bridges', constructed by Willoughby out of tuns and ladders, and to attempt an escalade from the river side while the King's other forces assaulted the breaches made by the cannon. Nevertheless, if we may believe Willoughby, the garrison said that they would not have surrendered if they had not been more afraid of the English behind them than of the French at the breach![20]

After this, with Châtillon's departure and the French foot dwindling to a mere handful of men, the English had even more of a part to play. At Alençon on 3 December they occupied the Monsort suburb. Then at 1 a.m. on 5 December, while the French were being repulsed on the other side, they stormed a ravelin just outside the town gate. This ravelin was

[19] *L. and A.*, I, 358–9, 484, 549–52; *H. M. C., Ancaster MSS*, pp. 298–9.

[20] *L. and A.*, I, 400, 541–2. Thou and the other French chroniclers, after mentioning that 4,000 English joined Henry at Dieppe and were present at the attack on the Paris suburbs, make no other mention of them or of their part in operations.

thought by both armies to be impregnable, for it was surrounded by a strong freestone wall beneath which ran a deep swift river. However, Willoughby and Sir Thomas Wilsford devised an 'engine' with an iron hook, with which Captain Lee and some sailors pulled down the drawbridge. Then, led by Wilsford, the English troops swarmed over, put to the sword the garrison of thirty-four or thirty-five men, and would have pulled down another drawbridge on the other side and stormed over it into the town itself if they had not mislaid their iron hook in the darkness. By the time next day that it, or another of the same sort, had been found and fixed, the town was already parleying and so Marshal Biron countermanded the attack that Willoughby had planned. Before nightfall the town surrendered, according to Lyly after four cannon balled with hay had been fired at them to save their honour. The castle held out for some days longer but that, too, surrendered on 14 December, after a couple of days' bombardment and without any other fighting. Neither town nor castle in fact offered much serious resistance, except for the ravelin where the English had a couple of officers killed and three wounded (as usual, losses – if any – among the rank and file were apparently not thought worth mentioning).[21]

The fighting at Alençon was the last that Willoughby's companies were to take part in. Willoughby himself and many English gentlemen were with the King at the taking of Falaise on 26 December, but the English troops were left seven miles away and were not called upon. Henry's need of them was a little less urgent now that 4,000 Norman infantry had just come to him as he entered their province. Besides, the English themselves had come almost to the end of their tether. Less than a hundred of them had been killed, but continued marching in cold, wet weather, with poor diet and worn-out shoes and clothing had caused so much sickness that even the best companies were now down to a bare third of their proper strength. On 19 December, when they marched fourteen miles in the day, we hear for the first time of large numbers dropping out and also, almost for the first time, of deserters. Men grew too feeble to carry their weapons and sometimes

[21] *L. and A.*, I, 402, 407, 543.

threw them away ten or twelve in a day, driving the carts over them to make them useless to the enemy. Willoughby did manage to provide some shoes and hose, but by now so many were sick or hurt or had lost their weapons that he doubted if there were 800 left fit for service.

Not unnaturally, therefore, the men were beginning to show 'a dangerous humour homeward'. Fraying tempers also brought friction with their French allies. In part this grew out of ancient national rivalry and 'Popish French humours'. But Henry IV's own rather happy-go-lucky, hand-to-mouth ways were also to blame. He protested that the sickness among the English troops was due rather to abundance than to scarcity of meat. He often found them, he said, eating hog's and goat's flesh half raw. However, Thomas Fludd, the English pay-master, complained that it was often eight or nine o'clock – and that in the short midwinter days – before they received their orders to rise. It would be another hour or two before they could set out upon, perhaps, a twelve or thirteen miles' march, often in foul and rainy weather and many of them shoeless and thinly clad. It might therefore well be midnight before even the strongest reached their quarters, only to find themselves then in empty, filthy houses with neither fire nor provisions. By that time they were so wet and weary that, once laid upon a wisp of straw, they would rather fast than rise and eat. Even when they found livestock or meat, they usually had to eat it 'fresh', without salt and often without bread or drink. And on the rare occasions when they were able to send to a town to buy things, they found everything priced at treble its value – shoes, for example, at six or seven shillings a pair.[22]

Fludd's complaints were echoed by Willoughby's cousin, John Stubbe. Back in 1579 the Puritan John Stubbe had had his right hand chopped off by the Queen's order, for writing a violent pamphlet against her proposed marriage to a Catholic French prince. But as he truly claimed – writing not too illegibly to Burghley with his left hand – 'no man more sincerely affecteth a French King of His Majesty's [religious] profession, nor more joyfully rejoiceth in his prosperity, than I do'. Even so he, too, described how their lodging was

---

[22] Ibid., 411–3, 548, 551, 553–4, 556: *H. M. C., Ancaster MSS*. pp. 300–1.

ofttimes under the open heaven, their meat is to seek till midnight, then eaten without salt, without bread, half raw, two hungry meals making the third a glutton, enough to cast down the whole and to kill the sick right out. It was no small damage that many of them walked, wearing their armour, barefoot almost one hundred miles. If therefore, the King will hereafter have good service of us in his wars and send us home honest men, fit to live in Queen Elizabeth's peace, we must be paid or victualled in some order and not put to continual forage.

The Swiss and Germans suffered no less from sickness, and so would the French but for the fact that 'when they come by their own houses or friends, they can go by great troops to refresh them'. Such deficiencies of organization might be passed over in a two week's march, but 'timely lodging and orderly diet' were essential 'in a whole winter's wars', as Xenophon and others truly taught.[23]

Hitherto the government at home seems to have had little idea of the true condition of the troops. Burghley, besides criticizing Willoughby for not writing more often, blamed Fludd for not coming over and bringing his accounts all neatly fair copied. Walsingham wrote to Willoughby, as late as 8 December, that all 'the better and well affected sort here' greatly desired the troops to continue in the King's service. 'Being lodged in villages as they are', he went on, 'their wants cannot be great, besides some reasonable relief hath been yielded unto them by the spoil of such towns as by their help, have been taken, wherein it is conceived their portion hath not been smallest' (Willoughby noted in the letter's margin: 'our shares the least'). Anyway, the good King Henry would assuredly in time, 'God blessing his actions', reward them most honourably. How little Walsingham knew Henry IV! And how well might Thomas Fludd wish that Her Majesty's Councillors could, without hurt, be with them, if only for twenty-four hours, to understand what the conditions really were.

By the time that Walsingham wrote, however, letters were beginning to get through again from the army. One from Sir William Drury to his brother-in-law Sir Edward Stafford was

---

[23] *John Stubbe's 'Gaping Gulf, with Letters, etc,* (ed. L. E. Berry), pp. 139–40.

shown by Stafford to the Queen. It was her sharp speeches to the French ambassador thereupon that drew from Henry the letter assuring her that her troops suffered rather from abundance than from scarcity of meat; that their victuals cost them nothing; that they had done well out of the booty of the Paris suburbs, Étampes, and Vendôme; and, in general, that they had been treated as well as his French troops themselves.[24]

Nevertheless, by Christmas even Henry had come to realize that no more useful service was to be had from Willoughby's Englishmen. Accordingly, on 28 December he decided to dismiss the lot and three days' later they marched into Dives to wait for shipping to transport them. Most of them had to wait some time, for the King's sudden decision to let them all go gave the English government no chance on this occasion to make arrangements for getting them home. French shipping was hard to come by and costly to hire, and to make matters worse the weather was stormy. Gradually, however, Willoughby managed to get, first, the sick and wounded across and then the rest of his troops, all except eighty who elected to stay on in the King's service. He himself seems to have been in no great hurry to get home. He was with Henry at the surrender of Honfleur on 15 January and it was apparently 23 January before he reported to the Queen at Lambeth.[25]

How many of the 3,600 men and 200 or so officers, whom he had led over to France in September, survived to get home in January, it is impossible to say. For, as far as we can tell from the surviving records, the companies were never mustered after they left England. The chief purpose of musters, after all, was to find out how many men each captain ought to be given pay or lendings for – it was the captain and his clerk who distributed the money to the men. Now, paymaster Fludd had given them a week's lendings before they embarked for France, but then Willoughby, not knowing how far or how long they would be gone, had told him to keep in hand the rest of the money for the 'Queen's month' and not issue it until

[24] *L. and A.*, I, 549–50, 556–7; *H. M. C., Ancaster MSS*, pp. 298–300.
[25] *L. and A.*, I, 558, 561; *H. M. C., Ancaster MSS*, p. 303; S. P. Domestic, ccxxx, no. 19; *Acts P. C.*, XVIII, 312–3.

they were back again near the sea coast. So the companies had received nothing more during their three months' service, except some special imprests made for the relief of individual sick or hurt soldiers. No pay or lendings meant no musters. At the end of December, near Caen, Fludd did make a full pay for the 'Queen's month', that is he paid the captains what remained due after deducting the one week's lendings, the special imprests, and the cost of certain victuals that he had provided for them. But from the amount that he then paid out, it seems reasonably clear that this payment, too, was made without musters and without 'checks', as if all the bands were at full strength.[26]

Besides the pay for the 'Queen's month', there was of course another month due from the French King, out of the £15,000 loan. The accounts of this 'King's month', as we may call it, do help us just a little in guessing how many men got home. On 6 December the French ambassadors handed back to the English Exchequer £4,657 4s., the sum needed to make one month's pay to 4,000 men. Out of this £4,657 4s. the Exchequer officials retained about £170 to pay for the hoys hired to bring the troops back in November. On 10 December they paid out another £825 to Bromley to provide apparel and on 28 December £32 to Quarles for seven days' victuals. The rest the Privy Council originally intended to send to the local authorities, who were to pay it out to the companies upon their return to London, Kent, Sussex, and Hampshire. On 4 February, however, a Council warrant directed Lord Treasurer Burghley to pay the money to Willoughby for him to distribute. Again the men were not mustered and presumably the pay was made in the accustomed manner through the captains.

This time it does look as if the captains were not given the amounts that would have been due for companies at full strength. For Willoughby, in a letter to Burghley, later spoke of their receiving £6,000 from Her Majesty and £3,000 'which Her Majesty lent the French King'. He was no doubt thinking in round numbers. Nevertheless £6,000 was the exact amount that had been issued to paymaster Fludd in September and

Beauvoir la Nocle on 14 February understood that between £800 and £1,000 of the £4,657 had still not been spent. If, besides this £800 or £1,000, we take away from that £4,657 the £825 issued to Bromley (what happened to that?) and the other £200 or so retained or paid out by the Exchequer, we begin to get down not too far from Willoughby's £3,000. This might suggest that payment to the captains for the 'King's month' was made as for companies at around two-thirds strength. Knowing the ways of Elizabethan captains, we might then not be very wildly wrong if we guessed that barely half of the original 3,600 men survived. Two years later the Privy Council wrote that 'Her Majesty is informed, and we do fear the same to be true, that few of the men returned again'.[27]

Most of this, however, is guesswork. All we really know is that, while few were killed in action, many fell sick and died, some of them even after getting back to England. Thus eighty or more came to Rye 'wonderful sick and weak, some wounded, some their toes and feet rotting off, and some lame, the skin and flesh of their feet torn away with continual marching . . . all of them full of vermin'. At a cost of £55 11s. 3d. the townspeople cleaned them up, fitted them out with fresh apparel, fed them, and sent surgeons to tend them. Yet of the eighty or more, they managed to save only forty-eight.

How much the men who did get back received of the pay that was due to them is another question that can hardly be answered. Twenty-five soldiers of Willoughby's company confessed, when they returned to London, that they had been paid in full for the Queen's month. Willoughby himself claimed that they had 'satisfied generally the soldier and at our return in Guildhall made payment to that regiment, and in every country likewise, to the good content of them and in such sort as few of them went after a-begging, but were bestowed in their own countries'. On the other hand, the eighty-odd sick and hurt at Rye arrived there 'all of them without money, without apparel to cover their nakedness'.[28] Whether these unhappy creatures at Rye were more typical than Willoughby's twenty-five contented fellows in London,

[27] Ibid., 558–9; *H. M. C., Salisbury MSS*, IV, 10; *H. M. C., Ancaster MSS*, p. 312; *Acts P. C.*, XVIII, 307–9; XXI, 260.
[28] *H. M. C., Ancaster MSS*, pp. 304–5, 312.

there is no way of telling. But we may guess that, whoever else suffered, few of the colonels and captains came home worse off for their adventure. And all but one of them did come safely home. The one who did not, Sir William Drury, died on 8 January of a wound received the day before in a duel over a private quarrel with his fellow-colonel Sir John Burgh. As he lay dying he asked that the Queen would be good to his wife and children and give the wardship of his eldest son to the boy's mother or grandmother.[29] But for the families of those rank and file who did not return, few in Elizabethan days spared much thought for them.

While the cost in human lives and human suffering can thus only be guessed at, the cost in money of English help to Henry IV during this first half-year of his reign is much more exactly recorded. Besides £2,350 worth of powder and shot, the Queen had lent him £20,000 in September and, thanks to the Londoners, another £15,000 in December. None of this £37,350 was likely to be soon repaid. On top of it, Willoughby's troops had cost her Exchequer £6,000, besides what the French ambassadors had handed back out of the second loan and what the counties had lost in the way of armour and weapons. Wilkes reckoned this last at over £3 a man, which would mean that London, Kent, Sussex, and Hampshire between them had invested about £10,000 in the expedition. No wonder the Earl of Sussex was anxious that Willoughby should see the Hampshire men safely returned 'with their armour, shot, and furniture', of which otherwise the county would have great want. Willoughby claimed that 'for my own regiment I delivered most of their arms ... and other regiments brought home some more, some less; which restitution of arms after so long a march and sundry services, I have not heard of any land soldiers [that] have done the like before.' Lord Cobham none the less complained to Walsingham of the losses of the Kentish bands' armour and furniture and wanted to know how they were to be made good since the county was unwilling to bear the charge anew. Altogether then, and if we add to all this the expense of the

---

[29] Ibid., p. 303; *L. and A.*, I, 560. Drury died owing the Exchequer £3,288 12*s.* 6¾*d.* for moneys collected as one of the receivers for Essex, Middlesex, and London – *Cal. S. P. Domestic, Addenda,* p. 461.

extra naval forces maintained during these months in the Channel, the total cost to the Queen and realm of this first assistance to the new Protestant King of France cannot have been much short of £50,000.[30]

It was undoubtedly money well spent and old John Stubbe had good reason to think it 'an honour to [have] been in this journey'.[31] Indeed, it is difficult to think of any other occasion, except the intervention in Scotland in 1559–60, when Elizabeth's help to her foreign friends bore such good fruit. Four thousand men may seem a tiny force to us in the twentieth century. But it was a substantial contingent in an army whose numbers, although they occasionally rose to between 20,000 and 30,000 horse and foot, fluctuated most of the time around or under 10,000. Moreover, with the Swiss and a few German landknechts, Willoughby's men made up the bulk of the King's infantry and its solid, continuing core. And for a good part of the time it had been money from Elizabeth's loans that had persuaded the Swiss and Germans not to sulk in their tents. Without English help, Henry could hardly have kept the field through the autumn and winter. With that help he was able to reduce to his obedience most of the country between the Seine and the Loire. He was able to keep his own cause so much alive between Brittany and the Seine that the threat of his progress to the great League cities – Paris, Rouen, Orléans – was soon to force Mayenne to risk challenging him to battle. English help in men and money during the last three or four months of 1589 did more than a little to make possible Henry IV's famous victory at Ivry in March 1590.

---

[30] *L. and A.*, I, 502; *H. M. C., Ancaster MSS*, p. 312; S. P. Domestic, ccxxx, no. 74; *Acts P. C.*, XXI, 259–61.

[31] *John Stubbe's 'Gaping Gulf', etc.* (ed. L. E. Berry), p. 141. I find it difficult to agree with Dr. C. G. Cruickshank (*Elizabeth's Army*, 1966 ed., p. 251) 'that the French would have got on quite satisfactorily without them'.

# IX

# Parma at Paris

For the next fifteen months after Willoughby's men returned to England in January 1590 the only English troops on the continent of Europe were the auxiliary and cautionary companies maintained in the Netherlands to help the Dutch in accordance with the 1585 Treaty. Moreover, for nine of those fifteen months, until September 1590, the Queen's Exchequer was not called upon to pay out by way of subsidies to Continental allies anything more than the weekly lendings of those companies in the Netherlands.

The country and the government certainly needed this breathing-space. During the two years 1588 and 1589, close on 24,000 English soldiers had been sent on official expeditions to Portugal and France, and maybe half of them never came back.[1] Those 24,000 were in addition to the 7,000 maintained in the Netherlands ever since the autumn of 1585, to the small garrison of 1,700 or 1,800 in Ireland,[2] and to the many hundreds of sailors on active service, official or otherwise, on the Narrow Seas and the English Channel and off the coasts of Spain and Portugal or out in the West Indies. To these we must further add the far greater numbers of the trained bands briefly mobilized in England against the 1588 Armada and more permanently burdening the county rates for their regular training and equipment. Elizabethan Englishmen, however, had come to believe that their country was over-populated and the Elizabethan government, in the callous fashion of all governments, may have been quite as much worried about money as about men. And as regards money, here, too, they certainly had good reason to worry. During the two years 1588 and 1589 the war had cost the Exchequer at least £522,000,[3] not to mention what it added – at least as

---

[1] The figures in C. G. Cruickshank, *Elizabeth's Army* (1966 ed.), p. 290, include only 6,000 for Portugal in 1589.

[2] *Acts P. C.*, XIX, 91-3.

[3] Against the Armada £161,185, according to the estimate in *H. M. C., Salisbury*

much again – to local rates, to ship money, and to other suchlike burdens upon the Queen's subjects.

It was fortunate therefore that during the first seven or eight months of 1590 affairs on the Continent developed in a manner that made little call for fresh English intervention. This was due, above all, to the remarkable success of Henry IV in France.[4] We have seen what he had been able to achieve, thanks very largely to English help, during the last few months of 1589. From then until well into the summer of 1590 he carried all before him. After taking Falaise on 26 December 1589, he went on to complete the reduction of practically all Normandy west of the Seine. Then in mid-February he moved south against Dreux and Chartres, whose surrender would complete his control of the land between the Seine and the Loire. The mounting pressure that this put upon Rouen, Paris, and Orléans, the three main bastions of the League, had already compelled Mayenne to take the field again. Remembering Arques, he was by no means eager to challenge Henry to another battle, despite the fact that his forces outnumbered the King's even before the Count of Egmont brought him 1,800 horse from the Spanish Netherlands. Nevertheless, Henry's siege of Dreux, at the heart of one of the capital's chief victualling-grounds, provoked such a clamour in Paris that Mayenne had to risk a fight.

The outcome more than justified his doubts. Henry's great victory at Ivry on 4 March left the League without a field army and its great cities, Paris in particular, with little apparent hope of any early relief if they should be besieged. For the next two months the royal army gradually closed in upon the capital. While the League's leaders, and even the Pope's Legate, put out more or less sincere peace feelers, the King's troops had by the beginning of May occupied all the

---

*MSS*, XV, 2; the Portugal expedition £49,000 – above p. 94; France £37,350 and another £6,000 for Willoughby's troops – above, p. 179; the navy in 1589 £60,000 – above, p. 134; the Netherlands from 12 October 1589 to 14 July 1589 £208,390 – *L. and A.*, I, 214; II, 170.

[4] For these events in France – *L. and A.*, I, 413–64 *passim*; II, 322–47 *passim*; the despatches of the Dutch agent in France, Taffin, in *Kronijk*, XVIII; *H. M. C., Salisbury MSS*, IV, 31, 36–7; Aubigné, VIII, 179–202; Davila, pp. 439–69; Thou, XI, 80–92, 114–33, 144–83; also P. de Vaissière, *Henri IV*, pp. 361–70; Lavisse, *Histoire de France*, VI, i, 312–22.

approaches and all the river crossings. Paris was cut off and for
the second time inside a year its inhabitants suffered all over
again the rigours of siege, bombardment, and starvation. On
13 July Henry drew his hold still tighter by occupying the
suburbs. He would not attempt an assault for fear that while
his men were scattered through the city's maze of narrow
streets, fighting and plundering, Mayenne might fall upon
them with the small army he was slowly gathering not far
away. And, indeed, an assault hardly seemed necessary.
Hunger was doing Henry's work just as effectively and not
much less swiftly. Already the streets were said to be paved
with dead bodies and at the street corners starving German
mercenaries stood whistling hungrily to dogs as emaciated as
themselves. Even Madame de Mayenne complained that she
had bread for only two more days, while the poorer
inhabitants made porridge of oat husks and a little honey or
else ate grass. One of the more colourful anti-Spanish rumours
had it that some were grinding up human bones to make
bread according to a recipe supplied by Mendoza. Henry, in
his gay humane fashion and to Elizabeth's considerable
annoyance, somewhat eased the besieged's victualling problems by letting several thousand women, children, old men,
and priests come out through his lines. Nevertheless, on
29 July letters to Mayenne were intercepted which warned
him bluntly that Paris could not hold out longer than mid-
August. In fact, by the end of July 1590 Paris looked to be
back in the same situation as in mid-July 1589. The King
looked to be upon the eve of decisive success and the days of
the Catholic League in France appeared again to be very
briefly numbered.

Yet once again Paris and the League were rescued at almost
their last gasp. This time, however, they were rescued not by
the dagger of a French monk but by Parma's army from the
Low Countries. For from the moment that the new King of
France had won his first big victory at Arques the affairs of
France had replaced the Netherlands rebellion and the
Enterprise of England as the first concern of Philip II and also,
however, unwillingly, of his lieutenant in the Low Countries.
France was, of course, Spain's hereditary enemy. Under a
Huguenot King she became the heretical enemy as well and

this brought a sharp change in Spanish policy. Hitherto Philip had been ready enough to give the Guises and the Catholic League underhand support and subsidies. He had allowed them to use some of his money to hire a few German infantry, landsknechts, discharged from Parma's army. But he insisted that his aid must be 'aid short of war'. Spanish troops were not to go in, not even if the Leaguers invited them to garrison French towns. All the same, after the assassination of the Duke of Guise in December 1588, Philip had warned Parma not to engage his troops at all deeply in the Low Countries lest they should be needed to succour the League in France. The stringent financial restrictions that followed were doubtless in part a deliberate device to ensure that this warning was heeded. Philip still avoided open intervention as long as Henry III lived, as long as France had a legitimate Catholic king. But with Henry III's death and Henry IV's accession, and more still after the death of the old Cardinal of Bourbon, the League's 'Charles X', in May 1590, everything changed. The French business, as Philip himself put it, was now the principal matter and Parma must be prepared to send – indeed, himself to lead – substantial military help openly to the League even though that meant standing strictly on the defensive against the Dutch.[5]

As a result all through the last months of 1589 and the first half of 1590 more and more circumstantial reports flowed in about the onslaught that would soon be falling upon the Huguenot King of France. There was a new treaty of alliance and subsidy made by the Spanish King with the League; Parma was preparing to march into France; the Pope was sending an army; the Dukes of Savoy and Lorraine would take their chance, jackal-like, to snatch for themselves sizeable morsels of French territory. Not all of this came true in 1590. Pope Sixtus V's ingrained jealousy of Spain and growing disillusionment with the League, and Savoy's prior involvement in none-too-successful operations against Geneva, delayed their intervention – and Sixtus V's death in August was to defer Papal action longer still. Egmont's ill-fated horsemen had been visible evidence of Spain's open engagement to assist

[5] *Correspondance de Philippe II*, III, 437–8, 441, 452; van der Essen, *Alexandre Farnèse*, V, 251, 259–61, 275, 277, 286–9; H. Forneron, *Histoire de Philippe II*, IV, 515.

the League militarily. But Parma himself had been held back by illness, by lack of money, by the mutinies among his troops, and by the necessity of securing Nijmegen against Maurice and Vere. Nor did he, and his officers and advisers, welcome the new policy. With the limited means at his disposal it might well result, as he warned Philip, in losing the Netherlands without gaining France. Nevertheless when Philip, after Ivry, categorically and repeatedly ordered him to lead his army himself to the aid of Paris and the League, the Duke dutifully, although still protesting, obeyed.[6]

So, before the end of July Parma's vanguard was past Amiens. On 12 August he himself with the main body arrived at Meaux, under thirty miles from Paris. Mayenne and the League's troops had been lying thereabouts for the past three weeks and the combined forces were now equal, or not far short of equal, to those with the French King. For a week Henry tried to hold them off with his horsemen alone, while his infantry kept Paris still besieged. But on 19 August Parma moved forward from Meaux and threw this cavalry screen back across the Biberonne river. He then dug in between Claye and Fresnes. There he was a bare six miles north of Lagny, the only real obstacle in the remaining eighteen miles down the Marne valley to Paris. To meet this threat, Henry had to call up his infantry, even though that meant raising his blockade of the capital. However, if he could force Parma to fight and could defeat him, it would then be possible to return and reduce Paris at leisure, and as always Henry's spirits rose at the prospect of a battle. So on 20 August he drew out his army in battle order on the plain of Bondi. But Parma, safe behind his entrenchments, refused the challenge. Next day therefore Henry advanced to Chelles, on the north bank of the Marne some five miles below Lagny. This forestalled Parma who, after some skirmishing, dug in again at Pomponne, a little upstream from Chelles, in an almost unassailable position behind a marsh. Then on 27 August, under cover of thick early morning mist which

[6] For the supposed terms of the new treaty – *L. and A.*, I, 572; *Kronijk*, XVIII, 19–20. For reports about Parma – *L. and A.*, I, 562–71, 579, 581–7; II, 586–8, 590–1. For the Pope – ibid., I, 448–50, 574–7, 668, 673–4, 686–8, 693–6, 703; II, 701, 708. For Savoy – ibid., I, 667, 670, 677–8, 685, 697, 702; II, 704–5.

both hid his troops' movements and muffled the noise of his siege guns, he passed men across the Marne on a bridge of boats and took Lagny by storm before Henry divined what was happening.

Thereupon the royalist army began to disband with a rapidity that surpassed even the previous summer's disbandment. Sir Edward Stafford, who had witnessed that earlier break-up and who was again in France as resident English ambassador, was none the less flabbergasted 'to see an army, such a one as I think I shall never see again, especially for horsemen and gentlemen, to take a mind to disband upon the taking of such a paltry thing as Lagny, a town no better indeed than Rochester'. Yet in fact it was hardly so surprising. Lagny itself was paltry enough, but with its fall the way down the Marne lay open and enough supplies could flow into Paris to remove any chance of the city's early surrender. At the same time it was only too clear that Parma meant, and well knew how, to avoid the risks of a pitched battle. For the French King's nobles, his 'horsemen and gentlemen', and indeed for his unpaid French infantry too, these were signals that it was time to go home. They had gathered as usual in the hope of fighting a battle or plundering a city – they ran to battle as to a banquet, Stafford said. Few of them, as he himself admitted, had a penny left in their purses, and around Paris victuals and fodder were both scarce and dear. Besides, back on their estates the corn was already ripe and the grapes would soon be ready to be harvested. Henry made one last desperate attempt, on 30 August, to enter Paris by escalade. But that came to nothing and before another week was out his army had dwindled to less than 2,000 horse and little more than 5,000–6,000 foot.[7]

So Paris was saved a second time. Nevertheless, as Palavicino remarked, it was still infinitely inconvenienced. The way down the Marne was indeed open, but royalist garrisons at Corbeil and Melun still blocked the Seine valley upstream as St. Denis, Poissy, Meulan, and Mantes blocked it

[7] *L. and A.*, II, 333, 346–56; *Kronijk*, XVIII, 258–68; *Lettres Missives*, III, 245–52; *Correspondance de Philippe II*, III, 512–5, 521, 528; Davila, pp. 468–76; Thou, XI, 183–92; *Mémoires de la Ligue*, IV, 324 ff.; also van der Essen, *Alexandre Farnèse*, V, 292–300; Vaissière, *Henri IV*, pp. 370–92.

downstream, while Pontoise and Senlis closed the Oise.[8]
Parma's next move therefore was to start clearing the Seine by
taking Corbeil. This was a weak place that should not have
withstood three hours' battering. But these were 'not ... the
Prince of Parma's batteries', for the Leaguers had failed to
provide the munitions that they had promised him and the
guns often had to lie idle for a day or two while more cannon-
balls were collected. Moreover, the League's French horse and
foot had disbanded no less rapidly than the King's had done
and were 'almost all gone quite', Stafford reported on 14
September. The scarcity of victuals drove Parma's own troops
to plunder indiscriminately and made them, especially the
Spaniards, increasingly hated by their French hosts. On top of
all this, in Parma's camp, as in the King's, sickness was
rife – 'not directly a plague, but a looseness and a burning
ague which one infesteth another withal' and of which many
died. Thus, although Parma sat down before Corbeil about 9
September,[9] it was 6 October before he managed to take it.

By then he had little hope of doing more to clear the
passages into Paris. He did escort a convoy of victuals in from
the west, through Étampes. But his army had dwindled to
under 2,000 horse and 8,000 foot; his French allies had mostly
gone home; and a rainy autumn was beginning to make
muddy roads difficult for his hundreds of supply carts and
waggons.[10] It was time to think of getting home himself,
despite the King of Spain's earnest desire that he should stay
in France. So, on 24 October, in company with Mayenne and
the remnants of the League's forces, he set out from Meaux on
the slow march back to the Netherlands. For the next month
the French King buzzed busily around his flanks and rear
with a few hundred horse and some mounted harquebusiers,
reinforced from time to time by local royalist troops from
Picardy and Champagne. But Henry could do little harm to
the retreating enemy, for 'all the several divisions marched

---

[8] *H. M. C., Ancaster MSS*, pp. 305–6.

[9] The date varies from source to source; this is Palavicino's – *L. and A.*, II, 358.

[10] Van der Essen, *Alexandre Farnèse*, V, 308, says '6,000 chariots et près de 3,000
chevaux' which, if he has not put the carts before the horses, must have caused serious
haulage problems. For what follows – *L. and A.*, II, 354–70, 375–80; *Correspondance de
Philippe II*, III, 533–5, 539–41; Thou, XI, 193–206; Davila, pp. 476–80; also van der
Essen, *Alexandre Farnèse*, V, 296, 300–10.

always drawn up in battalia and with their carriages and baggage on each side, which shut them up and enclosed them like a trench, and were so near that they might help one another mutually in a short time'. Boxed in by their baggage-waggons and with their horsemen cavorting around outside, they looked curiously like a nineteenth-century American waggon train trekking through hostile Red Indian country in the Wild West. And it meant that 'the army being always ready and disposed to fight, feared not to be catched and assaulted unawares'.[11] Indeed it was rather Henry who was 'catched', as for example in a skirmish on 15 November at Longueval (where three and a quarter centuries later so many much more bloody actions were to be fought). At the end of November Parma crossed the frontier back into the Netherlands with what was left of his army after its losses in France and after leaving a Spanish *tercio*, an Italian regiment, and 500 horse to bolster Mayenne.

Parma's intervention had not brought victory to the League, but it had snatched victory from the French King and brought the 1590 campaigns in France to stalemate. Moreover it made manifest a whole-hearted Spanish commitment to support of the League which threatened even worse effects for 1591. It was notorious that, now 'Charles X' was dead, Philip II was hoping to put his own daughter, the Infanta Isabella Clara Eugenia, on the French throne if not as Queen regnant in her own right, at least as Queen consort to some puppet French Catholic.[12] Admittedly this was likely to prove less easy than he imagined. For by no means all the Leaguers desired such an outcome to their rebellion. Just as there was a somewhat nebulous *Tiers Partie* among the royalists which was threatening to desert Henry IV if he did not speedily perform his promise to 'receive instruction' in the Catholic faith, so among the Leaguers there was a *Ligue française* which relished the prospect of Spanish domination as little as it relished the idea of a Huguenot king. Yet even if the King of Spain failed to achieve the French throne for his daughter and even if the divisions within the royalist and Leaguer parties cancelled one

---

[11] Davila, p. 478; cp. van der Essen, *Alexandre Farnèse*, V, 308–9 and the engraving there.

[12] Cp. *Correspondance de Philippe II*, III, 539.

another out, there would still remain the grave danger of a prolonged stalemate ending in the break-up of the kingdom of France. For on all sides the vultures were gathering. The Duke of Savoy was seeking men and money from his Spanish father-in-law to help him push his claims in Provence and to make him master of Marseilles. Some of his troops gave the Genevans a sharp set-back in August and in November he himself made a formal entry into Aix, where his supporters swore allegiance to him as Protector and governor-general of Provence. The Duke of Lorraine was not acting out of pure altruism or mere family solidarity in actively assisting Mayenne. And if Papal action had been held up by the deaths in quick succession of Pope Sixtus V in August and Pope Urban VII in September, the election of the strongly pro-Spanish Gregory XIV in December 1590 seemed to guarantee that Papal as well as Spanish money would be lavished upon support for the League in 1591.[13]

Nevertheless it was from Spain that the greatest danger threatened. Few Englishmen perhaps, except those engaged in the Bordeaux and Bayonne wine trade, worried very much when in July 1590 Philip II sent 2,000 landsknechts into Languedoc. But the sight of Parma's army marching to the Seine and Marne, with Paris and Rouen and Le Havre in the hands of his allies and with royalist Dieppe, Boulogne, and Calais perched precariously on the outer rim of a League and Spanish dominated Normandy and Picardy – this was quite another matter. Nor was this all. For a year and more there had been rumours that the Spaniards were preparing to send troops to aid Mayenne's cousin, the Duke of Mercoeur, and the Leaguers in Brittany. In April 1590 Henry IV had asked Elizabeth for ships to guard Brest and to seal off St Malo which had at last come out openly for the League. Early in June there were reports that a Spanish expeditionary force for Brittany had actually set out from Ferrol, but had been dispersed and driven back by bad weather. A month later two Spanish ships were caught spying out suitable landing-places in the neighbourhood of Belleisle. Finally, in October 3,000 Spanish troops under Don Juan d'Aguila landed at Blavet

[13] *L. and A.*, I, 570, 572; II, 704–5, 708–14, 717; Thou, XI, 216–29.

and immediately set to work to construct a heavily fortified base in that excellent harbour.[14]

Now Englishmen could not view with equanimity the possibility of Brittany falling into Spanish hands just when Spain's ocean-going navy was again becoming a force to be reckoned with. For with the fine harbour of Brest as a base at the windward end of the Channel, that navy would be a far deadlier menace than Medina Sidonia's ill-fated Armada. 'Then', as Sir Roger Williams said, 'must we at the least keep garrisons in all our ports and send our ships royal in good numbers always to convoy our merchants.'[15] But there was a worse danger still. What if Parma should come back again and the Spanish army from the Netherlands link hands with the Spanish troops in Brittany? Might not Elizabeth then face, in 1591 or 1592, a more formidable invasion attempt than that her father had faced in 1545? For if all northern France, as well as Flanders, should fall under Spanish control, then a new armada would have at its disposal not only Brest but all the French Channel ports as well. In particular it would have a Le Havre no longer cramped by the royalists' possession of Dieppe, Caen, and most of the rest of Normandy apart from Rouen. And Le Havre, the 'Newhaven' from which Francis I had launched the 1545 invasion, was the only place between Brest and Flushing capable of harbouring and serving as advanced base for a great fleet of large warships. It is true that by the time d'Aguila came into Brittany Parma was already on his way out through Champagne and that this worst danger had therefore passed for the moment. Nevertheless that was the nightmare conjured up by the happenings of this autumn of 1590, the nightmare that was to haunt Elizabeth and her advisers for several years to come and to bring in 1591–2 the supreme crisis of the struggle for western Europe.

It might perhaps also be true, as Palavicino maintained, that now Philip II had so openly committed himself to

[14] *L. and A.*, I, 525, 573, 658–9; II, 325, 589, 594–6, 600; Blavet, renamed Port Louis in 1618, is at the mouth of the river on whose opposite bank the modern port of Lorient stands. Williams reckoned it the best harbour in France for vessels of any burden, better than Brest with its rocks and foul entry; it was like Falmouth, but a better harbour – *L. and A.*, II, 486.

[15] Ibid., 467.

support of the League, he could not abandon that enterprise because, if he did, Mayenne would be overthrown and the Spanish Low Countries hard pressed; that despite Henry IV's faults and the disorders of his people, France was so great a kingdom and its nobility so concerned to expel the Spaniards that the war would go on; and that therefore Elizabeth could assure herself that the Spaniards would not harm her in Flanders or molest her in Ireland or elsewhere. Yet even Palavicino admitted that this depended upon Henry IV being able to keep the field, which meant his being assisted to hire a sufficiently large body of foreign mercenaries who would continue to serve him when his French troops went home to refresh themselves. If he could not be provided with such foreign forces then, as Ottywell Smith said, the wars would be long and the country, being so poor, might well become Spanish.[16]

This, indeed, was the crux of the problem. For as long as Henry IV did not possess the great cities of his realm, he could not have revenues enough to pay a large army. Yet if he could not keep a large army together, he could not get possession of his great cities. And it must be a large army. It must be large enough and strong enough to enable him to reduce some of those great cities which were the backbone of the League and at the same time hold off any force that Parma and Mayenne might bring to their relief. He needed, in short, men and money to keep him in the field and assure him the initiative as Willoughby's men and Elizabeth's money had done during the later months of 1589. But with the Spaniards now committed so fully to intervention against him, he would need in 1591 a very much larger force than Willoughby's. He would need something very like the German levy of 8,000 reiters and 14,000 landsknechts that de Buhy had asked Elizabeth to finance just before the assassination of Henry III.

Elizabeth, it must be remembered, had promised to provide £20,000 in cash and to pledge her own or the city of London's credit for another £60,000 to cover the expected cost of such a levy (about 250,000 crowns or £78,000). But then, of course, in September 1589 she had had to send that £20,000 not to

---

[16] Ibid., 451.

Germany, but to Henry IV himself at Dieppe, along with Willoughby's 4,000 soldiers and £2,350 worth of munitions. A month later she had to stand surety for another £15,000 lent to him by the Londoners. Meanwhile, however, Henry had sent Sancy to join Schomberg and de Reau in Germany to see what help he could raise from the Protestant princes without the leaven of any English money or credit. Their opening talks with John Casimir, the Administrator of the Palatinate, were encouraging. He assured them that the princes had already decided to lend 300,000 crowns to Henry III and that they would certainly not do less for the Protestant Henry IV. And in fact the princes did put about 100,000 (£32,800) at Sancy's disposal. Out of this he raised 1,500 reiters and a couple of regiments of landsknechts and a little later took over a few more reiters and another landsknecht regiment that the Duke of Nevers had been raising.

A levy of 2,000–3,000 reiters and 4,000–5,000 landsknechts was not a very impressive return for 100,000 crowns. It is therefore hardly surprising that, as Sancy wrote to Henry and Henry thereupon wrote to Elizabeth, the German princes were not likely to contribute enough for a second and more adequate levy unless money was also forthcoming from England. Elizabeth's response, however, was still limited to writing letters on 10 December to John Casimir, the Electors of Saxony and Brandenburg, the Landgrave William of Hesse, and half a dozen other German Protestant princes asking them to appoint a time a place for a meeting with an envoy of hers to discuss ways and means of helping the French King.[17]

At that moment a disaster happened which made the German princes less eager than ever to foot the whole bill for a second and larger levy. In mid-December 1589 the Duke of Lorraine's forces fell upon the troops Sancy had levied and which were lying in villages around Strasbourg waiting to be mustered. The landsknechts were scattered and the reiters fled to Basel, abandoning most of their baggage. Most of Nevers' levy, who were on their way to the muster, thereupon went home. Sancy's reiters and some hundreds of

---

[17] Ibid., I, 496–7, 706–8, 711–12, 714; Henry said that the Princes had put 150,000 crowns at Sancy's disposal – ibid., 496; Burghley later noted that they had paid £32,800 – ibid., II, 736.

landsknechts did eventually get through to join Marshal d'Aumont in Champagne, but his efforts had done Henry IV little good and his carelessness had wasted most of the German princes' 100,000 crowns.[18]

The news of the disaster spurred Elizabeth to do a little more than write exhortatory letters. By 21 January 1590 she had made up her mind to send Palavicino to Germany, and apparently some money as well. Matters still moved at quite a leisurely pace – after all it was midwinter and the Elbe frozen. On 11 February Lord Admiral Howard gave orders for one of the smaller royal warships, the 150-ton *Tramontana,* and either the *Charles* or the *Moon* pinnaces, to be made ready to take Palavicino and de Fresnes to Stade. A cipher key was prepared for him, by 21 February according to Burghley's endorsement. On that same day he named as his joint factors his servants Giorgio Battista Giustiniano and Francesco Rizzo, empowering them to receive in London the £15,000 that was to be delivered to him for Her Majesty's service. On 24 February Windebank told Walsingham that the Queen had agreed to his speedy departure.[19]

At about this time long and rather verbose instructions were drawn up for him – Burghley and Walsingham both had a hand in their revising. He was to point out to the German Protestant princes the danger that if Philip II once had France at his devotion by the Leaguers' help, he would soon be able to reduce the Low Countries and would then be rich and powerful enough to execute the Emperor Charles V's plot to reduce the Holy Roman Empire to a monarchy by suppressing the religion, regalities, and liberties of the princes. Palavicino was to deal with them therefore to provide Henry IV with an army competent to maintain him. He must do his utmost to obtain this without any contribution being required from the Queen, but if she had to contribute, it should not be more than she could bear, 'which haply may be to the sum of 50,000 crowns'. Besides this immediate counter to the danger of Spanish over-mightiness, Palavicino was also to propose

[18] Ibid., I, 715–17, 735; Thou, XI, 94–9; *Mémoires inédits de Michel de la Huguerye* (ed. A. de Ruble, 1880), III, 315–34.

[19] S. P. Domestic, ccxxx, nos. 20, 68, 84: *Cal. S. P. Domestic, Addenda,* p. 301; *L. and A.,* I, 730.

that the German princes should join Elizabeth and Henry in an offensive and defensive league. To this league the Kings of Denmark, Sweden, and Poland, the Catholic princes and the Free Towns of the Empire, the Swiss Cantons and the Venetians and other Italian states might be invited to accede – the Free Towns of the Empire would then naturally be expected to give up carrying victuals and munitions to the King of Spain's dominions.[20] The counter-league proposal was, of course, a repetition of that made the previous summer during de Buhy's negotiations and was a good deal wider and less confessional than the merely Protestant league that Henry IV had been suggesting through Beauvoir and de Fresnes.

Palavicino had to wait for a wind at Yarmouth until 31 March and then was forced by a strong north-wester to anchor off the Ems for a couple of days – another example of how much diplomatic communications between England and the Continent were at the mercy of wind and weather. He landed at Stade on 8 April and left the next day.[21] He called in briefly upon the Landgrave of Hesse and then joined de Fresnes, Schomberg, and Sancy at Frankfort-on-Main on 22 April. It was another ten days before he and de Fresnes were able to begin their negotiations with John Casimir, the moving spirit among the German princes in these matters. Casimir had earlier put off Schomberg and de Sancy on the ground that he was in mourning for his wife. The excuse must have looked a bit thin, for they had been far from a devoted couple, he a zealous Calvinist and she a Lutheran, and anyway she had died more than a month before. And, in fact, when Palavicino and de Fresnes did meet him, they soon learned that he and the other princes meant to have no more dealings with Sancy, through whose inexperience they reckoned the recent levy for Henry IV had cost twice as much as usual and had proved fruitless into the bargain. However, Casimir assured them that the princes were well aware of the dangers and well disposed towards another substantial levy, provided its raising and organizing were left in their own hands.

[20] Ibid., 725–8. This paper is undated and was placed with a later set of instructions of 30 November 1590.
[21] Ibid., 730. For this and the next two paragraphs – ibid., 724, 734–7, 741–5; II, 735; also L. Stone, *An Elizabethan*, pp. 159–63.

At the same time it was clear that most of those Protestant princes were still distinctly nervous about doing anything which might break the peace of the Holy Roman Empire or encourage the Emperor and the German Catholics to band together against them. This appeared also from their replies to the Queen's letters of 10 December, which Casimir had forwarded on 20 March. The idea of a public assembly to discuss and agree upon an anti-Spanish, anti-Papal, league was therefore out. For the levy, much would depend upon the Elector Christian I of Saxony, the wealthiest and most influential of the German Protestant princes. Lutheran Saxony, like the other Lutheran Electorate, Brandenburg, had usually been particularly careful not to risk upsetting the peace of the Empire. But the alcoholic Christian I, under the influence of his Chancellor Nicolas Krell, had since his accession in 1586 inclined more and more to aggressive policies. Casimir had already reached a considerable measure of agreement with him at a meeting on 2 March, and with the Landgrave also likely to help there seemed at first to be a good prospect that a complete and royal army would be ready by late August or mid-September. Casimir himself had promised £6,000 and the Landgrave, when Palavicino visited him again in mid-May, agreed to give a little under £5,000. Varying amounts could be expected from Brandenburg and from various other princes whom de Fresnes and Sancy were to visit.

Obviously, however, the great hope was that the Elector of Saxony would show himself ready to contribute handsomely. Palavicino must therefore have been a little disappointed when he visited Christian in the first week of June and found him willing to pay no more than £10,000 towards the £60,000 that would be needed for the proposed levy of 6,000 horse and 8,100 foot, all picked men, and some artillery. Even with the full £15,000 from Elizabeth, it would be necessary to call upon minor princes and the cities for contributions to make up the £60,000. More disappointing still was the Elector's unwillingness to come to any immediate decision about starting the levy. As he pointed out, Henry IV's victory at Ivry and closing in upon Paris had both happened since de Fresnes left France; indeed for all practical purposes since de

Fresnes and Palavicino left the English court. So, before the German princes put their hands into their pockets yet again, they must understand from the King himself what the state of France required and what he had in mind. They must make sure that this time their help would be really effective and would enable him to pacify his whole realm. Christian therefore urged Palavicino to go straight back to report to Elizabeth. Palavicino agreed. He left Dresden at once and was in England by 25 June – after a much quicker journey than on the way out.

.Elizabeth was by no means pleased with this outcome of his mission. She was already annoyed that he had taken so much for granted, that he had even told the Landgrave that she would contribute £15,000. In a letter drafted, but most probably not sent off,[22] before his return she had reminded him sharply of his instructions. He had no authority to offer any specific sum from her without first understanding what the whole cost of the levy would be and how much all the princes would contribute. She hoped therefore that he had not been so hasty as to make any offer in certainty but, in view of all the continuing expenses she had incurred in the French King's behalf, had done his utmost to acquit her 'of all new charges there or of some qualification thereof'. A postscript, intended probably to make this still clearer and to give him some firm guidance,[23] explained that she was willing for him to yield [*blank in manuscript*] thousand pounds or, rather than fail, even [*blank in manuscript*] thousand, to make the army ready. In the draft the exact figures are not filled in, perhaps because Palavicino arrived home before the

[22] *L. and A.*, I, 743–4. The date of the draft is clearly not before the beginning, and may well be near the middle, of June. It is endorsed as June and refers to the end of May being past. Palavicino was back in England by 25 June. Stone, *An Elizabethan*, pp. 160–2, assumes that the letter reached Palavicino and that his report (S. P. Germany, States, vi, fo. 44) was 'posted off' before he left Germany. But that report is endorsed as 14 July and there seems no reason to believe that this is an exception to the rule that endorsed dates on English State Papers at this period are almost invariably the dates of writing or despatch, not the dates of receipt.

[23] This seems to me the natural interpretation. But the drafting is ambiguous and Professor Stone (*An Elizabethan*, p. 161) considered that this postscript contradicts what has gone before and shows that the Queen, 'unable to determine what her policy should be, evaded the problem by shifting the responsibility for deciding whether or not to offer the money on to the shoulders of the ambassador'.

amounts had been decided and before the letter was ready to be despatched.

If Elizabeth at this juncture found it hard to make up her mind, that is not surprising. Her difficulty was much the same as the Elector of Saxony's. For the past three months she had been getting vague appeals, or piecemeal requests for help here and there, but no authoritative statement from Henry IV himself of his needs, position, and intentions. In April, as we have seen, he had written to ask for naval cover for Brest and St Malo. Earlier, before Ivry, he had sent Incarville to ask the Queen's permission to seek another loan from English merchants and to get help for Boulogne. The Queen commended the request to the lord mayor and aldermen. Also at the end of April she became responsible for the Londoners' previous loan of £15,000, made on 30 October 1589. She had given the city her bond for the repayment of this at the end of six months with £750 interest. But all that the Londoners could now be persuaded to lend, on 21 May upon a new alarm about Boulogne, was £2,000, also for six months. To this Elizabeth added twenty lasts of powder.[24] By then, and during the following weeks, reports kept coming in about Mayenne gathering forces and Parma preparing to join him to raise the siege of Paris. If they came forward, there would be no time to levy and bring in troops from Germany. Once again Henry would look to England for help. But what were his plans? What help would he need? Would he, indeed, need any help at all if there was truth in the reports that Paris was already treating and incapable of holding our for more than another few weeks or even another few days?[25]

There was also a further, and in some ways more worrying, question. Was Henry now thinking seriously of soon redeeming his year-old promise to 'receive instruction'? Within a few weeks after Ivry reports began to come in of meetings between Du Plessis and Mayenne's agent Villeroy and between Marshal Biron and the Pope's Legate. On 2 April the King himself had a long talk with Villeroy. On that very day Buzenval wrote to Walsingham – who probably did not live to read the letter – assuring him of the King's

[24] *L. and A.*, I, 517, 522–3, 528; Lansdowne MSS, lxiv, no. 42; ciii, no. 64.
[25] *L. and A.*, I, 456, 464, 585–7; II, 329.

constancy in religion and in hatred of the Spaniard. But Stafford's secretary, William Lyly, who was still attending upon Henry, was by no means so sure about it. And neither Buzenval nor Beauvoir could disguise the severity of the pressure that was being put upon their King by the Catholic princes of the blood royal, the royalist Cardinals of Vendôme and Lenoncourt, the Catholic royalists in general, and even by a few of his old Huguenot adherents. By yielding he would appease most of the Leaguers. He might well buy off the Pope and the Spaniard as well. Then Parma would be able again to give his undivided attention to crushing the Dutch and Philip would be free to take up again the Enterprise of England. French ports, too, might then be opened in greater or less measure to Spanish shipping.[26]

It was unfortunate that amid all this uncertainty Henry's ambassador resident in England, Beauvoir la Nocle, could do so little to help. He bombarded Burghley and the Queen with agitated memorials and requests for Palavicino to be sent at once to the King and then straight back to Germany. But he was as much in the dark as they were about his master's true prospects and intentions. So much so, indeed, that early in July he sent Jean d'Hotman to find out from Henry himself and from the Huguenots La Noue and Du Plessis what was really going on. Meanwhile some of his well-meant efforts can only have confounded confusion, as when he mixed urgent begging for assistance to the King with the expectation that within two days he would get news of the reduction of Paris.[27]

The root of the trouble was that Henry spent so much of his time on horseback and in almost perpetual motion. He enjoyed few things more than, as Biron and others complained, hazarding himself as a principal actor in actions fittest for a private captain, in making 'une de ses cavalcades en cheval léger' or charging at the head of a troop of horse. He found it great sport, but it was hardly good for generalship. It left him too little leisure, and even less inclination, for long-term strategic planning – not perhaps a very common inclination anyway among the generally 'kick-and-rush'-minded men-of-war of his day. Nor, of course, could he keep always at

[26] Ibid., I, 446–53, 521; II, 419.
[27] Ibid., 418–20, 427–8, 430–1.

hand an adequate and properly equipped secretariat to ensure full and regular despatches. The four Secretaries of State – Pierre Forget, Louis Potier, Martin de Ruzé, and Louis Revol who was primarily responsible for foreign correspondence – did usually follow the army and attend upon the King, but they and their clerks could not accompany him on his 'cavalcades'. And considerable handicaps could result even from following the army – a little later Stafford had to apologize for writing on the 'naughty paper' which was all that could be found in St Denis. Life might have been easier for the Secretaries if Henry IV had suffered from the same immobilizing complaint as his predecessor.[28]

Clearly, if Elizabeth wanted reliable information from Henry IV she had to send someone over to France to get it. She did apparently promise Beauvoir that she would send Palavicino straight on to France as soon as he arrived home. When, however, he arrived on 25 June she changed her mind, possibly because (as she told Henry) Palavicino was so wearied by the 'travail' he had endured that he needed to rest and recuperate. Sir Edward Stafford was to go instead, to resume his post as resident ambassador, to report the news from Germany, and to inform Henry of his election on St George's Day as a Knight of the Garter. But Stafford made difficulties. He was heavily in debt (not an unusual condition for him) and could not raise the money for such an embassy. Elizabeth, much displeased, swore that he should go at once 'or else she would lay him by the heels', though in the end she had to make a free gift of £500 on top of his ambassadorial stipend of £3 6s. 8d. a day. And Burghley persuaded her to send Palavicino over too, to make his own report on his German mission. Nevertheless as a result of these changes and delays Stafford's letters of credence were not drafted until 12 July. Palavicino's followed on 14 July, the date of his report about the costs of the proposed German levy and the contributions hoped for from the German princes.[29]

---

[28] Ibid., 368, 380, 438, 444. For a list of councillors attending on Henry IV in May 1591 – S. P. France, xxiv, fo. 192; see also E. Doucet, *Les Institutions de la France au 16e siècle*, I, 163–4.

[29] *L. and A.*, II, 418, 422–3; Lansdowne MSS, lxiv, no. 64; *Cal. S. P. Domestic, 1581–90*, p. 680.

His instructions were drawn up soon afterwards. They were on very much the lines that he himself suggested in a memorandum of 15 July. He was to inform Henry of his negotiations with Casimir, the Landgrave, and Saxony and to explain the Elector's 'frivolous objections'. It is very significant of the Queen's – and indeed Palavicino's – anxiety about Henry's religious constancy that Palavicino was to advise the King to make his Catholic councillors privy only to convenient parts of the Saxon articles, lest those councillors should conclude that he would get no timely help from Germany and should thereupon press him the more earnestly to establish his estate by professing their religion. Palavicino, too, in talking with the princes of the blood and Catholic councillors such as Biron and Aumont, was to blame the delay in the levy upon the great errors made by Sancy over the last one. He should also tell them that, after the King's victory at Ivry and his recovery of a number of towns, the German princes had been surprised to receive no letters or messages from him, not even a reply to the Saxon Elector's letter of congratulation of 3 April. They had accordingly presumed that he did not want a levy that summer and had sent Palavicino back to find out if this were so – a question which Elizabeth also wanted answered.

After getting Henry's answers, Palavicino might go straight back to Germany by land if that were thought both safe and desirable. Otherwise he was to return to England and go on to Germany by sea. In either event, when he got there he was to impress upon the German princes that Elizabeth had already spent far more in helping Henry IV since his accession than either he or Henry III had originally asked her to contribute towards a levy in Germany, as much indeed as the whole cost of the levy. Here the Queen's instructions differed sharply from Palavicino's memorandum of 15 July. For he had there asked for authority to assure the princes of the blood and the Catholic councillors, and above all Henry himself, of Elizabeth's willingness to contribute the full £15,000 set down for her in the Saxon estimate. But Elizabeth's anxiety about the prospects in France and about the King's religious constancy did not yet bite as deep as that. It is true that on 12 August, returning in a good mood from a successful day's hunting, she had a letter sent to Beauvoir with a haunch of venison for himself and an emerald for the King. And with the emerald she sent, not only her hope that when Henry wore it every blow he struck might fell an enemy, but also a reminder that an emerald was said never to break so long as faith was kept firm and intact.[30]

Poor Beauvoir needed cheering up. A little while back he had had an attack of colic during an audience with the Queen. His requests that she should raise her contribution in Germany to £20,000 had fallen on very deaf ears. Then on 5 August he heard that she had called an extraordinary meeting of her Council and he jumped to the conclusion that this was to discuss reports that, with Paris about to fall, Henry would need no help this year. The truth in fact was quite the opposite of his suspicions. For on 3 August Burghley had written to Thomas Wilkes in the Netherlands that the Queen was disposed to levy troops in England ready to assist Henry. As, however, this would take time, Wilkes and Bodley were to urge the States General to invade Flanders or Brabant immediately so as to distract Parma from France – as Bodley had actually been doing on his own initiative, though without much success. In the meanwhile public prayers were ordered to be offered throughout England for Henry's success.[31]

So far, until Elizabeth could learn what Henry needed, there seemed little she could do for him except pray. Learning what he needed depended upon Palavicino and Stafford who, though they landed at Dieppe on 1 August, were unfortunately unable to find an escort to take them to the King's camp until the 16th. They needed an escort anyway, but all the more because a rumour had spread that Stafford had brought with him a great sum of money. If was actually a coffer containing 700–800 horseshoes, but the weight of it when it was lifted out of the ship made men think it must be full of money. The news spread to Le Havre and other enemy towns and considerable bodies of League troops gathered to intercept the two ambassadors.

However, as the gates of Dieppe were shutting on the evening of 15 August a horseman rode in with letters

[30] *L. and A.*, II, 421, 424–6, 443.
[31] Ibid., 228, 427–8, 438, 443.

summoning all available troops to the King because Parma was within a few leagues of him and a battle was imminent. So Stafford and Palavicino decided to set out next morning with the eighty or so horsemen which were all Dieppe could spare. The journey was dangerous enough for Stafford, in a letter to Burghley, to ask that his mother and wife should not be told of it, they 'being women and natural'. It meant hard riding too, and by the time they reached St Denis on 20 August their horses were too spent to carry them the remaining two leagues to the King's camp on the plain of Bondi. Next morning Henry called to them at their window as he rode off to prepare for battle, inviting them in his familiar fashion to come as his friends to see and help him but not yet to treat of any matters. For the enemy were so near that they might well be interrupted in even a half-hour's talk, as the King had to be (or at any rate insisted on being) in every corner of the field.[32]

This was only a foretaste of the difficulties of negotiating with a soldier-king in the midst of a campaign. It was a week later before Stafford could write that they were beginning to discuss Palavicino's business. And just at that moment, as we have seen, Lagny was lost, the King's army broke, and his final desperate attempt to enter Paris by escalade failed. Amid all this clash of arms there was little time for diplomacy. So, immediately after the abortive Paris escalade on 30 August, Palavicino, suffering painfully from gout, rode off by easy stages across the Oise and the Seine to wait in comparative safety at Mantes until Henry could find time to attend to him. There Stafford, his horses worn out by their continual riding, joined him during the second week of September. Even then they did not expect Henry to come to them for another week, and before he arrived Palavicino fell ill with dysentery. Stafford, too, was in a very depressed mood. He was catching a cold, he complained, like the one he had last winter. He had spent all but £461 of the £1,160 he had brought with him from London and it was costing him £10–12 a day to live. Of his men, three or four were dead, fourteen or fifteen sick, and soon he would face the terrifying prospect of having to groom his own horse, dress his own meat, and wait upon himself! In fact by the time he reached Mantes he had already convinced himself that he must return home when Palavicino went. For the camp, as it would be running this winter, would be no place for an ambassador. An agent, at a mere twenty shillings a day, could do all that was needed.[33]

In the meantime, however, Stafford had written on 28 August that unless the Queen gave present orders to send men into Flanders to draw Parma home, Henry might not be able to wait for help from Germany. He might have to yield to his Catholic supporters, who were pressing him to a Mass and who were the stronger party. Palavicino took a less gloomy view and considered that it would suffice for the Queen to help the German levy generously. But Burghley's underlining and marginal notes to Stafford's remarks reveal that he took them seriously enough.[34] And the Queen seems to have shared his concern. For on 9 September Burghley drafted orders to be sent to various lords-lieutenant for a levy of troops for France. Three days earlier letters had been sent off to the States General, Council of State, and Count Maurice urging them yet again to distract Parma by an offensive in Flanders, through Ostend if they wished. To assist them, Elizabeth said, she was levying 4,000–5,000 men, with a month's victuals, in England. She was also ordering the English garrisons at Ostend, Bergen, and Flushing to send all the men they could spare to join Vere for the enterprise.[35]

Vere and other English officers in the Netherlands thought that something might well be done in this way to ease the pressure on the French King. But the States' finances and their small field forces had been almost exhausted by their operations around Nijmegen to cover the building of Fort Knodsenburg. Indeed, at the end of July Count Maurice had broken up his camp and sent nearly all his troops back to their garrisons to rest and refresh themselves.[36] By the time the Queen's letters arrived he was in the field again, but with no

[33] Ibid., 444, 448–50.
[34] Ibid., 445, 451.
[35] Ibid., 233; *H. M. C., Salisbury MSS,* IV, 54–61; Cotton MSS, Galba D, vii, fos. 231–5; S. P. Domestic, ccxxx, no. 64; *Acts P. C.,* XIX, 430–3; *Resolutiën der Staten Generaal,* VII, 41–2, 44; *Kronijk,* XVIII, 284–5.
[36] See below, pp. 210–2.

more than 300–400 horse and 2,000 foot apart from the English auxiliary companies. And he had already committed himself to operations to clear the Bommelerwaard and the country around Breda. So, although the States after several days' discussion replied encouragingly on 21 September, further letters from them on 29 September made it very clear that any major invasion of Flanders would have to be made by forces from England and at the Queen's expense.[37]

The expense was no doubt a discouraging factor. For, while she was awaiting the States' reply, Elizabeth had been asked by Beauvoir to make Henry IV yet another loan. He needed it in order to give his Swiss and German troops the pay that was due to them in September. Elizabeth had responded immediately with £10,000 for which Beauvoir gave his personal bond, as well as the King's, on 25 September. The money was sent over from Dover on the evening of 5 October and was at Dieppe next day. Incarville professed to be disappointed that it was not £30,000 but, like the £20,000 sent over in September 1589, it enabled Henry to keep in service the Swiss and German infantry who formed the enduring hard core of his army.[38] This meant that he was no longer in any immediate danger of destruction. At the same time Parma, though he had relieved Paris, had been bogged down for almost a month before Corbeil.

The worst of the crisis in France was thus over for this year and on 3 October at Gisors Henry and his council at last found time to discuss with Palavicino and Stafford the arrangements for getting a German levy in 1591. The outcome of these discussions was a decision to send the Viscount Turenne, one of the foremost Huguenot nobles and commanders, back with Palavicino to England and then on to Germany.[39]

At almost the same time, on 6 October, Elizabeth took up once again the idea of an offensive in Flanders. Orders were prepared to levy 3,000 men in England and letters were written to the States and Bodley urgently requesting Dutch co-operation. Next day, however, Wilkes delivered the States'

[37] *L. and A.*, II, 234–6.
[38] Ibid., 454–5, 459; *Cal. S. P. Domestic, 1581–90*, p. 689.
[39] *L. and A.*, II, 456, 460.

second and more discouraging answer of 29 September. News arrived, too, of the Spanish landing in Brittany. Thereupon the levy was cancelled and the letters to the States and Bodley were not sent. Nor did any troops from England go over to join Maurice when, with a mere 1,200 men, drawn mostly from the English auxiliary forces, he attempted to surprise Dunkirk on 19 October. Maurice, it is true, had not asked for any, since his purpose was not to overrun a province but merely to snatch a port from the enemy. He failed even to do that, for his enterprise was none to well managed and much too well advertised. Elizabeth's hopes for an effective offensive in Flanders thus petered out in a few plundering raids by the garrison of Ostend. As the enemy boasted, while Parma was relieving Paris, all that the Queen's forces could do was to 'take cows and sconces'. And as Burghley had sadly reflected more than a month ago, 'the enemy would not have lost such an opportunity against us'.[40]

Much of the blame for missing that opportunity must rest upon Elizabeth. No one else was in a position to take effective action to ease the pressure upon the French King. She was well enough aware of this. Before the end of June she knew from Palavicino that nothing could be looked for this year from Germany. Before the end of August Wilkes's return brought her quite unusually full and up-to-date information about the military intentions and limitations of the Dutch. She was equally well aware of the weakness of the enemy's forts and forces in Flanders, even before the Ostend garrison's raid past Nieupoort to East Dunkirk on 28 August. Even 4,000–5,000 men from England, with the Ostend garrison and perhaps a company or two from Flushing and Bergen, would have stood a fair chance of winning enough initial success to draw back a significant proportion of Parma's forces.

Admittedly, by October it was probably too late. But earlier such a stroke into Flanders might have had a decisive effect upon the situation in France. Of course Elizabethan England, with no standing army, had no ready-made expeditionary force which could be rushed across at a few days' notice. To levy, equip, and transport even 4,000 men must take at least

[40] Ibid., 14–16, 239–44; S. P. Domestic, ccxxx, nos. 87–90.

three or four weeks, as Willoughby's 1589 expedition had done. It is also true, as we have seen, that Elizabeth lacked reliable information about Henry IV's position and plans. It is none the less surprising that she waited until 9 September before deciding to order a levy of troops in England and that even then she made their despatch so dependent upon Dutch co-operation which, even if obtainable, must – as she well knew from past experience – be long in the obtaining. Had she ordered a levy of 4,000–5,000 men when she was first 'disposed' to it in early August, when Parma's intervention had become almost certain, those troops could have been at Ostend before he took Lagny. The effects could have been far-reaching. Even in September, when Parma was bogged down before Corbeil, an invasion of Flanders could still have made a considerable difference.

The opportunity missed in Flanders in 1590 was not perhaps as great as the opportunity missed by the Portugal expedition in 1589. But this time Elizabeth had only herself to blame for missing it.

# X

# Vere and Wilkes in the Netherlands

These events in France had brought a welcome relief to the Dutch. The financial restrictions that Philip II had imposed upon Parma had not only kept the Duke's forces mainly on the defensive. They also underlay, even though they did not directly provoke, the mutiny of the crack 'old tercio' of Spaniards on 24 August 1589. The danger of the enemy getting 'a good footing in Holland', which Sir Francis Vere had anticipated, passed away with that mutiny and the resulting withdrawal of Mansfelt's troops from the Bommelerwaard and from before Heusden. Unfortunately the States lacked the forces to take advantage of their enemy's troubles, even when the English companies returned from Portugal. Their main field force, Maurice's little army at Voorn, numbered only some 1,300 or 1,400 foot and half of these were Vere's Englishmen. Nevertheless from the beginning of September 1589 all quickly grew quiet along their main, southern, front, along the great rivers from Arnhem to the sea.[1]

Activity continued longer on their eastern flank, in the Overquarter beyond the Maas, where Schenk's death and the dispersing of his forces had somewhat disordered matters. More disorder followed when Count Mörs, the stadholder of Utrecht, Gelderland, and Overijssel, went to inspect a powder magazine at Arnhem and, owing to his page 'neglecting to look well to the candle', lost both the powder and his life.[2] Despite these setbacks, during the first week of October Count Overstein and Sir Francis Vere with 700–800 horse and 1,200 foot, 900 of them English, succeeded in re-victualling Rheinberg. They then routed a force of 3,000 Spaniards and Italians under Count Warembon, killing over 600 and capturing eleven ensigns and a lot of booty. Vere, who

---

[1] *L. and A.,* I, 7, 10–12, 79; Bor, xxvi, fos. 54–5.

[2] *L. and A.,* I, 16. Or was it an explosion of 'fireworks'?–Bor, xxvi, fos. 55–6. The Spaniards heard that a new petard burst – van der Essen, *Alexandre Farnèse,* V, 269.

had his horse killed under him and was himself wounded in the leg, wrote proudly home that, for the numbers, nothing better had been done by Greeks or Romans. After again victualling Rheinberg and putting in a fresh garrison, he and Overstein marched their men safely back to winter quarters in Gelderland and Holland. Thereupon, apart from some desultory activity beyond the Maas, both sides settled down for their six or seven months' hibernation. Mansfelt and Warembon kept Rheinberg blockaded and it fell into their hands in January 1590 when its victuals ran out. But their troops were in no condition to mount a serious threat to the United Provinces, especially after Vere with some English and Overstein with six Dutch companies were moved up to Doesburg and Doetinchem.[3]

The southern front did flare up briefly when, in one of the more spectacular episodes of the war, Maurice on 22 February 1590 surprised Breda. Some months earlier he had learned that boats carrying peat turves were admitted to the castle there without search and that one of the boats was owned and skippered by an old servant of his father. This skipper agreed to take aboard on one of his journeys only three lasts of peat instead of the nine he had promised the governor of Breda. He made up the rest of his load with Captain Héraugières and seventy or eighty picked soldiers, hidden underneath that top layer of turves. Early in the afternoon of 21 February he took his boat with its mixed cargo into the castle yard. On various pretexts he managed to avoid unloading it that day. Then, between midnight and one o'clock the soldiers sallied out from their cramped and dusty quarters in this Dutch version of the Trojan horse. They seized the castle, killing thirty of its garrison of 120, and signalled to Maurice who was waiting two leagues away with 1,700 men, 600 of them once again Vere's Englishmen. By five o'clock the Count was in the castle and by three that afternoon he had the town as well. During the next couple of weeks the States managed to scrape together a garrison of 1,200 foot and four cornets of horse to hold it.[4]

[3] *L. and A.*, I, 17–20, 28, 31–3, 47–51, 85; Vere's *Commentaries*, pp. 3–10; Bor, xxvi, fos. 55–6; *H. M. C., Ancaster MSS*, p. 304; *Resolutiën der Staten Generaal*, VI, 335–8, 501–4; VII, 8–15.
[4] *L. and A.*, I, 30, 58–61; *Kronijk*, XVIII, 113, 118, 122–5; Bor, xxvii, fos. 21–5.

It was a place well worth holding. Besides being strong in itself, it greatly strengthened the States' grip upon the river crossings from which the enemy might thrust into Holland and Zeeland. For Breda, Bergen, and Heusden could now put together 1,500 foot and 700 horse inside eight hours. This meant that the enemy's three remaining outposts on the lower Rhine–Maas waterline – Geertruidenberg, Roosendaal, and Steenbergen – were now virtually cut off. All three needed early re-victualling if they, too, were not to be lost. And their re-victualling now entailed a major military operation by a substantial part of Parma's forces. By drawing men out of the Brabant and Flanders garrisons and recalling some who were marching to join Mayenne in France, he managed to get Mansfelt into the field with 4,000–5,000 horse and foot. Sweeping round east of Breda, this force put supplies into Geertruidenberg on 15 March. Moving on round the north side, they seized the castle of Zevenbergen and built a small fort at Ter Heyden. Early in May they tried to strengthen these positions in Breda's rear by seizing the nearby Oordam fort, but despite a prolonged preliminary bombardment, their assaults were repulsed with considerable loss. All the while they had been continually harassed by sorties from Bergen and Breda. They were short of money and victuals and many of them were on the verge of mutiny. They had managed to re-victual their three outposts on the lower Maas and to link the most easterly and isolated, Geertruidenberg, through Ter Heyden and Zevenbergen to Steenbergen and Roosendaal. But they had done almost nothing to shake the States' hold upon Breda and at the end of the first week in May they had to move off eastwards to counter a new threat from Maurice at Nijmegen.[5]

For, thanks to Philip II's insistence that all possible forces must be concentrated upon France, Parma had not been able to provide Mansfelt with enough troops to secure more than one sector of the front at a time. While he was busy around Breda, the garrisons farther east and the cities of Flanders westwards were very inadequately covered. Moreover, the States now had almost complete control, not yet of the Maas, but already of the whole course of the Waal westwards of Nijmegen. Count Maurice therefore could move his forces laterally along this southern front by boat, which was far quicker and far less fatiguing for them than foot-slogging all those weary miles with full equipment as the enemy's infantry must do. Thus although Maurice was not strong enough to meet Mansfelt head on around Breda, he could move rapidly against other places whose safety Mansfelt could not afford to neglect. And at the end of April 1590 he suddenly moved east to threaten 'sHertogenbosch, Grave and Nijmegen. As Parma told Philip, these were key towns. 'sHertogenbosch was one of the most valuable taking-off places for attacks upon the Bommelerwaard and for thrusts into Holland. Nijmegen's loss would mean the loss of all Gelderland and thus of almost all contact with the hard-pressed Verdugo in Groningen. Grave was where the road from 'sHertogenbosch to Nijmegen crossed the Maas.[6]

Maurice's first move was to attempt a double surprise, by himself and Vere against Nijmegen and by Count Hohenlohe against Grave. During the night of 30 April Vere and Solms with Maurice's vanguard of 300 picked soldiers managed to creep up undetected and fix a petard to one of the gates of Nijmegen. But the thing 'took not fire in time, so that day being broken and we discovered, [we] were forced to retire'. Hohenlohe had even less luck. He found Grave forewarned and in arms against him. Retiring, he lost two fingers on his bridle hand in fighting his way through an ambush. Both surprises thus failing, Maurice brought together the two forces and settled down to build a fort on the north bank of the Waal opposite Nijmegen. This fort, besides being a continual thorn in Nijmegen's side, would also block the enemy's entrance into the rich pasturelands of the Betuwe and seriously threaten their communications with Zutphen and Deventer and on to Groningen. It was thus an enterprise that Mansfelt could not well ignore and by mid-May he, too, was on his way towards Nijmegen.[7]

In numbers the two little armies were not ill-matched. Maurice by the end of May had 600–800 horse and a little

[6] *Correspondance de Philippe II*, III, 512–14.
[7] *L. and A.*, I, 71–2, 74; *Kronijk*, XVIII, 202–4; Bor, xxviii, fos. 2–3.

under 4,000 foot, of whom some 1,300 or 1,400 were English. Mansfelt may have started out with nearly 7,000 horse and foot, but they were in poor heart and deserted daily and in July Parma told Philip that he had not 4,000 men to defend the whole Rhine–Maas area. Besides, by the time Mansfelt's troops crossed the Maas, they found Maurice's men well entrenched on both banks of the Waal on the west side of Nijmegen, with a pontoon bridge linking the two camps. The position was too strong for them to assault and after staying a fortnight within a league of Nijmegen, and putting some victuals into the town, on 3 June they retired back again over the Maas. During the rest of June and the first half of July there were occasional desultory skirmishes and Maurice's cannon periodically bombarded the town, without doing much harm. Under cover of this, the vital work of building the new fort, Fort Knodsenburg, went slowly forward. Slowly, because the States of Gelderland were still sulking over the loss of Rheinberg and failed to provide enough pioneers and labourers.[8]

In the end it was Gelderland that lost most by the delay. After blocking the enemy's entry into the Betuwe by the new fort before Nijmegen, Maurice had intended to bar their entry into the Veluwe and the Overquarter by seizing the fort before Zutphen and building another one opposite Deventer. It was too much to hope, security among members of the States being what it was, that these intentions could be kept reasonably secret through all the long weeks while Fort Knodsenburg was building. And in fact, before the work was finished, the enemy did intercept a letter in which the Advocate of Utrecht, 'Floris Thin, had discoursed of all matters'. Besides this, the Nijmegen operations had cost the States over 100,000 florins (£10,000) in extraordinary disbursements and money was getting short. For these various reasons Maurice therefore abandoned – or, more exactly, postponed – his Zutphen and Deventer plans and towards the end of July 1590 broke up his camp and sent almost all his troops to their garrisons to rest and refresh themselves.[9]

[8] *L. and A.*, I, 72, 74–5, 87; II, 3–5, 614; *Correspondance de Philippe II,* III, 512.
[9] *L. and A.*, I, 74; II, 3, 5.

All of them, that is, except Vere's twelve English foot-
bands. These, with 200 more English from Flushing, 200
from Bergen, and sixty boats Maurice brought quietly to
Arnemuiden in mid-August for an attempt to surprise Sluys.
This project, too, had hung fire long enough for the enemy to
get wind of it. Sir Robert Sidney thought that the States of
Zeeland had held it up because the plan originated with one
of Leicester's old followers, Colonel Nicolaas Meetkerke, and
was to be carried out by the English – in supporting it was
Maurice perhaps trying to make amends for 1587? At all
events, the Count, too, roundly criticized the Zeeland States
and on 15 August dined in very friendly fashion with Sidney
at Flushing. Nevertheless this Sluys project had also to be
given up as heavy rains and rising waters made the town
inaccessible. Vere's men went back to their billets in Holland
and the others to their garrisons. With the enemy's forces
likewise dispersing, major operations practically ceased.[10]

There was, however, still quite a lot of local activity, much
of it by the English garrisons and in direct response to
Elizabeth's demands for something to be done to distract
Parma from France. From Ostend Sir John Conway, now that
the enemy garrisons were so depleted, repeatedly sent out
small raiding parties who burned houses and barns and swept
in cattle from the neighbouring parts of Flanders. At the end
of August, to the surprise of some of his more aggressive and
discontented officers, he himself led 600 men in a bold raid
along the coast past Nieupoort. They burned most of the little
villages between there and Veurne and destroyed a great
quantity of hay and corn. While waiting near the village of
Oost Dunkerke for the tide to ebb and allow them to get back
across Nieupoort haven, they had to fight a brisk action
against enemy troops from Nieupoort and Dunkirk. Although
they had to abandon some of their booty, they returned safely
to Ostend with 750 head of cattle, a few score sheep and pigs,
and some horses. Conway reckoned that they had done
£40,000 worth of damage. Meanwhile, after the abandonment of Maurice's Sluys project, 200 of the Flushing garrison
raided the less watery parts of northern Flanders, burning

[10] Ibid., 7–8, 70.

houses and crops and bringing back a good haul of cattle and other booty. Farther east, from Bergen and Breda the States' horsemen raided deep into northern Brabant, past Herentals and Diest and as far as Tienen (Tirlemont).[11]

Farther east still, Sir Francis Vere with 600–800 English foot and six of the States' horsebands, in a brilliantly executed little operation, marched through the Duchy of Cleves, relieved Lütteckhoven, near Essen, and took two other forts near Wesel. On his return he wrote to the States that, with a little reinforcement, he could recover Rheinberg and all the places held by the enemy on the Rhine below Wesel. Those places, however, lay outside the Netherlands in the Duchy of Cleves and an embassy from the Rhineland princes, Protestant and Catholic, had just summoned both Parma and the States to restore them to the Duke and withdraw all their troops from the territories of the Holy Roman Empire. The States, very conscious of the expense of maintaining and periodically relieving such distant outposts, were ready enough to hand them over to neutral garrisons. They made some difficulty over Schenkenschanz, which commanded the Rhine a few miles above Nijmegen, but they hardly so much as considered Vere's offer.[12]

Instead, in mid-September he and his ten English footbands were called back to help Count Maurice, who was now in the field again. The Count had with him twenty-four cannon and demi-cannon, the greatest siege train the States had ever had. But, as usual, he was very short of men. Even when Vere's 1,100 joined him and another 250 English came from the cautionary towns and 400 or more foot and 250–300 horse from Bergen, he still had only 600 or 700 horse and between 3,000 and 4,000 foot. Apart from the 2,000–3,000 Friesland troops pinned down there by Verdugo, this was the greatest field force that the States could scrape together then. However, the enemy could not produce even those numbers with Parma away in France and half their best remaining troops on the verge of mutiny for the pay that the King of Spain was so slow to provide. So Maurice and Vere were able

---

[11] Ibid., 9, 70, 101, 126, 129–38; *Correspondance de Philippe II*, III, 522–3.

[12] *L. and A.*, II, 48, 50, 746. Vere gives a full account of this operation in his *Commentaries*, pp. 10–7.

unmolested to clear the passage of the lower Maas by rapidly taking Hemert, Hedel, and Crèvecoeur, the only enemy posts left in the Bommelerwaard. That accomplished, they moved south of the Maas to undo Mansfelt's summer's work around Breda. They took Elsthout, which had both constricted nearby Heusden and given Geertruidenberg a link with 'sHertogenbosch; Ter Heyden, which had obstructed the passage of supplies to Breda; and finally on 7 October Steenbergen. Thereupon Maurice once again dismissed most of his little army and, apart from his abortive attempt to surprise Dunkirk a fortnight later, that was the end of his campaigning for the year. With the enemy also inactive, there was, as Bodley put it, 'in a manner cessation of arms'.[13]

In these campaigns of 1590 in the Netherlands Vere and the English auxiliary companies had played a part very similar to that played by Willoughby and his men in France in 1589. They had made it possible for the States' forces to keep the field, to take some advantage of the enemy's distractions and weakness, and to lay solid foundations for more substantial success next year. Maurice and Vere had almost completely freed and secured the frontiers of Holland and Utrecht by driving the enemy out of all his bridgeheads on the north bank of the Maas from Hedel westwards. Geertruidenberg still somewhat impeded their free use of the lower Maas, while 'sHertogenbosch, Megen, and Grave on the south side and Batenberg on the north bank more effectively barred the way farther upstream. Nevertheless, all these enemy places on or near the Maas were themselves coming under a steadily growing pressure, as was Nijmegen, the only place on either side of the Waal that was not yet in the States' hands. This free passage up and down the Waal, moreover, made it possible for the States to move their forces across their southern front from flank to flank, from Heusden to Nijmegen and then across to Sluys and back again to Heusden, with an ease and rapidity that the enemy could not hope to match, as Parma and Mansfelt well knew.

These Netherlands operations in 1590, despite the smallness of the allied field forces, thus did much to reassure the English

---

[13] *L. and A.*, II, 9–13, 20, 611; *Kronijk*, XVIII, 307–8; Bor, xxviii, fo. 8*v*.

about the prospects of their Dutch protégés. As we have seen, they had long believed that the United Provinces could hardly survive unless something were done 'to give a head to their headless body and some good form to their unshaped commonwealth'.[14] This, they had thought, could only be achieved by establishing, or re-establishing, the executive authority of the lord general and Council of State as laid down in the Treaty of 1585, by restoring to them their full powers to expend the monies voted by the States General and to command and order the military forces of all the Provinces. With this should go a general reconciliation between the Provinces and between the factions within the Provinces, in particular between the States and Leicester's former followers; a settlement of accounts between the States and the Queen so that the way would be clear for a full pay to be made to the Queen's troops and for the reform of the abuses among them of which the States so often complained; and some agreement for the restriction of Dutch trade with the enemy, at least to Spain and Portugal.

Sir John Norris had outlined this programme to the States of Holland and to the Council of State back in November 1588 and Thomas Bodley had dealt about it more lengthily with the States General in January and February 1589. Neither had made any headway; nor did the overseer of musters, James Digges, procure agreement over the accounts; nor Noël de Caron achieve much in Holland and Friesland and Utrecht; nor Richard Allen at Utrecht, for the better treatment of Leicester's unfortunate adherents.[15] So, in discussions with Ortel, the States' agent in England, a new approach was considered whereby the settlement of the accounts would be left to Lord Burgh, Bodley, and Gilpin in the Netherlands while the States sent commissioners over to discuss with the Queen and her Council the reform of the United Provinces' government, the revision of the 1585 Treaty, and the regulation of Dutch westward trade.[16] Then, in April 1589, the loss of Geertruidenberg brought a new

---

[14] S. P. Holland, xxxv, fos. 302–7.

[15] For these various negotiations, January to July 1589 – *Cal. S. P. Foreign*, XXIII, vi–xviii, xxvii–xxxv.

[16] Ibid., pp. 137–8, 143–7, 191–2, 205; *H. M. C., Ancaster MSS*, pp. 268–70.

urgency to these problems and to English anxieties. So the Queen resolved that, instead of waiting for the States to send commissioners to her, she would take Ortel's advice and send 'a person of countenance' to them. The man chosen was Lord Buckhurst, who was thought to be particularly acceptable to the States – perhaps because he had fallen foul of Leicester during an earlier mission. [17] The States, however, had already decided to send three envoys – Jacob van Egmont, Sebastian van Loosen, and Jacob Valcke – to England. When the Queen and Council learned of this, they immediately jumped to the conclusion that the three envoys would come fully empowered. For had not Oldenbarnevelt recently spoken to Bodley in unusually friendly fashion of his desire to discuss 'the redress of all matters'? Buckhurst's mission was accordingly cancelled as unnecessary. [18]

Egmont and his colleagues had audience with Elizabeth on 23 May 1589 and began discussions with the Privy Council next day. At once it became evident that their commission was much narrower than the Queen had hoped. Their real and primary task was to seek redress for Dutch ships and goods seized by the English navy or privateers. While they were at it, they were in addition to reiterate all the old complaints about the weakness, unavailability, and abuses of the English auxiliary forces and to press for the prompt return of those companies that Norris had taken to Portugal. They were also provided with a lengthy justification of the States' past conduct and were to seek from the Queen a public declaration disavowing all those in the Provinces who formed or encouraged factions against the States' authority. But they had no powers to treat about important matters such as the remedying of the disorders in the Provinces' government, the provision of adequate field forces, or the reform of defects in the 1585 Treaty. During the next two or three weeks Buckhurst and other Councillors plied them with a host of detailed questions on these matters, only to receive answers that were vague to the point of impertinence. [19]

[17] *Cal. S. P. Foreign*, XXIII, 210, 235, 265.

[18] Ibid., pp. 218–19, 257, 264; *Resolutiën der Staten Generaal*, VI, 391–2, 395–6; *Kronijk*, XVI, 332–4, 378–90.

[19] *Cal. S. P. Foreign*, XXIII, 283, 287, 294–6, 309–10; Bor, xxvi, fos. 19–22.

Clearly little was to be achieved by negotiating with these envoys unless their commission were greatly expanded. So on 16 June the Queen instructed Bodley to require the States General to send Egmont and his colleagues full powers to deal with all these important questions. With these instructions went a list of 'general heads of matters fit to be treated between the Queen and the United Provinces' and lengthy notes elaborating those matters in greater detail. Bodley was to communicate the 'general heads' to the States General and to use the notes for his own guidance in less formal discussions.[20] Taken together, the notes and the general heads provided something very like a comprehensive statement of English policy towards the United Provinces at that time. The particular notes suggested that so long as the Queen kept her 5,000 footmen and 1,000 horsemen in the Netherlands, the States should be bound on their part to maintain, and to find money to pay, ordinary garrisons of at least 20,000 foot and 1,400 horse and to put into the field for four months every summer 2,000 horse and 7,000 foot. The civil and military authority of Her Majesty's general and the Council of State should be as ample as that enjoyed by any governor-general in Charles V's time. They should have 'the entire and absolute managing of all their contributions, moyens, convoys, and licences' and Her Majesty's general should have 'a voice negative' in the Council upon questions concerning her or her subjects. The Council's instructions should be approved by her and each Province should give its deputies in the States General full powers to treat and conclude with her, her general, and the Council of State on all matters except contributions and impositions. There was a long list of specific proposals for clearing accounts, for the better treatment of the English troops and for the better ordering of both them and the States' forces in matters of discipline, pay, and the avoidance of fraud.

When, however, Bodley communicated his instructions early in July 1589, the States General proved no less evasive than their envoys and, when pressed, fell back upon their stock delaying tactics of referring the matter to their principals, the

---

[20] *Cal. S. P. Foreign,* XXIII, 304–8, 325, 328–9, 333.

individual Provinces. Eventually, on 6 August they wrote to the Queen that they could not enlarge their envoys' commission and that they were recalling them as they needed their advice upon Bodley's proposals.[21] For various reasons Egmont, Loosen, and Valcke did not in fact leave England until mid-October. In the interval they discussed with the Privy Council and the judge of the Admiralty Court forty and more cases of seizures of Dutch ships and goods at sea or in English ports. They conferred with James Digges and were informed of the new orders that he was to take over for the payment of the English companies' weekly lendings by poll, that is only for those numbers actually present at the musters. They answered Willoughby's protests over the references to him in the States' placart against the Geertruidenberg garrison and they protested in their turn at the charges that he made against Oldenbarnevelt and Aerssens in the angry pamphlet he published in July. Upon leaving they were promised that the Queen would send over the desired declaration against factions – to be published when the States had answered Bodley's articles and after Buckhurst had settled all differences between them and the English.[22]

For it was to the idea of a mission by Buckhurst that the English government now turned again. Not very enthusiastically, perhaps: for in the discussions that went on all through the autumn and winter of 1589–90 there was a noticeable lack of urgency, besides some division of opinion among the Queen's advisers. There was once again some talk about the possibility of giving the States aid in money instead of men and even of making some Netherlands nobleman governor-general rather than appointing an English successor to Willoughby, who had ceased to be lord general at the end of July 1589. Burghley, having failed to persuade Willoughby to return to his post, had in August sounded Lord Burgh with equal lack of success. But by then Walsingham was already listing Count Maurice and Count Hohenlohe along with

[21] Ibid., pp. 369–70, 372–3; *L. and A.*, I, 254, 265; *Resolutiën der Staten Generaal*, VI, 402, 404; *Kronijk*, XVII, 32–40, 56–62.

[22] *L. and A.*, I, 257, 264, 272–80, 282–4. See also their correspondence in *Kronijk*, XVIII, 15–37, 62–7, 74–6.

Willoughby ('disliked of'), Lord Grey ('poor'), and Sir John Norris ('not in grace here'). In November a draft of instructions for Buckhurst contained the proposal that the States should restore their ancient form of government in some well-chosen head with a limited authority and assisted by a Council of State. In January it was suggested that a governor be chosen annually with the Queen's consent and that he and the Council of State should be given a sufficient authority and sole management of the revenues for the wars. And Walsingham, during these last weeks of his life, often discussed with Wilkes the possibility of getting the Queen to appoint Count Maurice as her lieutenant.[23]

It looks as if Walsingham may have half-persuaded the Queen. For her failure to appoint a successor to Willoughby suggests that she was already, as we know she was a few months later, resolved 'not to be at the charges of the maintenance of a general to command her forces and to exercise the authority granted by the Treaty'.[24] What is more, there is at least a hint that she was ready to consider the logical next step, the appointment of a Netherlander as governor. For at the end of December 1589 she had sent Deventer, now released and exiled from Utrecht, back to Holland with instructions to ask the States, Maurice, and Hohenlohe for advice on how to heal their divisions and improve their government; and to suggest that the Provinces might choose a governor to direct their public affairs and command her forces as well as theirs. The much hated Deventer was hardly the man to enhance Hohenlohe's already slender chances,[25] but Maurice's prospects were improving rapidly. He was already stadholder of Holland and Zeeland and was well on the way to being chosen stadholder of Utrecht, Gelderland, and Overijssel as well, while Holland and Zeeland were appointing a privy council to aid and advise him. Supported – or, according to most observers, governed – by Holland's Advocate Oldenbarnevelt, he stood head and

---

[23] *Cal. S. P. Foreign*, XXIII, 288; *L. and A.*, I, 78, 213, 268, 296, 306; II, 196.

[24] Ibid., II, 196; S. P. Holland, xxxviii, fo. 123. In February 1590 someone set down some notes to show how the Queen might have a general there without increase of charge – Cotton MSS, Galba D, vii, fo. 51.

[25] *L. and A.*, I, 287–8, 302–4, 311.

shoulders above all other possible candidates.[26] All this took some of the urgency out of the question of reforming the Provinces government. Indeed, on 6 March Gilpin wrote that the best plan would be to let the States run their course awhile. Their doings were now liked by their inferiors, while the enemy was too troubled by French actions to intend them much harm. In any event, he advised, Buckhurst should not come over until some less prestigious envoy had tested the prospects by presenting the Queen's demands in writing both to the States General and to the States of the various Provinces.[27]

It may have been partly in response to Gilpin's advice that on 15 March instructions were sent to Bodley to upbraid the States very sharply for their failure to answer the various important questions that had been presented to them over the past year or more, in particular about the Council of State's authority and the full observance of the 1585 Treaty. There were, however, other more cogent reasons for this move. At the end of January Lyly had reported from France the intercepting of letters to Mendoza about Spanish designs in Brittany. Then in February some of the Bergen troops captured a secretary of the Duke of Lorraine. On him were found letters in which the King of Spain told Parma, Mendoza, Tassis, and others of his negotiations with the Pope for sending aid on a large scale to the League in France during the coming summer. A figure of 40,000–50,000 horse and foot was mentioned as a desirable minimum. These letters were deciphered by Ste. Aldegonde, the former governor of Antwerp, and late in February or early in March he brought them and his decipherings for the Queen to see before he went on to show them to Henry IV.

Elizabeth therefore knew by early March that she might soon be faced by large and hardly deniable appeals for help from the French King. This made it more than ever necessary for her to limit her commitments in the Netherlands and to ensure that the Provinces had a government and forces able at least to hold their own without further English help.

---

[26] Ibid., 29, 45, 57.
[27] Ibid., 309.

Moreover, there were circumstantial rumours that Philip II, with his heart now set upon France, might try to buy off the United Provinces even at the price of offering them religious toleration. There was perhaps little likelihood that such offers would be made or, if made, would tempt the States, but news of them might well set off dangerous backslidings in weak, exposed, and largely Catholic Provinces such as Utrecht and Gelderland. The strengthening of the Provinces' government, and that quickly, thus appeared once again as an urgent necessity. Moreover at the end of April the States' mild and almost apologetic replies to Bodley's upbraiding suggested that they really were prepared, as they professed to be, to welcome the 'person of countenance' Her Majesty wished to send them. The time seemed ripe for Buckhurst and on 1 May the Privy Council instructed Bodley to inform the States General that he would be coming over soon.[28]

From the instructions drafted about this time it is clear that Buckhurst's mission would now have two main purposes. First and foremost he was to seek to reduce the Queen's military and financial commitments, provided he found the Provinces capable of defending themselves with that reduced English help. Second, he was to persuade the States to agree to an 'Explanation' of the 1585 Treaty that would remedy its defects and omissions; would define both parties' obligations (e.g. the size of the States' garrisons and field forces as well as the numbers of the English auxiliary troops); would settle past accounts and guarantee repayment of the Queen's expenses; and above all, would remedy the weakness of the Provinces' government by restoring full executive authority to the Queen's lord general and the Council of State.[29]

The inclusion of the Queen's lord general once again is at first sight rather surprising. Possibly the death of Walsingham on 6 April and the resulting increase of Burghley's activity in

[28] Ibid., 147, 324–6, 333, 573–8, 591; Cotton MSS., Galba D, vii. fo. 87; S. P. Domestic, ccxxxi, no. 15; *Kronijk,* XVIII, 61–3; *Resolutiën der Staten Generaal,* VI, 18–9; F. van Kalken and T. Jonckheere, *Marnix de Ste. Aldegonde,* pp. 55–6.

[29] *L. and A.,* I, 334–5. For the dating of these and later instructions, and for Wilkes's mission that followed – R. B. Wernham, 'The Mission of Thomas Wilkes to the United Provinces in 1590', in *Essays presented to Sir Hilary Jenkinson* (ed. J. Conway Davies), pp. 423–55.

foreign affairs had something to do with it.[30] For, while Walsingham seems to have been increasingly attracted to the idea of appointing Count Maurice as the Queen's lieutenant, Burghley clearly preferred an Englishman for that office. We may perhaps also detect here the influence of Thomas Wilkes. He had recent experience of the Netherlands affairs as Elizabeth's representative in the Dutch Council of State in 1586-7. With Buckhurst, however, he had fallen foul of Leicester in 1587 and it had taken him two years to gain the Queen's forgiveness. But in August 1589 he had returned to his duties as a clerk of the Privy Council. His knowledge of the Netherlands and his past links with Buckhurst ensured respect for his opinions, all the more perhaps 'because there are few of the [Privy] Council that understand the state of the Low Countries'. And as he showed now in various memorials to Burghley, Hatton, and Buckhurst, it was his very firm opinion that efficient executive authority could not be restored in the Provinces unless an English lord general was in place there to exercise the powers vested in him and the Council of State by the 1585 Treaty. Nor did he believe that this was a time to talk of reducing the Queen's commitment there.[31]

Now Burghley, Hatton, and Buckhurst were the three Councillors who, under the Queen, had charge of these Netherlands negotiations.[32] By convincing them Wilkes would go far towards getting his views adopted. And no doubt the task of convincing them, and the Queen, was made all the easier by the news from Lyly that Ste. Aldegonde was not only showing the King of France his decipherings but also suggesting to him and to Marshal Biron that the United Provinces might transfer themselves from Elizabeth's protection to Henry's. That news gave point to Wilkes's argument that, unless Her Majesty had an English lord general in place to give her a hold upon the Provinces' government, she would probably never recover what she had spent in defending them.

[30] After Walsingham's death the Secretary's office remained vacant until the appointment of Sir Robert Cecil in 1596. During those years the work of the Secretary was performed by Burghley with increasing help from Sir Robert.

[31] *Acts P. C.*, XVIII, 11; *L. and A.*, I, 316-18, 329-31.

[32] Wilkes and Bodley during the summer addressed their official letters to these three and Wilkes once referred to Hatton 'and the other two lords in commission for these causes'-ibid., II, 207.

It looks, too, as if it was a further development in this Ste. Aldegonde affair that produced the next turn in English policy and sent Thomas Wilkes off to the Hague instead of Lord Buckhurst. On 11 May Lyly reported that on the previous day Justinus of Nassau, Maurice's illegitimate half-brother and Admiral of Zeeland, had arrived in Henry IV's camp. His ostensible mission was to congratulate the King, somewhat belatedly, upon the victory at Ivry on 4 March. But Lyly strongly suspected that 'this Count de Nassau bastard' had really come from Maurice to follow up the earlier overtures of Ste. Aldegonde. Henry, perhaps, was hardly in a position to yield to such temptation and Lyly felt sure that it was not the work of the States, who would 'lose their greatness *ipso facto* by calling in a protector that is a King, French, and upon the same continent' for that 'must turn their authority into obedience'. What he suspected was that Viliers (Pierre de l'Oyseleur), 'our unnatural enemy', finding that Oldenbarnevelt ruled in the States and that the English amity did not serve his own purposes, was seeking to advance Count Maurice and that Maurice, whose marriage was motioned in France, hoped by becoming the King's lieutenant to 'become master where now he serveth'.[33]

Doubtless much of this was guesswork. Yet only a few months earlier Paul Buys had remarked to Gilpin that Maurice, though he dared not say anything, was growing weary of the present proceedings in the Provinces. And if there should prove to be truth in Lyly's guesses, then those Provinces might soon be split again between rival factions. Moreover, it was probably known by now that Richardot, who had gone on a mission from Parma to Philip and who had long been expected to be the bearer of the King's peace offers, was at last on his way back to Brussels, where an Imperial peace embassy was also expected.[34] If those offers were to be

---

[33] Ibid., I, 339, 361–6. The part of Ste. Aldegonde's correspondence printed in *Kronijk*, XVIII, 62–3, 130–1, 193–6, 204–8, 252–4, does not sound very sinister, though he did quote with approval the late Prince of Orange's opinion 'que la période où la catastrophe de nos maux gisait en cela quand l'interêt de notre cause serait tellement conjoint avec celui de la France que le Roi Très-Chrétien voudrait embrasser la guerre contre l'Espagne' – ibid., p. 195.

[34] *L. and A.*, I, 300, 591, 596. Richardot reached Spa on 13 June – Lansdowne MSS, lxiii, no. 44.

made when the Provinces were again torn by faction, they might well lead, and lead quickly, to their submission not to France but to Spain. Clearly Elizabeth now needed urgently to find out what truth there was in Lyly's guesses and, if truth there were, then to countermine such courses by using and binding to herself any leaders of the States, especially Oldenbarnevelt, who might oppose them. For this what was required was a skilled diplomatist, well informed about the Netherlands, rather than an impressive embassy by some 'person of countenance'.

And, sure enough, on 10 May Windebank told Burghley that the Queen had decided to send Wilkes instead of Buckhurst. Four days later Burghley instructed Bodley to inform the States General of the change. He might excuse it on the somewhat contradictory grounds that Buckhurst was indisposed and that as lord-lieutenant of Sussex he was indispensable if the armada preparing in Spain should come against England or to Le Havre. At the same time Bodley was to express the Queen's astonished displeasure at hearing, from Henry IV himself, of the offers made by Ste. Aldegonde, which she could not believe the States had authorized.[35] This would begin the countermining by bringing the matter into the open and putting the States and others upon their guard.

About the same time Wilkes was provided with a revised version of the instructions that had been drafted for Buckhurst.[36] A large part of these very lengthy and detailed instructions, part from the Queen and part from the Privy Council, remained unchanged. But there were certain substantial omissions, and some additions, which introduced a marked shift of emphasis. Thus the clauses about reducing the numbers of the English auxiliary forces or giving money instead of men were now omitted. For this was no time to suggest any diminution of England's commitment to the Dutch cause. On the other hand, new clauses explained that,

[35] Harleian MSS, 6995, no. 31; Cotton MSS, Galba D, vii, fo. 129; *L. and A.*, I, 338–9; *Resolutiën der Staten Generaal*, VII, 70–1. On 11 May Burghley had still been expecting that Buckhurst would go – Cotton MSS, Galba D, vii, fo.138.

[36] *L. and A.*, I, 340–2; also Wilkes's notes on his instructions and manner of proceeding – ibid., 345–7.

while treaty revision, the powers of the Queen's governor-general and the Council of State, the size of the States' garrisons and field forces, the settlement of accounts, the repair of Ostend's sea defences, restraints on westward trade, and all the other long-agitated questions remained the official and ostensible substance of Wilkes's mission, it had two other secret and more urgent purposes.

The first of these secret purposes was to discover the truth about the overture to the French King and to countermine it by using Wilkes's skill and credit with those opposed to its promoters, especially by trying to win Oldenbarnevelt and other leading men to be at the Queen's devotion – in some rough notes made about this time, possibly by Wilkes himself, it had been suggested that £300 a year, to be saved out of the troops' checks, might be bestowed in rewards and pensions to the four, five, or six most influential members of the States.[37]

The second, and even more important, secret purpose concerned the reports that Philip II was about to offer peace terms to the Provinces and that the Pope had granted him a dispensation to include the free exercise of their religion among those terms. The point of religion had hitherto been the only impediment to such a peace, and the Queen feared that, although the United Provinces were bound by the 1585 Treaty not to make peace without her consent, they might be sufficiently alienated from their former devotion to her to conclude an agreement with Spain upon such terms. So Wilkes's most important task was to observe and report what was done in this matter and to seek by all means possible to impeach it. To ease his negotiations he might give the States a declaration to publish in which the Queen disavowed all who stirred factions against them. He was also to publish, and communicate to them, certain new ordinances and instructions for the better conduct of the English troops' musters and payments.

These instructions and Wilkes's credentials, passport, and warrants were all completed and sealed by 28 May[38] and he

[37] Ibid., 336.
[38] Ibid., 342. The warrant for his entertainment allowed him 60*s.* a day, with an advance of £80 – S. O. Docquets, I, fo. 242*v.* There seems to be no record at all of his commission.

lost no time in getting on his way. Despite calms and light winds he was at Flushing by 4 June and at The Hague four days later. From that point onwards it becomes possible to follow the course of his negotiations in quite unusual detail. The originals of almost all the letters that he, Bodley, and Gilpin wrote home, and the minutes of those written to him by Burghley, are either among the State Papers in the Public Record Office or in the British Library. There, too, are copies or originals of the various writings which he and Bodley exchanged with the States General – these, together with the States' resolutions about them are all recorded in the registers of the States General, while a number of them were printed in full as long ago as 1862. Wilkes's letters to Sir Robert Sidney, just come over as governor of Flushing, are also in print. In addition to all this there is Wilkes's own letter-book, which contains not only his copies of his letters to the English and Dutch governments but also his notes of more private talks with various Dutch statesmen and officials – a very rare type of record for an Elizabethan embassy.[39]

With all this wealth of evidence it may seem surprising that, apart from a jeer or two from Motley, this embassy went until lately virtually unnoticed by historians. The fact is, however, that so far as the official and ostensible purposes of his mission were concerned Wilkes achieved little or nothing more than his predecessors. 'A sudden lameness in my arms and legs' forced him to defer his first audience until 13 June. On that day, limping along with the aid of a staff, he presented his letters of credence to the States General, outlined the official reasons for his coming, and asked that some of the States be appointed to treat with himself and Bodley, whom the Queen had joined in commission with him.[40] Three days later he presented to them, in writing as they requested, those points of his instructions that concerned the English troops' musters and discipline. With these he also presented the Privy Council's new musters ordinances. He and Bodley considered

[39] S. P. Holland, xxxvii and xxxviii; Cotton MSS, Galba D. vii; Harleian MSS, cclxxxvii; *Resolutiën der Staten Generaal*, VII; *Kronijk*, XVIII, 213 ff.; *Letters and Memorials of State* (ed. A. Collins, 1746), I, 301–7; *H. M. C., De L'Isle and Dudley MSS*, I, 107–10; S. P. Archives, xci, fos. 177–211.

[40] For a fuller account of these negotiations – R. B. Wernham, 'The Mission of Thomas Wilkes', pp. 439 ff. and references there.

that these matters would best sound the States' attitude to their mission in general. The results were not encouraging. It was 13 July before the States replied, and then with what was in effect an all-round refusal. On 17 July Wilkes and Bodley tried again. This time they presented the proposals about the restraints upon Dutch trade to Spain and Portugal. They also showed the Queen's declaration against factions. Again the States were uncooperative. They thought the proposed restraints on trade excessively harsh and they would promise no favour or leniency to Leicester's disgraced or banished followers. Wilkes therefore refused to deliver the declaration against factions and his negotiations came very near to deadlock. On 20 and 25 July he communicated in writing the remaining points of his instructions, including those concerning the power of the Queen's general and Council of State. These the States found altogether too important and fundamental to be resolved upon without consulting their principals. So, once again, they referred everything back to the Provinces. The Provinces were unlikely to answer before late September or October and whatever resolution the States General then made upon their answers would be final and not alterable by further argument. Wilkes was thus 'in a manner brought to a *non plus*' and on 29 July he wrote to Burghley begging to be called home. His request was promptly granted and on 18 August he took his formal leave of the States. Four days later he sailed from Brielle for England. So far as the outward and ostensible purposes of his mission were concerned, he came home empty-handed.

In other and less obvious ways, nevertheless, his mission marked a turning-point in Elizabeth's policy, or at least in her attitude, towards the Netherlands. He had at first suspected, as had the Queen herself, that the States' delays were due simply to their 'wandering dispositions' and French leanings, to the hope that Henry IV would soon take Paris, crush the League, and be able to think seriously about replacing Elizabeth as their protector. Conversations with Valcke, Aerssens, and Oldenbarnevelt in mid-June, however, radically altered his opinion. All three assured him of their own and the Provinces' devotion to Her Majesty, but blamed their past disorders upon former English governors' lack of political skill and ignorance of their affairs, or as Oldenbarnevelt put it bluntly, upon the violent proceedings of Leicester and Willoughby. They feared that a new English governor might only bring them back the old troubles. All three, moreover, emphasized how much better things now were, with the States' authority generally accepted, the English troops more available and more popular than for several years, and Vere, Lord Burgh, and the new governor of Flushing, Sir Robert Sidney, particularly well liked. Most significantly, too, Oldenbarnevelt had shown himself only lukewarm about publishing the Queen's declaration against factions. It might do good but, as all their divisions were now healed, it was no longer necessary. This betokened a new confidence and unity, and other signs pointed the same way. The growing prestige of Count Maurice, now stadholder of five of the six Provinces, and his close co-operation with Oldenbarnevelt and the States of Holland, were already providing a real and effective central authority to remedy the confusion that had arisen in past years from the multiplicity and equality of provincial, municipal, and personal commands of which the English had so often complained.[41]

All this became so clear to Wilkes that on 10 July he wrote to Burghley suggesting that if Her Majesty would give Count Maurice

the title of her Lieutenant-General to command with the Council of State as by the Contract is provided, and to commit the leading of her auxiliary succours in the nature of a regiment to some man of meaner quality, as the gentleman that now commandeth them in the field [Sir Francis Vere] or to Sir John Norris, there would not only not follow any prejudice thereby to Her Majesty (as things may be handled) but rather good, for that the States in that respect might be drawn to yield Her Majesty satisfaction in all matters of most importance required by Her Majesty of them.

And to tie the Count even more closely to her, she might well make him a Knight of the Garter.[42]

In this Wilkes was moving too fast for the Queen. After discussing his proposal with Burghley, Hatton, and some

---

[41] *L. and A.*, I, 351–6; II, 193–6.
[42] S. P. Holland, xxxviii, fo. 78.

others, she instructed Burghley to reply on 16 July that, while she did not dislike Maurice's growing credit and was willing to show him favour, she would not hear of appointing him as her lieutenant. Burghley himself now professed not to mislike such an appointment. He thought, however, that as it was unacceptable to Her Majesty, the best course would be to leave Maurice in his governments and to make a new bargain with the States whereby, as Ortel had once suggested, the Queen would give them 'a sum of money in commodities of the realm' instead of the great sums that she now paid to her auxiliary companies. The States could probably do more with half the money than was now done with the whole. Accordingly, and by the Queen's direction, Burghley told Wilkes to try 'obliquely to procure some offer of this nature by the States'.[43]

When, however, Wilkes sounded Oldenbarnevelt, who had inspired Ortel's original suggestion of providing money instead of men, he found the idea no longer favoured. Apparently Oldenbarnevelt suspected that the money might be paid for one half-year and then no more. Rumours – circumstantial, but ill-founded on this occasion – that the Queen was again treating for peace with Spain doubtless strengthened, if they did not beget, his doubts. Anyway, he argued that the show of Her Majesty's name and countenance was as beneficial to them as the succour itself and that much the best and most convincing demonstration of her support was the presence in the Netherlands of her general and a settled English army.

On the same grounds Oldenbarnevelt altogether rejected the suggestion of appointing Maurice as the Queen's lieutenant, when Wilkes tentatively put it forward unofficially and as his own idea. The fact was that the States and chief persons generally, grown greatly ambitious 'by the usurpation of their pretended sovereignty', would never suffer the Count to possess the authority granted by the 1585 Treaty to the governor and which they had refused to Her Majesty. They were afraid that by yielding that authority they would be bridled in their own government.[44] When they had made that

[43] Ibid., fo. 61, summarized in *L. and A.*, II, 197, 225.
[44] Ibid., 190, 224–5.

Treaty, so soon after William the Silent's death, most of them had still found it hard to conceive of sovereignty as other than personal, of their sovereign as other than a single person, a prince; and when Elizabeth refused to become their prince, they had still made Leicester their governor-general. That experience had brought about their final disillusionment with princely rule and had driven them to develop their own instruments of government, cumbrous and peculiar but by 1590 becoming increasingly effective. And, having tasted the sweetness of liberty and the temptations of power, they were determined never again to surrender them to kingly rule, whether Spanish, French, English, or even native Netherlandish.

This ruled out any likelihood of the States accepting Maurice as their governor-general, according to the 1585 Treaty or otherwise. It equally ruled out any real likelihood of the States transferring their allegiance to the King of France. They might use hints of offering their sovereignty as bait to hook his affections towards them. They might encourage the Queen of England to believe that they inclined to France: it would improve their bargaining position. They might even turn blind eyes to intrigues and propaganda by those who did favour a French course. But so long as they could defend their independence, they would never again become subjects of any monarch; or if they did, it would be with such strings and conditions 'as they will always be the masters and he have but the show of their sovereignty'. So Elizabeth, Wilkes was now convinced, might rest assured that the States would never become French and that so long as they had to fight for their independence they would never risk the loss of England's succour.[45]

For the same reasons the Queen need not fear that they would listen to the peace proposals which she heard that Richardot had now brought back from Madrid. Among these, she understood, was an offer that it should 'be lawful for them [the Dutch] both in their own Provinces to have exercise of their religion and others that have been banished to return to their native countries with freedom of religion'. That, as we have seen, was especially calculated to alarm her, all the more as intercepted letters from Moreo to the Spanish Secretary, Idiaquez, urged peace with the Dutch as a means to concentrating all forces upon France and pointed out that once Philip II had France at his commandment he could easily subject the Netherlands. Accordingly Burghley in his letter of 16 July had instructed Wilkes and Bodley to do all they could to secure the rejection of any such offers. He had deployed for them a whole broadside of arguments, but insisted, too, that they must work underhand and not appear too earnest. At the same time, in all their negotiations they should for a season deal calmly and 'doulcelie' with the States so as to retain them in good terms towards Her Majesty and in dislike of the Spanish faction.[46]

These instructions point the truth of Wilkes's remark that few of the Privy Council understood the state of the Low Countries. They show how far the Queen and most of her advisers were out of touch with the realities of Dutch opinion. The solid achievement of Wilkes's mission was to give her and them a better understanding, to make them better aware of those realities. Bodley and Gilpin were too close to things for their weekly or fortnightly despatches to bring home clearly the long-term trends and changes. Wilkes, who knew the Provinces well but had not seen them for three years, was able to put the picture in its true and changed perspective.

On the whole that picture was reassuring. The States, merchants, and chief men were quite unwilling to subject themselves to Spain or France or even to Count Maurice, though they were ready enough to co-operate both with the Count and with the English commanders. They meant to run their government themselves and the events of 1590 began to suggest that they were capable of doing so effectively at least so long as the Spaniards were distracted by the affairs of France. Bodley, it is true, still had doubts that 'the poorer sort' were so burdened with taxes as to be 'almost indifferent to embrace any change'. He also thought that 'the discontentments are so many among their martial people and such variances grown between province and province, the Council

---

[46] Ibid., 212.

of State and the General States, and some of the chiefest towns of Holland, that many men affirm, if the enemy for a time would surcease his wars, their state would come to ruin by civil distraction.'[47]

It does seem, however, that Bodley was making mountains out of molehills and that his pessimism was unduly influenced by memories of past unpleasantness and by the opinions of disgruntled men outside, or even opposed to, the States' government. The mutinies – at Schenkenschanz, Liefkenshoek, Wijk, Lillo, and Zwartesluis – had all been dealt with fairly easily six months or more ago; the controversies in Holland were appeased for the time being in October 1589; five Provinces had accepted or were soon to accept Maurice as their stadholder and Maurice was on reasonably good terms with the sixth stadholder, his cousin William Louis; and if some Councillors of State grumbled at the States' encroachments, they were by no means prepared to translate grumbling into hostile action. Nor did Wilkes share Bodley's fears that the heavy impositions and mislike of the States' government might drive the people to welcome a peace upon any reasonable offers. The impositions were now, by use, borne without grudging and the heaviest, being upon wine, did not touch the poor man, while the States' government was now accepted and settled as never before since their troubles began.[48] Moreover, at the end of October Bodley sent over copies of intercepted letters from Philip II to his ambassador with the Emperor, letters which revealed that he was in fact very far from considering any peace terms that included religious toleration. There was manifestly no likelihood of the 'reasonable offers' that Bodley thought might have moved the populace to welcome a peace.[49]

Elizabeth could therefore feel reasonably confident in taking Wilkes's advice, given not long before he came home, that the wisest course would be to 'leave things as they were at my arrival here; which, although they be not in such order as they should be, yet are they in course to continue without danger until the States themselves upon some other accident

[47] R. B. Wernham, 'The Mission of Thomas Wilkes', p. 454.
[48] *L. and A.*, I, 21–3, 64, 351; II, 214.
[49] Ibid., I, 738–40; II, 744.

may be drawn to seek Her Majesty and make offer unto her of that which she now demandeth'.[50] It was the same advice that Gilpin had given on 6 March. It meant steering English policy on to a new course, giving up at least for the time any idea of treaty revision, of restoring the authority of the Queen's general and the Council of State or even sending over a new general or of settling the accounts. But Elizabeth had probably grown lukewarm already towards all these, except the last. And with the struggle for western Europe likely to reach its supreme crisis in 1591, she must have sighed with relief at knowing that the United Provinces should be able to manage without either her 'counsel' or her 'extraordinary assistance'.

[50] S. P. Archives, xci, fo. 198.

234

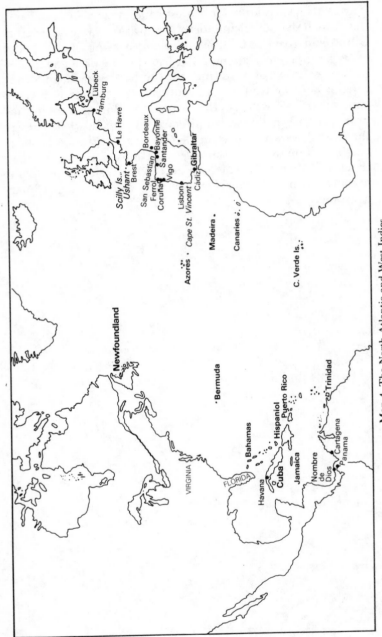

Map 4. The North Atlantic and West Indies.

# XI

# The War at Sea:
# Queen's Ships and Privateers

In both France and the Netherlands during 1589 and 1590 the central problem for Spain's enemies had been the inadequacy of the forces at their disposal. On what might be called the third front, in the war at sea, the trouble was not so much lack of forces. The Queen's navy royal was admittedly small, no more than a couple of dozen fighting ships and half a dozen pinnaces. But each year after the defeat of the 1588 Armada at least 100, in some years perhaps 200, ships fitted out by the Queen's subjects were at sea privateering and perhaps a dozen or more of these were sizeable and well-armed vessels capable of fighting alongside the Queen's warships against the galleons of Spain.[1] The trouble in the sea war was that a sixteenth-century government lacked the power to harness this private enterprise, operating primarily for profit, to a national strategic purpose. In any case, of course, from the assassination of Henry III of France in July 1589 onwards the diversion of the English government's resources to bolstering up his Protestant successor with both men and money ruled out any renewed attempt either to seize the Azores or to 'light a fire in the King of Spain's own house', a strategy already largely discredited by the failure of Norris and Drake's ambitious expedition.

So from that time forward the Queen and her advisers perforce contented themselves with the more or less self-financing naval strategy of sending out small squadrons of the royal warships to cruise around the Azores and between the Azores and Spain. In those waters they might hope to intercept the great carracks from the Portuguese East Indies with their rich cargoes of silks and spices or, better still, vessels of the West Indian fleets bringing the annual tribute of silver from the American mines.

---

[1] K. R. Andrews, *Elizabethan Privateering*, pp. 4–5.

Sir John Hawkins had been for years advocating attacking Spain by this 'method of Jason by fetching away his golden fleece'.[2] Now, as soon as the Privy Council discovered that Norris and Drake's force was incapable of setting forth again 'to destroy the King of Spain's ships and to intercept his fleet coming out of the Indies', they prepared to despatch Sir Martin Frobisher with two of the Queen's ships, a pinnace, and Hawkins's 200-ton privateer *Repentance* (renamed more cheerfully at the Queen's bidding as the *Dainty*). Frobisher's departure was delayed until mid-September by anxiety about Henry IV's position in Normandy. So instead of making for the Azores, he sailed straight for Cape St Vincent, the nearest point for intercepting the American convoy that was due to arrive immediately. There, although he was already too late for the East Indian carracks, he would, as it were, field at long-stop behind the Earl of Cumberland who, with the Queen's *Victory* and two 60-ton ships and a carvel of his own, was already at the Azores on a privateering venture.[3]

Cumberland[4] had arrived off Angra, on the middlemost island of Terceira, at the end of August, only a week after the homebound East Indian carracks had passed by that port on their way to Lisbon, which they reached safely in the first week of September. Then after taking the town of Horta on the island of Fayal, he was driven back by gales as far as St Michael's, the easternmost island of the Azores chain. Beating back westwards, in early October he missed by a mere two days six storm-beaten galleons bearing home four million ducats in silver and gold from Spanish America. A few days later, on 9 October he arrived off Angra just too late to catch another fifteen storm-battered vessels of the American convoy as they slipped into that well-defended harbour. Shortage of fresh water forced him to abandon his prey and then on 29 October to set sail for home. Driven as far north-west as

---

[2] The phrase is Fulke Greville's – *Life of Sir Philip Sidney* (ed. Nowell Smith, 1907), p. 90.

[3] For Frobisher, see S. P. Domestic, ccxxv, nos. 28, 32, 74; ccxxx, no. 92; *L. and A.*, I, 473, 512–13, 609; *Monson's Tracts,* I, 233–9; Hakluyt, V, 26–7.

[4] For Cumberland, see Hakluyt, IV, 355–80; V, 21–6; *Monson's Tracts,* I, 226–39; II, 325; *Cal. S. P. Venetian*, VIII, 467, 472; *L. and A.*, I, 609; *Further Voyages*, lxiii–lxiv; G. C. Williamson, *George, 3rd Earl of Cumberland*, pp. 41–64; Andrews, *Elizabethan Privateering*, pp. 72, 262.

Bantry Bay and then keeping 'a cold Christmas with the Bishop and his clerks, rocks that lie to the westwards from Scilly', it was 30 December before the *Victory* struggled into Falmouth. Despite the loss of one especially rich prize, said to have been worth £100,000, which foundered in Mount's Bay, Cumberland had very comfortably covered his expenses and cleared off some £6,800 of debts into the bargain.

He had, however, done little to 'intercept [the Spanish] fleet coming from the Indies'. Nor had Frobisher been much more successful. At one point he had sighted the fifteen sail that Cumberland had had to leave in Angra. But he was then alone in the Queen's *Golden Lion* and the fifteen kept so close together than he dared not attack them single-handed. He did at various times capture four other vessels, among them the admiral and vice-admiral. These latter two had been near to sinking during a very tempestuous passage and their commander, Alvaro Flores, had therefore landed at Angra the five million ducats' worth of silver (over £900,000 in Elizabethan money) that they had brought from Havana. Even without their silver they were worth £40,000–50,000, or so Walsingham wrote to Willoughby. Neither was brought back to England, for the vice-admiral was wrecked of Setubal and the admiral foundered off the Eddystone, almost within sight of Plymouth. Nevertheless the other two prizes were valued at £15,000, leaving a small profit over the £11,320 that Frobisher's squadron had cost.[5]

Nevertheless all this was but a small profit from the fairest opportunity Elizabethan England ever had to apply the 'method of Jason'. All through 1589 Spain had virtually no navy capable of putting to sea. Her losses in 1587 and 1588 had left her short of skilled mariners and compelled her to employ older ships in the 1589 Atlantic convoys. Those convoys were therefore more than usually vulnerable to that summer's bad weather. They were scattered widely by storms and dribbled home in dispersed groups separated from their escorting galleons. By the time they reached the Azores few of them were in any condition to stand up to a squadron of the Queen's navy.

[5] Hakluyt, IV, 379–80; IV, 26–7; *H. M. C., Ancaster MSS*, p. 300; *Monson's Tracts*, I, 239 (from Pipe Office Declared Accounts 2226).

Unfortunately all that did await them at the Azores – and much of the time at the wrong end of the Azores – was the Queen's *Victory* and three or four tiny privateers. And off the Spanish coast all Frobisher had was a couple of the Queen's ships, Hawkins's *Dainty*, and a pinnace. We must also remember that ship-to-ship signalling, communication beyond the range of a seaman's bellow, was virtually non-existent. Flag signalling was hardly known in those days before telescopes or binoculars had come into use. About all that could be done was to fire a gun or lower a topsail, while a consort once out of sight below the horizon was as good as lost.[6] Small squadrons such as those of Frobisher and Cumberland were therefore doubly handicapped. If their few ships kept one another in view, they covered too small a sea area; if they spread themselves, they might be individually too weak to attack when chances offered. The tragedy of 1589 was that what should have been at the Azores was not just the *Victory* and her three or four tiny privateers but the half-dozen Queen's ships and several score lesser vessels whose efforts Norris and Drake had spent to so little purpose at Coruña and on the coast of Portugal. Ships in those numbers could have covered all the approaches; a royal squadron of that power, with the larger of its accompanying privateers, could have overcome anything it was likely to meet that year.

Nevertheless these small makeshift forces of 1589 had done enough to encourage Elizabeth to agree by 1 December to Hawkins fitting out six of her ships for another voyage to the southwards, presumably to catch those five million ducats that Alvaro Flores had landed at Angra.[7] That they were still there was reasonably certain, for 'in winter time it is no dealing with the said island'[8] and if Hawkins could get away by late February or early March he should be in good time to catch them.

That, however, was just what he was not allowed to do. All through the autumn and winter intelligences had been coming in from all sides of Spanish preparations for a new

[6] M. Lewis, *Spanish Armada*, pp. 139–40.
[7] S. P. Domestic, ccxxix, nos. 2, 3; ccxxx, no. 35.
[8] *L. and A.*, I., 618.

armada to renew the Enterprise of England in 1590.[9] It is true that the reports of William Lyly in France, John Wroth at Venice, Gilpin at The Hague, and from Calais and Le Havre supported Beauvoir la Nocle's contrary opinion. He held that Philip II's eyes were now fixed upon France and that the preparations in Spanish ports were not great enough for an invasion of England, that what preparations there were were more likely to be for a landing in Brittany or perhaps a raid on Ireland.[10] The English government, however, could not be sure. It did try so far as possible to see through to whatever truth lay behind all this varied information. Just after the middle of February two papers (which naval historians do not seem to have noticed) were drawn up, listing under headings *pro* and *contra* the most recent evidence. This certainly did not suggest that 'the threat was feeble and distant', though it may be that the comparative speed with which England's naval forces could be mobilized led the Council to exaggerate the possible speed of Spain's recovery from the 1588 disaster.[11]

It is therefore hardly surprising that when on 23 February the Council discussed 'whether it be convenient that Sir John Hawkins shall proceed in his voyage', it was 'thought unmeet for him to go'. Naturally Hawkins was bitterly disappointed, 'out of hope that ever I shall perform any royal thing'. And indeed before the end of March that five million ducats' worth of silver had been safely removed to Seville. But this is not to say that Hawkins's 'perverse mistress had thrown away the chance upon a childish alarm', that 'any bogey was sufficient to frighten her into a passive defence'.[12] On the contradictory evidences available to her, it would surely have been a very unwise gamble to weaken the home defence forces by sending off to the Azores six of the Queen's best ships, a quarter of the royal navy's major fighting units.

Until well into the spring English defence measures by land

[9] Ibid., 610, 612, 615, 623; *Cal. S. P. Domestic, Addenda*, pp. 280, 292; S. P. Domestic, ccxxvi, no. 38; ccxxvii, no. 44.

[10] *L. and A.*, I, 486–8, 623–6; *H. M. C., Salisbury MSS*, III, 446–7, 448–9; IV, 1; *Cal. S. P. Domestic, Addenda*, p. 299.

[11] *L. and A.*, I, 628–9; cp. also S. P. Domestic, ccxxx, no. 69; J. A. Williamson, *Hawkins*, p. 456.

[12] S. P. Domestic, ccxxx, no. 80; ccxxxi, no. 2; Hakluyt, V, 29–31; Williamson, *Hawkins*, p. 456.

and sea took on an increasing urgency as the reports of Spanish preparations continued.[13] At the end of April a new alarm brought an extra flurry of activity. A Captain Hill then sailed into Milford Haven and reported sighting a mighty fleet of great ships off Cape Finisterre steering north-west towards Ireland. Within a few days, however, the mighty fleet was found to be a lot of hulks laden with salt going home round Ireland and Scotland because of the easterly winds in the Channel.[14] It was not the last time that a huddle of hulks on their way home to Hamburg or Holland was to be mistaken for an invading Spanish armada. All the same, this 1590 invasion scare was richly comical. For while the English were getting their fleet to sea and rushing to man their shore defences, there was an almost identical alarm in Spain and Portugal about an impending English invasion.[15] To the historian looking back and able to see what was happening on both sides of the water, it is a laughable enough situation and English naval historians have had a lot of fun with it.

Yet because the situation amuses us today, we should not assume that the fears of either the English or the Spaniards were necessarily ludicrous in 1590. For what the story really illustrates is how thick was the fog of war that enveloped both sides. It was not so very difficult to get reasonably reliable information about the size and nature of enemy preparations. It was much more difficult to obtain reliable information about their forwardness and intention. It was most difficult of all, given the slowness of sixteenth-century communications and the vagaries of wind and weather, to get news quickly enough for counter-measures to be mounted in good time. All this put a premium upon caution, upon preparing for the worst and preparing for it early. And that was just what both

---

[13] For these preparations, see especially the papers from February onwards in *Acts P. C.*, XVIII and XIX and in *S. P. Domestic*, ccxxx and ccxxxi; also *H. M. C., Salisbury MSS*, IV, 11–8; *L. and A.*, I, 314; *Cal. S. P. Spanish*, IV, 571–2, 575–7; *H. M. C., Foljambe MSS*, pp. 64–6.

[14] *Acts P. C.*, XIX, 78–9, 83–7, 91–100, 107; *S. P. Domestic*, ccxxxi, nos. 88–90, 93; ccxxxii, no. 17; For the shortage of mariners in Spain, see also *L. and A.*, I, 643; *Cal. S. P. Venetian*, VIII, 465, 469, 478, 480.

[15] *Cal. S. P. Venetian*, VIII, 477–8, 480–3, 486, 488; *Cal. S. P. Domestic, Addenda*, pp. 296, 298; *L. and A.*, I, 636, 638, 645–8; II, 638, 645–6.

the English and the Spaniards were doing during these early
months of 1590.

From the end of April, however, English fears began slowly
to die down and early in May it was decided to send out two
squadrons of the Queen's navy, six ships and two pinnaces
under Frobisher and six ships under Hawkins.[16] It has
generally been assumed that these two squadrons were
intended to operate in much the same way as Frobisher and
Cumberland in 1589, except that this time Frobisher would go
to the Azores and Hawkins act as long-stop off the south-west
corner of Spain. Frobisher's instructions are not known; but as
he did eventually cruise to the Azores, that presumably was
what he was meant to do.

Hawkins's instructions, however, have recently been found[17]
and they show that his primary task was to watch for the
armada gathering at Ferrol, not for the American treasure
ships. He was to lie off Cape Finisterre and 'if you shall
perceive that there be any strong fleet or army in any readiness
to set forward towards the coasts of England, France, Ireland,
or Scotland, then you shall attend and accompany them and
forthwith send some swift and nimble bark with intelligence
before'. If after a reasonable time he felt sure that there were
no preparations 'in any great forwardness and readiness to set
to the seas, then you may range the coast of Spain where you
shall think fittest to impeach such traffic in and out upon that
coast and restrain and impeach such as relieve the dominions
of the Spanish King either with victual, munition, or any
kind of furniture for his shipping or for his foreign traffic'. In
other words, Hawkins's job was first to make sure of the
Ferrol armada and then to cut off those supplies of timber,
corn, and naval stores from northern Europe which were as
essential for any rebuilding of Spanish naval power as the
American silver Frobisher would be waiting to intercept at the
Azores.

Clearly Elizabeth's concern now, as in 1589 with Norris and

---

[16] *Cal. S. P. Domestic, 1581–90*, pp. 663–6; *Monson's Tracts*, I, 242.

[17] By Dr H. A. Lloyd, among the Devereux Papers at Longleat – *Bulletin of
the Institute of Historical Research*, XLIV, 128. Hawkins's commission, 20 May 1590, is
on Patent Roll, 32 Elizabeth I, part iv, m. 33*d*; Frobisher's, 20 May 1590, ibid., m.
34*d*.

Drake, was the King of Spain's war fleet quite as much as his treasure ships. This is made clearer still by the fact that after Hawkins and Frobisher did put to sea, about 25 May, they were kept in the Channel or the Western Approaches until the end of June upon new reports that Bazan's armada at Ferrol might soon be ready to sail. They filled in the time by a number of pretty indiscriminate seizures of ships, friends and foes, and for months to come the Admiralty Court was to be kept busy and the Privy Council distracted by the outcries of irate Frenchmen, more or less innocent Dutchmen, and neutral but very angry Hansards. At the end of June, however, news came that a Spanish expeditionary force had actually sailed from Ferrol – for Brittany, not England – and had been driven back and dispersed by bad weather in the Bay of Biscay. Thereupon Hawkins and Frobisher were at last allowed to proceed.[18]

The achievements of the two squadrons, when once they were clear of the English Channel, were not particularly impressive. Frobisher made straight for the Azores and arrived off Terceira by 7 August. By then a number of privateers had joined him and his force had grown to twenty sail.[19] With that number of ships he could obviously spread his net a good deal wider than Cumberland had been able to spread his in 1589. And he should have been in fair time to catch the homeward-bound convoys from America and the carracks from the East Indies. For the combined fleets from the Spanish Main and from Mexico had been ordered to leave Havana together not later than 15 July so as to avoid the hurricane season and the losses and scattering that storms had caused in the previous September. On 29 April the King had extended the time to 31 July. The advice boat with this order only reached Havana, however, on the evening of 30 July. It was quite impossible to get the ships to sea at that short notice, all the more as some of them had only reached Havana on 19 July and after a rough passage across the Caribbean were in no shape to face an Atlantic crossing until they had had a thorough overhaul. So the authorities in Havana decided to hold the combined fleets there until the spring. For those fleets Frobisher would wait in vain.[20]

There was, however, still the King of Spain's share of the silver and gold from the Spanish Main and Peru. This had been shipped from Cartagena aboard two of the new *fregatas*, or *zabras*, which had already sailed from Havana on 13 July. These vessels, of a type which had first been employed for this purpose in 1588 as a temporary measure, were fairly small fast-sailing ships, equipped also with oars to help them in calms or other emergencies. They were well enough armed and manned to fight off attackers of their own size and at the same time swift enough to sail or row away from any that could outgun them. Unhampered by the slow merchantmen of the regular convoys, they could make the Atlantic crossing quickly enough to avoid touching at the Azores or anywhere else. They could take advantage of any opportunity for a quick, sure passage even very late or very early in the season. They could sail at short notice and with little of the advance publicity that clearing a convoy of three or four score heavily laden merchantmen must always entail. In all these ways their employment added enormously to the difficulties of intercepting the King of Spain's treasure from his Indies.[21]

Nevertheless, the two zabras carrying the 1590 treasure could hardly, even in the best conditions, have covered the three-and-a-half thousand miles from Havana to the Azores before Frobisher arrived off the Islands; and as it happened, they ran into heavy weather and made a slower time than usual. But this delay was in part a result of their keeping somewhat to the north of the normal route and by thus avoiding the Azores altogether they were able to slip past Frobisher without seeing or being seen by him. On 24 August they crept into Viana in northern Portugal. What a prize the English had missed may be judged by the fact that it took 1,125 pack animals to transport overland from Viana to Seville the bullion that those two zabras had brought safely across

[20] *Further Voyages*, pp. lxxvii–lxxviii, 258–9. As Dr Andrews (*Drake's Voyages*, p. 151 note 5) points out, it is clear from these letters that the fleet was held at Havana because of the lateness of the season and not from fear of Hawkins and Frobisher as has been generally supposed.

[21] For these *fregatas*, or *gallizabras*, see J. Lynch, *Spain under the Habsburgs*, I, 164–5; *Further Voyages*, pp. lxxi–lxxiii.

the Atlantic.[22] The other great prize, the five homeward-bound Portuguese carracks from the East Indies, also escaped him, all five coming safely into Lisbon early in September.[23]

It was, in fact, the privateers, not the royal squadrons, who enjoyed the only substantial success against the East India-men. This was the capture in September by the London-owned *Swallow* (70 tons) and Hawkins's privateer *Dainty* of the outward bound *Holy Ghost,* 'stuffed and laded as full of goods as possible might be' and some treasure as well. This enabled Hawkins to reflect philosophically to Burghley that 'thus God's infallible word is performed, in that the Holy Ghost said Paul doth plant, Apollos doth water, but God giveth the increase'. Elizabeth commented, when Burghley showed her Sir John's letter, 'God's death! this fool went out a soldier and is come home a divine.'[24]

There was point to her comment. For indeed it was the *Holy Ghost,* almost alone, that had brought in enough to cover the £17,275 that the two English squadrons had cost.[25] The American treasure zabras and the homeward-bound East Indian carracks had slipped through the English net. So, too, had the Spanish expeditionary force for Brittany. This, of course, was supposed to be Hawkins's quarry. But before the end of August some Netherlands ships encountered him, not on his station off Ferrol, but 'half the seas over' towards the Azores. His departure left Ferrol unwatched and the sea road to Brittany unguarded. So, in mid-September Don Juan d'Aguila and 3,000 Spanish troops went off unmolested to Brittany. At the same time Bazan and the Ferrol armada sailed out towards the Azores. Ten leagues short of those islands a violent westerly gale scattered his ships back to various ports in northern Portugal and north-western Spain without ever sighting Hawkins – Bazan, too, had missed his prey (if he ever meant to come face to face with it).[26]

[22] *Further Voyages,* p. lxxvi and note 4; *L. and A.,* II, 653, 674.
[23] *Cal. S. P. Venetian,* VIII, 505; *L. and A.,* II, 653; S. P. Domestic, ccxxxiii, no. 82; Hakluyt, V, 32–3.
[24] Hakluyt, V, 35–6; S. P. Domestic, ccxxxiii, no. 118; ccxl, no. 114; *Hawkins Voyages,* pp. 90, 93, 250; *Monson's Tracts,* I, 253.
[25] S. P. Domestic, ccxxxiv, no. 75.
[26] Hakluyt, V, 32–4; VI, 225; *Cal. S. P. Venetian,* VIII, 508–9; *Monson's Tracts,* I,

Why Hawkins had deserted his post off Ferrol, we can only guess. He can hardly have believed that there were no preparations there 'in any great forwardness or readiness to set to the seas'. Possibly, as his modern biographer suggests,[27] he thought that it was time to take over from Frobisher at the Azores. For he knew that Frobisher's ships would soon be running short of victuals (a shortage that did drive them back to Plymouth by 29 September), whereas his own squadron carried enough to last into November. But perhaps the most likely guess may be that in some way he got wind that the treasure zabras were coming round north of the Azores, wide of Frobisher. That would explain why in the last days of August he was already 'half the seas over' towards the Islands. For it was only on 24 August that the treasure zabras crept into Viana. And, of course, the carracks made Lisbon a week or so later.

Nevertheless he missed them all and by sailing out to the Islands he had not only allowed the Spaniards' expedition to reach Brittany but had also left the gate wide open for Bazan's armada. With that armada known to be at sea but in an unknown position and with forty Spanish ships reported at Nantes, it is hardly surprising than on 25 October, when Hawkins was already on his way home, the Privy Council wrote urgently to recall him to Plymouth 'with all the ships under his charge' for the defence of the Channel and the west country.[28] Altogether, strategically as well as financially, 'this voyage was a bare action at sea'.[29]

These southwards and westwards operations were not the only employments of the Queen's ships in these immediate post-Armada years. Half a dozen or more were regularly engaged, almost the year round, as the 'Channel Guard' in the Straits of Dover and the Narrow Seas. There they played their

251–2; *Cal. S. P. Domestic, Addenda*, p. 313; F. Duro, *Armada Española*, III, 69–71. According to Sir Richard Hawkins, his father's ships did once sight north of Cape Finisterre eight ships carrying stores to Brittany, but owing to a subordinate's laxness failed to stop them. This, however, may have occurred later, on Sir John's way home in late October – *Monson's Tracts*, I, 252.

[27] Williamson, *Hawkins*, p. 459.

[28] *Acts P. C.*, XX, 51–5; also S. P. Domestic, ccxxxiii, no. 112.

[29] *Monson's Tracts*, I, 241.

part in checking the flow of Spain's supplies from northern and eastern Europe. But they had also to keep an eye upon the Dunkirk, Somme, and Le Havre shipping and to provide escorts for English troops and supplies going to France. So their numbers were too few and their distractions too many for their control of westward traffic through the Straits and Channel to be anything but haphazard and intermittent.

It was the privateers whose numbers gave this blockade of Spain's northward traffic most of such effectiveness as it did achieve.[30] For although Elizabeth never declared war upon Spain and did not issue general letters of reprisal as she had done against France in 1563, from the summer of 1585 'there existed in reality what amounted to a general system of privateering against Spain'.[31] It became an alternative business for many of those London, south, and west coast traders whom the war now excluded from their accustomed markets in Spain, Portugal, and much of northern France. It became a common sideline for those who, even before the war, had been pushing their commercial enterprises past Spain into the Mediterranean and Levant and down the west coast of Africa. It attracted the adventuring gentry, especially those of the southern and south-western counties where traditions of privateering and piracy dated back to Mary's reign and beyond. It engaged a number of noblemen and courtiers and, more particularly, navy, admiralty, and customs officials from the Lord Admiral downwards.

The ships armed and put to sea by these private adventurers enormously outnumbered those of the royal navy. Dr. K. R. Andrews, in his account of Elizabethan privateering, identifies no less than 236 ships engaged in such voyages, some of them in more than one voyage, during the three years 1589–91. But of the 139 of those 236 whose tonnages are known, only five were above 300 tons and another eleven over 200 tons. Of the remaining 114 no less than ninety-eight were under 100 tons, twenty-nine of them under 50 tons.[32] It is

---

[30] For the privateers, see especially Andrews, *Elizabethan Privateering, 1585–1603*; see also E. P. Cheyney, *History of England*, I, chs. xxi to xxiii; R. W. Kenny, *Elizabeth's Admiral*, chs. ii and iii. The word 'privateer' was a seventeenth-century invention and not known to the Elizabethans.

[31] E. P. Cheyney, *History of England*, I, 471.

[32] Andrews, *Elizabethan Privateering*, pp. 32, 243–65.

unlikely that the picture would look very different if we knew the sizes of the other ninety-seven of the 236, for it is the tonnages of the larger vessels that are most likely to be on record.

The overwhelming majority of the privateers, then, were quite incapable of tackling the King of Spain's galleons. They had, for the most part, to be content with attacking relatively ill-armed merchantmen. Their role was commerce destroying or, rather, commerce plundering. The hope of profit set them forth and the return with profit kept them going. Hence, although three or four might sometimes work together, the privateers were always reluctant to hunt in large well-organized packs for fear there might be too many to share the spoils. And for the government to direct or co-ordinate their operations to any very specific and sustained strategic purpose was out of the question.

Nevertheless there were certain 'obvious hunting-grounds where the privateers would naturally congregate. Many of the smaller ships set forth by the lesser south coast promoters sought their prey near home, in the Narrow Seas, the Channel, and the Western Approaches. There they might hope to pick off League fishing smacks returning with their local catches or larger vessels bringing home cod from the Newfoundland Banks. They might also catch small traders running between Spain and the ports of Flanders, Normandy, and Brittany as well as Hanseatic and Dutch hoys, hulks, and flyboats that had slipped past the Channel Guard on their way with contraband corn, masts, and naval stores for Spain from the Baltic. Other privateers, bolder and often already experienced in pre-war Iberian navigation, gathered to windward of Cape Finisterre to intercept the coasting trade moving round to and from the Biscay ports. Farther south, by the Rock of Lisbon, others dreamed of rich East Indiamen and hunted the lesser traffic of the Portuguese capital. Farther south still, yet more cruised to the west and south-west of Cape St Vincent to catch unwary traders to and from Cadiz and San Lucar – twenty were already lying in wait there as early as March 1590, if we may believe Linschoten (who was then at the Azores).[33] By that time a few were beginning to look into the

[33] Hakluyt, V, 31.

western Mediterranean, despite the efforts of Spanish galleys to close the Straits of Gibraltar to all English shipping.[34]

The Mediterranean and African traders, members of the Turkey and Venice Companies (merged as one Levant Company in 1592) and the Barbary Company, were also prominent among the promoters of privateering voyages to the Atlantic islands, the Azores in particular. Here there was always hope that storm-scattered units from a New Spain and Tierra Firme fleet or weather-beaten Portuguese East Indian carracks or Brazilmen might be caught straggling in for shelter and supplies. By the summer of 1590 there were off Corvo, again according to Linschoten, 'at the least 40 English ships together'.[35]

The Azores and Canaries were natural stepping-stones to the West Indies and the Spanish Main. Along the immense length of coastline and the long chain of islands that encircled the Caribbean from Trinidad around past Panama and Mexico to Cuba and Florida the Spaniards were very thin on the ground except at a few focal points of local or transatlantic trade. Of these, Havana was by far the most important, strategically as well as commercially. For there was the great final 'marshalling yard' where not only the goods of all Spanish America and the West Indies but also the annual tributes of silver from Peru and Mexico were collected and despatched to Europe. Here was a pressure point where the 'method of Jason' might applied and the King of Spain's golden fleece might be stolen just as well as at the Azores or off Cadiz. Its chief disadvantage was its distance from England and for this reason the hope of establishing an advanced base on the North American mainland had been one of the primary motives inspiring the efforts of Raleigh and Grenville to plant a colony in Virginia. But the experience of planting a colony proved disappointing and in the crucial two or three years after the Armada, when Spain's maritime power was at its weakest, the privateers were able to reap reasonable profits around Cuba and Hispaniola without benefit of any advanced base. At the very least seven privateers were operating in those waters in 1590, at least another twelve or thirteen in 1591, and

---

[34] For actions near Gibraltar, see ibid., IV, 380–6.
[35] Ibid., V. 33–4.

the numbers increased 'in a more or less continuous crescendo from the year of the Armada until 1595'.[36] Between 1589 and 1591 they took a score or more prizes, mostly from the weaker and less valuable local shipping. They forced the Spanish government and local authorities to the expense of providing rather more adequate land and sea defences for such vital centres as Havana, Santo Domingo, San Juan de Puerto Rico, San Juan de Ullua, Puerto Bello, and Cartagena. But their strategic impact had been very limited. They had done almost nothing towards realizing Her Majesty's desire 'for the intercepting of the King of Spain's treasure from the Indies' and even less 'to distress the King of Spain's ships of war'.

However, of the 236 privateers known to have been at sea during the three years 1589–91, only twenty-one or twenty-two have been identified as operating in the West Indies. There may have been more but not, it would seem, a great many more. For the vast majority were certainly operating east of a line from Land's End through the Azores to the Canaries, many of them, indeed, in waters even more narrowly European. Here, too, so long as their enterprises were managed on reasonably efficient business lines, they for the most part earned at least modest profits. During these three years they took at the very least 300 prizes, worth fully £400,000.[37] By no means all were Spanish or Portuguese, but a very significant proportion were. For example, thirty-four of them were Brazilmen, a number equal to something like a quarter of all the ships normally engaged in that trade.[38] Coming on top of the heavy losses Spain's Atlantic merchant shipping and mariners had suffered from Drake in 1587, in the Armada in 1588, and from storms in 1590 and 1591, the privateers' depredations during 1589–91 gave a flying start to that 'wholesale destruction of the enemy's merchant marine' which was to become so evident to most observers well before the end of the century.[39]

Those depredations, however, did little to bring a quick end

[36] Andrews, *Elizabethan Privateering*, p. 163.

[37] Andrews (ibid., p. 125) lists 299, of which a score or more were taken in the West Indies.

[38] Ibid., p. 207.

[39] Ibid., p. 226, citing *inter alia* Sir Richard Hawkins's remark from Seville in 1598 that 'Spain is utterly without shipping or regard'.

to the war. The silver from the New World came home safely to Spain, indeed in record quantities, all through the fifteen nineties[40] and by the summer of 1591, as Lord Thomas Howard and Sir Richard Grenville were to discover, Spain again had a battle fleet in being capable at least of protecting the American convoys against English cruising squadrons.

If, however, the efforts of the Queen's ships and the privateers did little to bring the Anglo-Spanish war to a speedy end, their interference with the shipping of other nations did a lot to make bad blood between England and her Dutch and French allies and between England and the cities and princes of northern Europe. Before the end of 1585 Elizabeth had warned Hamburg that she meant to stop the Hansards carrying corn and other rather more obvious war materials to Spain and Portugal. She had also tried, though in vain, to persuade the King of Denmark to stop the export of those things from the Baltic westwards through the Sound. And in April 1586, Leicester, at her behest, had sought to ban all Dutch trade with the enemy, both with the Spanish Netherlands and with Spain and Portugal.

Now to the Dutch and the Hanse Towns especially, and in a measure to the Danes, the transportation of timber, pitch, tar, ropes, cables, iron, copper, and above all corn, from the Baltic regions to southern Europe, to Spain and Portugal in particular, was a principal foundation of the maritime trade upon which their prosperity depended. It was important also to Polish, Prussian, and Danish agriculture and to Swedish mining. For the Dutch, in addition, the sale of licences to trade with the enemy provided the revenue to maintain their naval forces, while the trade itself provided the profits from which their burghers found at least half of their other taxes.[41] Moreover, that traffic with southern Europe became particularly rewarding in this last decade or so of the sixteenth century. In part this was due to the increase in Spain's demand for masts and naval stores to rebuild her naval forces

---

[40] See, e.g., the table for 1503–1660 in J. H. Elliott, *Imperial Spain,* p. 175, based on E. J. Hamilton's tables.

[41] M. Malowist, in *Econ. Hist. Review,* XII, 177–89; H. Zins, *England and the Baltic in the Elizabethan Era; L. and A.,* III, 205–6.

after the 1588 disaster. In part it was due to the notable increase in southern Europe's demand for corn owing to the sharp decline in its own cereal production through a series of droughts and more long-term causes.[42]

So the inclusion of corn, timber, pitch, iron, and copper, and especially corn, in Elizabeth's list of contraband goods was particularly unwelcome to her eastern and northern neighbours. And the greatly increased numbers of English ships, royal and private, at sea in the Armada and post-Armada years gave her attempted blockade an increased effectiveness that provoked unusually loud and angry protests. Drake's commandeering of those sixty Dutch flyboats to serve as transports for the Portugal expedition, and his seizure of those twenty French and sixty Hanse ships off Lisbon with 'the whole summer provision of corn', showed that neither allies nor neutrals would be spared, whether they came through the Channel or around Scotland and Ireland. For the privateers who had swarmed out against the Armada, continued to swarm in the Channel and nearer Atlantic waters, ensuring that English interference with westward and southward traffic would not be limited to occasional spectacular seizures.

Moreover, as Walsingham on 28 January 1589 instructed Stafford to explain to Henry III, many

of the great number of ships of war that Her Majesty is forced to keep at sea for the annoyance of the King of Spain [were] adventurers [who] do ofttimes exceed their commission, spoiling of such as are in league with Her Majesty: who, being possessed thereof, have so many shifts to avoid the dangers of the law as it is impossible to reduce them to exact restitutions, though there do not want in Her Majesty and in the lords of the Council all the care that may be to yield satisfaction.[43]

The English Admiralty Court was notorious for its delays and its judgements were always liable to be challenged, appealed against, or simply ignored. Meanwhile the seized goods all too

---

[42] *Cal. S. P. Foreign*, XXIII, 172, 384; Lansdowne MSS, civ, no. 30. Poland's rye exports through Danzig, about 14,000 lasts a year in mid-century, were fast rising towards the 100,000 mark – *New Cambridge Modern History*, III, 401: Malowist's figures are rather lower for both dates – *Econ. Hist. Review*, XII, 184. For the whole subject, see F. Braudel, *The Mediterranean and the Mediterranean World in the Age of Philip II*, I, 584–606.

[43] Cotton MSS, Galba E. vi. fo. 379.

often disappeared, dispersed or sold profitably, though illegally, with the connivance of local officials. Not infrequently, too, when a ship was stayed, the skipper and crew might be held prisoners on board and terrorized, even tortured, until they signed statements, true or false, admitting enemy ownership or part ownership of their cargo. Even if restitution was eventually obtained, the costs of litigation and recovery might well amount to a third or more of the claim.[44]

The delays and ineffectiveness of the Admiralty Court, however, were nothing new. Privateering and piracy, too, were activities for which the English had long been notorious and complaints about them had made up a considerable and constantly recurring part of foreign ambassadors' correspondence long before 1588. Nevertheless the new intensity and seriousness of the complaints after 1588 did cause the Queen and Council to seek ways of soothing the anger of their allies and neighbours. For that anger could seriously damage England's own export trade. By far the greater part of that trade, probably as much as four-fifths of it, was in woollen cloth and probably as much as two-thirds of those cloth exports were carried by the Merchant Adventurers to Stade, Emden, and Middelburg, with perhaps another twelfth being taken by the Eastland Company through the Sound to Elbing. Since the war had closed the Spanish, Portuguese, and most of the northern French markets, these German and Dutch 'vents' had become even more important. If they, too, were closed, the great London merchants who dominated the Fellowship of Merchant Adventurers and the London and east coast members of the Eastland Company would be sharply pinched; the clothiers who supplied them might face bankruptcy; weavers and spinners in the west country, East Anglia, and the West Riding would be thrown out of work; and sheepowners would find sharply reduced sales for their wool. Something of this had already happened in 1586–7 after the closure of the Iberian markets.[45] Now, with war burdens

[44] Individual cases are too common and numerous to detail here. They appear with monotonous frequency in the Foreign and Domestic State Papers, the Registers of the Privy Council, etc. But see, e.g., Ortel's complaints, [13 March 1589] – *Cal. S. P. Foreign*, XXIII, 160–4.

[45] J. D. Gould, 'The crisis in the export trade', in *Eng. Hist. Review*, LXXI (1956), 212–22.

growing to their peak, the Queen and Council needed no reminding of how important was 'the vent of our English cloths ... that notable trade which of so long hath set a-work many thousands of poor people, being the principal cause maintaining the traffic of this realm'.[46]

The complaints that least disturbed the English government were probably those of the French Kings and their ambassadors. For Henry IV in particular needed English financial, military, and naval support too badly to bite as well as bark. Besides, with Rouen, Le Havre, and the Somme towns and in Brittany St Malo, Morlaix, and Nantes all supporting the League, commercial matters weighed less heavily in French Kings' minds and most of the harm the French could do to English trade was done already. Yet the very necessary goodwill of Dieppe, Boulogne, and Calais was often strained by seizures of their ships and maltreatment of their sailors, while down in the south-west Lussan at Blaye sought Spanish aid to close the Gironde to English wine ships and the merchants of Bayonne and St Jean-de-Luz repeatedly threatened reprisals against English traders there.[47]

With England's other allies, the Dutch, the matter was more serious. The United Provinces were both a valuable market themselves and also a useful staging-post to Germany and central Europe. But although irate merchants and seamen of Holland and Zeeland might persuade the States to increase their tolls or to niggle over defects in the quality of Merchant Adventurers' cloth,[48] the direct commercial threat was not the most serious aspect. It was the political consequences that appeared more dangerous. Seizures of their ships was one of the most effective ways of irritating the States into even greater obstinacy about the reform of their government and revision of the 1585 Treaty which the Queen and

[46] *Acts P. C.*, XVIII, 217.

[47] *Cal. S. P. Foreign*, XXIII, 35, 88, 314, 364; XXIII, 113, 177–8; *L. and A.*, I, 467, 500, 511–3; II, 416–17, 436–7, 464, 472, 485, 488–9, 525, 530, 534, 541; S. P. Domestic, ccxxix, no. 13; *Acts P. C.*, XVI, 415–16; XVII, 69; XVIII, 174, 252; XX, 324–5, 365; XXI, 345–6, 376. It is clear from Stafford's letters (*Cal. S. P. Foreign*, XXII, 80–1, 93) that Henry III's 'angry reply' of 6 February 1589 (NS) (Cheyney, *History of England*, I, 483) about the six French corn ships arrested at Dover was written for show, in case it should be intercepted, and did not at all represent the King's real feelings.

[48] *L. and A.*, I, 298–9, 313; III, 199–203; *Acts P. C.*, XVIII, 442; Cotton MSS, Galba D. vii. fo. 76.

her Council considered so necessary. And as Leicester had found, trade with the enemy could readily nourish dangerous divisions between the landward provinces and maritime Holland and Zeeland.[49] Proposals for some agreement to restrain or to regulate Dutch westward trade were therefore almost always included in the long series of negotiations begun by Sir John Norris in the closing months of 1588 and carried on through 1589 and 1590 by Bodley and Wilkes in the Netherlands and with Ortel, Egmont, and the rest in England.

Elizabeth at first demanded a total cessation of Dutch trade to Spain and Portugal, at least so long as the Portugal expedition was preparing or at sea. The States made their stock answer, that as they had no gold or silver mines the revenue from trade with the enemy was essential to them and that, anyway, banning that trade to them would simply divert it to the Hansards and other neutrals.[50] They did suggest in the autumn of 1588 and again through their agent Ortel in February 1589 that traffic to Spain and Portugal should be allowed only by passport from England or the United Provinces – the fees would enable them still to maintain their naval forces.[51] The English, however, doubted whether this would be compatible with England's treaties with other states – the King of France had protested against Leicester's 1586 prohibition on precisely this ground.[52] Moreover, ships coming from the Baltic and north-west Germany would pass by Dutch waters first and pay their fees to the States, who were certainly thinking of it as a means of raising revenue rather than of cutting off Spain's supplies. The five months' mission of Egmont, Loosen, and Valcke in 1589 thus produced little if any progress.[53]

Wilkes's mission in 1590 did, however, show some movement on the English side. The proposals that he took to the

---

[49] *L. and A.*, II, 79, 248; J. den Tex, *Oldenbarnevelt*, I, 184.
[50] *Cal. S. P. Foreign*, XXII, 324; XXIII, 38, 43, 67, 75–6; *Kronijk*, XVI, 239–45, 273–80.
[51] *Cal. S. P. Foreign*, XXII, 185, 215, 320; XXIII, 108–9; *Resolutiën der Staten Generaal*, VI, 385.
[52] *Cal. S. P. Foreign*, XXI, ii, 69–71, 74.
[53] For this mission – *Cal. S. P. Foreign*, XXIII, 257, 308, 333, 369; *L. and A.*, I, 258–63, 273–80, 320; *Acts P. C.*, XVIII, 37; *Resolutiën der Staten Generaal*, VI, 391–2, 396, 399; *Kronijk*, XVII, 14–40, 56–67, 74–6; Bor, xxvi, fo. 19–20, 58–9.

States were that no ship of over 300 tons and no more than ten of over 100 tons be allowed to go from the United Provinces to the King of Spain's dominions; that no more than forty be licensed to go at a time; that all should have to touch first at one of four specified ports, some of them in Holland and Zeeland, to be searched before being granted passports which would enable them to pass without further search or interruption. In each of the four ports a special officer appointed by the Queen should be joined with the States' officers. Any ship laden with prohibited goods by Netherlanders in Denmark or the Hanse Towns caught trying to sail to Spain would also be good prize.[54]

Forty ships at a time must have looked a pretty meagre ration if Lord Admiral Howard's statement may be believed, that there were over 200 Low Country ships, many of them very well armed, and 4,000 mariners in Spain even in January 1591 in the depth of winter.[55] Certainly Wilkes's proposals suffered the same unfruitful fate as the rest of his negotiations. A new mission to England, headed by Loosen and van den Warck, made equally little headway, for they demanded that ships sailing with the States' passports should be neither searched nor interfered with and they were not prepared to include corn and other victuals among the forbidden cargoes.[56] After further sharp protests by Bodley the States did in August 1591 offer to include corn grown in the Provinces. But even the Privy Council knew, and promptly pointed out, that very little corn was grown there and that none of it was exported anyway[57] – the corn that the Dutch took to Spain in such quantities was corn that they brought, as they also brought timber and naval stores, from Germany and the Baltic lands. In fact all through the long negotiations the States' attitude reminds one of the remark of the head of an Oxford college about an over-earnest colleague's efforts to win his support for a scheme he disapproved of: 'he would keep on arguing with me: silly man, he ought to have known that what

---

[54] *L. and A.*, I, 340 (xv), 341 (xvi); cp. *Kronijk*, XVIII, 240–2.
[55] *L. and A.*, II, 274.
[56] *L. and A.*, II, 250–1, 255, 265, 268, 276–9; *Resolutiën der Staten Generaal*, VII, 97–101; *Kronijk*, XVIII, 39–40 [misdated as 1589/90].
[57] *L. and A.*, II, 301–4, 308; *Acts P. C.*, XXII, 7–11.

I meant was that I wasn't going to do it.' It is true that these maritime arguments were not very likely to make a real breach between the States and the Queen or to bring total disaster to England's export trade. But equally they did nothing to make the States more co-operative at a time when the Queen was becoming increasingly anxious to persuade them to take a broader view of the war and divert more of their efforts towards helping the hard-pressed King of France.

With the Hanseatic Towns the controversies were complicated by their long-smouldering resentment at the whittling away during the past hundred years of their exceptionally privileged position in England.[58] This resentment had been fanned by the encroachments into their own north German and Baltic preserves by English merchants and shipping since the decline and eventual closure of direct English trade to Antwerp. Fortunately for England, however, the Hanse Towns were not easily to be provoked into concerted action. The profits that could flow from acting as host to the Merchant Adventurers offered an almost irresistible temptation to the German North Sea ports. First Emden from 1564, then Hamburg from 1567 to 1577, then Emden again (after the Baltic Hanse Towns had forced Hamburg back into line), and finally Stade in 1587 had in turn succumbed to it. Even now Hamburg was still angling to get the Adventurers back from Stade, just as inside the Baltic Danzig was trying to draw the Eastland Company away from Elbing. And if concerted action was thus improbable, one town acting alone threatened little danger.

Nor in these quarrels were the Hanse likely to find any effective allies in Scandinavia or the Eastlands. They did persuade the Emperor to press Stade to expel the Adventurers, but Stade evaded and eventually rejected his demand.[59] Nor were the Danes or the Poles likely to uphold Hanseatic commercial pretensions of which both had long been jealous. But in June 1589 Drake seized those sixty Hanse corn ships off the Tagus and in July Cumberland intercepted eleven more. This provoked a new bitterness in Hanse resentment and the

---

[58] For brief accounts of earlier Hanse relations with Tudor England – R. B. Wernham, *Before the Armada*, pp. 64–8, 71–3, 203–4, 226–7, 283–6, 346–8.
[59] *Cal. S. P. Foreign*, XXIII, 51–2, 197, 331.

Duke of Parma at once sought to exploit it for Spain's benefit. In the summer of 1589 he sent a mission to Bremen, Hamburg, Lübeck, Danzig, and Denmark and then in the autumn he wrote to the Hanse Towns and to the Emperor urging that the import of English cloth into the Empire should be prohibited until Hanse privileges in England were restored. The Merchant Adventurers should also be banned altogether from the Empire and he threatened Stade with loss of their privileges as Hansards in the King of Spain's dominions if that town continued to harbour them. He also offered to send ambassadors to treat with the coming Hanse assembly about avenging the wrongs done to them by England.[60]

The possibility of Spain, the Emperor, and the Hanse Towns establishing a sort of 'Continental System' against England's major export trade did cause the Privy Council a certain amount of alarm. The Councillors succeeded in convincing the very reluctant Queen – 'the only reason that moveth her to be so stiff therein is the profit', Walsingham told Burghley – to release Drake's and Cumberland's prizes and 'such goods as are not comprehended within the title of munitions'. They returned a comparatively soft answer to the wrathful protest of Maurice Timmermann, the Hanseatic representative in England and they set Walsingham's brother-in-law Robert Beale to write, in English and Latin, a public *Declaration of the causes* which led Drake and Norris to arrest those sixty ships off the Tagus. They also in a decree of 27 July 1589 listed the goods that they considered contraband:

cables, masts, anchors, cordage, pitch, tar, tallow, pikestaves, calivers, muskets, armour, powder, brimstone, saltpetre, bullets, copper, lead, match, ordnance not belonging to the ship, canvas and Danzig poldavys, bacon, corn, wheat, rye, barley, meal, beans, peas, and such like.

These and any 'mere merchandise' belonging to Spaniards or Portuguese would be confiscated.[61] Examination of the ships'

[60] *Correspondance de Philippe II*, III, 194, 450–1, 463, 465, 468; *L. and A.*, I, 704, 713.

[61] Harleian MSS, 6694. fo. 187, quoted in C. Read, *Burghley*, pp. 449–50; S. P. Domestic, ccxxv, nos. 24, 25, 43; *Acts P. C.*, XVII, 358–60, 380–2. The *Declaration*, it is now clear, was the work of Beale and not, as Cheyney (*History of England*, I, 495) surmised, of Burghley. Burghley began, but did not finish or publish, a paper on the question in 1591 – Lansdowne MSS, civ, no. 30.

papers of Drake's prizes, searching out and confiscating the contraband, retrieving a good deal of the 'mere merchandise' from those who had purloined it (Sir John Norris was one), all took time and it was 31 May 1590 before the last of the sixty was released.[62] Nevertheless the Council's close supervision of all this testified to its anxiety at the possibility of Hanse resentment throwing them into the arms of the Spaniards.

There was anxiety also about the attitude of the Danes. In September 1589 an envoy, Dr George Schumacher, arrived in London and over the next few months presented and sought redress for a list of complaints quite long enough to keep the Queen and her Council from taking Danish friendship too easily for granted.[63] Moreover James VI of Scotland had just married the young King Christian IV's sister and an ambassador of his at Stade was boasting much of his master's mighty leagues and consanguinities and that he 'would no longer be kept as a novice but would be known'.[64] It is improbable that Elizabeth or her Councillors ever suffered from nightmares at the spectre of Denmark and Scotland co-operating against them with a Hanse assembly hypnotized by Spain. Yet it was clearly politic to soothe the Danes and by 21 January 1590 Elizabeth had decided to send Dr Daniel Rogers to them.[65]

In the end it was not Rogers by Dr Christopher Parkins who was sent off in May 1590 on a mission that was to last fourteen months and to take him to Denmark, Lübeck, Stettin, Danzig, Elbing, Warsaw, Ansbach, back to Warsaw, Elbing, Königsberg, Danzig, and then again to Denmark.[66] To follow his

[62] *Acts P. C.*, XVIII, 19, 42–3, 52–3, 110–13, 159–60, 205; XIX, 48, 63, 185; *L. and A.*, I, 704, 713.

[63] *L. and A.*, I, 750, 756–74; II, 800–1; Cotton MSS, Nero B. iii, fos. 352, 358; S. P. Domestic, ccxxviii, no. 34; *Acts P. C.*, XVIII, 249; *H. M. C., Salisbury MSS*, XIII, 429–31.

[64] *L. and A.*, I, 702.

[65] S. P. Domestic, ccxxx, no. 20.

[66] *Cal. S. P. Domestic, 1581–90*, p. 665; *L. and A.*, I, 729. For his mission – ibid., I, 729, 782; III, 885; his negotiations in Denmark, June 1590 and May–July 1591 – ibid., I, 783–8; II, 797, 830; III, 884–5, 890, 894–6; at Lübeck, June–July 1590 – ibid., I, 746; II, 729–32, 738; III, 886; at Stettin, July 1590 – ibid., II, 738; III, 886; at Danzig, Elbing, Königsberg, Ansbach, and in Poland, July 1590–May 1591 – ibid., II, 807–8, 810, 812–14, 816, 820–4, 828–9; III, 846–9, 887–90. For Parkins, see *Dictionary of National Biography*, s.v. Perkins, Christopher, though this is not too clear about his various missions.

negotiations in detail would be tedious and not greatly profitable. For in its results his mission was a Baltic counterpart to Thomas Wilkes's 1590 mission to the United Provinces. It calmed the government's worst fears without achieving anything very positive. The topics covered were the familiar ones; the arguments for and against as familiar and as irreconcilable as ever. The Governors of Denmark and the King of Poland were at one with Lübeck and Danzig and Königsberg in emphasizing how essential corn exporting was to all of them. All, too, had their lists of complaints about the arrests and despoilings of their ships and goods.

But neither the Danes nor the Poles, nor for that matter the Dukes of Prussia and Pomerania, showed any interest in the Hansards' position in England or any sympathy for their efforts to drive the English merchants from Stade and Elbing. Had not Elizabeth's ambassador in Constantinople, Edward Barton, just (in June 1590) mediated Poland's peace with the Turks? Clearly there was little danger of any Baltic kings or princes joining the Hanse Towns in an 'Armed Neutrality of the North' such as England was to face two centuries later. Nor did the Hanse Towns themselves seem prepared to push their quarrels with England to extremes, despite the belligerent-sounding agenda for their assembly at Lübeck in June 1591. Danzig collected a list of thirty-one claims for seized goods, but seemed chiefly concerned to get the Eastland Company's residence back from Elbing. Lübeck, while 'blunt' about lost privileges and seized goods, professed to 'abhor' all idea of a league hostile to England and promised not to support Hamburg in any 'troublesome acts'. Parkins was convinced that there was nothing much to fear from any of the cities or from the Hanse assembly.[67] And he seems to have convinced the English government, for when on 31 December 1591 the Queen replied to the complaints sent over by Lübeck and the rest of the Hanses, she stood firmly by her declared policy. 'Their request to carry all things without exception is utterly against equity and reason', she told them; and if the growth of the Merchant Adventurers' trade damaged them,

[67] *L. and A.*, I, 825–7; II, 730–2, 828–9, 888; III, 849, 886–7, 905–6.

that was no reason for English merchants to be denied the liberty of traffic which all others enjoyed.[68]

Nevertheless the frequent seizures of ships and goods certainly did much to stimulate agitation and animosity against England's traders in north Germany and the Baltic lands. Also the Merchant Adventurers' bargaining power had been somewhat weakened when the government threw open the trade temporarily to non-members of the Fellowship during the 1586–7 crisis.[69] The interlopers' gains perhaps offset some of the Adventurers' losses, but England's main, eastward, export trade was certainly faced by increasingly difficult conditions as German, Dutch, and to some degree Danish, resentment mounted over interference with their westward navigation.

Yet although this eastward trade in cloth exports to the Netherlands, Germany, and the Baltic lands was still very much the main trunk of the tree of English commerce, the real growing-points were already to be discerned elsewhere, in the westward- and southward-pointing branches. And the naval war against Spain, the privateering war in particular, played an important part in spreading those branches farther and wider afield, not only across the Atlantic to the West Indies and the New World but to the Far East as well. For those who in 1589 had dreamed of opening the Portuguese empire to English traders, did not abandon hope when Norris and Drake failed them. That October a group of London merchants, among them leading promoters of privateering such as Paul Banning and Thomas Cordell, put to the Privy Council a scheme for an exploratory three-ship voyage to India and the East Indies. It was 10 April 1591 before their three ships actually sailed, under George Raymond and James Lancaster, both notable privateering captains. None of the ships and only fourteen of their men got home after three years of daring and desperate adventures. Yet Lancaster and his *Edward Bonaventure* had sailed eastwards as far as Malacca and then back as far as the West Indies before shipwreck overtook them. At least they had shown that English sailors in English ships could find their way to and from the Portuguese

[68] Ibid., III, 877.
[69] This lasted until April 1591 – S. P. Domestic, ccxxxviii, no. 122.

East. They had blazed the trail for England's East India Company that was to come into being five years later.[70]

Thus already in the three or four years after the 1588 Armada, with enterprises such as these, with the progress of the Levant Company, and with the growth of trade to Leghorn (newly established as a free port by the Grand Duke of Tuscany),[71] the first buds were appearing on what were to become in the next century the principal growth branches of England's overseas commerce. For the present the prospects thus opened combined with the profits of privateering to make the more enterprising of England's merchants and mariners willing supporters of the war against Spain. The very merchant interests which in 1580 had pressed the government to restore Drake's spoils to avert a breach with Spain, now provided some of the leading supporters of continued hostilities at sea. That, at least, may be set in the balance against the difficulties which their privateering and the Queen's contraband policy created with allied and neutral powers.

[70] Hakluyt, IV, 242–59, VII, 156–64; Cheyney, *History of England*, I, 439–43. Andrews (*Elizabethan Privateering*, pp. 214–16) regards the voyage, not unjustly, as an 'unmitigated failure'.

[71] *L. and A.*, II, 718.

## XII

## Plans for 1591 and Aid to Brittany

In the last chapter we discussed the actions at sea and the reactions to them among England's friendly or neutral neighbours during the years immediately after the 1588 Armada. However, from the return of the Portugal expedition and the assassination of Henry III onwards, the situation in France had become more and more the central, dominant concern of English policy. By the end of 1590 it was apparent that 1591 was likely to bring a crisis there no less serious for England, and indeed for western Europe, than that of 1588. By then Henry IV's foreign enemies were obviously gathering for the kill, while his Catholic supporters in France were growing daily more restive at his delay in performing his promise to 'receive instruction' in their faith. Moreover, the death of the old Cardinal of Bourbon, the League's 'Charles X', in May 1590 had – in Spanish and Papal eyes – left the throne of France vacant, which must tempt Philip II to press such claims as he himself or his daughter, the Infanta Isabella Clara Eugenia, could pretend. If the League, backed by Parma's Spanish army in the Netherlands and Aguila's Spanish force in Brittany, did no more than drive Henry back beyond the Loire, even that might well end in the virtual destruction of France as an independent great power, as a counter-weight to an over-mighty Spain. At the least it would put at the disposal of Spain's renascent Atlantic fleet all the harbours of Brittany, Normandy, and Picardy. England might then have to face a new Armada based upon Brest at the windward end of the Channel and free to make unhindered use of Le Havre half-way along – of that 'Newhaven' from which Francis I had launched his great assault upon Elizabeth's father in 1545.

To keep Henry IV in the field and north of the Loire therefore became more than ever the primary object of English policy in 1591.[1] That meant providing him with a

[1] As Burghley wrote – *L. and A.*, II, 752.

reliable army and especially with a large dependable mass of
infantry that would not melt away after a few weeks in the
field. Without such large and reliable forces Henry could not
hope either to hold off Parma or to take the great cities that
were the main bastions of the League. Yet until he could take
at least some of those great cities, he would never have the
revenues to provide the regular pay that alone could hold an
army together all through a campaigning season. For both
men and money, therefore, he had to look for the time being
principally to his foreign friends. And that meant principally
to England and to the German Protestant princes.

His first idea was to get a considerable army of Germans,
horse and foot, to hold off Parma while he himself with his
own troops, reinforced by an English contingent, reduced one
of the League's great northern bastions as he had so nearly
reduced Paris during the previous summer. But this time the
first objective would be Rouen, not Paris. Accordingly, at the
end of September 1590 he made a motion to Stafford to have
5,000 English foot and 1,000 pioneers, paid for two months by
Elizabeth, to help besiege Rouen. As soon as he had taken the
town he would pay them himself. Stafford thought quite well
of the idea and promised to further it all he could, if Henry
would 'murely' deliberate about it with his council and
'deliver me his intent for that, his ways and means and
likelihood'.[2] There was indeed much to be said for it. Rouen's
capture would go far to complete the blockade of the still-
straitened Paris. It would isolate, and soon bring in, Le Havre.
It would greatly strengthen the belt of royalist territory that
separated the Breton Leaguers from the main centres and
main forces of their party.

It seems likely, however, that there were other motives than
purely strategic ones behind this proposal. Back in October
1589, according to Ottywell Smith, Henry had sent for him
and told him that he would gladly besiege Rouen if he had
200,000 crowns (about £65,000) to pay his foreign troops.
Smith suggested that Henry should get Elizabeth to borrow
such an amount from some of the London merchants and
from the merchants of Lancashire, Yorkshire, Devon, and

[2] Ibid., 458.

Wales. Those of the latter regions especially would be ready to help because by Rouen 'doth stand all the trade and utterance of all the cloth that is made in those quarters'. Henry apparently liked the idea and was ready to promise that the money would be repaid out of the Rouen customs within eight months of taking the town.[3] He spoke about it to Stafford, too, but he had not immediately followed it up. Probably in that autumn of 1589 and during the ensuing winter he expected that his hoped-for German levy would enable him to take the offensive in 1590. Then after his great victory at Ivry in March, a direct attempt upon Paris looked more attractive. Parma's intervention, however, had frustrated that attempt and made a less ambitious, less direct approach look wiser – after all, Henry required forces to hold off Parma as well as to take the offensive against the League. Hence his revival of the Rouen proposal in September 1590. But this time there was no mention of loans from the English merchants, for recent experience of Henry's credit was unlikely to loosen their purse-strings. Yet it seems clear, although Stafford did not mention it in his letters home, that Henry did again hold out the bait of speedy repayment from the Rouen customs.[4]

It may seem somewhat odd that Elizabeth did not rise immediately and eagerly to this Rouen bait. Admittedly, the military situation in France had altered by the time Stafford's report arrived on 8 October. By then Elizabeth had just sent another £10,000 to Henry to help pay his troops, Aguila's 3,000 Spaniards had landed in southern Brittany, and reports, confirmed by intercepted letters, were beginning to come in that Parma was about to march back to the Netherlands.[5] Also, of course, Henry's proposal did not call for any immediate action. A siege of Rouen was not something to be

---

[3] Ibid., 480. It may be, of course, that the idea of besieging Rouen was suggested by Smith to Henry and not by Henry to Smith, – who may have thought royal authorship would lend it greater weight. For the dependence of these cloth-producing counties upon Rouen – A. P. Wadsworth and J. de L. Mann, *Cotton Trade and Industrial Lancashire* and T. Mendenhall, *Shrewsbury Drapers and the Welsh Cloth Trade*.

[4] Apart from the fact that this always seems to have been assumed in the negotiations, there is the report of a Spanish spy that Henry was offering the Queen certain towns as security for repayment – *Cal. S. P. Spanish*, IV, 586.

[5] S. P. France, xxii, fo. 60*v.*; *L. and A.*, II, 366, 459, 594.

started in midwinter. But there may well have been a more compelling reason for Elizabeth's lack of prompt response. It looks very much as if she had caught sight of another, and more attractive, possibility.

In November Palavicino and Stafford came back from France, bringing with them the Viscount Turenne, on his way as Henry IV's ambassador to arrange for the levy of a new German army to come into France next summer. Turenne received a magnificent welcome, so magnificent indeed that many suspected he must have Henry IV secretly among his suite. Much of the magnificence was, admittedly, due to the youthful enthusiasm of the Earl of Essex by whom Turenne was lodged, feasted, and entertained. For the 23-year-old Earl, who was beginning to bid for influence in the state as well as for favour at court, scented the possibility of winning in France in 1591 the military renown that he had missed in Portugal in 1589.[6] But the Queen, too, made much of Turenne and it was apparently in discussions with him between 20 and 25 November that her new idea took shape. Why not, she suggested – recalling perhaps a proposal made by Palavicino in October 1585 and by Leicester in July 1586 – why not bring the German army through the Netherlands instead of by the more usual route through Lorraine and Burgundy? The Dutch forces and the English auxiliary companies could give them a free passage over the Rhine and then could second them through Brabant into Artois and Hainault, open country rich in victuals. Entering France by Cambrai or St Quentin, they might catch Parma's army between themselves and Henry's forces. 'Shut up as in a strait' between them, unable either to return to the Netherlands or to enter further into France, the Spaniards might face a worse disaster on land than they had suffered at sea in 1588. And Henry would thereafter be free to reduce the great League cities and to rescue Brittany at his leisure.

Elizabeth put the idea forward with becoming modesty, as someone claiming no judgement in such martial matters. But Turenne, she gathered, was impressed by it; and indeed it does

---

[6] Lodge, *Illustrations of British History*, II, 418–21, 425–6; Devereux, I, 214; *H. M. C., Ancaster MSS,* p. 307; Collins, I, 317. E. P. Cheyney, *History of England,* I, 239, says surprisingly that Turenne met with 'little encouragement' in England.

show a grasp of essentials similar to that in the 1589 instructions to Norris and Drake. For just as the destruction then of what was left of the 1588 Armada would have freed England from all further fear of Spanish invasion, so the destruction now of Parma's army must have freed France from Leaguer rebellion and the Netherlands from Spanish domination. Whether the plan was as operationally practicable as it was strategically attractive must remain an open question. It bears a good deal of resemblance to the attempt of Admiral Coligny and William of Orange in 1572 to trap the Duke of Alba by a similar double assault. That attempt was of course rendered abortive by the St Bartholomew's Day massacre. The plan that Elizabeth put to Turenne, and to Henry IV, in November 1590 was never even attempted.[7]

For this Elizabeth herself was largely to blame. To begin with, although she hoped for so much from Turenne's German levy, she was still most unwilling to contribute anything towards its cost. Thus, the first draft of Palavicino's instructions for his return to Germany directed him to accompany and assist Turenne; to urge the German Protestant princes, and the Protestant cities also, to provide the money to put a substantial army in the field; but to do all he possibly could to prevent them calling upon Elizabeth for any contribution. He was to explain in detail what great sums she had already expended in direct military and financial aid to Henry IV during the past year, much of it made necessary by the Germans' slowness and hesitation in answering his appeals for help. These instructions were drafted on 20 November. Five days later, after discussions with Turenne, a clause was added to them outlining the scheme for bringing the army through the Netherlands. But there was still no mention of money from the Queen. It was not until 30 November, and under considerable pressure from Burghley, that she allowed the addition of secret instructions authorizing Palavicino, if he

---

[7] *L. and A.*, II, 469, 756. I agree with Professor Stone that the plan does seem to have been Elizabeth's own idea – *An Elizabethan*, p. 167. Palavicino had, however, suggested something similar to Navarre's envoy Ségur on 17 Oct. 1585 (NS) and Leicester, also to Ségur, on 25 July 1586 – F. H. Egerton, *Life of Thomas Egerton* (1828), pp. 433, 448. I think Professor Stone may somewhat antedate Turenne's preference for the Lorraine route.

found that the levy would not go forward without English money, to promise £10,000. He was, even so, to pretend that he was making the promise upon his own credit and that he must refer home for confirmation. Finally, and with even greater difficulty, Burghley persuaded the Queen to include in these additional instructions permission for Palavicino, if very hard pressed, to take up very secretly 'such a sum as £5,000' on top of the £10,000. But before handing over this extra £5,000 he must really write home to obtain special warrant under the Queen's own hand. And all these additional instructions were to be kept absolutely secret from Turenne and everyone else.[8]

It was, of course, perfectly true that Elizabeth had already spent a great deal in supporting Henry IV, over £62,500 in thirteen months apart from anything expected from her in Germany. It was not unreasonable of her to think that it was about time other Protestant princes took over a larger share of the burden. Also she was, as usual, short of money. During the previous twelve months she had raised £126,305 by the unwelcome expedient of selling Crown lands. Yet already nearly £103,000 of that money had been swallowed up by war expenditures and in November 1590 letters were going out, despite Elizabeth's reluctance, for levying another privy seal loan.[9] But such arguments as these were not likely to stimulate German generosity, least of all that of Lutheran princes and cities who felt no great love for a Calvinist King of France and a great deal of reluctance to antagonize their Habsburg Holy Roman Emperor, the King of Spain's nephew. Nor indeed does it look as if the Queen's financial straits can have been quite as desperate as her attitude would suggest: £8,000 of the required £10,000 or £15,000 had already been sent over by exchange to Frankfort earlier in the year. And it was the Lord Treasurer, Burghley, who persuaded her to allow Palavicino to offer any money at all towards the German levy. More than that, it was Burghley who persuaded her – bullied her, we might almost say – to reinstate in Palavicino's secret

---

[8] *L. and A.*, II, 753–8; S. P. Domestic, ccxxxiv, no. 11.

[9] *L. and A.*, I, 502; II, 455; S. P. Domestic, ccxxxiv, no. 20; ccxxxvi; ccxxxviii, no. 30; *H. M. C., Salisbury MSS*, IV, 64; *Acts P. C.*, XX, 185–7; Harleian MSS, 6996 fo. 67.

instructions the clause allowing him 'to make the sum to be
£15,000 in case of extreme necessity', a clause which she had
'rased' from his original draft.[10] On this occasion it does seem
that the Queen was being over-careful with her money.

What did more, however, to frustrate the Queen's plan for
the German army to march through the Netherlands, was her
decision to withdraw part of her forces thence to serve against
the Spaniards and Leaguers in Brittany. Here again she gave
her help with considerable reluctance. Early in December
1590, only a day or two after Turenne and Palavicino had
embarked for Germany, an envoy arrived from the Prince of
Dombes, the royalist governor of Brittany. This envoy, de
Mesnils, brought a request for munitions, weapons, and if
possible 2,000 men, to be sent over within a month. The cost
would have to be added to the King's debts, since Dombes had
no means of raising the money in Brittany. Yet in addition to
these requests by de Mesnils, he had sent other envoys to Sir
Francis Drake at Plymouth to suggest that the Queen should
send forces by sea to attack the shipping and cut off the
supplies of the Spaniards who were beginning to fortify a base
for themselves at Blavet. As there were two galleasses and six
great ships there, as well as 3,000 Spanish troops, this would
clearly call for very considerable forces, even if the Dutch sent
the five or six warships Henry had been trying to get from
them since the previous August. Not unreasonably, the Queen
wrote to Dombes on 17 December, after discussions with
Beauvoir and de Mesnils, that such forces could not be set
forth in so short a time and that midwinter was no season for
amphibious operations upon the exposed and rocky coasts of
Brittany. Moreover, now that Parma had returned to the
Netherlands, Henry IV should be able to send Dombes the
men and munitions he needed and to send them by land
better than she could by sea. Also as money would be involved, she needed to know from the King himself what was
required. In any case, she needed his authorization before she
sent English troops into one of his provinces – as she laughing-
ly but pointedly remarked to Beauvoir, he was not the
ambassador of the Prince of Dombes. She did finally agree to

[10] *L. and A.*, II, 757.

provide some munitions upon the security of bonds from certain rich Breton merchants, but that was all.[11]

Nevertheless, the threat from the Spaniards in Brittany could not easily be ignored. Sir Roger Williams indeed was writing, even while Turenne was in England, that it was more important to drive the King of Spain's troops from Brittany then to assure the German levy. For, he argued, 'it were better for us he had five other provinces than Brittany, for all the best ports of France is in that province and without [his] possessing either those ports or them of the Low Countries our dangers cannot be very great.' Besides, there was no guarantee that the German levy would enable Henry IV to destroy Parma who, like all good captains, would do his utmost to avoid the hazards of a pitched battle. Thereby he might win time for Henry's German levy to be answered by Spanish counter-levies and 'if we and our friends [thus] merchant wars with the Spanish King and his, their great means will eat our small'. They could well disburse six crowns to England's one. On the other hand, 8,000 men sent promptly would clear the Spaniards out of Brittany.[12] Williams's opinions on strategy tended to vary with his personal position and prospects, as he himself once admitted, but his friendship with Essex probably assured his arguments a hearing, even if anonymously, in the highest quarters.[13] And certainly his concern over Brittany was widely shared. Only the day before Williams wrote, Burghley was insisting that Henry IV must be required to be more careful to recover the Norman and Breton ports, since if the 'maritimes' were not kept from the King of Spain it would be labour lost to procure an army out of Germany.[14]

[11] Ibid., 471, 476–8, 482; S. P. Domestic, ccxxxiv, no. 23; ccxxxviii, no. 3; Cotton MSS, Caligula E. vii, fos. 349, 351. The envoys sent by way of Plymouth were delayed there by illness – *L. and A.*, II, 481. Henry IV was already seeking ships from the Dutch – *Resolutiën der Staten Generaal*, VII, 60–2, 207–8, 343–4; but it was 20 January 1591 before he wrote to the Queen and Beauvoir for 2,000 troops for Brittany – *Lettres Missives*, III, 331–4.

[12] *L. and A.*, II, 466–7.

[13] Ibid., 480, 536. Conyers Read's statement (*Burghley*, p. 477) that Essex was disappointed not to be given the command of the forces for Brittany seems based upon a misreading of Collins, I, 317. But the Earl was, of course, full of enthusiasm for Turenne.

[14] *L. and A.*, II, 752.

Just before Christmas Burghley succeeded in communicating his anxiety to the Queen. As late as 20 December,
according to Beauvoir, she was still determined not to send
troops to Brittany.[15] But then, on 23 December, she wrote to
Bodley instructing him, after privately consulting some
trustworthy members of the Dutch government, to urge the
States General and Council of State to agree to the withdrawal by sea of part of her forces. These were to go to
Normandy and Brittany, especially Brittany. She would not
take more than necessary, not more than a third of the foot
and none of the horse. Bodley was then to arrange with Vere,
Morgan, and Sir Edward Norris for 1,600 of the 'auxiliary'
forces to be sent to join others levied in England to help
Dombes expel the Spaniards from Brittany. If the States
refused, they should be told plainly that the Queen would
none the less call out what forces she thought fit, since these
were her natural subjects, paid by her, and the service would
be against the common enemy.

Having decided to send troops to Brittany, the Queen could
hardly avoid turning for at least some of them to her auxiliary
companies in the Low Countries. The troops would be going
into action straightaway and they were unlikely to have even
such French support as Willoughby's men had had in
September 1589. So a substantial proportion needed to be
trained and experienced men and the only place where such
men could be found was in the Netherlands. But from the
wording of the letter to Bodley, it looks as if Elizabeth and her
ministers were beginning to think further ahead. They, after
all, alone among the enemies of Spain, were able, were indeed
compelled, to view the war as a whole. While the Dutch and
Henry IV were both fully occupied on their own particular
fronts, England was involved in almost all theatres, in the
Netherlands, in France, at sea. Elizabeth was, as it were, in the
position – though without the authority – of a supreme allied
commander. When there were gaps in the defences to be
plugged or opportunities for offence to be exploited, it was to
her that the others turned. But if she was to be able to answer
their calls, she needed to have ready at hand a mobile,

organized force of experienced troops that, with the help of English sea-power, might be moved promptly from theatre to theatre. That in her letter to Bodley she spoke of Normandy as well as Brittany, of her right to call out her own troops as she saw fit, and of using them in service against the common enemy elsewhere, all suggests that there was, at least at the back of her mind, some such notion of treating a substantial part of the English auxiliary forces in the United Provinces as, in modern parlance, a mobile strategic reserve.

For some unrecorded reason the letter of 23 December had not reached Bodley even by 3 February.[16] Long before then the Queen had been persuaded to a more ambitious undertaking, to a combined operation commanded by Lord Admiral Howard, with Sir John Norris as general of the land forces, to expel the Spaniards from Blavet. The Lord Admiral was to have some of the Queen's ships besides twenty merchantmen and some fireships. The land forces were to be at least 6,000 men. Of these, 3,000 were to be levied in the southern counties of England and on 1 January instructions were drawn up for Norris to go over to The Hague to join Bodley in asking the States General and Council of State to agree to the withdrawal for two or three months, not of 1,600, but of 3,000 men from the English auxiliary infantry and, if possible, 2,000 of their own footmen as well – Williams's 8,000 men in fact. He was to point out that the States need not fear enemy attempts during that time, in view of Parma's recent losses in France and the mutinies among his remaining troops. If the States would not agree and if they refused passports for the English companies to move to their ports of embarkation, then Norris should order the troops away all the same. He might even discharge them, let them make their own way to Flushing, and there take them back into pay before shipping them to France. If the States would agree to his taking a smaller number only, then he might put them in hope that the Queen would send over some supply in case of need. And if he himself judged it unwise to take the full 3,000, he was to inform the Queen who would have the numbers made up in England.[17]

[16] Ibid., 258.
[17] Ibid., 261–3; S. P. Domestic, ccxxxviii, nos. 34, 63, 82; *Cal. S. P. Domestic, Addenda*, p. 320.

What was now envisaged therefore was no longer a limited operation of indefinite duration in support of Dombes, but a sharp decisive blow by a considerable force to destroy the Spaniards at Blavet before they could be reinforced or could take firm root. Norris himself may well have been the author of the project, for his 1 January instructions followed closely a list of 'points to be remembered in my instructions' which he had drawn up a few days earlier and which had set Burghley to work calculating ways and means. On 30 December, too, Norris had answered Burghley's doubts about the States agreeing to the withdrawals. The 1585 Contract, he argued, gave the Queen's lieutenant, and so the Queen herself, the chief superintending of the war. So, if Parma employed most of his forces in France, there was no reason why the Queen's troops should all be kept to guard the United Provinces. Anyway, the Brittany enterprise should be completed in two or three months, that is before the campaigning season opened in the Netherlands.[18]

The design for English strategy during 1591 was thus by now becoming clear. During the 'close season' for campaigning in the Netherlands and northern France, a force of some 6,000 men, half of them experienced soldiers from the English auxiliary companies in the United Provinces, half new levies from England itself, would be sent to help Dombes expel the Spaniards speedily from Blavet and southern Brittany. While they were striking a quick decisive blow there, Palavicino would help Turenne – if absolutely necessary with £10,000 or even at a pinch £15,000, of English money – to raise a large army of horse and foot in Germany. In the early summer the Dutch and the English auxiliary companies, by then back to full strength, would assist this German army to march through the Netherlands to the frontiers of France. There they would hope to trap Parma's army and the main body of the Leaguers between themselves and Henry IV's troops, reinforced perhaps by 4,000–5,000 footmen out of England. At the same time a squadron of the Queen's ships, accompanied by a score of so of armed merchantmen, would lie off the Azores in wait for the homeward-bound convoys and treasure ships

<hr/>

[18] *L. and A.*, II, 259–61.

from America. For the Queen and her ministers were ever mindful that, as Sir Roger Williams put it, the King of Spain's 'treasure comes unto him as our salads to us – when we have eat all, we fetch more out of our gardens; so doth he fetch his treasure out of the ground after spending all that is coined'.[19]

These plans outlined a reasonably coherent and balanced design for future operations. They did certainly call for a precision of timing and allied co-operation that it was optimistic to expect in the sixteenth century. Nevertheless they seem to have met with the pretty well unanimous approval – or at any rate acceptance – of the Queen's leading advisers. Of these, Burghley, the Lord Treasurer, was now more than ever the most influential in foreign affairs. For since Walsingham's death in April 1590 he had again taken on the work, though not the title, of Principal Secretary. He grumbled at the extra burden, at being 'so many ways answerable to the round world at home and abroad', and indeed such a concentration of business upon a gouty (or arthritic) septuagenarian did not make for efficiency and despatch. Yet he was by no means willing to unload the burden on to any other shoulders than those of his younger son, Robert Cecil. The Earl of Essex, perhaps with Hatton's support, was no less anxious to persuade the Queen to let William Davison resume the secretarial duties from which he had been suspended since Mary Stuart's execution in 1587. This produced a deadlock. For, while Robert Cecil's very limited experience and comparative youth – he was twenty-seven – made Elizabeth hesitate to appoint him, she could not forgive Davison for delivering Mary's death warrant and she was already hesitant about letting Essex fill important offices with his protégés. To appoint anyone else – Sir Edward Stafford, Henry Killigrew, Edward Wotton, Thomas Wilkes, and Edward Dyer were the names chiefly canvassed among the court gossips – would offend both Burghley and Essex. So the office of Principal Secretary remained unfilled and Burghley, with increasing help from Robert Cecil, continued to do the work.[20]

[19] Ibid., 467.
[20] Ibid., 29; S. P. Domestic, ccxxxiii, no. 109; *Cal. S. P. Domestic, 1591–4*, p. 97; Cotton MSS, Galba D. vii, fo. 26 and Vespasian C. xiii, fo. 288; *H. M. C., De L'Isle and*

Most of the diplomatic correspondence and foreign intelligences therefore now passed through Burghley's hands and he was now more than ever the most influential of the Queen's advisers upon these matters. With him it had always been a cardinal point of policy that England's security required the maintenance of a reasonable balance between the power of Spain and the power of France. It was the collapse of the French monarchy in the spring of 1585 that had eventually convinced him of the need for England to intervene against Spain by openly upholding the Dutch.[21] The apparent danger in 1591, not merely of Spain's aggrandizement, but also of France's extinction as a great power, now convinced him of the need to assist Henry IV whole-heartedly. Therefore, as we have seen, he strongly supported both the Brittany expedition and Palavicino's German negotiations.

Nothing suggests that Burghley had any doubts about the Azores operation either. That naval operation, however, was primarily the Lord Admiral Howard's affair. After all, his cousin Lord Thomas Howard was to be its commander and the two of them, together with Raleigh, were sharing its cost with the Queen. But the Lord Admiral himself was also to command the proposed Brittany expedition, at least until it got ashore, and there is no evidence at all to suggest that he was in any way opposed to the plan to bring Turenne's Germans through the Netherlands. Lord Chancellor Hatton's involvement in foreign affairs was of more recent date and perhaps still somewhat limited, but he, too, was to show himself a strong supporter of aid to Henry IV during the coming months. So also was Buckhurst, though he was perhaps better acquainted with the Netherlands. Of the other Councillors, Hunsdon, the Lord Chamberlain, was highly regarded by military men, but his long experience had been mainly in northern affairs. The rest seem to have played only a small part in the shaping of foreign policy. Sir Thomas Heneage had a hand in organizing foreign intelligences, but

---

*Dudley MSS,* II, 120; Collins, I, 303, 329; Lodge, *Illustrations of British History,* II, 416–17, 426–7; J. Strype, *Annals,* IV, 3–4; Devereux, I, 209–10; Sir H. Nicolas, *Davison,* pp. 181–3, 190–5; also Conyers Read, *Burghley,* pp. 464 ff.; F. M. G. Evans, *Principal Secretary of State,* pp. 53–4.

[21] R. B. Wernham, *Before the Armada,* pp. 369–71.

like Sir John Wolley and Sir John Fortescue, he was primarily an administrator. Archbishop Whitgift was fully occupied in making the Church militant at home. Henry Stanley, Earl of Derby, and Lord Cobham, the Warden of the Cinque Ports, were more concerned with local matters than with national policy – Cobham, too, was Robert Cecil's father-in-law. Sir Francis Knollys was patently approaching his dotage, and Sir John Perrot was on his way to the Tower under suspicion of treasonable activities in Ireland.[22]

Outside the Privy Council, Essex was certainly the most insistent of Elizabeth's advisers on military matters. As we have seen, he was a strenuous supporter of the Turenne project and of aid to Henry IV, while as Sir Roger Williams's pupil and patron he was not likely to oppose action in Brittany or at the Azores. Sir John Norris, who was to command the land forces in Brittany, had some doubts about the practicability of bringing Turenne's Germans through the Netherlands, but none about the necessity of helping the French King. Sir John Hawkins, no doubt, still wished Her Majesty to have as little to do with the Continent as possible, but he and Frobisher were now almost as much out of favour as Drake, less perhaps because of their limited success against the Spaniards on their recent cruises than because of the irritation they had caused among the Queen's friendly and neutral neighbours.[23]

Indeed, the person who seems to have been the least readily convinced about the urgency of helping Henry IV was Elizabeth. As she had shown in her 1589 instructions to Norris and Drake, and again in her precautions against the phantom armada of 1590, she took very seriously the maritime threat from Spain's Atlantic sea power. But she appears to have been less acutely worried than her advisers about the impending crisis in France. Like her father and grandfather, she seems to have had an instinctive confidence that European rivalries

[22] S. P. Domestic, ccxxxviii, nos. 17–19, 35, 37, 63, 82; *Monson's Tracts*, I, 72, 256–8; *Cal. S. P. Domestic, Addenda*, p. 320; *L. and A.*, II, 262. Hatton's part in foreign policy has been little studied. For a list of Privy Councillors at 20 December 1590 – *Acts P. C.*, XX, 136–7.

[23] Read, *Burghley*, pp. 472–3 and p. 584 note 40, seems to me completely justified in disregarding Camden's story (pp. 569–70) about the Queen's advisers being divided about policy towards France.

were too sharp and too deep-seated to allow Spain, or any other power, to establish or maintain a menacing Continental hegemony. The more obviously Philip II appeared to aim at such hegemony, the stronger and more widespread would be the Continental resistance to his ambition. Then, just as England had saved herself by her own exertions in 1588, so now surely the French royalists, the Dutch, and the German Protestants must exert themselves to follow her example. Saving Europe was, after all, first and foremost, their business. English diplomacy might well be active, as with Palavicino's mission, in encouraging their exertions. But before English money, and even more before English men, were thrown in to back English exhortations, long and vigorous argument was required to convince Elizabeth's reason of a necessity that her instinct doubted. All through 1591, in fact, the impression that English policy conveys is of Councillors and advisers pretty well agreed upon the imperative need for an active intervention in France, but having continually to push into action a Queen who hated war, who at fifty-seven was developing an old lady's fear that her money would not last out, and whose instinct whispered that in the impending crisis western Europe might eventually work out its own salvation without England exhausting herself by crippling exertions.

The first set-back to English plans for 1591, however, like the first setback to the plans for the 1589 Portugal expedition, was largely due to a quarrel with the Dutch. On 22 January 1591 the States General heard from Loosen and Warck – who, it may be remembered, were in England complaining about seizures of Dutch shipping – that Sir John Norris was coming over to get English troops for Brittany in addition to those promised to Turenne, to whose proposals they had given a somewhat cool welcome a month earlier. They immediately instructed their two envoys to use all means possible to stop Norris's mission. But it was already too late. He had landed at Flushing on 19 January. He reached The Hague on 25 January and, when on 27 and 28 January he met the States General and Council of State, he put his demands to them in his most uncompromising manner. He had the Queen's orders, he informed them, to take 3,000 of her troops for three months' service in Brittany. There was nothing of comparable importance for them to do in the Netherlands and, as Parma was preparing all his forces for France, no attack on the Provinces was likely for months to come. So the States should not only willingly release these 3,000 English, but should send 2,000 of their own men as well. And all must be done quickly. There was no time to waste on consulting the individual Provinces. If the States General would not consent, then Her Majesty 'sera occasionnée de suivre et exécuter ses propres resolutions'.

The States on 1 February met these blunt demands with a reasoned refusal. The best help, they said, that they and the English auxiliary companies could give to the French King was to put as many men as they could into the field to distract Parma at home. They had already almost completed their arrangements for doing just that, for levying more troops to provide a field force that would be able to clear their frontiers while the enemy was in France. Norris replied two days later with a formal declaration that his orders were to withdraw the 3,000 English without delay. He named the twenty foot-bands that were to go – the twelve that had been serving in the field under Sir Francis Vere, together with eight others from the Bergen garrison – and he required passports for them, their victuals, and shipping.[24]

This declaration caused general dismay, and not only among the Dutch. Buzenval, whom Norris had snubbed and whom the States blamed for seconding Norris's demands, foresaw an Iliad of woes. Gilpin wrote home that the States regarded Vere's companies, just replenished, as their greatest strength in the field and that their withdrawal would hinder everything. The eastward provinces, still largely Papist or of no religion, might suddenly fall away if they felt that the Queen could not protect them and if the reports proved true that ambassadors from the Emperor were coming with specious peace offers. Bodley, at a conference attended also by Lord Burgh and Sir Francis Vere on 4 February, tried to persuade Norris that his instructions required him to return to seek further order if the States rejected his demands. But Norris would not listen, even though his commission directed

[24] *L. and A.*, II, 269–71; *Kronijk*, XVIII, 392–9, 401–3. For the States' preparations – *L. and A.*, II, 20, 24; *Resolutiën der Staten Generaal*, VII, 243–5, 249, 393–4, 427–9.

him to use Bodley's advice. He hurried off letters ordering the twenty companies to be at Flushing by 15 February. If the Dutch refused them the means to march off quietly, then the captains were to discharge their soldiers and order them to make their own way to Flushing or Brielle, there to rejoin their colours. Vere, although he professed complete readiness to obey, knew not how this could be done if the Dutch refused them boats, victuals, and passes. And, indeed, it was a richly ludicrous idea that 3,000 English soldiers, a good many of them married to Dutch women and by no means all of them enthusiastic warriors, might stroll across from Gelderland and Bergen like tourists on a walking holiday and then faithfully rejoin their companies at Flushing.[25]

These problems, however, Norris left Vere and his captains to solve. He himself left The Hague for Zeeland on 5 February and was back in England a week later. With him he took a sharp letter of protest to the Queen from the States General and letters from Bodley supporting their arguments. Meanwhile the States forbade Bodley, Vere, Morgan, and all other officers to move any English troops from their garrisons without express orders from themselves or the Council of State. They also forbade their own officials to assist such movements with shipping, victuals, etc.[26] Most of the English commanders and captains were only too ready to take the States' prohibition as excuse enough for not obeying Norris's orders. Sir Thomas Morgan at Bergen was most reluctant to let any of his garrison go and foresaw, as did Gilpin, serious inconveniences if he had to make up his numbers with companies in the States' pay. Besides, his Netherlander and pro-Spanish father-in-law had just recently tried to seduce him into betraying Bergen to Parma, so he was particularly anxious to avoid doing anything that might strengthen the States' doubts about leaving him as governor of so important a place.[27] There were doubts, too, whether Vere's captains would be willing to serve under Norris. Some of the best of

---

[25] *L. and A.*, II, 24, 53, 269, 272–3, 277, 283–4, 760, 764; *Resolutiën der Staten Generaal*, VII, 361.

[26] *L. and A.*, II, 271–2, 277, 282, 284; *Kronijk*, XVIII, 403–6.

[27] *L. and A.*, II, 106, 108–10, 113, 286. In July Morgan had assured the Queen 'on the word of a soldier and a gentleman' that his governorship brought him no profit – ibid., 99.

them, while in England the previous year, had almost come to blows with him and his brother, a matter which seriously worried the Queen when she belatedly learned of it after Sir John had already gone over.[28] To make matters worse, Sir Edward Norris's high-handed usurpation of the contributions at Ostend and his unauthorized dealings with Bruges and other enemy places were even now involving him in long and bitter wrangles with the Zeelanders, the Council of State, and the States General.[29] Altogether, as Bodley wrote to Sir Robert Sidney on 9 February, it looked very much as if things were moving rapidly towards 'the ruin of the [English] companies, to the loss of those towns where the English only are in garrison, and to the general detriment of the state of these Provinces'. Fortunately Bodley had the courage as well as the good sense to step in and act upon his own responsibility. 'Because in this matter I am put in some trust and must answer my trust if I do not counsel for the best,' he told Sidney, 'I am fully resolved, whatsoever other course shall be taken by others, to direct mine own actions to the indemnity of this country.' Accordingly he wrote off to the English captains to suspend Sir John Norris's orders until they could hear further from Her Majesty.[30]

Fortunately, too, Her Majesty was as prompt to set things right now as she had been in 1589. Alarm at the rumours about the Emperor's peace envoys played some part in this.[31] But by Elizabeth's own account what chiefly moved her was the news of the States' intention to mount an offensive in strength in the spring to impeach or divert Parma's French enterprise. She was anxious that as many of the English auxiliary companies as possible should assist them in this

---

[28] Ibid., 270.

[29] Ibid., 143–5, 148, 156–8, 166; Collins, I, 315–16, 319–22; *Resolutiën der Staten Generaal*, VII, 149; *Acts P. C.*, XXI, 8.

[30] Collins, I, 315–16; *L. and A.*, II, 283–5.

[31] Norris's instructions of 13 February directed him to warn the States against them. But it was not until 1 March that the Queen sent Bodley a long paper by Burghley – the draft is endorsed as 20 February – on the subject. What moved her to send it then seems to have been a wild report from Sir Edward Norris, written from Ostend on 23 February, that the Duke of Aerschot, Count Charles Mansfelt, and President Richardot were meeting deputies of the States to discuss a peace, and that free traffic had been allowed to Dunkirk and Nieupoort – *L. and A.*, II, 288–91, 764; Read, *Burghley*, pp. 471–2.

offensive. So, although she could not do without some trained and disciplined bands for the service in Brittany, she would withdraw fewer than Norris had asked for. And as soon as she knew how many the States were willing to let go, provided it was not more than fifteen, she would send over an equal number, fully equipped, to take their place. The new bands would be made ready at once and the ships which carried them to Zeeland would take the old ones directly to Brittany. All this had been decided by 13 February. The States naturally welcomed the Queen's decision. When Norris returned and reported it on 8 March, they readily agreed that ten of the old auxiliary companies might leave for Brittany as soon as their replacements arrived. The Queen thus obtained her nucleus of trained and disciplined troops for the Brittany expedition. Also it became daily more obvious that there was no likelihood at all of the States listening to the Emperor's, or anyone else's, peace overtures. On the contrary, they were now definitely preparing for a spring offensive on a much larger scale than in previous years, though it would be centred upon Gelderland, Overijsel, and Groningen rather than upon Flanders as Elizabeth was urging.[32]

So far, so good. Nevertheless this decision altered the whole character of the intended operation in Brittany. It halved the strength of the striking force. Instead of 6,000 men, or 8,000 if the States would send 2,000 of their troops, there would now be only 3,000. For there would be only 1,500 English veterans from the Netherlands instead of 3,000, and only 1,500 of the 3,000 being levied in England since the other 1,500 would be going as replacements to the United Provinces. Moreover, instead of 6,000 or 8,000 men sailing for Brittany on 15 February, the 3,000 now going could hardly hope to get away until late in March and could therefore certainly not hope to return in time for the start of the Netherlands campaigning season. For it was 8 March before Sir John Norris got back to The Hague and imparted his new instructions to the States.

The States signified their agreement, with quite unaccustomed promptness, the very next day.[33] But in England things moved more slowly. This was not entirely, nor even chiefly,

[32] *L. and A.*, II, 24–6, 30, 287, 292–4; *Resolutiën der Staten Generaal*, VII, 362–3, 397–8.
[33] *L. and A.*, II, 292; *Kronijk*, XVIII, 409–11.

because the Queen and Council had to wait until mid-March to hear from Norris of the States' assent. The chief reason was, once again, the difficulty of communicating with the peripatetic King of France. As Elizabeth had told Beauvoir back in December, she could not well send English troops into a French province without the French King's explicit consent. She also needed more satisfactory undertakings about their conditions of service and the repayment of her expenses than Dombes and the Bretons could offer. So on 2 January 1591 Burghley, Hatton, and Howard had given Beauvoir a memorial to send to the King. This explained that, if the Queen were to send troops to help Dombes against the Spaniards, she would want first to know by the King's own letters where those troops should land; what arrangements would be made for their victualling; and what port and walled town would be assigned to them as a haven for their shipping and as a place of retreat – Brest seemed the most suitable. She would also want assurances that royalist forces, equal in numbers to the Spaniards and Leaguers, would join the English when they landed and that Henry would guarantee the full reimbursement of her expenses.

Beauvoir had sent off this memorial by 6 January. The Privy Council promised him that, while they waited for Henry's answers, everything would be made ready. And as we have seen, Sir John Norris was despatched to Holland immediately afterwards. Then on 9 and 10 January the Council instructed London and twelve counties to select, muster, and put in readiness their quotas towards a force of 1,500 men for overseas service. They were also to select and enrol, but not yet to muster or arm, the extra numbers that would be needed to bring the force up to 2,000 men and up to 3,000 men. On 31 January the 2,000 men were ordered to be put ready. Half might be drawn from the trained bands, who were normally exempted from foreign service. This would both increase the proportion of men with some military training and also ease the burden on the counties, which would already have provided these men's arms and equipment.[34]

[34] *L. and A.*, II, 481–3; *Cal, S. P. Domestic, 1591–4*, pp. 2, 7, 9, 10; *Acts P. C.*, XX, 204–6, 247–8, 255, 306–7.

Little more could be done until answers came from the States and from Henry IV. From Henry nothing had been heard by the end of January and by then several things had happened to make it even more necessary to know his mind. In Brittany Dombes' forces were as weak as ever and the Spaniards were making rapid progress in fortifying Blavet. Moreover, strong reinforcements of troops and ships were preparing in northern Spain and Elizabeth had secret information that when these reinforcements sailed, Parma was to enter France again and march straight across to Brittany to join them.[35] Nor was that all. In mid-January a messenger on his way from Turenne to Henry IV had talked with Norris at Margate. According to this man, Morlans, Turenne was under the impression, and he and Beauvoir had told the King, that Elizabeth had promised both to send forces to Brittany and also to send 4,000 new levies to the Netherlands to release her old soldiers for service with the German army. Beauvoir utterly denied reporting this. But clearly it was important to make sure that Henry IV understood the true situation.[36]

So on 27 January Edmund Yorke was given instructions, drafted by Burghley and checked by Elizabeth, to go over to Dieppe. There he was to find out where the King was and then to go to him and to get his answers to the 2 January memorial, to warn him of the danger that Parma might march across to Brittany, to deny Morlans' report, and generally to learn what he could about the situation in all parts of France.[37] Because of contrary winds it was 7 February before Yorke was able to embark at Rye and while he was there two more Breton envoys, Gabriel Huet and Pierre Gonaurt, arrived. Dombes had sent them to the King and the King had sent them on to England to beg for 5,000 or 6,000 men, paid for eight months, with munitions, cannon, and shipping. These two envoys presented their requests on 4 February and replied next day, as best they could, to a long string of questions from Burghley. But they had neither the authority, nor indeed the knowledge, to supply the answers

---

[35] *L. and A.,* II, 490–1, 599, 600.
[36] Ibid., 487, 492–3.
[37] The draft, in Burghley's hand, is endorsed with three trefoils, the revised copy with one – S. P. France, xxiii, fos. 48, 54.

and the assurances that the 2 January memorial required from the King himself. Nor could another envoy, La Tour, whom the King sent to Turenne by way of England at this time. La Tour's primary task in England was to ask the Queen to write to hasten the German army, as the King heard that Parma was coming back in March. He was also to press for aid to Brittany, but he, too, brought no satisfactory replies to the 2 January requests. Henry IV did manage to find time to write to Beauvoir about them on 8 February, but his answers and assurances were very hurried and vague.[38]

That was how matters stood when Sir John Norris arrived back from The Hague and reported the States' blunt refusal of his original demands. Altogether it was becoming every day less likely that it would be possible to strike a decisive blow against the Spaniards in Brittany and especially to strike quickly enough for the old companies to return in time for the opening of the Netherlands campaigning season. Burghley could still write on 6 February to Palavicino – sincerely? or just to encourage the Germans? – that Norris was sent for 3,000 men from the Netherlands to join 3,000 more from England. Elizabeth, however, seems already to have decided that the Brittany operations would have to be defensive and prolonged, not short and sharp. For in her instructions to Yorke she remarked that if the old companies were transported to Brittany, they would be unable to get back in time to join Turenne's Germans. And, of course, the orders sent to the counties on 13 February were for 1,500 of the 3,000 levied in England to go to the Netherlands instead of Brittany.

Even now it was another month before these men were actually ordered to the ports. Once again the delay occurred because Queen and Council could not take final decisions until they knew what Norris had agreed with the States and what Henry IV had replied to Yorke. It was mid-March before Norris's report of the States' reply of 9 March arrived; and it was 9 March also before Yorke returned from an adventurous journey to find the King who, to Elizabeth's considerable annoyance, had gone off to besiege Chartres. The requests that Yorke brought back from Henry made her even more annoyed, as we shall see. Nevertheless he did bring also letters patent empowering Beauvoir to sign agreements assuring repayment of the Queen's expenses in aiding Brittany.[39] So on 17 March the Privy Council sent out orders to ten counties for 1,500 men (or, in this case allowing the dead pays, 1,350) to embark at Harwich, London, and Sandwich for Flushing on 7 April, and to London and seven more counties for another 1,500 to take shipping at Portsmouth and Southampton for Jersey and Brittany on 11 April. During the next fortnight further directions followed about payment of coat and conduct money; provision of victuals and convoy at sea; musters and imprests; appointments of captains and which ten old companies were to come from the Netherlands – three from Flushing, three from Bergen, one from Brielle, one from Ostend, and only two from Vere's forces in the field. Finally, on 3 April Beauvoir signed with Burghley, Howard, and Hunsdon the contract for the repayment within twelve months of the Queen's expenses for the 3,000 men she was about to send to Brittany.[40]

This time all went to plan. Nine of the ten companies from England were at Flushing by 12 April – the tenth arrived on 17 or 18 April – and the ten old bands which they replaced were there ready to embark on 20 April.[41] But that was just a month from the time the orders of 17 March went out. It was not a spectacularly swift performance after all the preliminary preparations from early January onwards: in 1589 Willoughby's 4,000 men had landed at Dieppe a bare three weeks from the time when their levying was first ordered. By the time Norris and his troops landed near Paimpol, on the northern coast of Brittany, it was already 2 May, less than a fortnight before Count Maurice and Sir Francis Vere took the field against Zutphen. And Norris's troops no longer numbered even 3,000, for 600 of them had been detached under Sir Roger Williams to save Dieppe from being besieged by Villars with the Rouen and Le Havre garrisons.[42]

[39] Ibid., 506–8, 510–11, 514–15.
[40] Ibid., 529; *Acts P. C.*, XX, 361–4; XXI, 3–8, 12–17, 47–9; *Cal. S. P. Domestic, 1591–4*, pp. 21–5.
[41] *L. and A.*, II, 188–9, 550, 557, 560.
[42] Ibid., 517–19, 526, 528, 545.

As Norris found Dombes' forces hardly more numerous than his own,[43] there was clearly no possibility of a decisive offensive against Mercoeur and his Spanish allies. The most that could be done would be to keep Dombes in the field and the enemy away from the northern coast of Brittany. Instead of dealing a quick, decisive blow, the English troops in Brittany were committed, as the auxiliary companies in the Netherlands had so long been committed, to a prolonged holding action in support of an unreliable ally's very inadequate forces. The first item in the English government's strategic design for 1591 had gone very sadly awry.

[43] Ibid., 561.

# XIII

# The Genesis of the Rouen Expedition

While English plans for a quick decisive blow against the Spaniards in Brittany were thus being frustrated, the hope of seeing Parma and Mayenne trapped between Henry IV's army and Turenne's Germans was also evaporating. To some extent this was due to the difficulty of making contact with the peripatetic French King. Stafford, when he returned to England, had left his secretary, Edward Grimeston, to accompany Henry, but the King's wandering made communication between him and England always slow and often precarious. As we have seen, it was not until 8 February that he replied to Beauvoir about Turenne's route and the English Council's queries concerning the aid to Brittany. His letter can hardly have reached Beauvoir before the end of February and Edmund Yorke, sent to France at the end of January to discover Henry's plans and views, did not arrive back until 9 March.

What made communication so slow and difficult was that Henry had gone off, first, to try to close the eastern approaches to Paris by building a fort on the Marne and by taking Meaux and Pontoise; and then to deprive the capital of its westward 'granary' by besieging Chartres, 'the best magazine in France for corn'. For these purposes he had in January called Marshal Biron and the army away from Normandy, to the Marshal's considerable annoyance. The siege of Chartres proved disappointingly lengthy and while Henry IV and Biron were bogged down there, the League governors of Le Havre and Rouen, Villars and Tavannes, took the chance to reoccupy a good deal of eastern Normandy and to cut Dieppe's overland communications. At the same time the activity of League privateers from Le Havre and the Somme towns made the sea route to royalist Caen only a little less hazardous, as Edmund Yorke found when he went from Dieppe that way round to Chartres.[1] Henry's

---

[1] *L. and A.*, II, 385–8, 391, 395–8, 401–3, 506–8; *H. M. C., Salisbury MSS*, IV, 92, 97; *Lettres Missives*, III, 341–2, 360; Birch, *Memoirs*, I, 64.

preoccupation with Paris was thus causing him to neglect Normandy as well as Brittany, to risk the loss of those coastal areas that were most vital in English eyes. That preoccupation with Paris also suggested, and the letter of 8 February to Beauvoir seemed to confirm, that Henry's ideas of dealing with Parma differed sharply from Elizabeth's. In that letter he professed to expect Parma in March, long before Turenne's Germans would be ready to take the field. Not unnaturally, he was therefore no more than lukewarm towards Elizabeth's plan for bringing the Germans through the Netherlands, even if they were ready as soon as Parma. He would, he told Beauvoir, leave the decision to Turenne; but if they came that way, the Dutch must increase their contribution to pay for any delay this entailed in their arrival in France. That the Dutch would pay anything more than 100,000 florins that they had already, and rather reluctantly, promised was most improbable, as the Queen well knew from the despatches of Bodley, Gilpin, and Vere. Moreover, even if the States did increase their contribution, it was clear that their military plans were concentrated upon clearing the region between the Ijsel and the German borders and upon taking Nijmegen and 'sHertogenbosch, the links between that region and the obedient provinces of the South. The States and Maurice were under heavy pressure in this direction from Count William of Friesland, whose troops were an important element in the field army; and from Utrecht, Gelderland, and Overijsel who, though they contributed little, might refuse even that, might even come to terms with the enemy, if nothing were done to liberate and secure them now Parma was so preoccupied with France. There was therefore very little likelihood that Count Maurice, with the States' field army and Vere's English companies, would escort Turenne's Germans deep into Brabant, let alone on through Hainault to the frontiers of France. Elizabeth's dream of trapping Parma between Henry and Turenne was already fading fast.[2]

Worse still, it was becoming clear that Henry's general strategic ideas also differed disturbingly from Elizabeth's. What he seemed to have in mind for 1591 was to do over again

[2] *L. and A.*, II, 24–6, 30, 37, 271–3, 293, 316, 319–21, 505, 764; *Kronijk*, XVIII, 411, 420–1.

what he had done in the spring of 1590. Just as he had then
drawn Mayenne to battle and defeat by the pressure the siege
of Dreux had put upon Paris, so now he seems to have hoped
that his siege of Chartres and other operations to straiten Paris
would draw Parma and Mayenne forward to another Ivry.
But for this he needed forces, infantry in particular, more
numerous and reliable than he could himself provide. So in his
8 February letter he instructed Beauvoir to ask Elizabeth to
put ready at once in England the 4,000 men that Turenne
(mistakenly) told him she had promised to send to reinforce
Vere's companies and help escort the German army through
the Netherlands. If Parma entered France before the German
army was ready, those 4,000 should be sent over to reinforce
Henry's army instead; even if Parma was delayed, they should
still be sent over to help in some great enterprise in France.
Henry did allow that in the latter event they might perhaps
assist in escorting the Germans through the Netherlands as
Elizabeth had originally suggested. But it was obvious that
France, and not the Netherlands, was really where he wanted
them – and the Germans too, for he wanted the Queen to get
the princes of the Circles near the Rhine to mobilize their
forces to help the Dutch campaign and so leave Turenne's
levies free to march straight to France.[3] Henry, it seemed, was
leaving the initiative to Parma, was seeking to provoke him
into taking the offensive and trusting that it would then be
possible to bring him to battle more readily than in 1590. And
his preoccupation with Paris and Parma augured none to well
for his attention to Brittany and the Normandy coast.

The report and requests that Yorke brought when he
arrived back on 9 March did little to bridge these differences.
They made it still clearer that for Henry what mattered above
all was to make head against Parma, to gather the largest
possible forces to confront him when he tried to re-enter
France. So, in the requests sent by Yorke he again asked
Elizabeth to send him 4,000 foot, paid by her for the two or
three months before Turenne's Germans arrived. He would
meet them at Dieppe with 11,000 foot and 4,000 horse – so he
said – and he would then put 600 of the English, along with

[3] *L. and A.*, II, 505.

1,200 French foot, into St Quentin and another 300, with 600
French, into Corbie to defend the frontier. The rest, English
and French, he would hold ready nearby to check enemy
attempts to cross the Somme. He did say that, while they were
waiting for Parma, they might do what they could to clear the
Leaguers out of eastern Normandy and the coast towns. But
this hardly suggested that he was now seriously thinking of
any 'great enterprise' such as he had vaguely mentioned in his
letter of 8 February to Beauvoir. Moreover, he asked that the
4,000 English should include a good number of the veteran
companies from the Netherlands, even if this meant sending a
larger proportion of raw troops to Brittany. Clearly, he had
little enthusiasm for the plan of using English and Dutch
forces to bring Turenne's Germans through the Netherlands
and it was no less clear that he regarded Brittany as very much
a secondary matter, as an outlying corner of his realm whose
safety was of more immediate concern to his English ally than
to himself. And meanwhile there he was, he and his army,
bogged down far away before Chartres.[4]

It is small wonder, therefore, that poor Edmund Yorke got a
very rough reception from the Queen when he brought home
these requests.[5] Only two days before, on 7 March, she had
written to Henry complaining bitterly that since Parma's
withdrawal he had wasted his time on places of small
importance. If he had, instead, concentrated upon taking his
seaports, Paris would have been far less well provided and
places nearer the heart of his realm would have received
foreign aid less easily.[6] It is not very clear just what places
nearer the heart of Henry's realm Elizabeth can have had in
mind. But her other complaints went to the heart of the
difference between her attitude and his. For Henry the most
serious problem was obviously the likelihood that Parma
would come back and help the League in 1591 as he had done
in 1590. But when would he come? That was the crux of the
matter. Henry naturally felt himself obliged to prepare

[4] Ibid., 511; *H. M. C., Salisbury MSS,* IV, 92. All through the siege of Chartres Henry
was writing to Nevers that, as soon as that siege was over, he would come with his
army to Champagne: even farther, that is, from the 'maritimes' – *Lettres Missives,* III,
341–2, 358–9, 361–2, 369, 386.

[5] *L. and A.,* II, 511, 515. The Queen in fact refused to see him.

[6] Ibid., 514.

against the worst eventuality, to assume that Parma would be coming, if not actually in March, at any rate some weeks or even months before Turenne and the Germans. That, however, was an assumption which Elizabeth never really shared. She did not believe that Parma's army could recover so rapidly from the losses, diseases, and mutinies of the past year and the reports coming in from the Netherlands tended more and more to strengthen her disbelief.[7] She felt therefore that the time of waiting for Parma was likely to be long enough for Henry to take the initiative at least against some of the principal League strongholds in Normandy. If he could spend so much time and effort against Chartres, he might as easily and more usefully have stayed in Normandy and taken Le Havre. It was all very well for Edward Grimeston to write to Burghley that Chartres would prove the King's greatest conquest since he came to the throne, for it would 'famish Paris, bridle Orleans, and keep the whole country in subjection. If he had gone into Brittany or to Newhaven as your lordship writ, he must have retired himself into a corner of his realm and abandoned the heart of France unto his enemies.'[8] But those corners of his realm were precisely the parts of France where English interests were most deeply involved. Even from Henry's own point of view those corners, Normandy in particular, were important enough. For if the League were allowed to overrun Normandy, Spaniards in Brittany would be able to link hands with Spanish forces from the Netherlands. Henry must then perforce fall back beyond the Loire and be cut off from the English assistance in men and money without which he – and Grimeston too – confessed that he could not hope to make head against Parma.

It was just this danger that seemed to be impending by the middle of March 1591. By then Villars had taken Fécamp and shut up in its castle 400 of Dieppe's infantry who had been put in as its garrison. He had also taken the important castle of Blainville, 30 miles away. On 14 March he took Bacqueville, a bare dozen miles from Dieppe. De Chatte, the governor of Dieppe, now desperately short of infantry and

---

[7] For reports of Parma's losses – ibid., 366, 597, 625. See also, van der Essen, *Alexandre Farnèse*, V, 313–14.

[8] *L. and A.*, II, 514.

very discouraged, on 19 March got Ottywell Smith to write urgently to Burghley for 500–800 English troops. They might, Smith suggested, be taken from the 3,000 being made ready for Brittany. Or, better, why not send the whole 3,000? Paid for four months, they would recapture Fécamp, Harfleur, Caudebec, shut in Rouen and Le Havre, and in two or four months repay their cost out of the tailles of the surrounding country. Five days later, on 24 March, Smith and Incarville wrote still more urgently after the discovery during the previous night of a plot by some priests to betray Dieppe to Villars. Once again Smith suggested diverting the whole of Sir John Norris's 3,000 men from Brittany to Dieppe. To make the suggestion more attractive, he added that it would be a means to draw Henry IV to besiege Rouen. To make it appear more necessary, he reported that the *Great Brissac* and other warships of Le Havre were about to link up with twelve or thirteen sail from the Somme towns and with the Dunkirk privateers to blockade the Channel ports, while four galleasses and twenty-four galleys with 2,000 Spanish infantry were getting ready in Biscay to come to Le Havre at the end of . April. English warships, as well as English soldiers, were therefore needed if Dieppe was to be preserved and the Leaguers prevented from overrunning Normandy.[9]

Elizabeth's response to these rather exaggerated claims was prompt. Smith's letter of 19 March arrived on 24 March. By 26 March she had decided to detach to Dieppe 600 men from Norris's 3,000 and next day Beauvoir learned that Sir Roger Williams was to command them. On 30 March Williams received his instructions to hasten the men over from Portsmouth and Southampton to Dieppe. Once there, however, he was not to hazard them outside the town unless there were some special and manifest opportunity for some good exploit or unless the King's army or Halot de Montmorency's forces from west Normandy reinforced de Chatte so that there was a good chance of reducing the neighbouring country to the King's obedience.[10]

Williams and his 600 landed at Dieppe on 10 April, just in

---

[9] Ibid., 397, 517–19, 526; *Acts P. C.*, XXI, 3–4. Bodley, however, could hear of no unusual preparations at Dunkirk – *L. and A.*, II, 151.

[10] Ibid., 526, 528; *Acts P. C.*, XXI, 26–8.

time to break off the negotiations that the downcast de Chatte had begun with Villars.[11] It had been a near thing – or so it seemed – and the entire episode served to emphasize how necessary it was from the English point of view to draw Henry towards the Channel coast. It is true that Elizabeth was still struggling to avoid the commitments towards which that necessity was inexorably drawing her. How reluctant she was to be drawn, was manifest in the 'restraining orders' in Williams's instructions. Nevertheless she was under steadily increasing pressure from all sides. What we might call 'the Dieppe lobby' – Ottywell Smith, Incarville, de Chatte – were more insistent than ever upon the advantages to be gained by sending larger forces to Normandy and drawing Henry to besiege Rouen. They were now reinforced by Sir Roger Williams, anxious not to be sent off to serve under Norris and therefore no longer convinced of the supreme importance of Brittany. There were, too, influential London merchants – Alderman Hugh Offley, James Staper, Edward Smith, Ralph Leatherborough, for example – of whose desire to have their old trade to Rouen reopened the Queen's Council at least cannot have been ignorant.[12]

Then, at the very end of March another envoy, Antonie de Moret, sieur de Reau, had arrived from Henry himself to beg Elizabeth to hasten her aid to Brittany and to press her again for the other 4,000 infantry without which he would be unable to keep the field or fortify the frontier towns of Picardy against Parma. April, however, brought a variety of more encouraging news. Chartres had capitulated on 31 March and opened its gates to the King on 9 April. Thereupon, although Biron and the bulk of the royal army stayed awhile to clear the country around by taking Dourdan and other places, Henry with 1,200 horse immediately marched northwards to join Longueville's forces in Picardy and it was known that Caen had offered him 50,000 crowns and another 40,000 crowns' worth of wheat to come and besiege Rouen.[13] Moreover there now seemed a genuine opportunity for such an enterprise. For early in April Henry heard that Parma had sent 500 men to

[11] *L. and A.*, II, 404, 526, 545.
[12] Ibid., 536–9; *Acts P. C.*, XXI, 80–1, 103; *H. M. C.*, *Salisbury MSS*, IV, 87–8.
[13] *L. and A.*, II, 401–7, 410, 412, 516, 571.

Mayenne and promised another 500 but had warned that he would not be able to send any more before August. It is not certain when exactly Elizabeth received this particular piece of news – Grimeston reported it from Chartres on 10 April. But from the end of February onwards the reports coming in from the Netherlands about Parma's preparations suggested more and more strongly that he would concentrate, at least to start with, upon the defence of Brabant and Gelderland against the Dutch rather than upon another invasion of France to aid the League. Many, indeed, thought that he might well not move at all until he saw which way Turenne's German army was taking. News from France that Mayenne was again sending Villeroy to the King to discuss the possibility of a peace, also suggested that neither the League nor Parma would be ready to take the field in France for some considerable time to come.[14]

Hereupon the 'Dieppe lobby's' agitation for a siege of Rouen was redoubled. Sir Roger Williams weighed in with yet another disquisition to the Privy Council upon how to win the war. Conscious of shifting his ground on the supreme importance of Brittany, he began by admitting disarmingly that 'Sir John Norris will show your lordships no danger comparable unto his quarter; his brother Edward likewise; myself and others may also seek to enlarge the wars where we serve.' Nevertheless, he went on,

believe me, unless we can give great blows either on the Indian navy or in those countries where his [the King of Spain's] treasure comes or on the disciplined army (I mean on the Duke of Parma) or in the main of Spain or Portugal, be assured all the rest is consuming by little fires ... Let him be thoroughly warmed in any of the three actions, be assured his own estate will force him to any peace of conditions to your own desires.

But the first course would mean sending many of England's best ships, thoroughly manned, and a landing force of soldiers to strike at Havana and the other 'Indian' ports. The second would require 12,000 soldiers and 4,000 mariners: those numbers might give the law wherever they came in Spain or Portugal and could (as Williams professed to believe) enter

[14] Ibid., 32–3, 150, 159, 409, 533, 537, 601; *Correspondance de Philippe II*, III, 574–5.

Lisbon or Seville in less than thirty days, and 'doing that, your wars are ended'. For the third action, against Parma, the only sure means was through the French King. But a reinforcement of a mere 4,000 English troops and some cannon would enable him to beat Parma if the Duke dared to encounter him. If he did not dare, the King could assuredly take Rouen. Then other of the best towns would yield, the King's revenues would be so increased that he would be able to maintain his own wars, and Her Majesty's wars would be ended. For 'then the King of himself will make all Spain to shake with his own means.' So he must be drawn to besiege Rouen and to clear his sea coasts, which were dearer to England than the mainland. Otherwise, although he might take *bicoques* and win a wide country, he would only in time eat out his *plat pays,* ruin his nobles, consume Her Majesty's treasure, and leave Dieppe still dependent upon English help.[15]

In fact Williams and his friends were pushing, though not yet at an open door, at least at a door that was already ajar. For towards the middle of April – 'lately', Burghley and Hatton told Williams on 22 April – Elizabeth had sent de Reau back to Henry with a letter suggesting that he might come to besiege Rouen now that he had taken Chartres. She once again modestly disclaimed any expert judgement in these military matters. Her opinion about the ease with which Rouen might be recovered was founded only upon advertisements coming from that side and she would not wish to commit him to such an operation unless he had reason to hope for the speedy surrender of the town. But if he had reason to hope for that, then she would be ready to send over 3,000–4,000 soldiers and some shipping to help him in the siege.[16]

Over the exact nature of this promise there arose another Anglo-French misunderstanding similar to that about the help promised to Turenne in the previous November. Elizabeth did not mean to bear the cost of this new assistance of 4,000 men. She meant them, as Burghley and Hatton wrote in their letter to Williams on 22 April, to be waged by Henry. But either Her Majesty's French was less perfect than some of

[15] *L. and A.,* II, 536–9.
[16] Ibid., 533, 540.

her biographers would have us believe or else the French King's ambassadors, like Turenne earlier, were afflicted by wishful hearing. At all events de Reau and Beauvoir gathered that, when the Queen offered 4,000 troops, she would pay them at least for two or three months. It therefore came as a bad shock to Beauvoir to learn on 2 May that she intended nothing of the sort. Worse still, she was ordering Williams and his 600 to leave Dieppe and go at once to rejoin Norris in Brittany.[17]

This last decision was the result of a new alarm about Spanish reinforcements arriving in Brittany. Early in March 3,000 men had been sent thither from Spain but it was known that more than two-thirds of these had been driven back or drowned by a storm and that only a few hundreds had actually arrived. But on 29 April there landed back in England some Englishmen who had been taken at sea by the Spaniards between Spain and Brittany. They reported that on 17 April nineteen or twenty Spanish ships had landed another 2,800 men at Blavet. Seven of the ships stayed, they said, to guard the coast while the other fourteen [*sic*] went back to bring more troops from Spain to Brittany where there were already 7,000 Spaniards. The Englishmen's report was, in fact, to prove even less accurate than their arithmetic. As usual, however, it took time to ascertain the truth. And meanwhile the rumours grew – a Spanish fleet, twenty sail some said, was between Ushant and Land's End; they had sunk or burnt several merchant vessels; and they had attempted to take, if indeed they had not already taken the Isles of Scilly. None of these reports could be ignored. After all, the intelligence filtering in through various channels from Spanish ports left no doubt that a considerable fleet was beginning to gather at Ferrol; not yet an armada on the 1588 scale, but none the less quite a formidable force. Sir John Norris, too, had heard in mid-April from Jersey and from some Dutchmen just back from Spain, that besides the 3,000 Spanish troops lately sent to Brittany – the 3,000 presumably who had been mostly driven back by bad weather – another 8,000 were standing ready to embark at an hour's notice for Le Havre or Rouen.

[17] Ibid., 566–7. Beauvoir spoke little or no English. Once, at least, the Queen translated for him – ibid., 523.

Beauvoir himself may well have helped to sharpen the alarm. For it must have been towards the end of April or early in ' May that he communicated a letter of 9 April in which Henry IV sought to scare Elizabeth into hastening her aid to Brittany by passing on reports that the King of Spain had ordered Aguila to fortify Blavet as a refuge for the new forces he was sending thither and for the army he was preparing to send against England this summer.[18]

Elizabeth, whether or not she was scared, was certainly worried and depressed. During a visit to Burghley at his fine new house of Theobalds, from supper on 10 May to breakfast on 20 May, she was reported to be much moved and very melancholy at these various intelligences and rumours – Burghley himself was probably none too cheerful, for the royal visit cost him well over £1,000.[19] The Privy Council, too, took the situation seriously and as a result there was a flurry of activity similar to that of early 1590. On 16 May orders went out to the lords-lieutenant of the southern and eastern maritime counties as far north as Lincolnshire to have their trained bands reviewed and their beacons manned. The forces earmarked to come for the defence of the Isle of Wight, Milford Haven, and Anglesey from neighbouring counties were called to readiness. Sir George Carey was instructed to see to the Isle of Wight; the Earl of Sussex to Portsmouth; the Earl of Pembroke to Milford Haven; George Carey of Cockington and Sir William Courtenay to Devon. Edmund Yorke was to go to Ireland to alert the lord deputy. Raleigh was sent down to help Drake and Sir John Gilbert gather all the warlike shipping in the west country to guard those parts and help Sir Francis Godolphin hold Scilly. To reinforce them, Sir Henry Palmer was sent off to Plymouth with the Queen's ships of the Channel Guard, in whose absence the States of Zeeland were asked, and promptly agreed, to take over the watch on Dunkirk.[20]

[18] Ibid., 521, 533, 566, 603, 605, 679–85; S. P. Domestic, ccxxxviii, nos. 118, 152, 154, 159; *Acts P. C.*, XXI, 135–6, 140–1.

[19] S. P. Domestic, ccxxxviii, nos. 157–9; *H. M. C., Salisbury MSS*, IV, 115

[20] *Acts P. C.*, XXI, 131–40, 185–6; S. P. Domestic, ccxxxviii, nos. 154, 159, 182, 190; *L. and A.*, III, 171. The lords-lieutenant were ordered to stop all unlawful games such as bowls, dicing, and carding, and to see that archery practice was revived instead – *Acts P. C.*, XXI, 174–5.

Measures were also taken to re-victual and reinforce Lord Thomas Howard's squadron which had sailed from Plymouth early in April for the Azores to intercept the homeward-bound *flotas* from Spanish America. If the alarms of early May had come a month or so earlier, Howard might well have been kept in the Channel as Hawkins and Frobisher had been in 1590. After all, his five warships, and a sixth that had just gone or was just about to go with the Earl of Cumberland, were a significant portion of the fighting strength of the royal navy. For even after the 1590 additions the Queen's ships of 200 tons and upwards numbered no more than twenty-eight. Besides, the Privy Council knew by then that two of the new gallizabras had slipped through to Spain in August 1590 with the King's share of that year's output from the Peruvian mines and that in March 1591 four more had brought home another six or seven millions that had been held over the winter in Havana.

Even so, the 1591 Indies fleet remained a doubly tempting prize. For 'the great fleet' had not yet come with its treasure and other riches 'such as in no year heretofore the like hath been'. It would, of course, be swollen by the shipping of 1590 that had wintered in Havana. Indeed, a little later the Privy Council wrote of 'a great mass of treasure to be brought for the Spanish King from the West Indies this year to the value of 20 million at the least'. The chance of taking twenty million – something like £5,000,000 sterling – was not to be lightly passed up. And, anyway, by May Lord Thomas would in all probability be at the Azores and a thousand miles away. To recall him was hardly practicable. Yet if he was to stay out, he must be re-victualled. For the latest news the Council had, suggested that the Indies fleet might not now be coming until September or October and Lord Thomas's squadron had been victualled only for four months, that is only until late August. In mid-May therefore orders were given for three flyboats to take another two months' victuals out to him.[21]

The information coming in about Spanish preparations already made it clear that these victuallers would need an

---

[21] Ibid., pp. 140-1, 185-7; S. P. Domestic, ccxxxviii, nos. 19, 34-5, 150-2, 180, 188.

escort; indeed that Lord Thomas might need reinforcements as well as victuals. For besides the twenty sail of Spaniards rumoured to be off Scilly, it was known that there was more Spanish shipping lying between Cape St Vincent and Cape St Mary 'either to distress our merchants at their coming out from the Strait of Gibraltar or to defend the return of the Indian fleet'. Moreover in June it was learned that the Indian fleet was to return about the end of August 'strongly and well appointed' and including twenty-two or twenty-three 'armadas'. In addition the King of Spain was sending out other ships from Spain to meet them at the Islands or that way.[22] These other ships were presumably the galleons and great ships of Don Alonso de Bazan's fleet from Ferrol. Clearly, Lord Thomas with his five royal ships, two pinnaces, and perhaps a few small privateers, would be no match for a force of this strength. So, early in June two more of the Queen's ships, the 500-ton *Golden Lion* and the 300-ton *Foresight*, were ordered to make ready to sail by 2 July to reinforce Lord Thomas Howard and to convoy his victuallers, now increased from three flyboats to four.[23]

But a couple more warships, one of them not of the most powerful, were hardly an adequate reinforcement and by now a considerably larger operation was being considered. Already on 24 May Lord Admiral Howard had proposed bringing another eight of Her Majesty's ships and two pinnaces round to Portsmouth, ready for sudden service southwards.[24] Then

---

[22] *Acts P. C.*, XXI, 141, 185–6; S. P. Domestic, ccxxxviii, no. 152; ccxxxix, no. 52; *L. and A.*, III, 718; *H. M. C., Salisbury MSS*, IV, 103. The Council's information was remarkably accurate. The first ships of the Indian fleet arrived at the Azores on 6/16 September after being delayed by great storms. Bazan, when he caught Grenville and the *Revenge* at Flores on 31 August had some fifty-three sail with him, though not more than a couple of dozen of them were fighting ships – *Further Voyages*, p. 275; *Monson's Tracts*, I, 261–2; Hakluyt, V, 9, 36; F. Duro, *Armada Española*, III, 79. The information, it is clear, came chiefly from Châteaumartin and Edmund Palmer (who had a man at Ferrol on 28 February) and from the captured priest John Cecil *alias* Snowden – *L. and A.*, II, 666, 679–83; *H. M. C., Salisbury MSS*, IV, 115–16. A 'well-wisher of Her Majesty' had sent Burghley very accurate forecasts from Andalusia on 3 December 1590 – *L. and A.*, II, 673–4. Sir Robert Cecil had an agent in Cadiz – S. P. Domestic, ccxxxix, no. 87. On 29 June Châteaumartin reported fifty ships assembling in Ferrol to bring in Indies fleets; Palmer seems to have thought that they were for France – *L. and A.*, III, 711.

[23] S. P. Domestic, ccxxxix, nos. 20–4, 52, 58.

[24] Ibid., ccxxxviii, no. 171. The ships were those that 'are fit to lie there for all sudden service southwards or for France'. They were the 600-ton *Hope*, the 500-ton

on 11 June the Queen approved an arrangement made with the city of London for them to fit out by 20 July six of their more powerful merchantmen – the *Susan* (350 tons), *Centurion* (300 tons), *Mayflower* (320 tons), *Cherubim* (320 tons), *Margaret and John* (220 tons), and *Corslet* (200 tons) – and a pinnace, the whole victualled for five months. Fifteen other ports, from Barnstaple round to Newcastle, were to provide another eleven ships and five pinnaces. Those eleven ships were to be of not less than 100 tons apiece. They were to be victualled for three months and ready to join Her Majesty's ships at the Azores before 20 August. Instructions were also sent to Bodley at The Hague on 13 June and to Sir Robert Sidney at Flushing to invite the States of Holland and Zeeland to send ten of their warships. These ships, too, should be each of over 100 tons. They should be victualled for five months and be at the Isle of Wight to meet Her Majesty's navy by 31 July. For Her Majesty meant to 'employ forthwith the greatest part of her shipping in a special enterprise against the Spanish King' to intercept his treasure from the West Indies and she 'could be contented her neighbours and allies might be partakers of the booty if they shall list to assist her in the adventure'.[25]

Thus the aim was to assemble off the Azores before the end of August a force, including Lord Thomas Howard's squadron, of fifteen of the Queen's warships and at least twenty-seven English and Dutch armed merchantmen, besides smaller barks, pinnaces, and victuallers.[26] Of these, the fifteen royal ships and the six Londoners, with Hawkins's *Dainty* and Raleigh's *Galleon Raleigh* should be a reasonable match for Bazan's couple of dozen fighting units, and the rest should be able to deal with a very considerable proportion of the West Indies ships as they straggled in weary and weakened from

---

*Golden Lion, Vanguard,* and *Rainbow,* the 400-ton *Antelope,* the 360-ton *Swallow,* the 250-ton *Aid* and *Quittance,* and two pinnaces.

[25] Ibid., ccxxxix, nos. 27–8; *Acts P. C.,* XXI, 185–6; *H. M. C., Salisbury MSS,* IV, 119–24; XIII, 450–1.

[26] I assume that the plans did not include Cumberland, who had sailed to the Spanish coast in May with the Queen's *Garland* (660 tons), his own *Samson* (260 tons), the *Golden Noble* (260 tons) and four or five smaller craft and pinnaces. Apart from any difficulty in communicating with him, his victuals would be running very low by the end of August and, indeed, he probably started for home about then – *Monson's Tracts,* I, 269–77; G. C. Williamson, *Cumberland,* pp. 70–82.

their Atlantic crossing. And, incidentally, besides thus intercepting the King of Spain's treasure from the West Indies, the English were also hoping to deprive His Most Catholic Majesty and his Leaguer allies of their fish supplies from Newfoundland. Originally it had been intended to send the *Golden Lion* and the *Foresight* out to the Banks for this purpose. But now that they were diverted to escorting Howard's victuallers, Sir Henry Palmer and his squadron guarding the Western Approaches were to do their best to intercept the fishermen as they brought their catches home.[27]

These expeditions for Brittany and at sea committed Elizabeth to expenditures on a scale that does much to explain why, despite her desire that Henry IV should besiege Rouen, she was reluctant to pay the troops she was offering him for that enterprise. By the end of May £17,834 had already been issued to the treasurer-at-war, Sir Thomas Sherley, for the levy and transportation of the 3,000 men under Norris and Williams and for their weekly lendings until the end of September. And it was reckoned that they would cost another £3,575 for every month they stayed in France after September.[28] Lord Thomas Howard's nine ships – the original five Queen's ships and two pinnaces plus the *Golden Lion* and *Foresight* – and their extra two months' victuals meant another £18,000–£20,000 from the Exchequer besides what the Howards, Raleigh, and the Londoners adventured.[29] Sir Henry Palmer's ships and pinnaces, first in the Narrow Seas and then in the Western Approaches, must have cost at least £6,000–8,000 for their spring and summer service. Besides them, there were the other eight of the Queen's ships and two pinnaces that the Lord Admiral was moving round to Portsmouth. In the first days of May, too, the Queen heard from Palavicino that on 1 April he had paid out her £10,000

---

[27] S. P. Domestic, ccxxxviii, nos. 150, 171; *Acts P. C.*, XXI, 302–3; *Monson's Tracts*, I, 258. Palmer did bring in at least thirteen Frenchmen – *Acts P. C.*, XXI, 345–6.

[28] S. P. Domestic, ccxxxviii, nos. 173, 177; *L. and A.*, II, 529.

[29] By 15 September the Queen had already paid out £15,526 6s. 8d. – S. P. Domestic, ccxl, no. 14. A memorandum by the Navy Board officers put the total cost to the Queen at £18,085 11s. 8d., including £2,500 still owing of £4,000 advanced to Raleigh – ibid., no. 55. Later estimates in December were £16,150 5s. and £15,431 5s., besides the £4,000 to Raleigh – ibid., nos. 99 and 100. It was, of course, hoped that this expenditure would be more than offset by prizes.

towards Turenne's German levy. He was, moreover, being pressed very hard to pay over the extra £5,000. But that was more than Burghley dared to suggest to Her Majesty, who 'altogether condemned you for giving hope of £15,000'. Indeed, she wrote very firmly to Turenne on 9 May, and a little later to Casimir, that she must be excused from any further charge in view of her great daily expenses in Brittany, at sea, in Ireland, and at home during the past year. No prince who built up a treasure would wish to expend it all on someone else's business and it was high time that the Protestant princes and towns of the Empire shouldered more of the burden. Anyway, the much larger German army sent to France in 1587 had cost her only half as much.[30]

Nevertheless the pressures on the Queen to loosen her purse-strings yet further were great and growing. For one thing, the opportunity for some 'great enterprise' such as the capture of Rouen, was becoming more and more attractive. It soon became apparent that the danger in Brittany was neither so great nor so immediate as had been feared. On 5 May and again on the 16th, for example, Beauvoir received letters from Dombes which said nothing of any Spanish reinforcements having landed. Admittedly Norris did write a little later that the Spaniards had been reinforced and with the Duke of Mercoeur's Leaguers somewhat outnumbered his and Dombes combined forces, for Dombes had no more than 1,500 French, 500–700 landsknechts, and 400 horse. But Norris was writing to get back his 600 men detached under Williams to Dieppe and even he thought that with these and another 1,000 they could by the end of the summer drive the Spaniards out or at the least shut them up in Blavet. And, as an earnest of such hopes, he and Dombes on 23 May captured Guingamp, a strong town which commanded all Lower Brittany.[31]

Meanwhile Williams had been justifying his presence with those 600 Englishmen in Normandy. On various pretexts, principally that there was no suitable shipping at Dieppe and that it was too dangerous to march overland without a cavalry

[30] *L. and A.*, II, 778, 793–6. For Palmer, cp. S. P. Domestic, ccxxxviii, no. 36; ccxl, nos. 15, 45.

[31] *L. and A.*, II, 561–2, 568, 579; III, 416.

escort, he had managed to put off obeying the orders of 2 May to transfer his troops to Brittany. Then, on 19 May, after several earlier refusals, he agreed to risk Her Majesty's displeasure by marching out of Dieppe with 450 of his men to join 200 foot and 150 horse of de Chatte's for an attack upon two League regiments, 1,200 strong, that had approached menacingly close. They caught the enemy at St Saëns next morning and, although they had marched half a day and a night, the English stormed one barricade; charged 'so hard in their tails' that they carried a second as well; entered pell-mell into the great church despite its entrenchments; and eventually with the help of a cannon from Neufchâtel forced the enemy to surrender. The English lost only fourteen killed and twenty-four wounded. De Chatte lost no more than five. On the other hand, the two enemy regiments, mostly Italians and Lorrainers, were virtually wiped out – 400 or 500 killed, besides those slain by the horsemen in the woods; 200 prisoners and another 200 disarmed and released. They had been the strength of Rouen, Ottywell Smith said, and their loss was a great discouragement to the Leaguers there. De Chatte added that the inhabitants of Rouen were now all one against another in great disorder and mistrust. They had, moreover, knocked down a good part of their wall to make a ravelin and, as that was now level with the curtain and had no ditch, it would be easy to enter the city.[32]

So the chance of taking Rouen was alleged to be better than it had ever been. In its present state it would not be able to hold out long. Nor could it have any real hope of early relief. For, as with Paris in the previous year, the weakness of the League's forces meant that relief could only come from Parma. And it was clear by now that Parma would find it increasingly difficult to leave the Netherlands during the coming ·summer. Even if Turenne's German army did not come that way,[33] the Dutch were preparing an offensive that could not easily be ignored. Not for many a year had the States assembled such a camp as that which took the field under Count Maurice and Sir Francis Vere in the middle of

[32] Ibid., II, 569–78; III, 236, 239.
[33] It was common talk by now that it would come through the Low Countries – ibid., II, 32.

May 1591. It numbered fully 10,000 foot and 1,800 horse, including the 1,600 foot and 400 horse of Vere's English contingent. With them they had thirty-one siege cannon, bridging equipment, pontoons, and fifteen small warships to command the rivers. The troops, in sharp contrast to the penurious soldiery of the King of France – and even of the King of Spain – had been given a month's pay in advance with another three months already provided for.[34]

The initial achievements of this army were no less menacing than its numbers. On 13 May Vere, with the English and Gelderland companies, dislodged from Doesburg and marched towards Zutphen. Next morning he dressed up thirteen of his men 'like boors and boorins' and sent them, with other, genuine, boors carrying corn and victuals, to the fort that guarded the crossing over the Ijsel. These 'lusty and hardy young soldiers', as Vere described them, succeeded in seizing the gate and holding it till more of his troops came up and made short work of the fort's small garrison. On 15 May Maurice arrived with the main camp and invested the town itself. Four days later his thirty-one cannon began their battery and after three volleys the garrison of 400 to 500 surrendered.[35]

Maurice and Vere then marched north to Deventer, brushing aside an attack by a few of Verdugo's men on the way. The approaches were made and the battery planted by 29 May, but Deventer proved a harder nut to crack than Zutphen. After about a hundred volleys, a bridge of boats – or on three pipes – was pushed across the ditch and fifty of the English sent over it to view the breach. Unfortunately the bridge had not been made long enough by more than a good stride and although some thirty men did manage to jump across the gap and stand for an hour in the breach, they were in the end hotly repulsed with considerable losses. So the battery went on until nearly 5,000 rounds had been fired and powder and shot began to run low. But the garrison's losses were also heavy and at daybreak on 31 May they surrendered, Count Maurice lending his own coach to their commander,

[34] Ibid., II, 41; III, 2.
[35] Ibid., II, 43–4; III, 3; Vere, *Commentaries*, pp. 17–8; Bor, xxviii, p. 26.

his cousin Count Hermann van den Berg, who had 'almost lost his eyes with the wind of the cannon'.[36]

Thus in less than three weeks after the States' camp assembled, they had taken both Zutphen and Deventer and so cleared the Ijsel. The English could feel particularly pleased about their part in this rapid recovery of the two places which Rowland Yorke and Sir William Stanley had betrayed to the enemy four years earlier. But there was more reason than that for satisfaction. As Vere wrote on 3 June, 'the manner and means augment greatly the reputation of the country, for we have not heretofore used to batter towns of that strength nor to show so great numbers of men in so good sort.' Indeed the enemy had thought both towns too strong the States' army to attempt.[37] That it had attempted them, and attempted them with such rapid success, must increase the grave fears already felt among the enemy for the safety of Groningen, Nijmegen, and the entire area north of the Maas and Waal. Similar successes there would free even larger forces for even more dangerous attempts in Brabant and Flanders. And already Lord Burgh, who was in the field with Maurice and Vere, was writing home on 1 June that 'we intend to Groningen in Friesland, the hopes as great'. Parma could not turn his back on these dangers in the north, however strident his master's order that he should go to France, however limited the funds allowed him for other than French purposes, however difficult it might be therefore to appease the resultant mutinies among his ill-paid Spanish and German regiments. And, indeed, in the first days of June he set out with such forces as he could scrape together – a mere 6,000 foot and some horse – too late to prevent the loss of Zutphen and Deventer but hoping he might still save Nijmegen and Groningen.[38]

For most of the coming summer, therefore, the King of France was unlikely to have much to fear, or Rouen and the

---

[36] *L. and A.,* II, 46; III, 4–6; Bor, xxviii, fos. 27–8; Vere, *Commentaries,* pp. 18–19. According to Vere, Maurice was at one point so discouraged that he resolved to withdraw his cannon, but Vere persuaded him to try again next day. This could be true, but I have found no proof of it in letters written at the time.

[37] *L. and A.,* III, 7.

[38] *Correspondance de Philippe II,* III, 564–5, 568–70, 573–6, 579–81; *L. and A.,* III, 1, 8, 10; S. P. Domestic, ccxxxix, no. 35; also G. Parker, *Army of Flanders and the Spanish Road,* pp. 117, 246.

League much to hope, from the Duke of Parma. Henry, it seemed, was alive to the opportunity this offered. On 4 May de Chatte and Williams had letters from him, written before de Reau had brought him Elizabeth's proposals, in which he said that he would come to besiege Rouen if she would send him 4,000 men and ten cannon. Before the end of the month he was back in Normandy, at Mantes, and on 26 May his forces surprised Louviers, the chief place that victualled Rouen. Then on 3 June he sent de Reau back to England with definite instructions to thank the Queen for her help in Brittany; to assure her that la Noue and Lavardin were on their way there with another 1,400 foot and 400 horse; to explain in considerable detail why the King had so far been unable to attend to the maritime places as she desired; and to ask her for 4,000 foot, paid for two months, with 1,000 pioneers, thirty or forty miners, a dozen pieces of battery, and three of her ships and three pinnaces, to be used where she thought best – in other words against Rouen – if there were time to spare before Parma came. De Reau was also to ask her to send some of her Council to persuade the city of London to lend him 200,000 crowns for the payment of his Swiss and other troops. This would be repaid, as soon as Rouen was taken, out of the impositions, gabelles, and dues that they were wont to pay for their trade there.[39]

In face of these developments and under pressures from Beauvoir, the 'Dieppe lobby', and her more regular counsellors, Elizabeth's resistance to further expenditure gradually weakened. By 2 June Burghley was estimating the costs and drafting orders for the levy of another 600 men for Brittany. Next day Wilkes took a letter from him and a message from the Queen to Beauvoir, agreeing apparently to such a levy provided Beauvoir could offer sufficient guarantee that the King would eventually repay what it cost. On 5 June Burghley wrote to Edmondes that Her Majesty had been persuaded to let Williams and his men stay in Normandy and would also, he hoped, consent to send Norris his extra 600. Two days later she did consent and authorized the necessary expenditure of £4,153 6s. for their coat and conduct money,

[39] *L. and A.*, II, 410, 415; III, 234, 519; *H. M. C., Salisbury MSS*, IV, 116; *Lettres Missives*, III, 391-2, 399-400; Thou, X, 361-2.

transportation, and five months' wages. A week later the Privy Council for some reason, possibly to hear what de Reau had to say, ordered that the men should not be sent to their ports of embarkation until further notice. But eventually on 20 June they were ordered to go with all speed. They left in the last days of June and joined Norris in Brittany before the middle of July.[40]

So Norris got his extra 600 men and Williams stayed at Dieppe. There remained the more serious question of the augmentation of Williams's little force into a contingent large enough to persuade Henry IV to besiege Rouen. Elizabeth, we have seen, was quite willing to send the men. But could she be induced to pay them as well? And if she paid them, thereby making them her royal army and not just a number of mercenary companies in foreign pay, who should be their general? Here was undoubtedly another matter that prolonged her hesitation. For the young Earl of Essex was possessed of an almost fanatical desire for this command. His wiser friends urged him 'rather to seek a domesticall greatness like to his father-in-law [Leicester], which is plotted; but the Earl is impatient of the slow process he needs must have during the life and greatness of the Chancellor and Treasurer.' His marriage to Frances Walsingham, Sir Philip Sidney's widow, which the Queen considered a disparagement for one of his rank, and his failure to get Davison restored to the Secretaryship, had not made his 'domestical' prospects appear more rosy. Command at sea looked at this time very much a Howard prerogative. On the other hand, Essex had always admired, and been admired by, soldiers and there was no peer of the realm who could contest his primacy in this sphere.

Soldiering seemed therefore to offer the speediest and most congenial road to renown and influence. And where more speedily and more congenially than alongside that gallant hero of Protestantism, Henry of Navarre, Henry IV of France? As far back as November 1589 the Earl, writing to La Noue, had sighed for 'some opportunity by which we could together win honour and serve the common weal'. Turenne's visit in November 1590 enflamed his eagerness and in January 1591

[40] S. P. Domestic, ccxxxix, nos. 5, 11, 29, 32, 37, 70; *L. and A.*, III, 424, 428, 518; Birch, *Memoirs*, I, 67–8; *Acts P. C.*, XXI, 192, 194–9, 209–11, 217.

Beauvoir wrote that the Earl was determined to go to France. If he could get leave for a month or two, he believed that once he was with Henry he would be able to stretch the months to four at least.[41]

Essex was thus already straining hard at the leash when in mid-June de Reau arrived back with Henry's formal request for an English force to help him besiege Rouen and with instruction to put in a word for the Earl as its commander if that was likely to be helpful. Essex himself put in many words. Three several times, or so he told Beauvoir, he was on his knees before the Queen, each time for two hours at the least.[42] The sheer tedium of these rather ridiculous performances may have helped to wear down Elizabeth's resistance. But probably steady pressure from Burghley and other Councillors had more to do with it. Burghley later claimed 'to have been the principal furtherer in this voyage' and there seems no reason to doubt him. He had written to Edmondes, only a week before de Reau's arrival, that the Rouen enterprise was 'in mine opinion more profitable for sundry respects to be had than the recovery of Paris' and Essex at this time clearly regarded him as supporting it.[43] Nor is there any evidence that other Councillors were against it, certainly not Howard or Hunsdon who, with Burghley, were the three appointed to conduct the negotiations with de Reau and Beauvoir.[44]

Within no more than ten days of de Reau's arrival those negotiations were concluded, on 25 June. Even before that, on 20 June, Essex had written jubilantly to his steward Richard Bagot, 'I am commanded into France for establishing the brave King in quiet possession of Normandy'. Four days later the Council's letters went out to the city of London and twenty-one counties for the levy of 3,400 men, which with Williams's 600 would make up the 4,000 required.[45]

[41] Collins, II, 317; S. P. Domestic, ccxxxix, no. 70; Devereux, I, 209–14; Lodge, *Illustrations of British History*, II, 422.

[42] *L. and A.*, III, 520; *Lettres Missives*, III, 400; Devereux, I, 215.

[43] *Unton Correspondence*, p. 60; Birch, *Memoirs*, I, 67. But was there just a touch of sarcasm in Essex's letter of 28 July thanking Burghley 'for your wise, favourable, and fatherly instructions of which your lordship's letters are very full'? – *L. and A.*, III, 250; Devereux, I, 221.

[44] *L. and A.*, III, 525, 527.

[45] Devereux, I, 215; *Acts P. C.*, XXI, 220–5.

Agreement upon the main issue, that is the despatch of these 4,000 men to enable the King to besiege Rouen, had in fact been reached with the French ambassadors by 22 June. But then there was some further haggling over just which of Rouen and Le Havre's revenues were to be earmarked for the Queen's reimbursement. De Reau and Beauvoir also made a strenuous effort to include the 1,000 pioneers, thirty or forty miners, twelve pieces of battery, the warships for the Seine, and the loan of money which Henry had asked for, but which the English articles did not mention. But their effort was in vain.[46] Elizabeth had yielded so far as to undertake to pay her 4,000 men for two months from the date of their landing in France, She had also reluctantly appointed Essex as their general. Beyond that she would not go.

   She had driven a hard bargain. For by the agreement finally signed and sealed on 25 June, it was agreed that, in return for her sending the 3,400 men to join Williams's 600 – or a cornet of horse instead of 250 of these 4,000 footmen – her officers should collect and take away all the profits of all sorts of tailles, customs, taxes, duties, impositions, gabelles of salt, fourths of wines, etc. at and around Rouen and Le Havre as soon as either place as taken. And she was to go on receiving all these until she was reimbursed not only for her expenses for the 4,000 men under Essex in Normandy and the 3,000 under Norris in Brittany, but also for all the other expenses for which the French King was bound to her.[47] All this of course depended upon Rouen being taken. By providing the 4,000 men and their pay for two months, Elizabeth had at least provided what was essential if the enterprise was to be attempted.

   [46] *L. and A.*, III, 525–6.
   [47] Ibid., 518, 527–8; *Unton Correspondence*, pp. 8–10. Ottywell Smith told Burghley that the Rouen gabelle of salt was worth 400,000 crowns a year and the customs 300,000 – *L. and A.*, III, 551.

Map 5. Eastern Normandy and Picardy.

# XIV

# Normandy and Knodsenburg

'Your Majesty's army, I dare say, for the number is the fairest troop in Christendom', Essex reported to the Queen after reviewing his twenty-one companies at their first muster on French soil.[1] Considerable care had indeed been taken over their levying and equipment. Unusually, no contributions had been called for from the south-coast counties for this latest French service. They had already sent companies to Williams and to Norris, besides providing 3,000 of Willoughby's men in 1589 and having, as always, to carry the main burdens of home defence. London of course provided its usual share, 300 men on this occasion. But most of the men came from the counties north of the Thames. Two thousand were drawn from the midland and eastern counties and another 700 from as far north as Lincolnshire and Yorkshire. A company of 150 from the garrison of Brielle in the Netherlands, the four bands already with Williams in Normandy, and Essex's troop of 150 horse raised in place of another 250 foot, made up the total numbers to the equivalent of the promised 4,000, from which the usual ten per cent must be deducted for the dead pays.

In levying the twenty-one companies the lords-lieutenant had been specially exhorted to choose carefully men of able bodies and meet years and to see them provided with good and serviceable armour and weapons. Half of them were to be 'shot', twenty in every hundred armed with muskets and twenty-four with calivers. Of the rest – that is the remaining forty-six after deducting the dead pays – half a dozen were to be halbardiers and the other forty pikemen. The deputy lieutenants were to sign indentures with the captains, listing the details of the armour and weapons, to ensure that the captains rendered proper account for them at their return. They were also to send up to the Exchequer indented rolls, signed by the captains, giving the soldiers' names and weapons. Most of this was fairly normal practice. What was

[1] *L. and A.*, III, 256; Devereux, I, 223.

rather less usual was that the lords-lieutenant were directed to allow captains to take suitable volunteers in place of pressed men – although they were to see that those discharged did not pay anything for their dismission. Furthermore Her Majesty 'precisely with her own gracious speech' commanded that those who levied the troops should immediately warn the men's masters, or their township or parish, to keep their jobs or occupations open for them on their return so that 'they may be provided for how to live in their accustomed manner as they did before their departure, without suffering them for want of employment to wander abroad and fall into the misery of begging or of danger of punishment by the laws'.[2]

Thanks perhaps to Her Majesty's gracious speech and the Privy Council's exhortations, but more probably because of Essex's popularity with soldiers and would-be soldiers, volunteers did offer themselves in considerable numbers. As a result the Queen had, at the start, more men in her army than she paid for. The first muster showed all the bands, except Denton's from Brielle and Sir Thomas Baskerville's from Gloucestershire, as well up to strength, some even with a small surplusage. In addition to these mustered men, there were also volunteers not on the Queen's pay rolls. Essex's own foot-band, for example, contained no less than sixty-one – voluntary captains, lieutenants, sergeants, gentlemen, and pages – over and above the 200 men and ten officers paid for by the Queen. The horseband of 150, under his brother Walter, was likewise swollen by another fifty-eight such voluntary captains, officers, and other gentlemen, besides four pages and a number of spare horses. These were no doubt exceptional, but Hunsdon's youngest son, Robert Cary, one of the foot-band captains, tells us in his memoirs that 'I kept a table all the time I was there that cost me thirty pounds a week'. He also took over with him five great horses, a little ambling nag, and a waggon with five more horses to draw it. Sixteenth-century officers did not travel light.[3]

There were of course some defects. The Gloucestershire

---

[2] *L. and A.*, III, 64, 258; *Acts P. C.*, XX, 361–4; XXI, 25, 192, 220–4, 227–30, 232–4, 352–4; S. P. Domestic, ccxxxix, nos. 49, 60, 69, 98.

[3] Ibid., no. 93; *L. and A.*, III, 240, 258; *H. M. C., Salisbury MSS*, IV, 126, 129, 131; Cary, *Memoirs*, p. 12.

company, besides being eight under strength, contained a dozen diseased and unserviceable men. Also none of its men had coats. For whereas most counties paid twelve, fifteen, even twenty shillings a man and coats provided by the Privy Council cost 14s. 10d., the Gloucestershire county authorities, like those of Northamptonshire, had allowed only the 4s. 'coat money' which they could claim back from the Exchequer. Again, if Lord North may be believed, not only had the officers of Captain Swan's Cambridgeshire company taken money to release eleven of their pressed men, but the Captain himself had sold to a merchant in London all the poldrons, vambraces, and tags of the corslets delivered to him by the county. Scattered among the twenty-one companies there were also a few secret Catholics who had joined up as a means of escaping overseas. Sir Roger Williams noted further some bad characters whom England could not govern nor make honest men. Yet even he admitted that there were under Essex brave men in as good order as he ever saw. That other veteran, Edmund Yorke, likewise found the companies 'as fair and as strong as any in Europe'.[4]

Thomas Wilkes had another criticism. 'I have not known', he wrote to Sir Robert Sidney, 'so gallant a troop go out of England with so many young and untrained commanders.'[5] This, however, was hardly a fair comment on the twenty-one captains of the foot companies. At least ten of them had commanded companies in the Netherlands.[6] An eleventh, Thomas Grimeston, had been for four years lieutenant of a company there and a twelfth, Thomas Acton, corporal of the field in the Sluys relief force of 1587. Robert Cary, too, had served in the Low Countries, Henry Poore had commanded a company in Portugal in 1589, and Giles Helmebridge one under Willoughby in France later that year. As for the remaining six, our lack of evidence does not at all necessarily imply their lack of experience.

Nor does Wilkes's criticism seem wholly true of the higher command. Essex himself, at twenty-six, though young was not

---

[4] *L. and A.*, III, 256, 258, 267; *Acts P. C.*, XXI, 306–9; S. P. Domestic, ccxxxix, no. 141.
[5] Collins, II, 327.
[6] Namely Sir T. Baskerville, Sir J. Wingfield, Edward Cromwell, John Goring, John Shelton, Thomas Denton, George Barton, John Roberts, Lord Audley, Henry Swan.

entirely untrained. He had been general of the horse in the Netherlands under Leicester in 1585-6, besides his more irregular service in Portugal with Norris and Drake. Moreover, to advise him he had in his own regiment two very experienced captains in Sir John Wingfield, the unfortunate former governor of Geertruidenberg, and Sir Thomas Baskerville, who had been one of Willoughby's colonels in France and now filled the office of sergeant-major-general. As colonels of the other two regiments he had Sir Roger Williams, who was also marshal of the field, and Lord Audley, another of Leicester's captains in the Low Countries. Besides these, the Queen gave the young Earl two special advisers whose military experience stretched right back to the Le Havre expedition of 1562-3. These were Henry Killigrew, 'the oldest and most experienced member of the Queen's foreign service', and Sir Thomas Leighton, the governor of Jersey, who had some diplomatic experience and fluent French. Neither of these two elderly gentlemen much relished the appointment. Killigrew, as we have seen, enjoyed a lot of ill health, while Leighton suffered from gout. The Queen, however, insisted that bridling the impetuous young Earl would be a service of the mind rather than of the body and neither man was able to dodge the draft, as apparently Wilkes and Sir Thomas Sherley had done.[7] The new ambassador resident with Henry IV, Sir Henry Unton, was also charged to keep an eye on Essex and to advise him, commending him or, if necessary, remonstrating with him even though 'commonly young noblemen at the first do not embrace advertisements of things to be reformed'. Unton, a devoted follower of Lord Chancellor Hatton but also a friend of Sir Robert Cecil, was a

---

[7] *L. and A.*, III, 258, 552; *Acts P. C.*, XXI, 318-9; S. P. Domestic, ccxxxix, nos. 34, 90, 93; ccxl, no. 92; Cotton MSS, Caligula E. viii, fo. 89; *Cal. S. P. Domestic, Addenda*, pp. 326-7; Collins, II, 327; also Amos Miller, *Killigrew*, p. 223. Possibly Sir William Russell had also been considered, for Essex on 28 July begged Burghley 'to stay the Queen's purpose in sending any man out of Bedfordshire, for I know I were half revoked if he were but here'. It would discontent most of the men of quality in the army, who had been drawn to the service by Essex and would be loth to be left under another. Also the King would not be satisfied to have but a knight to attend him, who could not keep the English gentlemen from disbanding – *L. and A.*, III, 552. Russell was named in a list [of June 15?] of those who might have companies – S. P. Domestic, ccxxxix, no. 34. There is an account, sometime in June, of money due to him and his horse and footbands in the Netherlands – ibid., no. 68.

younger man. He was at this time no more than thirty-three or thirty-four years old; but he, too, had served under Leicester in the Netherlands.[8]

Essex's forces were made ready with reasonable speed as well as considerable care. There was a very brief hesitation on 15 July. That morning orders went out to hold the troops in their counties until further notice. This was apparently due to some report which cast doubt upon Henry IV's intention of besieging Rouen. Beauvoir, however, was able to back up his protests by assurances from de Chatte's secretary, Garnier, who had come over only two days before about the arrest of the Portuguese double agent Manoel d'Andrada at Dieppe and who affirmed that the King was diligently assembling his forces for the enterprise. So the morning's orders were cancelled that same afternoon and the troops came to their ports of embarkation by 20 July as planned. That was less than a month from the first ordering of their levy. That they took another week or ten days to reach Dieppe was probably the fault of the weather. Essex himself was held up at Dover for three days by contrary winds so tempestuous that he could not put out to the ships in the Downs. His companies, sailing (with one exception) from London and various east-coast ports, some as far north as Hull, must have been no less delayed, although the Norfolk company from Great Yarmouth shared with the Gloucesters, who sailed from Southampton, the distinction of being the first to land at Dieppe, on 28 July. All had arrived by 3 August.[9] And close on their heels, the Queen was after all sending the cannon that Henry wanted. She had granted them by August 8 and four pieces arrived from England on the 21st while two demi-cannon and a culverin came from Guernsey on 2 September.[10]

---

[8] *L. and A.*, III, 549–50; *Unton Correspondence*, pp. 3, 14, 76, 84, 217, and especially pp. 58–9.

[9] *L. and A.*, III, 250, 256, 537, 552, 579; *Acts P. C.*, XXI, 220–1, 266–7, 289–90, 292–3; Devereux, I, 222; *Unton Correspondence*, pp. 15–16, 21; S. P. Domestic, ccxxxix, no. 98. For Andrada's arrest – *L. and A.*, III, 533–6, 553–4.

[10] *L. and A.*, III, 266, 582; *Cal. S. P. Domestic, Addenda*, p. 327; S. P. Domestic, ccxxxix, no. 131; *H. M. C., Salisbury MSS*, IV, 137. Ottywell Smith on 31 July reported that three English ships had brought six pieces of great ordnance to Dieppe – *L. and A.*, III, 256. But if so, these cannot have come from the Queen, for Essex said that he did not get his artillery from England until his return from Noyon – *H. M. C., Salisbury MSS*, IV, 139.

The prospects for the Rouen enterprise still looked reasonably good when Essex and his troops landed at Dieppe. Two
or three weeks earlier Mayenne had come to Rouen and
replaced its governor, Tavannes, by Villars, who remained
governor also of Le Havre. Backed by his Le Havre troops,
Villars' authority was greater than Tavannes' had been and
he was able to press forward the defence preparations at a
somewhat faster rate. But much still remained to be done,
both in fortifying and in provisioning, if Rouen was to
withstand a vigorously conducted siege.[11]

From the Netherlands, too, the news about the Duke of
Parma still did not discourage prompt action against Rouen.
He had, as we saw, been too late to save Zutphen and
Deventer. Lacking the mutinied Spanish regiments, he was
also too weak and too worried about Turenne's German army,
to follow Maurice and Vere when they marched north against
Groningen. He did advance up to, and just across, the Rhine
at Rees, in the Duchy of Cleves, on 8 June. But there he stayed
for the rest of the month. As he expected, Groningen proved
able to defy the States' forces without his help. Verdugo, its
governor, though not allowed into the town by the burghers,
took up a strong position with 1,000–1,400 men under the
walls and by opening the sluices so flooded the country
around, or at least made it so miry, that Maurice could not
bring up his artillery and only with much difficulty his camp's
victuals. The attempt to besiege Groningen was therefore
abandoned. Instead, on 22 June Maurice took Delfzijl, on the
Ems estuary and Groningen's one link with the sea. On
28 June he took Opslach, a sconce a little to the south-west of
Groningen; on 1 July nearby Emmentil; and next day the fort
of Leverbort. These were the last of at least twenty forts the
enemy had held until recently in the province. Their capture
left Groningen itself almost blocked up, with no way to trade
or get supplies except overland through Coevorden, which
with Steenwijk was the only other place of any strength
remaining in enemy hands in that part of the Netherlands.
And Steenwijk was Maurice and Vere's next objective.[12]

[11] *L. and A.*, III, 245, 248, 255.
[12] Ibid., 8–13; *Kronijk*, XVIII, 442–7; *Correspondance de Philippe II*, III, 581, 585; Bor,
xxviii, fos. 31–2; also van der Essen, *Alexandre Farnèse*, V, 318–9.

Map 6. The Dutch Eastern Front.

The States' army arrived before Steenwijk on 5 July. But by then news was pouring in that Parma had come down to Nijmegen, crossed the Waal there, and entered the Betuwe to attack Fort Knodsenburg and rather more distantly threaten the States' important base at Arnhem on the Old Rhine. As Maurice had not yet summoned Steenwijk or planted his artillery or quartered his troops or in any other way engaged his honour, it was decided not to attack the town. Instead, he marched off southwards through Arnhem and over the Rhine there on a bridge of boats, 'to lodge the army in some convenient place whence by incursions we might molest the enemy' and lessen the pressure on Fort Knodsenburg. It was not thought worth risking a battle to save the fort for, if the enemy took it, they could only hold it as long as their army stayed there. Besides, Maurice no longer had enough forces to ensure victory if he did hazard a battle. He had had to leave Count William with his 2,000 men in Friesland and also to furnish garrisons for the thirty-two forts in Groningen that had yielded to the States. As a result he had, including Vere's Englishmen, no more than 5,000 foot and 1,300 horse as against Parma's supposed 6,000–7,000 foot and 2,000 or more horse.

Knodsenburg, however, offered a much stiffer resistance than either friend or foe had expected. It was a most up-to-date fort, 'very strong of rampart, water, parapet, mounts, and flankguards' and with a garrison recently reinforced to 700–800 men. When on 12 July, after 280 rounds from his eleven cannon, Parma sent his troops to the assault, they were repulsed with heavy losses and in the afternoon suffered more losses from a sortie by the garrison. Among the slain was the Count Octavio Mansfelt, old Count Peter's younger son. Two days later, on 14 July, Parma's cavalry suffered no less severely in an ambush planned and largely executed by Vere and the English. The captain and colours of Parma's own guard, several more captains and cornets, and according to Vere over 200 men, were captured.

At that moment Parma received a letter of 12/22 May from Philip II containing formal and peremptory orders to march to the aid of the League in France by 1 August (new style, i.e. 22 July by the old style) at latest. In the face of so categorical a command he dared not take the three weeks more that he reckoned he still needed to reduce Fort Knodsenburg. He may indeed have been relieved to have so good an excuse to break off an enterprise that had begun so inauspiciously. At all events, on 16 and 17 July, after consulting his council, he skilfully withdrew his forces and his artillery over the Waal to the Nijmegen side. A few days later the States' troops intercepted letters of 17 and 18 July from Guillaume le Vasseur, Parma's secretary of state, to the Abbé of St Vaast at Arras and to Juan Baptista de Tassis. The King, he told them, had sent Parma such express orders to go to France that the Duke, on his council's advice, was abandoning everything else and would return in three or four days towards Maastricht to prepare for his French journey, after taking measures to assure Nijmegen, Friesland, and those parts.[13]

These letters, of which Bodley sent copies home on 24 July, clearly answered the question *whether* Parma would be intervening in France again this year. But there was still the no less vital question of *when* he would be going. His enemies could not know that in his reply to Philip II on 14 July he doubted if he would be able to get away even as early as September.[14] They could, however, very reasonably suspect that he would need rather more than Le Vasseur's three or four days to assure Nijmegen, Friesland, etc. Moreover, there were other, rather more reliable, indicators of his intentions. Imminent intervention must be foretokened by large troop concentrations on the French frontier. A somewhat longer warning might be given by a settlement of the mutinies among the Spanish tercios, for Parma was not likely to enter France without at least some of his Spanish infantry. An even surer indication would be the departure of the forces he now had in the field around Nijmegen, for without them he could not enter France in anything like adequate strength. Now although by 31 July Parma himself with an escort of some horse and a few foot had left for Spa to recover his health, it was another week before the bulk of his troops began to

[13] *L. and A.*, III, 15–21, 678; *H. M. C., Salisbury MSS*, IV, 129–30 [which is clearly N.S.]; Vere, *Commentaries*, pp. 20–4; Bor, xxviii, fos. 32v.–34; *Correspondance de Philippe II*, III, 575–6, 585, 587–90.
[14] Ibid., p. 589.

draw slowly back up the Maas valley. And even then they went no farther than Venlo and Roermond, where they stayed until almost the end of August before moving on to Maastricht.

The principal reason for this slowness was obvious enough. For Parma to withdraw altogether so long as the States' army remained in the field between Arnhem and Fort Knodsenburg, would be virtually to deliver Nijmegen to them. Another reason was that just recently there had been renewed talk of Turenne's German army coming through the Netherlands and joining the States' forces in the Betuwe. When Parma had first appeared there, and was believed to dangerously outnumber Maurice and Vere, the States had suddenly taken up the idea. On 13 July they had offered Turenne, through one of his colonels, de Rebours, a second contribution of £10,000 if he would bring the Germans that way within the next twenty days and stay to help them for sixteen days. Nothing came of this, for the immediately ensuing defeat of Parma's horsemen and his withdrawal from the Betuwe quenched the States' brief panic interest in an operation for which they had never had much real enthusiasm. The letter that Maurice sent to Turenne, close on the heels of de Rebours, was so cold and perfunctory that Turenne refused to consider the project any longer.

Nevertheless its brief revival had given Parma pause. For besides getting a warning of it from old Count Mansfelt, he had also intercepted some of Turenne's letters just when the States were talking to de Rebours. He knew therefore that Turenne's Germans were almost ready to march. Now even if they did not march towards Nijmegen, they might well attack the levies, some 4,000–5,000 foot and almost as many horse, that he himself was seeking to raise in Lingen and around Cologne, as Le Vasseur's intercepted letters showed.[15] For a French campaign he needed these extra forces. He needed no less the 6,000 Swiss and Italian infantry and 800 horse, paid for by Pope Gregory XIV. Those troops, commanded by the Pope's nephew, the Duke of Montemarciano, were at this

[15] *L. and A.,* III, 22–5, 208, 679, 850; *H. M. C., Salisbury MSS,* IV, 129–30; *Resolutiën der Staten Generaal,* VII, 202–3; *Correspondance de Philippe II,* III, 588–90.

moment struggling up the 'Spanish Road' towards Lorraine. They, too, might be in need of help if Turenne decided to go that way.[16] By keeping his main forces around Venlo and Roermond Parma was in the best position to move against any of these various dangers.

It was not until mid-August that the threat to Nijmegen was temporarily removed and that Turenne's choice of route became clear. Maurice and Vere had not risked attempting Nijmegen, partly because heavy rains had dangerously swollen the Waal but more because they still believed themselves inferior in numbers to those forces of Parma's that remained within striking distance. So on 10 August the States resolved to put their men into garrisons for a time, though close enough together to be able to assemble again in two or three days. It was only after it became clear that the States' army had left the field, that Parma pulled his field forces back – and even so, only to Maastricht. Thirty or forty miles westwards, the Spaniards in Diest and Herentals remained as mutinous as ever. Away on the French frontier there were still no large troop concentrations. It was not until mid-August that Williams reported that Ascoli had brought 5,000 foot and a few hundred horse to reinforce what was left of the 4,500 disease-ridden and weary men Parma had left behind with Mayenne at the close of 1590. Now all these enemy dispositions were well enough known and the reasons for them well enough understood by the Dutch and, through the letters of Vere, Bodley, and Gilpin, by the English government too. Even the French King, though in sending de Reau back to England on 4 August he wrote of the League's boasts that Parma would be in France within ten days – even he did not believe that the Duke could come in any strength until at any rate the end of August.[17]

Essex, therefore, when he landed at Dieppe on 31 July, had reason to expect that the French King would be waiting with his army, ready for an immediate attack upon Rouen. It was thus with very considerable surprise and disappointment that he found no one there to greet him. There was no message from the King. There was no ratification of the 25 June

[16] *L. and A.*, III, 773, 781–2, 799.
[17] Ibid., 21–6, 675, 680, 698; *Correspondance de Philippe II,* III, 595.

agreement, without which the English troops were forbidden by the Queen's instructions to leave the immediate neighbourhood of Dieppe. Worst of all, there was no royal army and no sign of any preparation for an early siege of Rouen. Far from it: for the King, after pottering about rather aimlessly between Paris and Rouen all through June and early July, had gone off to besiege Noyon on the borders of Champagne and Picardy, taking Sir Roger Williams and his four English foot-bands with him. Why he should attack Noyon was not very apparent – unless, indeed, it was done, like the siege of Chartres back in the spring, to please his latest mistress, Gabrielle d'Estrées. Was that perhaps what Ottywell Smith was hinting at when he deplored that the King was so 'full of youthfulness and doth not regard the state as he ought to do, but pleasure carries him too much away'? Was it perhaps also the secret message that de Chatte's secretary, Garnier, was to convey to the Queen and Burghley but not to tell to Beauvoir?[18]

Whatever the reason, Henry IV was far away at Noyon and, although Essex sent three successive messengers to find him, it was 14 August before any answer came. That night Sir Roger Williams rode into Dieppe from Noyon. The news he brought proved almost worse than the previous two weeks' silence. The King had by now taken Noyon but, like Chartres, it had held out longer than he had expected. His troops, Williams's English among them, had sat down before the town on 15 July. They had beaten off two relief attempts by small bodies, one under Tavannes who was taken prisoner, the other under Aumale, and they began to batter with a dozen cannon on 26 July. Yet it was not until 9 August that the King was able to enter the town. It had cost him more to take than it paid in ransom. It had cost Williams's four foot-bands seventeen dead and forty-seven wounded, an eighth of their strength. And apart from the those English companies, the King's whole army, Grimeston wrote on 6 August, numbered according to its quartermaster no more than 6,680 foot and between 2,000 and 2,500 horse. That was little more than half

---

[18] *L. and A.*, III, 235, 242-3, 249, 252, 535, 546, 551; also P. de Vaissière, *Henri IV*, pp. 401-3.

the 11,000 foot and 4,000 horse Henry in February had talked to Yorke of bringing to meet an English 4,000 at Dieppe.[19]

Moreover Williams's report and the letters he brought made it clear that the King did not intend to make an immediate start with the besieging of Rouen. Although Mayenne, after making no serious effort to save Noyon, had dispersed his troops back to their garrisons and the Spaniards in Brabant remained as mutinous as ever, Henry still professed to believe that Parma would be entering France within two or three weeks. So he himself with a few troops of horse was riding eastwards towards Lorraine to hasten Turenne's German levies which were now on the march and coming that way. The rest of his army under Marshal Biron would march in a few days' time towards Normandy, there to join Montpensier's Norman troops and Essex's English. But not yet for a siege of Rouen. No: first they must take various smaller places such as Gournay, which guarded the overland approaches to Rouen from the east, and Caudebec which controlled the way up the Seine. All might then be ready to begin the siege of Rouen when the King arrived with Turenne's Germans. To arrange these matters more effectively, the King was very anxious that Essex should come to confer with him before he went off to meet Turenne or Biron set out for Normandy. Essex wasted no time in accepting the invitation. At noon on Sunday, 15 August, he rode off for Noyon with an escort of 300 English and French horse, leaving all his infantry at Arques under Sir Thomas Baskerville. It was to be quite an adventure, but his going was not altogether unreasonable, 'things', as Killigrew later wrote, 'standing so strangely as they did then here and the King so far off, without whom nothing could be made certain of that was looked for by Her Majesty'.[20]

Her Majesty was certainly looking for something very different. And it was not in Normandy alone that matters stood so strangely. In Brittany for the first couple of months

[19] *L. and A.*, III, 252, 254, 256, 259–60; *Unton Correspondence*, pp. 20, 23, 29–30, 34–5; *H. M. C., Salisbury MSS*, IV, 133; *Lettres Missives*, III, 446, 451–5, 463, 465–6; Thomas Coningsby's 'Journal of the Siege of Rouen' in *Camden Miscellany*, I, 13 – in this version of the first part of his Journal Coningsby is a day out in his dating: Saturday was 14 August, not 13 August, – *see Eng. Hist. Rev.*, XVII, 527–8.

[20] *L. and A.*, III, 257, 263–4; Coningsby, p. 13.

after Sir John Norris and his English troops arrived, things had not gone too badly. After the capture of Guingamp on 23 May, the Prince of Dombes and he had spent the month of June skirmishing with reasonable success against Mercoeur's superior numbers of Spaniards and Leaguers, first on open heathland between Guingamp and St Brieuc and then a few miles farther south around Quintin. But the 2,400 English footmen had had to bear the brunt of the action in these skirmishes, for Dombes could never bring together much more than 1,500 foot, 'and those the worst that ever I saw', Norris said. On 16 June the veteran Huguenot captain François de la Noue did at last join them, as the King had promised. But he brought with him only a hundred or so horse, not the promised infantry reinforcements; and it was upon infantry that 'the service in this strong country doth chiefly depend'. The extra 600 English foot did arrive on 13 July, but by then all except 120 of Dombes' French infantry and 300 of his cavalry had gone home to make ready for the harvest, and La Noue had been mortally wounded in an abortive attack upon the castle at Lamballe, about a dozen miles east of St Brieuc.[21]

Norris's report of all this reached the Queen while Essex and Unton were still in England. Her first inclination was to revoke Norris and his troops immediately. A letter from Dombes, however, caused her to pause. In it he assured her that Lavardin was already at Rennes with 150 horse and 800 foot; that another foot regiment followed; and that the Breton noblesse would be back by the end of August after they had seen to affairs on their estates. So the Queen contented herself with instructing Unton on 27 July to protest to the King and to Marshal Biron – though he was not to do so until 'after your first audience and not otherwise, because you shall not be ungrateful at the first'. He was to remind the King of his ambassador's promise 'that the King's forces there should be made double to ours'; to point out that in fact 'we are almost 1,000 for every their 100'; and to threaten that the troops must be called home unless they received better support.[22]

Ten days after sending these instructions to Unton,

[21] *L. and A.*, III, 416, 419–22, 425, 427–8.
[22] Ibid., 428, 430–1; *Unton Correspondence*, pp. 12–13.

Elizabeth set out upon a two months' progress towards the south coast. By 15 August she was at Lord Montague's Cowdray Park, 'within eight miles of the seaside' as Burghley wrote, a little optimistically so far as the distance went. She hoped that when she arrived on the Hampshire coast she would be able to keep in closer touch with Essex and her forces during their two months' service with the French King. She also hoped that her presence there might perhaps draw Henry himself over the Channel for a short visit, as indeed he actually suggested in a letter that de Reau was bringing to her. She could therefore find very little to please her in the budget of bad news which Williams had brought to Dieppe on 14 August and which was relayed home next morning by Essex, Unton, Baskerville, and Williams himself in letters that reached the English court on 20 August. Already on 16 August in consultation with the Privy Council she had resolved that, if the King did not follow the enterprise of Rouen, part of Essex's forces should go to Brittany. Two days later she wrote two letters, both in her own hand, to the King. In one she protested again at the weakness of his forces in Brittany and at Dombes' desire to march away from the coast inland to Rennes. In the other she protested that Henry by his own delays at Noyon was missing the opportunity offered by the mutinies that delayed Parma and by the disrepair of the Rouen defences. She had hastened her troops across only because de Reau had said that Henry was waiting for them and because Henry himself told her that his attack on Noyon was merely a feint to hide his purpose of besieging Rouen. She concluded this second letter 'avec mes prières à Dieu qu'il vous inspire le mieux en temps le plus convenable'.[23]

The letters that arrived on 20 August gave, of course, no hint of any such inspiration. Thus once again, on 22 August, the Queen instructed Unton to protest at 'these preposterous actions', and not only to the King but to the more experienced and faithful of his councillors as well.

We did always fear [she wrote] the ready performance of their promises when we understood that the King had directed himself to

[23] *L. and A.*, III, 263, 555, 561, 582; *Unton Correspondence*, pp. 33–41; *H. M. C., Salisbury MSS*, IV, 132–3; *Acts P. C.*, XXI, 386, 413; S. P. Domestic, ccxxxix, no. 159; J. Nichols, *Progresses of Queen Elizabeth*, III, 80–4, 90–122.

the siege of a town far off, from whence he knew not how to remove. Yet such was the importunity of the King and his ambassadors here, and the inclination of our Council to give more credit to the promises than we ourselves hoped to be performed with that speed that was promised, as we were in a manner led thereunto against our own opinion.

Now the King must waste no more time in amending his errors. As poor Unton had been suffering since 7 August from the double attack of.'a burning fever and the yellow janders', he was to write to Grimeston to make these protests for him.[24]

The events of the next few weeks did nothing at all to allay the Queen's discontent. Essex's journey to the King made her angry with him as well as with Henry. Indeed that journey was a very adventurous and risky undertaking for the Queen's lord general.[25] It meant a hundred miles ride through country mostly 'devotionated to the enemy' and often 'very apt, being somewhat close and upon straits betwixt hills, for ambushes'. Several times therefore they had to ride with their casques on – very tiring in the hot, dusty weather, though perhaps with casques on they were less pestered by the flies. Moreover, to get through in five or six days, as they did on the outward journey, meant very long days in the saddle. For their progress was limited by the many carriages and waggons that went with them, despite Essex's 'commandment that none should carry baggage but merely a shirt'. The Earl himself took his bed as well! They were away most mornings before six and seldom reached their night's lodging before dark, once it was not until two in the morning. However, when they came to Compiègne on the afternoon of 20 August they were not too weary to organize a party 'where a great number of ladies were gathered together, not without music and dancing'. Next day they rode on another eight miles to Attichy, where the King was waiting to greet them with a 'you are welcome' spoken in English. They spent four days with him, visiting the

[24] *L. and A.*, III, 261, 561; *Unton Correspondence*, pp. 32, 42–6, 48–9.

[25] The fullest and most vivid account is in Coningsby, pp. 13–23, though his dating is decidedly confused. There are much briefer accounts by Anthony Bagot – Devereux, I, 224–5; and Cary – *Memoirs*, pp. 12–15; see also *H. M. C., Salisbury MSS*, IV, 134.

badly battered Noyon and discussing future plans with him and Marshal Biron who was immobilized there by gout. Then, on their last evening together, 'the King with his nobles would needs leap, where our General did overleap them all' according to his loyal muster-master, Thomas Coningsby.

The return journey proved again arduous and hazardous. Again for much of the time they 'marched through the mere enemy's country, riding all day armed, the weather most extreme hot'. After four days – and passing regretfully by a convent where some of the nuns appeared 'coy and fine and otherwise, I think, than Mary Magdalen in their minds' – they came to Gisors. There next day Williams caught up with them with his four foot-bands, by now worn down to a bare 240 men. There, too, they found the way forward barred by Villars, who lay with 500–800 horse and 1,500–2,000 foot around Gournay, between Gisors and Dieppe. So they 'marched a clean contrary way to that we should have done', crossed the Seine at Vernon, and after a night march reached comparative security with de Rolet in Pont de l'Arche. 'By this means', as Robert Cary put it, 'God so blessed us that we escaped this imminent danger.' But Villars, who had drawn back towards Rouen, still lay with his very much greater numbers between them and Dieppe. So on 31 August Essex sent off messengers to de Chatte and Baskerville to bring up all the English foot-bands from Arques to rescue him. For the next three days he and his troop remained at or around Pont de l'Arche, waiting for their relief forces to arrive. Some of them spent the time 'in making of good cheer and playing at tennis'; but a good number were glad enough just to rest, for the 'journey was so hard that it hath destroyed divers young soldiers'.

On 4 September Essex, leaving his baggage in Pont de l'Arche, recrossed the Seine and joined de Chatte and Baskerville at Ry, half-way between Rouen and Gournay. There was a brief moment of danger next day when he divided his forces and sent his brother Walter and Sir Roger Williams back with all the horse and 700–800 of the foot to fetch the baggage from Pont de l'Arche. Villars came out, hoping to surprise one or other part of them on the march. But Essex, warned by his scouts, stood his infantry in battle order for four hours. Villars, seeing them ready for him, dared not attack and, when Williams and the horsemen returned, drew back into Rouen. For the tables were now turned and it was Villars who was outnumbered. The twenty-one English foot-bands from Arques, added to the remains of Williams's four, gave Essex close on 3,500 foot, besides 500–600 horse of his own and de Chatte's from Dieppe and Rolet's from Pont de l'Arche.

It is not surprising therefore that the Earl, though because of 'a very sharp fit of a fever' he had 'to be carried between two horses in a litter made of sticks', was reluctant simply to march back to Arques without striking a blow against Villars' forces. After all, their destruction or even their severe mauling would, as Unton said 'be a very great introduction to the action of Rouen for that they have no other succours for their defence than those by the which Villars doth now serve himself'. Mayenne had just dispersed his forces to their garrisons. Parma was still in the Netherlands. If Villars' forces were broken, the defence of Rouen would depend upon the burghers and they would not hold out long if Marshal Biron hurried forward with the King's army and the cannon. In the hope therefore of luring Villars out and trapping him, Essex on 6 September moved round north of Rouen to Pavilly. He meant to stay a few days there, eating up Rouen's supplies in the neighbouring villages, and then to move coastwards, threatening Fécamp, Caudebec, and even Le Havre as he went. The lure seemed to work, for on 8 September news came that Villars was advancing with all his forces. Leaving 2,000 foot at Pavilly, Essex moved out to meet him with 450 English and French horse and between 1,200 and 1,500 English foot, most of them 'raw men ... that had never seen enemies before', but able enough to beat twice as many of the enemy 'by reason of our advantage in weapons, besides the valour of our men, the which the world knows doth far surmount others', Williams boasted.

A mile from Rouen, however, they learned that Villars had in fact gone over the Seine to try to surprise Pont Audemer. In his absence, their approach threw the inhabitants of Rouen into panic and the magistrates sent off messenger after messenger to recall him. Indeed, Ottywell Smith, echoing apparently the advice de Chatte had given to Essex, later wrote that if they had approached along byways instead of in full sight of the town, they might at least have surprised one of the gates and possibly taken the town itself. Instead their horsemen found their way barred by barricades, Essex's brother Walter Devereux was shot through ·the head and killed in an ambush, and the whole 'bravado' petered out to little effect. Thereupon Essex and his little army made their way slowly and sadly back to Arques.[26]

The letters that the Earl found waiting for him when he arrived back at Arques on 10 September, brought him no comfort at all. Already, from the delayed batch of Burghley's letters that had been brought to him at Ry, he knew that he was deep in the Queen's displeasure for not answering a letter from her which had in fact been lost at sea and for not coming over to Portsmouth to visit her during her Hampshire progress, of which during his own cavalcade he had also heard nothing. Now, however, there was more serious trouble. For de Reau had meanwhile reached England, bringing indeed Henry's ratification of the contract of 25 June, but also a number of exceedingly unwelcome messages. It is not very clear why he had taken so long to get there. He had delivered the contract to the King at Noyon by 21 or 22 July. The ratification was ready for sealing by 29 July. Yet it was 4 August before his instructions were ready. Only on 5 August did he set off to get the ratification sealed by the Chancellor at Mantes before taking it on to Dieppe and England. After that it was 21 August before he reached Dieppe, and sixteen days from Noyon to Dieppe by way of Mantes was hardly a record-breaking journey even in the disturbed conditions of 1591. He landed at Portsmouth on 25 August and spoke there with the Lord Admiral and Sir Edward Stafford. Then, although he passed within less than two miles of where the Queen was staying, he took another seven days to find his way back to her.[27] She was by that time at Southwick, over the hill behind

---

[26] *L. and A.*, III, 271, 275–8; Devereux, I, 229–30, 233; Coningsby, pp. 22–3; *Unton Correspondence*, pp. 51, 53, 61–6; Cary, *Memoirs*, pp. 14–5; *H. M. C., Salisbury MSS*, IV, 167 [misplaced as December]; Coningsby, in *Eng. Hist. Rev.*, XVII, 530–1.

[27] *L. and A.*, III, 555, 562–3, 568; Devereux, I, 229–31; *Unton Correspondence*, pp. 46–7, 55. According to de Reau's instructions, the ratification had been sent to Mantes for sealing immediately after he arrived at Noyon but it was captured on the way and he

Portsmouth, in the house whose successor 350 years later was to be the headquarters from which General Eisenhower launched another, very much larger, Normandy landing.[28] There in 1 September 1591 de Reau delivered the King's letters and his own instructions.

Those instructions[29] were even more irritating to Elizabeth than de Reau's tardy arrival. They began with Henry's excuses for going off to besiege Noyon. It had, he said, taken longer than he had hoped to obtain the Queen's resolution – Burghley, we may guess in some annoyance, noted against this: 'the 25 June the contract sealed' – and he had not wanted to leave his troops idle. He tried to meet the obvious objection that they might have been better employed (as Williams had advised back in June)[30] against Caudebec, Gournay, and other places around Rouen, by the argument that his removal from Normandy might lull Rouen into a false sense of security.

The instructions then recited the King's fears about Parma. He believed that Parma had recently received money from Spain, had paid his mutinous troops, was expecting new levies from Germany as well as the Papal contingent from Italy, and would be in France before the end of August. In these circumstances Henry was not only unable to send any more troops to Brittany but, instead of coming to Normandy as soon as Noyon was taken, he must first go with his horsemen to meet Turenne's Germans. His presence would be needed both to hasten their march and to persuade their leaders to leave 3,000 of the landsknechts and 1,000 of their horse to help Nevers in Champagne. This had to be done to keep the lines open to Germany and prevent Duke of Lorraine from interfering. Marshal Biron in the meantime might lead the infantry from Noyon back to Normandy. There he would be able to seize some of the small towns around Rouen while

---

had to take a duplicate. This could well be true, for communications were very insecure. Yet it is curious that Grimeston, who was with the King, seems to have known nothing of this – *L. and A.,* III, 559.

[28] The house, a converted Augustinian priory, was burned down in 1750, as was its immediate successor somewhat later. The present house, built in 1841, is now occupied by the Royal Navy's School of Navigation and officially known as H. M. S. *Dryad.*

[29] *L. and A.,* III, 556–9, 582.

[30] Ibid., 235.

'waiting for the King and his Germans to come to begin the siege. For that siege, however, they would still need the English pioneers, miners, artillery, munitions, and shipping that Beauvoir and de Reau had asked for in June.

As if all this was not disturbing enough, de Reau had an additional instruction,[31] sent to him by the King on 12 August upon a new alarm about Parma. In this Henry said that he could not commit himself to any siege until he saw clearly what Parma meant to do. If the Duke entered France, the King must go straight to meet him and try to bring him to battle. And in that event Henry begged the Queen to allow him, if he thought it necessary, to use Essex's troops against Parma.

Elizabeth's answer was sharp and immediate. Late that same evening Anthony Ashley, one of the clerks of the Privy Council, brought it to the two ambassadors at Portsmouth. She 'flatly denied' the King's request that Essex's forces might serve against Parma or for anything but the siege of Rouen or Newhaven. She had so written to the King. She also wrote to Essex on 3 September 'that he do only obey our commandment . . . and observe the purposes for the which we sent him'. One of the two months for which her troops had been sent had already been wasted and she doubted whether anything could be done against Rouen in the time remaining. She was 'not only discontented but discomforted with all her actions intended by the going over of the Earl and her forces and wisheth with all her heart, though it were to the loss of double the sum of money spent thereon, that she had never assented thereto.' Burghley, whom she 'sharply charged to have been the principal furtherer in this voyage', did (by his own account) persuade her to one concession. In the unlikely event of the King besieging Rouen at once, with no more delay

and that before the end of the second month it may be probable that the continuance of our forces for the space of one month or forty days more might help to bring the enterprise to effect, we shall be contented that either the whole or part thereof shall remain, so as it may be made certain and plain beforehand that the French King will make like good payment to them weekly as we have done during

[31] Ibid., 560; cp. also *H. M. C., Salisbury MSS*, XIII, 451–2.

their abode. For otherwise we will not have any of them to abide longer than until they may be shipped after the end of the second month.

Killigrew, who got a sharp reprimand for letting Essex go off to Noyon, was with Leighton and Unton to make sure that the King really could produce the money and not just empty promises like those made to Willoughby in 1589. Poor de Reau, too, caught the lash of the Queen's displeasure. She would grant him neither audience to take his leave nor letters to carry back with him.[32]

The arrival of Francis Darcy on 10 September, with Essex's report on his conferences with the King, only increased the Queen's displeasure. For that report confirmed and re-iterated what de Reau had said. It did add that Henry had promised to send some of his Germans to Brittany. But it emphasized his poverty – 'all his certain revenue doth not answer the wages of his garrison soldiers, so as he hath nothing to maintain himself and his army but what he gets with the sword'. At the same time it gaily asserted that, if Marshal Biron kept his word, they would invest Rouen by 15 September, be joined there by the King and the Germans by 15 September, and be in the town eight days later.[33]

The Queen poured scorn on such hopes.[34] That the King would be at Rouen by 25 September or that Rouen could then be his in eight days, she found 'so far incredible as she marvelleth that either yourself [i.e. Essex] would think it likely or could be persuaded by others to make report thereof'. As Biron had delayed to besiege Pierrefonds castle near Noyon and meant next to besiege Gournay, he and his army were equally unlikely to join Essex before Rouen by 15 September. Essex himself was sharply reprimanded for his 'undutiful' and 'unadvised' journey to the King, 'leaving the army without any head or marshal and none else but a sergeant-major'. His 'bravado' before Rouen was condemned as 'a great oversight ... where to your own greatest loss, as a reward of your

---

[32] *L. and A.,* III, 563–5.

[33] Devereux, I, 225–9 [the date should read *stilo nostro*, not *stilo novo*].

[34] Unton did not share them either. On 13 September he wrote to Burghley 'that the siege is like to continue much longer' than the forty days. Burghley noted in the margin 'the siege longer than 40 days' – *L. and A.,* III, 571; *Unton Correspondence,* p. 68.

unadvisedness, you lost your only brother' – a most cruelly unkind cut, and some measure of the Queen's exasperation.[35] Yet even now the opportunity at Rouen was not entirely lost. The Spanish mutinies continued in the Netherlands and the Papal forces were reckoned to be still a long way off, so there was little reason to believe reports that Parma could be in France by 20 September. Accordingly, after the expiry of the two months for which Essex's troops had been promised, Elizabeth, the Privy Council wrote on 13 September, would still be 'contented that some part of her forces, but not all, shall remain for a month or two, only to recover Rouen or Newhaven and to no other purpose', provided the King could pay them. But Essex himself, 'considering how untowardly all this action hath fallen out under your government', was to come home on 26 September, at the end of those two months.[36]

The Queen's rebukes and his brother's death threw Essex into one of those violent oscillations from wild optimism to black despair which characterized his unstable nature and which explain both Elizabeth's anxious watch over him and her mistrust of him. The thought of being called dishonour-ably home 'wrought the strangest alteration in his body and mind that ever I knew in any in so short a time', Unton said. Killigrew heard from Leighton and others that 'he swooned often and did so swell that, casting himself upon his bed, all his buttons of his doublet brake away as though they had been cut with a knife'. And de Chatte and Ottywell Smith wished Her Majesty would write to command him not, in his desperation, 'to hazard so much his person and his soldiers'. Nevertheless Unton, Leighton, and Killigrew all supported the Earl's pleas that both he and the English companies might stay on in Normandy, especially as by 8 September Biron and the King's army were already at Gisors. They could not, however, yet offer any substantial evidence of the King's ability to provide pay for the English troops. In addition they revived the Queen's anger by going to meet Biron at

---

[35] It contrasts sharply with her kindly advice to the convalescent Unton to take care of his health 'which we desire as much to hear of as any friend you have excepting your own wife' – *Unton Correspondence*, p. 44.

[36] *L. and A.*, III, 573–4, 588.

Neufchâtel, going 'nine leagues to meet him that hath broken promise, and he to come but three leagues'. To make matters worse, Essex then agreed to bring his troops forward towards the Marshal as he began to besiege Gournay. Nor did the French themselves do much to appease the Queen's wrath. The ambassador Beauvoir would not risk coming near the court, but sent in a copy of a letter of 4 September in which the King repeated his request for the employment of Essex's troops against Parma. Henry, too, seemed as far away as ever, although there were uncertain reports in Normandy that he had met Turenne's Germans near Sedan and might be at Rouen by the end of September. Altogether, therefore, as Burghley wrote to Unton on 20 September, 'Her Majesty findeth herself to be so evil recompensed by the French King in delaying to come to Rouen when her men arrived, as she seemeth unwilling to have you to go to him or to be her ambassador. But God forbid that private respects should overrule public.'[37]

Burghley did his best to prevent such overruling. He had the support of Sir Robert Cecil, now a Privy Councillor, and no doubt of the other Councillors. They did persuade the Queen not to call Unton back to England. But they could not stop her from commanding the ambassador 'to go no furtherwards towards the French King, to do him that honour who had so apparently given her cause of offence'. The letters from Unton, Leighton, Killigrew, and Essex himself were read to her by her commandment, but 'in no way moved [her] to change her former purpose for revocation of the Earl and her forces; and therefore by her letters Her Majesty hath absolutely commanded the Earl to return'. Burghley and his colleagues did persuade her to concede that some part of the troops, perhaps 2,000 or 2,500, might stay under Leighton's command, provided assured arrangements could be made for their payment by the King after 26 September. This concession, however, Leighton and Killigrew were to keep absolutely secret to themselves until Essex had actually set sail for England, lest it should make him the more unwilling to

---

[37] Ibid., 270, 278–83, 565–6, 568, 570–1, 575, 577, 584–5; *Unton Correspondence*, pp. 66–70, 78–83, 87, 93–5, 104; *H. M. C., Salisbury MSS*, IV, 136, 139; Devereux, I, 233–42.

return home. All he was told was that there would not be enough shipping to bring back with him more than 1,000–1,200 of his troops. He was therefore to leave the rest in Leighton's charge until they, too, could be brought home. But he himself must come to England immediately.

The three drafts of the letter to Essex bear eloquent witness to Burghley's struggles. The first draft, in his handwriting, was a straightforward order of recall with a factual statement of the reasons. The second draft, endorsed with the trefoils that indicate its perusal by the Queen, added sharp criticisms of Henry's disgracing her, her general, and her forces by his faithless breach of his promises. The third and final draft added further sharp words against Essex himself for being 'blinded with French qualities'. A last sting in the tail referred him, lest he might plead ignorance or forgetfulness, to an accompanying 'declaration of the causes moving Her Majesty to revoke her forces in Normandy'. Like the Queen's letter, it was 'framed by her own direction' and 'she altered the same once or twice to make it sharper in taxing the French King' for his delays 'which she termed mockeries and contempts'. Essex was to remember it and to communicate its reasons to the King and any of his council. A copy of the declaration, dated 24 September, was sent also to Unton and Leighton with similar instructions. This declaration bitterly rehearsed the whole story of the agreements about the Rouen enterprise and the King's failure to keep his promises. To it was added on 28 September, again it seems at the Queen's special command, a further complaint about the further expense caused by the inability of the King's ministers to give any firm answer about the troops' pay after 26 September.

With this, and Essex's recall, it looked as if this much trumpeted expedition, this 'fairest troop in Christendom', might now return home without firing a shot in anger save in the unhappy 'bravado' of 8 September.[38]

---

[38] *L. and A.*, III, 578–81, 584–8; *Unton Correspondence*, pp. 88–96. The arrangements for the troops' return are outlined in *Acts P. C.*, XXI, 461–7. Strict order was to be taken for the return of weapons and armour as 'there can be no pretence alleged for any loss of armour or weapon in fight in respect the army hath not hitherto been employed in any actual service against the enemy'.

# XV

# A Summer of Disappointments

'We take courage here in court and expect some good issue of this summer', Thomas Wilkes had written to Sir Robert Sidney on 11 July 1591.[1] By the last days of September this hopeful mood had sadly changed. For by then it seemed that the English plans for the year's campaigns had failed in every particular. Neither the French nor the Dutch had warmed to the idea of bringing Turenne's German army through the Netherlands to join with Maurice and Vere so as to 'shut [Parma] up in a strait' between their combined forces and Henry IV's army in France. Instead while the Dutch, with Vere's help, had gone about their own business in the north-eastern Netherlands, Henry IV had been waiting defensively upon Parma's initiative. Now the recall of Essex and the threatened withdrawal of his troops seemed to spell the end of the attempt to profit in Normandy from Parma's inability or reluctance to leave the Netherlands.

Farther west, in Brittany, it was very much the same story. There, too, the plan for a decisive blow, the plan to send a substantial force to capture Blavet and expel the Spaniards, had fallen through. There, too, the Queen was now threatening to withdraw her forces because of the French royalists' failure to give them adequate support. Withdrawal from Brittany, however, was a more fateful matter than withdrawal from the Rouen enterprise. For the Queen and her Councillors were as convinced as Sir John Norris that without English support the Breton royalists would speedily collapse and the whole province fall into the hands of the Spaniards.[2]

Moreover there were awkward tactical difficulties about a withdrawal, more especially when in mid-August Lavardin decided to go home to Maine. Dombes, to keep in touch, thereupon resolved to march his depleted forces inland through Rennes to the Brittany–Maine border. When the

---

[1] Collins, II, 327.
[2] L. and A., III, 439–42.

French went, the English could not stay. For on the whole of
the northern coast of Brittany, from Leaguer St Malo to
beleaguered Brest, there was no walled port-town to shelter
them and on their own they would be too weak to keep the
field, or even to embark for home, in face of the combined
League and Spanish forces that Mercoeur had around Dinan.
Norris reckoned that to hold his own there, winter and
summer, without French help he would need 300 horse, 3,000
foot, 300 pioneers, and more artillery – or double those
numbers if the Spaniards received their expected reinforcements. It is true that a muster of his troops on 28 July had
shown them only two officers and ninety-seven men short of
their full numbers of 157 officers and 2,700 men, after
allowing the usual ten per cent for dead pays. But 500 sick
were included in these figures and although few of the sick
died, most of them became too enfeebled to be of much use
afterwards. Desertion, too, was made fairly easy by the small
boats that plied between Brittany and the Channel Isles. As a
result, Norris reckoned by 10 August that they were not above
1,500 whole men and Captain Francis Hall put the figure well
below that. The sickness, Norris said, 'was a thing ordinarily
incident to our nation and grown rather of plenty than want'.
Later on he was to write that 'all men of war do [know?], and
daily examples do show it, that three months being in the field
is enough to ruin the greatest army'. If that were true, clearly
his chances of either staying in the field or embarking his men
safely without French help were negligible. Where Dombes
went, there the English had to go also.[3]

So, on 21 August, after shipping his two cannon to
Granville, and the worst of his sick men to the Channel Isles,
Norris marched out of St Brieuc to join Dombes and Lavardin
on the road to Rennes. On 25 August Mercoeur moved south
from Dinan to intercept them. Two days later there was some
skirmishing around St Méen, twenty-six miles north-west of
Rennes. Lavardin with his horsemen and Norris with his
horse-band and 400 of the English foot pushed ahead early
and seized St Méen before Mercoeur could get there. But
then, instead of scouting forward to discover the enemy,

Lavardin went off half a league in the opposite direction. This left the 400 English foot and Norris's cornet dangerously exposed. For Dombes' horsemen had meanwhile scattered among the surrounding villages and the nearest of the remaining forces were still a long league and a half away when Mercoeur's whole army appeared within half a league of St Méen. Neither side, however, was exactly spoiling for a fight. So, when Norris with his handful of horsemen and the 400 English infantry boldly moved out to meet the enemy, Mercoeur 'in a very gentle fear' drew back. Two days later he moved a little westwards to the village of Eréac, where on 30 August Lavardin's harquebusiers surprised and cut up some of his outposts. After that, Dombes, Lavardin, and the English stood in battle order for three hours, Norris with a blue scarf fastened to the end of his pike in a personal challenge to Don Juan d'Aguila. But neither Spaniards nor Leaguers would be provoked to a battle 'and so for this time M de Mercoeur and we did part company'. Mercoeur went off to Nantes to discuss with an envoy from Spain Philip II's terms for further aid, while Aguila took his Spaniards back to Blavet and the League troops dispersed to their various garrisons.[4]

Thereupon Lavardin went home to Maine, glibly promising to return in three weeks to help besiege Fougères. On 4 September Dombes sent the English for a three weeks' rest at Châteaugiron. A mere five days later, however, they were off again to St Aubin-du-Cormier. From there some 300 of them went on to help Dombes take Châtillon castle on 13 September. By this time there were less than a thousand of them able to carry arms and most of those had been extremely sick. More of those who fell sick now died, among them the muster-master, Audley Danett; for 'the captains and better sort are as much troubled with it as the poorest'. Worn-out clothes, especially worn-out shoes and stockings, did nothing to improve their health. By mid-September, too, John Mole, the paymaster, had run out of cash even for their weekly lendings. Nor was it going to be very easy while they stayed on the borders of Maine, to get more through to them from Caen, the nearest place where French money could be had by exchange. These problems apart, however, they were reasonably safe for the time being. Mercoeur did take the field again and the Spaniards did receive some small reinforcements and supplies before the end of September. But their operations were on a small scale and limited to the neighbourhood of Nantes, twelve days' march away.[5]

Nevertheless, if Norris and his weak, unclothed, unshod troops had for the time being little to fear from the enemy, they were also doing nothing to achieve the purpose for which they had been sent out. While they lay upon the borders of Maine, the northern coast of Brittany was as much open to enemy attack as it had been before their landing. This point was sharply made when on 11 September four Spanish galleys and a few other ships from Blavet landed 500 men at Lannion. They burned a good part of the town before re-embarking for Morlaix. This was in fact no more than a raid, to scour the seas rather than to set on land, as Norris put it. Nevertheless Lannion, again according to Norris, had assisted the King's army during the past summer more than any other part of Lower Brittany.[6] That it should be so vulnerable to a handful of raiders coming in from the sea, demonstrated how precarious was the royal hold upon the vital northern coast of the province. And Norris's men were no longer able to stay within helping distance. In Brittany even that limited defensive purpose was no longer being fulfilled.

Further west still, out in the Atlantic at the Azores, there was disappointment yet more bitter. There, too, the hope of striking a sharp, decisive blow had proved vain. The Queen's intention to 'employ forthwith the greatest part of her shipping in a special enterprise against the Spanish King' had been frustrated by her inability to find the necessary shipping. Of the English ports to which the Privy Council had written, only Weymouth, jointly with Lyme Regis, offered a ship – the 120-ton *White Lion* which was already preparing in the Thames to go out privateering with the 170-ton London *Tiger* (not this time bound for Aleppo). The other towns with one accord made their excuses. None of them would admit to

---

[5] Ibid., 449, 451, 453, 456, 458, 460. For Mercoeur's siege of Blain castle, near Nantes – Moreau, pp. 98–102.

[6] *L. and A.*, III, 455–6.

having a ship of the required size in port at the moment. All claimed to be too impoverished by the decay of trade to be able to afford the £500 (Southampton's estimate) or £1,000 (Great Yarmouth's guess) needed to fit out such a vessel. York and Hull could not agree on how to share the cost. And almost everyone complained that so many mariners had been pressed already that it would have been difficult to find crews even if the ships had been available.[7]

The Dutch were equally unhelpful. To begin with, the Privy Council's letters of 13 June took nearly a month to reach Bodley and Sidney, nine or ten days just to get from Middelburg to them at Arnhem. When on 9 July Bodley imparted their contents to Maurice, the Count replied at once 'that he had no authority at all to dispose of the shipping of those Provinces unless it were at home'. It was a matter for the States General and they were unlikely to act without warrant from the particular Provinces. Anyway the States owned no warships of 100 tons or over and five of their largest were already serving on the French coast. Bodley suggested that, if they had no suitable shipping of their own, they might hire merchants' ships or induce the merchants to adventure for themselves. But the States General on 18 July answered as Maurice had foretold. They had no such ships; the time was too short; they could not decide without consulting the Provinces, which would take four or five weeks; and the Provinces were already overburdened by the cost of augmenting their own forces and sending assistance to Henry IV.[8]

Without those ships from the English ports and from the Dutch the 'special enterprise against the Spanish King' was hardly practicable. For those twenty-one were needed to tackle the Indies fleet with its twenty-two or twenty-three 'armadas' while the Queen's ships and the six Londoners dealt with Bazan's couple of dozen fighting ships and score of auxiliaries. So the eight royal ships and two pinnaces that the Lord Admiral had brought round from the Medway to Portsmouth were not after all employed upon any sudden service southwards. The *Golden Lion* and the *Foresight*

[7] *H. M. C., Salisbury MSS*, IV, 119–24.
[8] *L. and A.*, III, 171, 179; *Resolutiën der Staten Generaal*, VII, 371–2.

were sent off, together with the six victuallers, and they all joined Lord Thomas Howard sometime in August.[9] The six Londoners also went, but they were delayed, first, in the Thames when their crews refused to sail until they knew who was paying them, the Queen or the merchants; and then until 17 August by contrary winds at Plymouth. As a result, it was 4 September before these six quite powerful armed merchantmen arrived off Terceira, too late to be involved in the decisive action.[10] Moreover, in July Lord Thomas had sent home both his pinnaces, the *Moon* and the *Charles,* to hasten the victuallers and then on 23 July he had to send back the Queen's 500-ton *Nonpareil* because of 'the great infection in the ship'. By the end of August, therefore, he had with him, besides the six victuallers and the little *Bark Raleigh* and *Pilgrim,* only six of the Queen's fighting ships – his flagship the *Defiance*; the *Revenge,* with his vice-admiral, Sir Richard Grenville; the *Bonaventure*; the *Golden Lion*; and the two smaller *Foresight* and *Crane.*

Yet even with this force Howard could still hope for considerable success against the ships of the Indies fleet, if only he could catch them before Bazan's armada showed up. For after a stormy six weeks or more at sea – they had left Havana on 17 July – they were likely to be arriving at the Azores in scattered groups, some of them even singly, rather than in any close defensive formation. Howard, too, unlike Cumberland in 1589, was in the right place at the right time. On 31 August he was at Flores, the most westerly of the Azores, and with the wind now gone round to the east, he would be ideally placed to windward when the Indies fleet came in.

Here, however, Howard's luck ran out.[11] Just before or just

---

[9] The *Golden Lion* and the *Foresight* may have been the two Queen's ships damaged in a gale on 28 June. In July £210 was spent on repairing and setting forth these two and others. Possibly it was because they were delayed that on 20 July the Privy Council instructed Palmer with his squadron to meet the six victuallers at Cawsand Bay and waft them safely past Ushant out into the ocean seas – S. P. Domestic, ccxxxix, nos. 70, 144; *Acts P. C.,* XXI, 302-3. The Queen wrote on July 2, to Lord Thomas Howard by Thomas Vavasour, commander of the *Foresight,* that victuals were being sent – *L. and A.,* III, 724.

[10] S. P. Domestic, ccxxxix, no. 93; Hakluyt, V, 16.

[11] The most famous account of the following actions is that by Sir Walter Raleigh – Hakluyt, V, 1-15; see also Linschoten – ibid., pp. 37-43; *Monson's Tracts,* I, 253-6. Bazan's instructions for his fleet are calendared in *L. and A.,* III, 727. Some of

after noon[12] Captain John Middleton arrived in the little 50-ton *Moonshine* of London. He had been with Cumberland off the Spanish coast and there they had sighted Bazan's fleet westbound out of Ferrol. As the *Moonshine* was a fast sailer, Cumberland had detached her to check Bazan's course and then to go ahead of him to warn Howard.[13] But the bad weather, that for a week prevented Bazan from getting westward of Terceira, must have slowed down the *Moonshine* too. For almost as soon as Middleton arrived off Flores and delivered his warning, the leading ships of the Ferrol armada came in sight of Howard's anchorage. The English hastily weighed anchor – some had in their hurry to slip their cables – and beat up against the wind on a north-easterly course, more or less across the bows of the oncoming Spaniards. After some inconclusive exchanges of gunfire, all except the *Revenge* worked themselves clear. There, in the open sea and to windward of the enemy, they were in no great danger. For, as 1588 and many other actions had proved, in such circumstances the Queen's ships could easily outsail and outmanoeuvre the galleons of Spain.

Why the *Revenge* failed to get clear as well, remains something of a mystery. She was the last to weigh anchor and as vice-admiral would normally bring up the rear. Raleigh adds that Grenville also delayed to collect some of his men who were ashore foraging – foraging, not 'ninety men and more that are lying sick ashore', as Tennyson assumed in his

---

the more or less garbled rumours are summarized in ibid., 737 and in *Cal. S. P. Venetian*, VIII, 560–1. By far the best modern account is in A. L. Rowse, *Sir Richard Grenville*, pp. 286–331, which makes full use of an official Spanish relation; see also Oppenheim in *Monson's Tracts*, I, 256–68; F. Duro, *Armada Española*, III, 79–82.

[12] According to Raleigh: Monson says the night before. Oppenheim was inclined to prefer Monson, but Monson was writing thirty years later, Raleigh within a few weeks of the event and upon evidence of survivors and his timing seems to me to fit better into the context of events.

[13] Châteaumartin had written to Burghley from Bayonne on 28 July that Bazan was about to leave Ferrol with 45 great ships for Terceira to collect the Indies fleet – *L. and A.*, III, 727. The information was good, but like so much of the intelligence from S. W. France it arrived too slowly to be of much operational value. Bazan could reach the Azores long before Châteaumartin's news from Ferrol could get from Bayonne to London and then out to the Azores. It was much the same, as Burghley several times complained, with the intelligences of shipping movements between northern Spain and Brittany – e.g. ibid., II, 652–3; III, 731.

stirring versification of Raleigh's splendid prose. This seems likely enough. At all events, while 'the Lord Thomas with the rest very hardly recovered the wind', the *Revenge* was just too late to sail through before the trap closed. It would still have been possible for her to turn tail and run to leeward and this, according to Raleigh, was what her master and others urged Grenville to do, what indeed Grenville himself persuaded one of the victuallers, the *Golden Noble* of London, to do. But Sir Richard was not the man to run away from an enemy, especially as running away might mean losing touch with his consorts and leaving Howard short of one of his best fighting ships. Presumably, too, he believed that there was a chance that he might succeed in fighting his way through the Spanish fleet. Indeed it looks as if he had almost succeeded in doing so when the great *San Felipe,* a high-charged galleon three times the size of the *Revenge,* came across his weather bow and literally took the wind out of his sails, 'in such sort as the ship could neither make way nor feel the helm'.[14] Other Spanish ships were then able to come up, one after another and several at a time, and try to board her.

So began the famous last fight of the *Revenge,* a fight that went on all through that evening and all through the night as 'ship after ship, the whole night long, their high-built galleons came'. By morning the *Revenge* had fought off fifteen of them, sinking two and so damaging two more that they also went down before the day was out. But the *Revenge* herself by now could fight no more. All her powder was spent. Forty of her crew were dead, out of the hundred (besides ninety sick) who had taken her into the action. She lay there with 'her masts all beaten overboard, all her tackle cut asunder, her upper work altogether razed, and in effect evened she was with the water, but the very foundation and bottom of a ship, nothing left overhead either for flight or defence'. Grenville, himself mortally wounded, wanted to scuttle her. But he was overruled by his crew and the Spaniards were glad enough to compound with them, yielding 'that all their lives should be

---

[14] According to the vice-admiral of the New Spain fleet, Grenville 'would have fled like the rest if Martin de Bertendona's galleon [the *San Barnabe*], which got the wind of him, had not torn away his foresail with the bowsprit' – *Further Voyages,* p. 273.

saved, the company sent for England and the better sort to pay such reasonable ransom as their estate would bear'.

Meanwhile, what had happened to the other English ships? The Spanish account said that they

took to flight in disorder, some bearing west and others towards the Isles, taking advantage of the obscurity of the night, and others by different ways. Of whom up to now we do not know that they have collected together nor seen them, except for one very far off plying to windward, though we have gone with the fleet more than 40 leagues in the direction in which the *flotas* have to come.[15]

Raleigh, naturally, told the story rather differently. Howard, he says, wanted to turn back to the *Revenge's* assistance, but 'the rest would not condescend' so to commit the remaining five Queen's ships 'to an assured destruction, without hope or any likelihood of prevailing, thereby to diminish the strength of Her Majesty's navy and to enrich the pride and glory of the enemy'. Even so, the *Foresight*, commanded by Thomas Vavasour,

performed a very great fight and stayed two hours as near the *Revenge* as the weather would permit him, not forsaking the fight till he was like to be encompassed by the squadrons and with great difficulty cleared himself. The rest gave divers volleys of shot and entered as far as the place permitted and their own necessities to keep the weather gauge of the enemy, until they were parted by night.

The little *Pilgrim*, commanded by Jacob Whiddon – and set forth by Raleigh, though he does not mention it – still 'hovered all night to see the success. But in the morning, bearing with the *Revenge*, was hunted like a hare amongst many ravening hounds, but escaped.'

That was the last the Spaniards saw of them, the last, too, that we hear of them until the Queen's ships arrived back in England at various dates between 5 and 25 October, the *Defiance* perhaps even later.[16] It is possible that they came

[15] Quoted in Rowse, *Sir Richard Grenville*, pp. 317–18. The ships going west were probably the other victuallers running, like the *Golden Noble*, before the wind.

[16] The *Crane* on 5 October; the *Bonaventure*, 14 October; *Golden Lion*, 9 October; *Foresight*, 25 October. The *Defiance*, a bad sailer, was not home by 24 October and was not paid off until 13 December – *Monson's Tracts*, I, 256, 267. Ubaldini wrote from London on 23 October that Howard was still at sea – *Archivo storico italiano*, no. 464, p. 500: Ubaldini's letters are dated by the old style, and letters 5 to 8 (printed as 1590/1) clearly belong to 1591/2.

home by way of the Portuguese coast. That was the September rendezvous which Howard had given when he sent home the *Nonpareil* on 23 July. But it looks much more likely that, whatever their intentions on 1 September, they were soon separated by bad weather and straggled home, each ship as best it could. After all half their crews were already 'sick and utterly unserviceable' by the end of August. The *Bonaventure* then had 'not so many in health as could handle the mainsail'. The *Crane* by the time she got home had lost nearly all her men by sickness and the *Golden Lion's* sails had been blown from her yards.[17]

This would explain how it was that Robert Flick and the six London armed merchantmen failed to find them. For the Londoners sailed down the Portuguese coast before, on 29 August turning out towards Terceira where they arrived on 4 September. Thus while they were sailing westwards, as it were upon the base of the triangle, Howard's ships would be making for home north-easterly along the hypotenuse. For about a week Flick and his squadron cruised around the central islands, Terceira, Fayal, and Graciosa. There was no sign of Howard. Nor, fortunately, did they sight Bazan, of whose sailing for the Azores they had been warned on 30 August by one of Cumberland's company, the *Red Rose*. On 12 September the *Centurion*, which had fallen astern of the others, did meet forty-five of the Indies fleet, but the odds were obviously too great for her to attack them. Two days later, between Flores and Corvo, she rejoined her consorts, all driven that far west by 'extreme tempests'. Next day, 15 September, another violent storm separated Flick from the *Centurion*, *Mayflower*, and *Margaret and John*. After riding out this storm for some thirty-six hours, he sailed back eastwards with his own *Susan* and the *Cherubim* and *Corslet*, looked into Fayal and went on to Terceira. There, on 19 September, yet another tempest prevented him entering and drove him yet farther eastwards. It also forced some of the Indies fleet from the anchorage in Terceira Road and during the next couple of days the *Susan* managed to capture three of them, while the *Cherubim* took a fourth. But in pursuing their various prizes, the *Susan* and the

---

[17] Hakluyt, V, 3; S. P. Domestic, ccxl, no. 101.

other two ships 'lost the company each of other'. The *Susan's* crew also mutinied when Flick tried to stop them from indiscriminately plundering their prizes. So Flick, too, now turned for home, reaching Plymouth on 11 October. The *Cherubim* came into Portsmouth a week or so later and the other four apparently also returned safely. Although two of the *Susan's* prizes had sunk, after the more valuable parts of their cargoes had been transferred, the Londoners had at least captured four ships of the Indies fleet. That was more than Lord Thomas Howard and the Queen's ships could claim, for their five prizes had all been taken by 11 August, before the Indies fleet arrived.[18]

Indeed the combined achievement of Lord Thomas and the Londoners did not add up to a very impressive return for the £21,991 that the expedition had cost.[19] It just about paid for itself, but it inflicted very little damage directly upon the enemy. The Indies fleet did this year suffer, and suffer very heavily, but from the weather, not from the English. Already storms to the east of Bermuda had sunk a dozen of the seventy-three ships of all kinds that had sailed out of Havana on 17 July. Now during the great tempests of September at least another thirty foundered or were wrecked upon the rocky coats of the central and eastern Azores. To these must be added another twenty or more that had been lost off the Mexican coast on their way out and yet another thirteen that English privateers had captured in the Caribbean. In total, the year's losses did indeed amount to 'one of the greatest disasters the American trade ever suffered'.[20]

Bazan's armada suffered, too, in these late September storms, but nothing like so disastrously. After all, his ships had not spent months rotting in tropical waters nor been long enough at sea for disease to strike down their crews. The captured *Revenge*, or what was left of her, 'was cast away upon a cliff near to the island of Terceira, where it brake in an

[18] Hakluyt, V, 16–21; *H. M. C., Salisbury MSS*, IV, 157; *Acts P. C.*, XXII, 37–8, 44; *Monson's Tracts*, I, 267 note.

[19] S. P. Domestic, ccxl, no. 55.

[20] Hakluyt, V, 10–1, 14–5, 20, 39–43; *Further Voyages*, pp. lxxxv–lxxxvi, 270–9; *L. and A.*, III, 738–40, 748, 758; S. P. Domestic, ccxl, no. 97; *Cal. S. P. Venetian*, VIII, 560–1; *H. M. C., Salisbury MSS*, IV, 157; also Rowse, *Sir Richard Grenville*, pp. 318–19; Sir Julian Corbett, *Drake and the Tudor Navy*, II, 351.

hundred pieces and sunk to the ground'. She took with her all her Spanish crew and some of the English prisoners. A few of Bazan's warships also went with her, though certainly not the fifteen or sixteen that Raleigh claimed. Half a dozen is more likely. For of the fifty-five ships of all sorts Bazan had set out with from Ferrol, five stayed at the Azores and at least forty, perhaps forty-four, got home – twenty, or perhaps twenty-four, to Ferrol; eleven or twelve to Lisbon; and eight to San Lucar.[21]

Most of these had suffered some damage from the storms, some of them from the *Revenge's* gunfire. The *San Martin* and several others had lost masts, Bazan's flagship, the *San Pablo,* had been badly knocked about, and only five of the eleven or twelve galleons at Lisbon were in a fit condition to put to sea again immediately. But although widely dispersed and in need of greater or lesser repairs, the armada was very far from being permanently crippled. There was nothing much wrong with the ships that the dockyards could not put right long before the winter was past. Up in the Biscayan ports, moreover, there were six or eight brand-new 1,000-ton galleons just about to be commissioned. The shortage of mariners, seriously aggravated by the disasters to the American shipping, was an increasing handicap. Nevertheless, as more and more intelligences filtered through from Spain during the autumn and winter, the English were left in little doubt that King Philip's navy would be at least as powerful in 1592 as it had been in 1591. Intercepting the King of Spain's treasure from the Indies was no longer an operation for half a dozen of the Queen's ships and an assorted gaggle of privateers.[22]

Moreover, even in 1591, Howard and Grenville had been on a wild-goose chase. For there was no treasure aboard the Indies fleet that summer. It had all been left behind in the fortress at Havana, to be brought over later by the 'light armada', by those half-dozen new 200- to 300-ton, thirty-gun, gallizabras or frigates, that could outsail any enemy they could not fight off. And they, in fact, brought it home safely, all nine million pesos of it, early in January 1592. Intercepting

[21] Hakluyt, V, 10, 40; *L. and A.;* III, 737–8, 755–6, 758. The five left at the Azores were shallops left to watch for the 'light armada'.
[22] *Further Voyages*, pp. 270–9; *L. and A.,* III, 738, 753–6, 758.

the King of Spain's treasure was not only becoming far more dangerous but patently far more difficult. In 1591 Lord Thomas Howard's presence at the Azores had made Philip II hold the Indies fleet in Havana until Bazan's armada was ready to go out to the Islands to escort it home. And Spanish mariners did then 'all say that the late coming out of the Indies was the cause of the loss of the fleet going homewards'. But it was hardly necessary to risk a squadron of the Queen's ships just to force the Spaniards to escort their Indies fleet. The privateers made them do that anyway. Nor would it be sensible to risk the Queen's ships through the Atlantic's winter gales to catch so slippery a quarry as the gallizabras of the light armada. After the experience of 1591, it is small wonder that for the next few years the English government left the war at sea largely to the privateers.[23]

So in Normandy, in Brittany, and at sea nothing like the hoped-for 'good issue of this summer' had happened. There were, however, one or two comforting gleams amid the autumn's encircling gloom. The brightest came from the Netherlands, where the Dutch were now adding new successes to their capture of Zutphen, Deventer, Delfzijl, etc. and the repulse of Parma before Fort Knodsenburg. At the beginning of September Count Maurice assembled 4,000 men, again including Vere's Englishmen, and twenty-five guns. Taking full advantage of the States' almost complete control of the great rivers westwards of Nijmegen, he moved this force quickly across to the northern coast of Flanders. On 10 September he and Vere were before Hulst, a town not far inland and about half-way between Antwerp and Ghent. The enemy, although forewarned, could not collect a relieving force in time and on 15 September Hulst surrendered. Its capture brought with it £800 to £1,200 a month in contributions from the surrounding Land of Waes, besides a down payment of £7,000 'for ransom of the country from present spoil'. It also greatly tightened the Zeelanders' stranglehold on the Scheldte estuary and Antwerp's traffic. Altogether, in Vere's opinion, the capture of Hulst was as

---

[23] Ibid., 726, 739–40, 761, 765; *H. M. C., Salisbury MSS*, IV, 157; S. P. Domestic, ccxl, no. 97; Hakluyt, V, 20; *Further Voyages*, pp. lxxxvi–lxxxvii, 273–5; *Monson's Tracts*, I, 253–5; *Cal. S. P. Venetian*, VIII, 561.

profitable as anything they had done that summer. Moreover, he knew of no place more convenient for the invading of Flanders.[24]

An invasion of Flanders, however, welcome though it would have been to the English government[25] and probably to the Zeelanders, was something that none of the other Provinces would contemplate. Only two days after Hulst surrendered the States General wrote to Maurice telling him not to attempt anything else in Flanders. He was to bring the army back for a more useful service. This was the taking of Nijmegen, which was in such misery that its leading citizens – the burgomasters, Maurice told Lord Burgh – were prepared to deliver it up as soon as the States' army appeared before it. Maurice therefore sailed off thither from Hulst willingly enough, delayed only by contrary winds and by a mishap to the ships carrying his artillery which ran aground and had to wait till 23 September for a spring tide to float them off. By the end of the month the Count and Vere with the artillery and 1,500 horse and 8,000 foot were back in the Betuwe. By 6 October their bridge over the Waal was completed and that night the army lodged across the river within a mile of Nijmegen.

The circuit of the town was too great for them to enclose it strongly at all points. But by 8 October they had entrenched their own camp and built forts opposite the town's three gates. Verdugo, a few miles away around Grave with no more than 2,000–3,000 horse and foot, dared not attempt to raise the siege. Next day Vere made good the approaches for placing the cannon and on 10 October the magistrates forced the commander of the garrison, a bare 500 strong, to join them in a parley. The negotiations dragged on until next afternoon, by which time the States' cannon were planted and ready to begin their battery. The final surrender then followed quickly and some of Maurice's troops were admitted to the town that evening. The Count himself entered and took possession next morning. Despite the damage done in past months to many houses by the cannon of Fort Knodsenburg, it was, as Bodley said, 'a fair town and greatly beautified with ancient buildings of the Romans'. Its capture, moreover, snapped the most vital link between what remained to the Spaniards in the north-eastern Netherlands and the main body of the Obedient Provinces in the south.[26]

Maurice and the other 'sieurs et chefs de guerre qui se sont employés en campagne', Vere and Lord Burgh among them, had certainly deserved the official banquet which the States General gave them 'ainsi que l'on est accoûtumé de faire aux princes et sieurs qui retournent victorieux'.[27] Even the English government might feel some pleasure and not a little relief. Almost everyone, it was true, seemed agreed that in 1592 as in 1591 the States would again concentrate upon clearing the north-eastern Netherlands and attempting 'sHertogenbosch or Geertruidenberg. Nevertheless, if those enterprises succeeded, then, as Bodley pointed out to Burghley on 27 October, the country would be assured and the forces the States now had *in esse* would be enough to defend it. Her Majesty might be able therefore, if she so desired, to put over to the States' pay all or part of the forces she had in the field. Or, if the States were unwilling to take them over, she might safely discharge or withdraw them, for the Provinces' general means would suffice to make good any reduction she resolved upon. The Dutch successes in 1591 thus made it militarily (though perhaps not diplomatically) more feasible for the Queen to use Vere's companies as the mobile strategic reserve that hitherto she had lacked.[28]

More immediately, those Dutch successes must make it less easy for Parma to hasten away from the Netherlands to aid the League in France. And, of course, as autumn wore on and winter approached, every new delay must make field operations and marches across northern France more difficult and less attractive. Every week therefore that Parma remained in the Netherlands encouraged higher hopes that he would not be intervening in France, at any rate until the spring. As he

---

[26] *L. and A.*, III, 25-6, 33-6: *Resolutiën der Staten Generaal*, VII, 336-7; *Correspondance de Philippe II*, III, 601, 603-4; Bor, xxviii, fos. 36v.-39; Also van der Essen, *Alexandre Farnèse*, V, 325-8.

[27] *Resolutiën der Staten Generaal*, VII, 339, note.

[28] *L. and A.*, III, 37-8, 186.

remained at Brussels all through September and early
October, more and more doubts crept into the reports that he
was going to France. His forces for that expedition gathered so
slowly. The mutinies among his Spanish troops, momentarily
appeased in mid-September, broke out again almost at once
and his son Ranuccio was held for a while as a hostage. His
German levies were still east of the Rhine at the end of
October. The Papal army made very slow progress through
Lorraine in September, did not join Mayenne at Réthel until
late October, and then numbered less than 6,000 men.[29]

Besides all this, Parma was certainly taking his time over
the necessary arrangements for his absence, over the adminis-
trative arrangements, the dispositions of the forces left for the
countries' defence, and the organization of the provincial
contributions for their regular pay. It was well known that he
was most reluctant to leave the Netherlands and that he
regarded Philip II's obsession with France as disastrous.[30] It
was so well known, indeed, that as Sir Robert Sidney wrote,
'here are practices to stir up the Duke of Parma against the
King of Spain'. Burghley was apparently among the practis-
ers. For on 21 October he sent to Sir Thomas Morgan at
Bergen-op-Zoom a packet of letters to send on to Parma.
What they contained, we do not know. But Burghley was
anxious that in forwarding them Morgan should not let it 'be
known that they came from me'. Morgan duly had the letters
delivered to Cosmo Massi, Parma's secretary, who delivered
them to the Duke and promised an answer later. But, as
Sidney remarked, practices to stir Parma against the King of
Spain apparently took no hold with him and, so far as we
know, Burghley's practice took no more hold than the others.
Anyway, it was a hackneyed ploy. Walsingham had tried it
twice, in 1586 and 1587, and Palavicino had tried it again in
1588.[31]

[29] Ibid., 30, 34, 684-7, 698, 705, 799, 865, 875; *Correspondance de Philippe II*, III, 598.
[30] *L. and A.*, III, 684; cp. van der Essen, *Alexandre Farnèse*, V, 323-32.
[31] *L. and A.*, III, 703. Earlier this summer Sir Edward Norris had been discussing
with Pierre Corteken of Bruges 'how Her Majesty and the Duke of Parma might be
brought to treat of peace' – ibid., 128. For Walsingham's attempts – Conyers Read, *Mr
Secretary Walsingham*, III, 265-6; for Palavicino, L. Stone, *An Elizabethan*, pp. 263-5;
van der Essen, *Alexandre Farnèse*, V, 238-40; *Correspondence de Philippe II*, III, 361. Henry
III of France had apparently tried much the same practice in 1589 – ibid., p. 389. For

Nevertheless, although Parma would not stoop to treason, he was palpably dragging his feet. There might yet be time to take Rouen before he intervened. Thus all Elizabeth's advisers, at home and abroad, appear to have been unanimous in pressing her not to recall her troops so long as this opportunity remained. By the end of September they had persuaded her, as we saw, to allow at least 2,000 or even 2,500 to stay, provided that the French King could assure their payment and that they were used only for the siege of Rouen. She was, however, still adamant that Essex himself must come home. She could not trust him to wait patiently until her conditions were fulfilled.

Gradually, as October wore on, her conditions did come nearer to their fulfilment. That Henry had met Turenne and his German army was already known. That they were about to march, or were already marching, towards Rouen was repeatedly reported from France, though more in hope than of certainty. That Henry had delayed a little at Sedan to arrange the marriage of the Protestant Turenne to the young Protestant Duchess of Bouillon could not be held too seriously against him. The marriage would encourage the Huguenots and improve Turenne's ability to uphold the claims of the infant Condé, the Protestant heir presumptive to the French Crown, if Henry IV were killed. It would also strengthen the eastern defences against both Parma and the Duke of Lorraine and by so doing somewhat improve the chances of a successful siege of Rouen.[32]

The news from Normandy also grew a little more encouraging. In the first days of October Robert Cary arrived at Oatlands, where the Queen and court now were. He had been sent to report how Biron and Essex had taken Gournay on 26 September, were marching against Caudebec, and then hoped to come speedily before Rouen. Cary, and Captain Richard Turner who followed close on his heels, between them brought a batch of letters from Essex, Unton, Leighton,

reports of intrigues in 1591-2 by Michael Moody, Morley 'the singing man', and others to promote a marriage between Parma's son and Lady Arabella Stuart, see *Cal. S. P. Domestic, 1591-4*, pp. 99, 117, 209, 244, 255, 259, 520; *H. M. C., Salisbury MSS*, IV, 144, 156.

[32] *L. and A.*, III, 281, 287, 583; *Unton Correspondence*, pp. 101-2; Devereux, I, 252.

Killigrew, Williams, and Yorke. All of these contained glowing accounts of the brave conduct of the English troops, their captains, and their general before Gournay, though truth to tell the town's speedy capitulation once the cannon had breached its walls had given them little chance to do much more than parade a bold front. All the letters also expatiated upon the crucial importance of Gournay as forming, with Neufchâtel and Gisors, the essential shield against an enemy army seeking to relieve Rouen from the east.[33]

This was the news that Burghley had hoped might change the Queen's resolution to recall Essex and her troops.[34] It seems to have had that effect, although Cary in his memoirs[35] claims much of the credit for himself. On reaching the court, he says, he

spake with most of the Council before the Queen was stirring, who assured me that there was no removing of Her Majesty from her resolution, and advised me to take heed that I gave her no cause to be offended with me by persuading her for his stay, which they assured me would do no good, but rather harm. About ten of the clock she sent for me. I delivered her my lord's letter. She presently burst out into a great rage against my lord, and vowed she would make him an example to all the world if he presently left not his charge upon Sir Francis Darcy's coming to him. I said nothing to her till she had read his letter. She seemed to be meanly well contented with the success at Gournay,

however, and so Cary took advantage of the lull in the storm to launch into an impassioned plea for Essex. The Queen 'seemed to be something offended at my discourse and bade me go to dinner'. But she had not exploded again and almost before he had finished his dinner she sent for him, gave him a letter written with her own hand to Essex, 'and bade me tell him that if there were anything in it that did please him, he should give me thanks for it'. That afternoon Cary 'took post horse and made for France'.

The Queen's letter and another from the Privy Council, dated 4 October, gave Essex permission to stay in Normandy

[33] Cary, *Memoirs*, pp. 15–16; *L. and A.*, III, 279–80, 283–5; *H. M. C., Salisbury MSS*, IV, 139, Coningsby, in *Eng. Hist. Rev.*, XVII, 531–6.

[34] *L. and A.*, III, 584; cp. Hatton to the same effect – *Unton Correspondence*, p. 104.

[35] Cary, *Memoirs*, pp. 16–19.

with his troops for another month. Elizabeth gave this permission still very grudgingly. She had no disposition, the Council told Essex, to let him and his troops stay after the extra month or to increase their numbers. She expected him also henceforth to 'behave yourself in an honourable and comely sort as Her Majesty's Lieutenant and General of her forces' and not to hazard himself, as she heard he had done at Gournay, 'by trailing of a pike to approach the place like a common soldier'. He must, she commanded him in her own letter, henceforth attempt nothing without the advice and assent of Sir Thomas Leighton and some other captains of discretion and understanding. He must no longer heed the 'glorious windy discourses' of such as Sir Roger Williams, who had had the audacity to write 'to commend, yea, to extol', the bravado before Rouen. He must also make clear to Biron and the King's council that it was 'not to pleasure the King at all' that she was allowing her forces to remain. She was letting them stay only because the speedy winning of Gournay had so improved the prospect of speedily winning Caudebec and beginning the siege of Rouen and because their revocation now might both blight that prospect and discourage the German army the King was at last bringing to that siege.[36]

For once luck was with Essex. Darcy had arrived on 5 October with the orders for his recall. Two days later, in what looks like a desperate last minute gamble, the Earl and Marshal Biron set out with all their forces in the hope of seizing one of the gates of Rouen by intelligence with one of the town's colonels. Leighton warned Essex that this was probably a trap set by Villars, but they were in sight of the town before Biron discovered that indeed 'there was treason in their intelligence' and called off the enterprise. Essex, in fact, had narrowly missed being caught in another, and more disastrous, 'bravado' before Rouen. Early next morning, 8 October, he rode to the top of a hill near by and 'there upon a fair green in the sight of the town', he knighted no less than twenty-four of his officers and 'voluntary gentlemen'. Seldom can so few opportunities for valour have yielded so many knighthoods! Having thus given vent to his frustrations, Essex

[36] Murdin, pp. 644–5; *L. and A.*, III, 591; cp. also Hatton to Essex – Murdin, p. 646. For Williams – *L. and A.*, III, 277, 286.

rode off for Dieppe. Arriving there about ten o'clock that night, he 'stayed scarce to eat, but embarked for England'.[37]

In the darkness the 'little skiff' taking Essex home must have passed the ship bringing Robert Cary to Dieppe with the Queen's and Privy Council's letters of 4 October. According to Cary, they missed one another by a mere couple of hours.[38] Here again, though, luck was with Essex. Thanks to missing Cary, he had set off home as the orders brought by Darcy required and without even waiting for a warship or any other special shipping. He had also brought the English companies back to Arques, leaving Biron to besiege Caudebec without their help.[39] Such prompt, and perhaps rather unexpectedly ready obedience did a good deal to mollify the Queen – she had not yet heard about the knightings! Essex, too, proved more persuasive in person than on paper.

Several things helped to strengthen his arguments. On 6 October Beauvoir had delivered letters from Marshal Biron reporting the capture of Gournay and full of enthusiasm for a siege of Rouen. The Marshal had some doubts about the King's ability to pay Essex's troops, but he expected him to arrive with the Germans very shortly to begin the siege. Then, at an audience on 13 or 14 October Beauvoir showed the Queen the deciphered copy of another long letter from Henry IV. In this the King sought first at considerable length to explain and justify once again his tardiness in coming to Rouen. He repeated how important it had been for him to meet Turenne's Germans. He justified the further delay caused by his attempt to prevent the Papal forces and Lorraine's troops from joining Parma. He had in fact chased them into Verdun. But then de Reau arrived with the letters from Elizabeth and Beauvoir. So Henry had decided not to

---

[37] Coningsby, pp. 24–8 and *Eng. Hist. Rev.*, XVII, 536–7; *L. and A.*, III, 285.

[38] Cary, *Memoirs*, p. 19. Cary's dates and times, however, are rather confused and telescoped. He left Gournay on 27 September. He says that he then reached the court in four days, i.e. by 30 September or 1 October, arriving early in the morning and starting back for France that afternoon with the Queen's letter to Essex. But the Queen's letter is dated 4 October. Also, according to Coningsby (who here gets his days and dates right) Essex left Dieppe late on the night of 8 October and Cary arrived there next day. Cary's memory was not wholly reliable, e.g., he had Essex returning home finally only *after* Parma had relieved Rouen (p. 24).

[39] Coningsby, pp. 28–9; *L. and A.*, III, 285, 295.

follow up his advantage by further operations in Lorraine, in view of the Queen's annoyance over the delay in beginning the siege of Rouen. As he also heard that Parma was less ready than had been reported, he would leave a few forces to defend the frontier provinces and would hasten back to Normandy. He must let the Germans rest for six or seven days to provide themselves with necessaries. But as soon as they were ready, he would set out and he hoped to be in Normandy by the end of October (i.e. by 21 October by the English style). The Queen's help was essential to the siege of Rouen, so Beauvoir was to press her again for the pioneers, artillery, and shipping and to beg her to continue to pay her troops if the King should find himself unable to procure money for their entertainment.[40]

Elizabeth, so Burghley told Unton, 'found no kind of satisfaction' in Henry's explanations about the past and remained thoroughly sceptical about his promises for the future. 'Yet nevertheless she hath been contented, even against her own opinion in reason, to send the Earl of Essex back again.' From Dover on 16 October the Earl wrote dutifully to assure her that: 'I care for no cross of fortune so long as I find Your Majesty careth for me, neither can anything make me happy whan I do not hold a first place in your favour.' On 17 October he landed at Dieppe and next day wrote again, perhaps less tactfully and certainly less honestly. It was hardly tactful to ask Elizabeth to 'free me from writing to you of any matter of business. My duty shall be otherwise performed by advertising my lords of Your Majesty's Council'. And we must doubt his sincerity in beseeching that at his return 'no cause but a great action of your own may draw me out of your sight, for the two windows of your privy chamber shall be the poles of my sphere'.[41]

During this second half of October, however, Elizabeth could find rather more solid reasons for satisfaction than Essex's fulsome effusions provided. News of the taking of

[40] Ibid., 281, 285, 576, 589–90; *Lettres Missives*, III, 832–9. For the operations around Verdun – Davila, p. 512.

[41] *Unton Correspondence*, pp. 110–12; Devereux, I, 246, 249. According to Cary (*Memoirs*, p. 19) Elizabeth let Essex go 'with tears in her eyes' – but Cary, by then in Normandy, can have had this only by hearsay and recorded it years later from a by no means infallible memory (cp. note 38 above).

Nijmegen by Maurice and Vere made Parma's intervention in France look even less imminent. Marshal Biron's capture of Caudebec on 18 October, known in London by 23 October, cleared one more obstacle from the road to Rouen. By that day too, François d'O, the King's surintendant des finances, had arrived at Dieppe from Caen with enough money to give the English companies a fortnight's imprest and with promises of more to follow very soon.[42]

It was better news still that the King himself was at least really on the way. Although slowed down by his German troops, 'who if they march two days, will rest three', he was by 20 October back at Noyon. There on 22 October he gave audience to Unton, now recovered from his 'yellow janders'. From there, too, Sir Roger Williams, sent to him by Essex to learn his intentions, carried back a letter from Henry to the Queen, besides Unton's full reports of his audience and discussions. Williams left on 28 October, was delayed at Dieppe by storms and contrary winds until the morning of 2 November, and reached the English court a day or two later. With him he brought not only the King's letter, Unton's reports, and his own notes about the King's forces, but also the best news of all, that Essex and his troops had joined Marshal Biron's forces in at last actually beginning the investment of Rouen on 31 October.[43]

[42] *L. and A.*, III, 295, 301; Devereux, I, 251; Ubaldini, in *Archivo storico italiano*, no. 464, p. 501; Coningsby, pp. 29–31; *H. M. C., Salisbury MSS*, IV, 148–9, 150.

[43] *L. and A.*, III, 288, 299, 306, 598–602; *Unton Correspondence*, pp. 107, 114–25 [these two letters are in fact O.S., despite Robert Cecil's assertion]; *Lettres Missives*, III, 506; *H. M. C., Salisbury MSS*, IV, 157; Devereux, I, 256; Coningsby, pp. 29, 31–3.

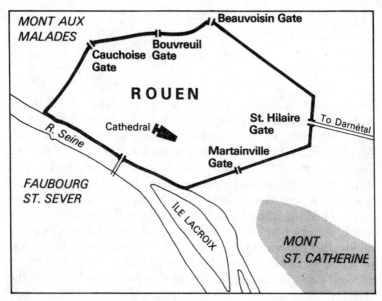

Map 7. Rouen.

# XVI

# The Siege of Rouen

So the siege of Rouen had actually begun. And the English, although now no more than 1,000–1,500 strong, had played their full part in the opening exchanges.[1] With Halot de Montmorency's 2,000 French foot and 300 horse they formed the vanguard of Marshal Biron's investing army. Coming down from Arques and swinging right-handed round west of Rouen early on 31 October, they took up their position on the slopes of Mont aux Malades. The village, a little north of the Seine, was 'not so far from the gates of Rouen as it is betwixt Savoy and the walls of London'. Halot's men, who had stood in battle to cover the Englishmen's advance, now moved up on their right to occupy the low ground between them and the river, while de Chatte with three regiments of French and one of Swiss formed up on Essex's left. Then Biron with the rest of the army, moving around left-handed, closed up to Darnétal and towards Mont Ste Catherine to complete the investment as far as the north bank of the river on the east side of the town. For the time being, until the arrival of the dilatory Count of Soissons, it was left to Rolet and the Pont de l'Arche garrison to do the best they could to seal off St Sever, Rouen's southern suburb on the peninsula across the Seine.

The Rouen Leaguers had apparently been caught off their guard. At all events they had no time to burn their suburbs or the nearby villages.[2] So the besiegers gained a most valuable asset. For, as Essex wrote, without the shelter thereby acquired in 'all these lodgings ... the town could not have been besieged in winter'. Villars, once alerted, did what he could to

---

[1] *L. and A.*, III, 306–8; Devereux, I, 254–60; Coningsby, pp. 31–3 (his dates are again shaky); Cary, *Memoirs*, pp. 20–2. For the English troops' strength – *L. and A.*, III, 289–90, 296.

[2] Thanks to Soissons' tardiness, Villars was able to burn the St Sever suburb on 9 November – Coningsby, p. 37. According to P. Benedict, *Rouen during the Wars of Religion*, p. 218, however, 'order was given to set afire and raze the faubourgs ... [and] the order was ruthlessly carried out'. So possibly the 'lodgings' Essex referred to were the nearby villages, such as Mont aux Malades.

hinder the investment, at first chiefly by sallies on the east side around Mont Ste Catherine, but then in considerable strength against Halot de Montmorency on the west. Twice small detachments from Essex's forces helped to regain ground that Halot's men had lost. The enemy then turned upon the English. 'They bent their whole forces upon us and came with great resolution to charge our quarter, drawing their best men from all other sides of the town upon us.' From noon until sunset the skirmish continued and, Essex boasted, 'this honour Her Majesty hath that her little broken troop made good the ground they first took, and got of the enemy when none else got and all that were charged lost some at one time or other.' There were there, he added, 'more men killed and hurt on both sides than in all the army besides, for it was without intermission and many times our soldiers came to the sword'. He did a little spoil this picture of long and bitter hand-to-hand fighting by mentioning that the casualties among his troops amounted to no more than six men killed and a couple of dozen wounded. Nevertheless, as the muster-master, Thomas Coningsby, gleefully recorded, 'it was a most pleasing day, to see horse and foot together by the ears on both sides. And so towards the evening we retired to our lodging which we possessed all that night in quiet without any enterprise against us.' The next two or three days were equally quiet and the English took advantage of the lull to entrench themselves strongly. There they did 'eat and drink that we can get and lie upon the straw and for many of us never better in our healths in all our lives and yet many times less contented'.

There were many, however who were far from sharing the muster-master's robust health[3] and Essex was begging earnestly for men and money, to be taken back into the Queen's pay, and to be sent at least 1,000 men to bring his numbers up to those of something more than a token force. For while he was as confident as ever that Rouen could be taken, he was no less sure that the success of the siege depended upon the

---

[3] By 18 October Ottywell Smith had already shipped 600 sick men to England and five days later there were thought to be another 600 at Dieppe. The Dieppe Papists were believed to be helping deserters to get passports – *L. and A.*, III, 300. It was said that 1,600 sick had gone by leave to England and another 500 run away – ibid., 318. Killigrew on 31 October put the number at over 1,700 – *H. M. C., Salisbury MSS*, IV, 155.

presence of an effective English contingent. They were now committed to that siege. The good of France depended upon its success and as 'Her Majesty, the Princes of Germany, and the States of the Low Countries have been seen to enter into this action, it is too great an honour for a proud vain Leaguer to be able to resist so great powers.'

Elizabeth, still reluctantly, now came to much the same conclusion. Ever since Essex returned to France she had been growing more and more angry at the continuing delays and lack of firm information. 'Les courroux de la Reine redoublent', Beauvoir wrote to Essex on 22 October. But now, at the end of the first week of November, news came that the siege had at least begun and Sir Roger Williams arrived with Henry IV's own answers and Sir Henry Unton's full report of his first audiences.[4] This at last gave the Queen some solid basis for reasoned conclusions, to 'build upon assurances and not continue her forces upon uncertainty'.[5] It seemed that Henry IV did after all mean business at Rouen. Anyway, as Parma still made no move, it was reasonable to give the enterprise one more chance now that the siege had actually been formed. At the same time, Unton's report reinforced the pleas of Essex and others for continued English assistance.

For while Henry, in talking to Unton on 21 and 22 October, had reiterated his determination to besiege Rouen, he had also explained frankly and at some length why and how much he had to look to his foreign friends for both men and money. For money, because most of his wealthier cities were in the League's hands and because such revenues as were left to him were almost wholly consumed in maintaining his cause locally. The local conflicts also tied so many of his French supporters to their own provinces, even to their own towns. Besides, the King, as he confessed to Unton, 'could not absolutely command his nobility and dispose of them as he would, for that they served without pay upon their own expenses and therefore would return at their pleasures to their

---

[4] *H. M. C., Salisbury MSS*, IV, 152; *L. and A.*, III, 598–602. The versions printed in *Unton Correspondence*, pp. 114–25, from the copies in Unton's letter book, vary considerably in details from the original letters. These 28 October letters, like the rest of Unton's, are dated O.S. and not, as Sir Robert Cecil thought, N.S. – ibid., p. 142.

[5] Devereux, I, 248.

houses'. These, of course, were no new problems and they applied to his Protestant supporters no less than to the Catholics.

But the Catholic royalists were by now beginning to find other matters that made them 'apt upon the least occasion to rebel'. It was more than two years since Henry had promised to listen to 'instruction' in their faith. Those two years had brought him no nearer decisive military success and had afforded little convincing evidence that his foreign and Protestant friends were likely to be able to give him the decisive backing that his domestic and Catholic partisans could not or would not provide. Already there were signs that a 'Third Party' might be forming around the Cardinal of Bourbon and the Count of Soissons, with Épernon's help. These, it was true, lacked the qualities to make them more than figureheads. But there were plenty of Catholic royalists of more weight who were beginning to think that they might be able to come together in a nationally minded Tiers Partie with those Leaguers such as Mayenne and Villeroy who were getting increasingly alarmed at the Spanish and demagogic proclivities of the Parisian leaders, the 'Seize'. If only Henry would redeem his pledge to 'receive instruction', this growing rift between 'Ligue française' and 'Ligue espagnole' might – or so it seemed to many – offer a real opportunity to rally to the 'Most Christian King' moderate and nationally minded Catholics from both sides. And they together, after all, comprised the overwhelming majority of Frenchmen. Ideas such as these, however, did nothing to sustain enthusiasm for a still Protestant King and they left him more than ever dependent upon foreign and mercenary troops.[6]

For the moment, certainly, all reports indicated that Henry was not particularly short of troops. Williams, indeed, even led the Queen to believe that there would be as many as 40,000 men before Rouen. In a more specific statement he spoke of 16,900 foot and 12,600 horse, besides the English and what Soissons and Longueville would be bringing – with the King 6,400 landsknechts and 8,000 reiters (Unton said 4,500)

[6] *L. and A.*, III, 481, 484, 489, 496, 501–3, 512; Thou, XI, 438–48; Davila, pp. 514–19; Cayet, XL, 359–401; Aubigné, VIII, 245–50.

and 400 French horse besides another 3,000 expected; with Marshal Biron 4,000 Swiss and 3,000 French foot and 400 horse; with Halot de Montmorency 1,500 foot and 300 horse; with Montpensier in Normandy 2,000 foot and 500 horse. There were, it must have seemed to Elizabeth, troops enough. The problem was to find the money to induce them to march and to fight, even to prevent them from going off home or going over to the enemy. 'My wants are so great', Henry told Unton, 'as I have not 500 crowns in my purse nor wherewithal to pay my army but the money which Normandy hath promised for the siege of Rouen.' His German troops were in open mutiny for their pay. In fact, he had to put off Unton's first formal audience on 21 October in order to go to deal with 'a great mutiny and sudden departure of his landsknechts and Walloons towards the enemy'. With the help of their commander, Christian of Anhalt, he persuaded them to resume their slow march to Rouen. There money might be found for them out of that promised 100,000 crowns from Normandy and what it was hoped du Plessis might bring up from Tours.[7]

With the Swiss infantry equally restless for their pay, however, Henry had to confess that there was unlikely to be anything to spare for Essex's Englishmen beyond the fortnight's imprest (£1,305) and some victuals that d'O and Incarville had just managed to scrape together. Yet without pay the English, too, would rapidly dwindle into an insignificant and ineffectual handful. Without them, the Germans and probably the Swiss as well would go home. Then, as Henry hardly needed to point out, it would be useless for him to attempt Rouen although, as Essex reiterated to Elizabeth, 'to leave Rouen for want when Rouen were half won, were both dishonourable and dangerous'. Nevertheless, unless she helped further, it might come to that, for 'the poverty of the King, the mutiny of the Almains, and the little assurance of the French

---

[7] *L. and A.*, III, 303–4, 339, 598. Unton's defence of Williams seems disingenuous, for Williams's early November estimates do not appear to have reckoned on forces from Montmorency, Conti, Aumont, or Bouillon. An estimate by him, which did include these and others and gives a figure of 40,000 foot and 8,600 horse, is endorsed by Burghley as 20 December. It looks very much like an attempt by Williams to explain away his original statement – ibid., 624.

Catholics do threaten the ruin of France if Your Majesty be not the conserver'.[8]

Elizabeth had no intention of becoming the conserver of France to the extent of footing Henry IV's bills to his Germans and Swiss. She wrote to Anhalt exhorting him to continue serving the King with his landsknechts and reiters. But she also strictly instructed Unton to give the Prince no hope at all that she would provide another penny towards their entertainment. Nevertheless on 9 November she did send Sir Roger Williams back with a promise that, provided the King could find the means to persuade the Germans to continue their service, she would send 1,000 of her seasoned troops from the Netherlands, paid for one month, together with 450 pioneers from England, to reinforce Essex's depleted force. They were to be employed only for the winning of Rouen and Essex himself should come home, though Cecil believed he would be allowed to go back again. This, of course entailed only a small increase in the Queen's expenses. The 1,000 soldiers would have to be paid whether they came to France or stayed in the Netherlands. So the only extra expenditures were for their transportation and for the levy, transportation, tools, and pay of the pioneers.[9]

It was certainly not all that the French King was hoping for. 'Conceiving her treasures to be infinite', he reiterated his requests to the Queen for a considerable quantity of powder, for pikes, for ships to help those of Dieppe block the mouth of the Seine, and for pinnaces to close the river at Rouen itself. He also raised again with Unton the idea of getting a loan of 200,000 crowns from the city of London. Unton did his best to discourage such importunity. He was not helped in this by Essex. 'Yet doth my lord general', he wrote to Hatton on 25 November, 'make him [Henry IV] believe and hope for great matters [from the Queen] which worketh sometimes the King's offence towards me.' By then Essex had gone over to England, promising, Unton added. 'to return with great forces. But if Her Majesty would stay him there, I doubt not to satisfy the King therein. And in my opinion it would every way further Her Majesty's service most.' That, indeed, seems

[8] Ibid., 301; *H. M. C., Beaufort MSS*, p. 167.
[9] *L. and A.*, III, 608–12; *Unton Correspondence*, pp. 140–6.

also to have been the Queen's opinion at this point, all the more as she was angry with Essex for his challenging Villars to single combat, a piece of knight-errantry that she sharply condemned as beneath the dignity of a peer of her realm and the lieutenant-general of her army.[10] She was, however, still under steady and united pressure from her principal advisers not to leave the French King in the lurch. Burghley, though he shared her annoyance at Henry's delays, had not yet lost hope of the Rouen enterprise. Robert Cecil, a Privy Councillor since August and beginning to take some of the Secretary's load off his father's shoulders, was in favour of pressing on with it. He was witness also to 'how much my lord of Essex owes' to Lord Chancellor Hatton in this action. Sir Roger Williams, too, 'hath done the cause good by plain dealing'.[11] Then on 20 November Essex had obediently set sail from Dieppe for England, bringing the news that a week earlier, on 13 November, the King himself had at last arrived before Rouen. The town was even then no otherwise invested than it was before his arrival. The river Seine, too, with the burned St Sever suburb on its west bank, was still open, though Soissons had now brought 1,200 harquebusiers and 300 horse to narrow the gap a little on that side.[12]

But the important thing was that the King had arrived and with him the prospect that the siege might now begin in earnest. Encouraged by this hope and the persuasions of Essex and her Councillors, Elizabeth did yield a little further. She had already by 18 November agreed to pay her troops and pioneers, new and old, in Normandy for two months more, at a cost for their lendings of £4,080. Now, on 30 November she instructed Captain Thomas Grove to take four of her pinnaces – the *Charles*, *Moon*, *Spy*, and *Sun* – to join in the Seine with the Dieppe shipping and some cromsters that the Dutch were sending. Next day, after Beauvoir had protested that

---

[10] *L. and A.*, III, 302, 310, 605, 616–17; *Unton Correspondence*, pp. 129–31, 165; Coningsby, pp. 37–9; *H. M. C., Salisbury MSS*, IV, 161; Cayet, XL, 355–7.

[11] *Unton Correspondence*, pp. 142–3. Sir Robert Cecil was sworn as a Privy Councillor on 2 August – *H. M. C., Salisbury MSS*, IV, 133. He wrote the Queen's letter sent by Williams on 9 November – *Unton Correspondence*, pp. 142–3.

[12] *L. and A.*, III, 317; Coningsby, p. 40. The French chroniclers' accounts of these early actions are very confused, at least so far as they concern the English troops – e.g. Davila, pp. 523–5; Thou, XI, 452–5; Aubigné, VIII, 250–1.

'Rouen ne se peut prendre avec les ongles', she agreed to Robert Bell buying twenty-five lasts of powder from her store upon the security of bonds from certain Frenchmen. The pioneers had landed at Dieppe on 27 November, 346 of them, armed with pikes and bills, many of them good men though the London contingent included some 'who had been sergeants of companies and many old soldiers which will never work'. They marched off to the camp before Rouen on 1 December.[13] The seven foot-bands were by then also on their way to embark at Flushing and on 29 November the Queen reversed her decision of three days earlier that they were not to march to the camp but wait at Dieppe. Thus, now that the King was there and the siege seemed really beginning, she had granted almost all Henry's original requests. Finally, on 4 December, after being swayed to and fro by the uncertainty of the news from France, she decided that Essex should go back, 'but with this condition that if he shall find this matter of Rouen "sperable", then to remain; if otherwise, to return hither'.[14]

It was not easy to judge how 'sperable' the siege was by the time Essex returned to Rouen on 14 December, after being delayed for a few days by contrary winds.[15] All through November and early December there had been frequent but desultory skirmishes, with little loss or hurt on either side, and from 18 November onwards the King had been slowly pushing forward his approaches to Mont Ste Catherine. By 25 November he was beginning to batter its outer defences with fourteen cannons and culverins. Two nights earlier, as he personally supervised the placing of his artillery, two French captains had been killed in his sight 'and he too near for a King'. On 26 November the Germans' commander, the Prince of Anhalt, was wounded painfully in the foot as he stood beside the King in the trenches. Yet despite the risks Henry IV was taking, his siege made little progress. Some blamed this upon his mistaken tactics. Sir Thomas Baskerville, for example, thought that he should have attacked both the town and Mont Ste Catherine at the same time. He would then

---

[13] *L. and A.*, III, 302, 319–20, 614, 621; *Unton Correspondence*, pp. 175–6, 188.

[14] *L. and A.*, III, 156–8, 189, 332; *Unton Correspondence*, pp. 174–6, 186.

[15] *L. and A.*, III, 335; Devereux, I, 265; Coningsby, p. 61.

have divided the enemy's forces and made then unable to defend either place effectively. Instead they had done nothing except against St Catherine's in all the five weeks they had been there. The Czech observer, Charles Zerotin, considered that Henry's great mistake had been to attack the almost impregnable St Catherine's fort instead of concentrating upon the vulnerable and ill-fortified city.[16]

The fact was, however, as Baskerville admitted, that Henry lacked the forces to press his siege more closely or more vigorously. According to Sir William Sackville, his sixteen regiments of French foot numbered no more than 3,000 men. His two regiments of German landsknechts were a bare 3,000 – and 'more poor people did I never see, nor worse armed and attired', the English muster-master, Sir Thomas Coningsby added. The three Swiss regiments were under 2,500 men. The English by now were also 'reduced into a brief army', with 'many companies of foot ... many captains, officers, and very few soldiers'. For although they still numbered at least 1,000, besides captains, officers, and gentlemen, most of them were sick 'and we have not to fight 300 able men'. So, in all, Henry had well under 9,000 foot, a bare half of the 16,900 foot, besides 12,600 horse, that Williams had so recently reported. It was a very small number to invest a city as large as Rouen. And indeed, the city never was truly invested. Apart from the failure, until early March, to close the river Seine or to hold effectively in winter weather the burned down St Sever suburb on the south bank, the encirclement on the north bank was far from watertight. Halot's troops, the English, and de Chatte's men formed a fairly continuous chain on the westward side. But between them and the forces of the King and Biron around Monte St Catherine there was a wide gap covered only here and there

---

[16] *L. and A.*, III, 321–2; Coningsby, pp. 33–61; *Unton Correspondence*, pp. 170. Zerotin wrote 'si l'on avait attaqué vivement dès le début la ville mal fortifiée, pleine de bourgeois, épouvantée de l'arrivée du roi, elle n'aurait pu résister à un assaut. Mais le château [i.e. St Catherine's], qui n'est abordable que d'un seul côté, est bien approvisioné; il ne peut être emporté que par de grandes forces et un effort héroïque ou bien un temps fort long et une patience soutenue. On a renoncé à l'un et à l'autre moyen. Non seulement nous n'avons pas pris le château mais nous avons perdu ce que nous avions gagné et après quatre mois inutilement employés nous avons dû renoncé à notre entreprise' – *Revue historique*, VII, 71.

by thinly held corps de garde, or outposts, too weak to prevent foraging expeditions by parties of the besieged.[17]

It was not, however, merely that the numbers were lacking. There was also a marked unwillingness to fight in those that were there. It was not until 2 December that Unton managed to patch up an agreement whereby the King gave Anhalt's Germans one month's pay (100,000 crowns in cash and 30,000 in wine) and promised them another month's at the latter end of January. On that they grudgingly undertook to serve until that second payment. But they had little faith in the King's promises and, indeed, Henry confessed to Unton that he knew of no means of performing his promise in January. So, as Unton wrote on 3 December, 'the French have no courage to attempt, the landsknechts until their pay will not, and the English are so few, poor, and sickly as they cannot effect anything of themselves ... And without English companies, the King hopeth for little good here'. He still hoped though, to get credit in London and a 30,000 crowns loan from Elizabeth, while Anhalt still pressed for a further contribution from her towards his troops' pay and, but for his wounded foot, would have gone over to England to urge it.[18]

The seven English foot-bands from the Low Countries did arrive at Dieppe, at the same time as Essex, on 10 December. 'For the number they are as brave men as is on the earth', but they, too, were disappointingly weak. A muster at Mont aux Malades seven days later showed only 734 officers and men, and 70 of them were 'newly entertained'. By then the 25 old companies mustered no more than 583 men, besides 192 officers, 62 'household servants', and 432 sick. So next day Essex reduced the 25 companies to 8, totalling 621 men and 50 officers, but including at least 36 sick men. New and old bands together thus amounted to some 1,400 officers and men – a not insignificant part of Henry's infantry, but by no means enough to 'effect anything of themselves'.[19]

Moreover, the arrival of the seven English foot-bands from

[17] *L. and A.*, III, 317–18, 323, 331; *Unton Correspondence*, p. 152; Coningsby, p. 51.

[18] *L. and A.*, III, 322–3, 328–9, 612, 617; *Unton Correspondence*, pp. 155–6; *Lettres Missives*, III, 531–2. It seems, too, that at least some of the King's Swiss had notions of getting pay from Elizabeth – *H. M. C., Salisbury MSS*, IV, 85–6.

[19] *L. and A.*, III, 332, 337–8; Devereux, I, 269–70; *Acts P. C.*, XXII, 98–103.

the Netherlands coincided with news that Parma with the
Spanish army from those countries was at last again entering
France. He had, it was reliably reported, kept his Christmas –
by the new style, that is – at La Fère. The strength of his forces
was variously estimated, but the lowest estimates put them at
7,000 foot and 3,000 horse. Even without Mayenne's troops or
the Rouen garrison, he would therefore be a match for the
forces that Henry had at the siege. The King did now summon
to him Conti and the troops from Poitou, Aumont from
Burgundy, Bouillon from Champagne, and Montpensier from
western Normandy. But even if they could cut loose from their
local entanglements, how soon could they reach him and with
what numbers in this deep midwinter season? Henry himself
looked for no more than 3,000 and his whole hope rested upon
Elizabeth. At eleven o'clock on the night of 3 December he
had visited Unton and 'stayed more than an hour, acquaint-
ing me and Sir Roger Williams with the estate of his weak
army and his resolution to attend the Duke of Parma before
this town [Rouen]. But without English he despaireth of all
good. If he die, he saith, he will be buried between an
Englishman and a Swisser. He greatly distrusteth his Almain
and French infantry. Now your lordship', Unton urged Essex,
'must help or else he will become a poor miserable King.' To
Burghley Unton wrote rather more apologetically that 'he
who serveth in my place can but behold the outward bark
of things abroad and rather guess than understand Her
Majesty's state at home'. Nevertheless, 'the occasions are
so extraordinary and the King's necessities so ordinary as
your lordship cannot expect better from hence.' He was,
Unton wrote three weeks later, 'a King without a crown and
he maketh wars without money'. Henry was pressing for the
English companies to be reinforced up to 5,000 men paid for
another six weeks. Without them, he said, he would be utterly
ruined. With them, he could take Rouen in the enemy's face
and defeat Parma in battle as well, 'being stronger in horse
than the Duke of Parma'.[20]

By now, however, Elizabeth's hopes of the siege and her

[20] *L. and A.*, III, 325, 331, 339, 623; *Unton Correspondence*, pp. 189, 239. Parma arrived
at Guise on 12/22 December and at La Fère by 17/27 December – *Correspondance de
Philippe II*, III, 617; also van der Essen, *Alexandre Farnèse*, V, 337.

patience with Henry were almost at an end. Already on 6 December she had instructed Unton to inform him that 'our great charges past have so smally profited him, as they have been used, that we are in small hope of any that hereafter shall be expended for him shall any more profit him than the former'. Burghley, too, was beginning to share the Queen's impatience.

I am most sorry to see the decayed estate of the King, [he wrote to Unton, also on 6 December] [yet] on the other side, knowing how much Her Majesty is so daily charged with these foreign wars, as the world may see it to our discredit both by selling of her own land and by borrowing of great sums of money, which being by you secretly communicated to the King, he ought to have more respect of Her Majesty than thus still to press her against her mind to yield more than is convenient to her estate.

Six days later on 12 December, and again on 15 December, Burghley reiterated 'Her Majesty's dislike of the King's letters and demands for further aid'. She believed the reports about the weakness of his forces to be exaggerated. She doubted whether Parma had yet left Brussels – men recently arrived from Flanders said he was still there. She 'hath great reason to think he cannot come hither to levy the siege in respect of want of victuals' in the devastated country he would have to advance through. Anyway, 'the unseasonableness of this time of year to send forces hither' must rule out any present English aid. It could not arrive in much less than two months and 'if the King win not Rouen before two months there is no hope to gain it'.[21]

On 13 December, too, Elizabeth informed Essex that she was sending Sir Thomas Leighton back to assist him and to see that he was not 'carried away with any other light devices or shows of braveries'. More especially, if the King left the siege of Rouen and went off to meet Parma, Essex and the English were in no circumstances to go with him. Indeed, if sufficient forces were not then left to keep Rouen besieged or well blockaded, he and his troops must return home. Ten days later she wrote with her own hand of her surprise that the Earl

---

[21] *L. and A.*, III, 334, 624; *Unton Correspondence*, pp. 193–4, 203–4.

had not come home already if the position and prospects were as desperate as the King's letters made out. Nevertheless, though she would strongly approve if he now decided to return, she left the decision to him and was determined not to recall him while the siege lasted and 'as long as one man is left behind'. Clearly she was washing her hands of the whole enterprise. Many of her Councillors, too, were beginning to feel that, at least, Essex was doing more harm than good by staying in Normandy. Burghley, Howard, and Hunsdon wrote urging him to come home now that the troops under his command were too few for a person of his rank and that 'Her Majesty will not be induced to increase the same by any supply'. They also urged Unton and Leighton so to advise him, even to get the King to persuade it, 'because we think the Earl's nature so desirous of martial service and the time now so proper for service [that] we doubt greatly that he will be hardly induced by persuasion without pressing him thereunto with much earnestness'.

The Queen's flat refusal of further aid threw Henry into despair when Unton informed him of it on 17 December. He could not believe that she would have come to such a decision if Unton had truthfully reported his state and needs. So next morning he told Unton that he was sending du Plessis over to England. He pretended it was 'only to acquaint Her Majesty with his broken estate and to crave her advice and counsel. But he intendeth thereby to draw some new supplies from Her Majesty.'[22] The arrival of Essex with the seven English companies from the Netherlands did, however, for the moment spur him to press his operations rather more vigorously against Mont Ste Catherine, whose capture would make it possible for him to leave Rouen blockaded while he turned to deal with Parma. Five of the seven companies had been placed between Darnétal and Rouen, on the opposite side of the city to the rest of the English troops at Mont aux Malades. On Christmas Eve, at Henry's bidding, 100 men from these five companies stormed an enemy trench and lodged themselves in part of the counterscarp of the 'hithermost' fort on Mont Ste Catherine. At the same time some

French and landsknechts under the Baron of Biron similarly lodged in another part. Next morning enemy counter-attacks won back both positions and although Essex brought up 200 fresh men and offered to regain all that had been lost, the French would not agree. Eventually, however, the King yielded to Williams's persuasions and during the night of 28–29 December the English 'won again all our first lodgings, whereof two of them are in the counterscarp and one in the trench which the enemy made to command ours'. They also tried to carry the fort by scaling, but their ladders proved to be a halberd's length too short.

A similar assault by the French a week later at the Porte St Hilaire on this east side of the city was repulsed with the loss of seventy men killed. Mining under the Martainville curtain wall and the Beauvais gate was also ineffective. Nor did the two batteries, one of fourteen guns and the other of seven, that had been planted by 19 December make much impression upon the Mont Ste Catherine forts, 'the forts being all of good earth and newly turfed'. The six or seven gun battery against the Porte St Hilaire also 'found the gate dammed up with earth' and had little effect upon it. On the south side the forces in the St Sever suburb met with a worse setback, for Rolet, the governor of Pont de l'Arche, was betrayed and taken prisoner in a plot to surprise the fort guarding the bridge over the Seine. On the river itself, the four English pinnaces and one of the Dutch cromsters came up daily to shoot at the town, but above the bridge the passage was still open.[23]

There was, indeed, still little attempt at a concerted, all-out, onslaught upon either Rouen or Mont Ste Catherine and Villars by well-judged sorties did much to disrupt or nullify the besiegers' piecemeal and spasmodic efforts. The Queen's siege guns, which had been brought up by water from Dieppe, had not yet been unshipped and the five English foot-bands at Mont Ste Catherine were now moved back to join their comrades at Mont aux Malades on the western side of the town. Then the number of the English companies was again reduced to eight. On 10 January these mustered sixty-six officers and 901 men, including forty or more of the sadly

[23] *L. and A.*, III, 333–4, 339–41; Coningsby, pp. 63–5; Devereux, I, 270–2; Davila, pp. 525–7; Thou, XI, 464; Cayet, XLI, 29–37; Aubigné, VIII, 252–4.

depleted pioneers now enrolled as soldiers. This reduction of the companies was Essex's last action as commander in Normandy. He had lost hope of reinforcements from England. He had almost lost hope of success at Rouen, for 'the expecting of the Duke of Parma makes the King afraid to do anything'. And the news that the Queen had made Buckhurst Chancellor of the University of Oxford, despite the dons' overwhelming preference for himself, reminded him that influence at home depended very much upon presence at court. So, on 8 January, after theatrically drawing his sword and kissing the blade, he set off for England. By then the King, too, had left, going off on 31 December with 1,000 of the reiters and 2,500 French horse to watch and harass Parma's army and to spoil the country through which it must march, while Marshal Biron with the infantry held Rouen still more or less besieged.[24]

Against this depressing background du Plessis had little chance of persuading Elizabeth to increase her help to Henry IV. On the day he landed in England (23 December), Burghley wrote to Unton and Leighton that 'the Queen's Majesty misliketh that du Plessis doth come hither and I wish he had not come, for he cannot profit, but offend'. Next day the Queen herself, in finally ordering Essex to come home, added that 'although we have understood of M du Plessis' purpose to come hither, yet do not deceive yourself to think that any motion whatsoever shall from us procure any manner of further charge, being of full opinion that this we do is merely spent in vain'. Du Plessis made the best case he could. The King, he said, besieged Rouen closely and meant to batter both the town and Mont Ste Catherine (a tacit admission of the justice of Baskerville's earlier criticism). But he had to provide garrisons for the frontier places in case Parma sought to divert him from the siege of Rouen by assailing them. He had also to garrison St Valéry and Neufchâtel, Gournay and Gisors, which covered the two possible lines of Parma's advance to Rouen. Besides this, many of his nearer supporters were tied down by wars in their own provinces – Bouillon with his large forces by the Duke of

[24] *L. and A.,* III, 341, 344, 347–8, 631, 642; Devereux, I, 271, 274–5; Murdin, pp. 649–60; *Unton Correspondence,* pp. 249–50, 256, 264.

Lorraine's siege of Stenay; Aumont making head against Nemours in the Bourbonnais and Auvergne; Conti joining Dombes to match Mercoeur and the Spaniards in Brittany. So, although Henry was determined not to abandon his siege of Rouen, he needed more forces, infantry in particular, if he was to keep Rouen invested and at the same time make head against Parma. That was why he had asked Elizabeth for 3,000 pikemen and 2,000 musketeers, paid by her for six weeks. Du Plessis did lower the request from this 5,000 men paid for six weeks to 4,000 men paid for five weeks. But he only met with a tirade from the Queen about Henry's time-wasting and about Essex 'making the King believe that it was he who arranged everything, but she would soon show him the contrary'. Threats that without these 4,000 English troops the siege must be raised and Rouen, Le Havre, most of Normandy be abandoned to the Spaniards, that Catholic pressure on Henry to change his religion would then increase dangerously, made little impression, though at one point du Plessis did for an hour or two hope that he had persuaded Elizabeth to grant 3,000 men.

In the end all that du Plessis obtained was a very sharp letter to the King, upbraiding him for his neglect of past opportunities, and a lengthy declaration of the Queen's grievances and her reasons for refusing further help in an enterprise that had now become a joke rather than a victory. What, she asked, had happened to the great force of 24,000 men under Marshal Biron that was to have attended to the siege of Rouen, in addition to the other troops, including the German army, that were to impeach Parma's entry? She could not believe that the King had not still enough forces both to besiege Rouen and to withstand Parma. Besides, if Parma was ready to come forward as speedily as Henry and du Plessis alleged, English reinforcements could not arrive quickly enough to make any difference, for in this winter time, it would take at least a month to levy, arm, and transport them. With a final sting in the tail, the declaration ended that the King only asked for more English in order to spare his own subjects. For on Christmas Eve had not three of the four places of attack upon the St Catherine's counterscarp been allotted to English captains and only one to some French companies?

Burghley, it seems, had done his best to obtain a better answer. He was, he told du Plessis, more troubled than he could say to see him leave unsatisfied. But they could only wait for the God whom they both served to change the hearts of the earthly princes whom they also served. Less piously resigned, du Plessis returned to France, landing at Dieppe on 25 January after being held up at Dover by contrary winds for fifteen days, a delay that hardly revealed any immediate divine inclination to change the Queen of England's resolution[25]

All through January and the first half of February 1592 Elizabeth's resolution remained unchanged, though Beauvoir lowered the French requests from du Plessis' 4,000 footmen to 3,000, to 2,000, and eventually to a mere 1,500. Burghley continued to urge her to yield to these demands. Essex, now back at court, piled on the pressure and also urged Unton to advise the King 'to solicit the Queen oftener in those things he seeks at her hands ... For there is not so much gotten of the Queen by earnestness as by often soliciting, according to the proverb *saepe cadendo*'. Elizabeth, however, 'saith I am too partial and doth not believe me'. He apparently made a tactical error, too, by informing her that the King meant to fall back upon Rouen where he would have the help of his infantry against Parma. He would therefore, she argued, need no more succour. Moreover, from the captains who came home with the Earl

she findeth the general opinion to be that Rouen is not likely to be recovered at all, by reason the King suffered them all this summer to strengthen themselves both with men and victuals and with the fortification of the fort of St Catherine which, if it had been attempted in July when Her Majesty's forces came over, might have been recovered in one month and long before the Duke of Parma's army could have come into France. [It still rankled, indeed, that] if the King had attempted Rouen when he went about Noyon and those other things afore the Duke of Parma was able to come into the field, he had won Rouen and been able to have now at this time beaten the Duke of Parma out of France.

For a brief moment, towards the end of January, the Queen did relent so far as to consider sending Henry 1,000 pikemen. Essex and Beauvoir wrote jubilantly off to tell him. But their letters and their jubilation were premature, for she immediately reverted to her former refusal.[26]

Up to that time, in fact, little had happened to move the Queen to heed the earnest pleadings of Essex and Beauvoir and the perhaps more subtle pressure by Burghley. At Rouen the siege went 'very slowly forward, for since the King's departure they have done nothing. The Marshal allegeth for his excuse his want of foot.' On the other side Parma showed no great inclination to rush forward to Rouen's relief. After some hard bargaining, he had induced the very reluctant Mayenne to let him put his artillery and a garrison into La Fère. Thereupon he had advanced from Nesle, just over the Somme, to Moreuil, on the Avre midway between Amiens and Montdidier. He had with him, according to English spies in his camp, 20,000 men at most, 4,000–5000 of them cavalry. Of these, only 2,000 foot and under 1,000 horse were French. Many of his men died or deserted for want of victuals, 'in respect the country is much harried and wasted'. At Moreuil he fortified his camp with his waggons and artillery, kept his horsemen within his infantry, broke down the bridge and entrenched at every passable ford on the river. When he marched he never moved more than two leagues a day and often only one, 'his army is so heavy in respect of his carriages'. Whenever he came to a wood, 'he maketh a stay of three hours, fearing some ambuscado of the King's and some treason of the French that are with him'. Many believed that he 'doth only temporise to weary out the King's nobility, knowing they cannot and will not continue at the most two months with the King after their arrival, and that either the reiters will mutiny or his infantry before Rouen disband, which they do daily'.[27]

---

[26] *Unton Correspondence*, pp. 281–2, 293, 316–19, 323, 330; *L. and A.*, III, 645–6.

[27] *L. and A.*, III, 349–55; *Unton Correspondence*, pp. 253–4, 257–8, 261–3, 266–7, 269–70, 278. Burghley's spy in Parma's camp was Adam Brissett – *L. and A.*, III, 352; *Unton Correspondence*, p. 266. A muster on 6 January showed Parma's army at 13,156 foot and 4,061 horse – van der Essen, *Alexandre Farnèse*, V, 336–7. The League, Lorraine, and Papal forces amounted to 8,700 men – Sir C. Oman, *History of the Art of War in the Sixteenth Century*, pp. 514–15.

On 19 January Parma resumed his slow and cautious advance westwards, towards Aumale on the eastern border of Normandy. There on 25 January his main forces surprised a reconnoitring party of 500 horse led, as usual, by the French King himself. Henry skirmished for three or four hours to cover the retreat of the rest of his horsemen and his baggage. But 'entertaining the skirmish too long . . . we and the enemy entered pell-mell into Aumale and the King was most unhappily shot into the lowest part of his reins'. The shot 'entered with obliquity downwards into the flesh and not directly into his body', so no vital part was hurt. There was some alarm 'because the King hath a weak body and is inclined to a fever naturally'. However, all was well. Within a couple of weeks he was on horseback again, though not without considerable discomfort. He had, none the less, had a very narrow escape. He might well have been, not just lightly wounded, but killed or taken prisoner if Parma had been more prompt to believe that he could have hazarded himself so rashly. But the Duke, as he said, had 'till then believed that he had to do with a captain-general of an army and not with a captain of light horse, which he now knew the King of Navarre to be'. It was all very well for du Plessis to plead that Henry had to do the work of a mere captain and make up by his valour for his lack of forces. The danger was that he seemed so frequently to confuse valour with foolhardiness.[28]

Nevertheless, the King's accident was bound to remind his friends very sharply of how much depended upon his life. Beyond him, as du Plessis was prompt to remind Burghley, only shadows and confusion were to be seen. Shadows, because there was no obvious male successor in the royal line other than the infant Condé and the untrustworthy Cardinal of Bourbon. Confusion, and worse, because as was known from Parma's letter of 7 January intercepted by the mayor of Langres, the Spaniards were putting heavy pressure on the League to assemble their States General and, despite the Salic Law, to elect Philip II's daughter, the Infanta Clara Eugenia, as Queen of France. This confirmation of the Spanish take-

[28] *L. and A.*, III, 356–7, 645; *Unton Correspondence*, pp. 278–80, 288–92; *Cal. S. P. Venetian*, IX, 10; Davila, pp. 532–4; Aubigné, VIII, 258–61.

over bid for the French monarchy could only sharpen concern for Henry's survival.[29]

Even if that bid failed, there was still the danger of a break-up of the French kingdom. The League leaders, in their negotiations with Parma, were demanding French provincial governorships and other offices as well as Spanish pensions. Among Henry IV's nominal supporters, the malcontent Cardinal of Bourbon and Count of Soissons were in contact with Épernon. He, like the royalists Montmorency, Matignon, and Bouillon and the Leaguers Mercoeur and Nemours, was building himself a semi-independent provincial principality. With the Dukes of Lorraine and Savoy also casting covetous eyes upon French territory and with Spanish troops in Languedoc as well as Brittany and threatening Gascony as well as Normandy, the prospects for the continued unity of France did not look good.[30]

In fact, affairs in France seemed to be rapidly approaching crisis point both politically and militarily during the four weeks immediately following Henry's misfortune at Aumale. This was made abundantly clear to the English government by three despatches of 8, 13, and 14 February from Unton which arrived together on 18 February.[31] These gave little hope of a successful outcome to the siege of Rouen. 'The scarcity in Rouen', Unton told Burghley, 'is not so great as it seemeth your lordship is advertised. For in our camp we pay thrice so much for all manner of victuals as they do in the town and we shall sooner famish in besieging them than they in being besieged.' If the fort on Mont Ste Catherine could be taken that might compel the town to capitulate, but 'other hope we have none'. To increase the pressure on that fort, Marshal Biron had brought the English troops across from Mont aux Malades to the Charterhouse, just to the north of Mont Ste Catherine and there was no doubt that 'the pressing of the fort doth hasten the Duke of Parma to advance'. The pressure, however, was not very skilfully applied. First the

[29] *L. and A.*, III, 683, 689–94; *Correspondance de Philippe II*, IV, 6. 10; Thou, XI, 461–3; van der Essen, *Alexandre Farnèse*, V, 337–40.

[30] *L. and A.*, III, 480–3, 487, 495–6, 499–500, 503, 506–9.

[31] *Unton Correspondence*, pp. 306–10, 323–7, 331–2. Only the first of these is among the State Papers. Williams also wrote that Rouen was 'no nearer to be forced than when your lordship [Essex] departed' – *L. and A.*, III, 359.

English miners hollowed out the earth under the rampart and then burned the wooden props with which they kept it up. 'The commanders believed that, without powder, it would all fall of itself.' Instead, 'it sunk down so gently that without opening itself or falling in pieces, it only sunk down upon the ground, the bulwark remaining lower but not broken.' The besiegers thereupon made another mine in the same place, this time filling it with gunpowder. Unfortunately, in the quiet of the night before it was due to be fired, the League officer of the watch heard the miners giving the final touches to their work. He had 'fireworks' thrown down to light up the moat to see what was happening and some of these touched off the mine. It carried away part of the bulwark, but the backward blast also burned and buried many of those who were waiting to storm the breach when daylight came. In the darkness and confusion no attempt was made to assault it and the defenders were given time to repair the damage with sacks of earth and faggots.[32]

Nevertheless, despite the pressure on St Catherine's, Parma still moved forward with slow caution. Neufchâtel and its castle, 'of great importance to the enemy in respect of his retreat and the safe passage of his victuals', held him up for four or five days. Then, on 7 February Henry IV, now astride his horse again and leading 4,500 cavalry and 500 foot, caught the enemy vanguard, all their light horse and some infantry regiments under the young Duke of Guise, at Bures, on the west bank of the Béthune river about five miles north-west of Neufchâtel. After an hour's engagement, Guise's men were routed, chased for three miles upon the spur, and driven back over the river with more than 200 killed. The Count of Chaligny, Mercoeur's brother, was captured by the King's jester Chicot and all Guise's baggage, plate, and money taken. Parma himself and Mayenne, who were also on horseback near Bures reconnoitring the way ahead, had almost as narrow an escape as the King had had at Aumale a fortnight

[32] This is Davila's account (p. 528); cp. Valdor, *Discours du Siège de Rouen*, pp. 38–40; Cayet, XLI, 37. It seems more probable than Unton's allegation that Marshal Biron had the mine sprung during the night. Unton admitted 'it hath never been seen among men of war that a mine hath played in the night or any breach assaulted but by day'. He was, of course, not present on the scene, but 15 miles away with the King at Clères – *Unton Correspondence*, pp. 324–5.

earlier. Once again the King had been in the forefront and thick of the action. Unton, who had as usual ridden all day alongside him, wrote that 'we all wish he were less valiant', adding wearily that 'we never rest but are on horseback almost night and day. I think never any ambassador lived in France with such charge, toil, and danger as I do.' He had no doubt, however, that 'this last service doth greatly encourage us and daunt the enemy . . . It is *bonum omen* against the battle which is shortly expected'.[33]

News of it, already uncertainly reported to Beauvoir in England by 10 February, may also have encouraged Elizabeth to think again about her refusal to send Henry any further aid. His prospects were, indeed, beginning to look a little less gloomy. His forces were growing as Aumont, Longueville, Soissons, and Bouillon all joined him. The Dutch were sending him 2,500 infantry under Count Philip of Nassau. He had money available, he said, to pay his Germans and Swiss, for La Trémouille brought 40,000 crowns and the Caen and Dieppe merchants had promised another 60,000, to be repaid to them from taxes at Bordeaux and in Poitou. Henry, moreover, seemed determined not to raise his siege, or at least not to raise it until the very last moment. He aimed to draw Parma forward and force him to a battle as near as possible to Rouen. And the success at Bures so encouraged Unton that he wrote 'if the forces come out of the Low Countries, and any from Her Majesty, I dare hazard my life the Duke of Parma will be beaten'. The outcome of a battle, however, could never be certain and Henry urgently needed more English infantry.[34]

Besides, more might be at stake than the fate of Rouen. For a time, at least, it seemed that Parma, rather than risk a battle, might seek to divert Henry from the siege of Rouen

---

[33] *L. and A.,* III, 358, 361-2, 622; *Unton Correspondence,* pp. 311-15; Davila, p. 535; Thou, XI, 468. Zerotin wrote on 11/21 March 'nous avons erré deux mois comme des Tsiganes', whereby Henry 'a tellement fatigué sa cavalerie qu'aujourd'hui au lieu de l'avoir sous la main et toute fraiche, il n'en a plus du tout. Tout est dispersé, l'un a perdu son cheval, l'autre son argent, un troisième est malade'. The infantry, too, unpaid, abandoned their posts to search the ravaged countryside for food till there was not a grain of wheat left outside the towns, except across the river – *Revue historique,* VII, 74.

[34] *Unton Correspondence,* pp. 268, 318, 323, 326, 332; *L. and A.,* III, 219, 354, 359-60, 363; *Lettres Missives,* III, 568.

by himself besieging Dieppe, the King's principal, indeed almost his only, direct channel of communication with England. The presence of Parma and Mayenne, with their vanguard under Guise, at Bures, north-west of Neufchâtel, on the road to Dieppe, suggested a move in that direction. When on 11 February they moved very cautiously forwards to near Bellencombre, the Dieppe option was still very much open. Even when on 14 February they turned south-west to St Saëns and Rouen then did become their more probable objective, Dieppe was still by no means entirely ruled out. After all, there had been numerous reports from Unton and others that Spanish troops were coming from Brittany to Le Havre. Parma, too, besides threatening to besiege Dieppe, was demanding that the League allow a Spanish garrison to enter Le Havre, the one practicable haven for a fleet of large ships, for an Armada, between Brest and Flushing. These threats to the Channel ports, which Williams, Smith, and Beauvoir were not slow to emphasize, probably weighed quite as much with Elizabeth and her advisers as the fate of Rouen or the possibility of a battle there against Parma, a battle which Burghley, for one, had always believed Parma would do his best to avoid. Indeed, fear that the Spaniards might get possession of Dieppe and Le Havre may well have been decisive in inducing Elizabeth to change her mind about further helping Henry IV. For the last of Unton's three despatches, that of 14 February, reported that Parma had just moved southwards to St Saëns, twenty-three miles north-east of Rouen. He was 'hastening all he can to succour Rouen ... or else to compel us to raise our siege to present the battle, which he may then accept or refuse at his choice'. Troops could hardly be levied and transported from England in time to take part in so imminent a battle – Elizabeth had made that point to du Plessis back in December. They might well, however, be in time to defend Dieppe, to take part perhaps in a second battle of Arques, and to head Parma off from Le Havre.[35]

---

[35] *Unton Correspondence*, pp. 280, 293, 322, 323–7, 330–1; *L. and A.*, III, 351, 364, 366, 463, 646. On 25 January Sir Henry Palmer had been ordered, upon these reports of Spaniards coming to Le Havre, to ply up and down between Le Havre and La Hogue to intercept them with H. M. S. *Rainbow* and the two cromsters *Answer* and *Advantage* and any other ships in this company or that he might meet – *Acts P. C.*, XXII, 206–7.

At all events, on 19 February, the day after Sir Robert Cecil had imparted the contents of Unton's three despatches to the Queen, she ordered the levy of 1,600 foot, 'which shall with all convenient speed be transported thither'. They were, moreover, to be chosen from the trained bands, contrary to usual practice. Burghley, in bed 'greatly pained with the gout', and Sir Robert hoped, very optimistically, that the men might embark by the end of the month. With the 870 English officers and men (besides 208 sick and hurt) already there[36] and the 2,500 the Dutch were sending, these 1,600 would near enough provide the 5,000 foot that du Plessis had said were needed to enable Henry both to face Parma and continue his siege of Rouen. Nevertheless, that the Queen's underlying concern was now for the Channel ports is suggested in her instructions to Sir Matthew Morgan and Sir Edmund Yorke, the two officers appointed to conduct the new levy to Normandy. She told them that on their way to Rouen they might, as they had offered, take any good opportunity of service against the King's enemies. And a later letter from Morgan and Yorke, explaining the reasons why they had not attempted 'the enterprise of A B C', shows fairly clearly that what they had in mind was to surprise Le Havre.[37]

---

[36] *Unton Correspondence*, pp. 336–40; *L. and A.*, III, 347, 647. Of the 1,600 men, 300 were to come from Sussex, 300 from Kent, 350 from London, 300 from Essex, 150 from Hertfordshire, and 100 from Middlesex. The Essex and Hertfordshire men were specifically ordered to be taken from the trained bands – *Acts P. C.*, XXII, 256–8, 274, 278–9, 296–7; *Cal. S. P. Domestic, 1591–4*, pp. 188, 192–3, 200–1. On 2 March the Privy Council wrote to the lords-lieutenant to make good with able men the deficiencies caused in the trained bands by the taking of these men for foreign service; and in July to levy a rate to replace the arms and armour – ibid., pp. 198, 201, 245–6.

[37] *L. and A.*, III, 377, 389. Beauvoir, however, on 8/18 March wrote to Henry IV that Wilkes said that the Queen heard from Unton that Henry was irresolute about the siege of Rouen and that his council advised blocking it instead. She thereupon nearly recalled the 1,600 men and was determined to order Yorke not to disembark at Dieppe unless he was sure that Henry meant to attack Rouen – Rymer, *Foedera, etc.*, VII, i, 116.

# XVII

# Parma's Relief of Rouen

When Elizabeth on 19 February decided to send those 1,600 men to reinforce her troops in Normandy, the immediate crisis at Rouen had already passed. Three days earlier, at dawn on 16 February, Villars had sallied out with 1,600 foot and 400 horse in 'the greatest and resolutest attempt that was done on our army since we lodged before this town'. For although Rouen was not yet in serious want of victuals, the continual sapping and mining were gradually weakening its fortifications. Also although only a few of its defenders were ever killed or wounded in any one sally, the frequent skirmishing was by now building up a dangerous aggregate of losses as well as depleting the stores of powder and shot. It is possible, too, that Villars, like Mayenne, was not anxious to owe his salvation wholly to the Spaniards. At all events, as Williams wrote to Essex, 'I never saw the League grow to the like resolution as they showed within these two days, come to the sword without fear.' Their resolution was well rewarded. They overran the besiegers' trenches, killing several hundred in them. They spiked some cannon, carried off others, filled in the trenches, 'gave vent to the mines, blew up the ammunition'. Marshal Biron received a bullet wound in the thigh and Larchant, captain of the King's guards, was slain as they came up with the Swiss and some landsknechts to restore the situation. Upon their arrival the English and French infantry rallied – Williams, indeed, claimed that, but for the English, all the guns would have been lost – and gradually Villars' troops were pushed back into the town and into St Catherine's forts. 'But the ammunition being blown up, the artillery taken, and all things put in confusion, the loss was inestimable and irreparable for a long time.'[1]

For the besiegers the set-back was certainly serious. It might well have been disastrous if Parma had followed his own

[1] *L. and A.*, III, 368; *Unton Correspondence*, pp. 333, 335; Zerotin, in *Revue historique*, VII, 72; *Kronijk*, XIX, 66–7; Davila, pp. 536–7; Thou, XI, 471–2; Cayet, XLI, 42–50.

instincts and fallen at once upon Biron's disordered infantry while the King with his cavalry was still some distance off. Villars, however, had promptly sent to inform Mayenne that Rouen was no longer in any immediate danger. Thereupon Mayenne and Guise, who 'both grew weary of the Spanish yoke', did an about-turn. Where before they had urged Parma forward, now they held him back. There was, they argued, no longer any urgent need to risk the uncertain outcome of a battle in difficult country against an entrenched enemy superior in horsemen. Let them rather draw off a safe distance until the unpaid nobles and gentlemen who made up most of the King's cavalry ran out of means to remain in the field – as in truth they were already beginning to do. Parma might well suspect the political motive behind this reasoning, but the tactical arguments were plausible enough. So, to the relief and astonishment of the King's supporters – 'we understand not the mystery', Unton wrote – Parma and his Leaguer allies withdrew rapidly on 18 February to Senarpont, on the Bresle. From there they continued to retire eastwards at a more lesiurely pace, followed and harassed by Henry IV and his horsemen, until they crossed the Somme at Pont Remy on 27 and 28 February. They had left behind some 600 French, Spaniards, and Walloons who on 27 February, in broad daylight, marched into Rouen through one of the many gaps in the besiegers' lines. This reinforcement made good the garrison's losses during the skirmishings of the past months.[2]

The news that Parma had drawn back and that Henry had not raised his siege gave Elizabeth some glimmers of hope that Rouen might yet be taken. Sir John Norris, it is true, took a gloomier view. He did not believe that Parma would let Rouen fall or that the King, with his fast-dwindling army, could prevent him relieving it. But Norris, on leave in England, was chiefly concerned to get the Queen to reinforce his own troops in Brittany, where he alleged that otherwise the situation would be irrecoverable. Unton, on the other hand, and many more in France and the Low Countries, believed, at least at first, that Parma was taking his forces back over the frontier. When at the beginning of March the Duke settled

[2] *L. and A.,* III, 368–9, 371, 373; *Lettres Missives,* III, 527–8; Davila, pp. 537–8; Thou, XI, 473–4, 476; Cayet, XLI, 51–2.

down to besiege Rue and threaten Boulogne, it still seemed that he was in no hurry to emerge from behind the Somme and its marshes to challenge the King again before Rouen. His army was considerably weakened by disease and his League allies, like the King's French horsemen, had largely gone home. Moreover, Mayenne was once more putting out peace feelers to the King. Villeroy was still in touch with du Plessis and other proposals were being made by La Châtre. These were not acceptable, 'but this is to be noted', Unton wrote on 5 March, 'that the Leaguers offer to chase out the Spaniards and to conclude this peace without comprehending them in it'. These various negotiations, however, made little progress and it was soon suspected that they were chiefly designed to raise the Leaguers' price with the King of Spain for accepting the Infanta as their sovereign. They were said to be treating also with Parma about 'the present delivery of all the maritime towns and places of account by the sea coast of France which the League possesseth into the King of Spain's hands and that they may receive Spanish garrison into them'.[3]

If these reports and suspicions were well founded, it was more than ever desirable that England should think about the defence of the French Channel ports and about keeping the French King near the Channel coast. The best way to do this would be to encourage him to continue and tighten his siege of Rouen, especially if Parma was really in such need of reinforcement and so committed to the siege of Rue. There might perhaps even be about enough forces to do it. For although the King's unpaid horsemen were disbanding fast, the promised 1,600 more English footmen were beginning to gather at their ports of embarkation and the 2,500 Dutch infantry under Count Philip of Nassau – 'very brave in their gold lace: it will shortly discolour' – were already at Dieppe. Besides, the King had now, for the first time, blocked the river Seine above as well as below Rouen with two forts upstream of the town and a flotilla of armed boats from Pont de l'Arche. Thus Rouen was beginning for the first time to feel the pinch of hunger and by 15 March Unton could write that 'we never had so good hope of Rouen as now, for they begin to suffer the miseries of our long siege'. And, to add to their troubles a full forty paces of the town wall fell down. On 21 February, too, the King and his council had resolved to batter the town in two or three places and simultaneously press forward their approaches to the St Catherine's fort, as Baskerville and others blamed Henry for not doing in the early days of the siege. Despite this resolution, however, Unton still feared that the King, as many of his Catholic followers urged, might merely seek to blockade Rouen 'and so to take it in time rather than presently to batter it, fearing the Duke of Parma's return to levy his siege when Rouen were in danger'. As the days and weeks passed this did seem to be his intention. The 21 February resolution was reaffirmed on 11 March, but its execution was still deferred until the English reinforcements should arrive – and these, delayed by contrary winds, did not reach Dieppe until 18 March nor Rouen until the 27th.[4]

With all these doubts about Henry's intentions, uncertain hopes about Rouen's fall, and fears lest Parma return, Elizabeth clearly needed much more definite information before deciding upon her attitude to the latest developments in northern France. Unton was too closely involved in day-to-day events for his reports to be entirely reliable or entirely consistent.[5] This was more than ever the case with the soldiers, with Sir Roger Williams or Sir Edmund Yorke. So, once again, as to the Netherlands in 1590, the Queen sent Thomas Wilkes to assess and report the true state of affairs. His credentials were drafted on 12 March and his instructions from Queen and Privy Council were drawn up on 16 March.[6]

'The matters to be communicated with the King', Wilkes

---

[4] *L. and A.*, III, 369–70, 375–8, 384–5, 390; *Unton Correspondence*, pp. 348–9, 371, 385; *Acts P. C.*, XXII, 318, 327–9; *Lettres Missives*, III, 574, 594; *Kronijk*, XIX, 69–70; Zerotin, in *Revue historique*, VII, 72–4; Davila, pp. 538–40; Thou, XI, 475–7; Cayet, XLI, 52–3; H. Lloyd, *The Rouen Campaign, 1590–1592*, pp. 145–52. On 14 March a Dutch captain doubted if the King would take Rouen in six months if he did no more than he was doing. By 28 March, however, the same captain thought that Rouen, because of famine, could not hold out more than another three weeks or month – *Kronijk*, XIX, 88–9, 106–7.

[5] He was also being sniped at by Sir Edward Stafford and Stafford's secretary Edward Grimeston who accused him of being lukewarm in the King's cause – *L. and A.*, III, 644, 671–2.

[6] *L. and A.*, III, 651, 654–8; *Unton Correspondence*, pp. 374–9.

was instructed, 'must be privately and confident[ial]ly with himself, considering how untowardly his affairs have proceeded by reason that divers Catholics that favouring not his greatness have given impeachment to his designs.' To avoid the 'jealousy' of Henry's Catholic councillors, however, Wilkes was to deal with the King and them of some matters in outward show. With the King himself he was to begin by yet another rehearsal of the Queen's complaints of Henry's broken promises, both about Rouen and in Brittany, and the waste of her troops and treasure in these two enterprises. Then the Queen required to know 'inwardly and without colour what success she may expect at Rouen'. The common opinion, which she shared, was that the King was unlikely to win it in a long time, if at all, and she feared that some of his councillors did not want him to win it and abused him with colourable but dangerous offers of peace. So 'Her Majesty plainly mindeth, except she may receive good satisfaction of these her doubts, she mindeth to revoke her forces.' Wilkes was also to demand that the King speedily send much greater forces to Brittany, if only to save what was still his. He was also to demand the cession of Brest, or failing Brest St Malo, as a base and place of retreat for her troops and caution for the repayment of her expenses. If these demands were not granted, then she must withdraw her forces from Brittany too.

With the Catholic councillors Wilkes was to raise two matters only. First, the prospects at Rouen and whether it was true 'that some of his councillors of good credit had no desire that it should be won'; secondly, the weakness of the royal forces in Brittany, 'and you may also, as you see cause, allege how unreasonable a matter it is to demand succours of Her Majesty out of England, which must needs come by sea, and to yield no port or town for the safety of her people and shipping'. Wilkes was also given various odd jobs to do if he had time – to look into the conduct of the English musters, to check that the French were duly victualling Grove's pinnaces, and to enquire for any English armour or weapons left at Dieppe.

Wilkes was at Dieppe by 23 March and before Rouen four days later. He and Unton then had to wait till the King returned on 31 March from another of his cavalcades to give them audience on 1 April. At that audience Wilkes presented the major points of his instructions. Henry in reply 'said that even from the first he never had any liking to attempt the siege of Rouen but was overruled therein by his council'. He had undertaken it only to satisfy Her Majesty. The initial delay in starting it had been due to the siege of Noyon. That siege he no longer justified as a device to lull enemy fears for Rouen. He now described it as an operation necessary to preserve Picardy, which was far more important than Rouen because its loss could give Parma free entry into France. The succeeding delays he attributed to trouble with his German troops about their pay, to the decay of the English numbers, and to the disbanding of his French troops.

So at last Henry confessed the truth to his English ally. The siege of Rouen had never held more than a poor second place in his thoughts. He had always regarded it chiefly as a bait to draw troops from Elizabeth and to lure Parma to battle. It was that battle that had always been his prime objective. It still was. For even now he was waiting to see what Parma would do before deciding upon his own course. Rouen, he said, could not hold out for more than another fortnight through lack of victuals. If Parma came within six leagues of the town during that time, he would give him battle and victory would open the town gates. If Parma did not come, then Rouen would be battered and carried by assault, if it had not already compounded.

Henry then admitted that his Catholic councillors were backward in the matter of Rouen and in all other things tending to advance his service. They urged him daily to become a Catholic. The League also insisted on that in their overtures and even proposed that he, when Catholic, should marry the Infanta, though they were also apparently prepared to agree to a settlement that did not include the Spaniards. To Wilkes and Unton, however, Henry protested that he would never forsake his religion and would ever make war upon Spain – protestations that the next few years were to prove as hollow as his earlier professed zeal for besieging Rouen.

As for Brittany, he knew how important it was for the Queen not to have so evil a neighbour as the Spaniard there and he would do all he could to defend the province. He had

sent Conti to assist Dombes and they were already assembling
their appointed forces to join with the English. In view of the
humours of some of his Catholic councillors, he could not
agree to yield Brest or St Malo in particular, but he would
assent to delivering the first port-town to be taken from the
enemy. Then, coming back to his own position, he begged
once again for reinforcement for his own army, for another
2,000 English footmen, paid for one month, in case Parma
should return to give him battle. With them, he would
undertake both to overthrow Parma and to take Rouen. And
taking Rouen might add 300,000 livres a year to his present
revenues – he seems to have forgotten that he had already
pledged a large part of the Rouen receipts to Elizabeth. But
Elizabeth, he said, 'made war at this time good cheap against
so great an enemy ... and [he] wished that he had such
another fool as Her Majesty had of him to make wars against
the King of Spain, that he might look out at the window, as
she doth now, and behold the tragedies between him and his
enemies now in action.'

Audiences with the King and council on 2 and 3 April, and
their written replies on 5 April, added little of significance to
the King's personal answers. He meant to take Rouen. He
would do his best to defend Brittany. To pay his forces there,
he wanted permission to try to borrow from the Queen's
subjects 20,000 crowns a month for some months upon the
credit of certain substantial French merchants. As for a place
of retreat for the English troops there – Wilkes had not named
any particular place to the council – the first place on the sea
coast to be taken from the enemy should be handed over to
them. There was, the King and his council said, little reason to
expect a peaceful outcome from the talks with various
Leaguers and so far nothing had been said about any accord
with the Spaniards. Certainly Henry would not enter into any
treaty with the King of Spain without Elizabeth's advice or
without including her in it.

On 6 April the ambassadors had a talk with Bouillon, who
told that the three-year-old Prince of Condé was to be
christened forthwith and that the good Catholics and those of
the Religion had laid plans to have him declared in Parlement
first Prince of the Blood. The Cardinal of Bourbon and

Bouillon were to administer his lands and the King was to see to his education, all this 'as a mean to provide for the succession and maintenance of the Religion and to bring them into a body, all to conjoin with the Queen of England in case of the King's death'.[7]

Finally, when Wilkes took his leave, Henry sent his thanks to Elizabeth for her picture which she had sent him and for her scarf which he would wear into the coming battle and for the rest of his life. If victorious in that battle, he would make a step into England to signify his love to her in person. Unton told Wilkes 'that the King hath in effect carried him about with him to the wars to feed the King's humour in talking and expressing his love to Her Majesty and to inform himself from the ambassador how Her Majesty would accept of the offer of his love unto her'. In all charges and fights he told Unton 'you shall see me adventure for the honour of my mistress, the Queen of England', as if he meant Unton to report his valour to draw on her liking. Elizabeth, at fifty-eight, was perhaps experienced enough to see through flattery of this familiar kind, all the more as it prefaced a final request that she would send him Sir John Norris with 3,000–4,000 men, to be employed only in the coming battle and then to go to Brittany.[8]

Wilkes took his leave on 8 April. Two days later the siege of Rouen was over. As early as 23 March Unton had reported the intercepting of letters from Parma and Mayenne summoning their forces to assemble at Montdidier on 29 March and revealing their resolve to relieve Rouen within three weeks at the farthest. Three days later a spy did report that it would be at least five weeks before they could come, if they came at all. Nevertheless, on 1 April the King and his council were expecting Parma within twelve days and for that reason dared not commit themselves to begin battering Rouen. Even so the speed of Parma's advance took them completely by surprise. Marching without baggage, he was within four leagues of Rouen on the morning of 10 April with 12,000 foot and 4,000

---

[7] *L. and A.*, III, 662–71. At this very time some Bordeaux merchants were borrowing 100,000 crowns privately in London, upon their own security, to provide pay for Henry's Germans – ibid., 652; *H. M. C., Salisbury MSS*, IV, 187–9.

[8] *L. and A.*, III, 672; also *Unton Correspondence*, pp. 448–50.

horse. The King's forces were then still lying scattered around the town, separated from each other by hills and valleys so that it took two hours or more to get from one group to another. Parma was advancing straight upon Anhalt's unsuspecting Germans around Darnétal. Fortunately for them Bouillon, reconnoitring with some horsemen, ran into the enemy's leading units and gave the alarm. The enemy, too, mistaking Bouillon's troop for the King's whole vanguard, halted and altered their march. So Anhalt's men were able to withdraw and even get their baggage away. The delay also gave Biron time to bring back all the royalist forces on the north bank of the Seine, withdrawing them past Darnétal and on towards Pont de l'Arche. The English, nearly 2,200 strong now that the new companies from England had arrived, acted as rearguard to cover the retreat. Directed by Sir Roger Williams, who had a horse shot under him and two bullets through his hat, they drew off with commendable steadiness and very little loss. At the same time the ships that had been blockading the river also withdrew, part upstream to Pont de l'Arche, the English pinnaces with the Dutch and Dieppe vessels downstream to Caudebec.[9]

Rouen was free. But Henry's hopes of bringing Parma to battle were not yet dead. For a day or two, though, it looked as if he had more reason to fear than to hope for such a contest. He had rather fewer troops than the enemy, no more than 300 French and 3,000 German horse and under 10,000 foot, most of these latter wearied, weakened, and dispirited after a five months' siege through a wet and sometimes snowy winter. He had summoned up another 3,000 French horse and 3,000 French foot, but it would be a week before these could join him. Meanwhile his army at Gouy was 'penned up in a corner' against the great loop made by the Seine by Pont de l'Arche. There they endured 'all manner of miseries, especially forage for our horses, which will force our army shortly to break'.[10]

[9] *L. and A.*, III, 396, 398–9; also Murdin, pp. 651–3 and *Unton Correspondence*, pp. 413–14, both with inaccuracies; *Lettres Missives*, III, 596–8; *Kronijk*, XIX, 86–7, 93–4, 104–5, 149–50; Davila, pp. 539–41; Thou, XI, 477–8; Cayet, XLI, 54–5; On 2/12 April Zerotin had not believed that Parma could come to Rouen before the end of the month – *Revue historique*, VII, 75–6.

[10] *L. and A.*, III, 394, 398, 400. The foot were 2,000 English, 2,000 Dutch, 3,500 Swiss, 1,400 landsknechts, and a mere 300 French.

Had Parma fallen upon them promptly, as he was expected to do, and indeed proposed to do, Henry's position could well have been desperate. He had a superior enemy force in front of him and the one bridge at Pont de l'Arche as his only means of escape to safety across the river. But once again Mayenne and the League's leaders held Parma back from striking a decisive blow. With Henry's forces gathering, the outcome of a battle would be uncertain, they argued, and it was more important to free the river communications between Rouen and Le Havre by capturing Caudebec. Again Parma bowed to his allies' counsels. He knew that they were negotiating, however insincerely, with Henry and he could not risk losing their support if he was to get a States General assembled to elect the Infanta as Queen of France. So Henry's enemies missed the best opportunity ever offered them of inflicting a truly decisive defeat upon him and of taking control of at least the whole of northern France.[11]

Instead, on 13 April Parma marched off in the opposite direction to besiege Caudebec. Next day, as he reconnoitred the town, he was hit below the elbow by a caliver or musket bullet. The bullet was only extracted after long and painful surgery and 'his sickly body and the accidents that usually follow such hurts doth give cause of doubt to his physicians'. He did fall into a fever and was forced to keep to his bed for the next few critical days, leaving the command to Mayenne. Caudebec, which was not capable of enduring a battery, surrendered on 17 April. By undertaking that siege, however, Parma had got himself into almost as dangerous a corner as Henry had been in at Gouy. More dangerous, indeed, for he not only had the unbridged Seine behind him but also by now Henry's army in front, an army growing daily in strength as horse and foot came to it in answer to the King's summons. This certainly seemed to be Henry's opportunity and 'our heads,' Unton wrote, 'are so full of the battle as we think of nothing else'.

The King and his army had left Gouy on 15 April. They marched past Rouen on its east side and by 16 April were about Anglésqueville, astride the Caudebec to Neufchâtel

[11] Ibid., 398, 501; Davila, p. 543; Thou, XI, 478–9; Coloma, p. 174; also van der Essen, *Alexandre Farnèse*, V, 348–9; Lloyd, *The Rouen Campaign 1590–1592*, pp. 183–4.

road, Parma's road back to the Somme and the Netherlands. Next day they made contact with the enemy vanguard under Mayenne and Guise in Yvetot and on 18 April drove it out of that place and back upon the main body, two or three miles to the south towards Caudebec. The King and Unton 'were of the first at the forcing of that village', from which Mayenne 'fled so fast as his horse was like to fail him for want of breath'. That night the King lodged in Yvetot. Some of his forces spread westwards to Valliquerville to cut Parma off from Le Havre. His vanguard now lay in a village a league to the south, within three-quarters of a mile of Parma's entrenchments and with 'Her Majesty's little numbers upon the head of all within half a mile of their army' as near the enemy 'as one side of Mile End Green from the other'. On the following day there were, according to Sir Edmund Yorke, only 'some little skirmishes of French to French, which are as a good base but not as a good play at football in England where men's necks, arms, and legs are broken; but here not a man hurt'.[12]

Part of the English forces was engaged in a rather more deadly two-hour skirmish on 20 April. They claimed to have inflicted losses of over seven score killed and wounded upon the Spaniards and Walloons at a cost to themselves of only eight or nine killed and forty-seven wounded. Williams, whom Henry again commended very highly – he 'fait acte d'un vrai César', Henry told the Queen – wrote that he 'never saw a braver skirmish nor our nation quit themselves more honourably and with few loss'. This action was one of many attempts to force Parma to a battle, but although his army was 'ranged in order of battle all day long, pretending to accept the battle', they utterly refused to come out and fight. On 24 April Henry tried another attack, this time upon the enemy's vanguard, Spaniards, Walloons, and some French, strongly entrenched 'in a little grove of wood under favour of their cannon'. The English, supported by the Netherlanders and some French, led the assault on one side of the wood, while a similar force of Germans, Swiss, and French moved against the other side. The Leaguers' French infantry ran

---

[12] *L. and A.*, III, 400, 402–5; *Lettres Missives*, III, 623; Davila, pp. 544–6; Thou, XI, 479–81; Cayet, XLI, 57–60; also van der Essen, *Alexandre Farnèse*, V, 348–52; Lloyd, *The Rouen Campaign 1590–1592*, pp. 184–6.

away and the Spaniards and Walloons, with their flank thus exposed, suffered considerable losses in falling back upon the main body of their army. They rallied, however, and by a sharp counter-attack regained the ground that they had lost. During the next night, 25–26 April, the English and Netherlanders with some 2,000 French were in arms from midnight until four a.m. expecting an enemy attack. But while they were standing to arms, Parma without sound of trumpet or drum had quietly withdrawn his troops, artillery, munitions, and baggage back nearer the Seine and in front of Caudebec. There he was known to have almost finished building a bridge of boats, defended by fortifications thrown up on either bank of the river.

Warned of this, Henry made yet another attempt to force a battle on 30 April. Drawing out 3,600 mounted men and 6,500 foot, including 1,000 English and 1,000 Netherlanders, he fell upon the quarter where most of Parma's horsemen were lodged. Unfortunately the Baron of Biron and part of the King's cavalry launched their attack prematurely. They broke through the enemy lines and charged on beyond, half an hour before the infantry could come up to consolidate this success. So the enemy escaped with only light losses. But now that the position was taken, 'all the French fell a-spoiling', leaving Captains St John and Edward Poore with 200 English to fight off, for a long half-hour, a counter-attack by 600 Spaniards who were continually being reinforced. Just when the English were beginning to give ground, Williams arrived. He rallied them and thereby held open the narrow passage which was the only way of retreat for the Baron of Biron and his cavalry.[13] 'Of a disorderly direction I never saw a journey prosper better – but all by reason the Spaniards played the great cowards', Williams wrote. As Unton told Burghley, 'the attempt was most desperate and resolved by the King to force the enemy to fight which nothing can work'. Parma once again had refused to be drawn to battle.[14]

[13] Taffin says it was Count Philip of Nassau and the Baron of Biron who beat off the enemy counter-attack – *Kronijk*, XIX, 275–9.

[14] *L. and A.*, III, 407–14; *Unton Correspondence*, pp. 434–6; *Kronijk*, XIX, 258–60, 268–73, 275–82; Davila, pp. 546–8; Thou, XI, 482–5; Cayet, XLI, 60–4. The French chroniclers' dates are not always accurate, e.g. they give Parma's withdrawal to Caudebec as 16 May (N.S.): Unton reported it on 1 May O.S. They give Parma's

Indeed, he was already passing his men in small groups over
to the west bank of the river in boats brought hastily
downstream from Rouen. The tempestuous weather – 'worse
weather there hath not been seen in winter than of late',
Unton wrote – somewhat slowed down the operation. But if
the storms either disrupted Parma's bridge of boats or made it
often too unsteady for safe use, they seem also to have
prevented the English pinnaces and the Dutch and Dieppe
shipping from interfering. At all events, on 3 May Parma
passed the rest of his troops and artillery over the Seine. The
bulk of the troops and all but three pieces of artillery were
safely across before the King's men, distracted by a rearguard
sally under Parma's son Ranuccio, began to realize what was
happening – although it had been obvious (at least to the
English) for some days that Parma intended to withdraw over
the river. By the time that the King's cavalry patrols had
closed up to Caudebec and a few light guns had been placed
on the hills overlooking the river, the three pieces of artillery
and the last few men of Ranuccio's rearguard were already on
their way across. After burning their boats and pontoons to
prevent pursuit, they hastened off to catch up the main enemy
army now marching rapidly away on the west bank of the
Seine towards Rouen and Paris.[15]

Henry had little hope of catching them. Unton blamed him
for spending the rest of that day and all the next morning over
reducing Caudebec where Parma had left a small garrison of
200 Spaniards and Walloons. If Henry had not 'amused
himself upon Caudebec', Unton complained, but had immediately crossed the Seine, he could have utterly overthrown

---

crossing the Seine as 12/22 May and 13/23 May (van der Essen, *Alexandre Farnèse*, V,
353–5, follows them; Lavisse, *Histoire de France*, VI, i. 352, and P. de Vaissière, *Henri
IV*, p. 410, date it as 6/16 May): Unton reported it on 5 May and Henry IV, in a letter
to Nevers, on 7/17 May (*Lettres Missives*, III, 635) and Taffin on 6/16 May as
happening on 3/13 May (*Kronijk*, XIX, 283–4). The chroniclers also say that Henry's
aim in these operations around Caudebec was to starve Parma out rather than to
force him to a battle. Unton, who was almost continuously at the King's side,
repeatedly stresses his anxiety to force a battle. Williams and Yorke reported
similarly. The English sources, and Zerotin, all agree that in the devastated
countryside the King's men were nearly as short of victuals and fodder as the enemy,
not as the chroniclers, that the King's men were well supplied.

[15] S. P. France, xxviii, fos. 15, 18, 20, 25; *Unton Correspondence*, p. 435.

the enemy. But with the few small craft at his disposal after Ranuccio had burned the boats Parma had collected, Henry had virtually no means of transporting his army, especially his cavalry and their horses, across the river at Caudebec. The nearest bridge over the Seine was at Pont de l'Arche, upstream past Rouen and close on forty miles distant by ways deep in mud after the recent heavy rains. Even if Henry had set off at once after noon on 3 May, he could not have arrived there in time to get across and intercept Parma. For by midday on 5 May Parma was already at Évreux, well past Pont de l'Arche and almost half-way to Paris. He marched in such haste that Unton had 'no hope our army can overtake him. Wherefore I fear the King will be forced to follow him only with his cavalry. And so he may once more take view of the enemy's march and upon fit occasion cut off some of them and conduct them out of his frontiers. This is as much, in my opinion, as the King can perform.'[16]

The King and his council at a meeting on 10 May came to the same conclusion. They knew that their army would break if it were pressed into a hard pursuit of the enemy. The nobles and gentry were clamouring to go home. The reiters and landsknechts were again mutinous for pay, pay which the King could not provide. The English and Dutch, who had borne the brunt of the last few weeks' fighting, were worn out, short of victuals, and deserting daily. So a vigorous pursuit of the rapidly retreating enemy was clearly not practicable. Instead, it was decided that Henry with 1,000 French horse and 1,000 mounted harquebusiers should march by Beauvais to attempt to shadow Parma after he crossed the Marne at Soissons or thereabouts. The rest of the army, what remained of it, under Marshal Biron should besiege Neufchâtel and then Honfleur, Fécamp, and other small places in Normandy whose capture would keep Rouen still straitened for victuals. In the event, the King never again even looked upon Parma and his retreating army. After recrossing the Seine at St Cloud on a bridge of boats, the Duke did allow his weary troops a fortnight's rest in the rich and unspoiled country of Brie and around Château-Thierry. Even by 16 May Henry with his

[16] S. P. France, xxviii, fos. 17, 25.

horsemen was only at Senlis, a good forty miles away and with the Marne, over which he had no bridge below Épernay, between them and the enemy. From there he turned north to Compiègne, apparently to gather the local forces of Picardy and Champagne around La Fère for a final attempt to harass Parma's retreat. But at Compiègne on 24 May bad news from Brittany gave him a reason – or perhaps an excuse – to break off his rather lukewarm pursuit and return to join Biron and the remains of his army in Normandy.[17]

The bad news from Brittany also put an end to Elizabeth's thoughts of reinforcing Williams and her troops in Normandy. So long, of course, as Parma had been on the Somme or the Seine, threatening a Spanish domination of the entire French side of the Channel, Queen and Council could not think of lessening English help to the French King in that principal theatre of the war. For, as Burghley said, 'in very truth upon the event of this present accident dependeth *salus nostrae republicae et totius Christiani orbis profitentis vere Christum'.*[18] Nevertheless, even now Elizabeth tried to find ways of assisting Henry in this very critical situation without increasing her own expenses either in money or in men. When Parma first approached Rouen in February she had been strongly attracted to a suggestion made by Bodley to Burghley from The Hague. At that time the Dutch States General were collecting the various Provinces' assents to an extraordinary contribution of £90,000 to finance their coming summer's campaign. Why, Bodley suggested, should they not this summer stand on the defensive at home and send another 5,000 or 6,000 Dutch and English foot to France, to bring the 2,500 they now had there up to 6,000 and the English up to 2,000? After all, if the French King did not prosper, the Dutch would not long enjoy the benefits of their own victories, and it was infantry that the King especially needed to enable him to prosper. Burghley put Bodley's suggestion to the Queen on 21 February and she greatly approved of it.[19]

So, while waiting for the States General to get final agreement to the £90,000 contribution, Bodley sought to

---

[17] Ibid., fos. 1, 13, 25, 31, 36, 51, 73; Davila, p. 550.
[18] *Unton Correspondence,* p. 431.
[19] *L. and A.,* III, 38, 42, 47, 195.

prepare the ground by discussing his suggestion with Olden-barnevelt and various other Dutch leaders. He knew that Count Maurice and the Frieslanders, and for somewhat obscure reasons the French ambassador Buzenval, would oppose it strongly. For Maurice and the Frieslanders hoped in 1592 by besieging Steenwijk, Coevorden, and eventually Groningen to drive the Spaniards from the north-eastern Netherlands, from all the rest of the area north of the Maas and Waal. The clearing of those quarters would free 6,000 troops from garrison duty and perhaps almost treble the States' means. The other Dutch leaders to whom Bodley spoke – to his surprise even Oldenbarnevelt – seemed, however, enthusiastic for his proposal. Accordingly on 6 April the Queen wrote to the States General, using Bodley's arguments to persuade them to send another 3,000 or 4,000 of their own troops to Henry IV and allow another 2,000 foot and 100 horse from her auxiliary companies to go with them. Bodley received this letter on 26 April. By then the siege of Rouen was over and Parma was penned in around Caudebec. The States would not therefore reply to the Queen until they saw the outcome of the actions between Parma and Henry.[20]

Then during the first week of May news came from Dieppe to the English court and to Beauvoir of Parma's withdrawal across the Seine at Caudebec on 3 May. The reports added, enthusiastically but erroneously, that Henry had crossed his own army over upon Parma's bridge of boats and had defeated a good part of the enemy's forces. Encouraged by this report, with its alluring hope of another Ivry victory, this time against Parma and the Spanish army, Elizabeth on 8 May definitely promised Beauvoir that she would send Henry 2,000 foot and 100 horse from her auxiliary companies in the Netherlands. These, Burghley remarked to Unton, 'may more speedily be sent from thence and of better soldiers than there can be levied and transported out of this realm'. That day and the next the Queen had letters written to the States General, Count Maurice, Bodley, Vere, Sidney at Flushing, Morgan at Bergen, and Norris at Ostend for the immediate despatch of these troops. On 7 and 8 May Edward Burnham was instructed to take these letters over to the Netherlands and to arrange for transports to be made ready at Flushing to carry the troops to Dieppe. Six companies of foot were to come from Vere's forces in the field, six from Bergen garrison, and one each from Flushing and Ostend, together with either Poley's or Parker's horse-band. In her letter to the States the Queen also once again urged them to send another 3,000 or 4,000 of their own footmen. Sundry overthrows lately given to Parma and his army, she wrote, made the total ruin of the French King's enemies seem possible if his lack of infantry could be speedily remedied.[21]

All this would not, of course, have meant any substantial increase in the Queen's expenses. She would have to pay these fourteen foot-bands and the horse-band whether they served in France or the Netherlands. Nevertheless, with the 1,000 or more still serviceable men already with Sir Roger Williams, and Count Philip's troops, they would have provided the King with a substantial nucleus of the infantry he so badly needed. But the question was whether Dutch opposition to their withdrawal could be overcome or evaded quickly enough, or indeed at all. This was Beauvoir's principal anxiety. He had letters from Buzenval and was also told by Noël de Caron, the States' agent in England, that the States' army was already in the field and far away.[22] Vere's six foot-bands and another two from Bergen and two from Ostend were already with that army before Steenwijk. So there was little likelihood of English or Dutch being drawn out promptly for France. Other letters amply justified Beauvoir's fears. One of 1 May from Bodley gave a very discouraging account of his dealings about the matter. Another, of 3 May, from Count Maurice alleged that the States had so denuded their forces to provide his army before Steenwijk that they had hardly enough left to defend their frontiers against the enemy who could still put 8,000 infantry and 1,500–1,800 cavalry into the field.[23]

[21] S. P. France, xxviii, fos. 23, 38; T. Rymer, *Foedera, etc.,* VII, i, 92–3; Cotton MSS, Galba D. ix, fos. 189, 191, 192; S. P. Holland, xliv, fos. 286–94; S. P. Flanders, v, fos. 78–81; *Acts P. C.,* XXII, 431–3.

[22] S. P. France, xxviii, fos. 29, 38.

[23] Cotton MSS, Galba D. ix, fo. 172; S. P. Holland, xliv, fo. 278.

It was the old problem of England lacking a mobile strategic reserve or any real standing army outside the companies in the Netherlands, and of her Dutch and French allies each concentrating their efforts upon their own local theatres of operations. It meant that unless the Queen was prepared to increase substantially her expenditure and her troop levies, any hope of providing timely help to Henry IV to crush Parma or renew the siege of Rouen was virtually moribund even before the bad news from Brittany killed it stone dead.[24] For although Burnham reached Flushing on 17 May, it was 24 May before the Queen's letters to the States General and Bodley reached Bodley, who was away with the Council of State at the camp before Steenwijk. By then Elizabeth, upon learning from Caron that the States' army was already in the field, so far modified her demands as to defer the withdrawal of her companies until after Steenwijk should be taken. Burnham at Flushing received a letter from Burghley on that 24 May, 'not to stir the companies until we do hear other order from your lordship'. On that same 24 May Burghley, writing from the court to Unton in France, added in a postscript that 'presently I hear of a great defeat given to the 2 princes [Conti and Dombes] by the cowardness of the lieutenants, whereof our nation hath, I fear, suffered great wrack. Such are the accidents of wars'.[25] This particular accident put an immediate end to all idea of reinforcing Williams's companies in Normandy.

[24] E.g. Sir R. Cecil to Sir T. Heneage, 23 May – *H. M. C., Salisbury MSS*, IV. 199.
[25] S. P. Holland, xlv, fo. 15; S. P. France, xxviii, fo. 157; *Unton Correspondence*, p. 466.

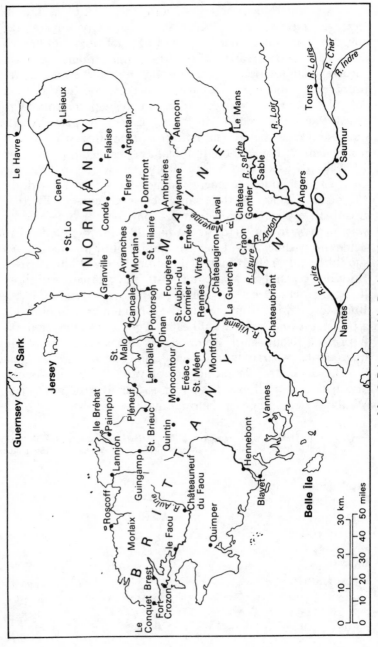

Map 8. Brittany and its Borders (1591–5).

# XVIII

## Disaster in Brittany and Abandonment of the Offensive

The defeat of the two princes, Dombes and Conti, occurred on 12 and 13 May before the town of Craon in Anjou on the border with Brittany. After Dombes had sent his forces home early in the previous December, Sir John Norris and his English companies had spent the winter billeted upon the villages of western Maine. By the spring they were reduced through sickness and desertion to a bare 900–1,000 men able to carry arms. Sir John had early in February sent his brother Sir Henry to plead with the Queen for the reinforcements that she had steadily refused him as long as the siege of Rouen lasted. He himself went back to England soon afterwards, leaving his troops under the sergeant-major Anthony Wingfield. Before he left, Dombes and Conti with their advisers had met at Laval and agreed to bring 7,000 foot, including the English, and 900 horse into the field on the borders of Anjou and Brittany by 19 February to besiege Craon, Fougères, Châteaubriant, or one of the other towns that blocked the passage between the two provinces. These numbers, however, were consciously inflated to almost twice the true figures to impress the enemy 'in respect of a false brother' in the princes' councils. Moreover it was the very end of March, instead of 15 February, before Dombes took the field and Conti was even slower. At length on 3 April Dombes approached Craon. Next day the English, with 100 lands-knechts and two Breton foot-bands, drove the enemy from the abbey and suburb of St Clement, on the right bank of the river Oudon which flowed along the west side of the town. Five days later Conti's first troops arrived from Poitou and Anjou. They began to entrench themselves on the other side of Craon, across the river from Dombes' men. Conti and the rest of his forces then arrived and after some desultory skirmishing the two princes settled down to a not very enterprising siege. Between them they had eleven cannon, but not enough powder and shot to begin a battery since Conti's intendant of finance had been captured on his way to arrange for extra supplies from Tours.[1]

Mercoeur was thus given time to gather a relieving army. By 11 May he was at Châtelais, within a league and a half of Dombes' troops. The little river Usure, a tributary of the Oudon, covered his front while the Oudon itself shielded his right flank against Conti. He had about the same number of troops as the two princes. So they at first resolved not to raise their siege, but to draw in all their horse and foot to camp 'close upon our guard and so to certify us in all our lodgings as that any one quarter should be able to withstand his uttermost charge till the rest might come to their relief'. The brunt of the first actions on 12 May fell, of course, upon Dombes' forces on the west side of the Oudon.[2] Upon the alarm that the enemy was approaching, about ten in the morning, he sent 150 of the English to help oppose their passage over the Usure. Wingfield reinforced these 150 with another 200 under Captain Wolf. Together they drove the enemy advanced parties from the hedges they had occupied. Then they reinforced some Frenchmen holding a mill that provided the principal passage over the river. Thereupon as all the enemy army approached, Wingfield sent forward all the rest of the English except those guarding the trenches before Craon. Two companies of French horse and 100 landsknechts joined them and together they deterred the enemy from attempting to cross the Usure that night.

The two princes now began to fear that Mercoeur would prove too strong for Dombes. They therefore resolved that night to withdraw his forces across the Oudon into Conti's quarter. About six a.m. on 13 May all the guards in the western suburbs were withdrawn, 'whereupon we drew off ours also in from the river and passed there into Prince Conti's quarter'. The enemy followed them over the Usure and then

---

[1] *L. and A.*, III, 460–78; S. P. France, xxviii, fos. 7, 105; *Lettres Missives*, III, 577–8; B. Pocquet, *Hist. de Bretagne*, V. 210–9, who reproduces a plan of the battle sent by Aguila to Philip II. The 'false brother' was La Courbe de Brée.

[2] For the Craon action – S. P. France, xxviii, fos. 52, 56, 71, 77, 105; Moreau, pp. 102–8; Davila, pp. 569–70; Thou, XI, 518–21; Cayet, XLI, 65–71; Aubigné, VIII, 290–6.

across the Oudon – on the bridge of boats that Dombes had omitted to destroy, according to Aguila and the French chroniclers; or by passing through Craon, according to one of the English accounts. Seven or eight hours' skirmishing ensued. The English came at least four times to push of pike and about noon drove the enemy from a well-trenched hedge from which they 'did beat upon all our battle, which made our great ones to stagger very much'. By then the princes had decided to abandon their siege altogether and to retire at once towards Château-Gontier, despite the warning of some of their more experienced officers about the dangers of a daytime retreat in the face of the enemy. Conti marched off first and Dombes followed him, through a country full of hedges, ditches, and narrow lanes. The English, having been engaged all the previous day and night and all this day, had run out of ammunition. So, at Wingfield's request, Dombes agreed that they should march away immediately after his own horse-band, leaving the landsknechts and French to 'make the retreat for us altogether and that M Liskarte with their horse companies should stand to assure them'.

The French chroniclers seem to assume that this was what happened. But by Wingfield's account, when Dombes' horse-band and the English marched off, the landsknechts at once marched off too and by cross ways thrust in front of the English. The French horse also ran away in disorderly fashion when the enemy horse approached them. They galloped through a lane where the English were marching and broke their ranks. Thus disordered and without powder or shot, the English were left to cover the retreat of all the rest. They twice made stands with their pikes, but each time had to give way before the storm of enemy shot to which they could not reply. Although Dombes and the few horsemen left with him charged three times, this 'did but give them passage who were before'. Conti, who seems to have taken little or no part in the fighting, escaped to Château-Gontier. So eventually did Dombes and most of the French forces. But two of their leading commanders were killed and seven of eight taken prisoner, while all their artillery, ten or eleven pieces including the English culverin, was lost. The landsknechts suffered heavy losses, while the English were broken and scattered far and wide. About 800 of them escaped, some to Château-Gontier, and then to Vitré, some to Laval, though not more than 600 remained in serviceable units. Their 'greatest loss was of our captains and officers who sustained the last brunt of all and deserved wonderful commendation in continuance of two days and a night, for the fight began on Friday about noon and ceased very little till Saturday three of the clock at afternoon.' Twenty of their officers were killed, three wounded, and six taken prisoner. Ten or eleven English colours were lost.

Mercoeur went on to occupy Château-Gontier, Laval, and Mayenne, while Conti retired to Angers and Dombes to Rennes, their armies broken. It looked as if all Brittany lay open to the Leaguers and their Spanish allies – Rennes, the provincial capital and royalist headquarters, all the little towns and seaports along the northern, Channel, coast, even Brest at the extreme western end of the province. In the end Mercoeur ignored these apparent opportunities and after a few weeks also withdrew back to Nantes.[3] But in the immediate aftermath of the battle of Craon the situation looked menacing indeed for the King's party and for the remnant of their English infantry.

News of the Craon disaster reached London on 24 May. It put the Queen altogether out of quiet, Cecil told Heneage next day. And four days later Burghley wrote to Unton that 'the evil news of Brittany maketh us so perplexed as we cannot take comfort of any hard accident to the Duke of Parma . . . I had rather both Paris and Rouen were left unrecovered than have Brittany lost'.[4] Their immediate reaction was to send Sir Henry Norris post haste by way of Caen to discover and report upon the situation in Brittany and the state and whereabouts of the English troops that had survived the battle. He took money to pay them, powder, muskets, calivers, and pikes to rearm them. On 3 June the Queen also wrote to Sourdéac, the governor of Brest, praising his loyalty to Henry IV and promising to send him help, as far as possible, if he needed it. More she would not do until she heard from the King just

³ S. P. France, xxviii, fos. 73, 188, 310, 318.
⁴ Ibid., fo. 66; *Cal. S. P. Domestic, 1591–4*, p. 222; *Unton Correspondence*, p. 466.

what the situation was, what he meant to do about it, and what help he needed from England.[5]

Another reason, too, persuaded her against any hasty resolution. On 1 June Unton wrote to Burghley in cipher and 'at large of the matter of peace and other advertisements of great importance'. Burghley never received this letter, but Unton no doubt reported its purport verbally when he came home in the middle of June. Anyway, other reports told of renewed peace talks between the King's ministers and the League, and perhaps with the Spaniards also.[6] If those talks were likely to prosper into a peace, then the King might well not need English aid against any of his subjects who still persisted in rebellion. It was of vital concern, too, to England that peace in France should not extend to a peace between France and Spain that would set Spain free to concentrate again upon the Enterprise of England or the suppression of the Dutch. Until these questions also were answered, English policy must remain in suspense.

One question was, however, already settled. The news from Craon put an end to all thought of substantially reinforcing Williams's forces in Normandy, the more so as Unton's report of an audience with Henry IV on 24 May showed clearly that the main brunt of defending Brittany was likely to fall upon Elizabeth. Henry then resolved to break off his not very promising pursuit of Parma and to return to the army in Normandy, there to take counsel on what was to be done about Brittany. He did not even turn down altogether Unton's urgent demand that he should himself lead an army into that province. So Unton did 'not doubt but with good handling Her Majesty may now obtain any reasonable matter for the conservation of Brittany, as also for a place of retreat for the English and I urge continually the yielding of Brest[7] into Her Majesty's hands, whereunto I find the King well inclined'. But Henry also pointed out the danger that Parma

[5] S. P. France, xxviii, fos. 90, 117, 139; *Cal. S. P. Domestic, 1591–4*, p. 223; *Acts P. C.,* XXII, 502–4; *H. M. C., Salisbury MSS*, IV, 202–3.

[6] S. P. France, xxviii, fos. 36, 51, 66, 133, 143, 164; S. P. Tuscany, i. fo. 79; *H. M. C., Salisbury MSS*, IV, 191–2.

[7] The version printed in *Unton Correspondence*, p. 463, has a meaningless 'the rest' instead of 'Brest' at line 22.

might now be encouraged to stay in France. Champagne and Picardy would then be in grave danger and those north-eastern frontier provinces, Henry emphasized, were to him 'of greater consequence than Brittany'. His argument was soon to be given yet more force when on 18 June the troops that Parma had left behind to bolster the League's cause captured Épernay and threatened Châlons. Clearly Brittany, so important in English eyes, was as usual taking very much a second place in the French King's thoughts. Parma and Parma's army still obsessed him. Clearly, too, he was about to make further calls upon Elizabeth for substantial aid, and not for Brittany alone.[8]

These new calls were to be voiced by a new special envoy, M de Sancy, who came over in Unton's company and was in London by 18 June.[9] Until he arrived the Queen would come to no firm and final resolutions. For the time being Williams and his troops were allowed to remain in Normandy. This was not altogether to Williams's liking. For a month and more he had been in an unusually gloomy mood. He was under the impression that 'some instruments of great men in this country' had wronged him in reports to Beauvoir, 'to the end that some of his should procure me a check from great ones in the court'. He also believed that some of his fellow captains gave out in England 'that I am too hot and cannot agree with the French'. As early as 26 April, while Parma was still at Caudebec, he had seen no reason 'but we should be all revoked until the King were forced to a battle, which cannot be at this voyage of the Duke of Parma, or else that His Majesty were in hope to recover some of his chiefest towns. And by such means Her Majesty might well stop her men and treasure until a dangerous action might happen'. A little later he wrote that the King would be deceived if he thought to draw four, three or two thousand Englishmen out of England every quarter of a year.

For the country will not be able to furnish him men and arms to be cast away in such sort as we have been hitherto since my Lord Willoughby first arrived here unto this hour. Also Her Majesty

[8] S. P. France, xxviii, fos. 73, 170, 195, 219; *Lettres Missives*, III, 842.
[9] S. P. France, xxviii, fos. 164, 176; *Cal. S. P. Domestic, 1591–4*, p. 238.

ought to consider that our armed pikes cannot continue these rolling "curvettes" so well as his light harquebus à cheval.[10]

Maurice Kiffin, the treasurer-at-war's deputy in Normandy, agreed. 'In the running camp in these parts' no supply of soldiers could serve and subsist for more than a month. 'Nothing consumeth our men more than such lingering kind of service and pilgrimage up and down.' There was no provision of carriage for arms and baggage, no manner of relief for hurt and sick men. It would be useless to reinforce them if they were to be marched up and down through 'this wasted forlorn country as they have been'. In less than three years 11,000 Englishmen, Kiffin said, had been consumed there and not 1,100 of them had fallen in fight.[11] The nineteen companies now there were no less sadly reduced. A muster on 24 May showed only 1,107 able men and even so the muster commissary, Thomas Powell, had to admit 'I am sure they have deceived me of very many men'. Some 400 Dutch and Scots from Count Philip of Nassau's force came to the muster and although Powell put back as many of them as he could, 'they changed the Scots' and Dutchmen's coats and put Englishmen's coats upon them'. There were also many English and Irish freebooters who mustered but did little service. Desertion, too, was rife. Two hundred able-bodied soldiers from Normandy arrived, without passports at Dover and another 200 at Rye early in May. In short, the nineteen companies were 'extreme weak' and when, as the Queen directed on 26 May, Williams discharged eleven of them and drafted their men into the remaining eight, those eight still mustered only 529 able men and 128 sick out of their supposed 1,125 effectives.[12]

The rapid decay of the English numbers from sickness, desertion, and the hardships of this service emphasized their need of a secure base on French soil to which they could safely retreat to refresh themselves and where they could heal their sick and hurt men and bring in and store their supplies. This was what Williams was now urging that the Queen should

[10] S. P. France, xxviii, fos. 31, 121, 135; *L. and A.*, III, 415.
[11] S. P. France, xxviii, fos. 58, 131, 133.
[12] Ibid., fos. 75, 78, 97, 166, 167; *Acts P. C.*, XXII, 448–9, 478–9.

demand if he and his companies were to remain in Normandy or Norris and his troops in Brittany. He saw 'no means for our nation to live in these wars, nor safety for Her Majesty's great expenses, without a town in her subjects' hands'. Quilleboeuf, half-way between Caudebec and Le Havre on the opposite bank of the Seine, was his first choice. It was not a town but it was reasonably well fortified and in two months could be made into a 'French Flushing'. But, as Williams soon recognized, there was no hope of getting Quilleboeuf (which Henry IV was trying to rename Henriquartville). It already had a royalist garrison and its temporary commander, the Huguenot du Fay, was being superseded by the Catholic Le Grand 'who doth not affect them of the Religion' and presumably liked Englishmen even less.[13] On 31 May James Colville of Ester-Wemyss, who commanded a small Scottish garrison in St Valéry-sur-Somme, privately offered that place to Williams 'as a retreat for you and all your nation'. But Williams had already written off St Valéry as a place commanded by high grounds and impossible to fortify to any purpose. Le Crotoy, however, on the opposite side of the Somme estuary, was 'commanded with nothing' and itself commanded the deep channel by which alone Amiens, Abbeville, and other Somme towns could obtain commodities from the seas. That, too, might within three months be made 'a French Flushing or at least stronger than a Brielle'. Besides paying the troops that garrisoned it, it could bring in fully £2,000 a year for the Queen, or four times that sum if she permitted trade with the League towns. At the end of June Ottywell Smith was to suggest making a base at Le Hourdel, also at the mouth of the Somme but on the opposite side to Le Crotoy and to seaward of St Valéry. Later Williams would take up that suggestion.[14]

For the moment, though, all these suggestions fell upon deaf ears in England since, with English eyes fixed upon Brittany, it was very doubtful whether any English troops would long be left in Normandy. On 9 June Williams and his men did obtain some relief. That day, at Unton's urgent request,

---

[13] S. P. France, xxviii, fos. 54, 73, 85, 87, 161, 184.
[14] Ibid., fos. 85, 125, 217.

Henry sent them and the Netherlanders with them back to rest and refresh themselves for twenty days between Dieppe and Le Tréport.[15] Grove, with the Queen's four pinnaces, had already sailed for England on 31 May and soon afterwards the Queen's ordnance was put ashore at Dieppe by the Flushing *Pelican* and *Grace of God* aboard which it had idly spent most of the siege of Rouen.[16] The remnants of the companies in Brittany had by now found a comparatively safe shelter in Vitré. English naval and military activity in France thus ceased almost entirely while the Queen and her Council listened to and decided upon the demands brought to them by Sancy.

The main purpose of Sancy's mission, like that of an agent named de Fourneaux who had already arrived from Dombes,[17] was to seek English military reinforcements for Brittany. What he first asked for was 6,000 footmen, 100 horse, and seven pieces of artillery with balls and 50,000 lb. of powder. This in itself was an unusually large demand and when Sancy and Beauvoir conferred with the Privy Council on 18 June, after Sancy's first audience with the Queen, the Councillors immediately whittled down the figure for discussion to 4,000 footmen and pointed out that it would be a month before they could be ready. Yet the request for Brittany was by no means the end of Sancy's demands. He also asked for 1,200 foot to follow the King in the Île de France, for eight or ten warships to serve against Lussan in the river of Bordeaux – all this at Her Majesty's expense – and for 400 pioneers, with promise of payment for these, to help to fortify Le Hourdel at the mouth of the Somme. In addition he suggested that other English forces, with cannon, should invade Artois from Ostend and take towns there with the help of such forces as the King had in Picardy. The Queen and her Councillors were obviously taken aback by the extent of these demands. They made it very clear on 18 June that they were not prepared to discuss anything more than the provision of a possible 4,000 men for Brittany. As the Queen pointed out in a written reply on 22 June, the demands were greater than any

[15] Ibid., fos. 164, 217.
[16] Ibid., fos. 111, 113, 145, 161, 169.
[17] Ibid., fos. 157, 159.

that had ever been made of her. They seemed very strange in view of the numbers of her people already wasted in various parts of France without any recompence or any assurance of any port-town for their safety. So strange that, were Sancy not in such high credit with the King as his letters of credence stated, she might well doubt whether the King was privy to such large requests.

But while the size of the demands was in itself enough to stop her acceding to them – to hire 6,000 French foot, it was estimated, would cost £90,096 a year[18] – there was another no less cogent reason. She heard 'that the French King and his subjects are inwardly accorded upon a peace and that the King hath such hope thereof as he is gone to lie near Paris with smaller forces than his enemies have in the same parts'. She would not mislike his making peace with his subjects, provided he expelled the Spaniards and yielded her such aid against Spain as she had shown to him. But if peace were made in France, she saw no need for her to give the King any new succours since he and his reunited subjects together would be well able to expel the Spaniards.[19]

Before this written reply was given to him, Sancy had already on 19 June begged that, if only the 4,000 men for Brittany could be granted and they could not be ready to leave in less than a month, at least the Queen would in the meantime reinforce Williams's eight foot-bands at Le Tréport up to 1,200 men. This would enable Longueville to fortify Le Hourdel. Then in five weeks' time these men could go off to join the rest of the 4,000 in Brittany. If that were done, Sancy would guarantee that the King would appoint the Huguenot Odet de la Noue as governor of Le Hourdel. He was also prepared to guarantee that one of the two places, St Malo or Morlaix, to be conquered in Brittany would be placed in the hands of someone the Queen named. This would be in addition to the place that was to be handed over to her as a place of retreat for her troops. The King, he added, reckoned on the Dutch succouring him with at least 2,000 men in Brittany and he asked the Queen to urge the States to grant this help. The King for his part was sending Marshal Biron to Brittany with forces.[20]

When the Queen's written answer to Sancy's original demands was delivered to him on 22 June, he took it – or affected to take it – as a flat refusal. Accordingly he asked to be sent back the very next day to inform the King as quickly as possible of this 'unexpected resolution'. The Queen, after checking that her Councillors had not said that 'la Reine ne peut secourir le Roi en cette urgente nécessité', explained through Burghley that she needed to know how far the King had already proceeded in his treaty with his rebel subjects before she could answer his requests. To that end she was considering sending an envoy urgently with Sancy to the King. After some further discussion, she offered on 26 June to send 4,000 foot and 100 horse to Brittany as soon as she understood that the King would make no peace with Spain without her allowance and would make peace with his rebels only if they promised to help him expel the Spaniards or at least in no way aid the Spaniards against him. The despatching of the 4,000 men to Brittany must further be conditional upon the Queen being given a port-town for her troops' safe retreat and for the reimbursement of her expenses, and upon the King putting into the field in Brittany 10,000 of his own footmen and a sufficient body of horse. Apparently the 2,000–3,000 men looked for from the Dutch might be counted in the 10,000. Sancy and Beauvoir would also be required to give renewed assurance for the repayment of all the Queen's expenses on Henry's behalf since September 1589, a sum now totalling £144,786 5s. 11d.[21]

Once again Sancy and Beauvoir came back on 27 June to beg that the 4,000 men for Brittany should be increased to the 6,000 they had originally asked for. At least 10,000 men were needed there, they said, to overcome Mercoeur's 6,000. The King could not provide more than 2,000 foot and 1,000 horse now that Parma's forces and the Duke of Lorraine's had united in Champagne and had taken Épernay. The two ambassadors also asked again that 1,000–1,200 of the 6,000

---

[20] Ibid., fos. 170, 180.
[21] Ibid., fos. 192, 206, 208, 227.

should be sent for six weeks to reinforce Williams's eight companies at Le Tréport to help fortify Le Hourdel. They would not mention the cannon and munitions, though without them the army in Brittany would be useless. Their requests were duly reported to the Queen. She agreed to let the seven cannons at Dieppe, with their munitions, go to Brittany but she would not increase the 4,000 men. Between nine and ten o'clock on that evening of 27 June Burghley sent the ambassadors a draft contract for these 4,000 men and the artillery, but nothing more. They returned the draft, with a few marginal additions and on 30 June at Greenwich between two and three o'clock they signed the formal contract with Burghley, Howard, Hunsdon, and Buckhurst. It was presumably with these four Councillors, under the very watchful eye of the Queen, that Sancy and Beauvoir had conducted the negotiations, with minor parts being played by Sir Edward Stafford and the Privy Council clerk William Waad, and we may perhaps guess Sir Henry Unton.[22]

The terms of the contract of 30 June followed fairly closely the Queen's answers of 22 June.[23] She promised to put ready enough footmen to bring her forces in Brittany up to 4,000 men. The artillery and munitions at Dieppe might go with them. But the troops should not go until certain conditions were satisfied. First, the Queen must be duly informed that the King would not make peace with Spain or include Spain in any agreement with his rebel subjects. Second, the 2,000 foot and 1,000 horse that the King could provide and the other troops coming from the Dutch should be ready to enter Brittany. Third, the King should bind himself to deliver to her such walled seaport as she or her general should require, or if he had none, then to deliver the next one that he should get. The Queen should retain the customs and trade dues of this port towards the repayment of what the King owed her but she should return the town to him when he sent her troops home. The King was to bind himself to repay the costs of the levy, transportation, and pay of the 4,000 and the value of the artillery and munitions. The Queen also asked that he should

[22] Ibid., fos. 190, 192, 206, 208, 215, 221, 232.
[23] S. P. Treaty Papers (France), vii, fo. 308.

ensure that there were at least 4,000 foot and 1,000 horse there in his pay to support her troops. Of the 4,000 English, 2,550 were to be drawn from the auxiliary companies in the Netherlands. The rest were apparently to be made up by transferring Williams's eight companies from Normandy to Brittany to reinforce the remnant of the forces there, and if need be by levying a few hundred men in England.[24] In sum therefore the new contract for Brittany committed Elizabeth to little real addition to her present expenses.

Yet despite the Queen's very apparent tight-fistedness, Beauvoir and Sancy on 1 July made one further effort to prise something more out of her. They asked Burghley to convey certain questions to her so that when Sancy took his leave of her in a day or two's time he might receive her answers to carry back to his master. They asked what about the 100 horse they had requested for Brittany? What about reinforcing Williams's eight foot-bands for a few weeks up to 1,200 men out of the 4,000 for Brittany? As the Leaguers' recent seizure of Pont Audemer and siege of Épernay, as well as du Plessis' return to Saumur, showed beyond doubt that the peace treaty had ended in smoke, would she not name a day when her 4,000 men would be on the frontiers of Brittany? Those from the King and the Dutch should be there in three weeks or a month, though as the Dutch States were short of men the King had only asked them for money to hire French or Swiss troops. Finally, as Quilleboeuf was in danger for lack of victuals, would Her Majesty send thither two of her pinnaces and a supply of victuals? Sancy and Beauvoir would bind themselves to repay the cost of the victuals within a month.[25] Elizabeth remained adamant. All these requests were rejected or ignored except that for two pinnaces for Quilleboeuf, which was also at first refused but then granted. They were to serve for two months, upon Sancy's promise to repay their cost – £298 5s. – within a month of their return to England. The pinnaces chosen were the *Charles* and the *Moon*.[26] It seems also that the Queen was prepared to allow eight ships and two pinnaces to be hired and fitted out to serve for three months in

[24] *Acts P. C.*, XXIII, 3–11; *Cal. S. P. Domestic, 1591–4*, pp. 242, 245.
[25] S. P. France, xxviii, fo. 237.
[26] Ibid., fos. 244, 248, 250, 252; *Cal. S. P. Domestic, 1591–4*, p. 243.

the river of Bordeaux provided that the King could procure the payment in London of the £9,434 that it was estimated they would cost.[27]

Elizabeth had driven a hard bargain. Yet after the experiences of the past twelve months in both Brittany and Normandy she could hardly be blamed for trying to insure against a repetition of those frustrations. It was reasonable enough to require that the French King's forces in Brittany should match her own for numbers and not leave the defence of the province entirely to her. It was reasonable enough to expect that if the King and his rebel subjects made their peace, he would not need further aid from her. It was entirely reasonable to expect that he would not make a separate peace with Spain without the Queen's knowledge and consent.

There was, however, more to it than this, The agreement of 30 June about Brittany marked a turning-point in English policy towards the Continental conflict, towards the fight to prevent Spanish domination of western Europe. For the past four years, with a comparative lull in 1590, Elizabeth had been persuaded, a little reluctantly perhaps, to undertake or support a series of offensive measures of a considerable magnitude. The 1589 expedition of Norris and Drake had been a veritable counter-Armada. The English auxiliary companies in the Netherlands had played a substantial part in Count Maurice's reconquest of most of the north-eastern Provinces. Willoughby's men and English money had done a good deal to pave the way for Henry's victory at Ivry in March 1590. It was hardly Elizabeth's fault that her plan for a major assault to expel the Spaniards from Blavet had dwindled to, at most, a defence of the northern coast of Brittany. It was not primarily due to shortcomings on her part that her plan to bring Turenne's German army through the Netherlands had not been attempted. Nor could the failure of the siege of Rouen be attributed to an English lack of offensive purpose. Alongside these continental projects and enterprises there had been the annual cruises by royal navy squadrons in search of the American and East Indian convoys. In 1591 Elizabeth had even planned to reinforce Lord Thomas

[27] Ibid., p. 242.

Howard and Sir Richard Grenville to enable them to confront Bazan's Ferrol armada as well as the galleons of the Indian Guard at the Azores. It was the professed inability of English ports to provide the necessary ships and the slow reluctance of the Dutch to co-operate that had frustrated this plan.

The results of this offensive policy had been most disappointing almost everywhere except in the Netherlands. The American and East Indian convoys had come through, with losses certainly but losses much more from the weather than from the English. The French civil war remained in stalemate, even if by distracting Parma and his army it had made possible Maurice's successes in the northern Netherlands. And now Brittany, the part of France that most vitally touched upon England's security, was in serious danger of being overrun by the League and their Spanish allies. For some months the Queen and her Councillors, Burghley in particular, had been growing more and more disillusioned about their French allies. Sancy's very considerable demands now finally tipped the scales against any continuation of offensive participation in the Continental war. The 30 June agreement marked a reversion towards a general defensive in that war. Henceforward English intervention was to be limited to areas and circumstances where English interests or English security was directly involved – Brest and the northern coast of Brittany, the Bordeaux trade, less urgently Dieppe and Boulogne and Calais. The decision to call upon Vere's companies in the field and upon the Bergen garrison for 2,550 of the 4,000 men promised to Sancy for Brittany likewise made it clear that in the Netherlands, too, the emphasis would now be upon holding Ostend and the two cautionary towns of Flushing and Brielle.

This return to the defensive was not due solely to the disillusionment occasioned by the frustrations of the past few years. There were also limits to what England could do or afford. A major limitation was, as usual, finance. During the two and a half years since September 1589 the Queen had expended over £144,786 in aid to the French King, £98,552 of it during the previous twelve months.[28] The cost of her aid to

---

[28] S. P. France, xxviii, fo. 227 and xxv, fo. 109. The £10,000 contributed to Turenne's levy must be added to the figures in these documents.

the Dutch was running at over £110,000 a year.[29] At the moment she was paying for 12,050 foot and 400 horse in the Netherlands and France at a monthly charge of £11,264. Besides these major expenses, the reinforcement of the small garrison of 1,786 men in Ireland had doubled the cost there during the summer months, from £2,266 to £5,000 a month. The Channel Guard, of seven ships serving in the Narrow Seas, and the four pinnaces in the Seine had been costing more than another £1,000 a month.[30] There was also the Queen's contribution to Lord Thomas Howard's squadron, though that was to be eventually repaid out of the prize money. Taken altogether, these extraordinary expenses upon the war totalled very little less than the whole of the Queen's ordinary annual revenue. They had been met partly from what remained from the sale of Crown lands to the value of £126,305 between November 1589 and November 1590, partly from the final instalment of the taxes granted by the 1589 Parliament, partly by yet another privy seal loan of £79,514 raised during 1591 from the Queen's better-to-do subjects. Of this loan £36,310 had been duly repaid by April 1592, but on 15 March Burghley had noted that repayment of the remaining £43,214, due between April and August, would have to be postponed for eight months. In the same paper he also noted the need to review the Low Countries' charges and to hasten the musters certificates of the companies in France. Clearly the government was getting very near to the end of its financial resources.[31]

Besides the expense of money there was the expense of men. The drain on the limited number of the seafaring population for service in the royal navy and aboard the privateers was already causing anxiety and had led to the compilation of a national register of mariners. The pressing of St Ives' fishermen had left the country for sixty miles around short of its staple victuals. Faced with shortages of that sort, some local officials, the Privy Council complained in a circular letter of 18 June 1591, had hindered the taking-up of mariners for the

---

[29] Sir Thomas Sherley, the treasurer-at-war, paid out £111,345 17s. 5d. in the year ending 11 October 1591 – S. P. Domestic, ccl, no. 81.

[30] *Cal. S. P. Domestic, 1591–4*, pp. 218, 221; *Acts P. C.*, XIX, 91–3.

[31] S. P. Domestic, ccxxxviii, no. 30; ccxli, nos. 100, 132.

Queen's ships. They had taken up too few or had warned the best and most serviceable 'to shun the prest'. In those notes of 15 March 1592 Burghley had pondered how fishing might continue and yet enough mariners be retained for service. He could only suggest hiring some from Holland and staying merchant shipping from putting to sea.[32] But it was the drain of men for the military forces sent to the Continent, to France especially, that aroused most resentment and caused the Queen and Council most anxiety. Besides the 4,000 under Willoughby sent over in 1589, another 10,000 at least had been sent to France during the past twelve months, Many of these 10,000 had died overseas, a few in battle but most from diseases aggravated, if not brought on, by the hardness of the service. During the siege of Rouen a mild, damp autumn had been followed by a cold, wet, and occasionally snowy winter and a no less wet spring. For the rest of the time in Normandy and most of the time in Brittany the troops had been wearied by long marches, without carts for their baggage or carriage for their sick and hurt, often short of food and without reasonable shelter for the night.

Desertion, which had been rare at first, was now rife both in Normandy and Brittany. Many of the deserters came home 'using most slanderous speeches of those Her Highness's service and entertainment'. As reports of the hardships and perils of that service spread, so did the reluctance of men to be impressed for France increase. Even in April 1591 Sir John Norris, admittedly not a man given to understatement, complained that half his troops from Somerset were the worst men and worst furnished that he had ever seen, so poor and weak that they would scarce endure the sea-crossing to Brittany. But the discontent was especially strong when, as in 1591 for Brittany and in February 1592 for Normandy, men were taken from the rather better-to-do, from members of the county trained bands. The Essex deputy lieutenants, writing to Burghley, their lord-lieutenant, on 4 March 1592 to deny any general dislike among such men chosen to go over to Rouen, nevertheless admitted that they had put others in place of some of those selected from the trained bands. That

---

[32] Ibid., ccxli, no. 100; *Cal. S. P. Domestic, 1591–4*, p. 73; *Acts P. C.*, XXI, 212–13.

hardly suggests great eagerness to be selected. It does not seem that anyone as yet openly challenged the legality of drafting men overseas as Sir John Smith was to challenge it at the Essex musters in 1596. The Privy Council, nevertheless, did consult Her Majesty's learned counsel in March 1592 before instructing the Sussex justices of the peace to have two deserters indicted for felony. This perhaps suggests that the Council was not entirely sure of its ground.[33]

Besides the men, there was their equipment. All these troops sent overseas had to be provided with coats, weapons, and armour by or at the expense of the counties they came from. Hertfordshire, for example, during the past twelve months had sent out 214 of their best corslets, 85 muskets, and 56 calivers, along with 355 of the best and most serviceable men from the 1,500 in their five trained bands. Indented rolls, giving each soldier's name and weapons, were required to be made between the deputy lieutenants of the counties and the captains who commanded the men levied, one copy being deposited in the Exchequer. Yet very few of the weapons and very little of the armour ever came back to the counties. Captain Docwra, for example, returned in February 1592 from his company of 135 men only 29 corslets and 2 headpieces, 8 morions, 15 damaged muskets, and a caliver. The county deputy lieutenants could make good these losses only by getting the justices of the peace to authorize the levy of another rate. It was all very well for the Privy Council to urge that this be done 'by a general and easy contribution'.[34] But it would come on top of the already considerable assessments for mustering and training the trained bands, watching the beacons that would signal the approach of an enemy fleet, and paying the provost marshal who now had to be appointed to deal by martial law with the wandering bands of deserters and vagabonds that the war multiplied.

These rates were not assessed without dispute nor collected without difficulty. There were many people in Sussex, for example, who refused to pay and were bound over to answer before the Privy Council. In Middlesex others tried to avoid

---

[33] Ibid., XXII, 338–9, 448–9; S. P. Domestic, ccxxxviii, no. 18, ccxli, no. 92; cclix, no. 27.

[34] *Cal. S. P. Domestic, 1591–4*, pp. 193, 200; *Acts P. C.*, XXI, 353–4, 463.

contributing on the pretence of being royal servants. Sussex also complained at the cost of the provosts marshal and was allowed to appoint a local, unpaid gentleman in each of its rapes to exercise the office.[35] In many counties the lacks were simply not made good. In Kent as early as the spring of 1590 the lord-lieutenant found 'how unwilling the country seems (I will not say unable)' to make good the armour and weapons lost by the 900 men it had contributed to Willoughby's expedition.[36] In Hampshire in June 1591 out of the 3,640 men from the trained bands of certain hundreds appointed to reinforce the Isle of Wight in the event of an invasion, only 2,866 were furnished with arms and these inadequately. The remaining 774 were entirely unarmed.[37] By March 1592 no less than thirteen English and Welsh counties had still not sent in the certificates of their forces that the Privy Council had urgently called for a year and a half ago. A further six had failed to mention in their certificates what quantities of powder, match, and bullet they held.[38]

Clearly Burghley had not been far wrong when he wrote to Unton on 14 March 1592: 'I assure you the realm here is weary to see the expense of their people for foreign services . . . But there I am assured no Frenchman will be touched with any sense.'[39] The weariness was widespread. Even the Earl of Essex, the most bellicose of those around the Queen, seems for the time to have turned aside from dreams of martial glory and begun to seek that 'domestical greatness' which many of his friends had long been urging him to aim at. The eclipse of Sir Walter Raleigh in June 1592 upon the discovery of his secret marriage to Elizabeth Throckmorton, one of the Queen's maids of honour, had removed Essex's chief rival among the courtiers. The death of Lord Chancellor Hatton in the previous November had left no one in the Privy Council to balance the influence of the Cecils as he and before him the Earl of Leicester had done. With a Queen 'ruling much

[35] Ibid., XIX, 34–5; XXI, 201–2, 319.
[36] P. Clark, *English Provincial Society . . . Kent 1500–1640*, p. 223.
[37] *Cal. S. P. Domestic, 1591–4*, p. 60; *Acts P. C.*, XXI, 135–6, 165–6.
[38] Ibid., XXII, 301–3. The thirteen were Somerset, Wilts, Monmouth, Pembroke, Anglesey, Cornwall, Chester, Devon, Huntingdon, Sussex, Rutland, Leicester, and Yorks.
[39] *Unton Correspondence*, pp. 376–7.

by faction' and liking to have a counterpoise even to Burghley, this opened the way for Essex to don the favourite-cum-councillor mantle of his stepfather Leicester if he could give proof of serious application to the business of state. By the summer of 1592 he was beginning to do that. He had drawn into his entourage the able Bacon brothers, Francis and Anthony, disgruntled at the failure of their uncle Burghley to promote their interests as energetically as they desired. Through Francis, Essex was beginning to draw in Thomas Phelippes, sometime Walsingham's chief clerk and spymaster, who under cover of his post as one of the London customs officials had kept up a good deal of his former intelligence activities.[40] This course was eventually to lead Essex into bitter rivalry with the Cecils, but as yet he seems to have remained on friendly enough terms with them. He may have suspected that Burghley had 'not so much favoured him in his absence as he expected' over the Oxford chancellorship. But in the summer of 1592 he was writing in friendly fashion to the old Lord Treasurer and they were clearly of one mind about the innocence of Sir John Perrot, the lord deputy of Ireland, accused of treasonable dealings with Spain.[41]

Weariness with the burdens of the Continental war and disillusionment over its fruits were indeed widespread in court and Council no less than among the county authorities and ratepayers and the unfortunates pressed into military service overseas. In more ways than one the summer of 1592 marked a turning-point in Elizabethan policy towards the war with Spain. Only the possibility of the French King's conversion to Catholicism and the imminent danger of a Spanish occupation of Brittany henceforward kept alive English interest in Continental military operations.

[40] S. P. Domestic, ccxxxviii, nos. 125, 137, 138; ccxxxix, nos. 114, 181; ccxlii, no. 33. Anthony Bacon had returned to England in February 1592 after a prolonged sojourn abroad – Birch, *Memoirs*, I, 70.

[41] *Unton Correspondence*, p. 264; *Cal. S. P. Domestic, 1591–4*, p. 218.

# XIX

## Delays and Inaction, July to December 1592

On 1 July, the day after the contract was made with Sancy and Beauvoir, the Privy Council despatched orders for the fifteen companies (2,250 men) from the English auxiliary companies in the Netherlands to make ready to move to Flushing, there to embark for Brittany. Eight of the ten English foot-bands in the Bergen-op-Zoom garrison were to go, along with seven of the nine in the field with Vere. In addition one was to go from Brielle and one from Flushing, but these were to be replaced by the bands of Sir Ferdinando Gorges and Sir Matthew Morgan from Williams's troops in Normandy.[1] Three weeks or a month later orders also went out to London and ten Midland counties to levy another 600 men, with armour and weapons, to embark at London and Southampton. These and the Low Country bands were to be ready to embark for Caen by 25 August.[2] It, was, however, 5 November before the first troops from England landed at Granville in western Normandy and it was almost the middle of January before the companies from the Low Countries arrived.[3]

There were a number of reasons for this delay. First, it will be remembered that the Queen's promise in the 30 June contract to despatch troops to Brittany was conditional. They were not to go until the King had given certain assurances. He was to undertake not to make a separate peace with Spain. He was to provide at least 4,000 foot and 1,000 horse in Brittany and to have these ready to enter the province. He was also to promise to deliver to the Queen a walled port-town and to bind himself to reimburse her expenses in the levy, transportation, and pay of her 4,000 men and her artillery. Sancy

[1] *Acts P. C.*, XXIII, 2–11; *Cal. S. P. Domestic, 1591–4*, p. 242; S. P. Treaty Papers (France), vii, fo. 316; S. P. Holland, xlv, fos. 61, 68.

[2] *Cal. S. P. Domestic, 1591–4*, p. 245; *Acts P. C.*, XXIII, 70–1, 132–6; S. P. France, xxix, fo. 10.

[3] Ibid., fo. 285; xxx, fo. 15.

had hastened back to France to get the King's confirmation of these promises. Unfortunately, after leaving Dieppe on 14 July, he fell seriously ill at Compiègne and was then delayed there still longer because the roads to the King, who was away at Épernay and Châlons, were too dangerous for him to travel. He 'related his negotiation by letters', but the King did not feel able to answer the Queen until he had talked with him. It was not until 24 August that Sancy eventually met Henry at Provins. Next day the King decided to send Bouillon's secretary, du Maurier, to England with his answers.[4] Du Maurier, and Sir Roger Williams who came with him, did not reach London until 15 September and it was 24 September before he and Beauvoir presented the King's answers to Elizabeth at Oxford. As Burghley remarked in a letter to Bouillon on 3 October, Sancy's 'delay in returning to the King by reason of his sickness hath greatly hindered the fruit of that service'.[5]

Sancy, however, was not responsible for the most serious and prolonged delays. For these we have once again to look to the Netherlands. There, to begin with, the States, Council of State, and Count Maurice had vigorously opposed the withdrawals from Vere's forces and the demand that they should make good the withdrawals from Bergen. Vere and his men during May and June had played an important part in the siege of Steenwijk and its capture on 24 June. Vere himself had been wounded in the leg at the first approaches to the town, in what had been, according to Sir Robert Sidney, 'the finest siege, by all men's saying, and where most art hath been shown, of all by far that ever was made of this side'.[6] Nevertheless it had cost Maurice upwards of 1,000 men killed and wounded, out of a force that had only numbered at the start 6,000 foot and 2,000 horse. So Vere's twelve foot-bands – he had recently been reinforced by two companies from Bergen and one from Ostend – made up a substantial part of the States' camp. The States were relying on them for their next operations, in which Count William with most of

[4] Ibid., xxviii, fos. 297, 325; xxix, fos. 14, 19, 50, 54, 70.

[5] Ibid., fos. 107, 109, 139, 143, 189.

[6] S. P. Holland, xliv, fos. 322, 324, 326; xlv, fos. 1, 7, 19, 23, 27, 39, 45, 47; Bor, xxix, fos. 19–22.

the infantry was to besiege Coevorden while Count Maurice mopped up the remaining small places held by the enemy in the surrounding country.[7]

On 11 July, while Maurice, the Council of State, and the provincial deputies at the camp were deciding upon this double enterprise, the orders of 1 July from the Queen and Privy Council reached Vere and Bodley at Zwolle. Maurice, the Council of State, and the deputies protested strongly against any withdrawals. It was, they added, too weighty a matter for them to decide and must be referred to the States General. On the other side, while Bodley went off to The Hague to argue with the States General, Vere firmly refused to march his men with the rest to Coevorden. Very reluctantly Maurice agreed to them going into garrison in several small towns just south of Zwolle until the States' answer was known.

At The Hague Bodley found the States equally unwilling to release the English companies and some loose drafting in the Queen's letter gave them the opportunity for a delaying answer. In that letter she asked the States, now that Steenwijk was taken, to release her troops 'pourveu que votre armée se puisse bonnement dissoudre et que nos gens qui vous y ont servi s'en puisse librement retourner'. Bodley tried to ride over this scribal blunder but, as he feared, the States' answer of 15 July took 'hold fast of that clause of Her Majesty's letter'. If the Queen withdrew those companies, they wrote, they would have to dissolve their army, waste the very large extraordinary contributions raised to provide it, and undo all the good resulting from the capture of Steenwijk. Bodley believed, however, that 'if Her Highness make an absolute demand, though perhaps they do not give an absolute allowance, they will be well enough content to use no further opposition'. Meanwhile it was a big point to have got Vere's companies back into garrisons.[8].

Her Highness did respond with an absolute demand as soon as she received Bodley's letter and the States' answer. She insisted that there was nothing conditional about her previous letter, that preventing the loss of Brittany was far more urgent

[7] S. P. Holland, xlv, fos. 77, 89, 91, 140; Verdugo, pp. 134–8.
[8] S. P. Holland, xlv, fos. 68– 89, 91, 106, 110, 121; *Resolutiën der Staten Generaal*, VII, 585.

than taking a petty castle like Coevorden, and that anyway the States had never before mentioned any further operations being intended after the taking of Steenwijk.[9] For some reason – Bodley blamed easterly winds and the slackness of the messengers – it was over three weeks before the Queen's letters reached The Hague.[10] In the mean time, upon a rumour that 2,000 enemy troops had crossed the Rhine and were moving in the direction of Coevorden, Vere at the request of the Council of State on 23 July marched his men to Doesburg – conveniently, it was a little further south, a little nearer to the seaside. There was another alarm a week later and more pressure on Vere to join the camp, but again it came to nothing and the town of Coevorden was taken by 8 August.[11] Steady progress was then made against the castle, though heavy rains hindered activity there. A newly raised German regiment, 1,000 strong with another 1,000 to follow, arrived in the camp on 22 August. By that time, however, reinforcements had also reached Verdugo, the enemy commander in those parts.[12]

Once again Maurice and the States begged Vere to march his men to the camp. After much hesitation he agreed, on condition that the Council of State promised in writing to allow his men to withdraw to their garrisons as soon as the present emergency was past, which he believed must be very soon. It was in fact already over by the time they arrived at the camp at daybreak on 28 August. Two hours earlier Verdugo had twice assaulted the besiegers' lines around Coevorden castle at a place where a local gentleman had informed him that they were weakly entrenched. Maurice, however, had been forewarned and the attacks were repulsed with considerable loss.[13] For another ten days Verdugo stayed within sight

[9] S. P. Holland, xlv, fos. 132. 152.

[10] Ibid., fos. 179, 181.

[11] Ibid., fos. 130, 134, 162, 168, 174; Bor, xxix, fos. 24–5.

[12] S. P. Holland, xlv, fos. 176, 179, 187; *Resolutiën der Staten Generaal,* VII, 553; Verdugo, pp. 139–48. Parma, recuperating at Spa, had been very critical of Mansfelt for not getting an army into the field to support Verdugo and relieve Steenwijk and Coevorden – *Correspondance de Philippe II,* IV, 64–7, 68–9, 78–80.

[13] S. P. Holland, xlv, fos. 189, 201, 213; S. P. Newsletters (Germany), xxvii, fo. 81; *Kronijk,* XIX, 410; Bor, xxix, fos. 27, 29–31. Sir Clements Markham, *The Fighting Veres,* p. 185, said (using G. van Prinsterer's *Archives de la Maison d'Orange-Nassau* (2nd series), I, 207) that Vere came up half an hour after the fight began, found the States' infantry giving way, and 'dashed into the thick of it'.

of Coevorden but, short of victuals and supplies, he made no further attempts to succour the castle. It accordingly surrendered to Maurice on 3 September. By then the States' camp had been further reinforced by ten or twelve more foot-bands under Count Philip of Nassau, just recently returned with his troops from Normandy.[14] Thereupon Verdugo's forces dispersed, some back to Groningen, others to Lingen, the bulk of them eventually back across the Rhine.[15] Vere, too, as soon as the castle was taken marched his companies back to their garrisons in and around Doesburg to await the Queen's orders to move to Flushing and embark for Brittany. There could never, he wrote to Burghley, be a better time, for the States now had enough men to hold their own without Her Majesty's companies and there was no appearance of any other enterprise this summer. Bodley, too, wrote that 'although the States will give no leave howsoever they shall be urged, but yet I stand not in doubt of any public impeachment'. They feared apparently that the English companies, once withdrawn, would never return, for there were rumours that they would be 'cassed' when the Brittany service was over. According to Sir Robert Sidney what most distressed the States was the high-handed manner of the withdrawals.

These men, [he wrote] how simple show soever they bear outwardly, have hearts high enough and look to be respected as they which hold themselves chief rulers of these Provinces which have so long maintained war against the King of Spain. And truly I do not think that secretly anything is so much undigested by them as the little respect, as they imagine, is had of them in England.

They had expected the Queen to proceed with them not by absolute commandment but by entreaty as she had done two years before when Sir John Norris had the first troops for Brittany. This insensitivity of the Queen and most of her ministers to the pride and self-esteem of the Dutch leaders was assuredly one of the major and continuing weaknesses of her Netherlands policy.[16]

All the same, the States did now virtually yield to the

---

[14] S. P. Holland, xlv, fos. 207, 215; *Kronijk*, XIX, 411–14.
[15] S. P. Holland, xlv, fos. 217, 219, 233, 235, 241.
[16] Ibid., fos. 166, 181, 215.

Queen's demands when on 2 September Bodley informed them of fresh orders, of 22 August, just received from her and her Council. These orders were for Vere's companies and those from Bergen to be at Flushing at the earliest moment possible – the Privy Council said optimistically by 6 September at latest – ready to embark for Caen at the same time as Norris's 600 men in England and Williams's bands from Normandy.[17] The States in reply complained bitterly once again of the inconvenience the withdrawals would cause, but as Bodley had anticipated they did not openly refuse to agree to them. All they asked was that Bodley should not send the orders on to Vere for just another two days, in which time a decision was likely to have been reached at Coevorden.[18] And, as we have seen, Coevorden castle surrendered to Maurice on 3 September. On the 6th Vere received the Queen's and Privy Council's orders from Bodley, who had held them back for two days as the States had asked. On the same day the Council of State wrote to the States of Utrecht to provide waggons to go with Vere's companies as far as the Vaert, near Utrecht, where boats would be made ready to transport them to Flushing. Bodley expected them to be at Rotterdam or Dordrecht 'ready for the first wind' by 13 or 14 September. All thus seemed set fair for them to get away little more than a week or ten days later than the Privy Council hoped.[19] This prospect was not quite fulfilled: Vere had to wait three days at the Vaert for three companies that were unable to leave Doesburg, Doetinchem, and Anholt until Dutch troops came to replace them. Then stormy weather and contrary winds prevented them from reaching Flushing for more than another fortnight. By then the delay was becoming serious, but not yet disastrous.[20].

At this point a new complication was introduced that was to lengthen the delay very considerably. It had been intended originally that all the troops for Brittany should go there by way of Caen, except for 300 of those levied in England who

---

[17] *H. M. C., Salisbury MSS*, IV., 224–6; Cotton MSS, Galba D. ix, fo. 252; *Acts P. C.*, XXIII, 139–43; S. P. Holland, xlv, fos. 211, 227; S. P. France, xxix, fo. 52.

[18] S. P. Holland, xlv, fos. 219, 229.

[19] Ibid., fos. 233, 235, 237; *Kronijk*, XIX, 414–16; *Resolutiën der Staten Generaal*, VII, 587–8.

[20] S. P. Holland, xlv, fos. 241, 243, 247.

were to sail from Southampton to Jersey and Guernsey to guard those islands while enemy shipping was in those parts. This was now altered and on 17 September orders were sent to Flushing for them all to go to Jersey.[21] The reason given for the change was an outbreak of plague at Caen. It was true that 'the plague rageth mightily in Dieppe' and that many were afflicted by the bloody flux at Caen where there was much fruit and the new cider was being made, which English soldiers could not be stopped from drinking.[22] There was, however, more than this behind the alteration of plan and discussions leading up to that alteration had been going on in England for several weeks.

The first step had been a proposal to add to the forces for Brittany another 1,000 men, levied in England but paid by the French King. The proposal may well have originated with Norris. For on 24 August, the day after his instructions and the confirmation of his commission were drawn up, he offered to discharge the Queen of the pay of an extra 1,000 men and also to discharge her and the counties of all their arming, coat, conduct, and transportation costs except for providing them with swords and paying anything over 4*s.* that a coat might cost. The bait that he dangled before her was an offer then to surprise and capture St Malo. This was an old dream of his. Back in early May, before the Craon disaster and while Dombes and Conti had 5,000 foot and 300 horse together in arms, he had boasted that he would undertake to put the Queen in possession of St Malo or Morlaix within six or eight months and to go very near to reimbursing her for all she had spent on the war in Brittany if she would send him over with another 3,000–4,000 English troops. Later there was talk of landing at Cancale, a small seaport about nine miles east of St Malo. Now, at the end of August or the beginning of September, Norris offered to the Queen and Privy Council – 'to us before our Council' – that even without the French King's promised forces, he would take St Malo if he might have these extra 1,000 men added to his 4,000. The 1,000 should be levied, armed, and transported at the Queen's

[21] S. P. France, xxix, fos. 52, 59; *Cal. S. P. Domestic, 1591–4*, p. 253; S. P. Holland, xlv, fos. 264, 270.
[22] *Acts P. C.*, XXIII, 209; S. P. France, xxviii, fo. 261; xxix, fo. 137.

charge – a modification of his 24 August offer – but he would procure means to pay them for two months from the time of their landing.[23]

Soon afterwards, upon reflection, some of the difficulties of such a project began to worry him. He had time to reflect as he waited wind-bound at Southampton with the 300 men for Jersey, now being augmented by the other 300 who should have sailed from London but because of the plague there had been diverted to Southampton.[24] To begin with, he could no longer expect much French help in an enterprise upon St Malo. The Prince of Dombes had succeeded his father as Duke of Montpensier at the end of May and the King had promptly appointed him to succeed the old Duke as governor of Normandy. His successor as royal lieutenant-general in Brittany was Marshal Aumont, who was preoccupied in Maine and Anjou and very unlikely to enter Brittany unless the English reinforcements first joined him.[25] Also, as Norris wrote to Burghley on 13 September, St Malo was very strongly seated, mostly environed with water, and well fortified on the landward side. To take it, he would need besides those extra 1,000 men, a good force of English shipping, and the English artillery from Dieppe and the Channel Isles, with powder and shot, to batter the town. Morlaix was not so strong, would not require warships, and would need less artillery and munitions. But it lay 'in the midst of the Duke of Mercoeur's strength' where the country people were generally armed and the gentlemen rich and wholly at his devotion. And against Morlaix even less help could be looked for from the King. Indeed, whether against Morlaix or St Malo, 'Her Majesty must look for no good but what is done by herself'. If she approved an attack upon either

---

[23] Ibid., xxviii, fos. 11, 35, 59, 65, 72; xxix, fos. 33, 127. For several drafts, 23 August to 5 September, by Burghley about this levy – *Cal. S. P. Domestic, 1591-4*, pp. 255, 265-6. But the levy was not actually ordered until 1 October: 200 each from Devon, Gloucestershire, and Somerset; 100 from Cornwall; 50 each from Dorset, Wilts, Sussex, and Kent; 40 from Oxfordshire; and 30 each from Berkshire and Buckinghamshire – *Acts P. C.*, XXIII, 223-6.

[24] S. P. France, xxix, fo. 101; *Cal. S. P. Domestic, 1591-4*, pp. 266-7.

[25] S. P. France, xxviii, fos. 111, 143, 145; xxix, fos. 50, 132. Marshal Biron was first appointed to succeed Dombes in Brittany, but he was killed before Épernay on 29 June – ibid., xxviii, fos. 234, 242.

of them, then the Low Country and Normandy companies and the artillery must come directly to the Channel Isles.

Burghley showed Norris's letter to the Queen. Not surprisingly she found that his doubts about St Malo and Morlaix were so many that she 'knoweth not what to say for it'. She would probably decide in a few days after speaking with the Lord Admiral, Beauvoir, and du Maurier who was on his way from the King. Burghley also doubted that, even if she granted the artillery, 'there will lack bullet for such an attempt'. This was on 16 September. But the Queen does appear then to have come to a decision upon one point. For it was on 17 September that the orders were sent to Flushing for the Low Country companies to go to Jersey instead of to Caen.[26] Three days later an addition to Norris's instructions was drafted though its contents, somewhat modified, were not sent to him until 26 September.[27] By then the Queen had received from du Maurier Henry IV's ratifications of the contract of 30 June. She had therefore a reasonable hope that any walled port in Brittany that Norris and the King's forces might recover would be duly handed over to her. But as usual the King was far more concerned about Parma, whom he expected to return to France about the end of October, than about Brittany. In fact the burden of his letters, and of his messages by Sir Roger Williams, was to beg for new succours for Normandy. As a result, his forces for Brittany were unlikely to exceed 2,500 foot and 1,000 horse, or 1,500 foot less than the contract required.

Accordingly the Queen now told Norris that he and his 600 men from Southampton, escorted by her six ships and the six Hollanders which were in the Solent, were to go to the Channel Isles. From there they were to land at whatever safe port in Brittany Norris thought suitable. But

for any attempt against St Malo or Morlaix, whereof we wish the former rather than the other and yet rather Morlaix than none, we must refer you to proceed therein as you shall find ability for the same by the French King's forces under the Marshal [Aumont] ready to join with you to attempt the same. And otherwise we think

---

[26] Ibid., xxix, fos. 101, 110; S. P. Holland, xlv, fos. 264, 270.
[27] S. P. France, xxix, fos, 149, 182; the 20 September draft – ibid., fo. 127.

it neither convenient nor feasible for you alone with our forces to take it in hand.

The companies from the Low Countries and Normandy and the artillery from Dieppe had also been ordered to the Channel Isles instead of to Caen, though the artillery was not to be transported into France for any purpose except to attack St Malo or Morlaix. The intention to attack either of these places must be kept very secret – and in correspondence St Malo was usually disguised as 'Trumpington' and Morlaix as 'Islington'. Finally, Beauvoir had been plainly told, and would so inform the King and Marshal Aumont, that the Queen did not mean to continue her forces or expend her money any further in Brittany unless the Marshal came into the maritime parts with the promised 4,000 foot and 1,000 horse. Elizabeth gave the King a similar sharp warning in a letter of her own of October sent by the returning du Maurier.

While Norris lay wind-bound at Southampton and just after the levy of the extra 1,000 men had finally been ordered on 1 October, news came of another disaster to the English troops already in Brittany who had survived the rout at Craon. Reduced to 500–600 men, these troops had taken part in Montpensier's victory over Mercoeur's recently arrived Lorraine companies in the suburbs of Dinan on 6 August. After that they had been lodged around Rennes. From there in September their acting commander, the sergeant-major Anthony Wingfield, marched them eastwards towards Domfront to meet 100 men, the remainder of a supply of 260 brought over from England by Lieutenant Morison in April, and to get apparel and pay from Caen. This meant marching past some of the enemy's strongest garrisons and through a wholly hostile population. Montpensier had therefore tried to dissuade Wingfield from attempting it and had offered to have the royalist garrisons of Normandy escort the men, apparel, and pay to Pontorson where it could be collected safely. Wingfield, however, would not listen. He got as far as Ambrières, between Mayenne and Domfront. There he halted for some days and then sent 200 of his 500 men forward to meet their supplies. Meanwhile Boisdauphin, the local League commander, had collected the garrisons of Dol, Fougères,

Château-Gontier, Claye, and Laval, 1,500 foot and 200 horse, with two field-pieces. With these on 22 September he fell upon Wingfield and his 300 men at Ambrières. The English resisted stoutly for over five hours and killed or wounded at least 200 of the Leaguers. In the end Boisdauphin offered them their lives and they surrendered upon those terms. The captains and officers, who were likely to be able to afford ransoms, were duly spared, but at least 100 of the rank and file were slaughtered in cold blood. Some 200 escaped – ran away during the fight, Wingfield bitterly complained – to Domfront where they joined the 200 who had been sent on ahead and Morison's 100 who had brought their supplies from Caen. Montpensier arranged for these to be brought back to Rennes by way of Pontorson.[28]

This new setback was a blow to Norris's hopes. He reckoned those men in Brittany to have been worth three times as many raw recruits from England. The death or capture of so many of their captains and officers was especially 'an extreme great loss'. Moreover men were running away daily from his 600 at Southampton. As early as 20 September the Privy Council had sent the lords-lieutenant of eight counties the names of 65 deserters who were to be rounded up and by 21 October a full hundred had run away. Most of those that remained had been miserably clothed by their counties and were 'in terms of mutiny for larger allowance'. However, by now it was in any case too late in the season for an attempt upon St Malo. The masters of the six Queen's ships at Southampton were unanimous that they could not remain in the waters around the Channel Islands during the winter, though they were confident that from the end of February they could keep St Malo completely blockaded.[29]

As hopes of St Malo fell, hopes of Morlaix rose – at least in the Queen's mind and for a short while. This was largely due to another envoy from Montpensier, de Poillé, who came to beg Elizabeth to hasten her troops and artillery over to Brittany. De Poillé was at Southampton on 7 October and

---

[28] Ibid., fos. 38, 155, 159, 178; *Acts P. C.*, XXXII, 361–2, 413–14. The Lorrainers had come to Brittany by way of Abbeville and Le Havre – S. P. France, xxviii, fos. 223, 286, 288, 291.

[29] Ibid., xxix, fos. 196, 212, 218, 239, 262; *Acts P. C.*, XXXIIII, 213–15; *Cal. S. P. Domestic, 1591–4*, pp. 280–1.

with Beauvoir at Hackney on the 11th.[30] He did not get an audience with the Queen – nor until the very end of November did Beauvoir – because on 12 October a servant of Mr Hoggins, Beauvoir's host, that day died of the plague in London. The man had spent the previous night in another part of Hoggins's house. He had had no contact with any of Beauvoir's household, but it was thought undesirable for either Beauvoir or de Poillé to come to court or to have audience with the Queen until all danger was past. De Poillé therefore gave his message to Burghley in writing on 16 October and the next day sent him answers to a long series of questions about Brittany. He mentioned recent successes against the Leaguers, such as Montpensier's defeat of the Lorrainers at Dinan and Sourdéac's defeat and capture of St Laurent at St Brieuc a little earlier. He gave a rosily optimistic forecast of the forces that would be waiting to welcome Norris. If he landed at Paimpol, Sourdéac would meet him there with 2,000 foot and 300 horse. As for the forces that the Breton royalists could put into the field, they might amount to 2,000 foot and 950 horse, besides the 500 remaining English and 300 landsknechts, the garrisons, and any regiments from Normandy. Against these Mercoeur might muster 1,800 French foot, 3,000 Spaniards, and 1,300 horse. But Mercoeur's forces would be all engaged in upper Brittany against Marshal Aumont who, when he had taken Rochefort and had been joined by St Luc, would have there at least 4,200 foot and 600 horse. So Montpensier and Norris would be able within a month to reduce all lower Brittany. The Duke would thereupon hand over Morlaix to Norris for a place of retreat. And, with a final burst of optimism, de Poillé asserted that Morlaix could be taken in a mere six hours.[31].

To Norris's disgust, Elizabeth swallowed – or at any rate took advantage of – de Poillé's optimism. On 20 October the Privy Council informed Norris that

Her Majesty, considering that with the number of 5,000 which she had now appointed to send over, you will not undertake to attempt

[30] S. P. France, xxix, fos. 167, 196, 202.

[31] Ibid., fos. 210, 214, 220, 222, 276; S. P. Treaty Papers (France), vii, fos. 318, 321. There are accounts of St Laurent's defeat and capture in S. P. France, xxix, fos. 38, 50, 424.

and recover St Malo, she hath of herself, much against our liking, appointed to make stay of the 1,000 men lately granted and will not by any our persuasion be induced to the contrary, whereof we are sorry. Howbeit, because we consider that the companies to come out of the Low Countries and out of Normandy are weak, we have obtained that 500 of that thousand shall go to complete the said companies.

In fact, by the time the orders reached Norris about 800 of the 1,000 men had already embarked. That number, the Privy Council believed, 'will do no more than fill up the other bands' to the 4,000 men and which was all Her Majesty meant to be charged with.[32]

It is perhaps a little doubtful whether all the Councillors were quite as opposed to Her Majesty's decision as their letter made out. Burghley, for one, had been wondering only a week earlier whether the Queen should continue aiding the King in Brittany, considering the loss of her people, the expense, and the King's neglect of that province. He was also wondering whether Ostend and Bergen would be safe if she eased her charges in the Low Countries by withdrawing her troops from there. Elizabeth had not yet come to quite such drastic conclusions. So, when on 28 October the wind at last turned into a not-too-unfavourable quarter, Norris was able to put to sea. He reached Guernsey two days later, moved on to Jersey the day following, and after being again wind-bound there put over to Granville in south-western Normandy, where he and the troops from England landed on 5 November.[33]

Meanwhile what had happened to the fifteen English companies due to come from the Low Countries? As we saw, the States by now had tacitly acquiesced in their withdrawal. They still grumbled a good deal about it, but their chief interest seemed to be whether and when they might expect the companies back. There was even some talk once again of the idea that Ortel had floated in 1589, that instead of troops in the Queen's pay 'they might hereafter be assisted with the

---

[32] *Acts P. C.*, XXIII, 247–8, 267. For Norris's annoyance – S. P. France, xxix, fos. 239, 246.

[33] *Cal. S. P. Domestic, 1591–4*, p. 279; S. P. France, xxix, fos, 267, 285.

imprest of some money and with a great deal less sum than is spent by Her Highness at this present'.[34]

As the States' opposition died away, however, a new difficulty arose. The companies arrived off Flushing towards the end of September, just in time to receive the orders of 17 September for them to go to Brittany by way of Jersey instead of by way of Caen. This caused a serious hold-up. The Zeeland shipping that had been chartered to take them to Caen was unsuitable for an autumnal voyage to the Channel Isles. The ship-masters denied all knowledge of those treacherous waters and all flatly refused to go there. Christopher Keynell, Sir Thomas Sherley's deputy, who had hired the ships, tried to find a couple of pilots to put aboard two of the ships which might then lead the rest, if need be under the compelling escort of Her Majesty's warships of the Channel Guard. But no pilots for Jersey could be found in the United Provinces and when in October some were sent from England, they had eventually to be sent home because it was still impossible to persuade the Dutch ship-masters to go to the Channel Isles.[35]

The Zeelanders were not encouraged to be more co-operative by the continued seizures or pillaging of their ships and goods by English warships and privateers. They were more especially angry over the rifling of the *Griffon* of Veere and the *Lune Croissant,* or *Crescent,* of Middelburg. Both had been taken earlier in the summer by the *Susan Bonaventure* (Captain Henry Thynne), the *Margaret and John* (Captain Greenfield), and the Lord Admiral's *Lion's Whelp* (Captain Mansfield). Several members of their crews had, it was alleged, been tortured 'avec des cordes nouées au front' to make them reveal where silver and pearls were stowed. From the *Griffon* 115 bags of money and pearls worth 18,000 ducats and cochineal and indigo worth another 4,800 ducats were stolen; from the *Crescent,* over £3,000 in money, pearls, and

[34] S. P. Holland, xlv, fos. 243, 299.

[35] Ibid., fos. 264, 266, 268, 270, 294, 317. Udall, the lieutenant-governor of Flushing, and Burnham had both suggested that English ships would be more suitable and cheaper – ibid., fo. 83, 85. Some of Caron's despatches about his arguments with Burghley concerning the withdrawals are summarized in J. L. Motley, *History of the United Netherlands*, III, 177–81.

other merchandise. Between sixty and eighty Zeeland merchants had shares in these goods and the whole Province was understandably angry. These were by no means the only recent seizures of Dutch ships or goods, but they were the ones that fell most sharply and most recently upon the Zeelanders.[36]

The Zeelanders were also none too pleased at being called upon to supply the places of the six English foot-bands withdrawn from Bergen. They had only done so, late in September, when Bodley told them that those English companies' weekly lendings would be stopped if they did not come away. This, of course, would have forced them to live upon the country.[37] Sir Robert Sidney, the governor of Flushing, was very worried lest the Zeelanders' annoyance over the withdrawals and over the seizures of their ships and goods might not tempt them to a sudden coup to seize possession of Her Majesty's cautionary town. He wanted twelve English foot-bands instead of the seven he had in garrison. He actually tried to stay one of those ordered for Brittany, a piece of insubordination for which the Privy Council rapped him sharply over the knuckles.[38]

At the beginning of November, however, Sidney received a very agreeable surprise. By then the English companies for Brittany, or at least those that came from the field, had been penned on shipboard for almost ten weeks, 'at first stayed by the wind and after by the changing of the direction of their landing from Caen to Jersey and now likewise will be forced to stay till some shipping come for them out of England'. The

---

[36] S. P. Holland, xliv, fo. 328; xlv, *passim; Resolutiën der Staten Generaal*, VII, 583. On 14 October the Privy Council wrote for Greenfield and Thynne to be apprehended and sent up to them – *Acts P. C.*, XXIII, 237-8. The Hollanders were no less aggrieved over the pillaging of the *Mercury* of Amsterdam by the same three English ships. Earlier in the summer the States General's agent Caron had presented a list of a couple of dozen Dutch ships seized or robbed, most of them during the past year – S. P. Treaty Papers (Holland), xxxiv, fos. 317, 319. About forty English sailors from the *Diamond* of Bristol were executed as pirates at Enkhuizen early in September despite pleas for mercy from Bodley and the Privy Council – ibid., fo. 321; S. P. Holland, xlv, fos. 213, 217, 239; *Resolutiën der Staten Generaal*, VII, 661-3.

[37] S. P. Holland, xlv, fos. 239, 274, 303.

[38] Ibid., fos. 93, 166, 341; *Acts P. C.*, XXIII, 297-9. Bodley found the 'English gentlemen' at Flushing 'much misinformed of the actions and affairs that pass in these quarters'. But even he thought it might be well to have some special care of the cautionary towns at this time – S. P. Holland, xlv, fos. 154, 299.

Zeeland ships they were embarked in still absolutely refused to go to Jersey. In the meantime all 'the men starve almost for want of clothes', since order had been given in the summer that their winter apparel was not to be delivered to them until they landed in Brittany. At this point, on 8 November, the States of Zeeland at Sidney's request took pity upon them. They did even more than he had asked of them. They 'very courteously' took the men into their towns and gave them service money to procure them lodging, fuel, and so forth.[39] Then on 9 December shipping from England, ordered on 18 November, arrived at Flushing. Thereupon the companies were mustered – the muster showed 1,623 officers and men present, including 49 sick, besides 33 absent and so a deficiency of 367 if the 8 officers of each company were included in its 150 pays. They were given their winter apparel and were embarked upon the ships. After another short delay waiting for a favourable wind, they arrived in the Downs by 25 December. By 10 January they had landed in Normandy and were on their way to join the troops from England. Those troops from England were by then getting on for eighty miles to the east of Granville, the port at which they had landed, and only some thirty-five miles south of Caen, making their roundabout way to join Montpensier and Aumont in Maine.[40].

 So, for considerably more than the second half of 1592 England's only contribution to the defence of Brittany had been the 800 men or less who had survived the defeat before Craon on 13 May. Even at the very end of the year Norris still lacked the final contingent of his forces, Williams's six foot-bands from Normandy. It was not because those English in Normandy had been much more active than the English in Brittany since the operations against Parma in early May. Early in July Williams had been sent back from a visit to England and ordered to take some of his troops with two of the Queen's warships, two of her pinnaces, and various vessels from Dieppe to relieve Quilleboeuf. The place was being besieged by Mayenne and Aumale with Villars and his Rouen

[39] Ibid., fos. 315, 317, 343.
[40] Ibid., fos. 368, 375, 381; *Acts P. C.,* XXIII, 311, 378–9; S. P. France, xxx, fo. 15.

forces.[41] But by the time Williams and the English ships reached Dieppe, St Pol with some troops from western Normandy and thirteen ships from Caen had already relieved and re-victualled Quilleboeuf. Thereupon the English ships and the pinnaces went home. Williams, hearing that Mayenne and Aumale were leaving the Seine for the Somme and gathering forces at Abbeville, called back his companies from their somewhat exposed position at Le Tréport to the comparative safety of Dieppe's suburbs. Most of the remainder of July he spent skirmishing, very much at arm's length, with the Rouen and Le Havre Leaguers in the Pays de Caux around Fécamp and St Valéry-en-Caux, neither side showing any excessive anxiety to come to close grips. Williams and his men, of course, had the excuse that they were under orders to be ready to embark for Brittany. Towards the end of July he moved his companies back to Le Tréport because plague was raging in Dieppe. From Le Tréport on 29 July they moved into the abbey at St Valéry-sur-Somme, which was still held for the King by James Colville of Ester Wemyss with his mixed force of French, Scots, and English.[42]

On 2 August Williams with 300 of his own men and 100 of Colville's attempted by a night march across the Somme marshes to surprise Le Crotoy. The attempt miscarried. 'By reason of our ill passage through deep mud and sands, the fire of our matches were discovered' and then the scaling ladders – as so frequently happened – proved too short. So, finding no way to enter, after rather less than an hour they withdrew, carrying with them two warships and two other vessels and leaving Le Crotoy 'never a vessel of war'. The English lost only three men, two of them poor soldiers and, as Williams callously put it, 'for the third, if he dies, it makes no great matter. He was a lackey of mine, which carried my headpiece.' It is small wonder that so many less-well-off Elizabethan Englishmen were so reluctant to be sent as rank-and-file soldiers into France or the Netherlands.[43] From St

---

[41] Ibid., xxviii, fos. 242, 252, 254, 258, 260; Cayet, XLI, 75–80. The two pinnaces were the *Charles* and the *Moon* – *Cal. S. P. Domestic, 1591–4*, p. 243.

[42] S. P. France, xxviii, fos. 254, 270, 286, 312, 320; xxix, fos. 3, 6, 35.

[43] Ibid., xxix, fo. 3. Williams sent his letter by a Mr God, but warned Burghley that 'your lordship must not think all his words be scripture'.

Valéry Williams was summoned back in haste to Dieppe by de Chatte when Villars with all the Rouen forces came to Neufchâtel. Once again, however, by the time they arrived, Villars was returning to Rouen. Williams thereupon camped in a reasonably strong house about half a mile from Arques.

All this time the 'Dieppe lobby' – Ottywell Smith, de Chatte, Incarville – had been stridently urging that Williams's companies should not be sent to Brittany, that they should instead be reinforced up to 1,200 men or more. With those numbers, Smith said, de Chatte would have forces to match those of Rouen and Le Havre. He would be able to collect enough taille from the neighbouring countryside to pay another 1,500 foot and six or seven horse-bands. Without them, he could hardly keep the field and Smith forecasted the most dire consequences for Dieppe and all Normandy if the English departed. As it was, he wrote on 27 July, 'every day is worse and worse'.[44] On 2 August the remains of Count Philip of Nassau's Dutch contingent sailed for home. About the same time it was decided in England – though the order did not reach Williams until 25 August – that two of Williams's companies, those of Sir Matthew Morgan and Sir Ferdinando Gorges, were also to be sent back to the Netherlands.[45]

For the moment the 'Dieppe lobby' made little impression. It was at this time that the proposal was made to levy another 1,000 men in England at the French King's expense. But this new levy was to be for Brittany, to be added to Norris's forces for his proposed attempt upon St Malo and by 21 August orders had been drafted and shipping prepared for Williams and his companies, less the bands of Morgan and Gorges, to embark at Dieppe. They were to be at Caen by 16 September to meet the other forces for Brittany.[46] Almost as if he knew of the St Malo project[47] and was seeking to outbid it, Ottywell Smith now dangled an even more tempting bait before the Queen and her advisers. On 25 August, just as Williams and de Chatte were setting out to take Neufchâtel by a night

---

[44] Ibid., xxviii, fos. 291, 293, 320; xxix, fos. 40, 44.
[45] Ibid., xxviii, fo. 103; xxix, fos. 10–15, 20, 52; Gorges' company left on 31 August, Morgan's on 30 September – ibid., xxix, fos. 29, 79, 200.
[46] Ibid., fo. 52.
[47] There is, however, no reason at all to suppose that he did know of it.

'escalado', the Privy Council's order for Gorges' company to go to Brielle arrived. Williams at once abandoned the Neufchâtel attempt because Gorges' departure would leave him with too few troops to provide an adequate guard for his sick men and his baggage. Ottywell Smith thereupon wrote off on 29 August in high indignation. This, he complained, was not the first occasion on which untimely letters from the Council had broken off a promising enterprise. And this particular enterprise had been more than just an attempt to take Neufchâtel. They would have gone on to surprise Fort St Catherine, the key to Rouen, where there were now only forty-five men in garrison.

Nor was that all. A week later Smith conjured up a practice against Rouen itself. One of the Rouen captains was offering to deliver a gate of the city to the Huguenot Baron of Bondville. They would 'have none but them of the Religion to do it', so they would not tell de Chatte. But they would need the support of Williams's troops. A Rouen for a St Malo. It was a very fair counter-bid and Smith certainly made full use of it to urge the necessity of keeping an English regiment at Dieppe. The neighbouring nobility were all lapsing into neutrality and once the English were gone, Villars would be at the gates of Dieppe. He was already preparing cannon to besiege the town as soon as Parma's army returned to France and de Chatte had offered to pay 600 English troops, but he could not even pay Captain Fournier's fifty horsemen adequately. Smith knew well that the Queen's charges these past six years had been as great as those of any prince in England before her and all the world marvelled where the treasure had been found. But God still sent it and if an English regiment were not kept about Dieppe the town would be in great danger. De Chatte was half-discouraged and said he would write no more for help when he could not be heard nor his letters answered. Smith himself feared more than he wrote and he asked Burghley to show Her Majesty his letters so that he should not be blamed for failing to warn beforehand.[48]

Ottywell Smith was clearly getting a little above himself. Back in April Burghley had described him as 'hasty in

[48] S. P. France, xxix, fos. 20, 23, 79, 83, 137.

hearing, light in believing, and as sudden in writing'. Now, on 7 September, he put him sharply in his place. The letters for Gorges' company to go to the Low Countries had not forbidden Williams to stir against Neufchâtel or St Catherine's. As for Smith's advice that 'if any such letter should be sent hereafter, that yet they should execute any great enterprise in hand before they should depart, . . . I think the enterprisers will therein use their discretion without your advice.' As for de Chatte needing a regiment of the Queen's troops, 'Her Majesty is to perform first her covenant with the French King to find 4,000 men in Brittany. And if the governor can procure from the King that some part of those numbers may be employed in Normandy, it is all one to Her Majesty in her charge. Or otherwise if the governor can procure from the French King or by his own means by the tax of that country' to pay a regiment regularly and to defray the cost of its levy and transportation, then Her Majesty would be prepared to let Williams stay there. Smith would do well to impress on the French how great Her Majesty's charges had been and were. They were 'so liberal in demanding and so forgetful in performing of promises. For I see it grown to a custom, whatsoever they would have in money, men, or munition, it must be demanded of Her Majesty. And methinketh you, being a natural subject of the country, should lay this overburden before their eyes and not feed their humours in their solicitations.' However, Burghley had read Smith's letter to the Queen and he had moved her that the English companies might remain and not be sent to Brittany until she heard from Sir Roger Williams, who had gone off to visit the King.[49]

When the King asked Williams to visit him, somewhere east of Paris, he had wanted him to bring his companies too. That Williams had not dared to do. He dared not carry them so far from the coast, especially as de Chatte feared an attack by Villars who was at Le Havre with all his Rouen troops. Williams had therefore left his companies at Arques and gone himself to the King with a mere fifteen horsemen. The King sent him back to England, as we have seen, with du Maurier,

[49] *Unton Correspondence*, p. 431; S. P. France, xxv, fo. 271.

who took the ratification of the 30 June contract, to beg for a reinforcement of English troops upon news that Parma would be returning to France at the end of October to support a League assembly at Soissons where they meant to elect a Catholic King. 'Il est temps', Henry said, 'et besoin plus que jamais que je soie assisté de mes amis.'[50] Henry also chose this moment to send Elizabeth a young elephant as a present. This seems to have done little to soften the Queen's heart. The elephant was likely to cost £200 or more a year to keep, it had grown by a third in the past year, it was growing still bigger every day, and would continue to grow 'this eight years yet'. We are not told whether the elephant was also white. But it is perhaps not altogether surprising 'that Her Majesty was not content with the sending of the elephant'.[51]

Williams was in England by mid-September and on 29 September he wrote to Burghley, Howard, Heneage, and Cecil in support of Henry's plea for more help. Once Parma entered France, all Normandy between Seine and Somme would speedily be lost unless the King could give him battle. That he could not do without good troops of Englishmen. Two thousand of them would rally many thousands of Frenchmen to him. In Brittany 4,000 would be too few to besiege any place of importance, yet 3,000 English should be ample to prevent the enemy taking any such place. On the other hand if the French King could not keep the field, 'scarce four times 6,000 will serve to countenance the Spanish and their parties, for they will force us to separate our forces into many places. Also it is not good to despair the poor King too much, fearing it may force him to join that party which he never meant to do'.[52]

This fear was already beginning to trouble the Queen and her Councillors more and more. But for the moment it was overshadowed by the news, which came a few days after

[50] Ibid., xxix, fos. 20, 31, 81, 107, 129; *Lettres Missives*, III, 844–8.

[51] S. P. France, xxix, fos. 95, 161, 230. In fact the Queen seems to have left the elephant's two keepers, Joos van Pelleken and Jasper Sterlings, to bear most of the cost of its keep. For in the spring of 1593 they asked to be allowed to take the elephant for four months or so to the United Provinces. No one there had even seen such an animal, so the two young men would be able to recoup some of their expenses by showing it there – S. P. Holland, xlvi, fos. 84, 116.

[52] S. P. France, xxix, fo. 157.

Williams wrote his letter, of the new disaster to the English remnant in Brittany at Ambrières. Once again therefore Williams and his six foot-bands – now little more than 400 strong, excluding the sick – and the Queen's seven pieces of artillery were ordered to embark for Jersey and from there to join Norris in Brittany. Norris, 'laying aside the remembrance of any former unkindness or other matter heretofore happened between you', was to admit Williams as marshal of the army in place of Sir Henry Norris who was to come home to attend upon the Queen at court.[53]

At the same time in her reply to Henry IV, sent by du Maurier, Elizabeth made it clear that her patience was almost at an end and that she had no intention of sending help elsewhere than to Brittany. She repeated the old complaints about the King's ill-timed leniency to the besieged Parisians in 1590, the mistakes and lack of enterprise at Rouen in 1591–2, and the neglect of Brittany. She felt herself 'à la fin de mes conseils, ne vous disant qu'au devant avez reçu'. She made no mention of giving aid anywhere except in Brittany and concluded by threatening again that if Henry failed to provide the forces there as promised by the Sancy contract, her troops would be called home. Burghley, replying at the same time to the Protestant Duke of Bouillon, protested his goodwill so long as the King upheld the Gospel, and regretted that he could not give an answer that smelt more of martial actions. He was sure that the Queen also bore Henry goodwill. Nevertheless,

in that she hath found her succours not used to the King's good but spent without any great fruit for want of taking opportunities of times and places, I find Her Majesty in some sort scrupulous to yield any further expenses than at this time she hath yielded for the service in Brittany ... And yet at this present Her Majesty hath increased those numbers promised to a fifth part more.

He omitted to mention that this extra fifth were to be in Henry's pay.[54]

The 'Dieppe lobby' did not give up trying. Ottywell Smith, despite Burghley's rebukes, returned to the attack with his

---

[53] Ibid., fos. 176, 230, 235, 237, 260, 281; *Acts P. C.*, XXIII, 246, 268.
[54] S. P. France, xxix, fos. 182, 189.

plea that the Queen would keep a regiment of Englishmen in Normandy. Williams, coming back to Dieppe from England, wrote to the Queen on 7 November that he had such intelligences that he could take Fort St Catherine or a gate of Rouen or Le Havre if she would have 800 men ready in Kent, Essex, or Suffolk to come over when he sent for them. He would attempt the enterprise within four days of the 800 arriving, so they would only cost her eight days' victuals and their shipping. It may perhaps be doubted whether the prospects were quite as good as Williams and Smith made out. Certainly some weeks later de Chatte's trumpet, Martin Audys, warned Burghley that Villars had learned of the project of 'divers brave-minded men' against Le Havre. Spies sent out from England – one of them 'could not speak one good word of French' – had behaved so ill that many people had been let into the secret. At all events neither Williams's hopes nor Ottywell Smith's fears as yet made much impression on the Queen.[55]

Nor did Beauvoir's advocacy of the demand that Henry IV now made for 3,000 more English troops to enable him to keep the field against Parma. There were, the ambassador said, 2,000 horse and 6,000–7,000 Spanish foot already on the north-eastern frontier of France in Artois and Hainault. The King's Germans had gone home long ago. So had his Dutch. His Swiss, down to less than 2,000 men, were leaving. Without 3,000 English, he could neither keep the field nor hold any place in Normandy or along the Seine. Elizabeth still answered that 'she cannot yield to be at any further charge'. She complained sharply about the King 'being occupied as he is in Champagne and other places distant from the seaside' without any regard for Normandy and Brittany.[56] This was true enough. Since Parma's return from Rouen to the Netherlands, Henry had spent most of the summer and autumn recovering Épernay, assuring Châlons-sur-Marne and Langres, building a fort on the Marne to restrict the victualling of Paris, and then moving south-westwards with what remained of his army by way of Étampes to Chartres. In his absence most of the nobility and gentry around Dieppe

[55] Ibid., fos. 288, 290, 292, 396.
[56] Ibid., fos. 306, 312, 326.

withdrew into neutrality, St Valéry-sur-Somme was taken by Aumale on 28 October and the castle of Pont de l'Arche was betrayed to Villars on 23 October.[57] The Queen did allow Williams to take his companies to help Longueville recapture St Valéry at the end of November.[58] But she still refused to listen to Beauvoir's pleas for troops – he now asked for only 2,000, paid for three or four months – to serve with the King. News of the Duke of Parma's death on 23 November merely hardened her determination, for she persuaded herself that no Spanish army from the Netherlands would now be coming into France. She was still resolved to pay no more troops than those promised for Brittany. As late as 12 December the Privy Council were instructing Sir Thomas Sherley and Sir John Hawkins to hire three hoys in the Thames and send them to transport Williams's companies to Brittany as no shipping was to be had at Dieppe.[59] Not until the beginning of the New Year did the Queen change her mind.

[57] Ibid., fos. 230, 258, 281, 283.
[58] Ibid., fos. 277, 279, 339; xxx, fo. 124.
[59] Ibid., xxix, fos. 379, 394; *Acts P.C., XXIII, 363-4.*

# XX

# The Great Carrack and the Spanish Blanks

In the Netherlands, Normandy, and Brittany the second half of 1592 thus brought a very sharp reduction in English military activity. The year also brought a marked reduction in offensive activity by the ships of the Queen's navy. Only two of them were engaged in operations outside home waters and one of these two, the *Foresight,* was among the smaller of the royal warships. The reasons for this slackening off – apart from the generally constricting effects of shortage of money – are to be found in the revival of Spain's ocean-going war navy and in the employment of the new elusive frigates to bring the treasure from America home to Spain. The events of 1591 had shown that a mere half-dozen of the Queen's ships could no longer be sure of holding the Azores station against Spain's resuscitated armada. Yet to send a very much more substantial part of England's fighting ships to the Islands, as had been thought of in the midsummer of 1591, would be a decidedly risky operation in 1592. In the summer of 1591 a squadron of the Queen's ships had been already at the Azores, the American convoys had been on their way there, and Parma was not in France. In 1592 to send the bulk of England's war navy away to the Azores might well tempt Bazan's armada, now reassembling at Ferrol, to strike north and seize command of the Channel just when Parma's army was in Normandy and Dombes and Norris were no longer able to defend the coastal areas of Brittany against Aguila and Mercoeur. Besides, although the homeward-bound convoys of merchant shipping from America might still be met at the Azores, the most tempting prize by far, the bulk of the American silver, now came in the fast frigates which no longer needed to touch at the Islands nor sail at broadly predictable seasons.[1]

For these reasons Sir Walter Raleigh who, with the

---

[1] *L. and A.,* III, 758, 761, 765; *Further Voyages,* p. lxxxvi; Birch, *Memoirs,* I, 75.

Howards and certain London privateering merchants, organized England's principal naval enterprise for 1592, did not aim at the Azores or the south-western coasts of Spain as had been done in 1589, 1590, and 1591. He aimed at the West Indies – perhaps at seizing Panama,[2] but more probably at intercepting the frigates at or off Havana. It was, as usual, a combination of royal and private enterprise, with two of the Queen's ships, ten sizeable privateers, and four pinnaces.[3] This was a force numerous enough to intercept the frigates in the narrower waters between Cuba and Florida and strong enough to overpower them. It was also to be sufficiently provisioned to winter in the West Indies so as to be at hand however late the frigates sailed.[4] Moreover, from April until at least the end of the summer it might hope for support from up to a score of other, independent, English privateers which would be in the Caribbean, among them three powerful vessels and two smaller ones that Cumberland was setting forth.[5]

In the event neither Raleigh nor Cumberland accompanied their squadrons nor did either squadron go to the West Indies. Cumberland, discouraged by a prolonged delay by adverse weather and possibly also by illness, stayed at home and left the conduct of his five ships to John Norton, who got no farther than the Azores.[6] Raleigh saw his squadron out past Cape Finisterre and then, in obedience to the Queen's command,[7] handed over to Frobisher, instructing him also to stay in the eastern Atlantic. Frobisher in fact stayed off the Spanish coast, taking a couple of fairly worthwhile prizes and catching a brief glimpse of one Portuguese East Indian carrack, the *San Bernardo,* 'at the Burlings in a dark night,

[2] Hakluyt, V, 59; also Camden, p. 598.

[3] *Cal. S. P. Domestic, 1591–4,* pp. 168–9; Lansdowne MSS, lxix, no. 21; Murdin, pp. 653–4; Monson's account of the voyage is in *Monson's Tracts,* I, 278–80, with Oppenheim's notes at pp. 281–96. The account in Hakluyt, V, 57–68 is more detailed. There are also a number of papers about it in Lansdowne MSS, lxix, lxx.

[4] E.g. the *Foresight* was sheathed, put in order, and victualled for eight months – *Cal. S. P. Domestic, 1591–4,* p. 143.

[5] *English Privateering Voyages,* pp. 173–223; *Further Voyages,* pp. lxxxvii–xciii, 280–304; Hakluyt, VII, 148–56; *Monson's Tracts,* I, 281; G. C. Williamson, *Cumberland,* pp. 83–112.

[6] Ibid., pp. 83–4; *Further Voyages,* p. xci note 10.

[7] Murdin, p. 663 (also quoted in Edwards, *Raleigh,* II, 44–6).

having sight of her lights the 7 of July' as she slipped by him into Lisbon.[8] Three of his ships, however, had left him and sailed off to the Azores.[9] Sir John Burgh in the *Roebuck* (250 tons) was the first to go. Joining forces at the end of July with three other privateers and four of Cumberland's ships, he forced a second East Indian carrack, the *Santa Clara*, to take refuge under Flores. Lack of wind made it impossible for the English to go in after her that day and by next morning, when the wind rose, the Portuguese had moved most of her cargo ashore. Then, as soon as the English moved in to board her, her crew set her on fire. So the *Santa Clara* and almost all her lading were lost. But some prisoners provided valuable information about another carrack, the *Madre de Dios*, that was following her.[10]

Just after this Hawkins's *Dainty* arrived, and next day the Queen's *Foresight*. The whole force then spread out to intercept the *Madre de Dios*. She was sighted early on 3 August, a giant ship of 1,600 tons or more and seven decks high. The *Dainty* reached and tackled her first, the other ships catching up one after another during the day, until at last, some time after midnight, she was forced to surrender. After a wild and happy night plundering the more portable and accessible parts of her cargo, everyone was eager to get home with their spoils before Bazan's armada arrived to catch them as he had caught the *Revenge* in 1591. Luck was with them. For although Bazan had sailed from Spain on 16 July, none of the English ships encountered him.

The *Madre de Dios* was easily the biggest and richest prize taken so far in the Spanish war. From her cargo almost all the precious stones, the ambergris, the musk, and other portable riches – said by the *Santa Clara's* purser to be worth

[8] *Monson's Tracts*, I, 287.

[9] According to the account in Hakluyt, V, 59, Raleigh had ordered such a division of the squadron. In view of what was known of the strength and dispositions of Spanish naval forces, this sounds unlikely. Moreover from the letter that Raleigh wrote upon returning to Plymouth on 18 May, Burghley and Howard certainly did not gather that there was to be any such division; they clearly expected the whole force to go to the Azores or the Canaries (*H. M. C., Salisbury MSS*, IV, 200). Also, although the *Foresight, Roebuck*, and *Dainty* did all go to the Azores, they did not go there as an organised squadron. They dribbled away one at a time, at different times and from different places.

[10] Hakluyt, V. 61–3; *Monson's Tracts*, I, 287–9.

£100,000 – were plundered by the English sailors before she was brought into Dartmouth. Yet what remained was still valued at £141,120 and the total value of what was saved or recovered must have been appreciably more. For out of it the Queen granted Cumberland £37,000, a profit of some £18,000 on his outlay. She allowed the London investors £12,000 as a return upon their £6,000 and Hawkins and others £7,000 or £8,000. To the untimely-married Raleigh[11] she allotted £24,000, rather less than he had spent. She herself kept the rest and the pepper alone, which formed the bulkiest part of the carrack's cargo, brought her in £80,000 when sold next spring to a syndicate of London merchants.[12] That was a most welcome windfall for the Queen's near-empty Exchequer.

It was the more welcome because, in addition to the problems of northern France, Elizabeth and her ministers had considerable anxieties nearer home. There was, it is true, little reason at this time to fear another Spanish invasion attempt on the scale of the 1588 Armada. Throughout 1592 most of the more reliable intelligences from abroad agreed that Spain's attention and energies were absorbingly concentrated upon France. Châteaumartin and Edmund Palmer during the early months of the year reported confidently that the naval preparations in Spanish ports were on a limited scale and designed merely to provide a force to escort the American flotas and the East Indian carracks from the Azores on the last leg of their journey home.[13] Palmer, admittedly, was complaining of lack of payment and of having his loyalty suspected.[14] Châteaumartin was already a double agent, using

---

[11] For Raleigh's marriage and imprisonment, see especially A. L. Rowse, *Raleigh and the Throckmortons*, pp. 150–69.

[12] For the *Madre de Dios* and her cargo – Hakluyt, V, 63–7; C. L. Kingsford, 'The taking of the *Madre de Dios*', in *Naval Miscellany* (Navy Records Society, XL), II; Purchas, XVI, 13–17; *Monson's Tracts*, I, 289–96; *English Privateering Voyages*, pp. 201–6; *H. M. C., Salisbury MSS*, IV, 301; J. Strype, *Annals* IV, 177–82; G. C. Williamson, *Cumberland*, pp. 85–103; E. W. Bovill, in *Mariner's Mirror*, LIV, 129–52. There are many papers about the enquiries into and disposal of the *Madre de Dios's* cargo in Lansdowne MSS, lxx and *H. M. C., Salisbury MSS*, IV.

[13] *L. and A.*, III, 755–6.

[14] He wrote on 20 January that he was already over £100 out of pocket and, as he had no money left, he would be unable to report any longer about the Spaniards' proceedings. There was apparently some suspicion of his loyalty because he had a

peace talks with Juan de Velasco, the Spanish governor of Fuenterrabia, as a cloak for serving and drawing pay from both sides.[15] But what Châteaumartin and Palmer wrote was borne out by other evidence. A report from 'a well-wisher of Her Majesty' and other letters from the coast of Spain told very much the same story. So, too, did examinations of merchants and mariners returning from Peninsular ports.[16] From the Netherlands Thomas Phelippes's spy William Sterrell,[17] although on 7 January he reported that the invasion was certainly intended for June, had come to understand by 13 February that the Spaniards were not strong enough to invade England during the troubles in France.[18] Reinold Boseley claimed to have seen a letter in which Cardinal Allen wrote that he would not be coming to the Netherlands until Michaelmas as nothing was intended for the year against England. Boseley also said that Sir William Stanley, who had come back to the Netherlands from Spain in August 1591, was raising a regiment of Walloons to go to France with Parma. And Stanley's employments were usually regarded as

---

Spanish wife. Also, according to Anthony Standen, he was 'subject to wine and over-familiar with merchants, a kind of people no way to be trusted and mortal foes to gentle blood or to such as they discover to have in them more than ordinary' – *L. and A.*, III, 719, 734.

[15] He was being paid 1,000 crowns a year by Elizabeth and 100 crowns a month by Philip II – *L. and A.*, III, 731; A. J. Loomie, *The Spanish Elizabethans*, p. 62. He had returned to Bayonne in June 1591 from a visit to England, with instructions from Burghley for replying to secret peace overtures from Juan Velasco, governor of Fuenterrabia. These came to nothing, but served him as a useful cover – *L. and A.*, I, 619–21; II, 644, 670; III, 715–16, 722. Most of the information he gave to the Spaniards was about French affairs – Loomie, *The Spanish Elizabethans*, p. 62. His reports to Burghley and Heneage seem to have been generally accurate, but often belated e.g. on 26 November 1591 he warned that Manoel d'Andrada had left Laredo and reached Rouen: Andrada had already been arrested at Dieppe on 4 July and sent to England – *L. and A.*, III, 237, 533–6, 747; cp. also Burghley's complaints – ibid., II, 652–3, 669.

[16] *L. and A.*, III, 755, 758. Who the agents in Spain were, is not clear. But cp. *Cal. S. P. Spanish*, IV, 599–602, 612–13, 643. In August 1591 John Arden and John Baker, whom Burghley had kept at the Spanish court, had returned to England – ibid., 719–20, 723. By February 1593 Arden was in Rome – S. P. Italian States, i, fos. 140, 150. A William Halfacre was sent to Spain as a spy in November 1591 – *H. M. C., Salisbury MSS*, IV, 158. Standen was at the Spanish court and said to be in great credit with the King and Secretary Juan d'Idiaquez, until January 1592 – *L. and A.*, III, 745.

[17] Alias Henry St Main, *alias* Franquelin, *alias* Robert Robinson, *alias* Jonnes.

[18] *Cal. S. P. Domestic, 1591–4*, pp. 169, 183–4. Wroth had reported similarly from Venice – *L. and A.*, III, 707.

reasonably reliable indicators of Spanish intentions regarding England.[19] As we have seen, events were to confirm that Spain's naval preparations in 1592 were almost entirely directed towards providing an escort for the homeward-bound flotas and carracks.

Indeed, as yet the Spaniards proved unable to muster even the limited number of additional ships and mariners required to carry out their long-threatened enterprise, in co-operation with Lussan, the Leaguer governor of Blaye, against Bordeaux and in the Gironde.[20] Land forces were almost equally scarce owing to the serious revolt in Aragon[21] that kept more than 15,000 of Philip II's troops occupied there in 1591 and well into 1592. This revolt grew out of the accumulated resentment and suspicion felt by some of the Aragonese nobility and gentry over the royal government's encroachments upon their feudal jurisdictions and their provincial privileges. The King's appointment of a Castilian, the Marquis of Almenara, as his viceroy in 1588 had brought his resentment dangerously near to an explosion. The spark that finally touched it off was provided by Antonio Perez. He, while Philip II's Secretary of State, had been responsible for having Don John of Austria's secretary Escovedo murdered in March 1578. In this he had acted with Philip's knowledge and consent and he possessed papers that could seriously compromise the King. Philip had gradually come to believe that Perez had wilfully misinformed him both about Escovedo and about the loyalty of Don John, had in fact tricked him into becoming an accessary to murder. So Perez was eventually imprisoned at Madrid, tortured, and in serious danger of his life. He managed in April 1590 to escape to Aragon. The privileges of that kingdom and its jealousy of Castile assured him of a favourable and public trial and, to forestall this, Philip had him transferred to the prison

---

[19] *Cal. S. P. Domestic, 1591–4*, pp. 208–9. But Stanley was bragging of a new fleet prepared in Spain and in March 1592 both Sir Roger Williams and Yorke wrote that 'we here [?hear] speak of a very great fleet in Spain'. But according to Williams some said it was for Ireland, though most for Brittany – *L. and A.*, III, 762.

[20] Ibid., 677, 733, 763, 768.

[21] J. Lynch, *Spain under the Habsburgs*, I, 337–45; J. H. Elliott, *Imperial Spain*, pp. 271–8; R. B. Merriman, *Rise of the Spanish Empire*, IV, 566–606; G. Marañon, *Antonio Perez*, pp. 248, 307. For information reaching the English government – *L. and A.*, II, 655–6; III, 720–1, 735–6, 751–2, 754, 759, 769.

of the Inquisition on a trumped-up charge of heresy. Thereupon Perez's supporters in Zaragoza stirred up a mob which stormed the Inquisition's prison, carried off Perez in triumph, and left the viceroy Almenara mortally injured. Their triumph did not last very long. For a few months the King temporized, but then at the end of October 1591 he sent in Alonzo de Vargas with an army of 12,000 foot and 3,000 horse that had been gathering earlier for an invasion of south-western France. Aragonese support for Perez, which had never spread much beyond the town of Zaragoza and a limited number of the lesser nobility, speedily collapsed although some resistance continued for a few months in the mountains.

Perez by then had fled over the border into Béarn, to the little court of Henry IV's sister, the Princess Catherine of Navarre, at Pau. From there in February 1592 he sent a small force of exiles and Frenchmen into Aragon. But they now found even less support than before and Vargas's troops soon chased the little force back into France. There was not much that the French King and his sister could do to keep the fire burning in Aragon. They had very few troops to spare in those parts and those they were able to put together had the great disadvantage in Catholic Aragon of being for the most part Huguenots. For obvious geographical reasons there was even less that Elizabeth could do to give direct help to the revolt, although in April Perez did send his devoted servant Gil de Mesa over with Châteaumartin to urge her to offensive operations against Spain. At least, however, the revolt in Aragon did much to delay Spanish intervention on behalf of the League in south-western France. It also provided further support for the opinion that Spain was unlikely to attempt any major invasion of England in 1592.

All the same, that did not necessarily rule out the possibility of smaller and perhaps more peripheral Spanish raids. Thomas Meade, a repatriated prisoner of war from the *Revenge,* warned in December 1591 that Ireland and Milford Haven should be well guarded. Sterrell, when reporting on 13 February 1592 that the Spaniards were not strong enough to invade England during the troubles in France, said nevertheless that there would be raids to surprise some port and so rule in England's seas. In May he, too, warned that the havens in Wales should be well looked to. Reinold Boseley, while in the Spanish Netherlands as a government spy, had been asked to persuade the supposedly malcontent Sir William Courtenay to deliver Weymouth to the Spaniards when they came. The cruise of two Spanish galleys and sixteen flyboats from Blavet along the north coast of Brittany as far as St Malo in August and early September 1592 lent a little substance to such rumours. It probably explains the report that Sir Walter Raleigh received in August from a man from Brittany that twenty enemy warships were between Scilly and Ushant, lying in wait for the returning Newfoundland fishing vessels. The Privy Council took the reports seriously enough to put some of the Queen's ships at readiness and to warn the deputy lieutenants of Hampshire, Sussex, and Kent to keep their beacons watched and their trained bands alerted to defend the coast and the Isle of Wight. The fortification of Plymouth was pressed forward[22] and at least half a dozen warships remained based upon Portsmouth instead of the Medway until very late in the year.[23]

It was not only in the Channel and Western Approaches that Spanish raids might be expected. Back in January 1592 Edmund Palmer had reported from St Jean-de-Luz that three or four small vessels were ready to leave Ferrol for the north parts of England to spoil the fishermen there. The commander was a mulatto, the son of a negro, who was said to have done much damage on that coast before and who swore to heave overboard any Englishmen he took. On this report the Queen sent ships northwards towards the Orkney fishing grounds. She required Newcastle and Yarmouth to fit out others in warlike sort to join with them. In addition, through her ambassador in Scotland, Robert Bowes, she got the Scottish council to send strict orders to the inhabitants of the Orkneys and of the north parts of Scotland that they should neither

[22] *Cal. S. P. Domestic, 1591–4*, pp. 143–4, 183–4, 196, 206–9, 225–6, 265; *Acts P. C.*, XXII, 344–8; XXIII, 160–1; Strype, *Annals*, IV, 162–7.

[23] In the autumn of 1591 there had been talk of keeping the fleet, or part of it, at Portsmouth, but Hawkins and Borough of the Navy Board had argued strongly against it – *Cal. S. P. Domestic, 1591–4*, p. 116. In 1592 half a dozen or so of the Queen's ships stayed there until late in the year – above, p. 298.

give any assistance to Spaniards and Leaguers nor allow them to land.[24] All through the summer of 1592 the Queen and Privy Council also devoted considerable attention to the defences of Ireland, although for the moment Ireland was deceptively peaceful and obedient.[25] Besides all these anxieties, justified or unjustified, about possible Spanish invasions, there was the usual crop of reports about plots to burn the Queen's ships, blow up the Tower of London, and other more or less hare-brained schemes.[26]

None of these enterprises, even if they were ever attempted, would in themselves have threatened any real danger to England's independence and security. The possibility that they might be attempted was, none the less, taken seriously because of the government's exaggerated, though quite natural, fear that even a small Spanish landing might find substantial support among the recusant Catholic minority in England. In this the government were to some extent deceived by their own intelligence reports. So many of these came from spies among the English Catholic exiles and reflected those exiles' highly exaggerated ideas about the strength of their likely support at home. Nevertheless there was some justification for alarm in the apparent success of the missionary priests. These men were being sent over in considerable numbers and a wide variety of disguises from the seminaries established by Cardinal William Allen and the Jesuit Robert Parsons at Douai, Reims, Rome, and most recently at Valladolid and Seville. Possibly their success was chiefly a matter of strengthening the faith of those who still clung to the old religion. But they did seem to a nervous government also to be winning numerous converts, especially among the gentry of Lancashire, Yorkshire, and – strategically the most dangerous – Hampshire and Sussex. To check their progress special commissioners had been appointed in every county in October 1591 to enforce the laws against recusancy and to ferret out Jesuits and seminary priests and their harbourers. They were

---

[24] *L. and A.*, III, 702; *Acts P. C.*, XXII, 398, 488; *Cal. S. P. Scotland*, X, 660, 735. For the depredations of a Spanish bark off the Scottish and Northumbrian coasts in 1590 – ibid., pp. 242, 335-6, 345-6, 353, 395-7.

[25] *Acts P. C.*, XXIII; *Cal. S. P. Irish*, IV; and C. Falls, *Elizabeth's Irish Wars*, pp. 168-75.

[26] E.g., *L. and A.*, III, 697; *Cal. S. P. Domestic, 1591-4*, p. 206.

also to examine any 'wilful recusants' about their reasons for not coming to church and 'upon any matters concerning their allegiance to Her Majesty and of their devotion to the Pope or to the King of Spain'. The success of these commissioners' efforts seems to have been somewhat limited, for a year later, in October 1592, Burghley was still making a note to consider how the 'general revolt' of the recusants, particularly in Lancashire, might be remedied.[27]

The danger seemed the greater because the English Catholics, both those in exile and those at home, were clearly beginning to scent the possibility that before long there might be a change to a regime more favourably disposed towards them. Elizabeth had already lived longer than any English monarch since Edward III and it was still very much an open question who would succeed her on the throne. It was a question that she always steadfastly refused to settle and which she would never permit her subjects to discuss publicly. Many of them, none the less, were growing increasingly anxious about it. The Puritan Peter Wentworth, for example, had run into serious trouble during the summer of 1591 over an unpublished manuscript on the subject and in 1593 he was to land in still worse trouble for attempting to raise the matter in Parliament. Some at least of the Privy Councillors – possibly even Burghley – seem to have felt a secret sympathy with Wentworth. For they, too, feared that Elizabeth's death might put the future of the English Protestant Church and commonwealth in jeopardy.[28] And what they feared, the Catholics hoped for. Nor were all the Catholics in exile content to wait upon the course of nature. There were still periodically reports, even if often rather second-hand and far-fetched, of plots to assassinate the Queen. For the reports of double agents, such as Reinold Boseley, from the confessions of one or two of the less steadfast missionary priests, and from intelligencers' reports a fairly clear picture of what the exiles were imagining emerged. The Pope, they were for example said to believe, wanted to reclaim England while the Spaniards were still engaged in France and before they could

---

[27] Ibid., pp. 112–15; Strype, *Annals*, IV, 78–89.
[28] *Cal. S. P. Domestic, 1591–4*, pp. 107–8; J. E. Neale, *Elizabeth I and her Parliaments, 1584–1601*, pp. 251–66.

spare forces enough to conquer England. So he was sending an Italian, who had been despatched to assassinate Henry IV, to assassinate Elizabeth instead. Thereupon Stanley would land with 10,000–12,000 men provided by the Pope. He would land in the part of England nearest Ireland. There, it was hoped, those other Stanleys, the Earl of Derby and his son Lord Strange, would join the invaders. Supported by most of Lancashire and the north, they would claim the crown against the Earl of Hertford, King James VI of Scotland, and any others whose pedigrees tempted such ambitions. In the ensuing division and confusion it would be easy for the Pope and Spain to send in larger forces and dispose of the kingdom as they pleased. The Spanish might wish to defer the whole affair until they had achieved their aims in France, but they could not deny the Pope the use of their ports as Stanley's enterprise was wholly at his charge. So that enterprise was intended to be executed in April 1593.[29]

This, if indeed it was the exiles' design, was largely moonshine. There was no sign at all of the 10,000–12,000 men the Pope was supposed to be providing for Stanley, and Stanley's regiment in Spanish service in the Netherlands was down to a few hundred dispirited men. There was little ground to doubt the loyalty of the Earl of Derby and Lord Strange and in fact on 30 October 1592 Elizabeth wrote to thank Derby for his efforts to discover those who favoured and maintained seminarists and Jesuits in Lancashire.[30] However, although we know all this today, it was somewhat less apparent to the government in 1592 who also had to be alert to the worst that *might* happen. Besides, there was another element in the situation that possessed, or so it seemed, a little more substance. This was the activity of the Scottish Catholic nobles and the attitude of the King of Scotland. Some of the exiles in the Spanish Netherlands – in particular Charles Paget, Thomas Morgan, and other one-time servants of Mary Stuart – were said to hope for substantial help from the

---

[29] *Cal. S. P. Domestic, 1591-4*, pp. 162, 208–9, 222, 227–8, 246, 259–63, 267, 269–71.

[30] Ibid., p. 283. A Richard Hesketh did come over in the autumn of 1593 to approach the Earl of Derby about turning Catholic and asserting a claim to the throne. He saw the Earl, who handed him over. Hesketh was tried and executed at the end of November 1593 – *H. M. C., Salisbury MSS*, IV, 381, 390, 408–9, 418, 421–4, 461–3; Birch, *Memoirs*, I, 145.

Scottish Catholics, even perhaps from King James VI himself. These hopes were encouraged by James's balancing policy between Protestants and Catholics. His independent power as King was decidedly limited and in seeking to avoid subjection to the yoke of the Presbyterian Kirk he did his best to keep alive – or at least did as little as he could to destroy – the Catholic faction headed by the Earls of Huntly, Erroll, and Crawford. His tolerance of these Scottish Catholic subjects was also inspired in part by a desire not to offend the Catholics in England who would, he hoped, also become his subjects upon the death of Elizabeth and whose numbers and militancy he, like the English exiles, considerably overestimated. He repeatedly showed a remarkable leniency towards these Scottish Catholic Earls. Back in February 1589 the English had intercepted letters from Huntly and Erroll to the Duke of Parma and the King of Spain. In these they lamented the defeat of the 1588 Armada and promised active support whenever the enterprise should be renewed.[31] Elizabeth sent the letters to James, with an expostulatory screed of her own. This drove the two Earls in April 1589 to take up arms. But when in the same month James marched in person against them, their rebellion flickered feebly out at the Brig of Dee. Yet upon their submission James, despite the clamours of the Kirk, condemned them only to the lightest of punishments. In September 1589 they were released from their loose imprisonment and allowed to retire to their Highland strongholds.

For the next few months, indeed through most of 1590, Scotland remained unwontedly peaceful. This was when James went off to Norway and Denmark to marry and fetch home his Danish bride, Anne, sister of the young King Christian IV. There were still periodical alarms about Catholic plottings. Late in 1589 there were reports that some of the leading Catholics were again sending messages to Parma, Philip II, and the Pope by means of the Jesuits William Crichton, Edward Hay, and Robert Bruce. A year later the English took a Spanish bark off Coruña. When it was brought into Sandwich, its crew said that they were in the following spring to have escorted two pataches with treasure

---

[31] *Cal. S. P. Foreign*, XXIIII, 56; *Cal. S. P. Scotland*, IX, 682.

from Spain for Huntly and his friends.[32] There were occasional rumblings of similar alarms during 1591. But for the greater part of that year the most remarkable events in Scotland were centred around a series of open defiances of royal authority by the turbulent, and dubiously Protestant, Earl of Bothwell, the nephew of Mary Stuart's third husband. Some of the nobility and some of the more extreme leaders of the Kirk were inclined to favour him, even to connive at his excesses. One who did so was the popular young Earl of Moray and James, in his weakness, commissioned Huntly to arrest him. Huntly, who was already feuding with Moray, went one better and murdered him on 8 February 1592. Once again James allowed Huntly to avoid trial and to go free after only another brief and loose imprisonment.

Then, during this summer of 1592, rumours and reports of Scottish Catholic plottings with Spain grew more insistent. Early in June Elizabeth instructed Robert Bowes to inform James that she had most certain knowledge that before the end of August forces were to be sent from Spain by the west seas into Scotland. Others were to follow by the east seas from the Low Countries. A great sum of money had already been sent to Flanders to pay these forces and to subsidize the leading Scottish nobles who were to be dealt with to band together to seize James and change the government and religion of their country.[33] James received this information very coolly, professing to doubt whether it really reflected anything more than the wishful thinking of the Jesuits and exiles. Bowes, too, understood that the Scottish Catholics were rather seeking to gather a party than having one already formed. He also heard that the King of Spain looked very coldly upon these projects. The Spaniards would do nothing until the Scots actually took the field and showed good hopes of success.[34] And, indeed, Elizabeth herself may well have exaggerated her fears in order to frighten James into dealing more firmly with Huntly and his supporters.

Certainly August came and went with no sign of any forces arriving from Spain or the Low Countries. Nevertheless the

[32] Ibid., X, 434.
[33] Ibid., pp. 682-3.
[34] Ibid., pp. 696, 721, 727, 764-5, 789.

rumours continued of Jesuits and exiles plotting a Scottish Catholic uprising, to be backed by Spanish aid in the spring of 1593. Other intelligences pointed in the same direction. An intercepted letter of 7 October from Havana said that eighteen frigates were building there and were to be ready for the voyage of England in 1593. On 22 October Richard Tomson wrote to Burghley that Spanish galleons were again beginning to gather at Ferrol. That was where, according to sundry Spaniards of commandment and good quality, the King of Spain assembled his navy when he intended any enterprise northwards, just as Lisbon was the base for operations southwards and westwards to escort home the Indies fleets, as in 1591. Ferrol was a safe haven from which they could be 'with two days' wind upon our coast'. It was, moreover, not frequented by foreign merchants, so intelligences from there could not so easily be obtained. Nevertheless it was known that some of the new-built galleons had already been sent there from Lisbon and many navy officers had been sent to levy 3,000 mariners and keep them together there to serve in the armada in February or March 1593. Furthermore some Scots who had traded to Spain and Portugal during the summer reported that many fugitive Scots, evil affected to their King and country, had come to Spain and were entertained by the Spanish King, who offered large sums to Scottish pilots and mariners to enter his service. Tomson therefore suspected that something was intended in the spring against Scotland or Ireland.[35]

A couple of months later, in the very last week of 1592, a discovery was made that seemed to lend force to this suspicion. Upon information sent by Bowes and the ministers of the Edinburgh Kirk, the minister of Paisley, Andrew Knox, with the help of Lord Ross and others, pursued and arrested a Catholic, George Kerr, as he was about to set sail from the Isle of Cumbrae for Spain. On his ship they found two great packets of letters. In one of the packets there were eight clean sheets of gilded paper on which no letter was written, but which were signed one by the Earl of Angus, some by Huntly, some by Erroll, and some by all three. These papers

[35] S. P. Spain, iv, fos. 133, 136.

were not addressed, but from the wording of the subscriptions they appeared to be addressed to a king or person of high estate. With them were eight seals of arms of each of the three Earls, so set down that they might be removed and affixed to the blank papers.[36] Kerr, under torture confessed that there was a plot, begun by the Jesuit William Crichton, for the Catholic Earls to aid a Spanish invading force. There were also some grounds for suspecting that James VI knew rather more about what was afoot than he admitted to Elizabeth's ambassador; that he might be weighing the possibilities of using Spanish aid to press his own claims to Elizabeth's throne.[37]

It seems very unlikely that James had any intention of backing the Scottish Catholic Earls in a Spanish-backed invasion of England. It may well be, too, that the Scottish Protestants made more of this affair of 'the Spanish Blanks' than the evidence justified. But one of the great difficulties that faced all sixteenth-century governments was the difficulty of assessing accurately their intelligences about their neighbours and enemies. It was particularly difficult to assess how much was real and how much was wishful thinking in the plottings of English exiles, Scottish Catholics, and the Jesuit henchmen of Father Parsons. Elizabeth therefore could not entirely ignore the reports that she might soon be faced with a Catholic invasion across her northern frontier into those parts of England where Catholicism was most widespread and recusancy most common. And clearly she did take the reports seriously. On 8 February 1593 the Privy Council wrote to the Earl of Derby that they were credibly informed that the

---

[36] *Cal. S. P. Scotland*, X, 828; T. G. Law, 'The Spanish Blanks and the Catholic Earls', in his *Collected Essays and Reviews* (ed. P. Hume Brown), pp. 244–76. F. Shearman, in *Innes Review*, III, 81–103, suggested that the whole affair was largely a Protestant fabrication; but cp. the account of this and later developments taken to Spain by the priest John Cecil in 1593 (though Cecil was by then working for Sir Robert Cecil) – *Cal. S. P. Spanish*, IV, 588–92 [which should be dated 1593, not 1591], 603–8; *Cal. S. P. Domestic, 1591–4*, pp. 474–5.

[37] In *H. M. C., Salisbury MSS*, IV, 214–16, there is a paper (possibly found with the 'blanks'?) in which James VI weighs the pros and cons of joining Spain in an attempt to conquer England. He comes down fairly firmly against any immediate attempt. The paper is headed and endorsed as 1592, but the date is altogether uncertain; nor is it altogether clear when it became known to the English government – not perhaps much before March 1594 (cp. *Cal. S. P. Scotland*, XI, 301). Cp. also *Cal. S. P. Venetian*, IX, 148.

Spaniards were conspiring with some Scottish nobles to invade England and that they were 'to pass the seas betwixt Ireland and England and in their way towards Scotland may surprise the Isle of Man'. Derby was therefore to look to the island's defence.[38] The revival of Spain's oceanic naval power could put Ireland also at risk and the weakness of the French royalists in Brittany made the west of England vulnerable. If these threats were to materialize in any substantial measure, England would have to draw in her forces for her own defence. The government must therefore think even more carefully than usual before committing English troops to operations overseas in the Netherlands or France. Yet without substantially increased military and financial support from England, Henry IV of France was unlikely to be able to resist the mounting pressures upon him to cut the ground from under the League by turning Catholic. From turning Catholic to making peace with Spain might be only a short step. If Henry took that short step, Spain then might well threaten England with invasion through Scotland or Ireland as well as with a new invading armada. How could Henry IV be held steadfast in the Protestant faith and in hostility to Spain and yet England's limited military and financial resources be husbanded for her own defence against a possible Spanish assault by sea or through Scotland? This was the problem that English policy faced at the opening of 1593.

[38] *Acts P. C.,* XXIV, 53.

# XXI

# Back to the Defensive

It looks very much as if the discovery of the 'Spanish Blanks' was the last straw that broke the back of Elizabeth's determination to limit her aid to Henry IV to the 4,000 men promised for Brittany by the contract of 30 June. Seen in the context of recent Scottish history, the affair seemed to offer final confirmation of the English government's intelligences about the likelihood of Spain making an attempt at invasion in 1593. If that was the prospect, Elizabeth could no more afford to let the League and its Spanish allies control the coast of Normandy and Picardy than she could allow them to control the north coast of Brittany. Nor could she well afford to drive Henry to despair by continuing to reject absolutely his pleas for aid outside Brittany. So, whereas at Beauvoir's audience on 24 December the Queen had flatly refused to give Henry any further help, early in January – little more than two weeks after the discovery of the Spanish Blanks – the Privy Council sent out orders for the levy of 1,200 men to serve in Normandy. Of these, 450 were to come from London, 150 each from Gloucestershire and Kent, 100 from Oxfordshire, and fifty each from Cambridgeshire, Buckinghamshire, Bedfordshire, Berkshire, Middlesex, Hertfordshire, and Essex. They were to embark by 12 February, the Gloucestershire men at Southampton and the rest at London. They were to be paid and raised at the Queen's expense: there was no longer any suggestion that the French King should pay them. This levy was, admittedly, a good deal smaller than the 3,000 men that Henry had been seeking. Nevertheless it was the number that Sancy had asked for seven months ago and it should be enough at least to assure Dieppe.[1]

The decision to send this levy to Normandy meant, of course, that Williams and his six companies were also to stay there. The Privy Council wrote to inform Norris of this on

---

[1] S. P. France, xxix, fo. 394; *Acts P. C.*, XXIV, 14–16. The letters ordering the levy passed the signet on 18 January – S. O. Docquets, I, fo. 388.

14 January. They told him that, although the Queen had resolved to increase her aid from 4,000 men to 5,000, in thirty-three companies, only twenty-two of these companies (3,300 men) were now to serve in Brittany. The other eleven (1,650 men) were to serve with Williams in Normandy. Five new bands were to be added to his present six, which were now to be brought up to full strength.[2]

This letter to Norris must have crossed one of 10 January from him. In that he repeated an offer from Montpensier to hand over Paimpol and the Île de Bréhat as a base and place of retreat for the English forces in Brittany. He suggested that the extra 1,000 men he had asked for, should be sent to take possession of these places. After getting Montpensier's written confirmation of the offer, he sent Colonel Anthony Sherley over to England on 1 February to urge the Queen to accept it and to act speedily to take advantage of it. Paimpol, he said, was 'but a small thing and newly fortified [Burghley underlined these words] but already so strong as M de Mercoeur durst not attempt it' when he was lately in those parts. The haven was better than any in Normandy and the Bréhat roads could receive most of Her Majesty's ships. Norris and the forces he had with him could not go to take these places because they had to stay in Maine to favour the entry of the royalist forces under Aumont and St Luc. Then they must besiege Laval and Château-Gontier to clear the way into Brittany. If, however, Sherley were sent speedily and secretly with the extra 1,000 men, he could take possession of Paimpol and Bréhat before the Leaguers gathered forces enough to move in. But as Paimpol was only just beginning to be fortified, he would also need 300 pioneers and a supply of tools for them, as well as carpenters, masons, smiths, and lime-burners. Furthermore, as the enemy might attack before the works were completed, he would need the Queen's artillery from Dieppe, with powder, bullets, and match and a month or two's store of victuals. Norris once again promised to discharge Her Majesty 'of all transportations, levyings, arming, and victuallings' of this supply. To secure serviceable men, who would not run away as Norris's last levy had done,

[2] S. P. France, xxx, fo. 95.

the 1,000 should be drawn from the trained bands. With them, and the help of Sourdéac from Brest, it might be possible to surprise Morlaix while Norris himself and the royalist forces drew off Mercoeur to the eastern frontier of Brittany. If, however, as he heard it rumoured – he had not yet received the 14 January letter – the Queen meant to send the extra 1,000 men to Normandy instead of to Brittany, Sherley was to 'protest that I shall be able to do Her Majesty no service'. Norris would then expect not to be blamed if any disgrace befell them. Sherley was also to press for the horse-band from the Netherlands whose departure Count Maurice had so far successfully frustrated.[3]

Norris's proposal did, it seems, for a brief while tempt Elizabeth. For in a letter to Williams on 12 February the Privy Council wrote that upon advertisement of some special service to be done in Brittany she had ordered the new levy to go to Norris. But she had, they added, now reverted to her original decision upon 'receiving very lately letters as well from the King as otherwise, requiring those forces for very necessary service in Normandy'.[4] Possibly she was put off by the extent of Sherley's demands, presented on 10 February. As Norris had instructed, he asked for pioneers and tools, guns and ammunition, and a store of victuals as well as the 1,000 soldiers. But the Queen also, as she told Norris, hesitated to entrust such enterprises as Sherley proposed to a mere 1,000 raw untrained or half-trained men without the backing of more experienced troops. Sherley had himself asked that all the men should embark at Southampton rather than London so that there would be a little time to fashion them to their arms before the shipping from the Thames came round to take them aboard. But above all, Elizabeth was anxious that Norris himself should move into Brittany instead of hanging about on its eastern frontier waiting for Aumont and St Luc. Accordingly on 12 February the Privy Council wrote to him that, although the Queen liked the enterprises that he had suggested Sherley should take in hand, she thought that Norris himself should undertake them with his troops. They

[3] Ibid., fos. 15, 70, 72. For Maurice delaying Parker's horse-band – S. P. Holland, xlv, fos. 229, 237, 243, 247, 262, 321, 329, 331; xlvi, fo. 64.
[4] *Acts P. C.*, XXIV, 57–8.

would be better performed by experienced soldiers than by fresh and raw men. Furthermore she marvelled that Norris should go so far out of the country towards Maine and Anjou and he was to threaten to return home unless Aumont arrived soon with the promised 4,000 foot and 400 [*sic*] horse. In any case, he was to discharge nine of the thirty-one captains now with him, as there were to be only twenty-two companies (3,300 men) in Brittany.[5]

On the day after the Privy Council wrote this letter to Norris, Beauvoir had an audience with the Queen. She assured him that the troops for Normandy would leave immediately if they had not already gone. But she also asked him to communicate certain complaints to the King. At his request he was duly given these in writing on 18 February.[6] They began with a list of Elizabeth's loans to Henry, amounting to £52,000 and all unpaid. These, it was admitted 'are money matters which the King is not able to satisfy, although all other strangers have been paid for their services. But the following are of another nature.' The first of these other complaints was that the English troops had never been allotted any place of retreat for their surety nor any port from which their sick and hurt might be transported home. This had resulted in the loss of many men. It had also bred a great murmuring among the English nation at home and made them more and more unwilling to suffer neighbours or friends to go into France. After this, the old grievances were rehearsed about the siege of Rouen, 'which if the King had come at his appointed time had been rendered before the Duke of Parma entered into Normandy'. Then followed complaints about Henry's failure to keep his 1592 promises to send 4,000 foot and 1,000 horse into Brittany and to deliver a walled port-town to her general there. In conclusion, it was stated that Her Majesty reminded the ambassador of these various errors, not as objecting her charges to the King by way of any reproof, but that he might be reminded thereof and hereafter either not make such promises or else see that they were better observed. Otherwise she would be moved to revoke her people to serve for their own country's defence.

[5] S. P. France, xxx, fo. 83; *Acts P. C.,* XXIV, 58–9.
[6] S. P. France, xxx, fos. 97, 103, 112.

Clearly, the total lack of any progress in Brittany was a major reason for Elizabeth reverting to her original intention and ordering the new levy to Normandy. She was growing tired of Norris's brave projects – St Malo, Morlaix, Paimpol – which he began to back away from as soon as they came to be seriously considered. She was impatient at his delay in entering Brittany and worried about the lack of French support there. By comparison the projects and persuasions of Williams and the 'Dieppe lobby' must have looked a good deal more substantial. And indeed the Privy Council in writing to Williams, also on 12 February, said explicitly that Her Majesty had reverted to her former decision to send the new levy to Normandy, for the reasons put forward in his letter of 6 February 'and especially for the special care you have to employ them without apparent danger to Her Majesty's honour in that service'.[7]

No letter from Williams dated 6 February seems to have survived. There is, however, an undated declaration by him to the Privy Council which he sent over by one of his captains, Sir Edward Brooke, about this time. In it he wrote that the Spanish Netherlands army under Count Charles Mansfelt was about to enter France. It would probably march straight to Paris to help Mayenne browbeat the League's States General, already assembled there, into choosing the Spanish King as their sovereign and Mayenne as his viceroy. Most Frenchmen 'lowed' not the Spaniards. But Mayenne, having a great party and a mighty army of strangers, would do what he listed unless Henry IV could match him with similar forces. That would require good troops of Englishmen and, if Henry lost the field, all would be lost irrecoverably without an army of 30,000 strangers, 10,000–12,000 of them English. Villars, now wholly Spanish, was already drawing Spanish troops into Le Havre and hinting broadly that within a year they would be invading England.

So, Williams urged, the Queen should now succour the French King with 2,000 men for as long as the Netherlands army was in France. Out of this 2,000, 600–700 might serve as a garrison for St Valéry-sur-Somme, which the King should be

---

[7] *Acts P. C.*, XXIV, 57–8.

required to yield to her as a base and place of retreat for her troops. With it he should also be required to yield to her the Somme customs and tailles. For 'debts is never so sure paid as with a gage ... Great matters of state, especially interest in kingdoms, passes all friendship. Cautionary towns, being well chosen, maintains always surety ... I find no such friendship in this people, but only through the King's person'. Finally, Williams held out the temptation of the Rouen enterprise. To judge from the Privy Council's letter it was this that especially impressed the Queen owing to 'the special care you have to employ them [her troops] without apparent danger to Her Majesty's honour in that service'. For Williams asked that, 'if your lordships will permit me, I will attempt one of the greatest enterprises that hath been attempted in all these wars. If I miss it, with God's grace I will not lose ten Englishmen. For I will thrust before us 300 French, all of the Religion in whom can be no treachery.'[8]

So the levy went forward and two-thirds of the men had arrived at Dieppe by the end of February. They had a rough crossing, which made them 'very sick, crying, as they tell me, for God's sake to be put on shore'.[9] To many of them this came as a crowning misery. Many resented being sent at all. Indeed, this levy seemes to have been made with more than usual difficulty and to have aroused more than usual resentment. There was a marked slackness, greater even than usual, in the county authorities over raising and equipping their contingents and the number of deserters was unusually large. All the evidence bears out the Queen's complaint to Beauvoir that her people were becoming more and more unwilling to suffer neighbours and friends to go into France. The Earl of Kent, lord-lieutenant of Bedfordshire, begged that his county should not be called upon to contribute any men or at most no more than 25 to this levy. The Privy Council very firmly rejected his plea. Their demand for 50 men, they told him, was 'very reasonable in comparison of the charge for like service laid upon the maritime counties, which have been more largely and oftener burdened than the inland counties'. Even so, Bedfordshire sent only 48 men and 19 of these were discarded

---

[8] S. P. France, xxix, fo. 406.
[9] Ibid., xxx, fos. 142, 144, 149.

as unable and insufficient, while most of the rest were 'very evil apparelled and their coats of very bad cloth and unlined'. Cambridgeshire sent only 49, of whom 10 were insufficient, one ran away, and most of the rest were 'ill and nakedly apparelled, wanting doublets, hose, stockings, shirts, and shoes, their cassocks being also of very bad cloth and unlined'. Oxfordshire did even worse, sending only 40, 12 of them very insufficient and ill-apparelled. Of the 49 sent from Hertford-shire, 14 were very defective and ill-apparelled – though there Burghley was the lord-lieutenant. Berkshire sent 48, of whom 18 were defective and 2 ran away. Northamptonshire sent only 123 instead of 150 and of these 32 were defective, 7 had run away, and most of the others were 'ill and nakedly apparelled'. The justices of the peace in Surrey and Middlesex had been ordered to help out with the London levy of 450 by pressing some of their 'loose and able' men, and the inhabitants of privileged and exempt places in and around the city, such as St Martin's and Blackfriars, had been com-manded to contribute men.. Nevertheless London produced only 375 men, 61 of them very insufficient and ill-apparelled.

Yet it does not look as if the standards expected of the counties by the Council were unduly exacting. For their lordships went out of their way to congratulate Buckingham-shire, Essex, and Middlesex upon each sending their full fifty able and sufficient men, 'furnished with armour, weapons, and other furniture fit for the wars . . . only wanting doublets, hose, stockings, shoes, and shirts'. When all the men, except those from Gloucestershire, were mustered on Tower Hill on 14 February by Sir George Carew, Sir Thomas Baskerville, and Sir Thomas Morgan only 922 appeared out of the 979 named on the muster rolls. Of these 922, no less than 167 were deficient in arms. Only 755 could therefore be handed over to Sir Edward Brooke to take across to Normandy.[10] Of the Gloucestershire 150, embarking at Southampton, about forty had run away or corruptly bought their discharge. On 20 February the officers at ports from Hull right round to Bristol were ordered to search all ships arriving from France for deserters from the forces in Normandy or Brittany who

[10] *Acts P. C.,* XXIV, 29–30, 47–8, 62–7; Lansdowne MSS, lxxiii, nos. 5, 6; *Cal. S. P. Domestic, 1591–4,* p. 315.

'withdraw themselves from those services in great numbers'. A month later John Wells, Her Majesty's post who had suffered that long imprisonment at Rouen in 1589–91, was appointed to arrest any deserters he found in London or its suburbs or in Middlesex or Surrey and to bring them before the lord mayor and justices for committal to prison. Meanwhile Sir Roger Williams was told that the counties were to make good the incomplete numbers and send them to him at their own expense. Of those already sent, the worst apparelled were to be used to fill up his six old companies, whereby they would have a supply of apparel with the rest. From the deficiencies in numbers and quality and in equipment and apparel it is clear enough that the counties had raised these 1,200 men for Normandy with no enthusiasm and that the men they levied had very little zest for the service.[11]

What made such attitudes doubly significant at this moment was that a Parliament had just been called to replenish the Queen's near-empty coffers. It assembled on 19 February and, as Sir John Neale has remarked, 'there was a new look about it'. The change was also apparent to men of the time. Robert Beale wrote to Burghley some weeks later, 'when I heard in what sort the elections of divers knights and burgesses proceeded, with no such readiness and desire as was wont to be in former times, I feared that there would have been a further backwardness than, God be thanked, hath now happened.'[12] Beale may have been referring as Neale suggests, to the sharp decline in Puritan influence in this 1593 House of Commons. The recent deaths of Leicester, Walsingham, Mildmay, and Warwick and the scourgings by Archbishop Whitgift and the Court of High Commission had certainly weakened Puritan influence in the country. Certainly, too, this 1593 House of Commons showed little enthusiasm for Puritan causes. Peter Wentworth found hardly any support for his attempt to raise the question of the succession to the throne. There was hardly a murmur when the attempt landed him in

[11] *Acts P. C.*, XXIV, 72–4, 77, 81–2, 129, 136–7. One of the deserters, however, George Scott, though caught and imprisoned, was released because he was 'the only stay and comfort' of his widowed mother and her seven other children – ibid., pp. 87–8.

[12] J. E. Neale, *Elizabeth I and Her Parliaments 1584–1601*, p. 243; Lansdowne MSS, lxxiii, no. 2.

the Tower. Nor was much fuss made over the disciplining of James Morice for introducing a bill against the procedures of the High Commission. Indeed, the most notable contribution of this Parliament to Elizabethan ecclesiastical legislation was to modify two anti-Catholic bills introduced by the government. One had its severer penalties toned down by both Lords and Commons, the other was transformed into an Act against Protestant sectaries.[13]

It looks, nevertheless, possible that Beale in speaking of the lack of 'readiness and desire' had in mind something more than a decline of Puritan spirit. It is possible that he was referring to a more general lack of enthusiasm, to the growing war-weariness in towns and counties that had most recently manifested itself in the unsatisfactory levying and slipshod equipping of those 1,200 men for Normandy. The story of the Commons debates about the subsidy bill seems to bear out such an interpretation. At the state opening of Parliament the Lord Keeper, Puckering, had made a powerful appeal for a prompt and liberal grant. In the past, he said, the Queen had asked only sparingly for money. Now, however, there were great and urgent reasons for her to call upon her subjects for financial help. The King of Spain was furiously bent upon revenge for the defeat of his Armada in 1588. He was cancelling out France by subsidizing the rebel Catholic League and by twice sending powerful armies to its support, as well as by inciting the Dukes of Savoy and Lorraine to other invasions. He now aimed at the French throne itself and had seized much of Brittany, a region more dangerous in his hands to England than even the Low Countries. He had built many new ships and had remodelled his old ones 'after the mould and manner of the English navy'. As a result he was believed to be now twice as strong at sea as in 1588. While thus threatening from the south, he was also conspiring with the Scottish Catholic nobles to invade from the north. This their recently intercepted bonds – the 'Spanish Blanks' – revealed. In addition his agents were still plotting to assassinate the Queen and to corrupt her subjects' loyalty on the pretext of religion. There were thus dangers from within as well as on

[13] For the foregoing–Neale, *Elizabeth I and Her Parliaments 1584–1601*, pp. 251–97.

every side without. The 'high wisdom and policy of Her Majesty in conducting these wars' had seen to it that 'others should fight for us'. By joining her forces to theirs she had spared much expense and many lives. Nevertheless, the present dangers were so great, and the need to provide against them was so evident, that she hoped Parliament would concentrate upon granting speedily the money to encounter them.[14]

The next week was taken up with the swearing in of the members of the House of Commons, with the election of Edward Coke as their Speaker, and the loss of one day owing to Mr Speaker's absence when 'extremely pained with a wind in his stomach and looseness of body'.[15] But on 26 February the Commons moved straight to the question of a grant. Sir Robert Cecil opened the debate with a speech on much the same lines as that of the Lord Keeper. He emphasized the double danger from the Spanish presence in Brittany and Spanish intrigues in Scotland. Sir John Wolley, Sir John Fortescue, and Sir Edward Stafford followed, all urging the necessity for a prompt and substantial grant. Then, after a rambling and not very relevant speech from Francis Bacon, the House appointed some 150 of its members as a committee to consider and advise upon the matter. This committee reported back on 28 February, suggesting a grant of a double subsidy and four fifteenths and tenths, the payment spread over four years. This was the same extraordinary sum as had been voted in 1589. In the debate that followed a few members, Raleigh among them, wished the bill to include a statement that 'those subsidies be to maintain a war impulsive and defensive against Spain', because since neither side had formally declared war, 'whether it be war or no war as yet we know not and the things that we take from the Spaniard is doubted by many not to be lawful prize'. Other members, concerned like their predecessors in 1589 that a grant of such size might establish, indeed confirm, a precedent wanted to have the reasons for it expressed in the bill. That the grant should be a double subsidy and four fifteenths and tenths

---

[14] *Eng. Hist. Rev.*, XXXI, 128 ff. A draft by Burghley is printed in J. Strype, *Annals*, IV, 174–6.

[15] D'Ewes, *Journals of all the Parliaments of Elizabeth*, p. 470.

payable over four years seems, however, to have been agreed without any serious question and another, rather smaller, committee was named to draft the bill.[16]

Before that committee could report there came an extra-ordinary intervention from the House of Lords. This followed a speech in the upper House by Lord Treasurer Burghley. His speech, again, had run on much the same lines as the Lord Keeper's at the opening of Parliament. He emphasized the King of Spain's determination to conquer first France and then England. He remarked upon the danger from Brittany and Leaguer Le Havre. He elaborated upon Spanish intrigues with the Scottish Catholic nobles. The King of Spain, he said, in return for those noblemen's bonds to serve him, had promised to send 25,000 men to the west of Scotland this summer. Five thousand of these were to stay to overrule the King of Scots and change the religion there. The other 20,000 with 10,000 Scots in Spanish pay, were to invade England. The Queen's need for money to oppose these attempts was urgent indeed.[17]

Presumably as a result of this speech, the Lords on 1 March sent to ask the Commons for a conference about hastening the subsidy bill. The Commons named a committee of sixty-four who met the Lords' committee that afternoon. At this meeting the Lord Treasurer told them that, whereas since the last Parliament met in 1589 the Queen had spent £1,030,000 upon the wars, the 1589 Parliament's grant of a double subsidy and four fifteenths and tenths had yielded only £280,000. Therefore in view of the present urgent necessity 'their Lordships will not give in anywise assents to pass any Act in the House of less than three entire subsidies to be paid in the next three years at two payments in every of the same years'.[18]

This was a truly astonishing intervention. For by Elizabeth's reign it had long been an accepted constitutional convention that the initiative over money grants and the

---

[16] Ibid., pp. 471–500, 507; also Neale, *Elizabeth I and Her Parliaments 1584–1601*, pp. 298–312.

[17] Strype, *Annals*, IV, 149–56.

[18] D'Ewes, *Journals*, p. 483. On 21 February, however, Burghley noted that the 1589 grant had by then brought in £297,124 3s. 9¼d. – H. M. C., *Salisbury MSS*, IV, 289.

decision about their amount should come from the Commons, the Lords merely ratifying what the Commons decided. That the Lords should peremptorily seek to dictate how much the Commons should offer was a remarkable constitutional impropriety. That it was done through the Lord Treasurer, in all probability at the behest of the Queen herself,[19] suggests how deep was the government's anxiety about the international situation and how desperate it felt the need for money. The intervention was, nevertheless, a blunder and much of the ensuing debates in the Commons was concerned with this invasion of their privileges. Sir John Neale has declared that those debates were wholly concerned with this issue and that there was no trouble over the size of the demand for three subsidies spread over only three years.[20] It is, however, difficult to agree with him on that point. Much of the long, vigorous, and sometimes acrimonious discussion that went on during the next two or three weeks was,[21] if not about whether to vote three subsidies instead of two, certainly about whether the three should be paid within three years or spread over a longer period at a more customary rate. The Privy Councillors in the Commons – Sir Robert Cecil, Sir Thomas Heneage, Sir John Fortescue, and Sir John Wolley – repeatedly 'put the House in remembrance of the great and urgent necessity' for the provision of money. They were supported at various times by Sir Edward Stafford, disappointed in his hopes of the Secretaryship but appeased by being granted for life the Exchequer office of remembrancer of the First Fruits and Tenths;[22] by Sir Walter Raleigh, eager to regain the Queen's favour and anxious about the safety of Plymouth and of Ireland where 'I think there are not six gentlemen ... of our religion'; by Sir Francis Drake, also concerned for the safety of the West Country; by Sir George Carey, who mentioned that 'Her Majesty is determined to send Sir Francis Drake to sea';[23]

---

[19] Neale, *Elizabeth I and Her Parliaments 1584–1601*, p. 303.

[20] 'Obviously there was no inclination to jib at the demand for heavier taxation' – ibid., p. 304.

[21] Ibid., pp. 303–12; D'Ewes, *Journals*, pp. 483–96, 499–500.

[22] S. O. Docquets, I, fo. 343.

[23] A commission had passed the signet on 18 January for Drake and Hawkins to take up three of the Queen's ships and twenty others for some adventure – ibid., fo. 389.

and by a good many more. But others were seriously concerned over the size and speed of the Lords' proposals. Sir Henry Unton, ambassador in France only a few months earlier and now member for Berkshire, was one of these, arguing that they must regard the people and their estates whom they represented, Sir Henry Knyvett was another. Francis Bacon, who in the 1589 Parliament had moved to insert that the double subsidy should not be regarded as a precedent, at one point won majority support for a proposal to spread the collection of the triple subsidy over six years, in other words to have it paid at the old accustomed rate of half a subsidy a year. Another member wished that, since 'according to men's valuation of subsidies are they at all other charges' for the wars, musters, and so forth, therefore a proviso should be added to the subsidy bill 'that by this subsidy no man should be raised as to the defray of other charges above the rate they were put at before'. After many debates, lasting sometimes well into the evening, the House eventually, and it seems still somewhat reluctantly, agreed to a proposal made earlier by Sir Thomas Cecil[24] that they should grant the three subsidies but have their collection spread over four years, one to be paid in each of the first two years and a half in each of the third and fourth years. Even now the debates were not quite ended, for there was further discussion and amendment to the subsidy bill's preamble.

At the dissolution of the Parliament on 10 April 1593 the Lord Keeper, replying in the Queen's name to Mr Speaker, gently chided those who 'in the cause of great necessity and grant of aid had seemed to regard their country and made their necessity more than it was, forgetting the urgent necessity of the time and dangers that were now imminent'. He added that 'this their doing Her Majesty imputeth more to their simplicity than any other ill meaning'.[25] Nevertheless, the long debates in the Commons, of which despite Sir Robert Cecil's stout denial she was undoubtedly well informed, must have shown her that she was drawing dangerously near to the

---

[24] Possibly at the Council's instigation – but only a year before he had been quarrelling sharply with his half-brother, the Privy Councillor Sir Robert Cecil – *Cal. S. P. Domestic, 1591–4*, p. 202.

[25] D'Ewes, *Journals*, p. 466; Neale, *Elizabeth I and Her Parliaments 1584–1601*, p. 320.

limits of her subjects' liberality as well as to the limits of her own resources. It is true that in face of the continuing expenses of the Spanish war and the new burden of Tyrone's rebellion in Ireland another Parliament four years later would vote her another triple subsidy, to be paid that time in three years; and that in 1601 her last Parliament granted four subsidies. Yet by this spring of 1593 it was clear enough that Elizabeth could hardly afford to continue intervening in Continental conflicts on the scale of the past few years.

Certainly she could not intervene on the scale that would be required to enable Henry IV, while remaining a Protestant, to overcome the League and establish himself on the throne as a generally acknowledged King of France. For three years and more he had tried to achieve this with the help of his foreign Protestant friends. The amount of that foreign help had been very considerable – a German army of 14,000–15,000 horse and foot, almost 15,000 English at various times and places, 2,500 Dutch, some Scots, and the regular contingent of several thousand Swiss. Yet all this had been cancelled out by the interventions of Parma's army from the Spanish Netherlands and Aguila's force in Brittany. Now the Germans had gone home in the summer of 1592 and there was no possibility of a new levy of any size in Germany. The two chief promoters of the 1591 levy, the Elector Christian I of Saxony and the Palatinate Administrator John Casimir, were now both dead and Saxony had succumbed to a strong Lutheran and anti-Calvinist reaction which was also threatening the young Elector Palatine and which had little sympathy for the Calvinist King of France.[26] The Dutch had also gone and no more could be spared from the States' forces to replace them. By the end of the year the Swiss had dwindled to a few hundreds. By then Henry's field army, operating now to the south-west of Paris between Étampes and Orléans numbered little more than 2,000 men.[27] He had no money to pay more troops and without the immediate prospect of a battle or a successful siege the French nobles and gentry of his party were slow to join him. They were also for the most part weary by

---

[26] S. P. Germany, States, vii, fo. 104; S. P. Holland, xlv, fo. 51; S. P. Newsletters (Germany), xxvii, fo. 76.

[27] *Kronijk*, XIX, 389–95; S. P. France, xxx, fo. 80.

now of the seemingly endless and hopeless conflict. They were no less weary of the burdens it imposed upon their purses and their time. Besides, most of them were pinned down by the local civil wars that raged in almost every province of France – Matignon in Guyenne, Montmorency in Languedoc, Épernon in Provence, Lesdiguières in Dauphiné and against Savoy, Conti in Poitou, Montpensier in western Normandy and Brittany, and much of the time Longueville in Picardy, Nevers in Champagne, and Bouillon around Sedan against the Duke of Lorraine.

Sir Roger Williams was therefore probably not far out when he reckoned that, even with Parma dead, Henry IV might need an army of 30,000 strangers, 10,000–12,000 of them Englishmen, to keep the field against Mayenne and the Spanish army. Assistance on that scale – needing replenishment every three or four months and in addition to the 4,000–5,000 men in Brittany – was clearly something that Elizabeth could not contemplate after all the expense and effort of the past years and with so uncertain a hope of eventual success.[28] After all, Henry IV always had the possibility of a political solution to his problems, provided he did not delay too long in adopting it. So long as the League had not in desperation sold out to Spain entirely, Henry could almost certainly cut the ground from under its feet and reunite France around the monarchy. All he had to do, provided he did not leave it too late, was to redeem his accession promise to 'receive instruction' in the Catholic faith. As a Catholic he would, of course, be a less compatible, and perhaps less dependable, ally for Protestant England. Yet as King of a reunited and independent France, if he could be held to continuing the war against Spain, he could do much to restore the former balance of power on the Continent. Upon that balance Tudor England's security and Tudor rulers' policy had been satisfactorily based until the collapse of the French monarchy in 1585. If it were restored, the worst of the crisis that had drawn England into open war would be over.

[28] Even in Queen Anne's reign 'it is clear that the annual demands for infantry recruits, about 12,000 every year, were more than the country could fulfill' – I. F. Burton, 'The supply of infantry' in *Bulletin of the Institute of Historical Research*, XXVIII, 57.

Elizabeth therefore made no great efforts to dissuade Henry IV from going to mass, however shrill her protests were to be after he did so. She concentrated instead upon ensuring that, whether Catholic or Protestant, he remained an active ally in the war against Spain – or at least that if he made peace with Spain, it should be a peace that embraced England and the Dutch as well as France.

To encourage Henry in these directions it might, of course, be advisable to continue giving him a measure of military assistance, particularly in those coastal areas most important to England's own security and most likely to provide jumping-off places for the anticipated Spanish invasion attempts. So, as we have seen, Elizabeth had agreed back in June 1592 to provide 4,000 men under Sir John Norris to help to defend Brittany against Spaniards and Leaguers. In January 1593 while reducing this 4,000 to 3,300, she had ordered the reinforcement of Sir Roger Williams's troops in Normandy up to 1,650 men. Besides this, she had in the autumn of 1592 allowed Beauvoir and Châteaumartin to arrange with Peter Houghton, the Hull customs officer, and various London aldermen and merchants to provide six warships, instead of the two that in recent years had escorted the English wine fleet to Bordeaux. They were also to serve for six months in the Gironde against Lussan, the Leaguer governor of Blaye, and his Spanish friends. These ships, however, were to be no expense to the Queen. Their cost was to be repaid by the collection of dues at Bordeaux. Moreover, in case the French King's promise for this collection should not be performed, all wines and other goods, except salt, coming into England from France during the year until Michaelmas 1593 were to pay an additional duty to cover Houghton's expenses.[29]

None of these English forces achieved anything very substantial. The six English warships provided by Peter Houghton arrived in the Gironde at the beginning of

---

[29] S. P. France, xxix, fo. 1; *Cal. S. P. Domestic, 1591–4*, pp. 251, 286; *Acts P. C.*, XXIII, 319–22. For the two escorting warships in 1590 and 1591 and the levy on imported wines to pay for them – ibid., XIX, 456–7; XXII, 16–17, 86–7. By mid-February 1593 Houghton had received only 7,006 crowns from the Bordeaux treasurers and was still owed 11,000. Burghley and Howard wrote to Marshall Matignon about it on 19 March – S. P. France, xxx, fos. 118, 226.

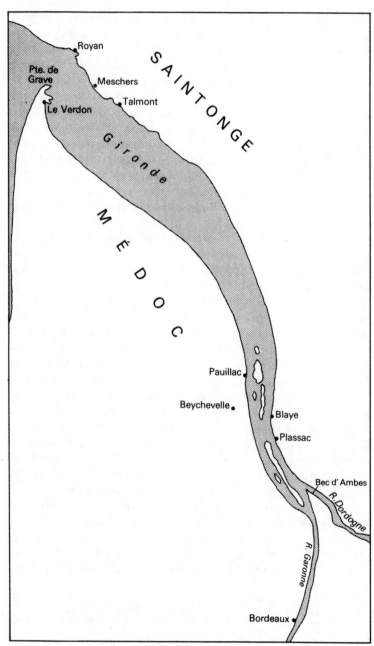

Map 9. The Gironde.

December 1592. Thereupon Marshal Matignon laid siege to Blaye. By 5 January his troops had taken the suburbs and lay under the town's walls while English and French warships blocked the river. The Leaguers of Marmande tried to succour the town by sending 800 men down the river in boats. But the English ships at the confluence of the Dordogne and Garonne prevented all but twenty-four men from getting through. Another relief attempt, by land, by Montpézat with the League forces from Périgord and the Limousin was crushed by Aubeterre and Thémines who were on their way to reinforce Matignon. By then Lussan's plight was growing serious and he sent off a four-ton shallop with one of his captains and a number of river pilots to Fuenterrabia to press the Spaniards to help.[30]

In response to this appeal Pedro de Çubiaur's squadron of fourteen Flemish flyboats and two pataches that had been running supplies and reinforcements to the Spanish troops in Brittany, set sail from the Passages on 6 April.[31] Two of the flyboats were of 150 tons, two of 120 tons, and the rest of fifty to sixty tons apiece. After being held up by contrary winds they eventually entered the Gironde on 12 April and anchored for the night off Verdon. Next morning they sailed past fourteen ships belonging to St Luc and commanded by La Limaille at Royan. Only a few shots were exchanged at long range between them. At five o'clock that afternoon they were at Blaye. On 14 April, while three of their ships landed munitions, victuals, and (it was said) 34,000 crowns for Lussan, the other eleven moved up against the six English warships off Plassac. These were the only ships Matignon had there at the time. The English, outnumbered by two to one, set off upstream for Bordeaux but were outsailed by Çubiaur's ships. After half an hour's pursuit three of them, those of Courtney, Brailford, and Wilkinson, were caught up with and boarded above the Bec d'Ambes, where the Dordogne falls into the Garonne. After an hour and a half or two hours' action Courtney repulsed the Spaniards who were attacking

---

[30] Ibid., xxix, fo. 366; xxx, fos. 1, 118, 256, 312.
[31] For what follows – ibid., xxx, fos. 312, 325; S. P. Newsletters (France) ix, fo. 167; also M. Wilkinson, 'The English in the Gironde in 1592-3' in *Eng. Hist. Rev.*, **XXX**, 280-2.

him. They drew off with blood running out of their scuppers 'as though it had been poured out with a bucket'. Two more laid Courtney aboard but were likewise repulsed and he put two others aground when they tried to get the wind of him. His own ship by then was badly holed and he had to anchor. Five more Spaniards came up, but when they were within shot cast about and left him 'lying in the ground upon the pass where there were none left to help me', for Brailford's ship had caught fire and sunk with all hands while the other four hurried on up to Bordeaux and 'like beasts left me', as Courtney complained. Two Spanish ships, one of them a 150-ton flyboat, were also burned. The remainder stayed masters of the river for the next three days.

Then on 18 April Matignon sailed down from Bordeaux with the four surviving English warships and twenty others. Next day La Limaille embarked on his ships at Royan while Matignon's attacked the enemy off Blaye. On 20 April La Limaille moved upstream, intending to anchor within cannon-shot of the retreating Spaniards. A little below Pauillac he received a letter from Matignon directing him to anchor there, off the east bank of the river so as to deny passage on the Saintonge side to the Spaniards who were a mile or so upstream in the pass of Beychevelle on the Médoc, or west, bank. An hour afterwards the fourteen Spanish ships set sail. Le Limaille allowed them to pass with no more than a brief and harmless exchange of gunfire. The reason is not at all clear. Perhaps the wind was against him. Courtney bluntly called him a traitor and Châteaumartin was puzzled why he made no effort to intercept the enemy. Certainly he showed little eagerness to engage, though he had two great ships, nine or ten others, and a frigate. He did weigh anchor and follow the Spaniards, exchanging a few more shots. 'But all was in pleasure', Courtney said, adding that 'if I had had two such ships as he, I would have clapped some of them aboard or else I would never have showed my face in England.' If he could have caught them, that is. For the fact was that the Spanish ships were better sailers than either the French or the English and they were 'always a tide down before us'. Off Castillon they anchored for the night and La Limaille followed suit, waiting for Matignon's two dozen ships to join him. At five o'clock next morning the Spaniards were away again. They anchored once more, presumably because of the incoming tide, near the Pointe de Grave, La Limaille's and Matignon's ships anchoring opposite them near Meschers on the east bank. After dinner, on the third or fourth hour of the tide, they weighed again and put out to sea. Twenty-four hours later more ships, from La Rochelle, entered the river to join Matignon, but by then the Spaniards were well on their way home to the Passages. They had lost a couple of their better ships, but they had supplied and re-victualled Blaye. Not long afterwards six Spanish pinnaces again crept up the river under cover of darkness with men and stores and in June Matignon abandoned his siege of the town.[32] Affairs in the river of Bordeaux were back where they had been before Peter Houghton's ships arrived.

In Brittany, too, little was achieved. After the companies from the Netherlands joined him in mid-January, Sir John Norris and his men spent the whole of the next five months in Maine, beyond the eastern borders of Brittany. He claimed that he could not march to Paimpol, as the Queen required, because Mercoeur might intercept him with much superior forces. He had to stay in Maine both for his troops' safety and to be ready to favour the entry into Brittany of any troops the King might send. When on 31 March the Queen suggested that he should march to Granville and there embark for Paimpol, he replied on 27 April that the French governor would not allow him to embark there without express order from the King. Anyway there would be no point in occupying Paimpol if there were no army in the field to cover it and the French alone could not provide such an army. Instead, he urged that another 1,000 men be sent to him to make good his forces' wastage through sickness and that 500 more be sent to occupy Paimpol.[33] Meanwhile he steadily evaded the Queen's and Council's repeated orders to reduce his companies from thirty-two to twenty-two. Not until June did he partially obey by discharging four of them.[34]

Towards the end of March St Luc did join him with

[32] *H. M. C., Salisbury MSS*, IV, 337–8.
[33] S. P. France, xxx, fos. 170, 241, 303, 315, 322; xxxi, fo. 9.
[34] Ibid., xxx, fos. 273, 277, 279; xxxi, fos, 56, 136; *Acts P. C.*, XXIV, 196–7, 242.

upwards of 2,000 foot and 100 horse, but Marshal Aumont still lingered away in Berri. There were occasional brushes with the enemy. On the night of 5–6 April an English foraging party, 600 strong, surprised a company of Leaguer light horse and four foot-bands at St Sulpice and put most of them to the sword. Four days later Norris and St Luc besieged the small town of La Guerche, which yielded on 13 April.[35] On their return a week later they were attacked by the Laval garrison while they were divided by a flooded river with one narrow bridge. Some 200 of them were forced back across the river, losing fifty or sixty men and four captains killed or drowned and one captain prisoner. Then the rest of the English troops came up and turned the tables on the enemy, who 'took over the hedges and threw away their arms', losing fully 500 killed or drowned according to the victors. Following up this success, the English entered the St Martin suburb of Laval on 22 April and there heavily repulsed an attack by Leaguer forces under Boisdauphin.[36]

None of this had much bearing upon the safety of Brittany, Elizabeth's main reason for providing Norris's forces. She was therefore growing more and more impatient with both the French and Norris. On 31 March, when proposing that Norris should go by sea to Paimpol, she had said that 'to continue our forces in this sort as they have been almost this twelvemonth, without service, and the one half of the time quite out of Brittany, we see no reason neither ought the French King to require such a continuance of charge at our hands'. Yet it was not easy to come to a firm decision. Brittany was of great importance. But 'such is the distance of time and space and so contrarious are the advertisements, as Her Majesty requireth to know from you further', the Privy Council wrote to Norris on 25 April, 'the true state of things and what you are like to have, not by possibilities but in certainty according to your judgement. For as things appear by your letters, both Her Majesty's honour and the reputation of you and her troops, to be thus meanly succoured, can hardly be conserved.' On 14 May definite orders were sent to

---

[35] S. P. France, xxx, fos. 237, 239, 258, 268, 336; xxxi, fo. 3.
[36] Ibid., xxx, fos. 315, 322, 336; xxxi, fo. 1.

him to withdraw to Granville and there await shipping to bring his forces home.[37]

A week later, however, on 21 May Aumont at last arrived in Maine. Norris at once told him that the Queen meant to revoke her troops because the French forces promised by the contract with Sancy had not been forthcoming. Aumont countered that he had come to the borders of Brittany with not much less than the promised numbers immediately after the contract was signed. He had found no English there and without them he was not strong enough to face Mercoeur and the Spaniards. (He did not mention that the delay of the English, so far as those summer months was concerned, was due to the delay in getting the French King's acceptance of the conditions of that contract.) Aumont went on that he had therefore retired across the Loire and had ruined his army in the unexpectedly difficult and eventually unsuccessful siege of Rochefort. He now had the foundation of an army and would shortly furnish the full promised numbers – he claimed to have 1,470 mounted men and 3,800 foot, though Norris doubted if he had more than 830 horse and 1,500 foot apart from an additional 390 horse and 1,200–1,500 foot that the Bretons might be able to produce.[38] He wrote off to the Queen and Burghley begging them to send another 3,000 men to bring Norris's forces up to the promised 4,000, 'without the which he doubted that safely he could not pass into Brittany or, being there, could not undertake anything to the advancement of the King's service'. Norris, too, was sure that Aumont would never to able to pass into Brittany unless the Queen's troops were supplied with at least 2,000 men. Even then they would still need a further 500–600 every six months to keep them up to strength. They were now, according to a muster on 13 June, 205 officers and 1,405 men but at least 300–400 of them were unable, from the after-effects of sickness, to march with their furniture or do any service with it. In fact, upon Aumont's arrival both English and French withdrew deeper into Maine, to Sille-le-Guillaume, half-way between Mayenne and Le Mans. There they

[37] Ibid., xxx, fos. 241, 295; *Acts P. C.*, 203–5, 239–43.
[38] For these estimates – S. P. France, xxxi, fos. 58, 131, 195.

idled the time away until they could hear the Queen's answer to the requests for a supply.[39]

Sir Roger Williams and his forces in Normandy could claim only a slightly more positive achievement. In February he had helped Rubempré take and raze an enemy fort across the Somme between Rue and Montreuil. He had then returned to Le Pollet and begun to take up seriously the project for surprising Rouen. On the night of 25 February he secretly met the Rouen captain and another who were to betray one of the town gates to him. Next day Sir Edward Brooke landed at Dieppe with the first contingent of the reinforcements from England.[40] Thereupon on 5 March, ignoring requests from the King and Longueville to join them in relieving Noyon, besieged by Count Charles Mansfelt and Spanish forces from the Netherlands, he moved to St Válery-en-Caux in a feint against Fécamp. He thus poised himself conveniently for the attempt upon Rouen. He now had 1,238 men, besides fifty-three sick, in eight of the completest companies, he said, that he had ever seen.[41] Yet he still needed French help especially in horsemen. He had hoped to get these from Le Grand at Quilleboeuf, but found that Le Grand had gone off to Caen. He had therefore to take de Chatte into his confidence on 15 March and together they planned to make the attempt on the 19th. This had to be put off to 22 March to coincide with the Rouen captain's watch night and on 24 March Ottywell Smith reported that it had been broken off altogether because La Londe, the Rouen sergeant-major, had got wind of it. That was, in fact, the end of the project, though the ever-hopeful Smith wrote on 18 April that the Baron of Bondville said it would be attempted within six weeks.[42]

It was on 24 March also that Williams and his troops marched away to join the King's little army across the Seine near Vernon. They stayed there in central Normandy all through April and May, helping to take Beaumont and Bernay.[43] By 30 May they had moved even farther south to

[39] Ibid., fos. 86, 122, 127, 129, 138; S. P. Newsletters (France), ix, fo. 171.
[40] S. P. France, xxx, fos. 76. 98, 142, 149.
[41] Ibid., fos. 152, 165, 172, 222.
[42] Ibid., fos. 177, 198, 205, 207, 222, 229, 260.
[43] Ibid., fos. 229, 260, 305; xxxi, fos. 23, 34, 60.

join in the siege of Dreux. Their numbers were then down to 1,100, though a couple of months earlier they had been 1,600 and, Williams said, most proper men and worth half all the other footmen in the King's army. If it had not been for them, 'we should have but too many relapse'.[44] They certainly played their full part in the siege of Dreux. On 5 June Captain Mosten with thirty men, supported by 100 more under Captains Masterson and Morrison, stormed over a drawbridge from the counterscarp into a ravelin flanking the town wall, while a similar number of French broke in at another point. Some forty or fifty English and as many French were then slain or hurt by gunfire from the town wall as they pursued the fleeing garrison of the ravelin up to the town gate. There, lacking cover, 'all the said captains continued, lying upon their bellies, some under the port, others under other shroud' until they were able to retire under cloak of darkness. As usual, initial hopes of taking the town and its castle speedily proved over-optimistic and it was not until 24 June, after a strong tower had been undermined and blown up, that the castle finally capitulated.[45]

Meanwhile, Williams's march southwards had left the coastal parts of Normandy and Picardy dangerously ill-defended. As he wrote, 'we are very negligent here, especially for those seaports'.[46] Fortunately, Count Charles Mansfelt's army from the Spanish Netherlands and such small field forces as the League could muster, were too weak to profit much by the situation. After taking Noyon on 30 March, Mansfelt had retired over the Somme. There in May he had taken Étaples and Hardelot castle and for a while seemed to threaten Boulogne. But he had not more than 6,500 or 7,000 men, too few to attempt that town. On 19 June he did come back across the Somme and take St Valéry-sur-Somme.[47] He had at least alarmed Elizabeth into making serious preparations to defend Boulogne. She had promised to send two lasts of powder. She had ordered the levying of 300 men in Kent

[44] Ibid., xxx, fos. 262, 287; xxxi, fos, 91, 116.
[45] Ibid., fos. 106, 109, 140, 175, 185, 201.
[46] Ibid., fo. 116.
[47] Ibid., xxx, fos. 234, 262; xxxi, fos. 32, 66, 90, 103, 178; *H. M. C., Salisbury MSS*, IV, 317, 319-20, 325; Thou, XI, 647-9; *Correspondance de Philippe II*, IV, 160.

and the making ready of eight of her ships – the 500-ton *Rainbow*, the 400-ton *Dreadnought*, the two 250-ton cromsters *Crane* and *Quittance*, and four pinnaces, among them the 60-ton *Moon* and the 50-ton *Spy*. The *Moon* did look in at Boulogne on 21 May to see what help the town needed.[48] The danger soon passed and most of these preparations were counter-manded. Yet whatever benefits Williams had brought to the French King at Dreux seemed to have been largely cancelled by the vulnerable situation his absence had created on the Channel coast.

Mansfelt's failure to make more of his opportunity was in part due to the Dutch. Back in December 1592 Elizabeth had urged the States to take advantage of Parma's death to seek to detach Flanders and Brabant from their allegiance to Spain. Bodley had poured cold water on this idea. He doubted whether the States could do much to provoke a revolt in any of the obedient provinces. He felt this especially because of 'the want they have of a person of authority by whom such motions might be made and directions given for good execution'. The most likely person, Count Maurice, seemed reluctant to involve himself in affairs of state and had only a limited command in military matters. It was the old English monarchical doubt about this 'headless commonwealth' and nothing came of the Queen's proposal.[49] Some Zeelanders, however, did suggest a combined attack upon Dunkirk, both to exterminate that nest of privateers and divert enemy attention from France. Some Hollanders, including Oldenbar-nevelt, took up the suggestion and through Count Maurice proposed it to Elizabeth, though without making the States General or Council of State privy to it. Elizabeth responded by sending Sir Francis Vere back in March 1593 from leave in England to urge Maurice and the States to make the attempt, though she also reiterated that she could not help. Maurice was somewhat embarrassed by this too public response to what had been a private and secret suggestion and he

[48] S. P. France, xxxi, fos. 80, 88; *H. M. C., Salisbury MSS,* IV, 318–19, 321, 324; *Cal. S. P. Domestic, 1591–4,* p. 348. Burghley seems to have been more sceptical about Boulogne's danger than Essex, Howard, and Cobham – T. Wright, *Queen Elizabeth and her Times,* II, 425. Apparently the *Golden Lion* and *Elizabeth Bonaventure,* which were to go out with Cumberland, also looked in at Boulogne – Birch, *Memoirs,* I, 102.

[49] S. P. Holland, xlvi, fo. 1; Cotton MSS, Galba, D. ix, fo. 334.

persuaded Vere to suppress the Queen's letters to the States. At the same time he made it very clear that an attack on Dunkirk was not something that the Dutch could undertake single-handed. In suggesting it they had reckoned upon substantial support from both English and French. The enemy would strain himself to the uttermost to relieve the place and the Dutch alone would have neither means to retreat nor sufficient forces to withstand him. They reckoned therefore that it could not be undertaken with less than 10,000–12,000 foot and 3,000 to 4,000 horse, where they themselves could put no more than 6,000 foot and 1,500 horse into the field. Thus although Henry IV had gaily promised them 2,000 horse, they would still need a very substantial English contingent, a contingent which Elizabeth had made very clear would not be forthcoming.[50]

By the time Vere reached Count Maurice, the Count and the States' field forces were already engaged in an operation that did something to attract the enemy's attention and forces away from France. This was the siege of Geertruidenberg, the last enemy bastion along the line of the great rivers.[51] The siege, begun on 18 March, was not easy and bad weather delayed it considerably. For almost a month, too, an enemy relieving force under old Count Peter Ernest Mansfelt camped within cannon-shot. But with Count Charles Mansfelt drawing troops away to France, the forces that his father could gather did not amount to more than 8,000 foot and 2,000 horse. Against the States' army of almost equal strength and very strongly entrenched, there was very little they could do.[52] Eventually therefore on 15 June 1593 Geertruidenberg surrendered. The States' control of the great rivers, of the Waal from the German border and of the Maas from just westward of Grave, was complete. Even so, this was only of indirect and limited assistance to Henry IV. Some part of Count Charles Mansfelt's caution was due to the distraction of his thoughts and the limitation on his numbers produced

[50] S. P. Holland, xlvi, fos. 52, 57, 96, 98, 103, 108, 110.

[51] Ibid., fos. 62, 70, 74, 86, 96, 108, 129, 152, 166, 172, 179, 181; Bor, xxx, fos. 16 *v.*–21. The terms of Geertruidenberg's surrender – S. P. Holland, xlvi, fo. 174.

[52] Ibid., fos. 123, 129, 141, 149, 166; S. P. Newsletters (Germany), xxvii, fo. 91; S. P. Newsletters (Holland), xlv, fos. 37, 41.

by the danger to Geertruidenberg. That was about all, and even for that Elizabeth could claim very little credit. Only 700 of her troops – 200 drawn from the Flushing garrison, 200 from Ostend, and two foot-bands from Bergen[53] – had taken part in the siege and these at the States' request rather than by her direct command.

Peter Houghton's ships in the Gironde, Sir John Norris's troops in Maine, Sir Roger Williams's companies in Normandy or before Dreux, Sir Francis Vere's little handful at Geertruidenberg – none of them had done much to encourage Henry IV to go on seeking a purely military solution to his problems.

[53] S. P. Holland, xlvi, fo. 117.

# XXII

# Henry IV's Conversion and After

By the early summer of 1593 it had become abundantly clear that the Huguenot King Henry IV of France could not hope to conquer his kingdom and destroy the Spanish-sponsored Catholic League by force of arms, either by native French arms or foreign Protestant arms, English, German, Dutch. It was also rapidly becoming clear that he might miss the opportunity for a political solution if he delayed much longer in performing the promise to 'receive instruction' in the Catholic faith which he had made at his accession nearly four years before. The great majority of both his loyal subjects and his rebels were by now thoroughly weary of war. Many of them were financially exhausted by its burdens. Considerable areas of the country, especially in Normandy and around Paris, had been devastated by the contending armies. Peasant insurrections were beginning in a number of regions to threaten the position and the possessions of the landed gentry and nobility. In these circumstances, while few except the more fanatical supporters of the ultra-Catholic Parisian 'Sixteen', were ready to accept a foreign prince for their king, a great many on both sides were prepared to acknowledge any reasonably eligible French claimant so long as he was a Catholic.

And there were other claimants or pretenders besides Henry IV. His nearest grown-up male relations,[1] his three first cousins, were all Catholics. The eldest, the Prince of Conti, was too feeble-witted to think of being, or to be thought of as being, a candidate for the throne. But the other two certainly had the possibility very much in mind. The Cardinal of Bourbon had been intriguing almost from the day of Henry's accession to gather a Third Party, a 'Tiers Parti', in support of his pretensions. The youngest of the three, the Count of

---

[1] The heir presumptive was Henri, Prince of Condé, the son of his deceased eldest first cousin. But Condé was only five years old and was being brought up as a Protestant.

Soissons, had an additional spur to his ambition in his resentment at Henry's adamant refusal to countenance his desire to marry the Princess Catherine of Navarre, Henry's sister. Besides these Bourbon princes of the blood, there were the princes of the House of Lorraine. They, too, had long been casting envious eyes upon the crown of France. The Duke of Mayenne coveted it for himself or, failing that, for his son. The young Duke of Guise looked to be also in the running and had a stronger popular following among supporters of the League. Even the Duke of Nemours was anxious to stake his claim if Mayenne should not stand. There were thus plenty of Catholic candidates, even apart from the Infanta Clara Eugenia whose claims her father, the King of Spain, was urgently pressing upon Mayenne and the League.

By the early summer of 1593 it was beginning to look as if one or other of these various candidates might be chosen as rival King to Henry IV by a considerable section of Catholic Frenchmen unless Henry soon carried out his promise to 'receive instruction'. For at the end of December 1592 Mayenne had at last summoned a League States General to assemble in Paris by 15 January. In a public declaration on 26 December he had invited the Catholic royalists to join them in working out a settlement of the nation's problems. Henry's Catholic councillors had trumped that card on 17 January by publicly inviting the Estates to send envoys to meet envoys from their side at some mutually convenient place between Paris and St Denis. The Estates hesitated for some time before accepting this counter-proposal. Mayenne and other leaders were away with Mansfelt's little army on the frontiers, the nobles and deputies arrived so slowly that it was some time before there was a reasonable quorum, and indeed the total attendance at the Estates never passed 128 (49 clergy, 24 nobles, 55 Third Estate) as compared with a normal 500 or more. Eventually, with the reluctant assent of the Pope's Legate, the Cardinal of Piacenza, on 22 February they agreed to the proposed conference, though asserting that they could not agree to any heretic being acknowledged as King of France. There was further delay, this time from the royalist side on the pretext that so many of their leaders were away campaigning, but in truth largely because the King had gone off to meet his sister at Saumur to break her inclination to a match with Soissons.

In the end both sides agreed to meet at Suresnes, just outside Paris, and the conference assembled there on 19 April. After ten or eleven days of talking it became clear that no settlement could be reached with Henry so long as he remained a Protestant. Had the Spanish agents – the Duke of Feria, Dr Inigo de Mendoza, Juan Baptista de Tassis and Diego d'Ibarra – now come forward with strong offers of support in men and money for, say, the Duke of Guise or the Cardinal of Bourbon, there could have been a considerable migration of Catholic royalists over the the League's side or at least to the Third Party. Fortunately for Henry, what the Duke of Feria did propose, almost demand, on 3 May was that the Estates should acknowledge the Infanta as Queen in despite of the revered Salic Law which traditionally ruled women out of the line of succession to the throne of France. Even two weeks later Tassis merely reiterated the demand while the lawyer Mendoza rehearsed at great length the best legal arguments he could find for the Infanta's claim as the elder daughter of Henry III's sister, Philip II's third wife. In the meantime Henry IV had taken the decisive step. After discussions with his closest friends and councillors, he published on 6 May a declaration announcing that he had resolved to 'receive instruction' in the Catholic faith. To this end he summoned bishops, theologians, princes and lords, and representatives of the Parlements to gather at Mantes on 5 July to witness and assist at his abjuration.

The League envoys at Suresnes were informed of Henry's decision on 7 May and were urged to expand the existing short-term local truce around Paris into a general truce for three months for the whole kingdom. In the Estates the nobles and the Third Estate were in favour of agreeing to this. So were most of the inhabitants of Paris, now that they had tasted the benefits of their local truce. The clerical estate, however, most of the Paris preachers, and above all the Legate, were violently against it. It was therefore agreed in the Estates to postpone discussion of the truce for a time. At this point the Spanish envoys again intervened on 3 June with a new proposal. Since the Salic Law forbade the choice of a

Queen regnant, they proposed the election of the Archduke Ernest, the Austrian Habsburg whom Philip II had just appointed governor-general of the Spanish Netherlands. Let him be King with the Infanta as his wife. Once again the Spaniards were giving too little and asking too much. The Estates answered them that they could no more elect a stranger than a woman to the throne. They begged the Spaniards therefore to agree to their electing a French prince, who should marry the Infanta. A week later, amid mounting agitation in Paris for a truce, Tassis did go a little way to meet this request. He offered that Philip II would give his daughter in mariage to a French prince provided that Philip chose the prince and the Estates elected the two of them together to the throne. This did for a time raise the hopes of the Duke of Guise, and even of Nemours and the Cardinal of Bourbon. But the concession, such as it was, was too little and it came too late. On 18 June the League rump of the Paris Parlement passed a decree forbidding the election of any foreign prince or princess or any infringement of the Salic Law. Thereupon the Estates told the Spanish envoys that the time was not seasonable nor their forces sufficient to make any election. Then, despite the angry protests of the Legate, they resolved to accept the general truce for three months that Henry had offered them.

That was resolved on 10 July. Five days later at St Denis Henry IV was formally received back into the Catholic Church by the Archbishop of Bourges.[2]

The conversion can hardly have come as much of a surprise to Elizabeth or her ministers. From at least the summer of 1592 they had been amply warned about Henry's poverty, the weakness of his forces, and the pressures upon him to 'receive instruction' in the Catholic faith. There had also been ample warning that a critical moment in the affairs of the Catholic

[2] For the foregoing, see, e.g. Aubigné, VIII, 298–301; Davila, pp. 562–614; Thou, XI, 666–787; XII, 1–33; Cayet, XLI, 202–470; L'Estoile, pp. 209–302; *Mémoires de la Ligue*, V, 266–402; Villeroy, XLIV, 320–41. Of secondary works the most adequate is still Mariéjol in Lavisse, *Histoire de France*, VI, i, 358–82; see also Poirson, *Histoire de Henry IV*, I, 334–456; M. Wilkinson, *History of the League*, pp. 136–44; P. de Vaissière, *Henri IV*, pp. 410–33; J. H. M. Salmon, *Society in Crisis*, pp. 234–75; A. G. Williams, 'The Abjuration of Henry of Navarre', in *Journal of Modern History*, V, 143–71.

League was fast approaching and that there was a growing possibility of the malcontent Catholic royalists joining to form a Third Party with those Leaguers whose devotion to Catholicism did not make them ready to submit to Spanish domination. Back in May 1592 the Grand Duke of Tuscany's trusted minister Lorenzo Guicciardini wrote to Burghley that the Italian princes and many of Henry's principal supporters were pressing him to go to mass for fear that otherwise the princes and nobility would fall away from him. Only a couple of weeks later Ottywell Smith heard from Huguenots at Henry's court that d'O, Le Grand, Soissons, and Torigny, in agreement with Villeroy, were plotting a 'second League' to make the Cardinal of Bourbon king. Early in September Edmondes wrote that 'the practice of the Third Party is more strongly afoot than ever' and that the Duke of Nevers and Chancellor Cheverny were also involved in it. Ottywell Smith added the names of Marshal Aumont and the Duke of Longueville to the intriguers and Sir Roger Williams urged that 'it is not good to despair the poor King too much, fearing it may force him to join with that party which he never meant to do'.[3]

By then the Queen and her ministers, too, were well enough awake to the possibility that Henry might go to mass. On 3 October, for example, in the answer she sent by du Maurier Elizabeth wrote to him that the only assured bond to hold the hearts of his subjects 'C'est la conscience qui, se corrompant vers Dieu, comme se peut-elle conserver solide vers le Prince? Aussi si le Roi n'ait les yeux fixes sur le Roi des Rois sans branle, comme doit-il attendre ou bon succés ou assuré consistance de telles mains?' Burghley on the same day assured Bouillon of English goodwill so long as the King maintained the Gospel. He might, however, tolerate his Catholic subjects and seek to win them by gentle means since 'in no Christian history can it be found that Christian religion was established with the sword'. (Burghley must have read some curious histories!)[4]

As the months went by, the warnings multiplied. On Christmas Day Beauvoir, in begging for another 2,000 men to

---

[3] S. P. Tuscany, i, fo. 83; S. P. France, xxviii, fo. 161; xxix, fos. 31, 95, 157.
[4] Ibid., fos. 182, 189.

join Williams's small force, remarked that the King's will was unalterable in the matter of religion. But, he added somewhat illogically, necessity might reduce him to such intolerable conditions 'qu'il sera contraint de quitter la partie'.[5] In the New Year Edmondes, writing about four times a month at rather irregular intervals,[6] sent home a flow of full and generally accurate information about the meeting and discussions of the League's Estates, the demands of the Spanish envoys, the attitudes of the Catholic royalists, and the progress of the Suresnes conference. On 26 April he heard 'from assured ground' that the King would shortly be 'forced to make that metamorphosis . . . His distress is such, joined with the practice of the Catholics, as will suffer him to shape no other course.' A week later on 2 May Edmondes tackled the King himself about these reports and drew from him an assurance that he had not yet come to a decision. He also promised that he would not decide without hearing Elizabeth's advice and that he would in any case make no peace with Spain. Four days later, however, he called Edmondes to him to tell him the results of the decisive council meeting about his conversion, 'saving only that he was determined to render himself a Catholic, which he would have rather understood than published by himself'. He again promised that there would be no peace with Spain and he told Edmondes that he would be sending an envoy to seek counsel of Elizabeth.[7]

Meanwhile another envoy, despatched earlier upon a somewhat different errand, had just arrived in England. This was Beauvoir's son, the Vidame of Chartres. He had been sent before the Suresnes conference opened and before Henry had decided about becoming a Catholic. His instructions, dated 19 March, look very much like a final attempt on the King's part to see whether he could extract a substantial enough assistance from his Protestant English ally to save him from an abjuration. They began with a lengthy apologia for the King's past actions in answer to the complaints that the Queen had

[5] Ibid., fo. 394.

[6] Except in February, when only one letter from him is extant. There are twenty-six letters from him in S. P. France, xxx and xxxi from January through June 1593; twenty of them are printed in *Edmondes Papers*.

[7] S. P. France, xxx, fo. 300; xxxi, fo. 7.

sent through Beauvoir on 18 February. This was followed by reference to Spanish intrigues at the League's Estates and to the expectation that a Spanish army of 14,000 men would soon enter France to support them. Henry would bear the brunt of this, but the cause was common so all his friends should assist him. He therefore wanted Elizabeth to grant him a fixed annual loan, assured for some years, of some notable sum upon which he could rely 'pour l'aider à faire un fond'. He would give all possible assurances for its repayment as soon as his affairs allowed. Meanwhile he begged the Queen's advice, which he would treat as a holy oracle, regarding the problems that beset him. Not long after the Vidame arrived in England, letters came also from the Huguenot Duke of Bouillon to the Queen, Burghley, and Essex. These emphasized the pressure of the Catholic royalists for the King's conversion and the likelihood that he would have to yield to it for lack of means. What then would be the fate of the Huguenots? 'Croyez-moi', the Duke concluded, 'que si bientôt vous ne nous aidez, nous sommes perdus et croyez que le mal est tel que la plume ne le peut écrire mais la bouche seule le pourrait exprimer.'[8]

None of this made much impression upon the Queen. She wrote to the King on 14 May, 'mon Dieu! vos grandes affaires me semble vous font oublier si grand et important faix que je porte et aussi bien comment mal employés tous que nous mandons sont pour faute d'être accompagnés et secondés'. She was therefore withdrawing Norris's troops from Brittany, though they might return when she was sure that the King and his servants would perform their promises. She had intended to send this answer back by the Vidame, but stayed him because she had just received Edmondes' letter of 6 May reporting the King's meaning to turn Catholic and to send an envoy to her about his decision.[9]

It was not until well into June that Henry in fact despatched his envoy, Morlans, and it was early July before Morlans eventually reached the English court.[10] In the

---

[8] Ibid., xxx, fos. 218, 308.

[9] Ibid., xxxi, fo. 29.

[10] On 30 May Edmondes wrote that Morlans was being sent. But his credentials were not written until 10/20 June and it was not until 30 June that Beauvoir was at last expecting his arrival – ibid., fos. 91, 114, 118, 189; *Edmondes Papers*, pp. 78–9, 81.

meantime agonized appeals came from a number of French Huguenots. Beauvoir, reporting some of these to Burghley on 17 May, insisted that help from England could easily bring Henry to break the promise which necessity had extracted from him. Without such help, 'necessitas coget eam ad turpiam'. Bouillon also wrote 'est-il possible que telles choses se traitent et que nos voisins dorment?' He, like Sir Roger Williams and Thomas Edmondes, pressed for the sending of a person of quality as special ambassador to argue against Henry's conversion and to lend support to the Huguenots. Ottywell Smith even suggested that the Queen should 'send over some learned minister that can speak French and that hath been accustomed to dispute with the Jesuits', to argue against Henry's Catholic 'instructors' – he thought Master Cartwright or Reynolds might be suitable! What was chiefly feared was that, although the King's Catholic councillors had given a written promise to do nothing at the Suresnes conference to prejudice the present position of the Huguenots yet, as Williams said, 'God knows how long it will continue from [becoming] wars on the rest of them of the Religion' and from developing into a peace with Spain that 'will grow to our wars and more dangerous wars than we look for'.[11]

None of these pressures could alter Elizabeth's determination to recall Norris and his men from Brittany. But she did at the beginning of June promise Beauvoir to add another 1,500 men to the 1,500 already serving under Williams with the King. In continuing to insist upon the revocation of Norris's forces, it looks as if she was once again going against the unanimous advice of her Councillors. Burghley certainly disagreed with her about it. He had always regarded the security of Brittany as a paramount English interest. Yet even he could not at this time persuade her to change her mind and, according to Sir John Wolley, no one else could either.[12] Her promise to reinforce Williams may owe something to the Earl of Essex's influence. He had been sworn as a Privy

[11] S. P. France, xxxi, fos. 7, 23, 63, 65, 106, 110, 116, 178. Thomas Cartwright, the chief Puritan opponent of Archbishop Whitgift in their Cambridge days, had been released only a year before after nineteen months in the Fleet prison and a trial before the Star Chamber – A. F. Scott Pearson, *Thomas Cartwright and Elizabethan Puritanism*, pp. 317-57.

[12] *Cal. S. P. Domestic, 1591-4*, p. 348; S. P. France, xxxi, fo. 170.

Councillor on 25 February and was clearly concentrating his attention upon foreign affairs and foreign intelligences. He was cultivating Antonio Perez, who had come over to England with the Vidame. He had drawn the brothers Anthony and Francis Bacon into his service. Through them he had already established a regular correspondence with Robert Bowes, the English ambassador in Scotland, and with a Dr Morison there. He had made overtures to Edmund Palmer down at St Jean-de-Luz and was beginning to detach from the Cecils one of Walsingham's chief intelligencers, Anthony Standen. Thomas Phelippes, another of Walsingham's old servants who was still keeping up more or less unofficially his secret service connections, was also beginning to direct his intelligences towards the Earl. Essex indeed seemed to be following Francis Bacon's advice to seek a 'domestical greatness' and with the Queen's encouragement was building up diplomatic and intelligence connections to rival the Cecils' Secretarial network. And there is little doubt that in him the King of France had a most staunch friend and advocate.[13] Nevertheless, Essex was still a little hesitant about challenging the Cecils too aggressively. He had hardly yet begun his uncompromising campaign to secure Francis Bacon's appointment as attorney-general and he was for some time clearly anxious not to arouse Burghley's jealously by too obviously attracting Standen away when he arrived in England this summer.[14]

Whatever Essex's counsel may have been, nothing was done until after Morlans' arrival to levy or prepare the 1,500 men promised to Beauvoir. When Morlans did at last arrive, he brought a message that was in part disturbing, in part

---

[13] Birch, *Memoirs*, I, 72–121; *Cal. S. P. Domestic, 1591–4*, pp. 271, 358; *H. M. C., Salisbury MSS*, IV, 331; Devereux, I, 276–304; Ubaldini, in *Archivo storico italiano*, no. 464, p. 538; G. Ungerer, *A Spaniard in Elizabethan England; the Correspondence of Antonio Perez's Exile*, I, 68 ff., 148 ff., 184 ff. Anthony Standen wrote on 20 December 1593, with his usual exaggeration: 'I see all matters of intelligence are wholly in his [Essex's] hands, wherein the Queen receiveth great liking, as by her words to the father and son touching this point is known'–Birch, *Memoirs*, I, 144. In notes sent to Thomas Phelippes [in June?] Essex said that Burghley only sought to compare Antonio Perez's judgement with his own experience, whereas he (Essex) sought to get somewhat out of him on which he might found some foreign action, for all his [i.e. Perez's] plots were to make the war offensive rather than be driven to make it defensive – *Cal. S. P. Domestic, 1591–4*, p. 358.

[14] E.g. Birch, *Memoirs*, I, 104; *H. M. C., Salisbury MSS*, IV, 388.

reassuring. The King sent him 'to give Her Majesty satisfaction both of the causes of necessity moving him to the resolution of his conversion, as also with assurance what course he will run with Her Majesty, wherein', Edmondes wrote, 'if solemn vows carry credit he meaneth great faith.'[15] In other words, while Morlans was sent to tell the Queen about the King's intended conversion rather than to seek her counsel about it, he brought fulsome assurances of Henry's determination to continue the fight against Spain.

The first part of his message, about Henry's conversion, drew wails of anguish from Elizabeth. To Bouillon she wrote 'je me trouve si à la fin de mon français que je ne sais que dire si non 'avertat Deus malum a quo lavabo manus meas'.[16] To Henry she wrote:

Ah! que douleurs, oh! quels regrets, oh! que gemissements je sentais en mon âme par le son de telles nouvelles que Morlans m'a conté. Mon Dieu! est-il possible que mondain respect aucun dût effacer le terreur que la crainte divine nous menace? pouvons nous par raison même attendre bonne sequele d'acte si inique? ... Ah! c'est dangereux de mal faire pour en faire du bien. Encore j'espère que plus saine inspiration vous deviendra.

And she signed the letter 'votre très assurée soeur si ce soit à la vieille mode: avec la nouvelle je n'en ai que faire'. It is perhaps possible, however, that this letter, so often quoted from Camden onwards, may have been only a draft reflecting the Queen's first overheated reaction to Morlans' report. For – soon afterwards? – she wrote another and less hysterical letter that Sir Thomas Wilkes was to take over to the French King,[17] while she herself turned to reading the Scriptures and translating Boethius's *Consolations of Philosophy* from the Latin.[18]

Just how strongly Elizabeth's Councillors shared her feelings is not altogether easy to discover. Certainly in sending Wilkes before she despatched any more troops she was

[15] *Edmondes Papers*, p. 81.

[16] S. P. France, xxxi, fo. 311.

[17] *H. M. C., Salisbury MSS*, IV, 342–3; Camden, pp. 611–12. The copies of both letters are endorsed as 'July' and as 'minutes'. But Elizabethan endorsers were seldom very precise in describing a paper as 'draft', 'minute', or 'copy'.

[18] Camden, p. 612.

following Burghley's advice. On 10 July the old Lord Treasurer had jotted down fifteen arguments to dissuade the King from a hasty conversion and to persuade his Catholic supporters not to force him to it. In another paper he argued that the King's conversion must be not only repugnant to the Queen's conscience but also dangerous to the security of her realm since he would then become subject to the Pope, her enemy. She must consider how to aid him against Spain and the Guises, but she might reasonably forbear to increase her forces until 'she may first impart her mind to the French King and be duly informed of his manner of proceeding' against his enemies and especially for the recovery of Brittany. In any case, if the King did turn Catholic, he should certainly get help from his Italian friends as well as from England.[19]

Wilkes's instructions, drafted by Burghley on 14 July, followed these papers closely. If he arrived in time, he was to use the arguments against the King's conversion both to the King and to his leading Catholic councillors. If he came too late for that, he should still express the Queen's deep regret at seeing Henry become subject to her enemy, the Pope. He should enquire into the probable effects of the conversion upon the King's power and prospects. He should ask what were his plans for freeing Brittany from the Spaniards and what French forces could be relied upon there. Until the Queen was satisfied on these matters and was assured of a port for her troops' landing and retreat, she could send no more forces to Brittany. Wilkes was also to ask for full assurance under the King's great seal that 'he will continue jointly with us in offence and defence against the King of Spain as long as the said King of Spain shall continue his enmity against us'. Finally, he was to inform Henry that the Queen was preparing, as he had asked by the Vidame of Chartres, another 1,500 men to go over and bring Williams's forces up to 3,000. They would be ready to be transported to France as soon as she received satisfactory replies from the King.[20] These, of course, were the 1,500 men that had been promised to Beauvoir early in June and now at last in mid-July definite orders went out for them to be levied. They were to be drawn

---

[19] S. P. France, xxxi, fos. 222, 228.
[20] Ibid., fo. 248.

from sixteen counties – because of the plague London was not included this time though it was to pay for and clothe 200 – and they should be ready to reach their ports by 13 August.[21]

Wilkes can hardly have left England when on 23 July news came[22] that Henry IV had gone to mass at St. Denis on 15 July. A week later came news of the conclusion of the general truce for three months between the King and the League. Among the terms of this truce was an article requiring that all foreign troops on either side should leave the country or at least be withdrawn into garrisons.[23] At once, on 30 July, the Privy Council countermanded the orders for the levy of the 1,500 men in England and both Queen and Council wrote on 31 July and 1 August instructing Sir John Norris to bring his companies home from Brittany as soon as shipping could be sent for him. On 4 August the Council wrote a little less definitely to Sir Roger Williams. He might himself come home and should arrange for the sick and wounded to be shipped over, but he was to leave the rest for the time being under Sir Edward Brooke at Le Pollet.[24] A few days later Isaac de Vaudray, sieur de Mouy, arrived from Henry IV. He brought a lengthy explanation of the reasons for the King's conversion and also demands for aid even greater than those that the Vidame had brought. He asked the Queen to continue and to reinforce her troops in Brittany; to provide money to entertain 4,500 Swiss foot to serve with the King; to lend in addition 10,000 crowns a month 'for some time'; to send the promised 1,500 English foot to bring Williams's troops up to 3,000 men; to keep some forces on the seas; and to get Dutch help to withstand the Spanish forces preparing against Brittany.[25]

These demands drew a sharp reply from Elizabeth. She

[21] *Acts P. C.*, XXIV, 401–2, 410–16, 419–21, 431–4; *Cal. S. P. Domestic, 1591–4*, pp. 362–3; *H. M. C., Salisbury MSS*, IV, 341.

[22] Ubaldini, in *Archivo storico italiano*, no. 464, p. 538.

[23] *Mémoires de la Ligue*, V, 397–402; Cayet, XLI, 463–70.

[24] S. P. France, xxxi, fo. 302; xxxii, fo. 5; *Acts P. C.*, XXIV, 431–4, 442–3; *H. M. C., Salisbury MSS*, IV, 341, 345. In mid-September ninety-five sick and hurt men were sent over. Contrary winds forced them into Gosport and the seventy-nine who survived were paid off at Fareham on 25 September – S. P. France, xxxii, fos. 137, 169; *Cal. S. P. Domestic, 1591–4*, p. 374.

[25] S. P. France, xxxii, fo. 28; Cotton MSS, Caligula, E. ix, fo. 116.

complained that after all the efforts she had made on Henry's behalf, he did not give her time even to draw breath before asking for still more. Most of what she had previously given had been wasted through his repeated failures to keep his promises. Therefore she must wait to see what answers he gave to Wilkes before she replied to his requests by de Mouy. Thereupon Williams was instructed to bring home all the English troops from Normandy, except any who might wish to stay there in the King's service and pay. The English cannon were to be brought over at the same time.[26] The Queen had sent Sir Edward Stafford to inform Beauvoir of this decision on the evening of 23 August. It gave the ambassador one of his (not infrequent) sleepless nights and next morning (St Bartholomew's Day) he described it, with some exaggeration, as the worst news since that other St Bartholomew's Day in 1572. He admitted that the Queen had plenty of excuse for her decision, but was it wise to spit at the sky and have it blown back in your face? The Vidame and Mouy protested in a similar vein. Then, by accepting a suggestion – or perhaps, as Henry suspected, by suggesting it themselves – that the Queen should be granted as a base Le Hourdel at the mouth of the Somme, they managed to persuade her to defer recalling her troops at least until she heard Wilkes's report of Henry's answers to her demands.[27]

Wilkes was home by the beginning of September, but the answers he brought did not entirely satisfy Elizabeth. Henry had explained the reasons for his conversion in much the same terms as de Mouy had done. It was a necessity that 'no verbal reasons' could have averted. In prospect it 'promised much, whereof there appeareth as yet no great effects more than that he hath in appearance assured his estate with those that were declining from him (I mean his Catholics) by breaking the neck of the Third Party'. He had also, as Elizabeth required, sent by Wilkes a 'bond of amity' under the great seal of France, promising to continue with her an offensive and defensive war against Spain and to make no separate peace. He therefore earnestly desired the Queen not to withdraw her

[26] S. P. France, xxxii, fos. 65, 72; *Acts P. C.*, XXIV, 484–5; *Cal. S. P. Domestic, 1591–4*, pp. 370–1.
[27] S. P. France, xxxii, fos. 66, 68, 70, 156.

troops and guns from Normandy. Yet there seemed little likelihood of his having enough French or mercenary forces either there or in Brittany to make further English help decisive when the truce ended. This was especially true of Brittany. He was unable to give a definite answer about granting the English a place of retreat there and Montpensier, if he were to take the command there, required the Queen to provide 3,000 English troops, monthly pay of 10,000 crowns for 2,000 French foot, and a loan of 50,000 crowns to raise more men and artillery and munitions[28] – this, of course, on top of the demands that de Mouy had made for Normandy.

Unsatisfactory as much of Wilkes's report seemed to her, Elizabeth still agreed not to withdraw her troops from Normandy until she had an answer from the King about the cession of Le Hourdel. On 5 September Burghley wrote instructing Thomas Edmondes to require of Henry that the English troops and artillery should occupy that place. There they could be easily provisioned from England and would be free from the demands and interferings of French governors – a month ago Williams had written that the Dieppe burghers would soon begin to regard the Queen's cannon as their own and Ottywell Smith had been outraged at French gunners using his Protestant Queen's powder and shot to shoot them off in celebration of the King's going to mass. If the King agreed to deliver Le Hourdel, Edmondes was to write to Brooke to stay there with his companies; if the King refused, then to bring them home to England.[29]

Edmondes received these instructions on 18 September and secured an audience with Henry four or five days later. The King blamed de Mouy and the Huguenots for putting such an idea into the Queen's head. There was, he said, not a single house at Le Hourdel. The place would have to be fortified, which would be a breach of the truce, now extended openly for another month to the end of November (NS) and secretly to the end of December. Besides, its cession would anger Nevers, whose land it was, and Longueville. Why did they not stay at Le Pollet, which was just as good a base? When Edmondes pressed for a more definite answer, the King grew

[28] Ibid., fos. 34, 51, 58, 63, 95–6.
[29] Ibid., xxxi, fo. 262; xxxii, fos. 3, 108.

very angry and spoke of being driven to seek undesired friends, not to the Queen's benefit. In the end they compromised. Henry wrote to Beauvoir to make one more effort to get Elizabeth to allow her troops to remain. If that failed, instead of orders for Brooke to depart being sent through Edmondes, Beauvoir should write direct to the governors to let the English troops and artillery go.[30]

Edmondes's report of his audience arrived on 3 October and it looks as if it touched off some debate among the Queen's advisers. For there is an anonymous October paper – by Essex perhaps? it hardly sounds like Burghley's work[31] – on 'The dangers that may ensue to Her Majesty and the realm by abandoning the present action of the French King'. This argued that if the truce in France developed into a peace, the League would be able to extract better terms if the English troops were withdrawn. If no peace resulted, then the King would be more at the mercy of the League and Spain. He might be driven to join Spain against England. Even if he only made peace with Spain, it would be dangerous. He might make a marriage alliance and, the young Prince of Spain being 'a child weak and full of diseases', that might bring the overwhelming danger of a union of the two monarchies. If he were overthrown, Guise and the rest would certainly join Spain against England. Even if he were not overthrown, the Pope might induce him to seek revenge upon the Queen for deserting him at so critical a time, especially after his sending his 'bond of amity' by Wilkes. The Huguenots would in any event be abandoned and perhaps persecuted into leaving France. And to withdraw from Brittany would mean a Spanish conquest of that province, a most evident danger to England.

However plausible these arguments may have looked and whoever put them forward, they had little effect. For just at this time a new and seemingly urgent need for Brooke's troops elsewhere occurred. This arose out of another alarm from Sir Edward Norris that Ostend was about to be besieged. There

---

[30] Ibid., fos. 156, 158; *Lettres Missives*, IV, 36–40.

[31] There are two copies of this paper. Neither is in Burghley's hand or annotated by him (*pace* J. B. Black, *Elizabeth and Henry IV*, p. 68 note) – S. P. France, xxxii, fos. 287, 414.

was rather more justification than usual for his anxiety. Count Charles Mansfelt was again assembling his forces in the villages around St Omer and gathering artillery and munitions at Gravelines. It was quite possible that his aim was Calais or Boulogne, both of whose governors had recently died, rather than Ostend. What he intended might well be some frontier demonstration there in favour of the League, since he was not strong enough to march to Paris. Nevertheless his forces *were* also within striking distance of Ostend and Sir Edward Norris had on this occasion some reason to clamour for supplies and reinforcements. And, indeed, an attempt from Ostend had been intended.[32]

Supplies of victuals and munitions were speedily organized from both England and Zeeland. But where were the reinforcements to come from? Sir Edward wrote (somewhat wildly) of 25,000–30,000 enemy troops, with 6,000 pioneers and eighty cannon, coming to besiege him. He reckoned that he would need at the very least 1,000 or 1,500 more men that the 1,074 foot (nine companies) and forty-nine horse that the last muster of his garrison showed. At the end of October the Queen did order three foot-bands to be sent to him from Flushing.[33] Yet even in the unlikely event of those bands being fully up to strength, they would still amount to no more than 405 men. The States of Zeeland also sent two companies, again not above 250 men at the best. It was hard to see where more could be found in the Netherlands. The English troops there had been seriously depleted by withdrawals for service in France. Flushing could not well spare any more of the seven foot-bands left there after the three had gone to Ostend. Brielle had only four foot-bands, few enough for its garrison. The two English foot-bands left at Bergen-op-Zoom had gone off with Sir Francis Vere and part of the States' field force to help Count William Louis defend Friesland and Overijsel against Verdugo and the reinforcements come to him from old Count Mansfelt's army in Brabant since the surrender of Geertruidenberg. And the rest of that army had been pinning

[32] Ibid., fos. 216, 244, 277; S. P. Holland, xlvii, fos. 89, 95, 99; *Cal. S. P. Domestic, 1591–4*, pp. 382–5; *Correspondance de Philippe II*, IV, 210.

[33] S. P. Holland, xlvii, fos, 94, 99, 123–4, 126, 129, 146, 154, 205; *Resolutiën der Staten Generaal*, VIII, 33.

down the remainder of the Dutch field forces in defence of Heusden, the Bommelerwaard, and Nijmegen.[34] It is true that during the latter part of October both sides were beginning to withdraw into winter quarters, but after a particularly hard summer's campaigning few of the States' field forces were by now in much shape for further active service.

The one force, at once sizeable and experienced, within reasonable distance of Ostend was that 1,200 men under Sir Edward Brooke at Le Pollet. So on 8 October orders were sent to Brooke to embark his companies as soon as shipping arrived. Ottywell Smith was told to ship the Queen's artillery with them. The Queen wrote on 7 October to inform the King of these withdrawal orders. Late on 16 October, before the orders arrived, Brooke received letters from the King asking him to bring his men from Le Pollet and march with him to relieve Fécamp which Villars was besieging in spite of the truce. But upon the King's approach, Villars raised his siege and entered into negotiations. So after marching out five leagues, the English returned to the little village of Appeville, half a mile from Dieppe.[35]

This march drew sharp reprimands from the Queen and Privy Council. On 24 October Brooke was told that shipping was on its way to Dieppe – it left Dover on 28 October – and that he and his men were to be ready to embark as soon as it arrived, regardless of any commands or entreaties from the French King. They were to go to Dover or the Downs, where some of the Council would be waiting to direct them with other companies to Ostend. Before these orders arrived Henry made yet another bid to retain the English troops. On 26 October he told Edmondes that if his negotiations with Villars came to nothing, he meant to press Rouen and Le Havre hard. To that end, if the Queen would allow her troops to stay, he was prepared to put them into Harfleur, with leave to re-fortify it. His offer must be kept very secret, for if Villars got wind of it he would break off his negotiations and burn Harfleur. On the morning of 30 October, however, the *Quittance* and four hoys arrived at Dieppe to carry the English

---

[34] S. P. Holland, xlvii, fos. 30, 34, 48, 64, 68, 70, 97; *Resolutiën der Staten Generaal,* VIII, 20–32, 61–8; Markham, *The Fighting Veres,* p. 190.

[35] S. P. France, xxxii, fos. 205, 220, 238, 240, 256; *H. M. C., Salisbury MSS,* IV, 404–5.

troops away to Ostend. Henry did not believe that Ostend was likely to be besieged at this time of year. Any offensive plans that the enemy had were, he thought, much more likely to be aimed at Boulogne. But in face of the categorical orders that Brooke had from Queen and Council, the King felt unable to detain them any longer, though he did still hold up the embarkation of the Queen's artillery. Yet even now he had not quite given up all hope. In a last desperate bid he instructed Beauvoir to offer Elizabeth possession of Harfleur, with permission to fortify it as soon as the truce ended, provided that by then she sent back Brooke's troops, reinforced to 3,000 men, to serve with himself and in addition to those needed to garrison Harfleur.

It was not a particularly tempting offer. Harfleur had a good haven that could take ships of up to 120 tons. The town was only slightly commanded by neighbouring hills. It was well situated both to cut off Rouen's trade and Le Havre's water supply. But it was at present unfortified. It was in a very advanced and exposed position, very close to Leaguer Le Havre and just across the water from Leaguer Honfleur. Villars, if he remained loyal to the League, was unlikely to leave an English garrison undisturbed in a position so threatening to both his governments. If he made his peace with the King, as seemed not unlikely, would the offer of Harfleur still hold? And even if it held, the Queen was specifically required not to levy any taxes or duties there by land or by sea. Apart from these not very attractive features about the offer of Harfleur, there were one or two other matters that did little to increase Elizabeth's readiness to listen to Henry's pleas for further help. One was that, after refusing Le Hourdel to her partly on the ground that to grant it would annoy the Duke of Nevers, he had almost immediately put a Huguenot in it without consulting the Catholic Duke.[36]

Another reason for doubt, rather more sinister-looking, was that, without informing her, the King had sent one of his servants, La Varenne, to Spain to look into proposals made secretly by an agent of Bernardino de Mendoza for peace with

[36] S. P. France, xxxii, fos. 265, 277, 279, 294–5, 308.

Spain and possibly a marriage between Henry and the Infanta. The mission itself could not be kept secret, though its purpose could only be guessed at. Henry tried to explain it away by saying that La Varenne had been sent in response to overtures from Mendoza to Marshal Matignon; that he had strict instructions only to listen and observe, not to propose or agree to anything; that he had brought back information which enabled Matignon to nip in the bud a plot at Bordeaux; and that, anyway, the matter was so slight that he did not think it needful to trouble the Queen with it – Bouillon said that the officials just forgot! As soon as La Varenne returned, Henry sent him over to make his own report to the Queen, but the incident did not encourage her to new efforts on the King's behalf.[37]

On 13 November she gave what proved to be her final answer. She wrote to Henry, and Howard, Hunsdon, and Sir Robert Cecil informed Beauvoir, that after the loss of so many men and so much money during the past years owing to her troops' lack of a base and lack of French support, she was no longer ready to respond to his appeals.[38] It was the end, apart from Brittany, of four years of active English military intervention in France. Outside Brittany, no more English troops were to serve in Henry IV's wars except for a couple of thousand that were to be sent over to Picardy under Sir Thomas Baskerville in October 1596 after the Spaniards' capture of Calais, remaining there until the Peace of Vervins in May 1598.

A final decision about Sir John Norris's troops in Brittany was still a good way further off. The recall orders of 31 July were slightly modified on 14 August. If Norris was already going with Aumont, as he was, to raise Mercoeur's siege of Moncontour, fifteen miles inland from St Brieuc, then he might stay for that special service. But once it was over he was to return and the Queen still refused to send the reinforcement of 2,000 men that he asked for. She also sharply reprimanded

---

[37] Ibid., fos. 193, 211, 306, 312; *H. M. C., Salisbury MSS,* IV, 367–8, 401, 421; XIII, 489; Birch, *Memoirs,* I, 133; Cayet, XLII, 80–3; Cheverny, *Mémoires* (ed. Petitot, XXXVI), p. 267; Du Plessis-Mornay, *Mémoires et Correspondance,* IV, 563; despatches of Calvert and Caron, quoted in J. L. Motley, *History of the United Netherlands,* III, 306–9.
[38] S. P. France, xxxii, fos. 308, 310.

him for trying to draw over to Paimpol the 600 men she had
recently sent to defend the Channel Islands against the thirty
sail of Spaniards said to be coming round from Blavet and
already past Le Conquet. She once again demanded to know
why he had not reduced his companies from thirty-two to
twenty-two (3,350 heads) as she had ordered months ago. She
complained bitterly that she had spent 400,000 crowns on the
service in Brittany, 150,000 since Norris had returned there,
and all to no profit. She did not blame Norris for the lack of
success during the past eleven months. For that she laid the
fault upon Aumont, as she had done in a very blunt letter to
him back in July.[39]

Before these new orders reached Norris, Mercoeur had on
16 August, raised his siege of Moncontour and accepted the
three months' truce arranged between the King and the
League. Operations in Brittany were thus suspended. Thereupon Aumont promised to put Norris's men into garrison in
Paimpol and the Île de Bréhat. Norris reported all this on
17 August. When his letter was received, 'upon these matters
and reading of your letters before Her Majesty and her
Council hath grown this day', Burghley wrote to Norris on
26 August, 'much diversity of opinion, Her Majesty a great
while utterly misliking your longer stay there by taking of
Paimpol'. She argued that by Norris's former letters it
appeared that the place was slenderly fortified and would
need constant provision, as well as pioneers and workmen, out
of England. Also he had described it as untenable against an
enemy siege unless she enabled the King to keep an army in
the field in Brittany. Further he had said that without another
great supply from England the numbers now there were too
few to do any good service when the truce ended. This 'Her
Majesty hath all this summertime refused, notwithstanding
all the motions made by the French King and his ambassador
here and the Marshal and you there, in which mind she still
continueth.'

Nevertheless, 'though Her Majesty held therefore these
arguments of long time, yet upon arguments made by her

---

[39] Ibid., xxxi, fos. 233, 297; xxxii, fos. 21, 32, 38; *H. M. C., Salisbury MSS*, IV, 336–7,
340, 353–4, 359–60.

Council to the contrary she changed her opinion.' For on the contrary it was alleged that Norris's return would make the enemy think that she was utterly abandoning the King's cause there. Paimpol and Bréhat, moreover, would give a good footing in the country. They had good communications by sea with the Channel Isles and England. If the English did not hold them, Mercoeur would certainly seize them when the truce ended. 'And so in conclusion it was advised that Her Majesty would continue her charge until the end of the truce.' Norris might take Paimpol and stay there 'as yourself shall think it fit and convenient. Or otherwise, if it should be refused you or you find it not convenient', then he should obey his former instructions and shipping would be sent to carry him and his troops home.

After sleeping on this decision, however, the Queen's doubts recurred. The next day she added more conditions. Besides coming away if Paimpol and Bréhat were refused to him, Norris was also to bring his troops home if those places could only be had with difficulty or if he were not given the sole command over them. The fact was, Burghley told Norris, that 'her mind is rather disposed to have you come away than to tarry, and yet she saith she yieldeth unto your tarrying because she findeth us that be of her Council to be of that mind'. It was a classic example of the perennial struggle between instinct and reason that made Elizabeth I such a problem to her more soberly rational Privy Councillors such as Lord Burghley.[40]

The decision whether to stay or to come home was thus virtually passed back to Sir John Norris. At first, while warning Burghley that the English troops' recall would be followed within a month by the melting away of the King's party and a Spanish conquest of Brittany, he thought that they could safely wait at Paimpol and Bréhat.[41] But when it came to actually handing over those places, Aumont very considerably modified his promises. He would not now yield the Île de Bréhat at all because of the opposition of its governor and of the Breton gentry. He would not allow any

---

[40] S. P. France, xxxii, fos. 42, 82, 84.
[41] Ibid., fos. 78, 80, 81.

fortifying at Paimpol either during or after the truce and the only remunerative impositions and customs dues there were not to be granted to the Queen. Elizabeth's immediate reaction to this news was once again to order Norris and his men to come home immediately. Sir John Hawkins and Captain George Fenner were ordered to provide shipping for them. By 20 September they had already chartered eight hoys of Ipswich, Harwich, and Colchester, which would be victualled and ready to sail, they promised, in another three days. Then once again the Queen's instincts yielded to the reasonings of her Councillors and the protests of the French ambassador. On 22 September the orders for the troops' recall were cancelled and the chartered shipping released. Norris and his companies were now to remain in Brittany until Beauvoir obtained answers from the King to the Queen's demand for the Île de Bréhat and for payment by him or the Bretons of any further troops she might be induced to send there.[42]

Meanwhile Norris, too, had put in another strong plea to stay and to be reinforced. On receiving Burghley's letters of 26 and 27 August on 28 September he wrote that he saw no reason why, as the King was unable to provide the forces needed, the Queen should not supply the defect rather than allow Brittany to fall into Spanish and Leaguer hands. He had repeatedly warned that no reliance could be placed upon the French. It was the Queen's persistent refusal to provide adequate forces of her own that had caused the waste of her past efforts. With 4,000 men and artillery he could do real service; he could even within a month win Morlaix. The Queen, however, would never listen to his advice or heed his warnings. In more than one earlier letter he had grumbled that she misliked both him and his service. The reason, he suspected, was the influence of one about her who would have had another man filling his post – was he perhaps thinking of Essex and Sir Roger Williams?[43]

Norris's grumblings, as we saw during the 1589 Portugal expedition, were usually the product of a very blinkered

[42] Ibid., fos. 103, 147, 149; *Cal. S. P. Domestic, 1591–4*, 371–2.
[43] S. P. France, xxxii, fos. 105, 178.

outlook. On this present occasion, too, he was also finding Paimpol a less secure base for his troops than he had hoped. He was therefore growing more and more anxious about their safety as the end of the truce drew nearer. As against his 1,800–1,900 men,[44] there were several hundred Lorrainers only four leagues away at St Brieuc, some of the League's French regiments about Lamballe, and the Spaniards–who might number 2,700 – only ten leagues away at Pontivy (his leagues do seem rather long ones). There were, of course, some Breton royalist forces that might help him, but they were neither numerous nor very certain. Paimpol, admittedly, had an admirable and uncommanded situation, but its fortifications were poor and weak. It contained no more than forty houses and those mostly in ruins, while the Île of Bréhat was worse, 'an open wild thing inhabited with a few poor fishermen' and yielding neither provision nor firewood. What was no less serious, the inner haven at Paimpol was dry at low tide and shallow at other times except with a spring tide, though there were always four or five fathoms at the entrance and around the Île de Bréhat. There were also continual reports that Mercoeur was again mobilizing and that the Spaniards were planning a surprise attack upon the English forces.[45]

Accordingly, although the duration of the truce was extended, as its ending drew nearer there was increased pressure upon Elizabeth to let her forces stay in Brittany and indeed to reinforce them. Marshal Aumont and St Luc both wrote to support Norris's pleas and the Estates of Brittany sent a special envoy, de Karanton, over to England. They all received the same chilly answer that in view of the repeated failure of French support for her troops – who were after all only auxiliaries, not principals, in the struggle – the Queen could no longer continue her aid regardless of the claims of her own country. Norris meanwhile was begging 'that we may no longer be delayed with irresolutions'.[46] On 11 December, ten days before the truce finally expired, he was sent his answer. At Burghley's suggestion, the Queen directed him to ship his

[44] Ibid., fos. 173, 269.
[45] Ibid., fos. 130, 178, 185, 195, 229.
[46] Ibid., fos. 218, 222, 227, 273, 283, 292.

companies to the Channel Isles. That would save them from the risk of another Craon disaster, yet would leave them conveniently placed to return into Brittany if better terms and more reliable promises could be extracted from the French. John Troughton was appointed to impress twelve ships from Southampton, Poole, Weymouth, and Lyme to carry the troops from Paimpol to Jersey and Guernsey with the help of such small barks as those Islands could provide. The ships should then (again as Burghley suggested) remain about the Islands for some time, ready to carry the troops either back to Brittany or home to England.[47]

Sir Edward Brooke's companies had already departed from Normandy and now Sir John Norris had orders to come out of Brittany. For the moment it almost looked as if, for the first time in nearly three years there would not be a single soldier in the Queen's pay left on French soil. It was not to turn out quite like that, for a new Spanish threat in Brittany was to keep English troops there for another twelve months. Nevertheless the turn of the year from 1593 to 1594 did witness a further development in Elizabethan England's withdrawal from involvement in French affairs.

Nor was a determination to limit commitments in France accompanied by any inclination to increase commitments in the Netherlands. Elizabeth had responded very promptly when Ostend seemed seriously threatened, whether or not she and her Council shared Sir Edward Norris's belief that the Spaniards coveted the town as a base for an invasion of England – 'to make a haven here able to contain a navy that shall command all these seas and land in England at their pleasure'.[48] But when, by mid-November, the threat to Ostend passed, neither Queen nor Council showed any disposition to add to the military aid that they had promised to the United Provinces by the 1585 Treaty. On 27 October the States General had written to Elizabeth, Burghley, Lord Admiral Howard, and Essex asking them to send over by the end of February or beginning of March 3,000–4,000 English troops, paid for four months. They needed them to help Count

[47] Ibid., fos. 366, 370; *Cal. S. P. Domestic, 1591–4*, pp. 392–3; *Cal. S. P. Domestic, Addenda*, pp. 357–8.
[48] S. P. Holland, xlvii, fos. 89, 124.

William Louis reduce the town of Groningen and the region
north of the Rhine and Maas, as Elizabeth had urged in a
letter of 22 August. At the same time they had to hold off the
main enemy field army in Brabant and Gelderland and the
great reinforcements said to be coming to the new Spanish
governor-general, the Archduke Ernest. Getting no reply to
their appeal, they wrote again in December, repeating the
request and adding that it should not prevent the Queen
sending another 3,000 to serve with the French King.[49]

At the same time the States sent Sir Francis Vere over to
raise an English regiment of 1,500 men at their expense and in
their pay. This the Queen granted readily enough when Vere
arrived. The men were to be levied from fourteen counties and
to embark 900 at London, 200 at Harwich, and 400 at
Southampton.[50] The earlier requests, for 3,000 men at the
Queen's expense, met with a less ready response. They had
been made, she wrote to the States on 10 January 1594, when
less was known of Spanish designs against her realm and when
there were fewer of her troops in the Low Countries than there
were now. Now that the eight 'Normandy' companies (nominally 1,250 men) had returned, she did not expect that the
States would expect another 3,000 men in her pay in addition
to the 1,500 in their pay that Vere was raising. Moreover, to
grant so large a request would distaste her subjects with her
government and incline them to believe that she had little
care for them, something that her enemies, the priests and
seminarists, were always insinuating. This would be the more
likely because, despite all the increase in strength and wealth
that her help had brought to the Provinces, she had never
been offered one penny's reimbursement of her great expenses
in their behalf. However, she would say no more on that point
since they had assured her that if she gave them help on this
one more occasion 'ne nous sera besoin de toucher une autre
fois à cette corde'.[51]

Thus Elizabeth not only looked upon Vere's 1,500 men and

---

[49] Ibid., fos. 21, 72, 113, 115, 179, 181; *Kronijk*, XX, 74–6; *Resolutiën der Staten Generaal*, VIII, 43–4, 103.

[50] S. P. Holland, xlvii, fos. 185, 189; *Cal. S. P. Domestic, 1591–4*, p. 411; *H. M. C., Salisbury MSS*, IV, 468–9.

[51] S. P. Holland, xlviii, fo. 23.

the eight 'Normandy' companies, with perhaps two or three more bands from the English garrisons, as providing the 3,000 men that the States had originally asked for. She was also hinting very broadly indeed that, when once this service was over, she would expect the Dutch to begin repaying their nine years' debts for her assistance.

# XXIII

# The Spanish Threat to Brest
# and the Taking of Groningen

'Never any King of this land was able to continue wars beyond
seas above one year.' So Dr Bartholomew Clark had written in
1586.[1] By limiting her military forces in the Netherlands and
France to strictly auxiliary roles, Elizabeth by the autumn of
1593 had managed to continue them beyond seas for a full
eight years. Nevertheless the difficulties and discontents over
the levyings of men for Brittany and Normandy in 1592–3,
and the twenty-four-days long debates in the Commons upon
the government's unprecedented demands for three subsidies,
to be collected within three years, had warned her that she
was nearing the limits of the burdens her subjects would
tolerate. Moreover, as Privy Councillors had repeatedly told
that 1593 Parliament, there were growing dangers nearer
home. Many of the reports coming in about Spanish naval
preparations were no doubt at present considerably exaggerated. Those preparations were still directed mainly to the
protection of Spain's American treasure and American trade
and to supplying the Spanish troops in Brittany. They did not
yet look like another 'Invincible Armada'. Even so the revival
of Spain's ocean sea power was real and was becoming
increasingly menacing. It looked all the more menacing
since the discovery of the Spanish Blanks had seemed to
reveal a maturing plot to make Scotland the base for
a combined Spanish and Scottish Catholic invasion of
England. James VI, too, did not appear to be over-eager to
take action against those northern Scottish earls whose seals
had been appended to the Blanks. There was, indeed, some
ground to suspect him of toying with Spanish and Catholic
overtures, if only as a means of heightening his bargaining
power with Elizabeth. And besides Scotland, there was
Ireland. Already in the spring of 1593 Hugh O'Donnell, one of

[1] *Cal. S. P. Foreign*, XXI, ii, 248.

the leading Ulster chieftains, had sent the Catholic Archbishop of Tuam to seek Spanish aid[2] and Hugh O'Neill, Earl
of Tyrone, was beginning to move cautiously towards open
rebellion.

Elizabeth therefore had good reason to look to her own
defence and to draw back from her military commitments on
the Continent. It was in part to find out how far she could
draw back with safety that in October 1593 she decided to
send Sir Robert Sidney on a special embassy to France. The
primary purpose of his mission was to give support to an
assembly of representatives from the Huguenot churches that
Henry IV had called together at Mantes. Bouillon, du Plessis,
Henry's sister Princess Catherine, and other leading Huguenots had begged the Queen to send a special ambassador for
this purpose.[3] On 26 October instructions were accordingly
drafted[4] for Sidney to go over to France and in concert with
the Huguenot leaders to urge the King to confirm and amplify
the liberties granted to them by former kings. He should warn
Henry not to let himself be misled into harsh measures by his
Catholic councillors who had seduced him into changing his
own faith. For a number of reasons, among them fresh
requests from Henry for further assistance 'in divers natures
and upon several conditions', it was another month before
Sidney was actually sent off. He then took with him revised
and expanded instructions, dated 20 November.[5] According to
these, his main purpose was still to support the Huguenots'
claims for at least their former liberties. He was also to urge
the King to decide upon their cause before he received either
allowance or rejection of his conversion from the Pope, who
could not then well object to an accomplished fact. Besides
this, Sidney was to take over the Queen's reciprocal 'bond of
amity', which would have been sent long ago had not
Beauvoir pressed for it to be delivered by an Englishman.

The most substantial addition to Sidney's instructions
directed him to discover upon what basis the King rested his
hopes of raising and paying the field army to which he wanted

[2] *Cal. S. P. Spanish*, IV, 608–12.
[3] S. P. France, xxxii, fos. 193, 213.
[4] Ibid., fo. 258.
[5] Ibid., fo. 330.

Elizabeth to contribute a contingent of her troops. For, the Queen's instructions added,

we never mean again to be taxed for sending over our men upon any conditions unless by more than their probabilities we may be ascertained of such forces to be adjoined and maintained as may (being well paid and like to keep together) not leave ours to the hazard of bearing the whole brunt of such and so potent armies as the King pretendeth will fall upon him.

Clearly, she was more than ever determined that, even if she were to continue to provide troops to support the French King, those troops should have a very definitely auxiliary role. How much, indeed, her mind was already moving back still further, towards its pre-interventionist ways of thinking, was manifested in a verbal addition to Sidney's instructions that she gave him at his last audience with her before he left court. If Henry, she said, showed himself obdurate or hostile to her pleas, Sidney might tell him that, if he did not show favour to the Huguenots, she would have to support their cause against him as she had done against the Valois kings.[6]

Sidney left court on 30 November, but was then held up at Dover for almost six weeks by contrary winds and storms in the Channel. After a rough crossing, he eventually reached Dieppe on 9 January.[7] There he stayed another couple of weeks awaiting an escort before moving on to Mantes and then to Chartres in time for Henry's coronation and 'sacring'.[8] The Huguenot assembly at Mantes had ended before he arrived there and leading Huguenots urged him not to speak too high in their behalf nor descend to any particular demands. Most of them agreed that the King had granted as much as the times would allow. Sidney therefore should only press for the enforcement of what the King had already promised and especially for the written confirmation of his verbal promise of matters additional to the renewed Edict of 1577. There was thus comparatively little that Sidney could

---

[6] Ibid., fo. 382. Not surprisingly, Sidney begged Burghley to get this confirmed for him in writing.

[7] Ibid., fos. 374, 380, 382, 384, 388; xxxiii, fos. 16, 21; *H. M. C., De L'Isle and Dudley MSS,* II, 145–6; Birch, *Memoirs,* I, 136–7, 146.

[8] S. P. France, xxxiii, fos. 38, 44, 50, 64, 83; *H. M. C., De L'Isle and Dudley MSS,* II, 146–7.

do about the chief original purpose of his mission. At his private audience on 11 February he did ask the King to show favour to those of the Religion. This Henry readily promised to do. He would also see that his promises were enforced. And he had, he said, left the Huguenots more places to preach in than they had men to preach. But he could only give a written act to confirm the verbal and additional promises he had made to them if his friends gave him enough military forces to dominate his realm. Once again he pressed his demand for 3,000 English infantry to join him in the field. With them he would hope to have 14,000 foot and 6,000 horse to oppose the gathering forces of Spain and the League, which he put at 18,000–20,000 men, though Bouillon doubted if they were as many as that. Without those English, he would be unable to keep the field or to keep his towns loyal. Certainly, Sidney felt, he was not yet so strong that the Huguenots need fear him, especially as the recent failure of the Duke of Nevers' mission to Rome had much sharpened the Catholics against the Pope. Nor was there any reason to doubt Henry's personal goodwill towards the Huguenots or his sincerity in promising that 'he will look through his fingers, as much as concerns him, if they do more than is allowed them'. For the time being at least there was no great cause to worry about the position and treatment of the Huguenots.[9]

In other ways, too, the reports that Sidney brought back were encouraging. The King, at his audience, reiterated his determination not to enter into any treaty with Spain without Elizabeth's privity. 'It is', he said, 'his occupation "espoiler les Espagnols".' He was eager to organize an offensive and defensive league among the enemies of Spain, if the Queen would agree to it. He wished also to ruin the House of Lorraine, but that again must depend upon what assistance his neighbours afforded him. Without their assistance, he must help himself as best he could. He had no present dealings with the Pope, but here, too, much would depend upon how far his neighbours helped him to strengthen his authority in France.[10]

Apart from the repeated demands for English troops, all

[9] S. P. France, xxxiii, fos. 64, 89, 103, 124; *H. M. C., De L'Isle and Dudley MSS*, II, 148.
[10] Ibid., pp. 147–8.

518 *The Spanish Threat to Brest and the Taking of Groningen*

this was eminently satisfactory. More satisfactory still were
Sidney's reports and the news brought by Thomas Edmondes
when he came home on leave early in March,[11] of Leaguer
towns and nobles coming over to the King. Even before the
truce ended on 31 December (New Style), Vitry had brought
over Meaux, which controlled the Marne valley approaches to
Paris, and Villeroy's son Alincourt had promised to yield
Pontoise, which dominated both the Seine and the Oise below
the capital. During January towns 'seem to come headlong
one upon another'. Lyons and Aix-en-Provence definitely
declared for the King and many more places and people were
treating with him. In February La Châtre brought over
Orléans and Bourges, Macon deserted the League, and
Villeroy came into the King's council. On 15 February the
Spaniard Juan Baptista de Tassis wrote to Philip II from Paris
that Henry, with what he by now possessed, was already a
powerful King of France.[12] Then on 12 March came the
greatest defection of all. On that day Henry IV entered Paris
amid the acclamations of the overwhelming majority of the
city's inhabitants. The city, as Davila said, had always been
the League's 'first basis and principal foundation', and
Henry's entry, as a more modern historian adds, 'marks in a
very real sense the end of the League'.[13] Sidney had entered
with Henry and could report as an eye-witness upon this
decisive development.

By the time Sidney reached home in April a veritable
avalanche of defections was under way following the example
of the capital. Villars had brought over – at a goodly
price – Rouen, Le Havre, Harfleur, Pont Audemer, and
Verneuil, so that with the surrender of Neufchâtel the whole
of Normandy would be for the King when once Montpensier
had reduced Honfleur. In Picardy, Abbeville, Peronne,
Montdidier, Roye, and Montreuil; in Champagne, Troyes,
Sens, and Chaumont; in Burgundy, Auxerre and Avalon;
Riom in Auvergne; in the west, Périgueux, Rodez, and Sarlat;
Agen, Villeneuve, and Marmande in Guyenne – all these were
by then returned to the King's obedience and Toulouse was

---

[11] S. P. France, xxxiii, fos. 101, 103.
[12] Quoted in Lavisse, *Histoire de France*, VI, i, 385.
[13] Davila, p. 643; M. Wilkinson, *History of the League*, p. 150.

secretly treating with him.[14] As early as 15 March Sidney had written to Burghley 'I think that by the end of this year, if the King live he will have no other enemy in France but upon the frontiers and in Brittany', especially if the Queen sent him the 3,000 English troops that he was asking for.[15] By April there seemed good reason to anticipate that this prophecy would be fulfilled even without the help of English troops. Accordingly, to the acute distress of Henry's ambassador, Beauvoir la Nocle, Elizabeth turned a completely deaf ear to his and his master's urgent pleas for those 3,000 English infantry to serve against Mansfelt and the Spanish forces from the Low Countries.[16]

As the summer of 1594 wore on, even Henry's calls for English help on his eastern frontier died away. He was just too late to prevent Mansfelt taking La Capelle early in May, but he countered by himself laying siege to Laon on 15 May. He hoped to take it within three weeks, although as so often happened this proved an over-optimistic expectation. It was 'a town of very great strength', perched upon a ridge rising steeply some 300 feet out of the plains of Picardy, and it held out for almost eight weeks. Nevertheless Mansfelt and Mayenne were not strong enough to raise the siege and their two attempts to send in supplies were both heavily defeated. In fact, when Henry sat down before Laon Edmondes, now back from leave, was able to report that he had 3,500 horse and 14,000–15,000 foot against the enemy's 1,200 horse and 10,000 foot at the very most. Henry himself admitted to Beauvoir that he had forces enough to fight a battle without abandoning his siege.[17]

By the latter part of June, it is true, Henry's forces were in usual fashion dwindling fairly fast. But Mansfelt's were dwindling even faster and by mid-July Edmondes reported them as a mere 4,000 foot and 300 horse. By then Mansfelt

[14] S. P. France, xxxii, fos. 372, 395; xxxiii, fos. 5, 12, 50, 54, 64, 75, 101, 136, 138; Birch, *Memoirs,* I, 170; Davila, pp. 627–41; Thou, XII, 107–54; Cayet, XLII, 112–44, 185–220, 231–8; L'Estoile, pp. 351–416.

[15] S. P. France, xxxiii, fo. 138.

[16] Ibid., fos. 196, 206, 240.

[17] Ibid., fos. 240, 277, 285; *Edmondes Papers,* p. 135; Cheverny, *Mémoirs,* p. 279. Even as early as April 1593 Count Charles had told Fuentes that he had only 4,300 foot and 800 horse – J. L. Motley, *History of the United Netherlands,* III, 258.

had left his army and gone back to Brussels, Mayenne and Guise were both treating with Henry IV, and Elboeuf was about to come over to him. Then, on 23 July Laon surrendered.[18] Another spate of defections from the League followed. Cambrai and Poitiers had already made their peace and before the end of August Château-Thierry, Amiens, Beauvais, Doullens, and away in Guyenne Lussan's Blaye also declared for the King. Noyon, St Malo, and Toulouse followed in September and early in November the young Duke of Guise was bought off, bringing with him Reims and all the rest of Champagne. At the same time the old Duke of Lorraine made his peace and transferred a number of his troops to the French King's service.[19]

By the end of 1594 Mayenne still kept an uneasy control over most of the duchy of Burgundy and over Soissons, Ham, and La Fère in Picardy. The Duke of Savoy still threatened the borders of Provence and Dauphiné. But, as Sidney had predicted, apart from Brittany the King had virtually no enemy in France except upon the frontiers. And this remarkable change in his fortunes had come about without any military assistance from England. For the last six months Henry had almost ceased to beg for such assistance. While Laon was surrendering he had suggested, rather tentatively, to Edmondes (as he also suggested to the Dutch) that French, English, and Dutch might combine to invade Artois and Hainault and partition those provinces between them. But Edmondes assured him that Elizabeth was unlikely to rise to such a bait. Having formerly refused to accept the sovereignty of the whole Low Countries, he did not imagine that she would now savour the taste of a part whereof she had refused the whole. Nor would she want to see the French settling a possession there or those of the Low Countries changing their dependency upon her to a dependency upon France which that proceeding would draw on. With the growing unity of France, in fact, the old deep-seated English fear of French

[18] S. P. France, xxxiii, fos. 305, 323, 345, 349, 365, 381. For the siege of Laon, see Davila, pp. 644–53; Thou, XII, 280–9; Cayet, XLII, 238–48.

[19] S. P. France, xxxiii, fos. 277, 365; xxxiv, fos. 4, 149; Davila, pp. 652–5; Thou, XII, 289–302. Mayenne was almost in despair, cp. the copies of his intercepted letters in *H. M. C., Salisbury MSS*, IV, 588–93, sent by Edmondes to Burghley on 26 September – S. P. France, xxxiv, fos. 149, 151.

expansion into the Netherlands was coming to the surface again, as it had done briefly after Ivry at the time of Ste. Aldegonde's offers and Wilkes's mission to Holland in 1590. This, no doubt, helps to explain the lack of response to Henry's later suggestion that Elizabeth should send troops to reinforce Bouillon who he left to defend his north-eastern frontier while the King himself went southwards to assure Lyons and those parts against Savoy, Nemours, and their Spanish allies.[20] Now that the French King was so largely master of his realm, the defence of France's frontiers was a job for Frenchmen, not for new, costly, and unpopular levies of Englishmen.

This had been Elizabeth's attitude ever since the autumn of 1593 – with one exception: Brittany, and in particular Brest. On the overriding need to keep the northern and western coasts and ports of Brittany out of enemy, especially Spanish, hands, the Queen and her Councillors were very well agreed. The problem was how to secure this without either assuming the role and the burdens of a principal in the Breton civil war or else risking the destruction of her forces if they were limited to an auxiliary role and an auxiliary strength. For the Breton royalists were very hard put to it to hold their own even against Mercoeur's Leaguers, let alone against Leaguers and Spaniards combined; and Henry IV was too busy elsewhere, and too penurious everywhere, to send them more than the most meagre and transient support.

On 11 December 1593, as we have seen, the Queen, at Burghley's suggestion, had tried to deal with this problem by ordering Sir John Norris to ship his troops across to the Channel Isles. There they would be safe from the enemy yet handy to return to Brittany if the situation on the mainland improved. About a fortnight later a letter of 20 December arrived in which Norris reported a request from Sourdéac for help to defend Brest against a probable enemy attack. The occasion of this appeal seems to have been the arrival of the Leaguer Count de la Maignane with 800–900 troops at Le Faou, about 15 miles inland at the landward end of Brest roads. It looks somewhat doubtful whether La Maignane

---

[20] *H. M. C., Salisbury MSS,* IV, 559–60; XIII, 513; S. P. France, xxxiv, fo. 196.

actually had designs upon Brest at this stage, for his next move, in January, was away southwards towards Quimper. Nevertheless Elizabeth wrote off to Norris on 28 December repeating her orders for him to withdraw to the Channel Isles but also commanding him to assure Sourdéac at once 'of your goodwill to give him succours of a convenient number which yourself will bring to him' – and the number 'we wish to be rather many than few'. Brest was so important that it should 'be either in our possession or at our commandment or at least sure to be kept from the enemy'. Norris, however, must be careful not, by taking great numbers there, to alarm Sourdéac into thinking that 'you seek to command that place'. Yet he must get the succours lodged where they would be secure against the enemy and with communications open by sea. On 11 January Sir Robert Sidney was sent instructions to inform Henry IV that the Queen had thus empowered Norris to aid Sourdéac. Sidney was to urge the King privately to hand over Brest 'for such time only as he will require our assistance'. She asked this only for the safeguard of her subjects and there was no reason for Henry to suspect that she coveted any of his possessions. After all, she had had plenty of chances to do that and had never taken them.[21]

Norris managed to disobey both of the orders from the Queen. He neither withdrew to the Channel Islands nor sent men to Brest. Of John Troughton's twelve ships that had set out to take him away, seven had been forced back to England by contrary winds. When the remaining five arrived in mid-January Norris decided that it would be impossible to embark at Paimpol until the next spring tide on 10 February. By that time Troughton's victuals had run out and he and his five ships had also had to go back to England. As for helping Brest, Norris was convinced that 'Sourdéac will never receive above 300–400 Englishmen' and those only into the weakly fortified town, not into the castle. And in fact when on 11 February Sourdéac's secretary brought his answer to Norris's offer of aid, he asked for only 200 men. By then, of course, there was no shipping available to carry even that number. On that same day, too, the King told Sidney that it was simply not in

[21] Moreau, pp. 120–5; S. P. France, xxxii, fo. 392; xxxiii, fo. 19. As the Queen had 'a rheum in the eyes' her 28 December letter was signed by her Councillors.

his power to grant Brest to the Queen. Sourdéac would go over to the League at once if he knew that he was to be replaced by a Frenchman, let alone by an Englishman.[22]

It was thus already becoming apparent that in demanding Brest Elizabeth was crying for the moon. The appeals that came to her from Brittany did little to change that picture. La Touche, sent over by Sourdéac in late January, reported that Mercoeur already had 900 foot and 200 horse at Le Faou and Châteauneuf (these were presumably La Maignane's troops), not four leagues from Brest, and expected to gather an army of 6,200 men. There were sixty sail of Spanish ships waiting to come from San Sebastian. They planned to build two forts on the two points of land that commanded the entrance to Brest roads and so to cut off the town from aid by sea. Sourdéac begged the Queen's assistance to prevent this happening. But, as the Queen told Sidney, there was no offer to admit her men into the castle, which alone was defensible, the town 'being a wild and open place'.[23]

Nor were offers from the envoys sent by the Estates of Brittany much more encouraging when they arrived early in March. They did offer to hand over both Paimpol and the Île de Bréhat and to allow their fortification. But they could not allow the Queen to collect the only worthwhile duties levied in those places and they wanted her to send not only more men, artillery, and munitions, but even money to help pay their own meagre forces. They had no power to make any offers at all about Brest and Beauvoir's suggestion that Paimpol and Bréhat might soon be exchanged for St Malo, which he said could be taken in a fortnight, bore little relation to reality.[24]

Elizabeth, who at the end of January had sent Oliver St John, one of the Gentlemen Pensioners, to report on the situation at Brest, did on 20 March give Norris leave to stay a little longer. He might stay until she heard what help the King would send and what cautions he would give for the repayment of her expenses and the safety of her troops. Even so, Norris was only to stay if he was sure that he could hold Paimpol and Bréhat or could get enough support from

[22] Ibid., fos. 22, 36, 40, 42, 80, 86, 89.
[23] Ibid., fos. 68, 114.
[24] Ibid., fos. 7, 77, 132, 139, 156, 172.

the French to hold them. He must not 'from us look for a man more than you have already' – some 1,895 officers and men, 355 of them 'unfurnished', according to a muster on 23 February. And he was given a sharp reprimand for wasting money and victuals by evading the earlier orders to return.[25]

Norris protested bitterly against this charge that he had deliberately avoided embarking his troops when the shipping came for them. He was particularly hurt that Burghley, upon whom he had always depended, had said at a Council meeting that 'he doubted whether if the ships did come I would come away'. On 7 April he sent his brother, Sir Henry Norris, to make his protest and excuses to the Queen and Council and to press for a firm and clear direction whether he was to stay in Brittany or to come away. There was, however, something disingenuous about the air of aggrieved innocence that he was putting on. For it is clear enough, both from his instructions to Sir Henry and from a letter he wrote to Sir Robert Cecil at the same time, that he was most reluctant to remove even as far as the Channel Isles. He begged 'that the cause of the drawing away Her Majesty's forces be not upon me, for I absolutely disclaim from it as a burden too heavy for me to bear'. He should not have to decide either 'to take upon me to defend myself and this ill-provided place from a strong enemy or else to confess that I do abandon it for fear'. Yet he was clearly most reluctant to abandon 'this ill-provided place'. If he left it, he said, the enemy would at once occupy it. Besides, no place held by 1,500 men could be taken suddenly. With the neck of the League apparently broken, too, a new phase in the war was opening. A person of quality should therefore be sent over to view the situation at first hand and decide whether or not to evacuate the troops.[26]

Was the person of quality that Norris had in mind possibly the Earl of Essex? Certainly the Earl had recently written to him that the Queen 'desired rather that place [Paimpol] should be kept than be abandoned but for the danger that we were in'.[27] It may well have been this letter that encouraged

[25] Ibid., fos. 109, 148, 152. For St John's mission – ibid., fos. 58, 114; Cotton MSS, Caligula E. ix, fo. 222.

[26] S. P. France, xxxiii, fos. 177, 179, 183.

[27] Ibid., fo. 189.

Norris to send back, for a second time, the shipping sent again to carry him and his forces away, an action that stirred Burghley, and Lord Admiral Howard, to renewed anger. On 29 April, too, Norris wrote to Essex that 'it were no policy for Her Majesty to refuse the King her succours now that his estate is so good and that he hath so good means to give assurance for the reimbursing of her charges'.[28]

Of Essex's zest for action there can be no doubt. Upon England's drawing back from continental military commitments after the conversion of Henry IV, he had begun, as we have seen, to concentrate upon the pursuit of 'domestical greatness'. During the winter his ardent advocacy of Francis Bacon for the office of attorney-general had brought him into conflict with the Cecils and earned him a sharp rebuff from the Queen. Elizabeth had not forgotten or forgiven Bacon's part in the 1593 Commons debates about the granting of the triple subsidy. She preferred Sir Edward Coke who, as Speaker, had played a very useful part on the government's side in those debates. Nor did she mean to let the domineering Essex bully her about her appointments. Nevertheless the Earl's zeal in gathering intelligences, with Anthony Bacon's help, was beginning to win him commendations from her.

It had also brought him in January and February 1594 a major detective triumph. He managed to unearth evidence of what he claimed was a Spanish plot to have Elizabeth assassinated by her own physician, the fashionable Portuguese Dr Rodrigo Lopez. Burghley and Sir Robert Cecil, and the Queen too, seem to have been at first sceptical about Lopez's guilt. Essex, however, threw himself into the investigation with a frenetic and obsessive enthusiasm that, while it did little to recommend him as a cool and level-headed statesman, did uncover or extract, partly by torture or threats of torture, a considerable quantity of plausible evidence. It was sufficient at least to convince many people at the time, including the Cecils and, very reluctantly, the Queen, that Lopez was guilty as charged. There were indeed plots of varying likelihood being dreamed up among the English Catholic exiles and some of the Spanish officials in the Low Countries. Some of

---

[28] *Cal. S. P. Domestic, 1591–4,* pp. 493–4; S. P. France, xxxiii, fo. 217.

these involved the entourage of the exiled Portuguese pretender Don Antonio. Some involved English and Irish serving
under or connected with the renegade Sir William Stanley
and his busy-headed lieutenant Jacques Franceschi. Some had
assassination as their aim, though it seems likely that in
several of them at this period the intended victim may have
been the fugitive Spaniard Antonio Perez or perhaps Don
Antonio, rather than Elizabeth. So far as Dr Lopez was
concerned, almost all modern historians have serious doubts
about his guilt and about the justice of his conviction and
execution. Nor has any evidence to prove him guilty yet been
found in the archives of Spain.[29]

The revelation of these alleged plots did help Essex along
the road towards his domestical greatness. He had by now
patched up his differences with the Cecils. In the spring of
1594 he and they joined forces to urge the Queen to appoint
his protégé and their relation Francis Bacon to the office of
solicitor-general. The result was no happier than that from his
single-handed pressure over the attorney-general appointment. One evening, indeed, Elizabeth sharply told the over-
insistent Earl to get off to bed if all he could talk about was
Francis Bacon and his claims. Nevertheless, he and the Cecils
were again on reasonably good terms.[30]

This was at the end of March 1594. At that very time things
were happening in Brittany that brought Essex and the Cecils,
indeed all the Queen's Councillors, into still closer harmony
and turned Essex's thoughts once again from domestical
greatness to martial glory. Over the necessity of saving
Brittany, or at any rate of saving Brest, from the Spaniards the
Councillors had all along been well enough agreed. Elizabeth
was still inclined to bargain for increases in the King's forces
and a place of retreat for her own. But few or none of her

---

[29] For the plots or alleged plots of Lopez, Emmanuel Luis Tinoco, Estevan Ferrara
de Gama, and of Patrick Cullon, John Amias, William Polwhele, Gilbert Layton,
young Edmund Yorke, Richard Williams, Henry Young, and the rest – *Cal. S. P.
Domestic, 1591–4*, pp. 390–1, 394–5, 406–51 *passim*, 455; *H. M. C., Salisbury MSS*, IV,
409, 483, 491–4, 515; V, 2; Murdin, pp. 669–75; Birch, *Memoirs*, I, 149–59; Spedding,
*Bacon*, VIII, 274 ff.; also A. Dimock, in *English Historical Review*, IX, 440–72; M. A. S.
Hume, *Treason and Plot*, pp. 115 ff.; G. Marañon, *Antonio Perez*, pp. 317–21; *Dictionary of
National Biography*, s. v. Lopez, Rodrigo; Conyers Read, *Burghley*, 497–9.

[30] *H. M. C., Salisbury MSS*, IV, 494, 525; Birch, *Memoirs*, I, 165–8, 170–2, 179–80.

advisers had sympathy for this brinkmanship. Of Essex's attitude there can be little doubt. Burghley, too, as we have seen, always regarded the defence of Brittany against the Spaniards as a vital English interest. It was he who had persuaded the Queen in December 1593 to order the withdrawal of Norris and his troops only as far as the Channel Isles. In February 1594, after Sourdéac's envoy La Touche had brought his report of Spanish intentions against Brest, the old Lord Treasurer had been considering various ways of financing more troop levies for Brittany without further burdening the Queen's Exchequer. One of these projects was for raising 3,000 men by 'a contribution to be granted towards the maintenance of certain foot, to be armed and furnished for six months, which is to be borne by men of wealth and by such as have livings of Her Majesty and by officers and gainful exercise in the law'.[31]

This unanimity in the Council produced a prompt and ready English response when news came that the Spaniards had actually begun to carry out the purposes which La Touche had earlier reported. In the latter days of March 1594 Spanish troops from Blavet entered the Crozon peninsula. There they began to build a fort on the headland of Roscanvel – known to this day as the Pointe des Espagnols – commanding from the southern shore the entrance to Brest roads. This was the first stage of the operation which Sourdéac had in January sent La Touche to tell Elizabeth that the Spaniards were planning. Of itself it would seriously impede access to Brest from the sea. If they were allowed to complete the second stage by building another fort on the opposite, northern shore, the town would be cut off entirely.

Elizabeth's immediate reaction to the news of the Spaniards' arrival in Crozon was to despatch Sir Roger Williams to Brest to view and bring back accurate information about the state of affairs there. By the time he returned to England, the Spaniards had completed their Fort Crozon, put a garrison of about 400 veteran soldiers into it under the brave and experienced captain Tomas de Paredes, and withdrawn the rest of their troops and their ships back towards Blavet.[32]

[31] *Cal. S. P. Domestic, 1591–4,* pp. 433–5.
[32] S. P. France, xxxiii, fo. 214; Moreau, p. 130.

But the worst of the danger was by no means past. Don Juan d'Aguila had only withdrawn to collect the reinforcements – 400 horse and 1,500 foot, Sir John Norris wrote to his brother on 7 May – that were just coming from Spain. He intended then, according to the confession of a Spanish prisoner, to return to besiege Brest. Eleven days later Sir John, in a letter to the Queen, boosted the numbers of these Spanish reinforcements to 4,000, though he now thought that Don Juan, who had come forward to Châteauneuf-du-Faou, was aiming at Paimpol and the English rather than Brest.

> I think [he added] there never happened a more dangerous enterprise for the state of Your Majesty's country than this of the Spanish to possess Brittany, which (under humble correction) I dare presume to say will prove as prejudicial for England as if they had possessed Ireland. It is very late for Your Majesty to help it, but it is truly said better too late than never.[33]

The Queen, and even more her Councillors, were well enough aware that the time was getting late and Sir Roger Williams's return from Brest at the end of April had already touched off a burst of activity. Williams himself was immediately despatched to the French King, along with Thomas Edmondes who was returning to resume his place as resident English agent at the French court. On 3 May Sir Henry Norris was hastened back to Paimpol with orders to take with him the hoys from Portsmouth carrying victuals, spades, picks, artillery, and munitions. He also took orders for his brother to take his troops to Brest, overland if he thought it safe to do so, otherwise by sea in the hoys to Le Conquet. Troops from the Queen's Netherlands forces would follow him there. If the enemy's shipping had possessed the haven and enemy troops had occupied the north shore opposite Fort Crozon, then Sir John should hasten home to advise on what further should be done.[34]

To get Dutch help and their agreement to yet another withdrawal of English troops, Thomas Bodley was sent back at the same time to The Hague. With him went Sir Thomas

---

[33] S. P. France, xxxiii, fos. 195, 236, 246. Châteaumartin, writing from Bayonne, put the Spanish reinforcements sailing from Pasajes at 300 horse and 1,000 foot – *H. M. C., Salisbury MSS,* IV, 474.

[34] S. P. France, xxxiii, fos. 208, 226.

Baskerville to bring the troops away, and Sir Robert Sidney to organize their shipping and embarkation at Flushing. Bodley's instructions, dated 3 May,[35] were to point out to the States General, the Council of State, and Count Maurice the danger from the Spanish threat to Brest, danger to Dutch westward trade as well as to English security. He was to ask them to send ships of war to reinforce the Queen's and to have them speedily at Portsmouth or Plymouth. He was also to ask them to assist Baskerville to take away the 1,500 men in Her Majesty's pay that she had promised them should serve in the field against Groningen. In addition he was to ask for the 1,500 English that Vere had levied at the States' expense and in their pay. There had obviously been some doubt about asking for these latter troops. For in a paper of notes on 2 May Burghley had queried 'whether the 1,500 levied and paid by Sir Francis Vere for the States shall be required or but the numbers in Her Majesty's pay?'[36] Bodley's instructions compromised on this. If the States would not freely grant the 1,500 in their pay, he should offer to set off the expense of their levy and wages against the States' debt to the Queen. If they refused even this, he was to acquiesce in their refusal but still to insist absolutely upon the withdrawal of the 'Normandy' companies and the other troops in her pay that had gone to the field. If Baskerville found that it would take a long time to get these men from around Groningen, he was to take 1,500 from Flushing, Brielle, and Ostend and bring them to Portsmouth, leaving Vere to return companies from the field to take their places in those garrisons. In England meanwhile, 1,100 men were to be levied from eleven counties. Her Majesty's ships *Merehonour, Vanguard, Rainbow, Hope, Dreadnought,* the new galley *Mercury,* and two pinnaces were to make ready to go under Sir Martin Frobisher to Brest. On 4 May the Queen wrote to assure Sourdéac that she was sending Norris with his troops and if necessary another 1,000 from England, as well as some ships of war to his assistance.[37]

[35] S. P. Holland, xlviii, fo. 185.

[36] S. P. Domestic, ccxlviii, no. 90.

[37] S. P. France, xxxiii, fos. 223, 226, 229; S. P. Holland, xlviii, fos. 204, 208; S. P. Domestic, ccxlviii, no. 90; *Cal. S. P. Domestic, 1591-4*, p. 503. In his requests to the States on 21 May, however, Bodley said nothing about setting off the pay of the 1,500 against the States' debt – *Kronijk*, XX, 224-7.

Baskerville found no great difficulty in withdrawing some two-thirds of the 1,500 men in the Queen's pay who were supposed to come away. The 500 appointed to go to the field from Flushing had not yet left when he arrived there. So he was able without much trouble to get them, or 480 of them. Another 100 came promptly from Brielle and 500 more from Ostend, making up a total of 1,080. By 4 June they had embarked, ready to sail as soon as the wind turned favourable, and by the 13th they were at Guernsey.[38]

The States had accepted these withdrawals from the English garrisons readily enough. After all, they did not need to be told by the Queen or Bodley how dangerous to their vital westward trade a Spanish occupation of Brest could be. But the request for the Queen's troops that had gone to the field and for the 1,500 that Vere had raised was a different matter. Some months earlier, when they had despaired of getting a favourable answer to their requests for English troops to help besiege Groningen, they had agreed with Count John of Nassau to hire 4,000 German foot and 300 horse. When they were eventually promised 1,500 from the English garrisons and the 1,500 of Vere's levy, they had hoped by adding to these Count John's Germans and up to seventy companies from their own garrisons to provide Count Maurice and Count William Louis with 13,000–14,000 foot and 2,000 horse for operations against Groningen and Verdugo.[39] But before the two Counts got into the field, 5,000 men from the enemy's army in Brabant slipped across the Rhine to reinforce Verdugo, who had been blockading Coevorden on and off since the autumn and was not far from starving it into surrender. At the end of April 1594 Maurice did force the enemy to retire from before Coevorden without even a show of fight. By early May John of Nassau's Germans, Vere's English levy, the eight 'Normandy' foot-bands from Ostend, and the two English foot-bands from Bergen-op-Zoom had joined him and on 12 May he and Count William had sat down before Groningen with 11,000 foot and 1,500 horse.[40]

[38] S. P. Holland, xlviii, fos. 204, 208, 216, 235, 251; S. P. France, xxxiii, fo. 301; *H. M. C., Salisbury MSS*, IV, 550.

[39] S. P. Holland, xlviii, fos. 44, 151; *Resolutiën der Staten Generaal*, VIII, 230, 241.

[40] S. P. Holland, xlviii, fos. 151, 173, 175, 181, 210, 214; *Kronijk*, XX, 72–3, 169, 174,

The besieged sallied fiercely, against the English on 20 May, against Count William's Frisians on 22 May, and against the English again on 30 May when Captain Wray and forty or fifty men were killed. Despite this, the States' troops took two sconces that guarded the approaches, brought up their artillery, and entrenched and fortified their own positions so strongly that it would be no easy task for the enemy to break through and relieve the town. Moreover, inside Groningen there was a growing faction that was ready to surrender. A parley was actually begun on 2 June, although it was broken off four days later after the suppression of a demonstration of those who wanted to capitulate.[41] Nevertheless, Verdugo was still in the field and not far away, and the besiegers were beginning to suffer from sickness brought on by the wet weather. Moreover, the States had to hold some troops in reserve in Holland, Utrecht, and Zeeland to match the Archduke's still considerable forces in Brabant and Flanders. So the besiegers of Groningen could not well spare the English companies, either those in the Queen's pay or those in the States' pay, nor could replacements for them be easily provided if they were to come away.

This was the answer that Bodley received after he presented the Queen's demands to the States General on 21 May. They made no difficulty about allowing the withdrawal of 1,500 men from the English garrisons, they would even supply their places if need be and would allow two or three companies to return from the camp to Flushing and Ostend if it were really necessary. But the other English companies now before Groningen, whether in their own pay or the Queen's, could not be spared without risking the ruin of that enterprise.[42] On this they were as adamant as they had been earlier with Gilpin in their refusal to consider any suggestion of their beginning to repay their debts to the Queen. No amount of argument from Bodley – who perhaps privately sympathized with their

---

188–9, 200–1; *Resolutiën der Staten Generaal*, VIII, 166, 168–9; Bor, xxxi, fos. 17–19; Verdugo, pp. 161–74.

[41] S. P. Holland, xlviii, fos. 225, 239, 241, 257, 262, 264, 272; Bor, xxxi, fos. 24 v.–27; Verdugo, pp. 175–83.

[42] S. P. Holland, xlviii, fos. 183, 230, 289; *Resolutiën der Staten Generaal*, VIII, 213; *Kronijk*, XX, 231–4, 278.

attitude – would alter their decision and the 1,080 men that Baskerville sailed away with were the only troops to go from the Netherlands to Brittany in 1594.[43]

Before they landed there Sir Roger Williams was back in England from his mission to Henry IV. He had reported to the King about his visit to Brest and had conveyed to him the Queen's request that he should send the Duke of Montpensier with 1,000–1,200 horse and 2,000 foot from Normandy to reinforce the Breton royalists and take command of their forces for the relief of the town. The Queen for her part offered to send a good number of her best ships and to reinforce her own troops in Brittany up to 6,000–7,000 or more under the command of some person of quality. After this service she would keep as many men there as the King did. On their way to the King, Williams and Edmondes had visited Montpensier, who was besieging Honfleur. The Duke professed to be eager to go to Brittany and was sure he could draw 3,000 foot and 500–600 horse thither out of Normandy. Henry IV, too, when Williams presented his requests at Laon about 6 June, agreed fairly readily to despatch Montpensier and forces from Normandy as the Queen asked. He did, however, point out that this was all he could do. He was being attacked from three sides at once and whereas Brittany was an isolated outpost the attacks from the Netherlands and Italy came from the areas of the enemy's main strength.[44]

Despite the limited help that Henry IV was able to offer, Elizabeth was at this time planning the operations for the relief of Brest on a very considerable scale. On 26 May, before she heard from Bodley or Williams or that Baskerville was on his way, she had again ordered Norris to withdraw to the Channel Isles rather than await a threatened Spanish attack at Paimpol. By the time this order arrived, however, the Spaniards had drawn back and Baskerville's companies were at Guernsey so Norris once again ignored the Queen's command. Instead he called Baskerville and his companies to

---

[43] S. P. Holland, xlviii, fos. 55, 80. On Burghley's instructions Gilpin had, from the end of March ceased to press for repayment – ibid. fo. 104. For Bodley's attitude – ibid., fo. 262.

[44] S. P. France, xxxiii, fos. 282, 285; *Edmondes Papers*, pp. 135–7.

join him at Paimpol.[45] So there were now at the least 2,700 English troops (though Burghley reckoned only 2,200) actually in Brittany. The royal forces there under Marshal Aumont were reckoned at 500 horse and 3,000 foot. From Normandy the King had promised to send Montpensier with 1,400 horse and 3,500 foot. To these another 3,000 foot from England were to be added. So a combined force of about 14,000 horse and foot was envisaged, with an English contingent of around 5,700. That is to say, it was for the English to be an operation on an even larger scale than Essex's 1591 Rouen expedition. And while the Lord Admiral was to be in charge of the naval squadron of up to twenty of the Queen's ships and five or six victuallers, the promised 'person of quality' in command of the English land forces was once again to be the Earl of Essex – so much for 'domestical greatness'![46]

In accordance with these plans orders went out on 14 and 16 July for the levying of 3,000 men from eighteen counties. With them were to go fifty pioneers levied by Sir Walter Raleigh from the tin miners of Cornwall. On 20 July a warrant was issued from the Exchequer to pay Sir Thomas Sherley, the treasurer-at-war, the sums needed for the coats, conduct, transporting, and wages of these 3,050 soldiers and pioneers. They were to go under the Earl of Essex and Lord Admiral Howard to join the troops already in Brittany under Sir John Norris, who was to hold the office of lieutenant-general, and Sir Thomas Baskerville, who would be sergeant-major. They came once again chiefly from the southern counties and East Anglia and were to be shipped from London, Harwich, Southampton, Weymouth, and Plymouth. There was also every intention of rushing them across to Brittany as early as possible, for they were to be at their ports ready to embark by 31 July for those going from Harwich and so in sequence westwards until those from Plymouth who were to embark by 5 August. The Dutch were asked to send ten of their warships to the Downs by 1 August. Even allowing for a

---

[45] S. P. France, xxxiii, fos. 261, 298, 301, 309; *H. M. C., Salisbury MSS*, IV, 550.

[46] S. P. France, xxxiii, fos. 313, 343, 354; *Cal. S. P. Domestic, 1591–4*, p. 529; *Kronijk*, XX, 263–5, 310–3.

fair amount of previous preparation, this would be quick work indeed.[47]

Few Elizabethan expeditions, however, got away without any hiccups and hesitations and this one was not to be an exception. As early as 19 July Burghley wrote in some alarm to his son Sir Robert Cecil that it was being 'blabbed abroad' that the intended journey to Brest would not take place. Part of his anxiety arose from delays in getting the shipping to sea and the army's victuals despatched. But clearly he was no less worried that the Queen's resolution might be faltering. Somewhat, he told his son, must always be attempted in great matters, for with no attempt no profit could follow but sometimes great loss. It is reasonably obvious that he hoped his son would put these arguments before the Queen, although (as he advised him) they should be put to her temperately so that they might not be taken offensively.[48] How different, incidentally, was this way of dealing with the Queen from Essex's hectoring and badgering! And, indeed, despite all Essex's enthusiasm for the Brest enterprise and all his pleas to be appointed to command it, the Queen now refused to let him take any part in it. She did her best to soften the blow. According to Anthony Bacon, who may well have had the story from Essex himself, she told him

that his desire to be in action and to give further proof of his valour and prowess was to be liked and highly commended. But that she loved him and her realm too much to hazard his person in any lesser action than that which should import her crown and state, and therefore willed him to be content, and gave him a warrant for £4,000 sterling, saying 'Look to thyself good Essex and be wise to help thyself without giving thy enemies advantage, and my hand shall be readier to help thee than any other'.

None the less when the news that the Earl was not going became public by 21 July, it cooled most of the heat of the enterprise, if we can believe Palavicino, who at his comparatively advanced age had hoped, somewhat ambitiously, to

---

[47] *Cal. S. P. Domestic, 1591–4*, pp. 528–9; *H. M. C., Salisbury MSS*, IV, 562–3, 565–6; *Kronijk*, XX, 312.
[48] *Cal. S. P. Domestic, 1591–4*, pp. 528–9.

command one of the Queen's ships under the Lord Admiral.[49] That the heat should have been somewhat cooled was no bad thing. Expelling the Spaniards from Fort Crozon was a job for professionals rather than for a noble amateur and his following of gilded youth zealous for stirring deeds and martial glory.

Within a few days of Elizabeth's decision not to let Essex go, it was also decided to reduce the numbers of the expedition. It looks as if this may have been due in considerable measure to Sir John Norris. He had often complained of the Queen's hesitations and indecision. Yet Queen and Council had no less often, and with no less justification, found it difficult to come to firm resolutions upon the decidedly variable information that came out of Brittany. And no small part of that variable information came from Norris himself. For example, as we have seen, on 7 May he had written to his brother that 400 horse and 1,500 foot had come from Spain to reinforce Don Juan d'Aguila; on 18 May in a letter to the Queen he had put those reinforcements up to 4,000 and had changed his mind about whether Brest or Paimpol was Don Juan's objective. Nor was that all. Five days later in a letter to Burghley, he was sending over, and apparently believing, a report that the *total* strength of the Spaniards was no more than 400 or 500 horse and 4,000 foot. So, in the hope of arriving at a more reliable and coherent picture of the situation in Brittany, the Queen on 24 June called him home to report. He was at Portsmouth by 8 July and at court a day or two later.[50]

Now, even when Sir John Norris had thought that the reinforced Spaniards might be 8,000 strong, and before he knew of Baskerville's arrival with the companies from the Low Countries, he had still believed that with Aumont's French and another 2,000 English it would be quite possible to raise any siege of Brest by Don Juan's forces.[51] Experience in the field during June can only have strengthened this belief. For just when he heard that Baskerville's companies had arrived

[49] Birch, *Memoirs*, I, 181; *H. M. C., Salisbury MSS*, IV, 563, 567.

[50] S. P. France, xxxiii, fos. 259, 317, 356. The Council wrote cancelling his recall on 26 June – ibid., fo. 319; but Norris either ignored their letter or left for home before it arrived.

[51] E.g., ibid., fo. 251.

in the Channel Isles, he had also heard that the Spaniards were advancing towards Brest again with the intention of building that second fort there. He had at once summoned Baskerville to join him as soon as possible. Then together they and such troops as Aumont had, began to march westwards from Paimpol in the direction of Brest (with the winds westerly at this season and a Spanish squadron of considerable strength reported off the haven, to go by sea was impracticable anyway). If they found the enemy too strong, they meant to return to Paimpol, the most suitable base for a further relief attempt. After a day's advance, they learned that Don Juan's forces lay directly in their path. But when Norris sent 800 men forward to reconnoitre the enemy they found that upon news of the new English forces landing, Don Juan, after reinforcing the Fort Crozon garrison, had drawn seven leagues back to Carhaix and abandoned his plan of building the second fort. Clearly, if this was the effect of some 2,700 English troops, together with Aumont's at present meagre forces, it was hardly necessary to send more than double the number of that 2,700.[52]

Accordingly on the evening of 26 July, a week after Norris came to court, it was decided to reduce the levy being made in England from 3,000 to 2,000 men. At the same time the total English numbers in Brittany were to be strictly limited to 4,000 foot, 100 horse, and fifty pioneers, instead of the previously intended 5,700 or the 6,000 or 7,000 or more that had been talked of back in May. The 2,000 were now to be ready to embark at their different ports at dates varying between 5 and 10 August. Norris was to be their commander – he was perhaps relieved not to be playing second fiddle under the shadow of the Earl of Essex. The naval forces were also to be under the command of a professional, Sir Martin Frobisher. He was to have six of the Queen's ships – the *Vanguard, Rainbow, Swiftsure, Dreadnought, Crane, Quittance;* two of her pinnaces, the *Charles* and the *Moon;* six London warships; and it was hoped, nine good Dutchmen. All the ships were to go straight to Brest haven, while the troops were to assemble at Paimpol and go to Brest overland now that

[52] Ibid., fos. 301, 309, 331; *H. M. C., Salisbury MSS,* IV, 562.

Don Juan's withdrawal had left the way open. These, in fact, were the final constituents of the English forces for the relief of Brest.[53]

[53] S. P. France, xxxiii, fos. 384, 386; S. P. Domestic, ccxlix, nos. 38, 39, 61, 86; Birch, *Memoirs,* I, 181. But apparently the *Swiftsure* and *Dreadnought* did not in the end go – Oppenheim, in *Monson's Tracts,* I, 304, from Pipe Office Declared Account 2231.

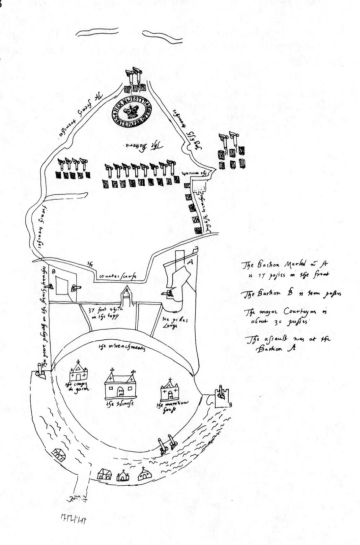

Map 10. Fort Crozon.

# XXIV

## The Capture of Fort Crozon

A full six weeks were to pass before the English forces that had been finally decided upon on 26 July were all assembled in Brittany. The Dutch naval contingent was even tardier. The Queen had asked the States General to send at least ten of their warships to Portsmouth by 5 August. It was in fact early September before any of them approached the English coast. Then only six of the ten arrived and by 22 September those six had got no farther than Plymouth.[1] Bodley had asked the States as early as 31 May to assist the Queen with ships of war in accordance with article 25 of the 1585 Treaty. He found them very willing. The 1585 Treaty, however, specified that when the Queen sent her ships against an enemy in the Channel or Narrow Seas, the States should send an equal number up to a total of twenty (or more according to her need and their power).[2] Now, Bodley was never told how many ships the Queen was setting forth and it was not until 14 August that he heard from Burghley how many she wanted from the States and when and where they should be sent.[3] Caron, the States' agent in England, had, it is true, reported on 15 July that Burghley, Howard, Essex, Hunsdon, and Cecil, had told him that the Queen was setting forth twenty of her ships and wanted the States to send ten of theirs, victualled for three months, to the Downs by 1 August (or to Portsmouth by 5 August). The States received Caron's report by 20 July. They thereupon decided to start making ready six ships from Holland and four from Zeeland, but they would not do anything more until they received a direct and definite request from the Queen. They did not consider a request made indirectly through their agent as good enough warrant – all the more as Cecil had asked Caron to hold back his

---

[1] *Resolutiën der Staten Generaal*, VIII, 216; S. P. Holland, xlix, fo. 159.

[2] *Kronijk*, XX, 225; Dumont, *Corps universel diplomatique*, V, 455; *L. and A.*, I, 314; II, 210.

[3] S. P. Holland, xlviii, fo. 281; xlix, fos. 64, 83, 98.

dispatch until the Queen was fully resolved and as Caron had miswritten the Queen's request for gunpowder at 20,000 lb. instead of 60,000 lb. Thus it was mid-August before Bodley had the information he needed to make a definite request. As he had anticipated, it took almost another three weeks to get the six Holland ships to sea and it was late September before Zeeland sent off two only of its ships instead of the four asked for by the States General.[4]

A side-effect of all this was a sharp dispute between Bodley and Burghley. The old Lord Treasurer – he was now seventy-four – wrote on 27 August that he considered Bodley had been sufficiently informed. 'I would you should understand', he added, 'my burden is great otherwise to answer far greater matters and that sometimes I am absent and sometimes sick, whereas if I had no other charge than to answer and instruct you, as you have nothing else to do but in your own negotiation, you might hear oftener from me.' Anyway, the States ought to have offered their ships 'and not with these trifling answers to delay it as they have done and so appeareth their unwillingness'. An additional aggravation to Burghley was that the post who brought Bodley's letters with news of the surrender of Groningen (on 12 July) had gone first to the Earl of Essex and 'dealt like a varlet with me to keep my letters so long after my lord had received his'. The rivalry between the Cecils and Essex to be first with foreign intelligences was clearly growing sharper and first call upon so important an overseas correspondent as Thomas Bodley was not lightly to be forborne.

This was not quite the end of the matter. Bodley was called home at the end of September and some weeks later Burghley accused him of 'making moan' to the Queen about his lack of definite instructions. Bodley answered that, on the contrary, the Queen had dragged the information out of him in close questioning about the reasons for the States' delays. He also sent the originals of the letters written to him by Burghley during the past summer to justify himself against the Lord Treasurer's strictures and to show what just occasion he had to

---

[4] Ibid., fos. 56, 81, 98, 140; *Kronijk*, XX, 310–3; *Resolutiën der Staten Generaal*, VIII, 214–6.

think that he was forgotten. He ended his letter by saying that if Burghley continued to hold so poor an opinion of him, he must ask to be clean discharged from his Low Country service. He was indeed already growing weary of that peculiarly wearisome service. This dispute with Burghley no doubt gave him a considerable push along the path to that withdrawal 'out of the throng of court contentions' which he was to make a couple of years later.[5]

We have, however, outrun the story of the Brest relief force. There had been a good deal of haggling with the French ambassador, Beauvoir la Nocle, over exact terms of the agreement about it and whether or not the Queen should provide artillery and munitions for the operations.[6] The final agreement bound the French King once again to repay, as soon as he was able, all the Queen's past expenses in his behalf. He was likewise to repay – if possible, at once – £2,985 for the present levy and equipment of the English troops, £4,971 a month for their wages, and £14,173 for the cost of the naval contingent. The Queen gave way to Beauvoir's protests so far as to promise six cannon and the munitions for them, though Norris was instructed to use French or Dutch munitions rather than hers. She insisted also that she would withdraw her forces altogether if the King failed to send at least 2,000 foot and 1,000 horse to reinforce the local Breton levies. Moreover, although the agreement spoke of saving Brittany from the Spaniards, in Norris's instructions the Queen emphasized that 'we do not mean that you shall use our forces for any other purpose but to such end as may necessarily and directly tend to the recovery of the fort and clearing of the said haven' of Brest. The only modification to this was that, as French support might prove inadequate and the fort might therefore not be taken, Norris in that event should look well to the preservation of Paimpol as a base, or else should lay hands upon some more convenient port, until the Queen could decide what course to take. The seizing of a more convenient port than Paimpol should be done, however,

---

[5] S. P. Holland, xlix, fos. 110, 243; *Dictionary of National Biography*, s.v. Bodley, Thomas.

[6] S. P. France, xxxiii, fo. 377; xxxiv, fos. 8, 11, 22.

as 'by yourself of necessity without any special direction from us'.[7]

The agreement with Beauvoir was concluded on 10 August. Two days later Sir John Norris went down to Portsmouth to gather together and embark the 2,000 troops and fifty miners levied in England. So far everything had gone quite well up to timetable. But at Portsmouth he was delayed for another fortnight by contrary winds, a delay perhaps more natural but hardly less predictable than that which was holding up the Dutch ships of war. While waiting there, his troops fell into 'many disorderous mutinies' and some 300 of them deserted, a loss which Norris blamed less on the delay than on 'the justices [who] did set forth such loose men as they found upon the highways and discharged those that had friends to speak for them'.[8] A more serious consequence was that the delay risked involving the English forces already in Brittany in another disaster. Towards the end of July Baskerville, at the request of Marshal Aumont and Sourdéac, had advanced from Paimpol to Lannion. Then towards the middle of August he and the Marshal had moved still farther westwards, towards Morlaix. The purpose of this advance was to lend support to an enterprise by Lezonnet, the governor of Concarneau, who had recently come over from the League to the King's party. His enterprise was aimed at Quimper, a town that was refusing to accept a new Leaguer governor or a Leaguer garrison, though it had not yet declared for the King. Lezonnet's attempt failed and although Aumont and Baskerville occupied the town of Morlaix, the castle there held out stoutly against them.[9] Mercoeur and the Spaniards, alerted by the danger to Quimper, now passed, were advancing in strength to relieve the castle at Morlaix and Aumont and Baskerville had no more than 3,600 foot and 500 horse between them. As early as 18 August Baskerville had written home for 1,000 of the troops newly levied in England to be sent over at once to reinforce him. He repeated the request more urgently on 26 August. Two days earlier the Privy Council had ordered Norris to send 1,000 of his men immediately to Morlaix. Norris made all

[7] Ibid., fos. 29, 38; *Edmondes Papers,* pp. 153–9.
[8] *H. M. C., Salisbury MSS,* XIII, 507; S. P. France, xxxiv, fos. 71, 74.
[9] Ibid., xxxiii, fo. 369; xxxiv, fo. 25; Moreau, pp. 130–53.

haste to get away and Frobisher agreed to go with him straight to Morlaix, if the wind allowed, and to ride with the whole fleet in sight of the town.[10]

Even so it was 29 August before Norris was at last able to put to sea. He then had to look in at Guernsey for pilots and on their advice sailed after all to Paimpol instead of to Morlaix. He arrived there on 1 September, 'with a giddy head, being newly landed, having been these four days at sea with contrary winds, by which means a great part of our fleet is left we know not where'. He had some 1,200 troops with him – the shallowness of Paimpol harbour, which had twice so effectively rendered embarkation of his forces impossible earlier in the year, seems to have offered surprisingly little obstacle to their disembarking now. Next day letters came from Aumont and Baskerville urging him to hasten to join them at Morlaix as the castle still held out, Aumont had no artillery except a couple of culverins, and Mercoeur was coming towards them with 6,000 men and would soon be joined by the Spaniards, though they were now no more than 2,600 strong. There was another brief delay at Paimpol because Aumont had failed to provide either victuals or waggons for Norris's men. So it was 5 September before Norris reached Morlaix with half his forces, the rest arriving next day. He was just in time. Mercoeur was already within four leagues of the town and had they arrived two days later, Norris claimed, Aumont would have received 'a great deal of shame by his unadvised enterprise'. As it was, the castle surrendered on 12 September, as soon as the English artillery was landed.[11]

The surrender of the castle touched off a quarrel between Norris and Aumont. They had for a time got on well together and Norris had at first felt that the Marshal would be better obeyed than previous commanders in Brittany had been. He had, however, soon come to endorse, although he did not inspire, the Queen's demands to Henry IV for the return of Montpensier. The young Duke, he thought, would show more favour to the Breton Huguenots, would perhaps also show greater deference to his own counsels. Certainly he hoped that

[10] S. P. France, xxxiv, fos. 59, 63, 73, 74.

[11] Ibid., fos. 94, 96, 98, 111, 115; *Edmondes Papers*, p. 169; Moreau, pp. 149–53, 161–5; Thou, XII, 306–9; B. Pocquet, *Hist. de Bretagne*, V, 248–52.

Montpensier, as governor of Normandy, might bring Norman troops in appreciable numbers to reinforce the Breton levies. On the other side Aumont suspected that Norris was behind the Queen's letter of July 1593 in which she complained so bitterly at his delay in entering Brittany. That autumn there was also a sharp dispute about Aumont's refusal to carry out his promise to hand over the Île de Bréhat to Norris or to let him fortify Paimpol. The quarrel was aggravated when Norris on his own authority used local people to assist in fortifying the town in defiance of Aumont's prohibition. Relations became so strained that when Norris was recalled to England for consultation in July 1594, Aumont immediately hurried off after him an envoy, the Sieur des Forges, to present his side of the matter to the Queen. He was also to complain of Norris poisoning her mind against him and allowing the ill-disciplined English troops to rob and pillage the poor inhabitants of the province.[12]

The Queen wrote on 11 August to assure Aumont that his charges against Norris had little or no substance, though there were evil minds on both sides of the water seeking to make trouble.[13] Thereupon, it seems, the Marshal was ready to let bygones be bygones. Black John Norris, however, was not a man who easily forgot or forgave. When he arrived at Morlaix on 5 September he found Aumont 'much out of countenance with his false complaints he had made of me, and offered divers messengers that he would write to Her Majesty what I would have him. But I would accept none of his kindness and have protested to him that I will seek my reason of him at the King's hands. And so I pray you', he wrote to Edmondes, 'let the King know when you shall think it fit.' It is therefore hardly surprising that Aumont, upon the taking of Morlaix castle, rejected Norris's demand that the town should be handed over as a base for the English in accordance with a promise Montpensier had made two years ago. He also refused to give the English the halfshare in the spoils of the castle to which another two-year-old agreement, with Sancy, entitled them. To widen their differences still more, Aumont was

[12] S. P. France, xxxi, fo. 137; xxxii, fos. 178, 335; xxxiii, fos. 183, 372; xxxiv, fos. 11, 84; Cotton MSS, Caligula E. ix, fo. 216.
[13] S. P. France, xxxiv, fo. 50; *Edmondes Papers*, pp. 253-9.

negotiating a truce with Mercoeur who, he believed, could be brought to promise not to assist the Spaniards if they were attacked during the truce. Norris suspected that this was merely a trick by Aumont to hinder Montpensier coming and by Mercoeur to win time for reinforcements to arrive from Spain. Norris at once wrote off complaining of all these matters to Burghley and, a few days later, to Edmondes as well, asking the latter in addition to press the King most urgently to send Montpensier to them.[14]

With Morlaix castle taken on 12 September, however, despite these quarrels, the way was clear to move against Fort Crozon. Frobisher and his warships had already moved into the bay of Brest and for eight or nine days had been bombarding the fort from the sea. The Queen's artillery had also been shipped there. For the rest of the land forces there was another week's delay while Aumont collected – or according to Norris, extorted – money from the townsmen of Morlaix and the English merchants trading there. He needed the money to pay his French troops.[15] Eventually, on 23 September, Yves de Liscoët with some 400 Breton horsemen and a few infantry began the investment of Fort Crozon on the landward side. Even now it was another ten days before any substantial force of infantry arrived to support them. The reason for this was that Aumont had carried them all, French and English, three days out of their way in the hope of securing Quimper. This strained relations still further between the Marshal and Norris, who wrote off now to Burghley that Aumont 'is the unfittest man to command an army that ever I saw'. To Edmondes he wrote that 'the Marshal maketh himself every day more hated than other, so that few will tarry with him'. It is clear none the less that Norris, who never found it easy to share command, was seriously blinded by the personal hatred he had worked up towards Aumont. For he had to admit that Quimper, which yielded after three days (on 1 October) on condition that it did not have to accept a garrison,[16] was a valuable flanking cover against any relief

[14] Ibid., pp. 169–70; S. P. France, xxxiv, fos. 115, 117, 129, 131.
[15] Ibid., fo. 129; *Edmondes Papers*, p. 178; *Lettres Missives*, IV, 268–9.
[16] For the siege of Quimper – Moreau, pp. 160–96; for the terms of its surrender – ibid., pp. 184–9.

attempt by the Spaniards from Blavet. And, although Norris omitted to say so, the truce that Aumont had just concluded with Mercoeur and the Leaguers meant that, for several weeks at least, relief for Fort Crozon could only come from the Spaniards. But in unspoken and reluctant approval of the Marshal's strategy, Norris when he marched off to Crozon with 1,000 of the English foot did leave the rest behind around Quimper under his brother Sir Henry and Baskerville.

Norris and his 1,000 English foot arrived before Fort Crozon on 2 October. Thereupon Frobisher landed four cannon and they hoped to begin their battery from the landward side by 6 October. To the Queen Norris wrote on 5 October that 'we have found the place in very good strength and hard to be approached by reason we are driven to bring our trenches forty score off, their cannon and muskets commanding so over the "explaned" places of the fort and the ground being rocky and hard to work.' He could not resist the temptation to argue once more for a larger operation than just the recovery of Fort Crozon. 'The King of Spain', he wrote, 'will not easily be brought to forsake this country.' Therefore the Queen should have 'some well fortified port in their country that upon any occasion Your Majesty may be the moderator for either party'. Still more unwisely, he went on to say that Fort Crozon would not be worth her keeping since 'not a boat of two tons can unlade anything into it' and it did not close Brest haven.[17]

This was a peculiarly ill-judged and ill-timed conclusion. Elizabeth was already growing restive over Henry IV's delays and hesitations about sending Montpensier and the promised reinforcements to Brittany. On 26 September Sir Robert Cecil had told Edmondes that 'surely if the King's forces for Brest come not, Her Majesty will not leave a man behind in the country'. She had ordered her Councillors to write to Norris 'absolutely to return', but then she heard from various sources that Fort Crozon was weak and would not stand a siege. She also heard from Norris that he was marching thither now that Morlaix castle had been taken. She therefore relented so far as to allow that, if by tarrying a few days Norris might reduce the fort with his own and the Marshal's forces alone or if he found

---

[17] S. P. France, xxxiv, fos. 162, 164, 166; *Edmondes Papers*, pp. 177–9.

that the King's promised reinforcements were on their way, she would not waste the chance of a good result by an over-hasty withdrawal. With Elizabeth in this mood it hardly needed Norris's low estimate of the value of, and danger from Fort Crozon to make her, as Burghley wrote on 16 October, repent somewhat of her charges in an enterprise of so little importance.[18] By then she knew that the King had decided that he could not spare Montpensier and that, although St Luc was to go to Brittany in his stead, he, too, was delayed by the King's lack of money to pay the troops he was to take with him.[19] So if the siege was likely to be a long one, Burghley told Norris, and the forces from the King did not come, she would prefer an honourable retreat to keeping her ships at sea in this season of the year and so large an army engaged to such small purpose. Nevertheless, although she utterly refused to send Norris the 500 men he asked for to make up his losses by desertion and sickness, she was sending his troops their winter apparel and Frobisher's ships another month's victuals. Meanwhile she advised Norris to do his best to agree with Aumont. All the same it is clear that her Councillors were once again having considerable trouble in keeping their mistress's hand to the plough.[20]

Meanwhile the siege of Fort Crozon went slowly forward.[21] Against Don Tomas de Paredes and his 300–400 seasoned Spanish infantry, Aumont and Norris brought forces numerically much superior. The French infantry never numbered more than 3,000, but a muster of the English on 7 October showed 4,603, men present in thirty-three companies – Norris once again had evaded the Queen's and Council's very firm orders to reduce the number of the companies.[22] This superiority in numbers, however was largely offset by the narrowness of the front on which they could be deployed. Fort Crozon was built on a triangular piece of ground at the end of

---

[18] Ibid., p. 177; S. P. France, xxxiv, fos. 173, 198.
[19] Ibid., fos. 149, 151, 153.
[20] Ibid., fo. 173; *Cal. S. P. Domestic, 1591-4*, p. 560.
[21] For the siege of Fort Crozon – S. P. France, xxxiv, fos. 184, 192, 208, 217, 235, 238, 239, 254; *Edmondes Papers*, pp. 177-9, 191-2; Moreau, pp. 198-203; *Monson's Tracts*, I, 303-9; Thou, XII, 311-5; Davila, pp. 656-8; Levot, *Hist. de Brest*, I, 78-83; B. Pocquet, *Hist. de Bretagne*, V, 255-61.
[22] S. P. France, xxxiv, fo. 179.

a peninsula. Steep and rocky cliffs made it inaccessible on its two seaward sides and the distance from cliff to cliff on the landward side was no more than 250 paces. Here it was defended by a curtain wall with a gate in the middle, and by a ditch and by flanking bastions at either end. The ground in front had neither hedge nor house, hardly so much as a shrub, to give cover to the besieger's approaches. If this was not already apparent enough, the fact was soon brought home when on 8 October the English sergeant-major, Anthony Wingfield, after repulsing an enemy sortie, approached too close to the fort and was killed, along with three others, by a single culverin shot. Nine more English were also killed that day by the enemy cannon.

The trenches had therefore, as Norris wrote, to be made some forty score paces, the better part of half a mile, back. Nor was entrenching easy, since in places there was little more than two feet of soil above the solid rock. A good part of the trenches therefore had to be fronted with turves and sandbags to a height of several feet and platforms for the artillery had to be built up in similar fashion. To make the work more difficult and life on the windswept peninsula even more uncomfortable, it rained and rained and rained. According to the Breton chronicler, Canon Jean Moreau, who was living only about thirty-five miles away at Quimper, there were no more than three really fine days during the whole five weeks of the siege. As a result the trenches were often knee-deep in water. It is small wonder that more and more of the besiegers fell sick and a great many of them died. To make matters worse, it was several weeks before the English received their winter apparel. So by 10 and 11 October Norris was already reporting the dwindling of his numbers and that 'our new men sicken apace'. The French suffered no less. Afloat, the crews of Frobisher's ships were also buffeted by the strong westerly winds that sometimes drove them to run for shelter in Brest roads.

In these circumstances it is hardly surprising that the besiegers were not able to mount their artillery and begin their battery until 23 October. Of the fourteen pieces then brought into action, two culverins were contributed by the French and two more were landed from the Holland warships. The six pieces that Norris had brought over together with two culverins from the *Vanguard* and two demi-cannons from the *Rainbow* put on shore by Frobisher, made up the remaining ten. They began by aiming directly at the ramparts, but although this brought down some of the turf and faggots with which the ramparts were covered, it made little real impression. So, after 300 shots at this target, they turned their fire upon the parapets. Some 800 shots at these did enough damage to encourage Norris to send 120 men from Sherley's and Sir Henry Norris's regiments under Captain Lister, with another 120 in support, to see whether it was possible to lodge in the enemy's ditch. Captain Lister's party was held up by the enemy's fire. Thereupon Captain Jackson and a number of others who had not been detailed to take any part in this reconnaissance, rushed forward to ease the pressure upon Lister's men by assaulting the bastion on their left flank. Lister's men gave up attempting to lodge in the ditch and joined in the assault. But the bastion had been only partially battered and the attackers were soon caught in the other flank by two enemy guns firing from the other bastion. Jackson was killed and the attackers were called off.

Then some more over-eager captains of the rearguard launched another unauthorized assault. It, too, was repulsed, with the loss of Captains Barker and Pretherch, Ensign Haines, and a couple of dozen others killed and three more captains and some soldiers wounded. 'All this hurt', Norris wrote, 'was caused by rash attempt contrary to their direction.' The attempt to lodge in the enemy's ditch had also to be abandoned. To confound the confusion, just as the assault was being made ten barrels of English gunpowder were blown up owing to the negligence of a cannoneer. About fifty people were burned, including Sir Thomas Knollys and four other captains, but by good fortune none of them badly. A week later the besiegers suffered another setback, this time on the right, in the French sector. In a rainstorm about eighty of the Spanish garrison sallied out against the French positions. They caught the French off their guard, killed the Sieur de Liscoët and twenty or more others, and destroyed part of the trenches. They were eventually driven back into the fort and the trenches regained – by Ensign Jackson and some English troops according to Sir John Norris; by the Baron of Molac and some French according to the French sources.

By now Don Juan d'Aguila and the main Spanish forces from Blavet, 3,000 strong, were advancing to the relief of Fort Crozon. They came forward slowly and cautiously, harassed in flank and rear by the royalist cavalry that Aumont had left around Quimper for this purpose. Happily, too, for the besiegers, Mercoeur, who had no wish to see Brest in Spanish hands, had evaded all Aguila's pleas to bring the League's forces to his assistance. Nevertheless, Aumont's troops 'forsake the field space'. His French infantry numbered no more than 600–700 until another 400 under de Tremblay and La Fontaine came to reinforce them on 5 November. Every night Norris had to help them out with 300 of his own men. Of the English fully 1,500 were sick or wounded. Altogether therefore the besiegers had very few more men than the combined numbers of those with Aguila and those in Fort Crozon. According to Norris, Aumont and his council of war now decided to abandon the siege. They sent orders to the guns to cease fire and to the miners to cease work on a mine they were excavating opposite the French positions. Norris counter-manded these orders and hastened, he said, to the Marshal, who was sick in bed. He told him that the English would not abandon the siege even if all the French did go away. This persuaded Aumont to change his mind and to agree to making a final, all-out assault upon the fort that day. The French sources make no mention of Norris's intervention or of Aumont's change of mind: Moreau, in particular, lauds the Marshal's resolution and boldness in deciding upon the assault when Aguila was already breathing down his neck. It does, however, seem just a little unlikely that Norris invented the whole story, much as he despised Aumont.

At all events, whether by Norris's persuasion or of his own volition, Aumont on 7 November launched a general assault upon Fort Crozon. The attack was preceded by a furious battery from all the fourteen cannon and by the explosion of the mine in the French sector. Then, about eleven o'clock in the morning, the assault was launched. On the right, wave after wave of French infantry was thrown back with consider-able losses and on the left the English, too, made slow progress, though with far fewer casualties. At a fairly early stage the fort's commander, Don Tomas de Paredes, was killed. His troops, however, fought on stoutly until they began to run out of shot and were reduced to firing odd bits of cut-up metal and even pieces of eight from their muskets and calivers. It was half-past four in the afternoon, and the winter sun was just setting, when the final break-through was made – 'in the end first entered by our English', according to Norris; by Romégou and his Gascons, according to Moreau; hard to say whether English or French were first, according to de Thou.

The Spanish garrison that had put up such a determined resistance was slaughtered almost to a man. Seventy or eighty jumped into the sea and were drowned, many of them knocked on the head by Frobisher's sailors – 'our mariners made them sink', Burghley wrote to Edmondes. A few escaped in the gathering darkness and hid among the rocks and ruins, only to be rounded up and killed in the next morning's light. Of between 300 and 400 men in the fort, a bare half-dozen were made prisoners. On the besiegers' side, the French lost, it seems, about 400 men, including Romégou and several other leaders; the English, some sixty men slain or hurt, the most notable being Sir Martin Frobisher who had come ashore to join in the assault. Frobisher was wounded, gangrene set in, and he died on reaching Plymouth. 'The loss was great of the man', Burghley wrote, 'for he was valiant both by water and by land.'

Norris generously reported 'that the gentlemen of France did their parts therein, with the loss of divers their lives, as honourably as ever he saw an assault attempted'. Yet even in the flush of victory he managed once again to ruffle Marshal Aumont's feathers. On the morning after the fort was taken, he sent off for presentation to the Queen three Spanish ensigns captured by the English troops. He had hastened them off before Aumont, as commander-in-chief, had time to ask for them and the Marshal was seriously annoyed by this slight to his prerogatives. He in his turn hastened off a letter to the Queen, praising the valour of the English but complaining about the three Spanish colours and about Norris's failure to punish his troops for their pillaging and for their ransacking of churches. He also complained that Norris, as a mere commander of auxiliary forces, failed to show due deference to himself as the chief commander.[23]

Besides these dissensions there was also a much less acrid difference of opinion between the two commanders about what could be done now that Fort Crozon was taken. Aumont wanted to pursue the retreating Don Juan d'Aguila back to Blavet. Norris, while approving the idea in the abstract, said that his troops were too weary and too weakened by sickness and wounds to undertake any such operation. They also needed money and clothes, for apparently their promised winter apparel had still not arrived. So he rested them for a time at Le Faou, at the inland end of the Brest inlet, before marching off towards Morlaix in case the French should after all decide to yield that town to the Queen. That they would yield it was most unlikely, for Aumont had the Estates, the Parlement, and the gentlemen of Brittany solidly behind him in defying Henry IV's orders to hand it over.[24]

In fact the delivery of Morlaix was no longer in question from the English side either, for as soon as the news of the taking of Fort Crozon reached England on 17 November – a neat Accession Day present for the Queen – Elizabeth determined to withdraw all her troops from Brittany.[25] The fleet had already come home and on 23 November orders were sent off to Norris for him and his troops to come too, as soon as shipping arrived to embark them. He was to pick out 2,000 'of the most able soldiers' and sort them into companies of 150 ready to sail to Ireland where O'Donnell and O'Neill, the Earl of Tyrone, were raising Ulster in rebellion and were in communication with the Spanish government. That the 2,000 were to go to Ireland was not to be made public – Ireland, after all, was little if any better than Brittany as a place to soldier in. The rest of the troops and the miners were to come back to England. Norris was also to try to get some of the guns captured in Fort Crozon and send them over to be displayed in London 'as a memorial of the victory'. And of course he was to take especial care to collect and bring home safely all the

---

[23] Ibid., fos. 254, 310; *Edmondes Papers*, p. 186; *H. M. C., Salisbury MSS*, XIII, 515.

[24] S. P. France, xxxiv, fos. 248, 272; *Edmondes Papers*, pp. 186–7; *Lettres Missives*, IV, 246–7.

[25] *Edmondes Papers*, pp. 191–2.

equipment, stores, weapons, and ordnance that were not needed to fit out and arm the 2,000 men for Ireland. Four days later, on 27 November, a warrant was issued to pay Sir John Hawkins, as treasurer of the navy, imprests of £2,225 for pressing and hiring twenty-five ships to carry the 2,000 to Ireland and £1,778 for another twenty ships to bring home the rest. Four months' victuals, at a cost of £5,600, were also to be sent for the 2,000. The shipping was to sail from Plymouth under the command again of Captain John Troughton.[26]

The orders for the troops to leave Brittany took a month to reach Norris, presumably because of adverse winds in the Channel. When they did reach him, on 23 December, he made one last effort to dissuade a withdrawal which, he wrote would 'amaze' Aumont and everyone else. For himself, he wrote to Sir Robert Cecil, 'I will ever be of an assured opinion that Her Majesty will be forced to give assistance to Brittany and that it imports as much her country to keep the Spaniard from the possession of Brittany as of Ireland.'[27] The French ambassador, Beauvoir la Nocle, too, made his protest when at the end of December he heard a rumour – the Queen's decision had apparently been kept more than usually secret – that Norris and his men were being recalled. Burghley did present the ambassador's written arguments to the Queen, but had to inform him that 'Her Majesty's answer was absolute that she would have her forces revoked . . . Other answer or hope of better I cannot give you, whereof I am very sorry.'[28] Whether Burghley's sorrow was genuine or merely polite, there is no means of telling, but on this occasion the Queen did stand firmly to her decision.

Even so, it was to be well past the middle of February 1595 before her troops actually embarked from Brittany. John Troughton with twenty-six of his ships arrived off Morlaix on 2 January, but was refused admittance to the harbour by the governor, was indeed fired upon by the town's great ordnance.

[26] S. P. France, xxxiv, fos. 248, 262, 264; *Cal. S. P. Domestic, 1591–4*, pp. 565–6.
[27] S. P. France, xxxiv, fos. 314, 316.
[28] The copy of Burghley's letter (S. P. France, xxxiv, fo. 274) was endorsed by one of his clerks as 30 November, but it is clearly a reply to Beauvoir's protest of 29 December (ibid., fo. 320).

He sailed off to nearby Roscoff and from there next day sent a man of his, Andrew Broughton, to inform Norris of the ships' arrival and to ask directions about embarking the troops. Broughton was taken prisoner by some Leaguer horsemen and although he, being a poor man unable to pay a ransom, was soon released, it was 6 January before he reached Norris at 'Kylyskin', four leagues from Morlaix. As Morlaix was closed to him and as Mercoeur was in the field again, Norris decided that the safest place to embark would be Paimpol (perhaps the water there had got deeper since the previous January). So he marched off to Paimpol and told Troughton to bring his shipping round to there .[29] By 8 January the troops were ready to embark, but Troughton could not get round so soon and when he did arrive he was further delayed by very adverse winds and by the delay in the arrival of the victuals from England for the men going to Ireland. Those 2,000 men were much the larger part of Norris's forces, which now mustered no more than 2,708 all told. Norris did at last reduce them, as he had been ordered to do months ago, from thirty-three to twenty-six companies. He himself thereupon managed with considerable difficulty to cross the Channel to Portsmouth, despite the very adverse winds. He arrived there on 3 February and it was another fifteen days before his troops finally embarked at Paimpol on 18 February.[30] Then for the first time in almost four years there was not an English soldier in the Queen's pay on French soil, not even in Brittany.

[29] S. P. Domestic, ccli, no. 2; *Edmondes Papers,* pp. 209–10.
[30] *Cal. S. P. Domestic, 1595–7,* pp. 6–8, 12.

# Conclusion

By the time the last English troops left Brittany in February 1595 the crucial phase of the struggle for western Europe was to all intents and purposes over. The central element in that struggle had been the attempt by Philip of Spain to gain control over the kingdom of France, even to acquire its throne for himself or his elder daughter. His attempt had depended for its success upon the existence in France of a substantial party allied to Spain and willing to further Spanish purposes. That party, the French Catholic League, was now destroyed, apart from a handful of great nobles clinging despairingly to their last footholds on the fringes of the kingdom – Mayenne and Aumale, already treating with Henry IV, in part of Burgundy; Mercoeur in part of Brittany; and possibly for a time a more dubious adherent in Épernon in Provence. Henry IV's domestic war against Spain and the League for the heart of his kingdom had become a straightforward national war between France and Spain, a war fought on the frontiers, on France's north-eastern frontier in particular.

In the Netherlands, too, with the fall of Groningen Spain had finally lost its hold upon the vital north-eastern provinces, its position upon the left flank of the main river defences of the Dutch republic. The Dutch now occupied all the territory north of the Rhine and Maas right up to the German border, except for a few small outposts such as Grol, Enschede, Ootmarsum, and Oldenzaal. They also controlled both banks of the great rivers from the German border to the sea and could thus move their forces laterally far more quickly by water than the Spaniards could march by land. The Revolt of the Netherlands was also becoming a straightforward war between the young Dutch republic and the still Spanish Netherlands, a war likewise fought out upon the frontiers.

The collapse of the French Catholic League and the fall of Groningen therefore initiated a new phase in the war against Spain on the Continent. France was beginning to re-emerge as a substantial counterpoise to the power of Spain. The old balance between the two great Continental military monarchies upon which Tudor England had been accustomed to rely, was beginning to come into being again and there was no longer any really serious danger of an over-mighty Spain dominating the whole of western Europe, of a Habsburg 'whole monarchy of Christendom'. The Continental war was reverting to a more normal pattern, becoming a war between independent states, not too unequally matched, fighting each other across their frontiers.

Admittedly, during the following three or four years the course of this war ran a little more in favour of the Spaniards than of their enemies. From Henry IV they took Doullens and Cambrai in 1595, Calais in 1596, and Amiens for a while in 1597. In 1595 they forced the Dutch to raise their siege of Grol and in 1596 they recaptured Hulst from them. Moreover the triple alliance of 1596 between England, France, and the United Provinces did not prevent Henry IV from making his peace with Spain by the Treaty of Vervins in 1598. On the other hand, by that treaty the Spaniards perforce recognized that it was now beyond their power to attain to the hegemony of western Europe. Nor did their prospects of reconquering the northern Netherlands look much brighter. The year 1597, when Philip II went bankrupt for a second time, had brought in January Count Maurice of Nassau's handsome victory at Turnhout over a Spanish army in the open field, and then in the autumn his conquest of the few remaining small Spanish outposts north of the Rhine and Maas – Grol, Brederode, Enschede, Ootmarsum, and Oldenzaal.

So the French monarchy was on its feet again and the Dutch had both reasserted their military prowess and finally secured the eastern flank of their defences. England's military assistance was therefore no longer required to assure the survival of the French monarchy nor, indeed, was it now in any very large measure essential to the independence of the Dutch republic. To a great extent Elizabeth could withdraw from the Continental war. And that was what, from the beginning of 1595, she did. A somewhat reduced number of English troops remained in the Netherlands, in the two cautionary towns of Flushing and Brielle, in Ostend, and in the field under Sir Francis Vere. But the English companies that had been withdrawn from Bergen-op-Zoom for service in

Brittany did not come back and in 1595 the Queen even pressed, though unsuccessfully, for the return of the regiment in the States' pay that Vere had raised in England the previous year. Moreover, in January 1595 she sent Thomas Bodley back to The Hague on the first of several missions to press the States to begin repaying the debts that they had incurred for her assistance since 1585. On this, too, the States long continued to stall, in fact until the King of France deserted them at Vervins in 1598 and they could not risk losing England's support as well. But already by 1595 in the Netherlands Elizabeth was not only limiting, and indeed a little reducing her present military aid, she was also beginning to send in her bill for past succours.

In her policy towards France the emphasis was a little different but the general drift the same. Henry IV's declaration of war against Spain in January 1595, and his appeal to Elizabeth to join him in vigorous hostilities, received only a vague and non-committal response. The Queen praised his declaration of war and assured him that if he royally invaded the King of Spain's dominions, he would not find her a cold or unresponsive ally. Nevertheless she had been 'the only party and actor' in open and actual hostility against Spain for many years and in many places, at great expense of men and money, while everyone else had stood upon the defensive. She and her subjects had therefore earned a rest. In Brittany her forces had done what they had been sent to do. They had taken Fort Crozon. They had restored the situation and given the King the upper hand in the province, despite the small assistance they had received from the French and the refusal of Morlaix as a base or even as a port of embarkation. The arrival of St Luc at Rennes with a number of regiments of foot and some ensigns of horse made the continued presence of the English even less necessary and they were to return as soon as shipping could arrive to carry them away. So from France the military withdrawal was total. Upon the French, too, there was pressure for some payment of debts, but the pressure was a good deal less urgent upon them than upon the Dutch. Marshal Aumont and the Estates of Brittany were asked to pay immediately for the Queen's gunpowder expended against Fort Crozon and the King himself was reminded that a good part of the cost of the shipping sent to the Gironde in 1592-3 was still not repaid. But although Elizabeth reminded Henry not infrequently of his other and larger debts, the obvious emptiness of his treasury, the enormous prices he was paying to buy off the League's leaders, and the continuing demands of his war against Spain made even the English Queen recognize that there was little hope of any immediate repayment of her expenses incurred in his behalf since he came to the throne in 1589. But only once during the remainder of her reign did she depart from her policy of non-involvement on land in France's wars and then only to a limited extent. This was after the Spaniard's capture of Calais in 1596. Then, in accordance with the triple alliance treaty, she sent English troops under Sir Thomas Baskerville. But in accordance with a secret clause of that treaty, the number of those men was limited to 2,000 and they were to be employed only to defend Boulogne and Montreuil or to fight under the King in person in Picardy. They remained there until Henry IV made his peace with Spain in 1598.

England's war with Spain, of course, went on and outlasted Elizabeth's reign. However, except for the limited force in the Netherlands and Baskerville's eighteen-months' stay in Picardy, it was now for the English a war fought no longer upon the continent but upon the seas and, in its later stages, in Ireland where Tyrone's rebellion offered the King of Spain an opportunity to do unto Elizabeth as she had done unto him in the Low Countries. On the seas it saw the ill-fortuned last expedition of Hawkins and Drake to the Caribbean and Spanish Main in 1595-6, the spectacular but hollow success of Essex and Howard at Cadiz in 1596, and the futile Islands Voyage of Essex and Raleigh in 1597. It saw also the even less successful Spanish armadas of 1596 and 1597, both scattered and shattered by storms before they could reach the Irish coast or enter the English Channel. In Ireland, at great expense of men and money – there were at one point 17,000 English troops there – and after a series of set-backs to a succession of English commanders, Mountjoy did succeed in crushing the rebels in Ulster and destroying their Spanish assistants at Kinsale. By then, however, the war between England and Spain had become a race between spent horses and one of the first acts of Elizabeth's successor James VI of Scotland was to bring the nineteen years' hostilities to an end by the peace treaty of 1604.

What had England contributed to the repelling of the threatened domination of western Europe by Spain? And what had her efforts cost her, not only in men and money but also in domestic harmony?

The most obvious and striking feature of English intervention was the almost total failure of the more ambitious offensive enterprises and plans. Some of these failed owing to the blunders and disobedience of the commanders. A most notable example was the expedition led by Norris and Drake in 1589. Had they obeyed the Queen's instructions and made the destruction of the remains of the 1588 Armada their first task, England would have been free from any fear of Spanish invasion for the rest of the war. Moreover, Spain's vital transatlantic traffic and its supply of treasure from the New World would have been at England's mercy. Philip II would then have been unable either to rebuild his navy, to pay his armies, or to subsidize his allies. And England would not have needed to annoy her Baltic and Scandinavian neighbours and her Dutch allies by interfering with their westward trade to Spain and Portugal. Indeed, had Drake and Norris in 1589 accomplished the purposes for which Elizabeth sent them out, there might well have been no threat of a Spanish domination of western Europe to draw England into Continental conflicts. Their failure to do what she had required of them was largely the outcome of her inability to control their actions when once they were beyond her sight over the horizon. And that inability was due to the limited nature of her financial resources which compelled her to entrust what she intended as a war-winning operation to a joint-stock enterprise that sought profit as much as, or more than, victory.

The Crown's financial limitations also go far to account for the failure of the plan to make a major attempt at the Azores in 1591 upon Spain's homeward-bound American fleets, even if it entailed a confrontation with Spain's fast-reviving sea power. The Queen lacked the numbers of ships needed for such an attempt and such shipbuilding as she had been able to undertake since the defeat of the 1588 Armada had considerably strained her finances. For the proposed large reinforcement of Lord Thomas Howard and Sir Richard Grenville she had therefore to call upon the English ports and her Dutch allies. The almost total failure of either to respond to her call put an end to the plan.

To some extent these financial limitations also helped to stultify the idea of a 'grand alliance' of England, France, the Dutch, Danes, German and Italian princes and cities which was tentatively put before Henry III in the spring and summer of 1589. Of course, the main reason why this proposal was still-born lay in the reluctance of even the German Protestant princes to jeopardize the peace of the Holy Roman Empire by active hostility to the Spanish cousin of their Habsburg Emperor or by an active anti-Catholic policy that might reopen the religious conflicts in Germany. Even when the question was of assisting the Catholic King Henry III of France, neither the German princes nor the Grand Duke of Tuscany was prepared to join an open anti-Spanish alliance. When after Henry III's assassination it was a question of helping the Calvinist King Henry IV, the Grand Duke pulled right out and the most that the German Protestant princes and cities would do was to contribute towards the cost of a French levy of German mercenaries. The contribution that Elizabeth felt able to make might have been, or so it would seem, somewhat more generous; but she could never have made it of a size to tempt them out of their cautious neutrality, particularly after the death of John Casimir of the Palatinate and the Lutheran reaction in Saxony that followed the death of Christian I.

It was also to some extent Elizabeth's unwillingness to face the cost of contributing extra troops to reinforce her auxiliary companies in the Netherlands that stifled almost at birth her plan to bring that German levy in 1591 through the Netherlands and so catch Parma's army and his League allies between it and the Anglo-Dutch forces from the one side and Henry IV's Frenchmen from the other. Whether such an operation would have been any more successful against Parma than the Coligny–Orange plan against Alba in 1572 may perhaps be doubted. But at least it was a plan that, like the plan for Norris and Drake's expedition in 1589, had decisive victory as its objective. It showed a broader vision and a better grasp of essentials than Henry IV's waiting upon Parma or Maurice of Nassau's concentration upon clearing his north-eastern provinces. It was this lack of enthusiasm among her allies more than Elizabeth's unwillingness to augment her Netherlands forces that prevented her plan from ever being attempted.

It is difficult not to conclude that a similar lack of enthusiasm on Henry IV's part was responsible for the miserable, long-drawn-out failure of the 1591-2 siege of Rouen. Henry clearly looked upon the siege as little more than a bait to draw Parma to battle, just as the siege of Dreux in 1590 had drawn Mayenne to battle at Ivry. This was an understandable attitude, though it was perhaps not altogether wise for a king as penurious as Henry IV thus to draw out time and leave the initiative to his opponent. It was certainly unwise of him to agree to, indeed to press for, English troops for an early siege of Rouen and then to go off to besiege Noyon and not even to begin to invest Rouen until three months after the English (promised by the Queen for two months' service) had landed. Had he, as he promised, been in Normandy with his army when Essex arrived at the beginning of August he might well, as Burghley later complained, have taken a still unprepared and partially provisioned Rouen long before Parma was able to move to its relief. And he would then have been a good deal better able, militarily and financially, to face a battle with the Spaniards and the League. Moreover, even when the siege was in progress, he never pressed it really hard or really closely. He was always looking over his shoulder for the arrival of the Duke of Parma and his heart was never truly in the siege operations. Indeed, there seems little doubt that he hoped to use those operations, not only as a bait to draw Parma to battle, but also as a bait to draw from Elizabeth English troops to serve him in that battle rather than just for a siege of Rouen. Always ready to promise, never very meticu-lous about performing what he promised, his conduct over the siege of Rouen did more than anything (except possibly his abjuration) to cool English zeal for his cause and to breed among Englishmen disillusionment with Continental military commitments.

Somewhat similar difficulties with the Dutch over the withdrawal of part of the English auxiliary forces were responsible also for the abandonment of plans for decisive attacks upon the Spaniards and Leaguers in Brittany in 1591 and again in 1594. The States' reluctance to release the English companies and the delays caused by their opposition meant that Norris's expedition to Brittany in 1591 was reduced to, at best, a long-drawn-out holding action instead of being a short sharp blow to expel the Spaniards. In 1594, too, fewer Englishmen could be withdrawn from the Netherlands than was intended and this helped a little to limit the English operations to the capture of Fort Crozon instead of the expulsion of the Spaniards from the whole province. It is, however, true that much of the States' opposition to the withdrawals, both those for the intended offensive in Brittany in 1591 and those for the more defensive purposes after the Craon disaster in 1592, was due to the Queen's very high-handed manner in ordering the withdrawals. As Sir Robert Sidney said their pride was wounded at being thus peremptorily commanded instead of being diplomatically entreated.

In part this high-handedness was the expression of a natural monarchical lack of respect for and inability to believe in a republican 'headless commonwealth'. But it was also the outcome of the Queen's attempt to treat her auxiliary forces in the Netherlands as the mobile strategic reserve of trained and experienced troops that she needed and which England's lack of a standing army made her unable to find elsewhere. To build such a standing army, or even such a strategic reserve, was clearly beyond her means amid the strains and stresses of the war; to have built it during the earlier years of peace would have been politically well-nigh impossible: witness the strength of the passive resistance to the organization of the trained bands in the counties and towns during the 1570s and earlier 1580s. Nevertheless, a more diplomatic and considerate approach might have made the Dutch less obstructive. There must still have been difficulties and delays owing to the cumbersome nature of their government and their determined concentration upon assuring their borders and especially upon clearing the north-eastern provinces across the Ijsel and Zuyder Zee. But in these dealings with the Dutch Elizabeth to a considerable extent brought her problems upon herself.

We must remember, however, that Elizabeth, the not-over-wealthy ruler of a small half-island of limited resources and manpower, found herself cast in the role of paymaster and, in effect, co-ordinator of an alliance of no less poor and weak states fighting the mightiest and wealthiest monarchy in Christendom. And although her more ambitious offensive plans and enterprises came to nothing, she and her Dutch and French allies did prevent Spain from establishing its control over the whole of western Europe, from acquiring the crown of France and destroying the Dutch republic. In this defensive achievement Elizabethan England had played a very considerable part.

To begin with, English intervention had saved the Dutch after Parma's conquest of Belgium and capture of Antwerp in 1585. It had done this, not so much by direct assistance in the defence of the United Provinces, though Leicester had delayed Parma on the Ijsel in 1586, but far more by diverting Spanish energies to the Enterprise of England. The preparations and waiting for the Armada, and also to some degree his deceitful peace negotiations, had kept Parma and the bulk of his army tied to the coast of Flanders all through 1587 and the first two-thirds of 1588. He had therefore not been able to take advantage of Stanley's betrayal of Deventer and Rowland Yorke's betrayal of Zutphen, which opened up the left, inland flank of the Dutch defences. Then after the Invincible Armada had come and seen and been conquered, it was largely English troops who denied him success at Bergen-op-Zoom. Moreover, the cost of that Armada, and the continuing expense of rebuilding Spain's oceanic naval power after its defeat, together with the expense of fortifying his ports and defending his coasts and his American traffic against English attacks, these coming on top of his military expenditures against the Dutch and in France, imposed an intolerable burden upon Philip II's finances. These things, taken altogether, were to bring him to virtual bankruptcy in 1597.

In the meanwhile, Elizabeth had done much to maintain Henry IV on the throne of France. Her loans and the 4,000

English infantry under Willoughby had enabled him to keep the field between Loire and Seine all through the autumn and winter of 1589–90. That had made possible his great victory at Ivry in March 1590, which destroyed the League's field army and compelled Philip II to send Parma with the Netherlands army later that year to save Paris. Thus forced to concentrate their efforts upon France, and indeed to bid for its crown, the Spaniards were able to offer no more than a weak defensive against the Dutch. Maurice of Nassau and the States' forces were therefore able to make their southern frontier secure by the capture of Nijmegen and Geertruidenberg and to clear their eastern flank almost up to the German border by taking Steenwijk, Coevorden, and Groningen. In these operations Sir Francis Vere and the English auxiliary companies made up a substantial proportion of the States' field force, particularly in the earlier years. And in France, while Henry IV was involved in his frustrating campaigns against the Leaguers and Spaniards, it was very largely English forces that kept his cause alive and the Spaniards at bay in Brittany.

In the end, of course, it was Henry IV's conversion to Catholicism in July 1593 that brought about the collapse of the League and put an end to Spanish designs in France. But that conversion would not have worked its magic if Henry had rushed into it immediately upon or soon after his accession, before almost all parties in France had grown weary of an indecisive war and before the naked revelation of Spanish ambitions had made most Frenchmen ready to acknowledge him if he became a Catholic. In the interval English men and English money had done much to prevent the war turning decisively against him. In particular they had done much to keep him north of the Loire, fighting for his crown in those northern provinces where alone he could stand forth as claiming to be indeed a king of all France, Thus, on the defensive side, Elizabethan England had done a great deal to frustrate a Spanish domination of western Europe, to secure the survival of the Dutch republic, and to re-establish the independence of the French monarchy.

These efforts had imposed heavy burdens upon both the government and the people of England. During a little over five years from September 1589 close on 20,000 English troops had been sent to France. At the same time there were a nominal 7,600 foot and 400 horse, auxiliary and cautionary, in the Netherlands. Deducting the usual ten per cent for 'dead pays', this should have left 7,200 real live soldiers. Although that number was seldom, if ever, realized, the drafts periodically taken over by captains to bring their bands to a more or less presentable strength justify our putting the troops serving in or supplying the Netherlands companies at well over 7,000, in addition to the 1,500 raised at the States' expense by Vere in 1594. Add to these the 19,000 soldiers mustered for the Portugal expedition and the total of English troops sent to the Continent during the seven years following the defeat of the 1588 Armada cannot have been much less than 47,000 or 48,000. Besides these, there were the sailors who manned the Queen's ships and the several hundred great and small privateering vessels. These sailors, though not countable with any exactitude, must have numbered several thousands and the wastage among them from disease was even greater than that among the land soldiers. Altogether the expense of manpower was quite considerable for a nation whose population can hardly have exceeded, if indeed it reached, four millions.

Moreover, almost all those troops sent over to the Continent had to be selected and collected, armed and clothed, by the local authorities of the counties and towns from which they were drawn. The repeated calls for such levies – there were ten major calls for France alone in the five years from September 1589, though not all from the same counties – took up a great amount of the time and energy of the country gentry who filled the offices of deputy-lieutenants, justices of the peace, sheriffs, and so forth. These men already had to see to the organizing, equipping, training, and occasional general mustering of the home-defence trained bands, as well as to the beacon watching, apprehension of vagrants and deserters, relief of maimed soldiers and deserving poor, hunting down of seminary priests, keeping an eye upon recusants, and all the other extra work that the war created or augmented. Their purses were called upon as well as their time and energy. The cost of the arms, armour, and clothing was considerable now that the musket or caliver and the pike were replacing bows and bills as standard weapons. And as we have seen, very few of the arms, little of the armour, and even less of the clothing supplied to those levies for overseas were ever returned. Drawn from the equipment of the county's trained bands, they had to be replaced and the replacements paid for by an additional county rate. The various demands, particularly those upon time and energy but also to quite a considerable extent those for money too, fell especially upon the more substantial people, the most administratively significant and politically conscious. We have seen how the growing demands upon them bred a diminishing zeal, a growing slackness and inefficiency in selecting and equipping the levies for overseas service.

Something of the same attitude carried over into their responses when called upon to help the central government financially, by privy seal loans (which were fairly promptly repaid) and by parliamentary taxes (for which, of course, there was no repayment). The government's expenditure was now far outrunning its ordinary income. Elizabeth had lent Henry IV of France £45,000 in hard cash since his accession in July 1589. With her £10,000 towards his 1591 German levy and the cost of the 20,000 English troops that she had sent to France, her total expenses in his behalf were already over £300,000 – in April 1593, before the final operations in Brittany, they had been estimated at £286,172. During the six and a half years from the defeat of the 1588 Armada to the end of 1594 her expenses in the Netherlands came close to £750,000. Then there were her contributions to the Portugal expedition and Frobisher's voyage in 1589, to Hawkins and Frobisher in 1590, to Lord Thomas Howard in 1591, and to various privateering enterprises – £46,000 to the Portugal expedition and an estimated £172,259 to 'voyages by adventurers'. Her share in any profits must, of course, be deducted from the cost of those maritime ventures. Yet even putting her net expenditure on these at no more than £50,000, her total expenses upon the war during those six and a half years cannot have been much less than £1,100,000, equivalent to a good half of her ordinary income during that time. The sale of £126,000 worth of Crown lands by no means filled the gap. Hence the demands for a double subsidy from Parliament in 1589 and a treble in 1593.

We have seen the hesitation and resistance that those demands met with in the Commons. Much of it no doubt arose from a mere dislike of paying higher taxes. Yet a number of members hesitated about agreeing to the demands in 1593 on the grounds explicitly that they must consider the people and their estates whom they represented. When one of those who acted in this way was the most recent English resident ambassador to France, Sir Henry Unton, it is difficult not to feel that this balancing of constituents' interests against the requirements of the war was not an at least implied criticism of government policy. The disfavour that Unton, like Francis Bacon, fell into thereupon with the Queen shows that Elizabeth certainly regarded it in this way. In the end, of course, the government got its grant from the Parliament and its troops from the counties. Nevertheless in both cases the process was becoming less smooth, a little more abrasive. Moreover the middle 1590s were a time of wet summers, ruined harvests, slack overseas trade (a direct result of the war), and widespread plague (much of it imported by soldiers returning from Continental campaigns). On top of all this, ever since 1588 hopes of decisive victory had again and again been dashed almost as soon as they were born. This was therefore for Englishmen a frustrating and depressing time and the depression was hardly to lift for the remaining years of Elizabeth's reign.

It was this frustration and depression that were chiefly responsible for a cooling of relations between court and people, between central government and the mostly unpaid but increasingly busied and burdened local authorities. The promoters of privateering, the army contractors, the gun-founders, and the shipbuilders were for the most part doing well out of the war. But to the rest of the nation that war meant steadily growing burdens, growing demands upon both their purses and their time and all in pursuit of a victory that often seemed within England's reach yet always eluded her grasp. Inevitably, even if often unfairly, the government that was directing and conducting the war got the blame for this repeated lack of success. Criticism of its policies and its strategies was spreading outside the inner circles of authority, beyond men close to the centre of power such as Essex and

Raleigh. Respect for the wisdom of the Queen and her Privy Council was being undermined by the frustrations that the war produced. Elizabeth personally remained widely popular and the Council retained its authority. But in the nation and in its Parliaments there was emerging a coolly appraising attitude towards its government that would set an increasingly searching examination for the statesmanship of its Stuart Kings.

# INDEX

Abbeville (Somme, France) 408, 437, 518
*Achates,* queen's ship 5, 86
Acton, Thomas 312
admiralty, high court of 242, 251–2; judge of 218
*Advantage,* queen's ship (cromster) 380n
Aerschot, Philippe de Croy, duke of 279n
Aerssens, Cornelis 218, 227
Africa 120
Agen (Lot-et-Garonne, France) 518
Aguila, Juan d' in Brittany 445, 474; lands at Blavet 189–90, 244, 262, 264, 296; Norris challenges 337; at Craon battle 403; and fort Crozon 528, 535–7, 550, 552
*Aid,* queen's ship 125n, 155, 298n
Aix-en-Provence (Bouches-du-Rhône) 189, 518
Alba, Ferdinand Alvarez de Toledo, 3rd duke of 14, 116, 266
Albert, cardinal archduke, governor of Portugal 116, 119–21, 123
Aldred, Solomon 149
Alençon (Orne, France) 172–3
Alincourt, Charles de Neufville, marquis of 518
Allen, Richard 215
Allen, William, cardinal 449, 453
Almenara, marquis of, viceroy of Aragon 450–1
ambergris 447
Ambrières (Mayenne, France) 430–1, 442
America 2, 6, 50, 95, 235, 248
Amias, John 526n
Amiens (Somme, France) 89, 185, 408, 520
Amsterdam (N. Holland) 56, 62, 84, 137
Andrada, Manuel d', 'David' 104, 120, 314, 449n
Anglesey 296
Anglésqueville (Seine-Mar., France) 391
Angers (Maine-et-Loire, France) 404
Angra (Azores) 236–8
Angus, earl of 458

Anhalt, Christian of 362–3, 365, 367, 390
Anholt (Nordrheinland-Westf., Germany) 426
Anjou (France) 401, 464
Anjou, Francis, duke of 23, 174
Anne of Denmark, queen of James VI 258, 456
*Answer,* queen's ship (cromster) 380n
*Antelope,* queen's ship 298n
Antonio, Don, king, pretender, of Portugal: plans to restore 14, 16, 18; and 1589 expedition 92, 98, 100, 111, 113, 115–22, 124, 126
Ansbach (Bavaria) 258
Antwerp (Belgium) 9, 23–6, 43, 135–6, 256, 347; greffier of 48
apparel, clothes: English crews needed (1588) 4; of Armada at Coruña 111; for Willoughby's troops 152, 168–9, 171–5, 177–8; for Brittany troops 337, 430, 436; for 1593 Normandy levy 467–8; for Brest relief force 547–8, 552
Appeville (Seine-Mar., France) 504
Aragon (Spain) revolt in 450–1
archery 296n
Arden, John 449n
*Ark Royal,* queen's ship 1
armour 257, 310, 467; to be returned to counties 152–3, 161, 334n; their losses 179, 418–9; Wilkes to search at Dieppe for 386; casques 111, 325; corslets 152, 156, 312, 418; morions 156, 418
Arnemuiden (Zeeland) 212
Arnhem (Gelderland) 34, 207, 317, 339
Arques (Seine-Mar., France) battle of 148, 151, 154–6; mentioned 160, 182–3, 380; other references 322, 326–8, 354, 358, 438, 440
Artaxerxes 72
artillery, cannon, guns: English: of 1589 expedition 19–21, 109–12, 121, 125; at Bergen siege 44, 46; French: requests for 282, 305, 308, 314, 330, 355; in Brittany 336, 528, 541, 545, 548–50, 553; for Rouen siege 371, 409; at Dieppe